THE EAST TENNESSEE VETERANS MEMORIAL

III THE III

EAST TENNESSEE

VETERANS MEMORIAL

A PICTORIAL HISTORY OF THE NAMES ON THE WALL

THEIR LIVES, THEIR SERVICE, THEIR SACRIFICE

JOHN ROMEISER with JACK McCALL

WITH A FOREWORD BY CARROLL VAN WEST

THE UNIVERSITY OF TENNESSEE PRESS
KNOXVILLE

Frontispiece and memorial photo on page xviii courtesy of
Robert Batey Photography.

Library of Congress Cataloging-in-Publication Data

Names: Romeiser, John Beals, 1948– author. | McCall, Jack H., author.

Title: The East Tennessee Veterans Memorial : a pictorial history of the
names on the wall, their lives, their service, their sacrifice / John B.
Romeiser, Jack H. McCall Jr. ; with a foreword by Carroll Van West.

Description: First edition. | Knoxville : The University of Tennessee
Press, [2020] | Includes bibliographical references and index.

Identifiers: LCCN 2019033196 (print) | LCCN 2019033197 (ebook) | ISBN
9781621902959 (cloth) | ISBN 9781621902966 (pdf)

Subjects: LCSH: East Tennessee Veterans Memorial. | Veterans—Tennessee,
East.

Classification: LCC F442.1 .R66 2020 (print) | LCC F442.1 (ebook) | DDC
976.8—dc23

LC record available at https://lccn.loc.gov/2019033196

LC ebook record available at https://lccn.loc.gov/2019033197

This book is respectfully and humbly dedicated to the service members of East Tennessee, whose lives and military sacrifice are commemorated by the East Tennessee Veterans Memorial, and equally to those whose lives are connected with them and who have never forgotten them: their families, friends, loved ones, and fellow military veterans and survivors of war.

CONTENTS

FOREWORD

Monuments and memorials are among the most important human expressions. From the pre-historic era to now, we always have had the need to mark our achievements, our travels, and our heroes, even where we failed. Monuments of course tell us more about those who created them than the actual event or person thus memorialized. Their messages can be mixed. We look at monuments and risk thinking of history as frozen, static, never changing. What mattered to past generations must always matter to the present, as well as to the future: why otherwise do so many monument makers carve the words "lest we forget" into their stone bases?

The word monument in the Volunteer state of the early twenty-first century is distasteful to many, as we have allowed too many groups to associate their views of exclusion, hate, and power with our monumental landscape. Extremes rule. One side wants to wipe the slate clean; the other side strives to make monuments the highest historic preservation priority and force feed their message anywhere and everywhere.

It need not be that way. Another path is available, as the authors of this important book re-mind us in their compelling exploration of the making of, and the stories embodied in, the East Tennessee Veterans Memorial. The memorial is a twenty-first-century creation, inspired by a 1999 journey by veteran J. William Felton of Knoxville to the D-Day cemeteries of France. After that visit, Felton dedicated himself to recognize individuals who have served the nation in the twenti-eth century and into present-day conflicts, and to extend the recognition to the families of service members from thirty-five East Tennessee counties.

This region of Tennessee includes the historic town sites of the Cherokees and early settle-ment towns of the late eighteenth century when the region was still North Carolina. From here during the American Revolution came the Over Mountain Men, who smashed a British-led loyalist force at the decisive Battle of King's Mountain. During the War of 1812, the region provided many of the state's military leaders, from John Williams in Knoxville to Gideon Morgan of the Cherokee nation.

In the American Civil War, most residents of East Tennessee remained loyal to the nation and served the American Flag with distinction, from the heroic efforts of the Bridgeburners in the first months of the war to the devastating 1863 battles in Chattanooga and Knoxville.

In the decades after the Civil War, officials and military officers in the nation's capital never forgot the region's loyalty, especially in upper East Tennessee. By the turn of the twentieth century the residents of northeast Tennessee had gained two living memorials, Lincoln Memorial College (now University) with its extensive Abraham Lincoln museum collection, courtesy of US General O. O. Howard, and the lovely campus of the National Home for Disabled Volunteer Soldiers, better known today as Mountain Home, in Johnson City, where aging Union veterans could find care and a chance to pass away with the honor they had long ago earned. The vastness of the simple stone markers for the soldiers at Mountain Home, centered around the American flag, is as striking as those thousands of crosses marking the American dead at Normandy.

This history came to mind as I read the many stories associated with the East Tennessee Veterans Memorial. The hand of the federal government, with over $1.7 million of support, was present at its creation, but like the projects of the turn of the twentieth century, it also had considerable local government and community support: the City of Knoxville provided the land, the University of Tennessee's Center for the Study of War and Society provided foundational research, and many veterans and their families added their support, their memories, and their best wishes to the project.

The end result—as an architectural statement—is impressive. On thirty-two granite pylons are the names of over 6,200 East Tennessee veterans who have served since World War I. These names include fourteen Medal of Honor recipients, from the internationally recognized Alvin C. York from World War I to Mitchell Stout from the Vietnam War.

More importantly the design by the architectural firm Brewer Ingram Fuller of Knoxville invites reflection and memory. The memorial is to be living tribute—open forever—but also adding the names of new veterans every Memorial Day. The creators state that their goals for the memorial are to "remember, honor, educate, and inspire," with the most important goal being education. Thus, they made the wise decision to take the names, find their stories, and share them through the pages of this book.

The stories come from a website that the East Tennessee Veterans Memorial Association has used to collect accounts, photographs, and documents from veterans and their families. The authors have taken this vast storehouse of information and selected over 350 individuals to represent the experiences of the thousands of names etched into the stone memorial who have served the nation from World War I to the Global War on Terror of the twenty-first century. The stories are not just of heroism and battlefield exploits but also the sense of profound loss felt by families at the time and for generations afterwards.

Hugh Johnston Luttrell (1895–1918) of Knoxville is one of those stories. An employee of a shoe company prior to his July 1917 enlistment, Luttrell fought during World War I, first in Belgium, and then died on the first day of the Somme Offensive in late September 1918, mere weeks before the Armistice that ended the war. Luttrell rose to the rank of sergeant, a promotion that pointed him towards officers' training camp. Luttrell wrote his family that he could not accept the plum assignment "as I love all of the boys and they seem to think the world of me. If I should leave I might never see them again and here I could die with them" (p. 23).

Devotion to duty and one's fellow warriors is a constant theme. The spouse of Sergeant First Class Stephen C. Kennedy (1969–2005) of Anderson County said that "going over there [Iraq] and doing what he was doing was right because it was for his family and it was for his country" (p. 253). During the brutal World War II Battle of Leyte Gulf in October 1944, Electrician's Mate Second Class James Kenneth Weaver (1917–1944) perished. This Bristol, Tennessee, native was one of ninety service men who died when their ship the Samuel B. Roberts received heavy shell fire and sank. Weaver's commanding officer wrote his wife, Carol Woolsey Weaver, "your husband was not only a hero—he manned his battle station and stayed there knowing that death was almost inevitable" (p. 98).

The stories of the service members who died as prisoners of war conjure the realities of combat turned into torture, brutality, and murder. The story of Private First Class James L. Badgette, an African American from Knoxville, speaks to another gruesome reality. Private Badgette (1921–1945) was a truck driver for the Transportation Corps serving in the Pacific Theater. He was thrust into battle in April 1945 when the army attempted to seize the island of le Shima off the coast of Okinawa. Japanese soldiers and civilians fought with a suicidal intensity; Badgette used his truck as part of a hastily erected defensive line. He died defending the position and his fellow soldiers, beheaded by a sword-yielding Japanese soldier.

Stories of life and death along the battlegrounds, naval battles, and the air attacks of both World Wars to Iraq form the core of the book's narrative. The authors devote one chapter to the three Tester brothers from Washington County, a Tennessee equivalent to the Fighting Sullivan brothers of Saving Private Ryan fame. The three Testers—Dent, Glen, and Earle—came from a single family who provided a total of five veterans to the nation. The three Testers died in World War II actions in different countries—North Africa, France, and Germany—but have been buried together in a rural cemetery in Belgium. Of the two hundred sets of brothers buried overseas in United States military cemeteries, the Testers are the only group of three.

The stories taken from the Korean War of the 1950s to the present are much more personal and include many more accounts from family members and comrades. For instance, Staff Sergeant Michael R. Conner (1947–1970) died when his electronics airplane crashed due to enemy fire. One of his crew members , Danny E. Russell, recalls that after the crash, "we slowly started to unpile each other, I discovered my good friend Mike, who had gone forward and had taken my seat, was killed. To this day I still ask GOD why. This man was married and all he could do is talk about his wife and the baby they were about to have" (p. 194]

In 2008 Shirley Bowman Kelly, the widow of Air Force Staff Sergeant James E. Bowman who died near Pleiku in 1968, admitted: "For a very long time, I could not speak of this event when I met new people nor read a written word about this country and this horror of war which devoured mine and my children's lives. . . . some how we have managed to go on, but we have never forgotten, nor has his memory dimmed in our hearts" (p. 317).

Some soldiers in the Vietnam War were fatalistic about what awaited them in southeast Asia. First Lieutenant Harry R. Stewart (1941–1967) of Johnson City wrote his family: "thank you and everyone else for remembering me in their prayers. Don't waste that precious stuff on my safe return. That is already decided. Ask instead, that I do my job well and that God be with me in the performance of my duties" (p. 212).

His thoughts of service and duty were shared by many other veterans featured in this volume. But the authors even include the stories of soldiers whom military officials executed during war, such as Private First Class Alvin R. Rollins (1924–1945) of Chattanooga, who was one of ninety-six service members sentenced to death and executed in the European Theater during World War II.

Reading the hundreds of stories contained in this volume can be emotionally draining, but it is rewarding to read the accounts of courage, bravery, devotion, and duty, and to realize that these service members are recognized for themselves and for their service to their country.

Built of stone and protected within a Knoxville public park, the East Tennessee Veterans Memorial will endure for decades, if not centuries. Let's hope the same proves true for the stories of the veterans and the words that are recorded within the pages of this book. Their stories educate, inspire, and, in this time of uncertainty and hate, they also reassure us that the best of our state and our nation can endure any challenge that comes our way. We are tough, determined, stubborn, and brave, and ready to face the next test.

Carroll Van West
MTSU Center for Historic Preservation
Tennessee State Historian

Preface

THE EAST TENNESSEE VETERANS MEMORIAL AND HOW IT CAME TO BE

Only the dead have seen the end of war.

—*George Santayana*

It is foolish and wrong to mourn the men who died.
Rather, we should thank God that such men lived.

—*Attributed to Gen. George S. Patton Jr.*

The idea for the East Tennessee Veterans Memorial was conceived in 1999 when J. William Felton III of Knoxville visited the Normandy beaches in northern France with his wife, Betty. Felton, a retired colonel in the US Army Reserves, was deeply moved by the thousands of white crosses and Stars of David in the Normandy American Cemetery at Colleville-sur-Mer marking the graves of those who never got a chance to return home and pursue careers, raise families, further their education, own their own homes, or otherwise participate in the opportunities and advances of post–World War II America. So, he vowed to return home and work for a suitable way to honor and remember those who died. During the ensuing months and years that Colonel Felton doggedly pursued his dream, the scope of the project was expanded to include on the physical memorial all the names of those East Tennesseans who died in military service from the beginning of World War I.

Proposals for the geographical spread for the project ranged from Knox County alone, to the surrounding counties, and even to the entire state. Finally, the thirty-five-county regional East Tennessee area was chosen. The counties are those of the eastern Grand Division of the state, plus Fentress and Sequatchie counties. Thus, the project's reach is from the Virginia border to the north to the Georgia border to the south, and from the North Carolina line on the east to the Cumberland Plateau to the west.

Early supporters of the East Tennessee Veterans Memorial included former Knox County mayor Mike Ragsdale and former US representative John J. Duncan Jr. At Mayor Ragsdale's request, the Knox County Commission approved $1.25 million for the project. Congressman Duncan was instrumental in gaining approval by Congress of a $475,000 HUD grant. Kimberly Lauth served as the Operations Consultant through the dedication of the memorial, provided the majority of the legwork in grant-writing and general fundraising, and still serves as a board member emerita.

On assuming his office, Knoxville mayor Bill Haslam promised to find a site for the memorial. In early 2006, Haslam recommended—and the Knoxville City Council approved—the 8,000-square-foot plot at the northern edge of Knoxville's World's Fair Park. Ground was broken for the memorial on November 10, 2006. Robert P. Murrian, a member of the East Tennessee Veterans Memorial Association (ETVMA) board and former United States magistrate judge, was the featured speaker. Albert K. Murrian, his father, was one of those from World War II whose name is inscribed on the memorial. Ensign Murrian's plane disappeared over the Pacific in May 28, 1945. His personal story is told by his son elsewhere in this book.[1]

Two years later, on November 15, 2008, the $2.5 million memorial had been completed and was dedicated and opened to the public. The list of names for the memorial was initially compiled and researched for the East Tennessee Veterans Memorial Association by Cynthia Tinker of the University of Tennessee's Center for the Study of War and Society. At the outset, the list totaled fewer than 5,000 names. At the conclusion of this meticulous process to check for completion and accuracy, the total is now over 6,200. The memorial itself was designed by architect Lee Ingram of the Knoxville firm Brewer Ingram Fuller.

The goals of the East Tennessee Veterans Memorial project are to remember, honor, educate, and inspire. Of those four noble objectives, education is the key. For, in educating our citizenry about the sacrifices and service this region has contributed to our freedoms and way of life, we also honor and remember. And this knowledge inspires us to honor and serve our nation and fellow citizens in the future.

The memorial has thirty-two granite pylons; each one is nine feet high, three feet wide, and one foot deep. Inscribed upon the memorial's series of granite monuments are the names of more than 6,200 veterans from thirty-five East Tennessee counties who have died in military service, beginning with World War I. The names of each of the fourteen Medal of Honor recipients from these counties are inscribed on the reverse side of the pylons. These Medal of Honor holders are James E. Karnes, Milo Lemert, James R. Talley, Calvin J. Ward, Alvin York, Raymond Cooley, Charles Coolidge, Paul Huff, Elbert Kinser, Troy McGill, Alexander Bonnyman, Charles McGaha, Ray Duke, and Mitchell Stout. The service and sacrifices of these men will be addressed in chapter 1.

The names of the fallen are inscribed on the pylons up to a height of fifty-four inches from the ground, making the names accessible for touching by all visitors, including those in wheelchairs. Each pylon contains about 220 names. Letters are approximately a half-inch high. The names are sorted by conflict and further sorted by county within each conflict and are randomly listed (non-alphabetical, non-chronological) within each county. Names continue to be added annually after a careful process of consideration. Dedication of these new names takes place with the Reading of the Names program that is conducted each Memorial Day at the memorial.

A three-foot-long granite bench is placed opposite each pylon for seated observation and contemplation. Walkways within the memorial are also in granite. A circular plaza that forms the entrance features an American flag on a fifty-foot pole. Since the memorial is lighted at night, the flag flies twenty-four hours a day. Another feature is a twenty-seven-foot-high bell tower. On each of the four sides of the tower is inscribed one of the Four Freedoms, as enunciated by President Franklin D. Roosevelt in a speech to Congress on January 6, 1941: freedom of speech and expression; freedom to worship; freedom from want; and freedom from fear.

Since its opening, the East Tennessee Veterans Memorial has become a frequent destination for school trips, for military service–related and veterans' groups, and for special events such as commissioning ceremonies and Boy Scout activities. Moreover, the memorial served as an important locus for several events held in connection with the 2014 Medal of Honor Convention and continues to be the site for the Memorial Day Reading of the Names and other community events. WBIR's recurring television news series, "Service and Sacrifice," hosted by television anchorman John Becker, has occasionally used the memorial as a backdrop for some episodes. Most poignantly, after the remains of Medal of Honor recipient Alexander "Sandy" Bonnyman were recovered on the Pacific atoll of Tarawa in 2015, seventy-two years after his death there in the heat of combat, they were brought back to the memorial for a memorial service before interment in the Bonnyman family's cemetery plot in Knoxville.

From the beginning, it was decided that there would need to be ongoing research and fact-checking to bring back the life stories behind the names on the memorial. To this end, a website was created that would allow researchers to update names, ranks, branches of service, dates of birth and death, and much more. At the same time, the East Tennessee Veterans Memorial Association's board made a deliberate decision to include accounts found in the press and in military archives, in addition to information shared by friends, family, and researchers. Another decision made was to allow families and friends to help create an online record for the service of those who did not die during the conflicts we remember, even though their names are not engraved on the memorial. A more recent change in policy allows families and others to petition the ETVMA board to engrave the names of those who gave their lives in peacetime but in special operations or training accidents. Their names can be found on the "Peacetime" stele under the heading "Other Military Operations." The database for the East Tennessee Veterans Memorial continues to be updated frequently, often daily.

One notable part of the memorial's mission has been to provide a photographic record of the men and women whose names the ETVMA honors and remembers. In the case of roughly one-third of the more than 6,200 individuals, we have been fortunate to have discovered and posted "featured images," which often consist of the official, in-uniform enlistment photo or, at other times, a carefully conserved and precious family snapshot or school photograph. For many, we have also included images of enlistment records, interment-headstone documentation, and grave and memorial markers. These photographs and documents are a vital source of many of the items and personal accounts that you, the reader, will find included in this book. We continue to receive new records, photos, and other information and post them as soon as they arrive.

At the time that their lives were taken—whether by bullet, bomb, torpedo, plane crash, train wreck, or disease—each of the service members whose names are inscribed on the plinths of the memorial reached the maximum of their potential, in a very final way. Not just their families, friends, and loved ones, but entire communities would never learn what their full human potential could have been. In a very real sense, then, the East Tennessee Veterans Memorial Association—much like Colonel Felton when he first envisioned the concept of the memorial on that day in 1999 in Normandy—has become the "caretaker" of the memories of these fellow East Tennesseans, on behalf of the communities of East Tennessee.

We ask the reader to bear in mind that the selected stories and photographs of the over 350 service members who are profiled by name in this book (all of whom are commemorated by the Veterans Memorial) are just a microcosm, and therefore a very small sampling, of the tragedies of loss. While some of the stories are clearly exceptional, and some are uplifting—whether in the heroism of these East Tennesseans or in the raw facts and history of how they perished—many of these stories have also been carefully selected to demonstrate the full nature of military casualties and losses, featuring both those who perished out of battle and those who fell in action or died of their combat wounds. In the chapters that follow, a host of selected stories of many of the over 6,200 veterans commemorated on the East Tennessee Veterans Memorial will be told. Ranging from participants in the First World War, now a century ago, to those fighting in Iraq, Afghanistan, and during the Global War on Terror, a wide range of men and women will be depicted. Some will be heroes or have heroic elements. Each of East Tennessee's Medal of Honor recipients will be included, as described above—the death of one near war's end was the origin for a bestselling nonfiction book by his nephew, and the death of three brothers in World War II may prefigure elements of the plot of the 1998 movie *Saving Private Ryan*. But not all deaths are necessarily heroic. Some might even be perceived to be, in a sense, anti-heroic.

Often this will not be easy reading. The causes of death vary greatly. Many of the stories summon up the ongoing grief and loneliness of families, loved ones, and fellow survivors of combat as their memories of these lost Tennesseans linger over the years, past the grim immediacy of the day when a death notice arrived via telegram or by solemn military detail, or the day when a soldier, sailor, airman, or marine was buried in a lonely cemetery. The faces, too, will often be quite poignant in their immediacy and, for lack of a better word, *recognizability*: these are American faces. These are East Tennessee faces. These could be your neighbors' faces.

★ ★ ★

A word as to sources and style: As noted earlier in the acknowledgments, many of the stories are originally derived from information first placed on the ETVMA website by a host of sources and contributors. That website has been under development for more than eleven years, with help from not just the aforementioned contributors (to include, in particular, the UT Center for the Study of War and Society's Cynthia Tinker; Dutch researcher and archivist Astrid van Erp; US Air Force veteran and researcher Allen D. Jackson; and long-time ETVMA Board member Jeffrey Berry), but also several retired military members, as well as numerous family members and friends of the deceased. To the extent that the ETVMA website was neither originally intended nor organized to become the basis for this book, we are sometimes at pains to determine exact citations for all the stories and photos selected for inclusion. Hence, please note that we cannot provide exact source citations or footnotes for all accounts, although we are satisfied through our own research and the assistance of the ETVMA's contributors who have labored to corroborate details as to the accuracy of the stories.

Also, many of the documents that have been subsequently added to the website—and which are also reflected in many of the biographies in this book—are ones that were available until recently only at the National Archives and Record Administration's facilities or at the National Personnel Records Center (formerly, the Military Personnel Records Center) in St. Louis, Missouri. These documents are now available online for a modest subscription fee from the "Fold3" military records project, an affiliate of the Ancestry.com genealogy service.[2] They run the gamut, from draft notices, unit rosters, and duty logs to Quartermaster Corps orders and chits for transportation of repatriated remains from overseas to the deceased service members' homes. Due to the relatively high volume of documents accessed from Fold3 by the ETVMA research team, sources and footnotes for these documents are not provided.

Explanations as to several stylistic conventions that we have adopted follow. First, whenever possible, the name of the deceased service member's town or city is listed, with the relevant county following in parentheses. Also, apart from correcting minor grammatical errors, all quotations from books, newspapers, and other sources are left as they were originally provided. The standard abbreviation for US Navy vessels is rendered as "USS" in this book, without periods.

Each of the stories recounted in this book will help to bring home the scope and magnitude of the ways America's wars and conflicts since the First World War have shaped the farms, towns, and cities of East Tennessee, and how the deaths of the region's soldiers, sailors, airmen, and marines have left their sometimes unseen—but nevertheless indelible—marks on generations to follow. This book concludes with the Roll Call of Honor, a comprehensive list of all 6,262 names currently inscribed on the granite pillars of the East Tennessee Veterans Memorial. The lists are arranged in order of conflict beginning with World War I and alphabetically by county.

The authors trust that this book will be a valuable resource to military historians, historians and students of Tennessee (especially East Tennessee) history, and genealogists, and offer a wealth of useful information to general readers. At the same time, it is the authors' fond hope that this book will serve as a cherished remembrance for family, friends, and loved ones of the lives and service of a legion of East Tennesseans who answered the call and made the ultimate sacrifice. If this book helps to keep the memories of these fellow citizens alive for future generations, further honoring the sacrifices of those men and women from or connected to this region, it will have provided great satisfaction to the authors and to the East Tennessee Veterans Memorial Association.

John B. Romeiser and Jack H. McCall Jr.

ACKNOWLEDGMENTS

A significant portion of the quoted material and many of the photographs in this book have been taken directly from the East Tennessee Veterans Memorial Association website, where they were submitted by family members, friends, genealogists, military veterans, and historians during the past eleven years.[1] Whenever possible, credit has been given in the text to the individuals and publications that originally provided these materials or shared them with the ETVMA. The inspiration for this book is in large part due to those who have worked tirelessly to make our online records such a rich, vital, and ever-expanding resource. Their online presence on our website is important, but, at the same time, providing a more permanent record in the form of a published work, via this book, strikes us as especially appealing and more of a long-lasting resource to be available to many.

Especially valuable resources have been the articles published in two of Knoxville's newspapers, specifically, the Knoxville *Journal*, which is no longer in print, and the *Knoxville News Sentinel*. This coverage began during the First World War and lasted through the more recent conflicts in the Middle East. We have also drawn upon reporting done by WBIR television, an NBC affiliate, especially the excellent "Service and Sacrifice" series launched in 2008 and moderated by anchorman John Becker, as well as a timely series on the Medal of Honor recipients of East Tennessee, which coincided with the national Medal of Honor Convention that convened in Knoxville in autumn 2014.[2]

Several individuals and staunch supporters who stand out in terms of their research efforts and major contributions to this book are Cynthia Tinker of the University of Tennessee's Center for the Study of War and Society, and Astrid van Erp, a volunteer researcher from the Netherlands who has been of inestimable value in terms of her painstaking work. Ms. Tinker, a US Air Force veteran and University of Tennessee staff member, was instrumental in identifying the initial roll of names to be included on the memorial at its onset; besides being critical to the success of ETVMA, her work was truly a labor of love and devotion to Tennessee and its veterans. Ms. van Erp is closely associated with the Fields of Honor Database, which has as its mission the compilation of information and photographs for all those buried or listed on the Wall of the Missing at the American Battle Monuments Commission cemeteries in Margraten, Netherlands; Henri-Chapelle,

Belgium; and Ardennes, Belgium. She has spent a considerable amount of her personal time verifying and adding documentation to the ETVMA website (especially as to East Tennessee's fallen in the World War II European Theater) from her own research. Jeffrey Berry, a longtime board member of the East Tennessee Veterans Memorial Association, also deserves special recognition: he has utilized his professional network of contacts in the funeral home industry to uncover information that has often been unavailable through traditional channels. Finally, Allen D. Jackson, a retired US Air Force service member, historian for the Tennessee Veterans Memorial Foundation, and researcher for several other organizations in the Tri-Cities area of upper East Tennessee, has, in many respects, been a co-contributor and supporter of this project from the very beginning. Scores of the accounts of service members chronicled here owe their existence to his dogged and detailed research. If we have failed to give Allan due credit where such credit is due, we ask for his forgiveness and understanding.

Likewise, we hereby express our appreciation to all who have contributed support, funding, materials, guidance, suggestions, and vision to the ETVMA and the memorial over the years. That list must include Kimberly Lauth; the members of the Board of the East Tennessee Veterans Memorial, who are listed in an appendix; architect Lee Ingram; Mike Fowler for his very significant role in the design of the landscape and hardscape; our webmaster, George Middlebrooks; the political leadership of both Knoxville and Knox County, Tennessee; the federal Congressional leadership of this district and of Tennessee for their crucial assistance in the early days of the project; and, last but certainly by no means least, the late Colonel William (Bill) Felton, who was the inspiration and vision behind the memorial, and his family.

The ongoing financial support of the East Tennessee Veterans Memorial provided by numerous board members, individual contributors and donors, and businesses over the years—to include support of the annual Medal of Honor Evening each May, with each dinner focusing on one of East Tennessee's fourteen Medal of Honor recipients—is also highly gratifying and has contributed immeasurably to the care, maintenance, and ongoing success of the memorial and its operations.

Our thanks are due in no small part to Scot Danforth, director of the University of Tennessee Press, to copyeditor Meg Olsen, and to the UT Press staff, who helped bring this manuscript to print; to Professor G. Kurt Piehler, director of Florida State University's Institute on World War II and the Human Experience and also the editor of UT Press's *Legacies of War* book series; and to UT Press's two independent readers—Dr. Lisa M. Budreau, military historian, author, and Senior Curator of Military History of the Tennessee State Museum; and Dr. Carroll Van West, the Tennessee State Historian—whose comments and suggestions added immeasurably to the quality and professionalism of this work.

Finally, co-author Jack McCall adds his own note of thanks and appreciation to his family for their cheerfulness and willingness to let him turn his time and talents outside of work and family life to assist in telling the story of the memorial and the souls that it strives to honor; and to Shelley Ward for her kind and cheerful assistance with word processing and formatting several sections of the manuscript. He also wishes to convey his deep appreciation to his colleague and friend, lead author John Romeiser—not only for the significant efforts he took in writing and re-searching the bulk of this work (photographs included), but also for his steady work in helping develop and curate the ETVMA's website, which has been a fruitful source for many of the stories and vignettes included in this book.

To each of these friends, supporters, colleagues, and allies, the authors express their abiding gratitude and appreciation.

The ETVMA's board members and officers, as of the date of this manuscript, are:

Scott Suchomski, President
Tim Eichhorn, Vice President
Charles Harr, Treasurer
Jenny Testerman, Secretary
Jeffrey Berry
Michael Crawford
Joleen Dewald
Ryan K. Dobbs
Logan Hickman
Eddie Mannis
Wes Stowers
Joe Sutter
George Wallace

UNCOMMON VALOR
The East Tennessee Medal of Honor Recipients

They went with songs to the battle, they were young,

Straight of limb, true of eye, steady and aglow.

They were staunch to the end against odds uncounted;

They fell with their faces to the foe.

They shall grow not old, as we that are left grow old:

Age shall not weary them, nor the years condemn.

At the going down of the sun and in the morning

We will remember them.

—From "For the Fallen" by Laurence Binyon

While memorializing the East Tennessee dead of America's armed conflicts and wars since World War I, the East Tennessee Veterans Memorial also honors the memories of those East Tennesseans who have received America's greatest military honor: the Medal of Honor.

The Medal of Honor is the highest award for valor in action against an enemy force that can be bestowed upon an individual serving in the armed services of the United States of America. It is generally presented to its recipients by the president of the United States of America, doing so in the name of the US Congress. Hence, it is occasionally called the Congressional Medal of Honor, although this is a misnomer; properly, its title is simply the Medal of Honor. Since 1918, its regulations specify that the Medal of Honor can only be presented to persons who, "while an officer or enlisted man . . . shall hereafter, in action involving actual conflict with an enemy, distinguish himself conspicuously by gallantry and intrepidity at the risk of his life above and beyond the call of duty."

Out of its 3,496 recipients to date (including 621 Medal of Honor holders who have received the decoration posthumously), fourteen holders of the Medal of Honor were from East Tennessee.

Of the fourteen, Milo Lemert, Alexander Bonnyman, Elbert Kinser, Troy McGill, Ray Duke, and Mitchell Stout received their Medals of Honor posthumously; of these, coincidentally, two men (Kinser and Stout) died in the same manner, by falling on an enemy hand grenade to save their comrades' lives. Among the fourteen are two East Tennesseans, Buck Karnes and Calvin Ward, who received the medal for a shared action, a joint attack they led on a German Hindenburg Line position in autumn 1918.

Also among the fourteen is one of America's greatest war heroes and most famous Medal of Honor recipients, and one of the Great War's most well-known enlisted soldiers, Alvin C. York.

In recognition of the heroism, service, and sacrifice, of these men, the ETVMA annually recognizes one of the fourteen East Tennessee recipients with a Medal of Honor Dinner held in early May. The ETVMA served as one of the leading sponsors for the Annual Conven-

tion of the Congressional Medal of Honor Society in 2014, and the East Tennessee Veterans Memorial served as the backdrop for several activities for that convention. The memorial also served as a public visitation location for the remains of Medal of Honor recipient First Lieutenant Alexander "Sandy" Bonnyman Jr. in September 2015, after his remains were located on the Pacific atoll of Tarawa, almost seventy-two years after he fell there on November 22, 1943.

Numerous books have been written on the Medal of Honor and its individual recipients. Because of the wide availability of other, more detailed sources on most of these men and their life experiences than space permits in this book, what follows is essentially a précis of their life experiences, along with the relevant Medal of Honor citation for the combat actions that led to each man's recognition.[1]

WORLD WAR I

Sergeant James E. (Buck) Karnes was born on July 20, 1889, in Arlington, Tennessee, and died of natural causes on July 7, 1966. He was from Knoxville (Knox) and served with Company D of the 117th Infantry, 30th Infantry Division, in Belgium and Northern France. He is buried at Greenwood Cemetery in Knoxville. Karnes's Medal of Honor citation reads as follows for the actions he and a fellow Medal of Honor recipient took in assaulting a Hindenburg Line machine gun position. While the citation is brief, it gives a hint of the violence of this short but desperate foray: "Near Estrées, France, October 8, 1918: During an advance, his company was held up by a machine gun, which was enfilading the line. Accompanied by another soldier [editors' note: this was his

Sergeant James E. (Buck) Karnes.

First Sergeant Milo Lemert at his home in Fort Wayne, Indiana, enjoying a well-deserved leave.

Near Bellicourt, France, September 29, 1918: Seeing that the left flank of his company was held up, he located the enemy machine gun emplacement, which had been causing heavy casualties. In the face of heavy fire he rushed it single-handed, killing the entire crew with grenades. Continuing along the enemy trench in advance of the company, he reached another emplacement, which he also charged, silencing the gun with grenades. A third machine gun emplacement opened up on him from the left and with similar skill and bravery he destroyed this also. Later, in company with another sergeant, he attacked a fourth machine gun nest, being killed as he reached the parapet of the emplacement. His courageous action in destroying in turn four enemy machine gun nests prevented many casualties among his company and very materially aided in achieving the objective.

friend and fellow Medal of Honor recipient for this same action, Calvin J. Ward], he advanced against this position and succeeded in reducing the nest by killing three and capturing seven of the enemy and their guns."

First Sergeant Milo Lemert was born in Marshalltown, Iowa, on March 25, 1890. He was a farmer before his enlistment on June 25, 1917, at Crossville (Cumberland), Tennessee. He trained at Camp Sevier, South Carolina, and Camp Merritt, New Jersey. Lemert served with Company G, 119th Infantry, 30th Division. He sailed to Europe on May 11, 1918, arriving on May 26, 1918. Lemert was killed in action at Bellicourt, France, on September 29, 1918, during the action for which he would posthumously receive the Medal of Honor, and he was buried at Crossville City Cemetery, Crossville, Cumberland County, on July 31, 1921. He was the husband of Nellie V. Lemert of Crossville. Lemert's Medal of Honor citation reads:

Sergeant Edward R. Talley was born on September 8, 1890, at Russellville (Hamblen), Tennessee. He served with Company L of the 117th Infantry Regiment, 30th Division, in Belgium and France. He died of natural causes on December 14, 1950, and is buried at Bent Creek Cemetery, Whitesburg, Hamblen County.

Like each of the preceding citations, and much like several others to follow, Talley's citation is quite brief. Even in its brevity, it gives the reader a clear sense that many actions which gave rise to conduct and bravery meriting the Medal of Honor in the First World War were the result of the "doughboys'" valiant—and often desperate—efforts to silence the curse of Allied infantrymen across the Western Front, the Germans' hated Maxim machine gun: "Near Ponchaux, France, October 7, 1918: Undeterred by seeing several comrades killed in attempting to put a hostile machine gun nest out of action, Sgt. Talley attacked the position single-handed. Armed only with a rifle, he rushed the

Private Calvin John Ward.

Corporal Alvin C. York.

nest in the face of intense enemy fire, killed or wounded at least 6 of the crew, and silenced the gun. When the enemy attempted to bring forward another gun and ammunition he drove them back by effective fire from his rifle."

Private Calvin John Ward was born on October 30, 1889, in Greene County and died on December 15, 1967.[2] He was from Morristown and served with Company K of the 117th Infantry, 30th Infantry Division, in Belgium and Northern France. He is buried at Glenwood Cemetery in Bristol, Tennessee. Ward's brief Medal of Honor citation mirrors that of his friend Sergeant Buck Karnes, who as noted earlier teamed up with Ward to fight the action for which both received the Medal of Honor: "Near Estrées, France, October 8, 1918: During an advance, Pvt. Ward's company was held up by a machinegun, which was enfilading the line. Accompanied by a noncommissioned officer,

he advanced against this post and succeeded in reducing the nest by killing three and capturing seven of the enemy and their guns."

Corporal Alvin C. York was born on December 13, 1887, in Pall Mall (Fentress), Tennessee, and died on September 2, 1964, in Nashville. He was the son of William Uriah York and Mary Elizabeth Brooks and the husband of Grace (his beloved "Miss Gracie") Williams. York served with Company G of the 328th Infantry Regiment, 82nd Division. He died of natural causes and was buried at Wolf River Cemetery, Pall Mall.

Originally a conscientious objector at the time he was drafted to serve, York went so far as to file a draft appeal with the local draft board in Fentress County. The well-known 1941 Warner Brothers movie *Sergeant York* made the East Tennessee farmer perhaps the most famous of all the doughboys. Gary Cooper won an Oscar for the movie's title role. The movie shows York coming of age in his home valley, then going off to fight the Germans in France. The brevity of York's citation is nevertheless suggestive of the astonishing deeds of his largely (but not entirely) single-handed action early in the Meuse-Argonne Offensive, along a machine gun-studded French valley: "Near Chatel-Chéhéry, France, October 8, 1918: After his platoon had suffered heavy casualties and three other noncommissioned officers had become casualties, Cpl. York assumed command. Fearlessly leading seven men, he charged with great daring a machinegun nest which was pouring deadly and incessant fire upon his platoon. In this heroic feat the machinegun nest was taken, together with four officers and one hundred twenty-eight men and several guns."

Omitted from the sparse text of the citation is the fact that, in the process of this incredible firefight, York famously used the turkey-hunting skills he had learned in Pall Mall to knock off the German gunners in sequence. Further omitted is the fact that Corporal (later Sergeant) York—accompanied by seven other doughboys, who had watched him and supported him during his assault, after nine other Americans, including York's closest Army buddy, Murray Savage, had been cut down by vicious German fire—marched 132 prisoners back to the American lines.

Upon York's return to his unit, his brigade commander, Brigadier General Julian R. Lindsey, supposedly said, "Well, York, I hear you have captured the whole damn German army." York's reply was brief but priceless: "No, sir; I got only 132." York's actions silenced a substantial number of German machine guns, enabling the 328th Infantry to renew its attack to seize a critical railroad line essential for German resupply in that region of the Meuse-Argonne sector, and aiding AEF units seeking to free the equally famous "Lost Battalion" of the 77th Division, isolated and cut off behind German lines in the same general sector of the Argonne Forest.

After his famed action on the ridges outside Chatel-Chéhéry, Alvin York became one of the most highly decorated US and Allied enlisted men of the Great War. When later asked by General Lindsey how this action was possible without himself becoming a casualty, York responded simply and humbly: "A higher power than man guided and watched over me and told me what to do."

WORLD WAR II

First Lieutenant Alexander Bonnyman Jr. was born in Atlanta, Georgia, on May 2, 1910, and grew up in Knoxville (Knox), the son of Scottish immigrant and industrialist Alexander

First Lieutenant Alexander Bonnyman Jr.

Bonnyman Sr., who was the chairman of the Blue Diamond Coal Co. After attending the J. A. Thackston School in Knoxville and, later, boarding school in New Jersey, the younger Bonnyman, who was known as "Sandy," played on the football team at Princeton University. He was briefly an aviation cadet in the Army Air Corps in the early 1930s but "washed out" before earning his pilot's wings. He later married, had three daughters, and bought a copper mine in New Mexico before entering military service in World War II in the Marine Corps.

Bonnyman, a combat engineer officer, landed on the South Pacific island of Betio, one of the small islands comprising the Tarawa atoll, on November 20, 1943, as a member of the Shore Party of the 2nd Battalion, 8th Marines, 2nd Marine Division. On the third day of fighting at Tarawa, Bonnyman led an ad hoc demolition team in assaulting a sizeable Japanese bomb shelter. He was eventually able to reach the top of the shelter and help flush out several of the enemy. As the Japanese began to fight back, Bonnyman remained in a forward position and was eventually killed, but not before he had killed several Japanese troops.

He was buried on Betio, but the site of his burial was lost for many years; at one point, it was claimed that his remains had been buried at sea. In 2015, Sandy Bonnyman's remains were finally located on Betio by the non-profit History Flight group, and his remains were brought back to Knoxville for burial next to his parents in Berry Highland Memorial Cemetery on September 27 of that year.[3] Sandy Bonnyman's Medal of Honor citation reads as follows:

> For conspicuous gallantry and intrepidity at the risk of his life above and beyond the call of duty during the assault against enemy Japanese-held Tarawa in the Gilbert Islands, 20–22 November 1943.

Acting on his own initiative when assault troops were pinned down at the far end of Betio Pier by the overwhelming fire of Japanese shore batteries, 1st Lt. Bonnyman repeatedly defied the blasting fury of the enemy bombardment to organize and lead the besieged men over the long, open pier to the beach and then, voluntarily obtaining flame throwers and demolitions, organized his pioneer shore party into assault demolitionists and directed the blowing of several hostile installations before the close of D-day.

Determined to effect an opening in the enemy's strongly organized defense line the following day, he voluntarily crawled approximately 40 yards forward of our lines and placed demolitions in the entrance of a large Japanese emplacement as the initial move in his planned attack against the heavily garrisoned, bombproof installation which was stubbornly resisting despite the destruction early in the action of a large number of Japanese who had been inflicting heavy casualties on our forces and holding up our advance.

Withdrawing only to replenish his ammunition, he led his men in a renewed assault, fearlessly exposing himself to the merciless slash of hostile fire as he stormed the formidable bastion, directed the placement of demolition charges in both entrances and seized the top of the bombproof position, flushing more than 100 of the enemy who were instantly cut down, and effecting the annihilation of approximately 150 troops inside the emplacement. Assailed by additional Japanese after he had gained his objective, he made a heroic stand on the edge of the structure, defending his strategic position with indomitable determination in the face of the desperate charge and killing three of the enemy before he fell, mortally wounded.

By his dauntless fighting spirit, unrelenting aggressiveness and forceful leadership throughout three days of unremitting, violent battle, 1st Lt. Bonnyman had inspired his

Staff Sergeant Raymond H. Cooley.

a hand grenade. The enemy, however, threw the grenade back at him before it could explode. Arming a second grenade, he held it for several seconds of the safe period and then hurled it into the enemy position, where it exploded instantaneously, destroying the gun and crew. He then moved toward the remaining gun, throwing grenades into enemy foxholes as he advanced. Inspired by his actions, one squad of his platoon joined him. After he had armed another grenade and was preparing to throw it into the second machinegun position, six enemy soldiers rushed at him. Knowing he could not dispose of the armed grenade without injuring his comrades, because of the intermingling in close combat of the men of his platoon and the enemy in the melee which ensued, he deliberately covered the grenade with his body and was severely wounded as it exploded.

By his heroic actions, S/Sgt. Cooley not only silenced a machinegun and so inspired his fellow soldiers that they pressed the attack and destroyed the remaining

men to heroic effort, enabling them to beat off the counterattack and break the back of hostile resistance in that sector for an immediate gain of 400 yards with no further casualties to our forces in this zone. He gallantly gave his life for his country.

Army Staff Sergeant Raymond H. Cooley served with B Company of the 27th Infantry, 25th Infantry Division, in the Pacific Theater of Operations. He was born on May 7, 1916, and was killed in an automobile accident on March 12, 1947. He was thirty-one. Cooley is buried at Cumberland View Cemetery, Kimball, Marion County, Tennessee. His Medal of Honor citation reads as follows:

> Near Lumboy, Luzon, Philippine Islands: February 24, 1945. He was a platoon guide in an assault on a camouflaged entrenchment defended by machineguns, rifles, and mortars. When his men were pinned down by two enemy machineguns, he voluntarily advanced under heavy fire to within twenty yards of one of the guns and attacked it with

Technical Sergeant Charles H. Coolidge, in later years.

enemy emplacements, but also, in complete disregard of his own safety, accepted certain injury and possible loss of life to avoid wounding his comrades.

Technical Sergeant Charles H. Coolidge, of Signal Mountain (Hamilton), Tennessee, was born on August 4, 1921, and served with the 141st Infantry, 36th Infantry Division, in Europe. At the time of this writing, the only still-living Medal of Honor recipient from Tennessee, Coolidge did not receive his medal from the president upon his return to the United States—Franklin D. Roosevelt having died in April 1945—so on June 18 of that year, he was presented with the Medal of Honor by Lieutenant General Wade H. Haislip. Coolidge's citation describes a struggle in the Vosges Mountains in Eastern France that stretched over four days, as the Army edged closer to the Rhine River and Nazi Germany:

> Leading a section of heavy machineguns supported by 1 platoon of Company K, he took a position near Hill 623, east of Belmont-sur-Buttant, France, on 24 October 1944, with the mission of covering the right flank of the 3d Battalion and supporting its action. T/Sgt. Coolidge went forward with a sergeant of Company K to reconnoiter positions for coordinating the fires of the light and heavy machineguns.
>
> They ran into an enemy force in the woods estimated to be an infantry company. T/Sgt. Coolidge, attempting to bluff the Germans by a show of assurance and boldness, called upon them to surrender, whereupon the enemy opened fire. With his carbine, T/Sgt. Coolidge wounded two of them. There being no officer present with the force, T/Sgt. Coolidge at once assumed command.
>
> Many of the men were replacements recently arrived; this was their first experience under fire. T/Sgt. Coolidge, unmindful of the enemy fire delivered at close range, walked along the position, calming and encouraging his men and directing their fire. The attack was thrown back. Through 25 and 26 October the enemy launched repeated attacks against the position of this combat group but each was repulsed due to T/Sgt. Coolidge's able leadership.
>
> On 27 October, German infantry, supported by two tanks, made a determined attack on the position. The area was swept by enemy small arms, machinegun, and tank fire. T/Sgt. Coolidge armed himself with a bazooka and advanced to within twenty-five yards of the tanks. His bazooka failed to function and he threw it aside. Securing all the hand grenades he could carry, he crawled forward and inflicted heavy casualties on the advancing enemy.
>
> Finally, it became apparent that the enemy, in greatly superior force, supported by tanks, would overrun the position. T/Sgt. Coolidge, displaying great coolness and courage, directed and conducted an orderly withdrawal, being himself the last to leave the position. As a result of T/Sgt. Coolidge's heroic and superior leadership, the mission of this combat group was accomplished throughout 4 days of continuous fighting against numerically superior enemy troops in rain and cold and amid dense woods.

A highway and a park in Chattanooga are named for Coolidge.

Corporal Paul Bert Huff, from Cleveland (Bradley), Tennessee, was born on June 18, 1923, and died on September 21, 1994. He is buried at Hillcrest Memorial Gardens in Cleveland.

Huff was a squad leader in Europe with A Company, 509th Parachute Infantry Battalion, which had been attached to the US 5th Army. His platoon was staked out on the Anzio beachhead after making an amphibious landing on January 22, 1944. During the evening of February 8, the Germans took a small hill across from the American positions near the village of Carano and began shelling the GIs early the next morning. Huff volunteered to lead a six-man patrol to check out the Germans' exact location and strength. His Medal of Honor citation is a reminder of the fierce determination of the Allies to escape the brutal killing fields of the Anzio beachhead and its nearby ring of hills and eventually move to liberate Rome from the Nazis on June 6, 1944, notably the same day as the Allied landings in Normandy, France:

> For conspicuous gallantry and intre-pidity at risk of life above and beyond the call of duty, in action on 8 February 1944, near Carano, Italy. Cpl. Huff volunteered to lead a six-man patrol with the mission of determining the location and strength of an enemy unit which was delivering fire on the exposed right flank of his company. The terrain over which he had to travel consisted of exposed, rolling ground, affording the en-emy excellent visibility.
>
> As the patrol advanced, its members were subjected to small arms and machine-gun fire and a concentration of mortar fire, shells bursting within five to ten yards of them and bullets striking the ground at their feet. Moving ahead of his patrol, Cpl. Huff drew fire from three enemy machineguns and a 20mm weapon. Realizing the danger confronting his patrol, he advanced alone under deadly fire through a minefield and arrived at a point within seventy-five yards of the nearest machinegun position.
>
> Under direct fire from the rear machine-gun, he crawled the remaining seventy-five yards to the closest emplacement, killed the crew with his submachine gun and de-stroyed the gun. During this act he fired from a kneeling position which drew fire from other positions, enabling him to estimate correctly the strength and location of the enemy. Still under concentrated fire, he re-turned to his patrol and led his men to safety.
>
> As a result of the information he gained, a patrol in strength sent out that afternoon,

Corporal Paul Bert Huff.

> one group under the leadership of Cpl. Huff, succeeded in routing an enemy company of 125 men, killing twenty-seven Germans and capturing twenty-one others, with a loss of only three patrol members. Cpl. Huff's in-trepid leadership and daring combat skill reflect the finest traditions of the American infantryman.

Paul Huff was the first American para-trooper to be decorated with the Medal of Honor, and he opted to have the medal pre-sented to him in newly-liberated Rome by the US 5th Army's commander, General Mark Clark, surrounded by his 509th buddies and comrades-in-arms. Huff remained in the Army after the war, rising to the rank of command sergeant major; he retired from active duty after having served with the 1st Brigade of the 101st Airborne Division in Vietnam and as the command sergeant major of the US Third Army. A parkway in his hometown of Cleveland is named for him, as is an Army Reserve center in Nashville.

Sergeant Elbert L. Kinser was from Greeneville (Greene), Tennessee. He was born on October 21, 1922. He enlisted in the military in December 1942, serving with the 3rd Battalion, 1st Marines, 1st Marine Division, the famed "Old Breed" division of the Marines. After he was graduated from boot camp at Parris Island, South Carolina, the young Marine deployed to the South Pacific and fought in battles ranging from Guadalcanal to Peleliu. By the spring of 1945, he had been promoted to the rank of sergeant and was the leader of a rifle squad. He was killed in action with Japanese forces on May 4, 1945, after having survived the first month of the bloodbath at Okinawa. Kinser is buried at Solomon Lutheran Church Cemetery, Greeneville, Greene County.

US forces claimed victory at Okinawa in late June 1945. In August, the war ended, thanks partly to the atomic bombings of Hiroshima and Nagasaki—attacks that were themselves partly influenced by the extensive casualties suffered on Okinawa and the expectation that these heavy American losses would pale by comparison to the anticipated losses of an invasion of Japan's home islands.[4] The war was concluded, and men returned safely home just three months after Kinser made the ultimate sacrifice for his country. His Medal of Honor citation reflects the incredible selflessness of his sacrificial deed:

> For conspicuous gallantry and intrepidity at the risk of his life above and beyond the call of duty while acting as leader of a Rifle Platoon, serving with Company I, 3d Battalion, 1st Marines, 1st Marine Division, in action against Japanese forces on Okinawa Shima in the Ryukyu Chain, 4 May 1945. Taken under sudden, close attack by hostile troops entrenched on the reverse slope while moving up a strategic ridge along which his platoon was holding newly won positions, Sgt. Kinser engaged the enemy in a fierce hand grenade battle.
>
> Quick to act when a Japanese grenade landed in the immediate vicinity, Sgt. Kinser unhesitatingly threw himself on the deadly missile, absorbing the full charge of the shattering explosion in his own body and thereby protecting his men from serious injury and possible death. Stouthearted and indomitable, he had yielded his own chance of survival that his comrades might live to carry on the relentless battle against a fanatic enemy.
>
> His courage, cool decision and valiant spirit of self-sacrifice in the face of certain death sustained and enhanced the highest traditions of the U.S. Naval Service. He gallantly gave his life for his country.

Sergeant Troy A. McGill was from South Knoxville (Knox), where he was born on July 15, 1914. He enlisted in Ada, Oklahoma, after his family moved there, and served with G Troop of the 5th Cavalry Regiment, 1st Cavalry

Sergeant Elbert L. Kinser.

Sergeant Troy A. McGill.

of eight men, occupied a revetment which bore the brunt of a furious attack by approximately 200 drink-crazed enemy troops.

Although covered by crossfire from machineguns on the right and left flank he could receive no support from the remainder of our troops stationed at his rear. All members of the squad were killed or wounded except Sgt. McGill and another man, whom he ordered to return to the next revetment. Courageously resolved to hold his position at all cost, he fired his weapon until it ceased to function.

Then, with the enemy only five yards away, he charged from his foxhole in the face of certain death and clubbed the enemy with his rifle in hand-to-hand combat until he was killed. At dawn 105 enemy dead were found around his position. Sgt. McGill's intrepid stand was an inspiration to his comrades and a and a decisive factor in the defeat of a fanatical enemy.

Master Sergeant Charles L. McGaha was from Cosby (Cocke). He was born on February 26, 1914, and, tragically, was killed by a robber at his taxi company in Columbus, Georgia, on August 8, 1984. He was seventy years old when he was murdered. McGaha served with G Company of the 35th Infantry Regiment, 25th Infantry Division, in the Pacific during the February 7, 1945, action near the village of Lupao on Luzon, in the Philippines, for which he received the Medal of Honor. McGaha's citation omits the fact that he was also a survivor of the attack on Schofield Barracks at Pearl Harbor on December 7, 1941. To have survived that infamous attack, then, four years later, emerge from a vicious tank battle only to die years later at the hands of a common criminal is a supremely sad irony. He is buried at Union Cemetery, Newport, Cocke County.

Division, in the Pacific. He is buried at Knoxville National Cemetery. In his honor, a stretch of Interstate 40 through Knox, Sevier, Jefferson, and Cocke Counties is named the Troy A. McGill Memorial Highway. On March 4, 1944, McGill fell in action with the Japanese on Los Negros in the Admiralty Islands, a lesser-known engagement that was part of General Douglas MacArthur's "island-hopping" campaign in the southwest Pacific and advance towards the liberation of the Philippines. His Medal of Honor citation reads:

> For conspicuous gallantry and intrepidity above and beyond the call of duty in action with the enemy at Los Negros Island, Admiralty Group, on 4 March 1944. In the early morning hours Sgt. McGill, with a squad

He displayed conspicuous gallantry and intrepidity. His platoon and one other from

Company G were pinned down in a roadside ditch by heavy fire from five Japanese tanks supported by ten machineguns and a platoon of riflemen. When one of his men fell wounded forty yards away, he unhesitatingly crossed the road under a hail of bullets and moved the man seventy-five yards to safety. Although he had suffered a deep arm wound, he returned to his post.

Finding the platoon leader seriously wounded, he assumed command and rallied his men. Once more he braved the enemy fire to go to the aid of a litter party removing another wounded soldier. A shell exploded in their midst, wounding him in the shoulder and killing two of the party. He picked up the remaining man, carried him to cover, and then moved out in front deliberately to draw the enemy fire while the American forces, thus protected, withdrew to safety.

When the last man had gained the new position, he rejoined his command and there collapsed from loss of blood and exhaustion. M/Sgt. McGaha set an example of courage and leadership in keeping with the highest traditions of the service.

KOREA

A veteran of World War II, Sergeant First Class Sergeant Ray E. Duke was a member of Company C, 1st Battalion, 21st Infantry Regiment, 24th Infantry Division. He was born on May 9, 1923, and was from Whitwell (Marion). He was seriously injured in Korea on March 7, 1951, and returned to duty on March 23, 1951. On April 26, 1951, near Mugok, Korea, when he learned that several of his men were isolated by the enemy, he led a daring assault to recover his cut-off troops. Although severely wounded by mortar fire, he continued to direct his platoon's fire upon the advancing enemy. When the platoon was forced to withdraw, he directed his men to leave him and get to safety. He later died while a prisoner of war—ironically enough, on Veterans Day—on November 11, 1951. His remains were repatriated, and he is buried at the Chattanooga National Cemetery. Ray Duke's posthumous Medal of Honor citation is as follows:

> Sfc. Duke, a member of Company C, distinguished himself by conspicuous gallantry and outstanding courage above and beyond the call of duty in action against the enemy. Upon learning that several of his men were isolated and heavily engaged in an area yielded by his platoon when ordered to withdraw, he led a small force in a daring assault which recovered the position and the beleaguered men. Another enemy attack in strength resulted in numerous casualties but Sfc. Duke, although wounded by mortar fragments, calmly moved along his platoon line to coordinate fields of fire and to urge his men to hold firm in the bitter encounter.

Master Sergeant Charles L. McGaha.

Sergeant First Class Sergeant Ray E. Duke.

VIETNAM

Sergeant Mitchell William Stout was born on February 24, 1950, in Knoxville (Knox). His hometown later became Lenoir City (Loudon), and he also counted Sanford, North Carolina, as a home. He entered service in Raleigh, North Carolina, and served with Battery C, 1st Battalion, 44th Artillery, 108th Artillery Group, I Field Force Artillery, in South Vietnam. He is buried at the Virtue Cemetery, Concord, Knox County.

The action resulting in Stout's posthumous Medal of Honor bears striking similarities between his death in combat and that of Raymond Cooley some twenty-five years earlier, as both men fell on hand grenades to save their buddies from certain death or dismemberment. Stout's death on March 12, 1970, occurred in defense of Firebase Khe Gio, which guarded a bridge

Wounded a second time he received first aid and returned to his position. When the enemy again attacked shortly after dawn, despite his wounds, Sfc. Duke repeatedly braved withering fire to insure maximum defense of each position. Threatened with annihilation and with mounting casualties, the platoon was again ordered to withdraw when Sfc. Duke was wounded a third time in both legs and was unable to walk. Realizing that he was impeding the progress of two comrades who were carrying him from the hill, he urged them to leave him and seek safety. He was last seen pouring devastating fire into the ranks of the onrushing assailants.

The consummate courage, superb leadership, and heroic actions of Sfc. Duke, displayed during intensive action against overwhelming odds, reflect the highest credit upon himself, the infantry, and the U.S. Army.

Sergeant Mitchell William Stout.

astride the vital Route 9 near Cam Lộ and an enormous karst outcropping known as "The Rockpile," Route 9 being a critical supply artery for South Vietnamese and US forces running through central South Vietnam. Stout's citation reads:

> Sgt. Stout distinguished himself during an attack by a North Vietnamese Army Sapper company on his unit's firing position at Khe Gio Bridge. Sgt. Stout was in a bunker with members of a searchlight crew when the position came under heavy enemy mortar fire and ground attack. When the intensity of the mortar attack subsided, an enemy grenade was thrown into the bunker. Displaying great courage, Sgt. Stout ran to the grenade, picked it up, and started out of the bunker. As he reached the door, the grenade exploded. By holding the grenade close to his body and shielding its blast, he protected his fellow soldiers in the bunker from further injury or death. Sgt. Stout's conspicuous gallantry and intrepidity in action, at the cost of his own life, are in keeping with the highest tradition of the military service and reflect great credit upon him, his unit and the U.S. Army.

At the date of this writing, Mitchell Stout is the only member of the US Army's Air Defense Artillery to have received the Medal of Honor. The Interstate 75 bridge across the Tennessee River near Loudon is named in his memory, as is the main post gymnasium at Fort Bliss, Oklahoma.

2

THE MEN OF THE 30TH DIVISION IN WORLD WAR I

In a wood they call the Rouge Bouquet

There is a new-made grave to-day,

Built by never a spade nor pick

Yet covered with earth ten metres thick.

There lie many fighting men,

Dead in their youthful prime,

Never to laugh nor love again

Nor taste the Summertime.

For Death came flying through the air

And stopped his flight at the dugout stair,

Touched his prey and left them there. . . .

—From "The Wood called Rouge Bouquet,"
by poet and AEF Sergeant Joyce Kilmer, 165th Infantry,
42nd Division, killed in action in France on July 30, 1918

Tennessee's "volunteer spirit" was vividly demonstrated in the groundswell of enthusiasm that accompanied America's entry into the World War I. Tennessee's National Guard contingents formed a substantial basis of the 30th ("Old Hickory") Division, which served alongside British and Australian troops in breaking the Germans' vaunted Hindenburg Line defensive system at the Saint-Quentin Canal, as well as engaging in fighting at Ypres and in the Somme region.

The 30th Division was created on July 18, 1917, and was formally activated into federal service in August 1917 at Camp Sevier outside Greenville, South Carolina. The division was principally composed of National Guard units from North and South Carolina and Tennessee and was nicknamed after the famed and illustrious soldier and president, Andrew "Old Hickory" Jackson, who was born near the North/South Carolina border and rose to fame in Tennessee, where he provided some regional flavor to the tightly-knit group of soldiers that he led during the Indian wars of the early nineteenth century and at the famed Battle of New Orleans in 1814.

The 30th Division served overseas with the American Expeditionary Forces during World War I and, on September 29, 1918, distinguished itself in the Somme Offensive by smashing its way through the famed and so-called "impregnable" Hindenburg Line, a victory that hastened the end of World War I. The 30th was one of two AEF divisions of the US II Corps, which, unlike most other American divisions, was detached to serve alongside troops of the British Empire in the Ypres area of Belgium and the Somme River region of northern France in the wake of Germany's massive spring 1918 offensives on the Western Front. It fought in several actions alongside British troops near the bitterly contested Belgian town of Ypres and, in late September 1918, was one of the Allied divisions that assaulted the Hindenburg Line at the heavily defended Saint-Quentin Canal near

the French village of Bellicourt. Elements of the Old Hickory Division (including its assigned 55th Field Artillery Brigade) also participated in the Battles of La Selle, St. Mihiel, and the Meuse-Argonne offensive. During these battles, its men garnered twelve Medals of Honor.

After World War I, the 30th Division was deactivated from federal service and its members reverted back to their National Guard roles in their respective states. During World War II, the 30th would again play a pivotal role, both in the Normandy Campaign during the summer of 1944 and during the Battle of the Bulge in late 1944 and early 1945.[1]

Carl D. Brandon was born on September 6, 1897, in Lovelace (Greene). He was the son of Andrew J. Brandon and Cora M. Pierce. He was living in Fall Branch (Washington) with his family when he enlisted in the Tennessee National Guard in Bristol on May 8, 1917. Brandon was assigned to Company H, 3rd Infantry, Tennessee Army National Guard, headquartered at Bristol. He would die in fighting at the Hindenburg Line on October 8, 1918, at the age of nineteen. The following account of Brandon's service is by historian and retired United States Air Force veteran Allen D. Jackson:

The 3rd Infantry, after being called to active federal service, became part of the 117th Infantry Regiment, 59th Infantry Brigade, 30th Infantry Division. Private Brandon stayed with Company H, 2nd Battalion, and was promoted to private first class on September 1. After that, his unit was dispatched to and arrived in Camp Sevier for training on September 8. There, they would join units from North and South Carolina, as well as other elements from Tennessee, to form the core of the 30th Division.

Brandon's skills as a soldier improved and, due to his potential as a leader, he was promoted to corporal on September 18, 1917.

Private Carl D. Brandon.

Brandon departed Camp Sevier on May 5, 1918, with Company H for Camp Merritt, in Cresskill, New Jersey, to await transportation overseas. After boarding the SS *Northumberland* in Brooklyn, they set off for Liverpool, England, on May 11 and arrived on May 23. After disembarking the ship, he and the four infantry regiments of the 30th Division boarded troop trains and were taken to the port cities of Dover and Folkestone for the channel crossing over the next couple of days. Company H arrived at the port city of Calais, France, on the 25th. As the 30th Division's elements arrived piecemeal in France, just as they had done into England, they journeyed the short distance to the various towns and villages known as the Éperlecques Training Area. Brandon was billeted with the 117th at Nortbécourt and began Phase "A" training with the British 39th Division on June 19, 1918.

The training phases that followed under the watchful eyes of British instructors were much the same for all of the subordinate units of the "Old Hickory" Division as they were for Company H and the 117th. Phase "A" initial field training lasted until the morning of July 16. Phase "B" began the same day for the 30th Division, with a three-day march into Belgium. On arriving at the Poperinghe area near Ypres, the 117th was billeted in one of the numerous camps and was integrated over the next month into actual battlefield operations and trench warfare conditions with active combat units. Phase "B" was completed on August 10, and Phase "C," the last training phase, was cancelled and the 30th was declared combat-ready. Operational orders came in on the 14th, and the 30th Division was to relieve the British 33rd Division starting the night of August 16 in the Canal Sector near Ypres, Belgium. The Ypres-Lys Offensive began on August 19, 1918, and the

30th would be in the thick of the fighting to the very end of the war. Brandon and the 30th were given a breathing spell after being relieved from the Ypres-Lys Offensive on September 5 and entrained to the St. Pol area; Companies F, G, and H of the 117th were billeted at Beauvois, France, to resupply, do more training, and get a little rest from all the heavy artillery explosions. On the 17th, the 30th Division made the move to the Puchevillers area, where they came under the operational control of the 4th British Army, as would the American 27th Division, to join in the Somme Offensive of 1918.

Brandon was hit by shrapnel and died of those wounds on October 8, 1918, the first day of the Battle of Montbrehain. He had participated in two unit campaigns—the Ypres-Lys Offensive in Belgium and the Somme Offensive

Private First Class Milburn Moffitt.

in France. Brandon also fought in the Battle of Bellicourt on the Hindenburg Line. He was twenty-one years old and was first interred at the British Military Cemetery at Fricourt, France, and later moved to the Somme American Cemetery, Bony, France, after his parents decided that their son should stay with his brothers in arms.

Private First Class Milburn Moffitt was born in October 1899 in Magnetic City (now known as Buladean), Mitchell County, North Carolina. Moffitt was the son of William M. Moffitt and Sarah E. "Sally" Rominger. He later moved over the mountain with his family to Hampton (Carter), Tennessee. Moffitt was working as a farmer when he and two of his brothers enlisted in the Tennessee National Guard at Hampton on July 18, 1917. He was assigned to Company E, 3rd Tennessee Infantry Regiment, based at Hampton. He stated his age as eighteen years and eight months when he enlisted. In fact, he was only seventeen years and eight months old. Just seven days later, Company E was activated and called into federal service.

Company E, as well as all the other companies in the 3rd Tennessee, deployed to Camp Sevier to form part of the new 30th Division, arriving on September 8, 1917. As noted above, the 3rd was reorganized into the 117th Infantry Regiment under the 30th's 59th Infantry Brigade. Moffitt stayed with Company E, 2nd Battalion.

Like Carl D. Brandon of Company H, Moffitt departed Camp Sevier on May 5, 1918, with Company E for Camp Mills, Long Island, New York, to await transportation overseas. Milburn was killed in action on October 8, 1918, the first assault day of the Battle of Montbrehain, while engaging German forces at Prémont. He had participated in the Ypres-Lys Offensive in

Belgium and the Somme Offensive in France. Milburn also fought in the Battle of Bellicourt on the Hindenburg Line. He was first interred at the British Military Cemetery at Fricourt, France, and later moved to the Somme American Cemetery in Bony, France. After his parents decided that Moffitt should come home, they requested that he be returned to Buladean, North Carolina, for interment but reconsidered afterwards, and he was interred at the Mountain Home National Cemetery on April 19, 1921.

Moffitt's older brother, James Jessie, and his younger brother, Robert Hobart, also served in Company E of the 117th. Robert was wounded in action; like Moffitt, he had "fibbed" about his age, enlisting at age sixteen years and six months old, to serve with his brothers.

Sergeant Claude B. Phillips was born in the town of Loudon (Loudon), Tennessee, but later moved with his family to Knoxville. He died at the age of twenty-three. An article in Knoxville's *Journal and Tribune*, dated October 21, 1918, told of his service and death; the article is representative of many others to follow in Knoxville's and the region's newspapers as the Great War raged:

> Sergt. Claude B. Phillips, aged 23 years, son of Mr. and Mrs. W. L. Phillips, 132 New York avenue, Lonsdale, is officially reported killed in action, during the battle waged by the 117th Infantry against the Huns, September 20. An official telegram from the war department was received Sunday by Mr. and Mrs. Phillips, advising them of the fatality.
>
> Sergt. Phillips enlisted in the machine gun company of the 117th Regiment, commanded by Col. Cary F. Spence, of Knoxville. At the outbreak of the war between the United States and Germany, young Phillips expressed a desire to enter the service. He told his father that he would rather volunteer and enter the service than to be drafted. He was personally acquainted with

Sergeant Claude B. Phillips.

Col. Spence and Capt. Bob McMillan before the organization of the 117th Regiment was started.

Mr. Phillips had worked with his father at local marble mills and became a proficient stone-cutter. He was at one time employed by the Fenton Construction Company and some of his best work was done on the interior of the Holston National Bank, while that building was under construction. Mr. Phillips, father of the dead soldier, came to Knoxville eight years ago and lived in South Knoxville for a long time. He was then employed at the plant of the Ross & Republic Marble Mills.

Sergt. Claude Phillips was born at Loudon, Tennessee and he received a liberal education, having attended the schools at Columbus, Miss., and Tate, Ga. He was a member of Maxwell lodge, Free and Accepted Masons, of Knoxville.

After going to the training camp at Greenville, S.C. [i.e., Camp Sevier], Sergt.

Phillips returned to Knoxville for a visit to his relatives and while here he talked enthusiastically of the part the 117th expected to take in winning the war. Mr. and Mrs. Phillips received a letter from their son in September and recently his mother received a Liberty bond for $100 and an allotment.

Wendell Phillips, a brother, was a member of the 13th U.S. Cavalry that was part of General Pershing's division in Mexico. He is now assigned in the U.S. base hospital at West Baden, Ind. Sergt. Phillips is survived by his parents, one brother, Wendell, and five sisters, as follows Mrs. Will Roberts of Oakwood, Misses Lucille, Maudie, Willie and Katherine Phillips.

After receiving the official notice of his son's death on the battlefield, Mr. Phillips said, "I am proud of the fact that I had a son to sacrifice to help win the just war against the Germans. It is extremely sad to realize that my son has given his life. I may yet have to answer the call to aid in winning the war, that is, if the age limit should be raised."

Phillips was initially buried at the Somme American Cemetery in Bony, France. His body was returned to the United States, and he was buried in Arlington National Cemetery.

Private Claude L. Mingle was born on July 20, 1895, in Maryville (Blount) and was living and working as a machinist for the William J. Oliver plant in Knoxville before entering the service. He was married to Ruby Vineyard. Mingle volunteered his services to the US Army on April 16, 1917, as a member of Company D, 117th Infantry Regiment. He was later transferred to the Machine Gun Company and the Supply Company of the 117th. He took part in the Ypres Defensive and, on September 29, 1918, while assaulting the Hindenburg Line near Bellicourt, he was killed in action. Mingle was awarded the Distinguished Service Cross on December 10, 1918, for conspicuous bravery. His citation reads:

Private Claude L. Mingle.

The President of the United States of America, authorized by Act of Congress, July 9, 1918, takes pride in presenting the Distinguished Service Cross Posthumously to Private Claude L. Mingle ASN 1306628, United States Army, for extraordinary heroism in action while serving with Machine-Gun Company, 117th Infantry Regiment, 30th Division, A.E.F., near Bellicourt, France, 29 September 1918. When enemy machine guns suddenly opened fire on both flanks of his platoon, Private Mingle bravely refused to take cover, but delivered effective rifle fire on the enemy, putting out of action one of the machine guns before he was mortally wounded. War Department, General Orders No. 37 1919.

An article in Knoxville's *Journal and Tribune* dated November 10, 1918, provided addi-

tional details on the circumstances of his death, from quite an unusual source:

Papers taken from the pockets of Private C.L. Mingle, who was recently killed in France, have been forwarded to his widow by Sig. F. Coupland, of the Australian Expeditionary Forces, who found the body on the battlefield.

Following is the letter Mrs. Mingle received from Private Coupland:

"You will no doubt be surprised to have a few lines from me. I felt it my duty to inform you of how your husband met his death, although it grieves me to have to do the same. It was on Sunday, September 29, while the Americans did most excellent work and then opened out to let us through. It was while doing this that I came across your husband, lying dead. He was wounded in the stomach and must have died almost instantly. I took his letters and papers off him and am sending them along with this letter. The American Red Cross was over the battleground later on, so you can rest assured that he will get a decent burial, of which the military authorities no doubt will inform you. As to where he was buried, I am not allowed to mention names or places, as perhaps you are aware, but that is what our authorities do in similar cases."

Private Mingle is buried at the Somme American Cemetery, Bony, France.

Private David (Davie) E. Ott from Rockford (Blount) was born in March 1897. He served with the 119th Infantry Regiment, 30th Division. He died on September 29, 1918, at the age of twenty, but his remains were not recovered. He is listed on the Tablets of the Missing, Somme American Cemetery, Bony, France.

Private Ernest C. Carter was born on November 14, 1895, in Chucky (Greene). He was killed in action in France on October 7, 1918.

Private David (Davie) E. Ott.

Knoxville's *Journal and Tribune* published his last letter to his mother on November 10, 1918, just one day before the declaration of the Armistice ending World War I:

"Somewhere in France. October 1918

"I guess it is with the greatest pleasure in my life that I can now write you. I am well and O.K., except wearied from having no sleep in four days and nights and at least 25 miles on a bike in the past day and night.

"I got to sleep last night for the first time in five nights. I am now at a rest camp. I am just back from a real battle. I suppose you read in the papers of the success of the Australians and Americans on the Hindenburg line. Believe me that is some line and I have been across it and all around the canal. It is at least 200 feet from the top of the bank to the water and has bridges nearly one mile wide.

"You read where the Germans made high explosives out of their dead. I never believed it, but now have seen it with my eyes. One of the vats was captured and there they were, some partly cut up to put in and others had been [there] for days. It was one more sight. It is something to be proud of to come out of such a push. You know everybody had been watching for the Hindenburg line to go down. I hear that the Berlin papers praise the North Carolina, South Carolina and Tennessee troops for their good work.

"We were with the good old Australians, the best fellows in the world, and they think the same of us. We went through all kinds of shell fire. The ground is absolutely torn to pieces and in the towns there is not one

Private Floyd T. Koontz.

Private Francis M. Davis.

Private Grayson Caylor.

brick upon another, so to speak. We were in rain and mud all the time and lots of time the mud was almost knee deep I tried to sleep in the muddy trench with a shelter half under me and the rain coming from the sky. I never

got scared. A piece of shell missed my head only about a foot. It would have cut down a big tree. The experience is enough to make a fellow fear nothing by god. The prisoners looked pleased and would gladly carry back the wounded. I am feeling very well except I have not got well filled yet."

Private Floyd T. Koontz was born in 1896 in Jefferson City (Jefferson) and enlisted in September 1917 as a member of Company B, 117th Infantry Regiment, 30th Division. Camp Gordon, Georgia, and Camp Sevier, South Carolina, were his training stations prior to sailing for France in May 1918. He was killed in action on September 29, 1918, in the first day's fighting on the Hindenburg Line near Bellicourt. He died at the age of twenty-one and is buried at the Somme American Cemetery, Bony, France.

Private Francis M. Davis was from Fentress County (coincidentally, Alvin C. York's home county) and served in Company F of the 117th Infantry. He died of wounds on October 27, 1918, having been evacuated to England. He is buried in Arlington National Cemetery.

Private Grayson Caylor was born in Blount County on June 23, 1896. He served in Company B of the 117th Infantry. He died at the age of twenty-one on October 8, 1918, and is buried at Caylors Chapel Cemetery, Townsend, Blount County.

Sergeant Hugh Johnston Luttrell was born on March 9, 1895, in Knoxville (Knox) and, like several others recounted in this chapter, was killed in action on September 29, 1918, during the first day's combat in the Somme Offensive near Bellicourt. He was a member of Company D of the 117th Infantry after his enlistment on July 23, 1917. He went through training at Camp Sevier and after his arrival in France. In the earlier fighting in Belgium, he was unscathed, only to fall during the first day's combat against

Sergeant Hugh Johnston Luttrell.

the Hindenburg Line. The November 9, 1918, Knoxville *Journal and Tribune* recorded his fate, as well as a connection to one of the Medal of Honor recipients profiled in the preceding chapter:

Sergt. Hugh J. Luttrell, of [C]ompany D, 117th Infantry, was killed in action according to a letter received by his parents, Mr. and Mrs. H. M. Luttrell, 807 North Fourth Avenue, from Sergt. Harry T. McLean, also of Knoxville. Further confirmation of the death was made in a letter from Ernest Karnes [i.e., "Buck" Karnes, who is discussed in this book's chapter on East Tennessee's Medal of Honor recipients] to his mother, Mrs. J. H. Karnes, North Broadway. The actual date of the death and official announcement has not been received by the family of the deceased.

In a recent letter to his family, Sergt. Luttrell, who is in Capt. Harry Custis' company, told of an offer from his captain to send him to officers training camp. Sergt. Luttrell expressed his intention of refusing the offer in order to stay with the men he had under him. He wrote, "My captain told me today he was going to send me to training camp for officers, but I believe that I will turn it down as I love all of the boys and they seem to think the world of me. If I should leave I might never see them again and here I could die with them."

Sergt. Luttrell enlisted in the old Third Tennessee Regiment, which is now the 117th Infantry, in July 1917, and left shortly afterward with Col. Carey F. Spence. In leaving, young Luttrell gave up prospects for a successful business career and left a wide circle of friends in all parts of the city. Although only 23 years of age at the time of his death, he had made a good record for himself by his work in the stock department of the Haynes-Henson Shoe Co. He graduated at the Knoxville High School in 1913 and for some time afterward was connected with the Little River Lumber Company at Elkmont, Tennessee. Following this he spent two years with the Haynes-Henson Company.

Following is the letter received from fellow Sergt. McLean regarding the death of Sergt. Luttrell:

"Dear Mr. Luttrell and Family
I want to extend to you my sympathy over the loss of your dear son and brother. He has given his life for his country and didn't fear going into battle. Hugh was one of the most popular men in this company and he was a friend to all. Always ready to help those who need help. In the loss of Hugh you have lost a noble son and brother and the boys in the company have lost one of their best friends. Your friend, Sergt. Harry T. McLean."

Sergeant J. Auls Fagg was from Maryville (Blount). He too was killed in action on September 29, 1918, during the first day's fighting against the Hindenburg Line and was buried

Corporal John F. Acuff.

Private John L. Bentley.

at Old Piney Cemetery, Maryville. He served with Company B of the 117th Infantry.

Corporal John F. Acuff was born on October 6, 1893, in Ooltewah (Hamilton), then the seat of James County, on October 6, 1893. Born into a rural family, he spent his formative years as a farmer before registering for the draft on June 5, 1917. He was killed in action at St. Souplet, France, on October 18, 1918, and is buried at the Chattanooga National Cemetery. He served with Company M of the Old Hickory Division's 117th Infantry.

Private John L. Bentley was born in Knoxville and died at the age of twenty-one. Before he enlisted, Bentley was employed by the American Zinc Company of Tennessee at Mascot and had earlier worked as the bookkeeper for a local wholesale firm. After enlisting in the medical detachment of the Second Tennessee Infantry, Tennessee National Guard, in July 1917, he was transferred to the 119th Infantry at Camp Sevier. He sailed to France in May 1918 and went through the training period without accident. He lost his life in action on September 1, 1918, during the 30th Division's operations in Belgium alongside British forces. Bentley was initially buried at the British Cemetery at Poperinghe, Belgium, near Ypres, but was returned for burial to the Knoxville National Cemetery. An article from Knoxville's *Journal and Tribune* on October 6, 1918, told of his last letter to his wife, as well as noting one kind of heartbreaking confusion that could arise in relaying the word of a soldier's death:

> John L. Bentley . . . was a member of the medical department of the 119th Infantry Regiment. He formerly boarded at 112 East Jackson Avenue. His wife, formerly Miss Minnie Talver, is living with her mother, Mrs. Lucy Butcher, Hume Street. Mrs.

Bentley received a telegram from the war department informing her that her husband was killed about September 1. However, it is stated by a friend of Mr. Bentley that another letter was received from him under the date of September 12. Mrs. Bentley said Saturday that she believed there was an error in transmitting the information.

The last letter Mrs. Bentley received from her husband was dated August 30. He informed her that he had been in action on the firing line. He expressed the opinion that the fighting would end and that his regiment would return in time for him to be at home for Christmas.

[The Bentleys] were married December 18, 1917. His regiment was ordered to Camp Sevier, Greenville, S.C., where they remained for a long time. The organization left for overseas last April. Mrs. Bentley went to Greenville and was there when her husband left.

Marker for Sergeant John M. Carr at Somme American Cemetery, Bony, France.

Sergeant John M. Carr was born in Knoxville (Knox), the son of Mr. and Mrs. Andrew J. Carr. He had been a member of the Tennessee State Militia before the war, serving on the Mexican border during General Pershing's 1916 punitive expedition against Mexican politician and warlord Pancho Villa. Once America joined the Great War, Carr reenlisted on July 20, 1917, in the Third Tennessee Infantry (federalized, as noted earlier, as the 117th Infantry). Like the rest of the men of the 117th, he was assigned to Camp Sevier, South Carolina, for training before being deployed overseas. A non-commissioned officer in the 117th's Machine Gun Company, he embarked for France on May 11, 1918. Sergeant Carr was killed in action on October 9, 1918, during joint American-British-Australian operations north of Montbrehain, France, and received the Distinguished Service Cross:

> The President of the United States of America, authorized by Act of Congress, July 9, 1918, takes pleasure in presenting the Distinguished Service Cross to Sergeant John M. Carr, ASN 1306503, United States Army, for extraordinary heroism in action while serving with Machine-Gun Company, 117th Infantry Regiment, 30th Division, A.E.F., near Montbrehain, France, 9 October 1918. While leading his section upon a hostile machine-gun nest Sergeant Carr fell mortally wounded, but he inspired his men by urging them on and giving detailed instructions to the soldier whom he placed in command to succeed himself.

Carr was twenty-three years of age and was survived by his parents; three younger brothers, Cecil, Taylor, and Fred, each of whom also were serving with the AEF in France at the time; and by another brother and a sister. He is interred at the Somme American Cemetery, Bony, France.

Sergeant Lawrence W. Cockrum.

Private First Class Joseph L. Housley was born on March 18, 1888, in Rhea Springs (Rhea), Tennessee. He worked in sawmills in Seymour (Blount) before entering the service at the age of twenty-nine on June 5, 1917. He died on October 7, 1918, in France, while serving with Company M of the 117th. Housley was initially buried at the Somme American Cemetery, Bony, France. He was reburied at the Chattanooga National Cemetery.

Lawrence W. Cockrum was born in Talbott (Jefferson) and volunteered in July 1917 as a member of Company G, Second Tennessee Infantry, later absorbed into the 117th Infantry on its federalization. He was transferred from Camp Sevier to the 117th's Headquarters Company, with which he sailed to France on May 11, 1918. He took part in all of the fighting of his unit in the Ypres sector of Belgium, but lost his life near Bellicourt on September 29,

1918, during the first day of the Allied attack on the Hindenburg Line. He died at the age of twenty-six. He is buried at Arlington National Cemetery. The Knoxville *Journal and Tribune* of October 22, 1918, provided this account:

> Sergt. Lawrence Cockrum, formerly in the employ of the Hall and Donahue Coffin Co., Knoxville has been killed in action in the campaign against the Huns in France, according to an official telegram received in Knoxville Monday night.
>
> Mr. Cockrum was born and reared near Talbott's Station, Jefferson County, and came to Knoxville at an early age and found employment at the factory of Hall and Donahue Coffin Co. He became a skilled workman in the finishing department and held the position for sixteen years. A year or two ago he was given employment in the undertaking establishment conducted by the same firm. He was widely known in Knoxville and East Tennessee.
>
> Manifesting deep interest in educational matters, Mr. Cockrum was an untiring student and reader. Working during the day he spent his evening hours pursuing studies and obtained a splendid education. He brought one of his sisters, Miss Dora Mae Cockrum, to Knoxville and they resided at the residence of Mrs. Annie Condon Shea, 304 Fourth Street.
>
> When the war started between the United States and Germany, Mr. Cockrum enlisted for Foreign Service. He was with the 117th Infantry, commanded by Col. Cary F. Spence, at Camp Sevier, S.C. and it is presumed by his local friends that he was still with that command when he fell on the French battlefront.
>
> When informed of the death of Sergt. Cockrum, John Donahue, former employer of the young man, said, "I am deeply grieved to hear of his death. He was a model young man and worked faithfully here from his boyhood days until he responded to the call of the nation."

Private First Class Lester P. Harris.

The following chronicles the Great War experiences of one East Tennessee doughboy who did not serve with the 30th Division but on an entirely different part of the Western Front, alongside a different Allied army than the British and Australian compatriots of the Old Hickory Division.

Private First Class Lester P. Harris was born on December 31, 1893, and raised in Johnson City (Washington). He was the son of William Pond Harris and Ida Florence Potter. Harris's father was the founder and owner of the Harris Manufacturing Company and the Harris Flooring Company. He attended the Michigan Agricultural College in East Lansing, Michigan, for two years prior to transferring to the Ivy

League and graduating Columbia University, New York City, New York, in the class of 1918. Harris was a member of the Phi Gamma Delta Omega Chapter and the Athenaeum Society. After the United States declared war on Germany and men were being called up, Harris, along with nearly half the 1918 class, was allowed to graduate early to join national service. He volunteered with the Red Cross on June 8, 1917, to serve with the French Army for six months; he completed his passport paperwork that same day, with a request to sail for France on June 30.

Harris finally sailed from New York Harbor for France on July 20, 1917. Just after this, on July 30, his brother in Johnson City received a letter from the local draft board, instructing Lester to report for his physical examination on August 2. Harris's brother informed the board on July 31 that Lester had already left for overseas service and that the Red Cross' headquarters had been notified to follow up with the draft authorities to verify this fact.

After arriving in France, Harris received advanced training in the operation of ambulances and as a corpsman (medic). As a non-combatant, he had to learn a lot of the battlefield actions from other corpsmen who had been there for a bit, or on his own. In September 1917, it was agreed upon by the Red Cross, the French Army, and the United States that all Americans of fighting age would be transferred to the newly-formed United States Army Ambulance Corps Service (USAACS) headquartered at Noyon, France. Harris enlisted in the United States Army as a private on October 5, 1917, at Noyon and was assigned to Special Services Unit (SSU) 648 and attached to the 67th Infantry Division of the French Third Army. SSU 648 would serve with the French troops until the end of the war. He was promoted to Private First Class on December 28, 1917.

Harris participated in the unit campaign of the Montdidier-Noyon Operation (June 9–13, 1918) and at the engagement of Château de la Folie. Not long after this, around midnight on July 4, a German air raid was conducted on the crossroads near the village of Catenoy, where SSU 648 was resting for the night at a relay station. Harris and three others were sleeping in their two ambulances when his was struck near the rear by one of two bombs dropped by one aircraft, trapping Lester and two others. Just after they were removed from the ambulances, both vehicles exploded into flames. Harris was severely wounded in both legs, especially his knees, and died from those wounds five days later on July 9, 1918, in a French Army field hospital near Catenoy. He was twenty-four years old and was first interred at a nearby military cemetery and later reinterred at the Somme American Cemetery in Bony, France at his family's request. He also has a memorial marker at Monte Vista Memorial Gardens in Johnson City.

For his actions and bravery in the face of the enemy, the French government awarded him the Croix de Guerre. The city of Johnson City renamed a street in his honor that is now called the Lester Harris Road.

First Lieutenant Levi S. Morehouse was born on December 31, 1892, in Fulton, New York. When he entered the service, he was living in Tellico Plains (Monroe). He was assigned to the 117th Infantry Regiment, 30th Division. He died on October 7, 1918, and is interred at the Somme American Cemetery, Bony, France. Monroe County archivist and genealogist Joy Locke has researched Morehouse's story in great depth. The following excerpt quotes

First Lieutenant Levi S. Morehouse.

some of her findings, to which the ETVMA is indebted:

A lady from New York recently visited the [Monroe County] Archives. She was passing through and noticed a name on our World War I monument on the Courthouse lawn. "Why is my great-uncle's name on the WWI monument for Monroe County?" she asked. "He was born and raised in New York."

An investigation revealed that Levi Sherman Morehouse was indeed born and raised in Volney, Oswego County, New York by his parents, Alfred Fremont and Elvira Blakeman Morehouse. Levi lost his mother in 1909 while he was in his fourth year of high school, and entered St. Lawrence University's School of Agriculture in 1910, graduating in 1912. Three years after his mother's death Levi's father married Lena Babcock, who embraced her husband's children as her own. Lena was a relative of the Babcocks who owned a huge lumber business in the mountainous area of Monroe County, Tennessee during the early 1900s. When Levi's father died in 1914, Lena's brother, Clarence Babcock, who lived in Knoxville, and who was also very close to the Morehouse children, asked Levi to come to Tellico Plains, and oversee a huge farm that he owned there. Levi consented, and thus became a citizen of Monroe County. He joined the Tennessee National Guard, Company M, 3rd Infantry, and spent some time in Texas. He returned to Monroe County, but at the outbreak of World War I, the 3rd Tennessee Infantry was called into Federal Service in July of 1917.

A letter Morehouse wrote to his family in New York recalled his departure from Tellico Plains:

Dear Ones at Home,

Friday morning, about 1130, the train pulled out of Tellico Plains, bearing her soldier boys away. Everyone in Tellico was at the Station. The mills closed, also the schools, to turn out and pay a last tribute to the youth of Monroe County. The crowd looked almost mute. Good-byes were said very quietly, with little demonstration or sign of emotion, but you could feel it in the air. There were many wet eyes, but the tears were not allowed to flow. Yet everyone was determined that the boys should leave amid cheers and shouts of encouragement. Finally, when all was ready, a great hush fell on the crowds, tense with pent-up emotion. Then as the train slowly moved out, the air was rent with cheers and shouts, hats flew in the air and handkerchiefs floated on the breeze. Thus, we left those who will always be dear to the memory of Fighting M Company to wend their way slowly back home, some to break down and weep now that the boys were out of sight, and others to begin the long, long watch for the return of husband, sweetheart, or brother. For life would be barren indeed, were it not for the hope that someday the hero will return."[2]

On May 8th, 1918, Morehouse's company set sail overseas, serving in France and Belgium. On October 7th, 1918, Lieutenant Morehouse was killed in action at Fraicourt Farm, one mile northeast of Brancourt, France, by a "whiz-bang" or a three-inch (German 77mm) shell, which exploded ten feet in front of him. A letter from Morehouse's first sergeant to Clarence Babcock, dated October 15, 1918, detailed his lieutenant's death:

Corporal Hall, whose home is in Madisonville, was the last man in the Company to see Lt. Morehouse alive. He placed this Corporal in a hole for protection and went to have a consultation with some other officers of the 117th Infantry. He did not return . . . He must have been killed instantly and did not suffer. His body was not mutilated[;] a small piece of shrapnel had pierced his heart.

—Your Friend, R. B. Cable, 1st Sgt. Commanding Company M.[3]

Sergeant Robert Johnson.

Lieutenant Morehouse was survived by his sister, Cora Morehouse Wilcox, and a brother, Carl Elihu Morehouse, both of New York.

Sergeant Robert Johnson was born on August 24, 1887, and was from Hartford (Cocke). He entered the service on August 21, 1917, in Asheville, North Carolina, when he was twenty-nine. At the time, he was living with his wife and child in Crestmont, North Carolina, where he was employed as a brakeman by the East Tennessee and Western North Carolina Railroad Company, affectionately known as the "Eat Taters, Wear No Clothes" line. He had previously served in the Army as an infantry private during a six-year tour of duty in the Philippines after the Spanish-American War. After further training, he departed for Europe on May 17, 1918, and arrived on June 7, 1918. He served with Company A, 113th Machine Gun Battalion, 30th Division. He was yet another East Tennessean to be killed in action in France on September 29, 1918, during the first day's assault on the Hindenburg Line and was buried at Clark Cemetery, Hartford, Tennessee.

Private William M. Austin lived in Newport (Cocke) before his family moved to Knoxville. He resided in Knoxville for a few years before joining the Army. Austin enlisted on September 15, 1917, and served as a member of Company B, 113th Machine Gun Battalion, 30th Division. After training at Camp Sevier, he went to France in May 1918. He took part in the fighting in Belgium but, like Robert Johnson of his battalion's Company A, was killed in action on September 29, 1918, on the first day of the Allies' attack on the Hindenburg Line near Bellicourt. He died at the age of twenty-three. Austin is buried in the Knoxville National Cemetery.

Although he died in late September 1918, Austin was one of the last men to be reported

Private William M. Austin.

killed in World War I. He had formerly resided with his mother, Mary Austin, at 968 Jacksboro Street in Knoxville. Mrs. Austin received an official telegram from the War Department on Friday, November 8—just three days before the Armistice took effect—announcing the death of her son.

3

EARLY MILITARY AVIATORS
Kiffin Yates Rockwell and Charles McGhee Tyson

Oh, I have slipped the surly bonds of earth,

and danced the skies on laughter-silvered wings;

Sunward I've climbed and joined the tumbling mirth of sun-split clouds—

and done a hundred things you have not dreamed of—

wheeled and soared and swung high in the sunlit silence.

Hovering there I've chased the shouting wind along

and flung my eager craft through footless halls of air.

Up, up the long delirious burning blue

I've topped the wind-swept heights with easy grace,

where never lark, or even eagle, flew;

and, while with silent, lifting mind I've trod

the high untrespassed sanctity of space,

put out my hand and touched the face of God.

—American-Canadian military pilot, John Gillespie Magee Jr.

Fewer than eleven years separated the onset of World War I in August 1914 from the initial flight of Orville and Wilbur Wright's Flyer on the sands of Kitty Hawk, North Carolina, on December 17, 1903. The Wrights had once hoped that their invention would make war impossible and serve as an instrument of peace by bringing humanity together. The technology of aviation, however, would advance rapidly during the four years of the Great War, as did the growth of the airplane from an unarmed craft used mainly for reconnaissance and scouting to fast pursuit (fighter) aircraft, bombers, ground-attack planes, and seaplanes. The Germans' use of lighter-than-air Zeppelin dirigibles and, by 1917, multi-engined Gotha and Staaken bombers to target the civilians of London and other Allied cities brought warfare one step closer to the grim concept of total war. It also resulted in British and French counter-efforts to develop their own strategic air forces, with the goal of bringing an enemy to its knees by devastating its industrial base and hitting its civilian population.

The early aerial combat activities in the skies of Europe were closely observed by others, among them US Army colonel (later, brigadier general) William "Billy" Mitchell, who drove relentlessly to transform the Army Air Service from part of the Army Signal Corps (in which the Army's aircraft and aviators resided from 1908 until May 14, 1918) into a modern air force after America's entry in World War I. (It would not be until September 18, 1947, however, that Mitchell's vision of having a truly independent branch of service would come to fruition with the creation of the US Air Force from the Army Air Forces, itself the successor to the Army Air Corps, which itself succeeded the Army Air Service in 1926.) Young men, seeking adventure, the opportunities posed by the new technology of aviation, or what was then perceived as a more noble, romantic, or glamorous way to fight for one's country than toiling in the mud and blood of protracted trench warfare on the Western Front, sought eagerly to join the infant air services of the US Army, Navy, and Marine Corps.

Among the young Americans fascinated by aviation was an East Tennessee newlywed, Charles McGhee Tyson. In deciding to pursue the life of a military aviator, he may have been partially influenced by the legend and mystique of a group of celebrated American pilots already at war, who did not wait for Congress to declare war on Germany on April 2, 1917, instead preferring to join the French Air Service to raise their own all-American squadron of "knights of the air." Joining the colorful and disparate characters who formed this unique

Kiffin Yates Rockwell.

squadron—the famed *Lafayette Escadrille* (more formally in French service, *Escadrille N.124*)—was another one-time East Tennessean, Kiffin Yates Rockwell.

Both Rockwell and Tyson would perish in action. While the name of one of these aviators continues to be recalled in daily life in East Tennessee one hundred years after his death over the North Sea, the other—once lionized by many in both the French and American media and the public of both nations during his brief life and service as a pilot for France—has seemingly been largely forgotten in his homeland.

Kiffin Yates Rockwell with his Nieuport 17.

KIFFIN Y. ROCKWELL:
THE "ARISTOCRAT OF THE AIR"
AND HERO OF TWO NATIONS

Kiffin Yates Rockwell was born on September 20, 1892, in Newport (Cocke), the son of James C. Rockwell and Loula Ayres.[1] His father, a Baptist minister, died shortly after Kiffin's birth; the family soon moved to the home of his maternal grandfather in South Carolina, and later to Asheville, North Carolina. After completing his preparatory schooling at the Orange Street School in Asheville, Kiffin enrolled at the Virginia Military Institute in 1908 and, for a time, later attended Washington and Lee University, where his brother Paul was also a student. Kiffin left college in 1911 and worked for an advertising agency in Atlanta until summer 1914.

Within days after war erupted between France and Germany in early August 1914, both Rockwell brothers decided to fight for France and serve in the French Army. Setting sail for France, the Rockwells enlisted on their arrival in the *Légion Etrangère*, the famous French Foreign Legion. Paul was severely wounded in November 1914 and was invalided out of the French military, becoming a civilian war correspondent, while Kiffin continued to serve in the trenches as an infantryman with the Foreign Legion. Kiffin was wounded by an exploding shell in December 1914; following his hospitalization and recovery, he served with the 1st Regiment of the Moroccan Division. After being shot in the thigh on May 9, 1915, and a period of convalescence, Kiffin sought to transfer to the nascent French aviation branch, the Service Aéronautique. By late summer 1915, he got his wish, writing to his mother on September 8, 1915: "I have at last gotten what I have been trying to get these past two months. I am transferred to the aviation as a student-pilot. That is a jump from the lowest branch of the military service to the highest. It is the most interesting thing I have ever done, and is the life of a gentleman, and I am surrounded by gentlemen."[2]

After completing his initial flight training, in early 1916 Kiffin became one of the first seven founding pilots of a new French squadron equipped with the latest Nieuport pursuit airplanes, *N.124*, initially known informally as the Escadrille Américaine, because it was manned principally by expatriate American volunteers. After protests were brought by the German government over the apparent violation of the laws of war by neutrals fighting for the Allied cause, the French helpfully renamed the squadron the Lafayette Escadrille, and a legend would soon be born, one in which Rockwell took a prominent role. In May 1916, he became the first member of the *Escadrille*—and the first American pilot—to shoot down an enemy plane not far from the squadron's airfield at Luxeuil-les-Bains, France; when the news of his victory broke in Paris, it created "a tremendous wave of excitement."[3] Due to his comradely nature and bearing, he would in time be popularly nicknamed the "Aristocrat of the Air," and Kiffin Rockwell became the toast of two nations, aided in some ways by his brother Paul's reporting on the *Escadrille* for the *Chicago Daily News*. At least one of the traditions of this squadron—a unit noted for its varied styles of uniforms and flight gear and its lion cub mascots "Whiskey" and "Soda," as well as by its colorful and larger-than-life group of pilots—is directly attributable to Rockwell. Following his first victory, Kiffin opened a celebratory bottle of aged bourbon brought him by Paul. After taking a drink, he recorked the bot-

tle with instructions that it not be opened again until the next pilot had scored a victory; "every man who brings down a German is entitled to one good slug" from the "Bottle of Death."[4]

Rockwell flew combat patrols over Alsace and near Verdun during the horrific fighting there throughout 1916; he reputedly fought in some 140 dogfights during his service with the *Lafayette Escadrille*. He was wounded yet again, but on his discharge from the hospital, he resumed his tenure with the *Escadrille*. On September 23, 1916, his luck ran out: while diving on a German Aviatik or Albatros two-seat observation plane, he was shot in the chest by the observer/machine-gunner and apparently died instantly; he was twenty-four years old. He was still a sergeant at the time, but he had been recommended for a battlefield promotion to second lieutenant; at the time of his death, he had scored two victories in aerial combat. Rockwell was buried in the cemetery at the squadron's base outside Luxeuil-les-Bains, and he was posthumously decorated as a knight (*Chevalier*) of the *Légion d'honneur*, France's highest military decoration.[5] Of Rockwell, his commanding officer, French captain Georges Thenault, said: "His courage was sublime. . . . The best and bravest of us is no longer here."[6] Afterwards, Kiffin's friend and fellow Lafayette pilot, Edmond Genet, wrote to a grieving Paul Rockwell: "If you can console yourself at all, console yourself in the fact that your brother's end came while he was heroically defending this big cause, for which we all are willing to give our lives, in the face of the enemy. . . . Try to brighten up, dear Paul. Your brother has found a glorious end—a soldier's death—and, 'tho it has come far too soon and unexpected, such a death should tend to soften the hardness of the personal loss and bereavement. May you find it so."[7]

Kiffin Rockwell's life is remembered by his-

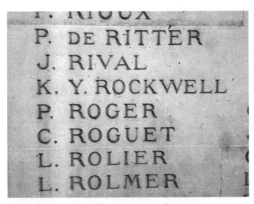

A detail from the wall in memory of France's honored dead at the Pantheon in Paris.

Charles McGhee Tyson.

torical markers in two states: one in his first hometown of Newport, Tennessee, and another stands on Merrimon Avenue in downtown Asheville, North Carolina. Similarly, a VFW post in Newport and an American Legion post in Asheville are both named in his honor. He is also memorialized at the Robert E. Lee Memorial at Washington and Lee University and at Virginia Military Institute. Rockwell's remains were exhumed from the military cemetery at Luxeuil after the war, and they are now entombed at the *Lafayette Escadrille*'s memorial at Marnes-la-Coquette near Paris, where his name appears among those of the sixty-eight American volunteer aviators who fell in the service of that squadron. Rockwell's name is also inscribed on the walls of the Panthéon in Paris alongside other French patriots and the tombs of the "immortals of France," notables like Madame Curie, Victor Hugo, Rousseau, Voltaire, and World War II resistance hero Jean Moulin. Rockwell was indeed a hero of two nations.

CHARLES MCGHEE TYSON

Charles McGhee Tyson was born on August 10, 1889, at Clifton Springs, New York, to Lawrence Davis and Bettie McGhee Tyson. With a father like Lawrence Tyson—a West Point graduate, seasoned veteran of the Plains Wars with Native American tribes including the Apache under Geronimo, one-time professor of military science at the University of Tennessee, and commanding officer of the 6th Tennessee Volunteer Infantry during the Spanish-American War—one might have foreseen that young McGhee Tyson might have military service in his future, even before America's entry into World War I. McGhee Tyson was two years old when his father assumed the duties of being the chief military science instructor at UT, in the process of which the elder Tyson moved the family to Knoxville, the home of his wife's family. Mrs. Tyson was related to Knoxville pioneer and city founder James White via her father, prominent industrialist and railroad executive Charles McClung McGhee, and her mother, *née* Cornelia Humes White. While McGhee Tyson was very much a child from a privileged and historic family background, he came to be a young man who nevertheless felt a strong sense of duty and obligation. Amy McRary of the *Knoxville News Sentinel* wrote of his school days:

> McGhee Tyson followed the path of many upper-class young men in the early 20th century. At 16 he was sent to boarding school at St. Paul's School in Concord [New Hampshire]. After graduating, he enrolled at Princeton University in 1908. He wasn't initially much of a student at Princeton, according to the 1926 "The Roll of Honor," a book published by The St. Paul's School Alumni Association to remember school alumni who died in the Great War.
>
> "Tys" had a tough Princeton freshman year, says the book, before more advanced courses interested "his really brilliant mind." From then on, his "academic standing was distinctly credible" even though he didn't spend lots of time studying. He more enjoyed rowing and playing golf. Musically gifted, he played several instruments. "He never loafed but in college he played harder than he worked," notes his "Roll of Honor" biography. But the memorial notes Tyson graduated in 1912 "well up in his class" with a bachelors of science. By all accounts, the book noted, he "was just what a fine American boy should be."[8]

After his graduation from Princeton, he returned to Knoxville to work for his father, who was now the owner of two local textile firms, the Knoxville Spinning Company and the Tennessee Mills Company. By early 1917, McGhee

Tyson was the vice president and general manager of both firms, where co-workers and colleagues recalled that he was by no means snobbish; rather, he was a businessman who was sincerely "interested in welfare work among his men and labor conditions in the plants," and he was regarded with great affection by many of his employees.[9]

Then came Congress's declaration of war on Imperial Germany on April 2, 1917, provoked by its waging of unrestricted submarine warfare against American and neutral shipping, acts of sabotage on American shores, and a secret telegram from the German foreign ministry to Mexico intended to fuel hostilities on the southern border of the United States. Just three months later, in July, McGhee Tyson enlisted as a Seaman Second Class in the United States Navy Reserve. He was twenty-seven years old. While his son sought to become a naval aviator, Lawrence Tyson applied to return to active military duty; the governor of Tennessee appointed him as a brigadier general over the troops of the Tennessee National Guard. After the Guard's federalization, General Tyson became commanding general of the 59th Infantry Brigade of the 30th Division, which, as we have seen in the preceding chapter, embarked for field service in France in May 1918.

Following initial training at the Massachusetts Institute of Technology and naval air stations at Pensacola and Newport News, McGhee Tyson was detached from the aviation service for a time. Because of his prior executive ability, the Navy ordered him to Washington and tasked him with ordering and loading supplies for a collier (coal cargo ship), the USS *Jason*. Nevertheless, his request to be allowed to join an aviation unit in the field was granted, and he sailed for the European theater on August 8,

1918.[10] Before departing for "over there," however, McGhee Tyson married his sweetheart, Betty Carson of New York, a longtime friend of his sole sibling, Isabella. The newlyweds were, in fact, still on their honeymoon in early August when Tyson's departure orders assigned him to report to a US Naval Air Service post in Killingholme, England, located due east and south of the industrial cities of Sheffield and Hull, respectively. Tyson and his bride spent his last ten days in America in Knoxville.[11] He had requested and had been granted leave, but he turned it down the morning of October 9, 1918, after volunteers were urgently sought for a critical mission over the North Sea.

In an effort to halt ongoing German U-boat depredations on Allied shipping, both the British and US navies were laying a cordon of naval mines in strategic areas of the North Sea, including by aircraft. Tyson volunteered, serving as the machine-gunner on a four-man mine-laying flight two days later. On the morning of October 11, 1918, taking off in heavy fog, the heavily loaded airplane had barely reached one hundred feet above the ground when its pilot lost control. The aircraft crashed into the water, killing Tyson and two others of the crew. Betty Carson Tyson and he had been married for only three months before she was widowed. His death at the age of twenty-nine was one of the lead stories atop the *Knoxville Sentinel*'s front page, and the news of his loss "brought tears even to the eyes of strangers. Scores who waited anxiously around newspaper bulletin boards for developments on the Western Front lowered their heads and grew silent."[12]

Charles McGhee Tyson perished exactly one month to the day before the Armistice marked the end of the war on November 11, 1918. His remains were brought to Knoxville under naval escort and buried with full military honors on November 26, 1918, at the Old Gray Cemetery. In an obituary, one of Tyson's closest friends noted that he would always remember him as "a boy who had the courage to do the hard thing he thought was right."

Knoxville's first municipal airport, dedicated in 1930, bears Tyson's name at the behest of his widowed mother, Bettie, General Tyson having died in 1929. Following the airport's move from Sutherland Avenue to Blount County in 1937, the name was retained. Knoxville civic leader Mrs. W. C. Ross wrote at the time: "I should think the Gold Star mothers of [East Tennessee] would rejoice over perpetuating the name of one boy who fell in the World War, with the feeling it was, in a way, a recognition of what other youths gave too."[13]

4

EAST TENNESSEANS IN WORLD WAR I
AND THE GREAT INFLUENZA EPIDEMIC

There was a little bird,

its name was Enza;

I opened up the window,

and in flew Enza. (In-flu-enza.)

—*American children's rhyme of the*
Spanish influenza pandemic of 1918[1]

When one thinks of military deaths and casualties in so many wars, it is commonly assumed that the vast majority of deaths are attributable to wounds due to combat action. Across the centuries, however, the principal killer of troops and sailors was not battle; it was disease. The experiences of the last year of World War I, during the 1918 global influenza outbreak, cruelly drive home this medical reality of warfare.

Both on the home front and in the combat zones of 1918, the greatest single killer of the Great War was not artillery, machine guns, or poison gas. It was something far more insidious and invisible. By some estimates, half of the doughboys, Marines, and sailors who died in Europe fell not to enemy fire but to the influenza pandemic of 1918–1920. Sometimes referred to as the Spanish flu, the "plague of the Spanish lady," and the "grippe," the epidemic had begun to dissipate almost as quickly as it appeared by the time the Armistice was signed on November 11, 1918.

On March 11, 1918, the first cases of what would become the influenza pandemic were reported in the United States, when 107 soldiers rapidly became ill at the Army's Camp Funston training camp near Fort Riley, Kansas. It was the beginning of the worst pandemic in modern history. The flu that year killed only 2.5 percent of its victims, but more than a fifth of the world's entire population caught it; it is estimated that between fifty million and one hundred million people died in just a few months. Historians believe at least 500,000 died in the United States alone.

The influenza outbreak swept through military bases in the United States. The virus was an exceptionally deadly strain that struck young, previously healthy adults particularly hard. Once their bodies were weakened, many were vulnerable to secondary infections such as pneumonia, often leading to death within a mere matter of days after the onset of symptoms were noticed. By late spring 1918, there were influenza outbreaks in fourteen of the largest Army training camps in the United States. After temporarily subsiding, a second more deadly wave of influenza appeared in late summer 1918. By mid-September, it had developed into a mass outbreak. Many servicemen caught the influenza virus in the United States and boarded troopships bound for Europe, unaware of their infected condition. Crowded quarters on the ships provided an ideal environment that readily enabled the flu to spread. Some soldiers did not survive the two-week voyage. Others fell sick during the crossing and were taken directly to hospitals in Britain and France when their vessels entered port.

Healthy soldiers arriving in France in late 1917 and in early 1918 immediately went into battle, distinguishing themselves in infantry charges, artillery exchanges, and trench warfare. However, if they were not already infected by the virus, many contracted it in the close

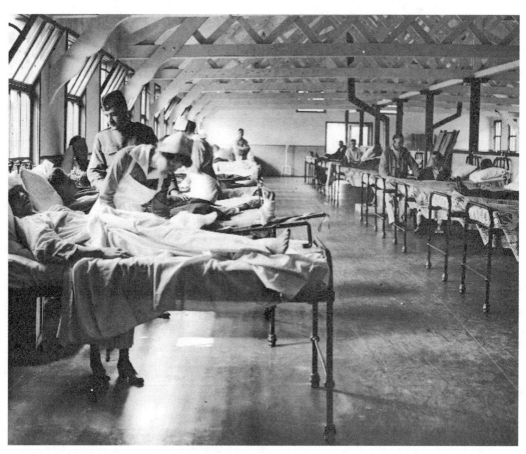

American Red Cross Hospital in Liverpool, England, 1918. National Archives.

Camp Wadsworth, Spartanburg, South Carolina, in 1918.

quarters in which they were confined. As has been pointed out, others contracted the disease onboard ship before even arriving in England or France. A third group became ill so quickly in the United States that they never had time to go overseas. They died in the field hospitals of their training camps. Others were buried at sea before even reaching land.

An extract from the annual report by the Army Surgeon General focused on the situation at Camp Hospital No. 53 in Le Mans, France—just one of numerous camp and base hospitals—and described the inadequacies of the facility for the huge patient load. Cross-infections were rampant. The report added that pneumonia cases accounted for over 80 percent of the total deaths at this one camp hospital, as a complication of influenza. Other recorded cases included outbreaks of measles, mumps, and a small number of instances of meningitis.[2] Worsening the military situation was the fact that the autumnal wave of the pan-demic coincided with the launch of the Allies' fall offensives—the British, Australians, and the US 30th Division, largely comprised of Tennesseans and Carolinians, at the St. Quentin Canal, and Pershing's American First Army in the Meuse-Argonne sector—intended to crack, once and for all, the Germans' vaunted Hindenburg Line.

In all, 1,089 service members from the thirty-five counties of East Tennessee died or were killed during World War I. The largest numbers were from Hamilton (146) and Knox (139) counties. Sequatchie County had the smallest number of casualties, with only six. It is likely that many of the deaths occurred owing to the influenza outbreak.

The 57th Pioneer Infantry Regiment was particularly affected by the influenza epidemic. As the letter from Henry F. Forte in Arl B. Kelly's story will recount below, this unit—one with several East Tennesseans in its ranks—never had an opportunity to see action in

France, and its men succumbed in droves to the flu. As historian David Tschanz observed:

> Of the 100,000 stricken in the AEF over 8,000 died. The overall mortality rate among those developing pneumonia of 32% was an average only—in some units, as Pershing wrote—"It reached as high as 80%." On September 28, the 57th Pioneer Infantry Regiment of the 31st Division was struck—three days later 200 had died. While wounds were not communicable, influenza is so in the vortex of chaos and death that ambulances drivers and hospital aides were ordered always to segregate influenza cases from the wounded. But drivers under artillery fire didn't quibble about diagnoses as the litter bearers shoved their burdens in the back. Thus, the wounded were exposed to the disease which often hastened their deaths.[3]

What follows in this chapter are some of

Corporal Wesley M. Furches.

the most poignant stories of those soldiers and sailors from East Tennessee who perished in the great influenza outbreak of 1918.

Corporal Charles S. Lacey hailed from Hopson (Carter). He was born in 1893 and died of throat and chest complications due to influenza on November 3, 1918, at an Army general hospital in Rouen, France. He was initially buried at Saint-Sever Cemetery in Rouen and later was reinterred in his family's cemetery in Carter County. He served with Company E of the 117th Infantry Regiment, 30th Division, and fought in the battles of Bellicourt, Prémont, the Hindenburg Line, the St.-Quentin Canal, and Ribeauvillé.

Corporal Wesley M. Furches was born in 1894 in Embreeville (Washington). He served with the 324th Infantry Regiment, 81st Infantry Division, and fought during the Meuse-Argonne

Corporal Charles S. Lacey.

Seaman Second Class Joseph S. Bachman Jr.

offensive. He died overseas of pneumonia on October 26, 1918, at age twenty-four and is buried at Bumpus Cove Cemetery, Embreeville.

First Lieutenant Benjamin J. Cogdill was born on January 28, 1881, at Ogle's Crossroads (Sevier). He was educated at Harrison Chilhowee Academy and was graduated from Lincoln Memorial University's Medical Department in 1906. He practiced in Sevierville, Pigeon Forge, and Vestal before being commissioned in the US Army Medical Corps. Cogdill gave up his medical practice in January 1918 and was assigned to duty as first lieutenant with the 3rd Development Battalion, 155th Depot Brigade at Camp Lee, Virginia. He contracted pneumonia at camp in October of the same year and died a few days later. He is buried at the Pigeon Forge Baptist Cemetery, Sevier County, Tennessee.

Seaman Second Class Joseph S. Bachman Jr. was born on March 3, 1897, in Bristol (Sulli-

van). He was a Seaman Second Class and died on October 17, 1918, at a Naval Base Hospital in Virginia of influenza. He enlisted in the US Naval Reserve at the age of twenty-one on March 19, 1917. According to the October 19, 1918, Knoxville *Journal and Tribune,* Bachman had left "with several other Bristol boys" for naval training at Norfolk about a month before he died; he was educated at Davidson College.

Jasper York (Scott) was a sergeant with Company L of the 47th Infantry Regiment, 4th Infantry Division. York developed influenza and died as a result of pneumonia at Camp Greene Base Hospital in Charlotte, North Carolina, before he could even be deployed to active battle in Europe. According to his grandnephew Leo York, Jasper York was born in December 1891 in Cordell to Andrew and Lucinda Newport York. One of nine brothers all serving in the US military in all branches during the Spanish-American War, World War I,

Private Arthur N. Bacon.

and World War II, Jasper was unmarried. When he died February 9, 1918, his body was shipped home, and Jasper was interred in the York Cemetery in Cordell.[4]

Arthur N. Bacon was born in 1894 in Riceville (McMinn). He was a farmer and left his home on July 22, 1918, for initial training at Camp Gordon outside Augusta, Georgia. He stayed at Camp Gordon one month and thirteen days; was transferred to Camp Merritt, New Jersey; and then was sent to France on September 26, 1918, as a private with the AEF. He was on the troopship seven days and fell ill with bronchopneumonia (another frequent medical indication for many of the Spanish flu's victims) the day before the ship landed in France. He was evacuated to Base Hospital No.

65 in Kerhuon (Brittany), France, where he survived for just three days, dying on October 7, 1918. Bacon is buried at the Oise-Aisne American Cemetery, Fère-en-Tardenois, France.

Private Lacy O. Smith was born on June 12, 1896, in Mullens Cove (Marion). He worked as a farmer before his induction into military service on October 25, 1918, at Camp Wadsworth, Spartanburg, South Carolina. He served with the 62nd Pioneer Infantry and died at the camp's base hospital of bronchopneumonia. He is buried in Whitwell Cemetery, Marion County.[5]

Private Grant Vandeventer was born on March 12, 1900, in Knoxville (Knox). He entered military service on August 27, 1917. As an enlisted man in Company I, 117th Infantry,

A view of the Kerhuon, France, hospital center. Courtesy of the US Army Medical Department's Office of Medical History.

Private Lacy O. Smith.

30th Division, he trained at Camp Sevier and sailed for overseas duty on May 11, 1918. He took part in all battles of his unit until October 1918, when he was removed from the lines after having been gassed. As a result of contracting the Spanish influenza, followed by pneumonia, Vandeventer died on December 10, 1918, at the age of eighteen at a base hospital in England. He is buried at Brookwood American Cemetery, Brookwood, England. One can only wonder if the gassing that he had suffered in combat only exacerbated the risks of Spanish flu to his weakened lungs.

Private Arl B. Kelly was born on April 2, 1897, in Cocke County and was assigned to Headquarters Company of the 57th Pioneer Infantry Regiment on September 4, 1918. Prior to sailing that same month, he was stationed at Camp Wadsworth, South Carolina. He contracted pneumonia while on the transport USS *Leviathan* (the well-known prewar ocean liner *Vaterland*, which was seized at the beginning of the war from Germany) and died at sea on October 4, 1918. He is buried at the Knoxville National Cemetery. An article in the October 18, 1918, Knoxville *Journal and Tribune* noted that "Mr. Kelly was a Christian and a patriotic young American. Before leaving for the army camp he told his father that he must not worry about his leaving because he was willing to sacrifice all for his country." Arl's cousin Pat Kelly advised the ETVMA that Arl was married to Tula Leford and added that reputedly the 57th Pioneer Infantry had "the most casualties of any unit from Tennessee," although the regiment never saw combat.

Pat Kelly's reminiscences of his cousin's fate are corroborated by the 1975 letter, provided to ETVMA by Captain Kelly and reprinted below, from the US Army Military History Center at Carlisle, Pennsylvania. In it, Henry F. Forte of Nashville recounted his own experiences as a private in the 57th Pioneer Infantry:

> I was drafted in the U.S. Army on September 5, 1918, as a private soldier at Camp Greene, North Carolina, and I remained a private all the way through. We were attached to the 57th Pioneer Infantry and sent to Camp Wadsworth, South Carolina where the entire 57th was assembled. We were camped there until September 24th, 1918, leaving there for the next day for Camp Merritt, New Jersey. We stayed there just long enough to get our overseas equipment, but we received no training what so ever [sic]. Can you imagine sending us as soldiers overseas without any training? We stayed 3 days at Camp Merritt and boarded the largest and fastest ship on the water in those days, the *Leviathan*, the German ship that the U.S. captured on our Atlantic Coast when we declared war on Germany. We sailed on September 29th and arrived at Brest, France on October 8th, 1918. . . . [In early November,] we were designated as "Casuals." This

is where we separated from the 57th Pioneer Infantry to Company K, 329th Infantry, 83rd Division. . . . We [were] on our way back to the U.S.A. on January 23rd, 1919.

Your direct question was "Did the Pioneers see actual combat service?" [T]he answer is no, although we were called Dough Boys. The only type of duties we were in was slopping around the mud like a bunch of frogs.

I almost forgot the worst part of it all. I almost died from Spanish Influenza and men in our outfit were dying like rabbits from that disease, especially while on the *Leviathan* going over there.[6]

Of course, one of the dead aboard the *Leviathan* was Arl Kelly, who had perished before seeing France or any action.

Sergeant Charles D. Johnston Jr., of Knoxville (Knox), was born on November 25, 1894, to C. D. and Mary A. Johnston. He attended Knoxville High School, later going to Tusculum College where he became a well-known athlete, winning many track-and-field events across East Tennessee and southwest Virginia. He left college early to join the Square Drug Company of Knoxville. Johnston volunteered for the Army on June 7, 1917. As a member of the University of Tennessee's Ambulance Unit, he received military training at Allentown, Pennsylvania, embarking for France on December 25, 1917. As a member of the AEF's contingent of the Army Ambulance Service, Sergeant Johnston saw service with the 7th, 8th, and 10th French Armies in Sanitary Section Unit (SSU) No. 533, and he was a participant in all battles of his command until his death on September 26, 1918, at the age of twenty-four, as a result of influenza. An article in the Knoxville *Journal and Tribune* recounted his family life and prior service on the front:

Thursday, Mrs. Johnston, wife of Sergt. Johnston, received a letter from Sergt. Willard Wiley, of Knoxville, stating that he had received a postal card which Sergt. Johnston had started to write him, but was finished by a Major, stating that Sergt. Johnston had died in hospital. Miss Louise Currier also received a letter from a friend in the same section stating that Sergt Johnston had died in a hospital.

The last letter received direct from Sergt. Johnston was by his mother. This letter, dated September 16, 1918, stated that he had been through a baptism of German machine gun fire, but luckily escaped, that he had been in rain for several days and had not had his clothes off for eight days. Sergt. Johnston died Sept. 22.

The delay and absence up to this time of official notice of his death, is probably due to the fact that since June 10th of this year, he has been attached to the 10th French [A]rmy under General Mangin. . . . He joined the U. of T. ambulance corps last year, went

Private Vestus Kesterson.

into training at Allentown and sailed for France last January. . . .

He was married July 3, 1917, to Miss Annie Katherine Dunn, of Knoxville and to this union a son was born last May, whom the father had, of course, never seen, having been in France at the time of the birth. When last he wrote, Sergt. Johnston held the rank of corporal but was pleased that he had been recommended for promotion to the rank of sergeant, notice of which promotion he had not received before his death.

Johnston is buried at Old Gray Cemetery, Knoxville.

Private Vestus Kesterson was born on June 14, 1897, at Mohawk (Greene). The son of John and Nancy Kesterson and husband of Cassie Lou Voiles, Vestus entered the service on September 5, 1918, at Greeneville and

Private Lina N. McCourry.

Corporal Hobart D. Willocks.

trained at Camp Wadsworth, South Carolina. Like Arthur N. Bacon, who had succumbed two days earlier, he died on October 9, 1918, at Base Hospital No. 65 in Kerhuon (Brittany), France, of bronchopneumonia, that frequently identified manifestation of the effects of influenza. Kesterson is buried at Fairview Baptist Church Cemetery, Mohawk, Greene County, Tennessee.

Leonard F. Marine was born on August 3, 1895, in Blount County. The son of Joseph M. Marine and Mary Ann Belle Whitehead Marine, he married Lou Emaline Payne in 1917 or 1918. Prior to joining the military, he worked on the family farm in Rasar, Tennessee. Marine became sick with influenza during transportation back to the States and died at sea on October 2, 1918, only five days before the birth of his first son, Leonard H. Marine. He is buried in Happy Valley Missionary Baptist Church Cemetery in Tallassee, Tennessee.

Hobart D. Willocks, of Maryville (Blount), was the son of Martha Melvina Gardner and John S. Willocks. A corporal in the 117th Infantry Regiment of the 30th Division, he did not live long enough to see combat: Willocks died of bronchopneumonia at the base hospital while still in training at Camp Sevier, South Carolina. He is buried in Magnolia Cemetery, Maryville.

Lina N. McCourry (also spelled McCoury) (Unicoi) was born on August 1, 1897, in Glen Ayre, North Carolina, and was married to Nervie McCourry. He was a private with Company L, 61st Pioneer Infantry, a sister unit to the ill-starred 57th Pioneer Infantry. He was inducted into the military on November 6, 1918. McCourry died of pneumonia on December 3, 1918, in Spartanburg, South Carolina (likely at Camp Wadsworth), less than a month after the Armistice brought a ceasefire to the war. He is buried in the Garland Family Cemetery, Limestone Cove, Unicoi County.

Private William (Will) Phillips was born on May 21, 1898, and died on October 11, 1918, at age twenty. He was born in Jonesborough (Washington). He died of the Spanish influenza on board a troopship en route to France. He was attached to Company D, 5th Infantry Replacement Regiment. He is buried at the Oakland Cumberland Presbyterian Church, Oakland Drive, Limestone, Tennessee. The inscription on his grave marker reads: "Away from home and friends of his youth,/ He heard the call of justice and truth,/

He died as a soldier./ He died at his post." In a letter to his brother Frank, composed while he was still in Camp Gordon, Georgia, Phillips wrote: "Well, I guess I will start to France tomorrow. I am all ready to go and want to go. It seems like the quicker I go, the quicker I come back home. Say Frank, I had my life insured so if I don't make it back, you get it. I took out $5,000 insurance."

In the parlance of the day, the $5,000 government life insurance policy provided by the federal government to the doughboys was reputed to be enough to pay for the purchase of a typical family farm—hence, the euphemism for a soldier's death, like that of Phillips: "He bought the farm."

5

LOST AT SEA AND IN THE AIR

East Tennesseans Who Perished in the Atlantic and the Pacific during World War II

Eternal Father, strong to save,	Oh Father, hear an humble prayer,
Whose arm hath bound the restless wave,	For those in peril in the air! Amen.
Who bidd'st the mighty ocean deep,	
Its own appointed limits keep.	Oh Trinity of love and pow'r,
	Our brethren shield in danger's hour,
Oh hear us when we cry to Thee,	From rock and tempest, fire and foe,
For those in peril on the sea! Amen.	Protect them where so e'er they go.
Eternal Father, lend Thy grace	Thus evermore shall rise to Thee
To those with wings who fly thro' space,	Glad hymns of praise from land and sea!
Thro wind and storm, thro' sun and rain,	Amen.
Oh bring them safely home again.	

—*The Navy Hymn*

Of the scores of East Tennesseans who perished during the Second World War, a remarkable number of sailors and soldiers from the region were among those who died in the sinking of several famous ships. These include the USS *Oklahoma*, lost at Pearl Harbor; the troopship *Dorchester*, sunk in the Atlantic and notable for being the shipwreck that inspired one of the nation's most well-known incidents of devotion and sacrifice by military chaplains; and at war's end, the USS *Indianapolis*, sunk just days after having delivered atomic bomb components to Tinian atoll. The stories of these men, and those of two East Tennesseans who by remarkable coincidence were crewmen on the last American bombers fated to fall over Germany and Japan, are explored in this chapter.

ENSIGN ALBERT K. MURRIAN, LOST IN THE PACIFIC

Among those Americans whose lives were lost in the vast reaches of the Pacific Theater of Operations, one young pilot from Knoxville disappeared along with the rest of his crewmen in his Navy patrol bomber, almost three months before the end of the Second World War. His son and only child, who grew up to become a Navy officer himself and a distinguished Knoxville lawyer and federal magistrate judge, recounts his father's life and service.

My father, Albert Kinzel Murrian, died in the line of duty in World War II. I would like to offer this information in honor of his memory. My Dad was born on January 26, 1922 in Knoxville, Tennessee. His parents, John Hendry Murrian and Helen Ault Murrian, were living at 127 Jennings Street at the time. He had an older brother, John Jr., and

younger brother, David. John Jr. is deceased and David lives in Antioch, Tennessee.

My Dad was known as "Al." His parents moved to North Knoxville when he was young and he was graduated from Central High School. He was in the band and selected to be drum major. He was a gifted musician and played the trumpet and cornet. He played in several dance bands. He attended Maryville College where he was also in the band and drum major. His sport was wrestling.

My Mom, Mary Gilbert Eppes, who was also raised in Knoxville, was visiting my Dad at Maryville College on December 7, 1941. They heard the news about Pearl Harbor on the radio and immediately knew that their lives would never be the same.

My Dad volunteered for Naval Aviation Cadet training and left Maryville College. He and my Mom were married in May 1944 while he was still in training at Pensacola Naval Air Station. He qualified to fly the PV1 Ventura [patrol bomber] and the PBY [Catalina] amphibious plane.

I was born on April 1, 1945 while my Dad was in the Pacific. He saw my picture before he died, because it was returned with his personal belongings. When he and his crew went missing in action on May 28, 1945, he was attached to Patrol Bombing Squadron 133, Asiatic Area and flying the PV1.

My middle name, "Phillip," comes from a man he flew with, Phillip Olson. Mr. Olson survived the war, and I have visited with him and his wife in Beverly, Massachusetts. He is now deceased. He told me how he and other pilots spent days searching the area where my Dad's plane is thought to have gone down.

My Dad was awarded the Distinguished Flying Cross, Air Medal, Purple Heart, American Campaign Medal, Asiatic Pacific Campaign Medal, and WW II Victory Medal. His father had been awarded the Distinguished Service Cross, French Croix de Guerre, Purple Heart, British Military Cross

Ensign Albert Kinzel Murrian.

and other medals for his bravery and distinguished service in World War I as a member of a Tennessee Army National Guard Unit.

I have a letter signed by President Truman that states in part that my Dad "stands in the unbroken line of patriots who have dared to die that freedom might live, and grow, and increase its blessings. Freedom lives, and through it, he lives—in a way that humbles the undertakings of most men." I believe that to be true.[1]

Ensign Albert Kinzel Murrian is remembered at the Honolulu Memorial to the Missing (often known as the Punchbowl), in Hawaii.

GLENN S. MORTON, LOST OVER BURMA

The China-Burma-India ("CBI") Theater was created by the Allies in late 1941 to counter Japanese incursions into China and, to a lesser extent, Burma (now Myanmar) and other

Technical Sergeant Glenn S. Morton.

Southeast Asian countries and provide logistical support to Chiang Kai-shek's Nationalist Chinese forces. It was also designated symbolically to provide moral support to China, in recognition of its years of lonely, unassisted combat against the Japanese since 1937. In October 1944, the CBI theater of operations came to an end, at least formally, when it was divided into the India-Burma theater and the China theater.

Technical Sergeant Glenn S. Morton was among a small number of East Tennesseans (the most famous of whom was the legendary coach of the University of Tennessee's football team and Army engineer officer, Brigadier General Robert R. Neyland) who served in this far-flung and lesser-known theater of operations. Morton was born on December 2, 1923, in Maryville (Blount) and served with the 493rd Bomb Squadron, 7th Bomb Group (Heavy), 10th Air Force, in the CBI. On October 22, 1944, he was on board a B-24J Liberator flying out of Pandaveswar, India, on a mission to Moulmein, Burma. He was the radio operator for his crew. Five minutes after dropping their bombs, the five-plane formation was attacked by eight to twelve Japanese fighters. Second Lieutenant Kenneth A. Hill, piloting another Liberator on the same mission, provided this report on the fate of Morton's plane:

> Five minutes after leaving the target at approximately 1202, the formation was jumped by from eight to twelve fighters. All I saw were Oscars [Nakajima Ki-43 fighter aircraft]. Lt Blair was flying in number two position on Lt. Young. Major Bradford was flying number four position directly behind Lt. Young. Lt. Bodmer was in number three position, and I was flying number five position. When the fighters were first sighted the formation tightened up considerably. On about the third or fourth pass, Lt. Blair's #2

engine caught on fire. He pulled out slightly to the left, and feathered the engine. The fire went out and Lt. Blair made a diving left turn into the clouds. He was not seen afterwards. Five minutes later Major Bradford appeared to be trying to look back to see what had happened to the other aircraft. . . . His aircraft went down slightly and to the left. He pulled up just under Lt. Bodmer, who was flying to the front and left of him. As he pulled up directly under the other aircraft, Lt. Bodmer pulled up and out. After Major Bradford had moved back into position Lt. Bodmer again took his own position. Almost immediately the same thing happened to Major Bradford. He pulled up under Lt. Bodmer, and his left vertical stabilizer went into Lt. Bodmer's bomb bay doors. Apparently #3 and #4 props of the other aircraft cut the tail of Major Bradford's ship off, just behind the waist window. The ship pulled up violently and fell off into what appeared to be a spin. At the same time Lt. Bodmer's aircraft lost one bomb bay door, and fell off on the right wing, did a half turn spin, and spiraled down. Both aircraft hit the water about 200 yards apart and exploded. No parachutes were seen to open.

The stricken bomber was last seen near Bilugyn Island in the Gulf of Martaban, off the

Glenn S. Morton appears in center of crew of his B-24J Liberator.

Bay of Bengal. Its missing crewmen's remains were never recovered, and they were officially declared dead as of October 4, 1946.

Crewmembers of the lost B-24J Liberator were:

Pilot, 1st Lt. Arthur J. Bodmer Jr.

Co-Pilot, 1st Lt. Joseph W. Coffman Jr.

Navigator, 2nd Lt. Ernest R. Ford Jr.

Bombardier, 2nd Lt. Fred H. Reed

Engineer, T/Sgt. Herbert P. Slesrick

Radio Operator, T/Sgt. Glenn S. Morton

Assistant Engineer, Sgt. Carter P. Bedard

Armorer-Gunner, Sgt. Clifford H. Grierson

Armorer-Gunner, Sgt. Marvin L. Caffery

Armorer-Gunner, S/Sgt. James J. Soptick

Glenn S. Morton is commemorated on the Tablets of the Missing at Fort Bonifacio, Manila American Cemetery, Philippines. He was awarded the Distinguished Service Cross, Air Medal, and Purple Heart.

THE SINKING OF THE *HMT ROHNA*

The HMT (His Majesty's Transport) *Rohna*, a British vessel carrying American troops, was blasted open by a German Henschel Hs-293 guided missile in 1943 off the coast of Algeria during the course of Operation Torch, the Allied landings in Vichy French-occupied North Africa. Around noon on November 25, 1943, *Rohna* and four other troopships left Oran in French Algeria. At sea, they joined Convoy KMF 26, which was passing on its way from Britain to Alexandria, Egypt.

Off Bougie, Algeria, the next day, the convoy was attacked by about thirty *Luftwaffe* Heinkel He-177 heavy bombers escorted by Junkers Ju-88 aircraft, followed by between six and nine

HMT *Rohna*.

torpedo bombers. The big Heinkels carried Hs-293 radio-guided "glide bombs," an early air-to-surface guided missile, some sixty of which they launched at the convoy. Unlike the Nazis' pulse-jet-powered V-1 cruise missile and the larger V-2 guided missile that were typically directed to their targets by pre-set gyrocompasses, the Hs-293 had to be steered by radio onto its target. The convoy's combined anti-aircraft fire seems to have impeded most of the attackers' attempts to direct their glide bombs on-target; unfortunately, the *Rohna* was the only casualty. One of the Heinkels released a glide bomb that struck the *Rohna*'s port (left-hand) side, at the aft end of her engine room and Number Six troop deck. Men poured on-deck, many of them badly wounded. The *Rohna* sank in a half-hour with a loss of 1,015 men, more than half of the total 1,981 American military personnel aboard her. The attack is the largest loss of US troops at sea due to enemy action in a single incident.

Private First Class Jesse W. Poteet.

A further thirty-five of the *Rohna*'s occupants later died of their wounds.[2]

Four East Tennesseans perished in the *Rohna*'s loss on November 26, 1943: Private First Class Jesse W. Poteet (Bradley), with the 853rd Engineer Battalion, who was born on February 14, 1915, in Whitfield County, Georgia; Technician 4th Grade Robert Fleming Pace Jr. (Hamilton) with the 31st Signal Construction Battalion; Sergeant Thomas O. Tyner (Hamilton), Army Air Forces; and James D. Tester (Washington) with Company I, 320th Infantry (see chapter 9 for his family story). All are memorialized at the North Africa American Cemetery, Carthage, Tunisia.

LAST HEAVY AMERICAN BOMBERS LOST OVER THE PACIFIC AND EUROPE

Captain Henry B. Baker was born on February 26, 1917, in Greeneville, Tennessee. Baker served as a navigator in the 20th Air Force's 45th Bomber Squadron, 58th Bombardment Wing, 40th Bomber Group, flying a B-29 Super-

fortress out of Tinian Island in the Central Pacific. It was a B-29, the *Enola Gay*, that also dropped the first atomic bomb on Hiroshima, Japan, on August 6, 1945. On August 14, 1945, Japan surrendered unconditionally to the Allies, effectively ending World War II. The mission of Baker and his fellow airmen on August 30, 1945, was to drop relief supplies of food and medicines to desperate Allied POWs awaiting liberation at Camp Fukuoka, on the northern shore of Japan's Kyushu Island.

In dense fog and pouring rain, Baker's B-29 attempted to cross the Sobo Mountain range but clipped a mountain peak and crashed, bursting into flames. The bomber's wreckage was located on Mount Sobozan, near the boundary of the villages of Miyazaki and Oita Ken. All twelve crewmembers aboard the bomber were killed. Their remains were recovered, but only three bodies were definitely identified: Baker, Corporal John D. Dangerfield, and Staff Sergeant Walter R. Gustaveson. Since 1995, the tragedy has been commemorated annually by the Japanese citizens of nearby towns and villages at a Monument for Peace—dedicated

Boeing B-29 Superfortress.

in memory of the twelve victims of the crash and a Japanese pilot who died in an unrelated incident—in the nearby town of Takachiho. A local publication from a town near the crash scene envisioned the crew's last thoughts as follows:

> With the feeling of finally being able to return to their hometowns, Chief Pilot Henry Baker and eleven other crewmembers attempted to fly just over the mountain ridge extending from Kyushu's Mt. Sobo to Mt. Katamuki. All were experienced in flying bomber aircraft over long distances. All fought in the war, risking their lives for their country. However, even these soldiers of the victorious country were probably in slight disbelief that they had survived the war. They were positioned according to their seating arrangements on board their [airplane]. They sat unaware of the tragedy about to occur only seconds after entering the dense fog mixed with light rain. Some of these men were possibly lighting a cigarette; again, some may have been gazing at a picture of their loved ones whom they thought they would be able to see soon.
>
> Not having to worry anymore about the attacks by persistent small Japanese Army fighter planes or about flak from anti-aircraft guns, they were quietly performing their last duty, flying through the skies of Kyushu. Their plane attempted to fly over an area about as high as the mountain ridge connecting [two high mountains] near the peak of Mt. Shoji. Right at that moment, a dreadful disaster occurred. A section of the plane made contact with the top of the ridge, instantly causing the plane to crash and be engulfed in flames. Not even the slightest chance of escape was possible.[3]

Captain Baker is buried at the Andrew Johnson National Cemetery, Greeneville, Tennessee. Baker's B-29 may have been the last US bomber lost in active service in the Pacific

Theater during World War II—much like his fellow East Tennessean, Howard Goodner, who was on the last American bomber lost in Europe during World War II and who is profiled in the next account.

Crewmembers of the lost B-29 Superfortress were:

Pilot, 1st Lt. Jack Lee Riggs

2nd Lt. John G. Cornwell

1st Lt. Alfred F. Eiken

1st Lt. George H. Williamson

Capt. Henry Brown Baker

S/Sgt. Henry N. Frees

Cpl. John D. Dangerfield

S/Sgt. Solomon H. ("Solly") Groner

S/Sgt. Walter R. Gustaveson

Cpl. Bob L. Miller

Sgt. John M. Hodges Jr.

Sgt. Norman E. Henninger

Howard Glenn Goodner was born in Etowah (McMinn) on March 2, 1924; he was the son of M. Ernest Goodner and Callie Howard, and he grew up in Cleveland (Bradley). He was attending college at Western Kentucky University in

Marker commemorating the death of Captain Henry Brown Baker.

Technical Sergeant Howard G. Goodner's fated plane, the *Black Cat*. Courtesy of the Air Museum in Britain.

1942 when he volunteered for service with the Army Air Forces, and on March 23, 1942, he shipped off for induction at Fort Oglethorpe, Georgia, to join the USAAF.[5] In time, he was assigned to the 8th Air Force, one of the principal tools of the Allies' bombing campaign over Germany. He served in the 787th Bomber Squadron (Heavy) and, later, in the elite 784th Bomber Squadron (Heavy), both squadrons of the 466th Bomber Group of the "Mighty Eight," based at Air Station 120 at Attlebridge, England. Rising in rank to become a Technical Sergeant, he served as a radio operator on several Consolidated B-24 Liberator bombers.

On April 21, 1945, Sergeant Goodner and the rest of the aircrew with which he served, piloted by First Lieutenant Richard J. Farrington and accompanied by command pilot Captain Louis C. Wieser, boarded a B-24J nicknamed of the *Black Cat*, serial number 42–95592, on a bombing mission against a rail viaduct in Salzburg, Austria. The *Black Cat* did not survive this mission: the aircraft was struck by flak at an altitude of over 20,000 feet over Regensburg, Germany and, within seconds, the bomber caught fire, entered into a spin, and disintegrated. The Davis wing, mounted high on the *Black Cat*'s fuselage (and being a chronic structural defect of the B-24 aircraft series),

folded and broke free from the bomber's fuselage as she plummeted to earth. Of the *Black Cat*'s twelve crewmen, only two—the bombardier and one of the waist gunners—survived. The *Black Cat* had the fate of being the last American bomber to fall in the air war over Europe; it was the last of over four thousand B-17s and B-24s of the 8th Air Force to be downed in combat between 1942 and 1945.[6] When Goodner and his nine fellow airmen lost their lives near Regensburg, only sixteen days remained before the surrender of Nazi Germany. To compound the tragedy, Goodner's family and the other nine crewmembers' families began to learn of their deaths as word of V-E Day was breaking.[7]

Goodner's remains were repatriated from Germany, and he was buried in December 1948 at Hillcrest Memorial Gardens in his hometown of Cleveland. The memory of Goodner's funeral—in particular, of being in a room at his grandmother's house, filled with colors and flowers and sobbing adults—was one of the earliest childhood recollections of his then two-year-old nephew, Thomas Childers.[8] Himself an East Tennessean who later became a history professor at the University of Pennsylvania, Childers set out to explore the fateful mission of the *Black Cat* and the death of his uncle in the early 1990s. That quest led to an award-winning book, *Wings of Morning: The Story of the Last American Bomber Shot Down Over Germany in World War II*. In his research, Professor Childers adduced the fate of his uncle: not wearing a parachute, he free-fell to earth, his body landing in a field outside the Bavarian village of Scharmassing. His death was witnessed by Maria Wittig, a teenager in 1945, who recalled Goodner as being "athletic looking, fair-skinned, handsome."[9]

In 2005, as part of a commemorative series of aviation-related stamps and in honor of the sixtieth anniversary of the *Black Cat*'s loss, the United States Postal Service introduced a limited-edition stamp, featuring a Liberator with the *Black Cat*'s distinctive livery and "nose art." An excerpt from a *Washington Post* article provided additional details from the stamp's first-day-of-issuance ceremony in Vienna, Austria, as to how the stamp came about and also how Professor Childers came to research his uncle, Technical Sergeant Goodner:

> Today, when more than 60 million of the stamps go on sale at post offices across the nation, customers might assume the aircraft pictured on it is a generic model of a plane that has long since faded from use. Only a few know its story of heartbreak, and how it has continued to reverberate in the lives of a few for so long. . . .
>
> [The families of the ten crewmen who died] were informed of their loss on May 8, V-E Day, when the rest of the nation rejoiced. "The plane being shot down at the very end of the war—it has haunted my family for so many years, and I finally went to Germany and found the crash site," says Thomas Childers, Goodner's nephew, whose 1995 book, *Wings of Morning*, chronicled the story of the plane and its crew. "This farmer started scratching around in the dirt, and he pulled out a 50-caliber machine gun bullet. I was speechless. Every year when they plow, parts of the plane come to the surface." . . .
>
> If not for Childers's curiosity, the *Black Cat*'s history would have almost certainly been lost. After his grandmother died in the small town of Cleveland, Tenn., in 1991, Childers went to clear out her house before it was sold.
>
> He found a musty case of letters—more than 300—that Howard Goodner, her son, had sent during the war. Childers was a historian of German culture and politics by then, and to find such a cache of original documents from World War II was striking.
>
> He put down his academic research and took up the story of his uncle's flight crew. . . . In his research, he discovered that the *Black Cat* was the last bomber shot down over Germany before peace was declared, lending the story its tragic footnote. When he discovered that the crew wasn't originally scheduled to fly that day—and that bad weather should have forced them to cancel before takeoff—it only added to the pathos.
>
> He wound up in Bavaria, where he met [Maria] Wittig. He did not tell her that Goodner was his uncle, only that he was researching the history of the plane. When she tapped Goodner's picture, as the airman who came to earth in the field, he felt a tingle on the back of his neck. . . .
>
> [T]he surviving members of the 466th Bomb Group, of which the *Black Cat* was a part, began petitioning the U.S. Postal Service to memorialize the *Black Cat* on a stamp. It was a long shot.
>
> "We get 50,000 people a year who say, 'I've got the best idea ever for a stamp,'" says David Failor, executive director of stamp services for the U.S. Postal Service. "We actually release about 25 or 30 subjects for commemorative stamps each year. You can figure the math."
>
> The ceremony yesterday marked the official release of the stamp's one-year run. Looking at the plane on the stamp—the sunlight warm on its silver wings, a river glinting in the green fields below—lends a bittersweet irony to one of Goodner's last letters home.
>
> He was on a three-day break at a resort in Mundesley on the British shore. There were dining rooms—not chow lines—soft beds, hot water, a golf course. He walked on the beach, played darts at a local pub. He loved it.
>
> "Just hoping the war ends soon," he wrote to his family, "and we can all get home again."
>
> The letter was dated April 8, 1945.
>
> Howard Goodner had 13 days to live.[10]

Though his bomber was the last to fall from

Postage stamp honoring the B-24 Liberator shot down just short of WWII victory. Courtesy US Postal Service.

Crew of the *Black Cat* with Howard Goodner, kneeling, second from right, and pilot Richard Farrington, standing third from right. Photo by Jonathan Newton. Courtesy of the *Washington Post*.

European skies, Howard Goodner would not be the last East Tennessean to perish in the Second World War, as will be seen.

The crew members of the *Black Cat* on its fatal mission of April 21, 1945, were:

Pilot, 1st Lt. Richard J. Farrington

Command Pilot, Capt. Louis C. Wieser

Co-Pilot, 1st Lt. John A. Regan

Navigator, 2nd Lt. John Perella Jr.

Navigator, 1st Lt. George E. Noe

Bombardier, 2nd Lt. Christ D. Manners (*survived*)

"Mickey" (H2X navigational and bombing radar) operator, 1st Lt. John C. Murphy

Flight Engineer, T/Sgt. Jerome Barrett

Radio Operator, T/Sgt. Howard Glenn Goodner

Waist Gunner, S/Sgt. Albert Seraydarian (*survived*)

Waist Gunner, S/Sgt. John C. Brennan

Tail Gunner, S/Sgt. Robert E. Peterson

MILLER W. BEALS:
OUT ON THE DEEP BLUE SEA

Fireman Second Class Miller W. Beals was born in Sulphur Springs (Washington), Tennessee, on August 10, 1919, the son of Alley Marshall

Fireman Second Class Miller W. Beals.

Beals and Tennie Miller. He worked as an automobile mechanic at a Johnson City dealership to support his wife and two daughters before entering service. He enlisted in the Navy on April 4, 1944, in Chattanooga and completed basic training at Camp Peary outside Williamsburg, Virginia. As a new Seaman Second Class, Beals came home on leave before shipping out to Pearl Harbor for duty. On July 27, 1944, he reported aboard the USS *Bush* (DD-529), a *Fletcher*-class destroyer, along with twenty other men whose last named started with the letter "B." Soon after, Miller Beals and the *Bush* set sail to join in the war in the Pacific. For the *Bush*, it was to rejoin the fight: she had already distinguished herself in the Pacific, including in service during the Cape Gloucester landings and off New Britain and New Guinea.[11] On August 5, 1944, Miller was reassigned to the *Bush*'s Engineer Division. Bearing the rank of Fireman Second Class, Beals crossed over the Equator on August 12, 1944, two days after his twenty-fifth birthday; as Navy custom dictates, he was transformed from a "Pollywog" (one who has never crossed the Equator) to a "Shellback."

Beals' first action was during the Morotai landings on September 15, 1944. He participated in four unit campaigns—Leyte, Luzon (to include the Mindoro and Lingayen Gulf landings), Iwo Jima, and Okinawa. At Okinawa on April 6, 1945, the *Bush* was assigned to radar picket duty, meaning that she was part of a screen of destroyers and destroyer escorts providing radar detection against aerial intrusion for the rest of the fleet. The destroyer had already downed one Japanese *kamikaze* suicide aircraft when she was hit by another. The first of three *kamikazes* hit the *Bush* at 3:15 p.m. on the starboard (right) side between the stacks, exploding in the forward engine room. The second hit at 5:25 p.m. on her port side, also

between the stacks, starting a fire that nearly severed the ship. Twenty minutes later, a third *kamikaze* hit, also to port, just above the main deck, and its impact sprayed the *Bush* with debris and fire. Even after this third strike, it was believed the *Bush* might be salvageable, but as heavy swells rocked the vessel, she began to cave in amidships.

As the *Bush* broke apart, the captain gave the abandon-ship order. Beals was seen in the water after the abandon-ship command was given; he swam to one lifeboat, but finding it to be full, he told those aboard that he would swim to the next life raft. He never made it there. Beals is listed on the Tablets of the Missing, at the Honolulu Memorial (often known as the Punchbowl), Hawaii, and is memorialized at the Fairview United Methodist Church Cemetery, Section 2, Row 2, Grave 32, in Jonesborough, Tennessee.

When he died, Miller Beals was twenty-five years old and was married to Daisy V. Dixon; they had two daughters. After the war, a shipmate of Beals visited the family and told them how courageous Beals had been. Daisy penned a poem after Beals's buddy's visit and having received official news of her husband's death. It was printed in the *Jonesborough Herald & Tribune* newspaper:

Miller W. Beals and Daisy Beals, with daughters Peggy (left) and Carol (right), 1944, along with the Purple Heart given to the Beals family.

My darling in Heaven, waiting for me
Where there is no more pain and war.
And I'll be with you soon, my dear,
And we will part no more.
They said you lost your life, my dear,
Out on the deep blue sea, but I know
Where you are, sweetheart, you're up home
Waiting for me.
In the letter you ask your buddy to write,
He told of your great love for us.
And how true, darling, you were to me,
Just like I was to thee.
And he said in battles you were so brave,
Always doing your best,
And God said, Miller, you've stood enough,
Come on home to rest.
Darling this is so hard to bear,
For we love and miss you so
We can never meet again on earth,
But we will in Heaven, I know.

THE LAST FLIGHT OF *MR. FIVE BY FIVE*

East Tennesseans Vaughn Reaves, of Greene-ville (Greene), and Cecil M. May, of Trade (Johnson), were both crew members on a B-17G bomber, serial number 42–29955, nicknamed *Mr. Five by Five*, an aircraft of the 427th Bomb Squadron, 303rd Bomb Group (Heavy), known as the "Hell's Angels." (Coincidentally, at least one more East Tennessean—Knoxvillian Walter Dooley—was lost in action while serving as the co-pilot of a B-17 in this same bomb group.) *Mr. Five by Five* departed from Molesworth, England, on a mission to Bremen, Germany, on November 26, 1943. The airplane was last seen ten kilometers west of Texel Island, off the Dutch coast, when it dropped

Kneeling, second from left, Vaughn Reaves, and second from right, believed to be Cecil May.

out of formation, wheels down. No parachutes were observed when *Mr. Five by Five* crashed at Den Helder, Netherlands. All of its crewmembers were killed in the wreck, and the bodies of nine crewmembers were never recovered. Both Reaves and May were twenty-two years old at the time.

Previously, Reaves and May had served on the B-17 *Vicious Virgin*, which performed a daring air raid on Le Bourget airport outside Nazi-occupied Paris along with over one hundred other bombers on August 16, 1943. The picture of Reaves and the man believed to be May was taken after that mission. While it cannot be confirmed that this is actually May, it seems highly probable that it is. According to Gary Moncur, archivist for the 303rd Bomb Group: "As of now, we believe Cecil May is on the front row, second from the right, but that is unconfirmed. Our guess is based on his small size, as required for the ball-turret, and his not wearing a Mae West [i.e., inflatable life preserver] and chute. They did not fit in the ball [turret], so they would have been lying outside it nearby. The photo was taken immediately after that mission."[12] Service as a gunner in the tightly-cramped confines of the ball turrets fitted to the bellies of B-17s required a man of small stature as a matter of necessity.

Vaughn Reaves was born on March 27, 1921, and enlisted at Camp Forrest, Tennessee, outside Tullahoma on July 4, 1942. He is memorialized at the Netherlands American Cemetery, Margraten, the Netherlands. May is memorialized at the Cambridge American Cemetery, Cambridge, England. The crewmembers of *Mr. Five by Five* were:

Pilot, Capt. Addell A. Cote

Co-Pilot, 2nd Lt. Clarence C. Bixler

Navigator, 1st Lt. Wilbur R. Barnhill

Bombardier, 1st Lt. John W. Hull

Engineer/Top Turret Gunner, T/Sgt. John R. Arter

Assistant Radio Operator/Ball Turret Gunner, S/Sgt. Cecil M. May

Radio Operator/Gunner, T/Sgt. Vaughn Reaves

Tail Gunner, S/Sgt. Paul Gunsauls

Right Waist Gunner, S/Sgt. John M. Micek

Assistant Engineer/Left Waist Gunner, S/Sgt. Theodore Gomes

NORMANDY, AT SEA AND IN THE AIR

East Tennesseans were heavily involved in the liberation of northwestern Europe from Nazi control as part of the massive land, sea, and air effort called Operation Overlord. Casualties during the Normandy campaign took place

Gunner's Mate Second Class William H. Carney Jr.

prior to and over about a two-and-a-half-month span, ending with Paris's liberation on August 25, 1944. While most East Tennesseans who fell in combat during France's liberation were from the Army's ground forces, there are two notable exceptions, whose stories are chronicled below. In all, 135 East Tennessee servicemen died from wounds or were killed outright in the lengthy and bloody Normandy campaign.

Gunner's Mate Second Class William H. Carney Jr. was born on April 4, 1919, in Dayton (Rhea). He was killed when his ship, *LST* (Landing Ship Tank) *523*, hit a mine and sank off the coast of France on June 19, 1944, roughly two weeks after D-Day. Assigned to the Western Task Force's Follow-Up Force B sailing from Falmouth, *LST-523* and her crew made two round trips to the Normandy beachhead, each time delivering supplies and removing the wounded. On her third trip, with the troops and material of the 300th Engineer Combat Battalion embarked in addition to her crew of 195 and a forty-man medical staff, *LST-523* struck a mine while maneuvering from the Utah Beach anchorage to the beachhead. The force of the blast split the LST in two pieces, and she sank rapidly; ninety-four men of the 300th Engineers plus forty-one of her own crew went down with her. The LST sank not far from the Pointe du Hoc promontory, site of the 2nd Ranger Battalion's famous D-Day assault on German fortifications. For her actions, *LST-523* earned one Battle Star. The Purple Heart was posthumously awarded to Carney. He is listed on the Tablets of the Missing at the Normandy American Cemetery, Colleville-sur-Mer, France.

Lyon Elkin Agee Jr. was born in Randolph, Cumberland County, Virginia on September 25, 1924, the eldest son of Lyon Elkin Agee, Senior and Pearl M. Evans. He lived in Mag-

Second Lieutenant Lyon Elkin Agee Jr., center.

nolia, Mingo County, West Virginia before the family moved to Johnson City (Washington). He graduated from Science Hill High School, class of 1940, and attended the State Teachers College (now East Tennessee State University) in Johnson City for two years before entering service. Agee enlisted on May 29, 1942, in Knoxville and was sent to the Army Air Forces Classification Center in Nashville, where he was selected as a pilot trainee.

After pre-flight training, he was chosen to become a fighter pilot, and he earned his flight wings at Napier Field, Alabama, on August 30, 1943. On graduation, Second Lieutenant Agee was assigned to the 512th Fighter Squadron (FS), 406th Fighter Group (FG) and honed his skills at Key Field in Meridian, Mississippi, Dale Mabry Field near Tallahassee, Florida, and Congaree Army Airfield near Columbia, South Carolina. He entered into a competition in 1943 and took away the Highest Aerial Gunnery Medal. The medal for this competition was struck from a 1943 silver half-dollar.

Agee and the 406th FG shipped off to England from New York harbor aboard the British vessel *Stirling Castle* on March 13, 1944. On arrival, he joined the 303rd Fighter Wing, 9th Air Force, at the Ashford air base in Kent. Agee started flying combat missions on May 9 out of USAAF Station 417, a former Royal Air Force station in Ashford. His assigned aircraft was a P-47D Thunderbolt, serial number 42–75345/ L3-G, featuring a standing puppy dog painted on its nose.

On June 22, 1944, his five-man flight, Blue Flight—with Agee flying as "Blue 4"—was assigned to do low-level bombing and strafing runs on German units in the Cherbourg area. At 1:50 pm, he called his wingman, First Lieutenant Creighton Smith, "Blue 3," and reported he had been hit and needed assistance. Blue 3 acknowledged, but then Smith took a hit from an antiaircraft round in his engine, so he now

had his own problems. Smith last reported seeing Agee flying at about five hundred feet, heading in a northerly direction over the English Channel steering towards England, with his engine smoking badly. He never made it to England, nor was he ever seen again; he apparently crashed in the Channel.

Agee received the Air Medal with three Oak Leaf Clusters and the Purple Heart. Two days after his disappearance, he was promoted to First Lieutenant; he was declared dead on June 23, 1945. His name is inscribed on the Tablets of the Missing, Cambridge American Cemetery, Cambridge, England. He was nineteen years old at the time of his death. His younger brother, Bill (Billy) E. Agee, also served in World War II with the Army.

First Lieutenant James B. ("J. B.") McKamey was born on August 10, 1921, in Bluff City (Sullivan) and moved with his family, first to Boones Creek and then to Johnson City (Washington). He was graduated from Science Hill High School, in the class of 1939 and completed two years as a JROTC cadet. He attended the State Teachers College (now East Tennessee State University) in Johnson City for his freshman year, 1939–1940. While at State Teachers College, McKamey learned to fly as a member of the school's Civilian Pilot Training Program. After that, he attended Milligan College in Carter County for his 1940–1941 year.

McKamey enlisted on May 23, 1942, at Knoxville. He was accepted for service as an aviation cadet; after passing the required tests at the Army Air Forces Classification Center in Nashville, McKamey was dispatched to the San Antonio Aviation Cadet Center at Kelly Field in San Antonio, often referred to as "Kelly on the Hill." Over 10,000 cadets there awaited their final evaluation as to their position of

First Lieutenant James B. ("J. B.") McKamey.

B-26 Marauder *Bad Penny,* in front.

training—pilot, navigator, or bombardier. Of these, only 400 would be selected to start training in an experimental flying course. Due to the lack of pilot instructors, this brand-new course was intended to produce a fully-qualified pilot and instructor in just over ninety days (thirteen weeks), versus the normal nine months of pre-flight, primary, basic, and advanced flight schools. McKamey met the strict requirements and excelled in all the tests. He was selected to be one of the 400, members of a group nicknamed "Hap Arnold's Guinea Pigs," in honor of the chief of the Army Air Forces, General H. H. "Hap" Arnold.

At Hunter Field, Savannah, Georgia, he was reassigned to the 497th Bomb Squadron, 344th Bomb Group (Medium), 99th Bomb Wing, 9th

Air Force, in December 1943. Equipped with Martin B-26B Marauders, McKamey's crew left Hunter Field on January 26, 1944, and arrived at USAAF Station 169-S (formerly RAF Base Stansted Mountfitchet), thirty miles northeast of London, on February 8. McKamey and his crew completed their first combat flight on March 6, bombing a German airfield at Bernay-Saint-Martin, France. They continued attacking airfields, V-missile sites, marshalling yards, U-boat pens, coastal defenses, and other targets in France, Belgium, and Holland until the beginning of May.

The unit's mission changed to preparation for the Normandy landings by striking vital bridges and transportation targets in France. On D-Day, June 6, 1944, the 344th was the lead group for the entire 9th Air Force, attacking German coastal batteries at Cherbourg and along Utah Beach. On D-Day, McKamey and his crew flew in a Marauder named the *Bad Penny*. While passing over Utah Beach, *Bad Penny* was hit by flak (anti-aircraft fire) at 6:09 a.m. McKamey pulled out of the formation, his craft's right engine and bomb bay on fire. He hit the bailout alarm, and three crew members left the B-26's rear. They were killed by German machine-gun fire as they floated down. McKamey, the co-pilot, and the bombardier stayed with the *Bad Penny* to get her back past the Allied flotilla, salvo (dispose of) the undropped bombs, and bail out themselves, but she exploded around three and one-half minutes later, falling into the English Channel near the coastline at Montebourg, France. The three crewmen remaining aboard the stricken bomber were never seen again; the bodies of the three who were shot while bailing out by the Germans were later returned to their loved ones for burial.

McKamey was twenty-two years old at the time of his death and had participated in the Air Offensive-Europe and Normandy campaigns. He was decorated with the Air Medal with three Oak Leaf Clusters and a Purple Heart. While listed as Missing in Action, he was promoted to first lieutenant. He, along with John Keehley and Jess Scott, are listed on the Tablets of the Missing at the Normandy American Cemetery, Colleville-sur-Mer, France. He also has memorial markers at the Arlington National Cemetery and at Monte Vista Memorial Gardens in Johnson City.

The crewmembers of the *Bad Penny* on June 6, 1944 were:

Pilot, 2nd Lt. James B. McKamey, Johnson City, Tennessee

Co-Pilot and Flight Officer, 2nd Lt. John F. Keehley, Rochester, New York

Bombardier (assigned Tail Gunner), Sgt. Jess M. Scott, Lakeland, Florida

Radio-Gunner, S/Sgt. Salvador J. Zuniga, San Diego, California

Engineer-Gunner, S/Sgt. Manuel H. Larini, Sonora, Arizona

Tail Gunner (sitting in for Sgt. Scott), Sgt. Howard L. Finn, Chicago, Illinois

PEARL HARBOR

The Japanese attack on the United States naval base at Pearl Harbor, Hawaii, in the early morning of December 7, 1941, dramatically pulled the United States out of its non-interventionist stance into the far-flung wars that were already raging in Asia and Europe. The attack led directly to this country's entry into World War II. Proclaimed by President Franklin D. Roosevelt as a "day which will live in infamy," the surprise attack resulted in the deaths of 2,008 sailors, 218 soldiers and airmen, 109 Marines, and 68 civilians in less than two hours. In all, 2,403 Americans died; more than 1,000 others were wounded. These were just the initial wave of a long list of Americans—and East Tennesseans—who would perish over the next three years and nine months, until the Pacific war officially ended with the signing of peace in Tokyo Bay on September 2, 1945.

The largest loss of life at Pearl Harbor occurred with the sinking of the USS *Arizona* (BB-39) by Japanese bombers. The explosions of the vessel's forward ammunition magazines killed 1,177 of the 1,512 crewmen onboard at the time, over half of the lives lost during the entire attack. The *Arizona* wreck

USS *Arizona* (BB-39) sunk and burning furiously, December 7, 1941. Her forward magazines had exploded when she was struck by a Japanese bomb. At left, men on the stern of USS *Tennessee* (BB-43) are playing fire hoses on the water to force burning oil away from their ship. Official US Navy Photograph, National Archives.

remains at Pearl Harbor to commemorate the men of her crew, lost that December morning in 1941, and its sunken hulk is designated as a National Historic Landmark. Onboard the battleship that fateful day were eight East Tennesseans: James L. Bridges, Gordon B. King, Charles L. Echols, and John B. McPherson (all Knox County), James M. Robertson (Hamblen), Charlie L. Burnett (Sevier), John W. Farmer (Hamilton), and Charles D. Byrd (Sullivan).

Robertson, from Morristown, served as a machinist's mate first class. He was posthu-

mously decorated with the American Defense Service Medal, World War II Victory Medal, and a Purple Heart Medal. A memorial marker is located at Liberty Hill United Methodist Church in Morristown; every year on Memorial Day, VFW Post 5266's Honor Guard places a wreath and honors his memory with a twenty-one-gun salute and taps. Charlie L. Burnett was from Seymour and held the rank of seaman second class. John W. Farmer, coxswain, hailed from Chattanooga. Charles D. Byrd of Kingsport served as a seaman first class.

Aboard the USS *Oklahoma* (BB-37) on De-

USS *Oklahoma* (BB-37) passing Alcatraz Island, San Francisco Bay, California, during the 1930s. This black-and-white image is from a hand-colored photograph. Courtesy of the USS Oklahoma Association, 1975. Collection of Irvin Barrett, US Naval History and Heritage Command Photograph.

cember 7 were five from East Tennessee—Seaman Second Class William V. Campbell (Carter), Fireman Third Class Warren H. Crim (Sullivan), Watertender First Class Kenneth O. Burger from Athens (McMinn), Seaman First Class William Brooks (Claiborne), and Fireman First Class Paul E. Saylor from Johnson City (Washington). The battleship, a veteran of World War I service, took three torpedo hits almost immediately after the first Japanese bombs fell. As she capsized quickly to her port side, two more torpedoes struck home, and some of her crewmen were strafed while abandoning ship. In less than fifteen minutes, the *Oklahoma* rolled over until halted by her masts touching bottom, with her propellers and keel exposed.

A total of 429 of the *Oklahoma*'s crew died

in the attack; the Navy's efforts to remove the remains of those trapped inside the ship after her sinking were both grim and herculean. One of those killed, Catholic priest Lieutenant (j.g.) Aloysius Schmitt, was the first American chaplain of any faith to die in World War II, having helped at least twelve men escape through a porthole before he drowned. Unlike the *Arizona*, which remains an underwater memorial, the *Oklahoma* was salvaged but sank yet again during a storm while being towed on its way to San Francisco. Its whereabouts under the Pacific remain unknown.

Non-Navy personnel Private Robert C. Duff and Sergeant James Strickland Jr. were also killed during the Pearl Harbor attack, most likely in the course of the fierce bombing and strafing of the Army's aviation facilities located at Hickam Field on Oahu. Duff served with the 18th Bomb Wing of the USAAF. A native of Elizabethton (Carter), he is now buried in Union Cemetery, Leesburg, Loudoun County, Virginia. Sergeant Strickland, who hailed from Erwin (Unicoi), was the son of Mr. and Mrs. James E. Strickland Sr. He was a graduate of Erwin High School, where he played on the varsity baseball, football, and basketball teams. He had been in the service since November 1939, when a group of twenty-six Erwin students collectively enlisted in the armed forces. He was an NCO in the Army Air Forces' Ordnance Department; he was assigned to the USAAF's 23rd Material Squadron, serving like Private Duff at Hickam Field when the Japanese assaulted Hickam and other air bases across Oahu on December 7.

All of the East Tennesseans who perished at and around Pearl Harbor on December 7, 1941,
received the Purple Heart posthumously and, with the exception of Duff, are memorialized on the Tablets of the Missing at the Honolulu Memorial (often known as the Punchbowl), Hawaii.

THE PLOESTI AIR RAIDS

On August 1, 1943, as part of Operation Tidal Wave, five bomb groups from the 8th and 9th Air Forces—the 44th, 93rd, and 389th from the 8th, and the 98th and 376th of the 9th—were assigned to bomb nine oil refineries around Ploesti, Romania, north of Bucharest. In 1943, the Ploesti refineries provided about sixty percent of Nazi Germany's oil supply, making it critical to the *Wehrmacht*'s war effort. It was the only American air action of the war in which five Medals of Honor were issued.

Consolidated Liberator, on its bomb run over the Ploesti oil refineries, August 1, 1943. 44th Bomb Group Photograph Collection.

All five bomb groups that took part received Presidential Unit Citations. The B-24D Liberator heavy bombers flew low to avoid radar detection and dropped time-delayed bombs. Out of the 177 B-24s that took part in the raid, 167 managed to attack their targets. Fifty-seven Liberators were lost in total: fifty-four over Ploesti and three more crashing into the Mediterranean. Three East Tennesseans died on the desperate aerial mission to destroy the Ploesti refineries: Staff Sergeant Roy E. Carney (Fentress); Technical Sergeant Leon D. Pemberton, Harriman (Morgan); and Staff Sergeant Jim M. Crumley, Johnson City (Washington).

Sergeant Carney was assigned to the 345th Bomb Squadron, 98th Bomb Group (Heavy), the "Pyramiders," flying out of Benghazi, Libya. He was the tail gunner onboard a B-24D Liberator, serial number 41–11886, nicknamed *Lil' Joe*.

The aircraft had a large fuel leak in the bomb bay prior to target, pressed on, and bombed the target with the Liberator bursting into flames from leaked fuel. The pilot pulled the aircraft into a climb to enable the crew to bail out. Six crewmembers bailed out, but only two survived their descent, and *Lil' Joe* exploded and crashed. Its pilot and radio operator were pulled from the wreckage, badly burned, and became POWs. Roy Carney is listed on the Tablets of the Missing, Florence American Cemetery, Florence, Italy. He received posthumously the Distinguished Flying Cross, Air Medal with four Oak Leaf Clusters, and Purple Heart.

The crewmembers of the *Lil' Joe* on the Ploesti raid:

Pilot, 1st Lt. Lindley P. Hussey (POW)

Co-Pilot, 2nd Lt. Donald Jenkins (KIA)

The crew of the *Lil' Joe* with their plane—note pith helmets to shield them from the Libyan sun. Courtesy of the American Air Museum in Britain.

Bombardier, 1st Lt. Allan E. Peterson (KIA)

Navigator, 2nd Lt. Phillip E. Nelson (KIA)

Engineer, T/Sgt. Lloyd T. Fowlkes (KIA)

Gunner, S/Sgt. Raymond A. Heisner (POW)

Radio Operator, T/Sgt. Edmond T. Terry (POW)

Gunner, S/Sgt. James E. Turner (POW)

Gunner, S/Sgt. Roy E. Carney (KIA)

Technical Sergeant Leon D. Pemberton, missing in action since August 1, 1943, served as radio operator aboard aircraft B-24D, serial number 42–40663, nicknamed *Maternity Ward*. Pemberton initially was not assigned to the mission on the morning of August 1, 1943, but fate interceded, and he was assigned at the last minute to the aircrew of the *Maternity Ward*, due to three of its crewmembers being ill. He received posthumously the Distinguished Flying Cross, Air Medal, and Purple Heart. Pemberton is memorialized at the Sicily-Rome American Cemetery, Nettuno, Italy, outside Anzio.

The crewmembers of the *Maternity Ward* on Pemberton's last mission were:

Pilot, 1st Lt. John Vernon Ward

Co-Pilot, 1st Lt. Andrew L. Anderson

Navigator, 2nd Lt. Beverly S. Huntley

Bombardier, 2nd Lt. Harry C. Crump Jr.

Engineer, T/Sgt. James J. Toth

Assistant Engineer, S/Sgt. Kenneth L. Turner

Radio Operator, T/Sgt. Leon D. Pemberton

Assistant Radio Operator, S/Sgt. Harold W. Scott

Gunner, S/Sgt. Robert Earl Long

Armorer Gunner, S/Sgt. William J. Fay

Staff Sergeant James M. "Jim" Crumley, Johnson City (Washington) enlisted January 28,

Staff Sergeant James M. "Jim" Crumley.

1941, and arrived in England on May 27, 1943. He was assigned to the 330th Bomb Squadron, 93rd Bomb Group (Heavy), 201st Bomb Wing, 8th Air Force. He was a waist gunner on B-24D-75 AC# 42–40609, *Jersey Bounce*, flying out of USAAF Station 104 Hardwick, near Norfolk, England. As with the other B-24s that attacked Ploesti on August 1, 1943, his unit was temporarily moved to North African airfields for the raid.

Crumley's plane, piloted by Lieutenant Worthy Long, was in the right-wing position of the second element over Ploesti. By the time this element appeared near the target refineries, the enemy's flak and air-defense systems were fully activated. While approaching the target, Romanian fighters attacked Long's plane from the rear, killing the tail gunner, Staff Sergeant Havens, the crew's first casualty on the raid. Besides the damage to the tail, there was damage to the nose, and wind whistled through the fuselage. Then, the number four engine was knocked out, and a shell blew up the control pedestal in the cockpit. Two "flak towers" (anti-aircraft gun towers) ripped up each side as the B-24 raced between them, and the number one engine caught fire. Somehow, the pilots managed to coax the *Jersey Bounce* down into an open field where she slid into a berm; the nose broke away and rolled with Lieutenant Norman Adams, the bombardier, still inside. He was unable to hear for three days after the crash. The *Jersey Bounce*'s pilot and co-pilot escaped through the broken nose but suffered burns that required hospitalization. The surviving crewmen were taken prisoner before the last bomber had flown over Ploesti. Lieutenant Lipton, the navigator, was struck in the chest and was burned while trying to exit the plane. He died of his wounds. Staff Sergeant Crumley was killed by flak before the crash. He was twenty-five. Of the ten-man crew, six were killed in action, and four became prisoners of war.

Crumley received posthumously the Distinguished Flying Cross, Air Medal, and Purple Heart. He is interred at the Ardennes American Cemetery, Neupré, Belgium, and he also has a memorial marker at Oak Hill Cemetery in Johnson City.

Crewmembers of the *Jersey Bounce* were:

Pilot, 1st Lt. Worthy A. Long (POW)

Co-Pilot, 2nd Lt. John O. Lockhart (POW)

Navigator, 2nd Lt. David Lipten (KIA)

Bombardier, 2nd Lt. Norman C. Adams (POW)

Waist Gunner, S/Sgt. James M. "Jim" Crumley (KIA)

Waist Gunner, S/Sgt. Ignatius J. Deicidue (POW)

Tail Gunner, S/Sgt. Leycester D. "Dee" Havens (KIA)

Engineer Top Turret, T/Sgt. Maurice J. Peterson (KIA)

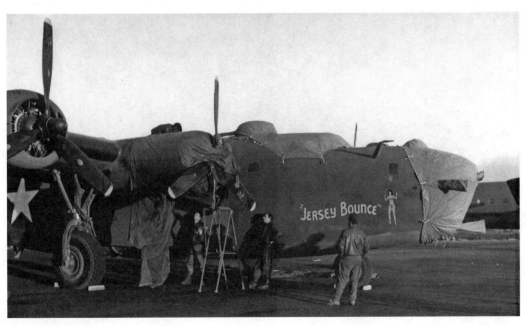

B-24 *Jersey Bounce.*

Radio Operator, T/Sgt. Frederick E. Fagan Jr. (KIA)

Gunner, S/Sgt. Marion J. Szaras (KIA)

THE BATTLE OF SAVO ISLAND

The Battle of Savo Island took place in early August 1942 during the Pacific war between an Allied naval force assembled to support and defend US Marine landings at the start of the Guadalcanal campaign and a flotilla of seven Japanese cruisers plus one destroyer commanded by Vice Admiral Gunichi Mikawa. Mikawa's aim was to ambush a joint American-Australian naval force that had been placed in a blocking position to protect the transports and cargo ships supporting the landings of the 1st Marine Division on Guadalcanal and the adja-

cent islands of Tulagi, Gavutu, and Tanambogo. Attacking under cover of darkness in the early morning hours of August 9, Mikawa succeeded in achieving near-total surprise, leading some of the surviving US sailors to give the vicious nighttime engagement the bitter nickname of "battle of the sitting ducks."

The Japanese suffered only light damage; on the Allied side, three American heavy cruisers, USS *Vincennes* (CA-44), USS *Quincy* (CA-39), and USS *Astoria* (CA-34), were sunk along with an Australian heavy cruiser, HMAS *Canberra*. The channel in which these vessels went down, Sealark Channel, earned the grim sobriquet of "Ironbottom Sound"; among the other lost vessels of both sides, its waters would also claim the USS *Juneau* two months later. Some 1,270 Allied seamen lost their lives in the Battle of

Map of Savo Island and Ironbottom Sound showing locations, from left to right: USS *Astoria*, USS *Quincy*, and USS *Vincennes*.

USS *Astoria*.

USS *Quincy*.

USS *Vincennes*.

Savo Island, and 709 were wounded. Yet, having wrought havoc and substantial damage to the Allied warships, Mikawa's force broke off the action and retired; the Americans' transports and cargo vessels remained unharmed.

Twelve East Tennessee seamen perished during the lopsided naval battle. Onboard the *Vincennes* were Seaman First Class Oscar J. Bennett, Erwin (Unicoi); Steward's Mate Second Class Samuel Cantrell, Knoxville (Knox); Seaman Second Class French A. Finnell, Cleveland (Bradley); Coxswain Edwin Hines, Johnson City (Washington); Seaman First Class Thomas L. Merriman, Dunlap (Sequatchie); Seaman Second Class Robert D. Rainwater (Carter); and Fireman Third Class Clyde E. Stephens, Chattanooga (Hamilton). Three more sailors perished aboard the *Quincy*—Apprentice Seaman Dallace Cable (Johnson); Seaman First Class Chester E. Hamby (Cumberland); and Fireman First Class Jim Taylor, Johnson City (Washington)—and Chief Car-

penter's Mate Edward S. Osborn, Frankfort, Ohio (whose wife was from Knoxville), served aboard the *Astoria*. All twelve are remembered on the Tablets of the Missing, Fort Bonifacio, Manila American Cemetery, Philippines.

Historian and retired United States Air Force veteran Allen D. Jackson extensively researched Fireman First Class Taylor, as he has done with many of the fallen from the Tri-Cities area. Excerpts from Jackson's research capture the perilous events that befell Taylor, his fellow sailors, and their ships during the Battle of Savo Island:

> The Japanese attacked both the southern and northern Allied Forces. Those in the south were attacked first, and even after the ships in the north were notified and saw the flares, the sailors on these ships did not awaken their captains or sound general quarters. At 1:44 a.m. the Japanese cruisers started firing torpedoes at our forces to the north. *Astoria* did sound general quarters first at 1:49 a.m., and the Japanese forces

Seaman Second Class French A. Finnell.

The Taylor brothers, left to right: Stokes Taylor, Jim Taylor, David Taylor, and Ben Taylor

turned on their searchlights at 1:50 a.m., exposing our three cruisers. Our northern force was caught in the middle of the lights and cut down by a massive Japanese cross-fire. The captain of the *Quincy*, Samuel N. Moore, got to the bridge very quickly and ordered his crews to commence firing, but the gun crews were not ready, and within minutes she was hit heavily by the Imperial Japanese Navy cruisers, *Aoba*, *Furutaka* and *Tenryu*, and set ablaze.

Captain Moore then ordered the *Quincy* to charge the eastern Japanese forces, but while attempting to do so, was hit by two more torpedoes from the *Tenryu*, causing severe damage to her. She did manage to fire a few main gun salvos, hitting the Japanese cruiser *Chokai*, killing or wounding around thirty-six men. At 2:10 a.m., *Quincy* was hit again by incoming shells, killing almost all the bridge crew including Captain Moore.

The *Aoba* fired another torpedo at 2:16 a.m., and the remaining operational guns of the *Quincy* went silent. At 2:38 a.m., she sank bow first, taking Jim and another 369 of his fellow shipmates down with her. The *Quincy* was the first ship to be sunk in the area now known as Ironbottom Sound. The USS *Vincennes* followed her down twelve minutes later, at 2:50 a.m., and the *Astoria* at 12:15 pm. [HMAS *Canberra*] was heavily damaged and was scuttled on the 9th to Ironbottom Sound.

Tragedy befell Jim Taylor's parents, John and Lilly, again two years later, in 1944, when Jim's brother, Corporal Stokes M. Taylor, was killed in Belgium during the Battle of the Bulge. Stokes Taylor received the Distinguished Service Cross posthumously. Two other Taylor brothers, Ben and David, survived their World War II service.

THE LOSS OF THE USAT *DORCHESTER*

At 12:55 pm on February 3, 1943, about one hundred miles from the coastline of Greenland on a cold, moonless night, a German torpedo hit the US Army Transport (USAT) *Dorchester's* starboard side. The power and lights went out immediately. The vessel was transporting a contingent of Army and Army Air Force personnel, having departed from St. John's harbor in Newfoundland as part of SG-19, a six-ship convoy. Although ordered to sleep with their lifebelts on, many troops did not do so because of their discomfort from the heat trapped within the ship's hull from her boilers. After the torpedoing, the passengers came up to the deck to find a scene of stark contrasts. According to survivors' accounts, the ship's skipper, Captain Preston S. Krecker, assisted his men in abandoning ship, and he went down with the ship in doing so. Both the water and the air temperatures approached freezing. Under such conditions, hypothermia set in rapidly among those forced to take to the water, and the troopship sank within twenty-five minutes. Of 904 aboard the *Dorchester*, only 230 were saved from the icy waters by Coast Guard cutters.

The *Dorchester's* sinking is well known;

US Army Transport *Dorchester*.

among its passengers and crew lost at sea were four Army chaplains, who gave up their own lifejackets to save others and, when last seen, they were singing hymns, their arms linked together, and went down with the ship. These were a Methodist minister, the Rev. George L. Fox; Jewish Reformed rabbi Dr. Alexander D. Goode; a Roman Catholic priest, Father John P. Washington; and a Reformed Church in America minister, the Rev. Clark V. Poling. Known as the "Four Chaplains" or the "Immortal Chaplains," their loss has been commemorated in books and documentaries, with a unique medal awarded by Congress in 1960, and with a postage stamp. In memory of their heroic sacrifice, by act of Congress, each February 3 is "Four Chaplains Day."

Four East Tennesseans were lost at sea on the *Dorchester*. They are Yeoman Third Class Peter T. Zecchini Jr., US Coast Guard (Campbell); Private Joel R. Barlow, US Army (Greene); Private Carson A. Ricks, US Army Air Forces (Meigs); Private George D. Plemons (Roane); and Private William T. Cannon Jr., US Army Air Forces (Washington). All five East Tennesseans were recognized with the Purple Heart posthumously and are memorialized at the World War II East Coast Memorial. Unknown to many because of its location within the continental United States, this unique memorial stands in Battery Park in New York City. The memorial commemorates those soldiers, sailors, marines, coastguardsmen, merchant marines, and airmen who met their deaths in the service of their country in the western waters of the Atlantic Ocean during World War II. Its axis is oriented on the Statue of Liberty. On each side of the axis are four gray granite pylons, upon which are inscribed the name, rank, organization, and state of each of the 4,611 missing in the Atlantic.

As will be seen later in this book, the loss of one of these East Tennesseans—Peter Zecchini—would be keenly felt by one of his family members who was also serving on active duty. The consequences of Peter's death may have been one of several contributing factors to the death, some two years after the torpedoing of the *Dorchester*, of his sister, Julia M. Zecchini, whose own story is recounted in chapter 13.

THE SINKING OF THE SS *LEOPOLDVILLE*

On Christmas Eve 1944, the troopship SS *Leopoldville* made her final crossing of the English Channel. The former Belgian passenger liner carried 2,235 men of the 66th Infantry Division from Southampton, England, to Cherbourg, France, reinforcements critically needed for the then-ongoing Battle of the Bulge. Five and a half miles from shore, the *Leopoldville* was struck by a torpedo fired by *U-486*. Several hundred troops were killed in the initial blast. The exact number of casualties was 763 dead, of which 493 were never found. Although the ship sank slowly, a combination of errors, delays, oversights, and communication problems resulted in the deaths of so many.[13]

Five East Tennessee infantrymen died in the sinking of the troop transport: Private Fay Cannon (Greene), Private First Class Daniel H. Brown (Hamilton), Private Burl W. Ailey (Jefferson), Private First Class Robert R. Miller (Knox), and Technical Sergeant Forrest D. Taylor (Knox). Each man was assigned to the 262nd Infantry Regiment, 66th Infantry Division. All, with the exception of Taylor, who is buried at Greenwood Cemetery, Knoxville,

SS *Leopoldville*.

Private Fay Cannon.

Technical Sergeant Forrest D. Taylor.

Tennessee, are remembered on the Tablets of the Missing, Normandy American Cemetery, Colleville-sur-Mer, France.

THE LAST FLIGHT OF THE
TENNESSEE TODDY

The *Tennessee Toddy*, a Boeing B-17G bomber, serial number 43–38854, departed from England early in the morning of March 24, 1945—relatively late in the air war in Europe—on a bombing mission to Hopsten, Germany, 400 kilometers west of Berlin. Its strategic location on the main routes for Allied heavy bombers meant that Hopsten played an important role in the anti-aircraft defense of the Third Reich's embattled capital. A unit of the world's first operational jet fighters, the Messerschmitt Me-262, was deployed at the Hopsten airfield. By April 6, 1945, British forces captured the airfield without a fight—unfortunately, just two weeks after the *Tennessee Toddy* was destroyed by anti-aircraft fire. On the day that the *Tennessee Toddy* was downed by German flak guns, and two East Tennesseans aboard her perished, the war in Europe had less than a month and a half until its end.

Two East Tennesseans were aboard the *Tennessee Toddy:* Second Lieutenant Sherrill R. Williams (Anderson), a seasoned combat pilot, and Technical Sergeant Ralph W. Smith (Greene), top turret gunner. They served with the 751st Bomb Squadron, 458th Bomb Group, based in Glatton, England. Williams was posthumously decorated with the Purple Heart and the Air Medal with two Oak Leaf Clusters; Smith received the Purple Heart and the Air Medal with one Oak Leaf Cluster. In all, six members of the B-17's crew died; three survived as POWs after bailing out of their crippled bomber. In an article in the June 21, 1987, issue of *The Atlanta Journal and the Atlanta Constitution*, J. Edwin Smith records the final hours of the *Tennessee Toddy*:

> The night before he flew his 20th and final mission over occupied Nazi Germany, [Sherrill] Williams spent the early evening hours of March 23, 1945, in England trying to keep the minds of his B-17 crew—the eight other men of the *Tennessee Toddy*—off the next day's bombing run over Hopsten. "When we were down in the mouth, Sherrill could always cheer us up," recalls Burnard Klimoski, Williams' waist gunner. "Sherrill always took everything with a grin. It means a lot to have someone like that with you."
>
> "I remember Sherrill speaking of his child and what a wonderful little girl she was. He had one of her baby shoes with him (in the cockpit), and he wrote down all the missions we went up on the sole. He was proud to be her father and said there was no other kid like her in the world."
>
> The next day at 7 a.m., with a light drizzle falling on the runways of Glatton airfield near Conington, he boarded his plane. Silently, Klimoski watched as Williams penned "Hopsten" on the sole of his little girl's baby shoe, then the waist gunner braced himself for take-off as Williams eased the B-17 through the rain and down the runway.
>
> Hours later, at 21,000 feet over Munster, the *Toddy* approached the target. "The bomb door bays were opened," Klimoski recalls. "Lieutenant Williams told us, 'Watch out for fighters.' Then we took a hit. Flak."
>
> There was a flash where anti-aircraft fire tore into the right wing, nine feet of which was torn off by the explosion. The aircraft peeled off to the right, turned over on its back and went plummeting out of control.
>
> At 10:13 a.m., the *Tennessee Toddy* went into a spin and broke in half. On that morning, 44 days before the war would end, life ceased for six American airmen—the pilot, Williams; the co-pilot, Earl Downey; the

flight officer, Benjamin Bushey; and sergeants Ralph Smith, Eugene Bussard and Anthony Demaro.[14]

Both Williams and Smith were interred at the Netherlands American Cemetery in Margraten, Netherlands.

TYPHOON COBRA

One of the worst battles faced by the US Navy's Third Fleet in late 1944 was not a naval engagement between its forces and the Imperial Japanese Navy; it was with the forces of nature, as the fleet encountered a massive typhoon off the Philippines' eastern coast. Sometimes known as "Halsey's Typhoon," this ruthless storm was later fictionalized by Navy veteran Herman Wouk in his novel (and its later movie adaptation) *The Caine Mutiny*. Among the nearly eight hundred sailors and officers lost in this typhoon were two East Tennesseans. The typhoon, informally named "Cobra," hit on December 16, 1944, as the Third Fleet, commanded by Admiral William F. "Bull" Halsey, headed east into the open Pacific to refuel and replenish supplies from tankers and cargo ships to the fleet's aircraft carriers, battleships, cruisers, and destroyers, out of range of the Japanese airplanes, including the deadly *kamikaze* suicide airplanes, based in the Philippines. The fleet had been supporting the successful US invasion of the Philippines.

Early on December 17, Commander George F. Kosco, Halsey's chief meteorologist, advised the admiral of a storm well to the east and "likely to turn north." Unfortunately, Kosco was dead wrong, and the Third Fleet sailed straight into the heart of an intensifying storm front. During the next twenty-four hours, Halsey ordered other course changes that sent "many of

USS *Hull.*

USS *Monoghan.*

the ships into the core of the typhoon, with sixty-foot waves and sustained winds estimated at higher than 145 miles per hour." A worse course of action for a fleet encountering the equivalent of a Category 5 hurricane, far from the security of sheltered harbor facilities in which to weather a severe storm, could hardly have been imagined. The resulting losses to Third Fleet included 3 destroyers capsized and sunk, over 25 other ships damaged (at least 9 of those being heavily damaged and requiring significant repairs), and 146 planes on aircraft carriers destroyed when they broke loose and slid across decks, sometimes starting fires when their fuel tanks split open. After the storm ended, 790 officers and enlisted men were either dead or washed overboard and presumed killed. Halsey's illustrious naval career survived the court of inquiry that followed. While the court held that Halsey had committed an error of judgment in sailing the Third Fleet directly into Typhoon Cobra, Halsey was not formally sanctioned. He resumed command of the Third Fleet in spring 1945.[15]

As a result of Typhoon Cobra, three East Tennesseans were reported missing in the Pacific Ocean since December 18, 1944, each being a crewman of two of the sunken destroyers. They were Radioman Second Class Lester Cantrell Mullins of Harrison (Hamilton) and Seaman Second Class Louis McKeehan from Elizabethton (Carter), both of whom served on the destroyer USS *Hull* (DD-350), and Seaman Second Class Carlus B. Moore of Bristol (Sullivan) of the destroyer USS *Monaghan* (DD-354). A total of seven officers and fifty-five enlisted men of the crew of the *Hull* survived the disaster. The majority of the personnel saved (five officers and thirty-six men) were rescued by the USS *Tabberrer* (DE-418), which engaged in

a painstaking and vigilant search for survivors. All three men are listed on the Tablets of the Missing at Fort Bonifacio, Manila American Cemetery, Philippines.

THE SINKING OF THE USS *HELENA*

Not long after Guadalcanal was secured in early 1943, the Allies learned that Japanese forces were constructing a sizeable air base on the Central Solomon island of New Georgia, some two hundred miles northwest of Guadalcanal and within striking range of Henderson Field and other American bases. The next step in the US advance in the South Pacific area therefore became Operation Toenails, an effort to seize the New Georgia island group, in order both to neutralize the Japanese air presence at the Munda Point field and, through a strategy of "island-hopping," tighten the perimeter around Japan's largest base in the area: the naval and air facilities at Rabaul on the island of New Britain. Among American naval losses during this phase of the Pacific war was the USS *Helena*, sister ship of the ill-fated *Juneau*.

The light cruiser *Helena* (CL-50) was built at the New York Navy Yard and commissioned on September 18, 1939. The *Helena* was the first ship to receive the Navy Unit Commendation for her actions in the battles of Cape Esperance, Guadalcanal, and Kula Gula. Of ten American cruisers lost during World War II, *Helena* was the second-to-last, the final being the USS *Indianapolis*. The cruiser performed patrol and escort duties in the area around Guadalcanal until the end of February 1943, when she was dispatched to Sydney, Australia, for an overhaul. Afterwards, *Helena* returned to battle off the coast of New Georgia to shell Japanese po-

USS *Helena*.

sitions in preparation for Operation Toenails, the New Georgia campaign, which began on June 20, 1943. She continued to support the Army's and Marines' landings, and just before midnight on July 4, she moved into the Kula Gulf with an escort group to support another Marine landing there. Shortly after midnight on the July 5, her big guns opened up in her last shore bombardment. The landings were completed successfully by dawn, but in the afternoon of July 5, 1943, a run of the "Tokyo Express" (the nickname given to Imperial Japanese ships delivering equipment, personnel, and supplies at night to avoid Allied air attacks) was anticipated, and so the escort group turned north to meet it in what would be called the Battle of Kula Gulf.

By midnight on July 5, 1943, *Helena*'s group was off the northwest corner of New Georgia, a flotilla that included three cruisers and four destroyers. Racing down "The Slot" (the channel

between Rabaul and the various islands in the Solomon chain) to face them were three groups of Japanese destroyers forming another "Tokyo Express" run, totaling ten enemy ships. Four of them peeled off to land troops in a counterattack against the Marines. By 1:57 a.m. on July 6, the *Helena* commenced firing; unfortunately, she had expended all her flashless powder and was forced to use a type of gunpowder that produced immense flames when fired, making her a perfect target at night. Just seven minutes after she opened fire—silhouetted by her own gunfire—*Helena* was torpedoed by the Japanese destroyers *Suzukaze* and *Tanikaze* off Kolombangara Island, adjacent to New Georgia. In the next three minutes, two more torpedoes hit her. Almost at once, she began to jackknife, and the *Helena* sank on the early morning of July 6, 1943; 174 sailors were lost when she went down.

Three East Tennesseans perished in her

Seaman First Class General P. Douglas.

Seaman James A. Dyer.

sinking: General P. Douglas (Campbell), Fred B. Howell (Unicoi), and James A. Dyer (Washington), all holding the rank of seaman first class. Two of the three—Douglas and Dyer—were recognized with the Silver Star for gallantry in action. Dyer and Howell are memorialized at the Manila American Cemetery, Fort Bonifacio, Philippines, as is Douglas. However, an amazing discovery, sixty-three years after he was lost at sea, would bring Douglas's remains back home to East Tennessee at long last.

Seaman First Class General P. Douglas was born on July 26, 1922, in Newcomb, Tennessee, to Walter and Bertha Douglas. He enlisted in the Navy just ten days after the Japanese attack on Pearl Harbor, and he served on the *Helena*. Although 700 were rescued, 150 crewmen went missing, including Douglas, who died two weeks before his 21st birthday. He was officially declared dead on August 10, 1945. In a strange twist of fate, Douglas's dog tag and remains were located in the South Pacific, more than fifty miles from where the battle took place and sixty-four years after his death. For years, his sister Regina made multiple inquiries about her brother's fate. He remained MIA until 2006, when a native beachcomber on Ranongga—a Solomon island west of Kolombangara and some fifty miles distant from the site of the Battle of Kula Gulf—discovered a dog tag protruding from the sand along with human remains. Local officials notified the US Department of Defense, which dispatched a team from the Joint POW/MIA Accounting Command (JPAC) in Hawaii to excavate the area. The JPAC team discovered more remains and a metal four-leaf clover that Douglas typically carried. JPAC theorized that Douglas's body may have washed to shore on Ranongga where it was buried by local inhabitants, and his impromptu grave was later opened up by the action of erosion. Unfortunately, his sole surviving sibling, Regina Douglas, died in November 2007. S1C General Douglas's remains were finally buried beside her in the Douglas family plot at the Gollihon Cemetery in Sneedville on January 26, 2008.[16]

James A. Dyer from Washington County was also aboard the *Helena*. He was born on March 4, 1922, in Johnson City, enlisting in the Navy in Nashville on February 15, 1942. After basic training in San Diego, Apprentice Seaman Dyer was dispatched to Pearl Harbor for assignment and joined the *Helena*'s crew. In

addition to being memorialized at the Philippines American Cemetery in Manila, there is a memorial marker at the Monte Vista Memorial Gardens in Johnson City. Like General Douglas and Fred Howell, James Dyer was declared dead on August 10, 1945.

THE ORDEAL OF THE USS *INDIANAPOLIS*: TWENTY-TWO EAST TENNESSEANS LOST AT SEA IN THE FINAL DAYS OF WORLD WAR II

The torpedoing of the USS *Indianapolis* (CA-35) resulted in the greatest single loss of life in American naval history, with approximately 300 crew members going down with the ship and another 580 dying in the water from dehydration, exposure, saltwater poisoning, and shark attacks. Only 317 of its original crew of

USS *Indianapolis* off the Mare Island Navy Yard, California, July 10, 1945, after her final overhaul and repair of combat damage. Photograph from the Bureau of Ships Collection, National Archives.

1,196 survived the ordeal. The heavy cruiser was torpedoed just after midnight on July 30, 1945, by the Japanese submarine *I-58*. The *Indianapolis* sank in twelve minutes, but it took four days for her survivors to be spotted purely by accident by a crew on routine air patrol and for the Navy to learn of the sinking. Traditionally the flagship of the Fifth Fleet, the warship was en route to Leyte Gulf in the Philippines from Tinian Island, having just delivered components for "Little Boy," the atomic bomb that would be dropped on Hiroshima on August 6, 1945. The crewmembers that perished were all awarded the Purple Heart and are memorialized at the Manila American Cemetery, Fort Bonifacio, Philippines.

Twenty-two men from East Tennessee were on the *Indianapolis* representing eleven different counties, from Hamilton and Marion in the southwest to Hawkins and Sullivan in the northeast. Knox and Marion Counties had the largest losses, with five from Knox and four from Marion. In terms of population, Marion County's losses on the *Indianapolis* were proportionally the most severe. These East Tennessee crewmembers held a wide array of duties and ranks, from ship's cook, boilermaker, and fireman to lieutenant commander and ship's dentist.

While many of them did not know each other before boarding the ship, it would stand to reason that, in a total crew of 1,179—almost a small town on the water—some of these East Tennesseans would likely gravitate to one another. For a community as small as Marion County, it seems entirely possible that its four lost men—Ralph H. Holloway, Thomas H. Jordan, Clifford C. Owensby, and Aulton N. Phillips Sr.—knew each other as civilians and perhaps even enlisted together. Many of the men onboard were married; some had children, like Winston H. Watson from Madison-

Lieutenant Commander Earl O. Henry.

Lieutenant Commander Kyle C. Moore.

Seaman Ralph H. Holloway.

Seaman Clifford C. Owensby.

ville (Monroe), born on December 13, 1919. He was married to Edna Dailey and left one child, a daughter, Martha Annetta, to survive his loss.

Three enlisted sailors from Knox County were aboard the *Indianapolis*—Seaman Second Class Stanley F. Jones, Seaman Second Class Joseph R. Sampson, and Seaman First Class Carey L. Underwood—as well as two officers, Earl O. Henry and Kyle C. Moore, both lieutenant commanders. Born in 1911, Henry served with the Navy Dental Corps; Moore was born in 1908 and earned a Silver Star along with the Purple Heart. Henry's life and service have been extensively documented and remembered by his son, Earl Henry Jr., who was born in 1945, just six weeks before his father perished on the Indianapolis at the age of thirty-three. The younger Henry described the weeks before he

was born and before his father, whom he never knew, vanished:

> My father received photos of me aboard the USS *Indianapolis* at Guam, the last port of call before the tragic sinking of the ship. Through a personal phone call, Captain [Charles B.] McVay expressed to my mother how excited my father was as he showed the baby pictures to anyone who would look.
>
> In response to my birth, my father paid the highest compliment to my mother with this handwritten note addressed to Earl, Jr. as an expression of the quality of "Dad" he planned to be. My mother received this after his death: "To Earl Jr.—If I make as good a Dad as your Mother *does* a Mother, son, you'll be O.K."[17]

Besides being a skilled and much-admired dentist, Earl Henry had a fascinating avocation as a bird watcher, bird caller, bird painter, and ornithologist. He started studying birds at the age of twelve and taught himself taxidermy, creating a collection of eighty-seven species that now belong to Ijams Nature Center in Knoxville, which also named an ornithology trail in his memory.[18] In addition, he could imitate the calls of more than sixty birds, and he often entertained the *Indianapolis*'s crew with his imitations, bringing down the house. Henry began painting birds as a serious hobby during the last three years of his life. *Knoxville News Sentinel* columnist Sam Venable wrote: "Simply stated, here was a walking, whistling, brush-wielding genius who happened to fill teeth Monday through Friday. Not bad work for a kid from Knoxville who died at sea, thirty-three years young."[19]

The loss of the *Indianapolis*, one week before the A-bombing of Hiroshima, was one of the last combat losses of the US Navy, not just during the Second World War but to this day. While its sinking haunted the memories of the families and loved ones of its lost crew members, its skipper, Captain McVay, carried

a mental weight for the torpedoing of his beloved ship to his dying day. Although he was promoted to rear admiral, the taint of a postwar court-martial alleging failure to take evasive action ("zigzagging") to protect against Japanese submarines like *I-58* haunted him, and McVay committed suicide in 1968. In a sense, McVay was another victim of the *Indianapolis*, alongside his twenty-two dead East Tennessee shipmates.

THE SINKING OF THE USS *JUNEAU*

In one of the most bitterly contested areas of the Pacific Theater, one of the first Allied victories—and the first major American amphibious operation of the war in either Europe or the Pacific—was the foray launched by US Marine, naval, and Army forces to take the islands of Guadalcanal, Tulagi, and Florida from the Japanese. Originally expected to be a brief engagement, Operation Watchtower became a campaign that took some seven months and

USS *Juneau* in New York Harbor, February 11, 1942. Photograph from the Bureau of Ships Collection, National Archives #19-N-28144.

resulted in the deaths of approximately 7,100 Allied and 19,000 Japanese combatants. Lying in the Solomon Islands of the South Pacific, east of New Guinea and northeast of Australia, Guadalcanal's strategic location made it a lodestone for attention by both sides. Sealark Channel (soon to be known as "Ironbottom Sound") and the other sea lanes surrounding Guadalcanal—which would be dubbed *Gadakanaru*, the "Island of Death," by the Japanese—saw multiple naval engagements. In one of the savage sea battles that contributed to the sinking of sixty-seven warships on both sides, four East Tennesseans would perish aboard the USS *Juneau* (CL-52), a ship that became legendary not just for its own combat prowess but also for the legend of five fighting brothers from Iowa.

On the night of November 12–13, 1942, the light cruiser *Juneau* was part of Task Force 65, intended to stop a Japanese fleet headed for Guadalcanal. The Japanese goal was to bombard the island's sole airfield (later named Henderson Field) from the sea and then land enough of their troops to retake it from the Allied forces. During the ensuing naval clash, later named the Naval Battle of Guadalcanal, the *Juneau* and USS *Atlanta* were credited with sinking two enemy destroyers. However, the *Juneau* was struck by a torpedo from the destroyer *Amatsukaze* and was forced to retire from the action. With only one propeller functioning, the *Juneau* proceeded to escape through Ironbottom Sound, along with the damaged heavy cruiser and Task Force 65's flagship, USS *San Francisco* (CA-38), *Juneau*'s sister ship, the cruiser USS *Helena* (CL-50), and two destroyers.

At about 10:00 a.m. on November 13, the Japanese submarine *I-26* fired three torpedoes at the *San Francisco*. Missing their intended target, they continued towards the *Juneau*.

After dodging the first two torpedoes, the *Juneau* was struck by the third—in almost exactly the same location as the previously inflicted damage—straight into *Juneau*'s ammunition magazine. The direct hit caused a catastrophic explosion that split the cruiser in two, and she sank in twenty seconds. There was little time for *Juneau*'s sailors to escape. Of her 683 crew members onboard, only ten survived. Four East Tennesseans were aboard the *Juneau* on that fateful morning. Seaman First Class Harold W. Massengill of Morristown (Hamblen); Coxswain John C. Baker and Seaman First Class Garnet H. Bowlin, both of Chattanooga (Hamilton); and Mess Attendant First Class Marvin R. Jones of Sweetwater (Monroe) were killed in the explosion or died later from drowning and injuries. All four are listed on the Tablets of the Missing at Fort Bonifacio, Manila American Cemetery, Philippines.

Perhaps the *Juneau*'s most famed crewmembers were the five Sullivan brothers of Waterloo, Iowa, all of whom were lost when the ship went down. As a direct result of the Sullivans' deaths (and the deaths of four of the Borgstrom brothers within a few months of

The five Sullivan brothers. Courtesy of U.S. Naval Historical Center.

each other, two years later), the War Department adopted the Sole Survivor Policy in 1948, allowing the surviving sons of families who had already lost a family member in wartime to be exempt from military service. This policy continues in effect to this day.

One *Juneau* survivor, Allan C. Heyn, Gunner's Mate Second Class, provided a poignant account of the sinking and the ensuing pandemonium:

> [A]nother night went on and the next day, this gunner's mate … said that there was a hospital ship there and we were going to go over to it. There was three of us, him, me and another fellow, and he said that we should swim over to it and leave the doughnut [life raft]. We didn't know whether to or not. You hated to leave it there because you knew if you got out in the water, you were gone. So he dove in the water and swam off and he just kept swimming out over the water and he wouldn't turn around. You could see the sharks going after him and he swam and kicked and swam. And he hollered to us to come and get him with the raft, to paddle towards him but he kept swimming the other way. We paddled towards him and finally he got tired. He turned around and came towards us and he got back before the sharks got him.

Heyn was finally rescued on November 22, 1942, ten days after the *Juneau*'s sinking:

> [A]bout noontime that day a PBY [Catalina seaplane] flew over and circled around and then it went away again. Well, I gave up. I figured, well, I guess it's just like all the other planes, they ain't gonna bother, they figure you ain't worthwhile coming for. Or maybe they didn't know what I was because I was all black. I might have been a Jap for all they knew. A couple of hours later they come back and they flew around me and they dropped smoke bombs all around me.

Well, that built up my hope a lot and I took off my shirt and I waved at them and they waved back at me and then they went off and I could see them way off flying. And I figured, well, they must be guiding the ship to me. And that's what they were doing because it wasn't long before I could see the mast of a ship coming over the horizon and it was the USS *Ballard* [a destroyer]. They lowered a small boat and came out and picked me up and took me aboard there and that's about all, for I went on into sickbay.[20]

Regrettably, none of her East Tennessee crewmen were among the tiny number of the survivors of the *Juneau*'s sudden demise and the agonizing odyssey of those who survived to be shipwrecked on life rafts, like Allan Heyn.

In an amazing finale to the story, wreckage from the Juneau was discovered on March 17, 2018, by the expedition crew of the research vessel *Petrel*. The *Atlanta*-class light cruiser was found 4,200 meters (about 2.6 miles) below the surface, resting on the floor of the South Pacific off the coast of the Solomons.[21]

THE MYSTERY OF THE *USS* PICKEREL

Two young sailors from Maryville (Blount)— J. W. Wayne Pierce and Elmer H. Russell—were aboard the USS *Pickerel* (SS-177), which went missing in the Pacific on May 6, 1943. Pierce, a seaman second class, was born January 21, 1922, in Champaign, Illinois, and Russell, also a seaman second class, was born six months earlier in Maryville on July 25, 1921. Given their ages and the fact that they were Maryville residents, it seems likely that they knew one another and may have perhaps even enlisted together. The two sailors, along with fellow crewmembers— seventy-four in all—were reported missing in

Seaman Second Class J. W. (Wayne) Pierce.

Seaman Second Class Elmer H. Russell.

USS *Pickerel* (SS-177), circa 1937. Courtesy of Bureau of Ships Collection, National Archives.

action on May 6, 1943, and officially declared dead on August 10, 1945. They are remembered on the Tablets of the Missing, National Memorial Cemetery of the Pacific, Honolulu, Hawaii.

The loss of USS *Pickerel* during her seventh war patrol is one of the many mysteries of World War II. Having sunk five Japanese ships and damaged another two freighters and eight sampans on her earlier patrols, the submarine left Pearl Harbor on March 18, 1943. She topped off with fuel at Midway on March 22; departed for the waters around Honshu, Japan; and was never heard from again. The *Pickerel* was stricken from the Naval Vessel Register on August 19, 1943.

The *Pickerel*, commanded by Lieutenant

Lieutenant Commander Augustus H. Alston Jr.

Commander Augustus H. Alston Jr., was the first US sub to be lost in the Central Pacific area. According to submarine researchers Paul Wittmer and Charles Hinman, anti-submarine attack reports submitted by the Japanese at the end of the war listed one attack that could conceivably have been made on the *Pickerel*. This occurred on April 3, 1943, off Shiranuka Lighthouse, located on Honshu's northern tip. While this position fell outside the area assigned to the *Pickerel* on its last patrol, no other US submarines were near the area of the attack. Further, a special notation was made on the Japanese records to the effect that they are inaccurate for the month of April 1943. Thus, there is every reason to speculate that, if the *Pickerel* did survive the April 3 attack, she may have been attacked later in her own area, and the attack may not have been reported. The most probable cause of the submarine's loss

is that she was sunk by enemy depth charge attack. Operational casualties or mine explosions represent other possibilities but are not thought to be likely.[22]

WALTER E. DOOLEY AND FDR'S POTATO PEELER KIDS

First Lieutenant Walter E. Dooley, of Knoxville (Knox), was born on November 4, 1920, to Mr. and Mrs. Charles Dooley and grew up in a comfortable, middle-class family on Cumberland Avenue adjacent to the University of Tennessee. He enlisted on September 5, 1941, at Fort Oglethorpe, Georgia, three months before Pearl Harbor. A 1938 Knoxville High School graduate, Dooley studied engineering at the University of Tennessee, but duty called; by 1942, he was in flight school in Texas. He eventually became a member of the 359th Bomb Squadron, 303rd Bomb Group (the famed "Hell's Angels"), 8th Air Force. At the age of twenty-two, Dooley was flying missions on a B-17F nicknamed *FDR's Potato Peeler Kids*, based at Molesworth, England. Dooley was on his sixteenth mission when his aircraft failed to return from a bombing mission to Kiel, Germany, one of the *Kriegsmarine*'s principal U-boat harbors. An excerpt from a Memorial Day tribute by Randy Kenner of the *Knoxville News Sentinel* chronicles his life and final hours:

> It's a holiday sometimes known more for its cookouts, big movie openings and weekend trips then for its solemn ceremonies. But Memorial Day has been a day for honoring fallen soldiers since the 19th century. Which is why it's the most important holiday for someone like Walter Dooley. On May 13, 1943, Dooley had just co-piloted a B-17 Flying

First Lieutenant Walter E. Dooley, top row, second from left.

Fortress on a raid over France so uneventful that a crewman reported, "We could have slept or played cards."

At the time Dooley was 22 years old, a Knoxville native who was his father's youngest son, a faithful friend to a trio of buddies he'd known since junior high and a good natured, handsome man to a female cousin who adored him. He was also two semesters shy of an engineering degree from the University of Tennessee and so extraordinarily lucky that he had parachuted to safety from a plane on one occasion and helped bring a bullet-riddled one home on another. But less than a day later, on May 14, Dooley and the 10-man crews of roughly two dozen unescorted American bombers were

fighting for their lives above the North Sea after a raid on the submarine pens at Kiel, Germany.

"I remember there were about 40, probably 40 fighters attacked us," Irl Baldwin of Albuquerque NM, said. "As I recall they met us over the water and followed us all the way home." Baldwin was an Army Air Force Captain who was leading the formation in his plane, "Hell's Angels." At the other end of the group, Lt. William J. Cline was flying just ahead of the last plane in the formation, *FDR's Potato Peeler Kids*, piloted by Bales and Dooley. Cline who now lives in Bakersfield, California, no longer has a clear memory of what happened that day, but his diary entry for it notes his plane dropped its bombs at 12:02 p.m., "and things started to happen. Running fight for an hour or so."

Walter Dooley grew up as the youngest of four children in a house on Cumberland Avenue near where a gas station now stands. The Dooley's were, by the standards of the depression, fairly comfortable. Walter's father, Charles Dooley, had a good job. Sam Fincannon, who met Walter Dooley in the early 1930s at Boyd Junior High School, said "He was . . . a happy-go-lucky guy, and he made pretty good grades." Dooley and Fincannon were also good friends with Ed Dougherty and Charles Benzinger during junior high. "Ed and Walter and Sam and I ran around together," said Benzinger, 77, the only one of the group who still resides in Knoxville. The four, all 1938 graduates of Knoxville High School, went on to UT. . . .

When the group arrived at UT, their social lives tended to revolve around the fraternity three of them joined, and they shot pool at a hall on Cumberland. But their world was about to change. Much of the world was already at war by 1939, and the little group of friends knew they would probably be drawn into it. "We thought we were going to be heroes and all that sort of thing," Daugherty said. "It seems to me, as I look back on it, that Knoxville was sort of a country town back then. And we were sort of country boys. The war was the biggest thing to come along, and we wanted to be in it." Dooley was the first to go, which broke up the group forever. . . .

In late 1942, after training in Texas, Dooley was assigned to the 303 "Hell's Angels" Bombardment Group, which flew out of a base in Molesworth, England. It was a dangerous place to be. Nearly all the pilots were in their early 20s, and the losses were horrendous. The group flew without fighter cover early in the war, and at least 24 of the original 50 pilots had been shot down by June of 1943. Dooley nearly shared their fate in a January 1943 raid over Germany in which his plane was so badly damaged he

had to get a new one. In a radio interview after the incident he said he was, "anxious to go after them again."

LAST MISSION: Walter Dooley was on his 16th mission on May 14th, 1943. He was back from a recent leave in London and had written home, telling his parents of his pleasant rest. He and Bales were "Rear-End Charlie" that day, meaning they were the last plane in the group. They were part of a four-plane formation led by Capt. Jack Roller with Cline flying to Roller's right as they cruised toward Kiel, along with five other groups of B-17s in what was the biggest raid of the war up to that time. . . . Lt. Col. Harry D. Gobrecht, a pilot and the squadron historian, wrote in his book "Might in Flight," that the bombers were met by 100 to 150 German fighters. A running battle ensued that lasted through the bombers' run on the target and most of the return flight to England. Dooley's plane was in the thick of it, and Cline chronicled the result in a series of stark sentences. "Bales . . . got his left stabilizer (the left horizontal section of the tail) shot up," Cline wrote in his diary. "He was 'Rear-End Charlie' about 50 miles off the coast, got hit by a (fighter). Seven chutes and he ditched . . . blew up in the water." No one was recovered.

Walter Dooley was awarded the Air Medal with Two Oak Leaf Clusters and the Purple Heart. He is memorialized by a stone in his memory in Knoxville's Greenwood Cemetery near his parents' graves. He is also listed among the missing at the Cambridge American Cemetery, Cambridge, England.

Crewmembers of *FDR's Potato Peeler Kids*, all of whom were lost on the May 14, 1943, sortie, were:

Pilot, Capt. Ross C. Bales

Co-Pilot, 1st Lt. Walter E. Dooley

Navigator, 1st Lt. Daniel A. McColl

Bombardier, 1st Lt. Rhude M. Mathis

Flight engineer/top turret gunner, T/Sgt. Raymond H. Kilgore

Radio operator, T/Sgt. Raymond K. Winter

Waist gunner, S/Sgt. Jack D. Snell

Tail gunner, S/Sgt. Edward A. Van Ravenstein

Ball turret gunner, S/Sgt. Joseph G. Zsampar

Waist gunner, S/Sgt. Francis W. O'Reilly

THE WAR BENEATH THE WAVES

USS Scorpion, USS Grayling, USS Grampus

While assuming a more limited role in the European Theater and the Battle of the Atlantic, Allied submarines played a major part in the war in the Pacific by seriously disrupting Japanese shipping. Submarine warfare arguably spelled the end of Japan's fighting ability. Nearly 1,300 Japanese merchant ships, as well as one battleship and eleven cruisers, were sunk by US submarines. A total of 52 American submarines, representing 18 percent of the 288 boats in the Navy's Submarine Service, were lost during World War II, resulting in approximately 3,630 Navy personnel missing in action.[24]

Seaman First Class Hollis F. Bell, Foster Crossroads, Oneida (Scott), volunteered for the US Navy and was assigned to the submarine USS Scorpion (SS-278). Scorpion was launched July 20, 1942. Its first patrol was a mining mission near Honshu in April 1943. She laid twenty-two mines off the coast, then commenced a search for enemy shipping, which would prove to be devastating for Japan. The Scorpion fiercely assaulted enemy vessels in a series of submerged torpedo attacks and surface gun battles. She sank two freighters, four sampans, and two patrol vessels. She also encountered tragedy on board when Lieutenant Commander

USS Scorpion.

Seaman First Class Hollis F. Bell.

Reginald M. Raymond, her prospective commanding officer, was fatally wounded by an enemy bullet as he fired a Browning Automatic Rifle from the ship's bridge during a surface engagement. On her next patrols, *Scorpion* inflicted even more damage on enemy shipping. Each of these three patrols earned her a battle star.

Scorpion departed Pearl Harbor on December 29, 1943, under the command of Commander M. G. Schmidt. She stopped at Midway to top off with fuel and departed Midway on January 3, 1944, to conduct her fourth war patrol. On January 5, 1944, she attempted to rendezvous with sister ship USS *Herring* (SS-233) to transfer an injured man. Heavy seas prevented the transfer, and *Scorpion* continued west to her assigned area, which was in the Northern East China and Yellow Seas. She was not heard from again after her departure from

Fireman First Class Curtis D. Clark.

the rendezvous area. Assumed to be the victim of a Japanese mine, she was declared lost on March 6, 1944. The *Scorpion* went down with seventy-seven officers and men.

The last sentence on Bell's memorial stone at the Foster Crossroads Baptist Church Cemetery reads: "He Lived in Honor, Beloved By All Who Knew Him And Died For His Country And Will Never Be Forgotten." He is also memorialized at the Manila American Cemetery, Fort Bonifacio, Manila, Philippines, and was decorated with the Purple Heart posthumously.

Fireman First Class Curtis D. Clark was born on May 15, 1924, in Erwin (Unicoi). He was reported missing in action on September 24, 1943, and officially declared dead on January 3, 1946. The USS *Grayling* (SS-209) had begun her eighth and last war patrol in July 1943 from Fremantle, Australia, but was not heard from again after September 9, 1943. The ship was officially reported lost with all hands on September 30, 1943, after having recorded five major kills totaling 20,575 tons in or near Tablas Strait, Philippine Islands. Even today, the exact cause of the loss of *Grayling* is unknown, but on September 9, 1943, the Japanese passenger-cargo vessel *Hokuan Mary* reported a submarine in shallow water west of Luzon. The ship made a run over the area and noted an impact with a submerged object. It is assumed that the object was *Grayling*. The submarine was scheduled to make a radio report on September 12, which she did not make, and all attempts to contact her failed. The *Grayling* was lost with seventy-six officers and men.

Curtis D. Clark is memorialized at the Manila American Cemetery. Also serving on the *Grayling* was Radioman Third Class Donald L. Keplinger, a fellow resident of Erwin, who was born on April 5, 1923. It is reasonable to spec-

Motor Machinist's Mate Second Class
Richard E. Corum.

Moffett (DD-362), a *Porter*-class destroyer, on December 16, 1940, as an apprentice seaman and was soon promoted to seaman third class. On August 1, 1941, shortly before his transfer to the USS *Mississippi* (BB-41), a *New Mexico*-class battleship, he received a rating change to fireman third class. The next month saw a promotion to fireman second class.

Early in 1942, Corum volunteered for a new duty assignment and was accepted. He was to become a submariner. He shipped out of San Francisco on March 7, 1942, en route to Pearl Harbor on the USS *Wharton* (AP-7), a troop transport ship. Arriving at Pearl Harbor on March 16, his submarine had not returned from her first patrol in which she sank two enemy vessels, so he signed aboard the USS *Tambor* (SS-198) to continue training and await the arrival of the USS *Grampus* (SS-207), a *Tambor*-class fleet submarine. The *Grampus* arrived to re-outfit on April 22, 1942, and Ernest signed aboard. She sailed immediately on her second patrol to Fremanle, Australia, and Ernest was promoted to fireman first class on May 1, 1942.

The second patrol, as with the third, was uneventful, but the *Grampus* changed ports to Brisbane, Australia, and Ernest received a rating change and a promotion. On his fourth and fifth patrols, the *Grampus* sank three more enemy vessels, and Corum was promoted to motor machinist's mate second class. Their sixth patrol began on February 11, 1943, and the *Grampus*, along with the USS *Grayback* (SS-208), her sister submarine, were to patrol in and around the Solomon Islands.

On the afternoon of March 5, 1943, she and the *Grayback* entered the Blackett Strait to destroy any enemy vessels that would try to escape. That night, two Imperial Japanese

ulate that they were friends from childhood and that they signed up for the same duty. He, too, is memorialized at the Manila American Cemetery in Fort Bonifacio, Manila, Philippines, and was decorated with the Purple Heart posthumously.

Motor Machinist's Mate Second Class Richard E. Corum was born in Nashville (Davidson) on December 23, 1918, and raised in Jonesborough (Washington). Corum was working for a Kingsport milk distributor when he enlisted in the Navy in Nashville on October 17, 1940. He completed basic training at Norfolk Naval Base, Norfolk, Virginia; he was assigned to the USS

Navy destroyers, *Minegumo* and *Murasame*, entered the strait to resupply the Japanese base at Vila on Kolombangara in the Central Solomons island chain. What happened next remains a mystery today. The *Grayback*, around fifteen miles away from the *Grampus*, never saw or heard the two enemy destroyers, but it is assumed that *Grampus* did and that she must have been caught on the surface; *Grayback* never heard any depth charges explode, suggesting that the fight likely was on the surface. The next day, both *Minegumo* and *Murasame* encountered Task Force 68 and were sent to the bottom of Blackett Strait with only two survivors. Any reports that may have been created on the engagement with the *Grampus* also went down with those ships. A large unexplained oil slick was reported in the Blackett Strait on March 6, 1943.

After no radio transmission was received on March 6 and 7 and in the absence of reports or sightings, the *Grampus* was reported on March 22 as lost with all seventy-one crewmembers. On June 21, 1943, she was struck from the Naval Vessel Register; on March 23, 1944, Richard Corum and his other seventy shipmates were declared dead. Richard was twenty-four years old and received the Purple Heart posthumously.

Corum was the son of the Reverend Richard E. Corum and Ethel E. Ramsay. His mother was a librarian and teacher at Jonesborough High School and was the town's postmistress when she received the official letter of her son's death. In addition to his memorial at the Manila American Cemetery in Fort Bonifacio, Manila, Philippines, he also has a memorial stone in the Maple Lawn Cemetery, Jonesborough.[25]

AN EAST TENNESSEAN AT THE "LAST STAND OF THE TIN CAN SAILORS": THE BATTLE OF LEYTE GULF

The largest naval engagement of the Second World War, and quite probably of all time, was a series of naval battles collectively known as the Battle of Leyte Gulf, fought off the Philippines islands of Leyte, Samar, and Luzon, October 23–26, 1944. This titanic naval struggle was waged by the last major surface ships of the Imperial Japanese Navy's Combined

US Navy destroyer escort USS *Samuel B. Roberts* (DE-413), circa June 1944. Courtesy, US Navy Naval History and Heritage Command.

Fleet, thrown into a final desperate effort to halt Douglas MacArthur's initial beachhead in the Philippines and cripple the US Navy's 3rd and 7th Fleets. The Combined Fleet not only failed to achieve its objectives, but it suffered extraordinary losses in men, ships, and aircraft that essentially crippled its fighting power for the rest of the war. This success for the US Navy came at a cost, however, and the engagement saw heavy American losses, as well. One East Tennessee family would receive not just the dreaded knock on the front door accompanying the feared telegram on behalf of the secretary of the Navy, but also an amazing letter penned by their lost son's skipper as his own token of respect for one of his lost men.[26]

Electrician's Mate Second Class James Kenneth Weaver was born on March 27, 1917, and was raised in Bristol (Sullivan). He was a 1937 graduate of Bristol (Tennessee) High School; coincidentally, among his high school classmates was a certain Ernest Ford, later known as "Tennessee Ernie" Ford. He was the son of Mr. and Mrs. James Edward Weaver of 1229 Windsor Avenue, on the Tennessee side of Bristol, and he married his sweetheart, Carol Woolsey, on November 3, 1940, in Johnson City. Weaver would be one of the "plank owners"—the initial commissioning crew—on the destroyer escort USS *Samuel B. Roberts* (DE-413), called the "Sammy B." by her crewmen, commissioned on April 28, 1944, under the command of Lieutenant Commander Robert W. Copeland.

Weaver was one of ninety men lost when the "Sammy B." went down on October 25, 1944, in a vicious naval engagement later known as the "Last Stand of the Tin Can Sailors." During MacArthur's landings on Leyte Gulf, the *Samuel B. Roberts* formed part of Task Unit 77.4.3. Known as "Taffy 3," this was a screening force whose ammunition was principally intended

for ground support missions—not for shooting it out with enemy battlewagons. Taffy 3 was comprised entirely of destroyers and destroyer-escorts (nicknamed "tin cans," for their lack of heavy armor plating), and CVE-class escort carriers, better known as "jeep carriers." None of these relatively small and lightly armed-and-armored ships were prepared to face the full might of the Center Force—the twenty-three-ship Japanese battleship and heavy cruiser force, including the gigantic *Yamato*, the world's largest battleship, with nine 18.1-inch guns. That is, however, what transpired on the early morning of October 25 during the portion of the actions at Leyte Gulf known as the Naval Battle Off Samar.

Shortly after dawn October 25, 1944, as the *Samuel B. Roberts* and a small force of other "tin cans" were protecting Taffy 3's escort carriers off the coast of Samar, the Japanese Center Force suddenly appeared on the horizon and, in a matter of minutes, opened fire. In a desperate effort to hold at bay the Japanese battlewagons and cruisers, save MacArthur's toehold on the Leyte beachhead, and defend the vital jeep carriers, the destroyers and destroyer-escorts of Taffy 3 launched a daring torpedo attack on the many-times-larger (both in pure size, as well as in numbers) Japanese ships. Although scoring a torpedo hit on one and at least forty gunfire hits on a second enemy vessel, the much-smaller *Samuel B. Roberts* was hit by three salvoes of incoming shells. The third was a salvo of 14-inch shells from a battleship (likely the battleship *Kongo*), which her skipper Copeland later recalled "just ripped the ship wide one," and another survivor described as rippling through the ship "like a puppy being smacked by a truck." One shell tore a hole thirty to forty feet long and seven to ten feet high in the port (left) side of her engine rooms—the very place that formed Kenneth Weaver's battle station. In Copeland's words, the shell "blew . . . all to hell" the engine rooms. Hull filling rapidly and unresponsive to controls, the "Sammy B." was abandoned and rapidly sank; even as she did, Japanese gunners still fired at the ship. Her survivors clung to a handful of life rafts in shark-infested waters for over two days before they were finally rescued. The *Samuel B. Roberts*'s skipper, Lieutenant Commander Copeland, survived.

Weaver's wife, Carol Woolsey Weaver, received the dreaded telegram from the Secretary of the Navy, announcing the change in her husband's status from missing to presumed dead: "It is with deep regret you are now advised that although the body of your husband was not recovered, the executive officer of the ship in which he served has reported that the circumstances of his disappearance have led to a conclusion of death. I extend to you my sympathy in your sorrow and hope you may find comfort in the knowledge that your husband gave his life for his country upholding the highest traditions of the Navy."

This official telegram was not the only communiqué that Mrs. Weaver would receive about her husband's death; she also received a personal letter from her husband's skipper, Lieutenant Commander Copeland. Unlike the formal language of the secretary's telegram and many other condolence letters from COs to their men's survivors and grieving families, Copeland's letter was not formulaic. Remarkably candid, this letter left the widow neither in doubt of her husband's fate nor cause for any lingering hopes, yet it was tinged with the highest respects for Copeland's lost crewman:

> The truth isn't nice but it is still the truth. Kenneth was on the main switchboard in the number 1 engine room . . . the second most important job for an electrician's mate aboard the ship. . . . We received 6-inch explosive shells in both the number 1 and number 2 engine rooms and there was only one survivor for the former, none for the latter. I talked with the one man to get out of number one engine room; he was down on the lower level and was blown into the bilges. He was of the opinion that all [the] others in the engine room was [sic] instantly killed. He barely escaped through all the live steam that filled the engine room and although he saw several bodies, none were identified.
>
> I regret the finality of the tone of the letter, but I cannot in good conscience tell you anything but the truth. I can assure you that your husband was not only a hero—he manned his battle station and stayed there knowing that death was almost inevitable, in fact, I don't yet know how any of us escaped, in fact, he was also as an outstanding man aboard ship from the day he first reported. All of the officers held him in very high regard, not only for his ability, but for his outstanding character and forthright conduct. I know you will suffer untold grief in your loss, but I do hope that you will take pride in the fact that your husband although dead (I could not officially declare him such as his body was not identified) was an American hero, so much more to be proud of than one who was a shirker or disloyal to his trust.
>
> My very sincerest sympathies to you and all the family and friends who have suffered sorrow in his loss.[27]

James Kenneth Weaver is commemorated on the Tablets of the Missing at Fort Bonifacio, Manila American Cemetery, Philippines, and was posthumously honored with the Purple Heart.

6

PRISONERS OF WAR IN WORLD WAR II

It's easy to be nice, boys
When everything's O.K.
It's easy to be cheerful,
When you're having things your way.
But can you hold your head up
And take it on the chin.
When your heart is breaking
And you feel like giving in?
It was easy back in England,
Among the friends and folks.
But now you miss the friendly hand,
The joys, and songs, and jokes.
The road ahead is stormy.
And unless you're strong in mind,
You'll find it isn't long before
You're dragging far behind.

You've got to climb the hill, boys;
It's no use turning back.
There's only one way home, boys,
And it's off the beaten track.
Remember you're American,
And when you reach the crest,
You'll see a valley cool and green,
Our country at its best.
You know there is a saying
That sunshine follows rain,
And sure enough you'll realize
That joy will follow pain.
Let courage be your password,
Make fortitude your guide;
And then instead of grousing,
Just remember those who died.

—*"Can You Take It?," anonymous poem found on a cell wall in Dulag Luft, the Luftwaffe's
central POW processing and interrogation camp near Frankfurt, Germany*[1]

Under the Geneva Convention of 1929, prisoners of war (POWs) were to be removed promptly from the area of combat and, if wounded, be given adequate medical care. They were to be housed and fed adequately. Under interrogation, prisoners were required to give their captors no more than their names, ranks, and serial or service numbers. In both theaters of the Second World War, however, these and other basic rights and protections for prisoners and responsibilities of their captors often fell by the wayside; in the Pacific Theater in particular, such protections seemed elusive at best, non-existent at worse. This chapter chronicles many East Tennesseans who died in the POW camps of the Axis powers in both the European and Pacific theaters of war. The fates of those who died aboard Japan's notorious "hellships" will be explored in chapter 8.

The International Committee of the Red Cross, as the so-called "Protecting Power," was allowed to inspect conditions in the permanent prisoner-of-war camps. The Geneva Convention of 1929 also stipulated that officer POWs were not to be used as common laborers and that non-commissioned personnel were allowed to do only supervisory work. Japan signed the convention but did not ratify it, and its military widely viewed the precepts of the Geneva Convention as being contrary to the Japanese "warrior spirit," the *samurai* code of *Bushido*. The Soviet Union refused to even sign the convention, not imagining that troops of the Red Army would ever have to surrender. As a result of these and other factors, the reality during World War II was quite different from the legalities called for under the Geneva Convention and other international laws of armed conflict. Allied service personnel taken prisoner by the Japanese were often neglected, mistreated, starved, and dealt with harshly, as the personal histories below will show.

The German military's prisoner of war camps were, by and large, more humane than the Japanese camps when it came to most Americans, although the prisoners' existence in the German camps was still difficult and challenging, especially during the last months of the war. The Germans established two kinds of camps, the *Oflag* (*Offizierlager:* officers' camp) for officers and the *Stalag* (*Stammlager:* main camp) for NCOs and enlisted troops. For Allied aircrew captured by the Germans, the *Luftwaffe*

administered its own *Stalag Luft* (*Stammlager Luftwaffe*) camps, which were separate from those administered by the German Army for ground troops. However, the life of a "kriegie" (the American POWs' nickname for themselves, from *kriegsgefangener,* "prisoner of war" in German) was still rigorous, full of deprivations, and dangerous enough for some East Tennessee POWs to die in German custody.

Conditions were far more threatening and dangerous for any Allied prisoners who fell or were transferred into the custody of the *SS* or the *Gestapo*, the Nazi secret state police. A number of Jewish-American POWs and other GIs deemed to appear Jewish were transferred to the Berga concentration camp to serve as forced laborers under *SS* watch, while some Americans and other Allied servicemen were transferred to the Mauthausen concentration

Chief Electrician's Mate Houston E. Edwards.

camp in Austria, to be beaten, worked, or starved to death under inhumane conditions.

Chief Electrician's Mate Houston E. Edwards, of the Goin community (Claiborne), served aboard the submarine USS *Perch* (SS-176), which was scuttled on March 3, 1942, after being seriously damaged in a prior engagement with Japanese naval forces. The *Perch* bore the dubious honor of being the first US submarine lost in the war. Subsequently captured by the Japanese, Edwards was interned as a prisoner of war in the Makassar Prisoner of War Camp, Celebes, Indonesia, where he died on or about July 10, 1944. The camp was described by Dutch history sources as follows:

The 1,100 or so [Dutch East Indies] POWs who fell into Japanese hands [in the Celebes region of what is now Indonesia] were concentrated in the infantry barracks in Makassar in February, March, and April 1942. Also interned here were about 1,700 Dutch, British and American navy staff, among whom [were] survivors of the Battle of the Java Sea. In April 1942 there were about 2,870 POWs in this camp. In June and July 1942 small groups of POWs from the Lesser Sunda islands arrived in Makassar. Mid-October 1942 some 1,000 POWs were put on transport to Japan. Small groups of officers were taken to Japan and Surabaya in April 1942 and October 1943 respectively.

The POWs in the infantry barracks were put to work, among other places in the harbour of Makassar, in a lime factory on Matuangin road, on Mandai airfield about 15 kilometres to the northeast of the city, and from January to September 1943 in the nickel mines of Pomelaä in Southeast Celebes. Executions were carried out several times in the camp. . . . In June and July 1944 the approximately 1,700 remaining POWs were taken to a new barracks camp, located in a boggy coconut plantation just south of Makassar.

From March this Mariso camp, also known as Bamboo Camp, had been built by the prisoners themselves. Due to the harsh regime, malnutrition, heavy forced labour and the unhealthy environment at least 330 POWs died here before the liberation.[3]

An article published in his wife's hometown newspaper, the *Portsmouth* (New Hampshire) *Herald*, revealed Edward's fate when it was discovered after war's end:

[Mrs. Edwards] has been notified by the Navy department that her husband, Houston E. Edwards, chief electrician, USN, died July 10, 1944, as a prisoner of the Japanese in the Dutch East Indies and was buried in the cemetery of the Makassar Celebes prison camp. The Naval man was reported missing in action with the crew of the USS *Perch*, March 1, 1942, when the ship was lost in the battle of Java, but it was learned later that he was taken prisoner by the Japanese March 3 of the same year and held captive at Makassar Celebes until his death.

He had been a member of the crew of the *Perch* since its commissioning nine-and-a-half years ago at the Electric Boat company plant at Groton, Connecticut. A native of Goin, he had served in the Navy for 18 years, having enlisted in the service as a boy of 16. Much of his duty was on submarines and he was a member of several Portsmouth-built boats, including the *Dolphin* and the *Cachelot*.

He married the former Miss Stella Drobisewski of Portsmouth nearly 10 years ago. The couple had one daughter, Victoria Edwards. . . . Mrs. Edwards was with her husband in Manila until November 1940, when all Americans were warned to leave the territory, and then she returned to Portsmouth.[4]

Chief Electrician's Mate Edwards's remains were returned to Tennessee on June 12, 1948; he is buried at the Knoxville National Cemetery.

Machinist's Mate Third Class Hubert D. Thornburg.

Second Lieutenant John F. Hay.

Machinist's Mate Third Class Hubert D. Thornburg (Greene) was born on March 22, 1919. He entered the service when he was seventeen. While he was serving on the old "four-stacker" destroyer USS *Pope* (DD-225), the Japanese bombed Pearl Harbor. The *Pope* was then based at Manila Bay; she left the Philippines for the East Indies and joined the American, British, Dutch, and Australian ("ABDA") joint fleet. Following the Battle of Java Sea against a superior force, the venerable *Pope* was assigned to escort to safety the damaged British heavy cruiser HMS *Exeter*, along with the destroyer HMS *Encounter*. At 7:30 a.m., March 1, 1942, the ABDA flotilla encountered a Japanese force of two heavy cruisers and three destroyers. The Allied force began a running battle to safety. It is believed the *Pope* sank the Japanese heavy cruiser *Ashigara* with torpedoes during this action. The *Exeter* and *Encounter* were sunk shortly after 11:40 a.m. The *Pope*, however, continued to fight on.

At 12:30 p.m., the *Pope* came under attack by twelve aircraft and was severely damaged. The ship was scuttled and, as she was sinking, was hit by gunfire. The crew abandoned ship and was taken into captivity the next day. The Japanese picked Thornburg up at sea, and he was put into a prison camp at Batavia, Java. Confined to this camp for three years and three months, he died from starvation and dysentery on January 30, 1945. His body was returned to Greeneville in 1949 and is buried at Bethesda Cumberland Presbyterian Church Cemetery in northern Greene County.[5]

Second Lieutenant John F. Hay (Hamblen)

was born on November 8, 1919, and died as a POW on October 10, 1942. He was with Company C of the 192nd Tank Battalion, which fought valiantly during the defense of the Bataan Peninsula. He was imprisoned at the infamous Camp #1 POW facility at Cabanatuan on Luzon in the Philippines, which at its peak held some eight thousand American prisoners; compared to Imperial Japan's other camps, Camp #1 had one of the highest number of prisoners and was the largest such camp in the Philippines.[6] A July 9, 1943, article in the *Kingsport News* told of his death: "Lieutenant John Frederick Hay of Morristown, who was reported prisoner of war of the Japanese, has been reported by the War Department to have died in the Philippine Islands subsequent to the fall of Bataan. The Government received its information from the Red Cross, but no dates have been given. Lieutenant Hay was the son of Dr. and Mrs. Samuel H. Hay of the pastorate of the First Presbyterian Church of Morristown. He is survived by his parents and two sisters, Miss Rachel M. Hay and Mrs. T. Moffatt Burriss."[7]

According to a 1930 census, Private Evans E. Overbey (Carter) was born around 1913 in Tennessee and was the only son of William and Maggie Overbey, originally of Elizabethton. He entered the service from Coeburn, Virginia, his last official residence. Overbey served with the 93rd Bombardment Squadron, 19th Bombardment Group, at Clark Field. He too was a prisoner at the Cabanatuan camp, surviving the Bataan Death March but later dying of malnutrition and lack of medical care. He is memorialized at the Manila American Cemetery, Fort Bonifacio, Philippines, and is now buried at Mountain Home National Cemetery in Johnson City, his remains having been identified by forensic scientific tools in 2015 and repatriated to East Tennessee in June 2016.

Private George W. Purdy.

Private John I. Kerns. Courtesy of Gunner Ed Sere, USMC, ret.

Private George W. Purdy (Loudon) was born August 10, 1917. He enlisted on March 11, 1944, and served with a company of the 109th Infantry Regiment, 28th Infantry Division. He was captured in Germany on January 11, 1945, and died as a prisoner of war at Stalag IV-B, in Muhlberg, located in the German province of Saxony, on May 10, 1945. Stalag IV-B was one of the largest German POW camps. At various times, the camp held Polish, French, Russian, British, and Australian soldiers, among those of other nationalities, and some 7,500 Americans arrived in Stalag IV-B in late December 1944 and January 1945 as prisoners taken during the Battle of the Bulge. Purdy was one of this sizeable influx of POWs. Private Purdy's remains were repatriated, and he is buried in the Steekee Cemetery, Loudon, Tennessee.

Private John I. Kerns, Copperhill (Polk), was originally from Lincoln, Nebraska. He served with the 2nd Marine Raider Battalion, which was carried aboard the submarine USS *Argonaut* (SS-166) to assault Makin atoll in the Gilbert Islands. The date of his loss is believed to be August 18, 1942, in connection with the Marines' raid on Makin. This raid was among the first American offensive ground combat operations and amphibious assaults of World War II. Its primary aim was to destroy Japanese installations, take prisoners, gain intelligence on the Gilbert Islands area, and divert Japanese attention and reinforcements from the Allied landings underway at Guadalcanal and Tulagi. Kerns was captured on Butaritari Island, Makin Atoll, and taken to Kwajalein, where he was executed. His Navy Cross citation, written before the actual circumstances of his death were fully known, follows:

The President of the United States of America takes pride in presenting the Navy Cross (Posthumously) to Private John I. Kerns, United States Marine Corps (Reserve), for extraordinary heroism and conspicuous devotion to duty while serving as a member of a volunteer boat crew in Company B, 2nd Marine Raider Battalion, during the Marine Raider Expedition against the Japanese-held island of Makin in the Gilbert Islands on 17 and 18 August 1942. Fully aware of the hazards of an imminent enemy attack, and with complete disregard for his own life, Private Kerns, with four others, volunteered to take a boat to a point outside a reef and shoot a line ashore to assist in evacuating those men remaining on the beach. Caught on the sea, he was defeated in his valiant efforts by the violent strafing of his boat by withering enemy machine-gun fire. His great personal valor and loyal spirit of self-sacrifice were in keeping with the finest traditions of the United States Naval Service. He gallantly gave up his life in the service of his country.

Private Cornell Dillon.

Of course, not properly reflected in the above citation is the reality that, in fact, he had been taken prisoner by the Japanese and executed on Kwajalein. Private Kerns is memorialized on the Tablets of the Missing, National Memorial Cemetery of the Pacific, Honolulu, Hawaii.

Private Cornell Dillon (Roane), of Company C, 192nd Tank Battalion (the same tank company as Lieutenant Hay), was born in 1919 in Ozone (Cumberland), in the shadow of the Cumberland Mountains. After both his parents died, Cornell and his siblings were placed into the Tennessee Industrial School in Nashville. His oldest brother died in an industrial school at the age of twelve. His younger brother, Fred, joined the Marines in 1940 at age sixteen. Dillon was living in Roane County when he was inducted into the Army in 1941. He trained at Fort Knox, Kentucky, and Camp Polk, Louisiana. Upon arrival at Camp Polk, Cornell was assigned to the 753rd Tank Battalion.

After arriving in the Philippines, he was assigned to the 192nd Tank Battalion at Fort Stotsenburg, adjacent to Clark Field and northwest of Manila, where the 192nd lived in tents since their barracks were unfinished. The tank crews spent much of their time doing maintenance, loading ammunition belts, and "decosmolining" (removing grease from) their tanks' guns. On December 8, 1941, seven hours after Pearl Harbor, the battalion's companies were ordered to Clark Field's perimeter to guard against Japanese paratroopers. At 12:45 p.m., the field was bombed by Japanese planes. This massive air attack took place ten hours after the attack on Pearl Harbor; it largely decimated the bulk of American and Filipino air power in the Philippines, most of which were caught on the ground.

Dillon became a prisoner of war after the battles for Luzon and Bataan ended on April 9, 1942. He embarked on the Bataan Death March, starting at Mariveles on the southern tip of the Bataan peninsula. Most POWs were already sick with dysentery and malaria and had had little to eat for days. They were neither allowed water or food nor given breaks. Those who fell during the march were often shot, decapitated, or bayoneted. At San Fernando, the POWs were packed into small wooden boxcars used to haul sugar cane. Once they reached the hamlet of Capas, many POWs were left to suffer in the stifling and human waste-filled boxcars. Those who could do so then walked the last ten miles to Camp #4—the also infamous Camp O'Donnell—located near the Luzon village of Tarlac.

The majority of Camp O'Donnell's prisoners were never liberated. Most died as prisoners of war before the Japanese finally shut down the camp in January 1943. This was one of the most brutal POW camps, with as many as one in six Americans held there dying, for a death toll of approximately 1,500 Americans and over 26,000 Filipino POWs dying at O'Donnell during its existence.[8] Cornell Dillon was one of these victims. He died May 27, 1942, of dysentery at Camp O'Donnell, only seven weeks after his capture. He is buried at the Manila American Cemetery, Fort Bonifacio, Philippines.

Private Ted E. Vitatoe (Roane) was born on January 1, 1915, and died as a POW on December 14, 1944, in the Palawan Massacre. In order to prevent their rescue by the advancing Allies, Japanese camp guards herded 150 POWs held at the Puerto Princesa POW camp (also called Camp 10-A) on the Philippine island of Palawan into three covered trenches, ostensibly dug as air-raid shelters, which were then set on fire

Puerto Princesa Japanese Prisoner of War Camp, the Philippines.

Private Ted E. Vitatoe.

using barrels of gasoline. As prisoners tried to escape the flames, they were shot down. Some temporarily escaped by going over the edge of a cliff that ran along one side of the trenches, but most of these were later hunted down and killed. Marine survivor Corporal Rufus Smith described escaping from his shelter as "coming up a ladder into Hell." The four American officers in the camp, Lt. Cmdr. Henry Carlisle Knight (US Navy Dental Corps), Captain Fred Brunie, Lieutenant Carl Mango (US Army Medical Corps), and Warrant Officer Glen C. Turner, had their own dugout, which the Japanese also doused with gasoline and torched. Mango, his clothes on fire, ran toward the Japanese and pleaded with them to use some sense, but was machine-gunned to death.

About thirty to forty Americans escaped from the massacre area, either through the double-woven barbed-wire fence or under it where some secret escape routes had been concealed for use in an emergency. They fell or jumped down the cliff above the beach area, seeking hiding places among the rocks and foliage. Marine Gunnery Sergeant Douglas Bogue recalled: "Maybe 30 or 40 were successful in getting through the fence down to the water's edge. Of these, several attempted to swim . . . but were shot in the water. I took refuge in a small crack among the rocks, where I remained, all the time hearing the butchery going on above. They even resorted to using dynamite in forcing some of the men from their shelters. I knew [that] as soon as it was over up above they would be down probing among the rocks, spotting us and shooting us. . . . Shortly after this they were moving in groups among the rocks dragging the Americans out and murdering them as they found them. By the grace of God, I was overlooked." Ted Vitatoe did not, however, escape from the slaughter. In 1952, the remains of 123 of the Palawan Massacre's victims were transferred to the Jefferson Barracks National Cemetery near St. Louis, Missouri, where they lie in a mass grave.[9]

Pharmacist's Mate Third Class Deenah R. McCurry, Erwin (Unicoi), whose first name is also sometimes listed as Deanah and Danah, died while a Japanese prisoner of war. McCurry was assigned to the US Naval Hospital in the Philippine town of Canacao when the war began. He was captured after Manila fell in early 1942 and was sent to an unstated camp where 9,012 other American POWs were held. Deenah's capture was first reported to the International Committee of the Red Cross on

May 7, 1942, and the last report was made on December 23, 1944. Based on these two reports, Deenah apparently was imprisoned for at least 961 days—two years and nine months—one of the longest durations of American POW captivity recorded in the war. After surviving the sinking of the "hellship" *Oryoko Maru* (the sinking of which is described in chapter 8), Deenah died on December 23, 1944, while being transported overland from Olongapo to San Fernando, Philippines. Somehow during his captivity, he maintained records of personnel captured, at great risk to himself, until he was killed by the Japanese. He is buried at the Manila American Cemetery at Fort Bonifacio, Philippines.[10]

While not falling neatly into the category of a POW story, the account below is compelling enough to be worthy of attention in completing this chapter. The circumstances surrounding the death of Private First Class James L. Badgette are still not fully known. However, the narrative furnished by his family members touches on one of the little-discussed injustices of Army regulations during World War II, namely, the disparities in the treatment of African-American vis-à-vis Caucasian service members.

Badgette, the son of Bessie and Lafayette Badgette Jr., was born on December 30, 1921, in Knoxville (Knox). When twenty-two, he was inducted into the Army on June 15, 1944, at Fort Benning, Georgia, during the height of the war. Once on active duty, Badgette was assigned to the 126th Port Company, Transportation Corps, as a truck driver. Nearly 75 percent of all Transportation Corps drivers were black—due, in large part, to a semi-institutional opinion then held at high levels of the Army that African Americans lacked the skills and courage to be effective combat soldiers (this, despite the legacy and heroism of the "Buffalo Soldiers" of the Indian and Spanish-American wars and the "Harlem Hellfighters" of the prior world war). As a result of this erroneous belief, the Army relegated many black soldiers to relatively "safe" service and supply outfits, where they were used as clerks, cooks, laborers, and truck drivers. Convoys of the Transportation Corps' African American drivers rolled all day, every day, keeping the frontlines supplied with food, weapons, ammunition, and fuel; its port companies (like the 126th) served as stevedores and logistics workers at docks and shipping facilities.

In March 1945, the 126th Port Company was deployed to the Pacific Theater to support Operation Iceberg, the invasion of Okinawa, which would be the last and bloodiest battle of World War II in the Pacific. The Japanese province of Okinawa and the smaller islands surrounding it lay just south of the Japanese home island of Kyushu. At this point in the war, the decision to force Japanese surrender by dropping atomic bombs on the cities of Hiroshima and Nagasaki had yet to be made, and the capture of Okinawa and its surrounding islands were a vital last step towards the planned invasion of Japan's home islands.

On April 16, 1945, US forces attempted to seize Ie Shima, an eleven-square-mile island off the northwest coast of Okinawa defended by over two thousand Japanese soldiers and several hundred civilians. The 126th Port Company landed there, along with parts of the 77th

Okinawa Peace Memorial Park. Mabuni, Okinawa.

Private First Class James L. Badgette.

the line and exploded satchel charges. Some of them came within fifteen feet of the command post and engaged the Americans in vicious, close-quarters, hand-to-hand combat. It is believed that during this attack, Badgette, then only twenty-three years old, with less than a year in the Army, was beheaded by a sword-wielding Japanese soldier. By dawn, most of the enemy had been killed within the American lines, and by 4:30 p.m., Ie Shima was declared secure. Although official records show May 24, 1945, as Badgette's date of death, it is believed that was actually the date on which his remains were positively identified.

Badgette was posthumously awarded the Purple Heart. His remains were finally returned to the family in Knoxville during the summer of 1949 and were interred at the Knoxville National Cemetery. Badgette is one of the 240,000 names forever inscribed at the "Cornerstone of Peace" memorial in Mabuni, Itoman-shi, Okinawa.[11]

Infantry Division and other elements of the US Tenth Army. The GIs fought a vicious battle on Ie Shima against a determined and suicidally reckless enemy. The "GIs' buddy," beloved war correspondent Ernie Pyle, died on Ie Shima, shot while accompanying a group of 77th Infantry Division troops.

At 5:30 a.m. on April 21, three to four hundred Japanese soldiers, along with women armed only with spears, attacked a battalion command post positioned just under the rim of a hill known as "Bloody Ridge." Here, the Americans' battalion commander, staff officers, clerks, cooks, and truck drivers formed a defensive line along the crest of the hill. In a suicide attack, Japanese soldiers rushed into

7

THE GIs' GREAT CRUSADE IN EUROPE

Remembering the East Tennesseans Who Fell in the European Theater of Operations during World War II

Soldiers, Sailors, and Airmen of the Allied Expeditionary Force:

You are about to embark upon the Great Crusade, toward which we have striven these many months.

The eyes of the world are upon you. The hopes and prayers of liberty-loving people everywhere march with you.

In company with our brave Allies and brothers-in-arms on other Fronts you will bring about the destruction of the German war machine, the elimination of Nazi tyranny over oppressed peoples of Europe, and security for ourselves in a free world.

Your task will not be an easy one. Your enemy is well trained, well equipped, and battle-hardened. He will fight savagely.

But this is the year 1944. . . . The United Nations have inflicted upon the Germans great defeats, in open battle, man-to-man. Our air offensive has seriously reduced their strength in the air and their capacity to wage war on the ground. Our Home Fronts have given us an overwhelming superiority in weapons and munitions of war and placed at our disposal great reserves of trained fighting men. The tide has turned. The free men of the world are marching together to victory.

I have full confidence in your courage, devotion to duty, and skill in battle. We will accept nothing less than full victory.

Good Luck! And let us all beseech the blessing of Almighty God upon this great and noble undertaking.

—*General Dwight D. Eisenhower's order of the day to all members of the Allied expeditionary forces on the D-Day landings in Normandy, June 6, 1944*

The ranks of the GIs in North Africa, the Mediterranean, and Northwest Europe were swelled by East Tennesseans, both draftees and volunteers, many of whom fell in the vicious combat required to liberate Europe from over four years of Nazi oppression. This chapter surveys the experiences of a number of those who perished in the fighting that accompanied the Allied "crusade in Europe" as American, British, Canadian, Free French, Free Polish, and other Allied forces liberated millions

Captain Paul F. Harkleroad.

of oppressed people across the European continent, the Mediterranean, and North Africa.

Among those killed during Operation Overlord, the June 1944 Normandy landings, were Paul F. Harkleroad (Sullivan), John D. Hall (Hamilton), Broadway V. Sims (Carter), and Ed C. Davis (Bledsoe). Captain Harkleroad, a native of Kingsport, was graduated from the University of Tennessee's School of Engineering. Harkleroad's unit, the Army's 5th Engineering Special Brigade, was tasked to clear the Normandy beaches of German-built obstacles designed to slow or halt an invasion. He was killed in action on D-Day, June 6, 1944, by a mortar explosion as he stepped onto Omaha Beach. The same shell also killed his commander, Lieutenant Colonel Lionel F. Smith, and fellow staff officer, Captain Allen H. Cox Jr. A monument stands on the bluffs overlooking Omaha Beach, listing the names of all the men who gave their lives from the 5th Engineering Special Brigade. Harkleroad is buried at the Normandy American Cemetery, Colleville-sur-Mer, France.[1]

Technician Fifth Class John D. Hall was assigned to the 1st Battalion, 506th Parachute Infantry Regiment, 101st Airborne Division. He died in the very early hours of June 6, 1944, during the initial phase of the D-Day invasion of Normandy. He was a passenger on a Douglas C-47A troop transport that departed from Upottery, Devon, England, on the Allied parachute drops in France that preceded the amphibious landings on the D-Day beaches. Hall's transport plane was hit by German flak and crashed in flames near the Norman village of Picauville; all sixteen paratroopers and four Army Air Forces crewmen aboard died. Originally buried near Carentan, France, Hall's remains were returned to the United States in 1948 for final interment. He was posthumously awarded the Purple Heart. He is buried at the Chattanooga National Cemetery.

Technician Fifth Class Broadway Sims served with the 377th Field Artillery Battalion, 101st Airborne Division, and died June 11, 1944, on "D +5," five days after D-Day. He was buried at the Normandy American Cemetery, Colleville-sur-Mer, France.

Private First Class Edward C. Davis was assigned to the 119th Infantry Regiment, 30th Infantry Division. Much like its World War I incarnation, the "Old Hickory Division" was largely comprised of National Guardsmen from the two Carolinas, Georgia, and Tennessee. The division went into Normandy across Omaha Beach on "D +5," secured the Vire-et-Taute Canal, and crossed the Vire River on July 7, 1944. The division was selected to be the spearhead of the Allies' Operation Cobra breakout from the Norman hedgerow country into open country beyond the town of Saint-Lo. However, on July 24 and 25, the 30th Division suffered devastating "friendly fire" losses: on both days, a planned carpet-bombing of the battlefield by the Army Air Forces went grotesquely off-target, when marking smoke used by the planes' lead bombardiers shifted away from the intended targets of the German frontline positions and back towards the US lines. As a consequence, several Allied bombloads on both days fell "short," landing squarely on the frontline GIs waiting to advance. The Old Hickory Division and its neighboring units lost over one hundred dead, including the most senior American general to fall in action in the ETO, the visiting head of Army Ground Forces, Lieutenant General Lesley J. McNair. Davis was killed in action on July 25, 1944, and is interred at the Normandy American Cemetery, Colleville-sur-Mer, France.

One of the fiercest and costliest battles between the US Army and the Germans occurred just prior to the Battle of the Bulge, as the drive into Germany was beginning. Not far from Aachen, the ancestral home and last resting place of Charlemagne, stood a series of thick, almost impenetrable evergreen woods. The most notable of these was the Hürtgen Forest. The battle for that forest was started in September 1944 by Lieutenant General Courtney Hodges' First Army and continued until December; it ended up being one of the worst American reverses in northwest Europe. Command Sergeant Major Benjamin C. Franklin, who served with the 16th Regiment, 1st Infantry Division, from November 1942 in North Africa until the end of the war in Europe, recorded his vivid memories of what he called the worst pitched battle he had been engaged in:

> And the memory is still fresh in my mind. We had a lot of rain, a lot of mud, and it's turning very cold. [...] And the Hürtgen Forest is a thirty-mile area of forest. We were trying to get in a position to jump across the Rur [also spelled Roer] River to cut off the German industry that is located in the Ruhr Valley. What is preventing us is that we have a line here, and a line here, that the Germans control—the Hürtgen Forest. So there's a town called Hamich that is the key town at the eastern end of the Hürtgen Forest. The trees are unlike most German forests. The trees are very close together, sometimes only a couple of yards. Most German forests are ... very organized, but this Hürtgen Forest was not. It was almost like a Smoky Mountain Forest. Very disorganized, very close together. But you cannot use tanks, which is our best weapon, you cannot use [the] Air Corps, because they can't see what they're doing. So it ends up the infantry has to do the fighting. The woods themselves are superfluous. They're worthless. Why we wanted them, I don't know, other than to straighten out the line to give us a jump off so we can cross the Ruhr. So the 1st Infantry Division, the 4th Infantry Division, the 9th Infantry Division, and I'm sure a couple other infantry divisions, all had to go in and try to clear out the Hürtgen. We suffered 33,000 [casualties] in a battle the lasted about five weeks. I remember distinctly that the Germans would put shell after shell on us, but they knew any place a shell hit in the tree, you could be way over there and shrapnel would hit you and you can't lay down because ... so you stand up against the tree and just hope that they don't hit your tree. Then our own artillery [was] coming through, and occasionally we'd send a tank down the tank trail, down the fire trail; they'd knock the tank out. It was terrible, terrible fighting.[2]

While Franklin survived his Hürtgen Forest ordeal, two East Tennesseans who fought there were not so fortunate: these were First Lieutenant Willis N. Tucker (Knox) and Lieutenant Colonel Charles E. Etter (Hamilton).

First Lieutenant Willis N. Tucker.

Willis N. Tucker attended Knoxville High School and enlisted on June 27, 1941, in Fort Oglethorpe, Georgia. He was killed in action by the explosion of a booby trap in the Hürtgen Forest on November 28, 1944. At the time of his death, he was assigned to B Company, 12th Infantry Regiment, 4th Infantry Division. Tucker was a University of Tennessee graduate and an outstanding varsity athlete who ran track and also played football for UT's legendary football coach, General Robert Neyland. An article by Fred Brown of the *Knoxville News Sentinel* reports on a long-overdue UT tribute to Tucker, more than sixty years after his death in Germany:

Mike Sanders arrived in Knoxville on Friday to pay tribute to a father he never knew. Sanders and his mother, Hazel Hicks, will join other families whose relatives played football at the University of Tennessee in the 1940s and who died in combat during World War II. Tonight, in pre-game ceremonies before the Vols take on Air Force, the four families will be recognized with a sign inside Neyland Stadium and a banner in the north concourse. The four players—Clyde "Ig" Fuson, Rudy Klarer, Bill Nowling and Willis Tucker—were killed as World War II was coming to its violent end in Europe. All four were in the U.S. Army, and all four were in combat in France and Germany.

Sanders [was only] 2 years old when his father, Willis Tucker, was killed. Through the years growing up in Mississippi, his mother never told her son about the Knoxville man she married until he was a grown man with a family of his own. "Back then, they wanted to protect you," says Sanders. "I didn't get to see a photo album until my other father (Jimmy Sanders) died not too long ago," he says. Neither Sanders nor his mother knows where his father is buried and whether he's in an American cemetery in Germany or France. Tucker was killed in action Nov. 28, 1944, in Germany just before the Battle of the Bulge, says Sanders. . . .

Tucker and the other three UT football players who died were all top athletes and even reached stardom under iconic UT football coach Gen. Robert "Bob" Neyland. Tucker, a graduate of Knoxville High School, wore jersey No. 61; Fuson, a native of Middlesboro, Ky., wore No. 62; Klarer, of Louisville, Ky., wore No. 49; and Nowling, from St. Petersburg, Fla., wore No. 32.

During the war, after the four UT players died in action, the university retired the four jersey numbers. In later years, the numbers returned to the jersey rotation. In the 1980s, the UT Athletic Department permanently retired them.

Tucker was one of the finest track stars of that era and became a lineman with UT in 1940. . . ." This is my first visit to Knoxville," says Sanders. "And we are excited about this and these guys," he says.

And, it gives him a chance to possibly learn more about the father he never knew, No. 61.[3]

Tucker was initially buried at the Henri-Chapelle American War Cemetery in Belgium and is now interred at the Knoxville National Cemetery.

Lieutenant Colonel Charles E. Etter was born on December 6, 1913. After graduation from law school, he worked as an attorney in Chattanooga. Etter joined the Army in 1941 and served as an infantry officer in the European Theater of Operations. He was the commanding officer of the 41st Armored Infantry Regiment. On November 16, 1944, the 41st was the spearhead of the 2nd Armored Division (the famous "Hell on Wheels" tank division) assault on the Germans' Siegfried Line fortifications, located on the northern edge of the Hürtgen Forest and east of the Roer River, and captured the hamlet of Puffendorf. As the 41st continued its push into Germany, it came under an intense artillery and mortar attack. Etter was killed in action in Immendorf, Germany, on November 18, 1944, and is buried in the Netherlands American Cemetery, Margraten, Netherlands. He was awarded the Silver Star, Bronze Star, Purple Heart, and Croix de Guerre with Palms, and for his valor in action, he was nominated for the Medal of Honor.

EAST TENNESSEANS AT THE BATTLE OF THE BULGE

Among the Americans who fought and were wounded, captured, or died in the massive and unanticipated final German counteroffensive launched on December 16, 1944, were a host of East Tennesseans. Called by the Germans "Operation Watch on the Rhine," this counteroffensive was known to the Allies as the "Battle of the Bulge," due to the massive bulge-shaped incursion opened by the drive of two Nazi pan-

zer armies into the Allies' lines in Belgium and Luxembourg. This push was intended to break through to the port city of Antwerp, thereby driving a wedge between the US and British armies. The fighting during the Battle of the Bulge was famous for the stand of the encircled 101st Airborne Division's "Screaming Eagles," alongside other American units, at the embattled Belgian crossroad of Bastogne, liberated around Christmas Day by advance units of Lt. General George S. Patton Jr.'s Third Army, during one of the coldest Northwest European winters in then-recent memory.

This battle was also infamous for the vast numbers of American troops taken prisoner in the shock and surprise of the German offensive's opening days—one of whom was onetime University of Tennessee mechanical engineering student Kurt Vonnegut, later author of the novel *Slaughterhouse-Five*, based partly on his ordeals as a POW in Dresden during the Allied bombing of that city in February 1945—and also for the massacre of captured American prisoners-of-war by *SS* troops at the Baugnez crossroad located near the Belgian town of Malmedy. It took until January 25, 1945, to reclaim and liberate the areas seized by the Germans, who threw over 400,000 troops and 1,214 tanks into the fighting. Of 610,000 Americans involved, some 89,000 became casualties, making it the largest and bloodiest battle fought by American forces in the Second World War.

Sergeant Willie B. Beaty was born on January 1, 1921, and grew up in Fentress County. The son of Thomas S. Beaty and Ida Parsetta Hinds Beaty, he enlisted on July 16, 1942, at Fort Oglethorpe, Georgia. He served as a member of Company G, 3rd Battalion, 505th Parachute Infantry Regiment, 82nd Airborne Division. The NCO and squad leader of a light mortar squad, he was killed in action during the Battle of the Bulge in the village of Grand-Halleux, Belgium, on December 22, 1944. The story of his small unit's fight against a sizeable contingent of Hitler's vaunted *SS* is representative of some of the most desperate fighting of the Battle of the Bulge and how small units of GIs found themselves fighting doggedly against often much larger German *panzer* (tank) and *panzergrenadier* (armored infantry) units in the first phases of the Nazi counteroffensive.

Two days after the Germans launched the Battle of the Bulge, Sergeant Beaty and the rest of the paratroopers of the 505th Parachute Infantry, part of the famous "All-American" Division, loaded into open-topped cargo trailers. They were trucked from their camps in northern France (where they had been on "R&R" after Operation Market-Garden, the abortive September 1944 British and American thrust into the Netherlands) to Belgium. In the haste to move the 505th and its fellow units of the 82nd Airborne to blunt the German tide, the paratroop companies set out without suitable quantities of ammunition; C or D rations (often, just one day's supply); antitank weapons like bazookas and antitank guns, vital for lightly-armed parachute infantrymen to face the panzers; and—perhaps most critically, in light of the frozen winter conditions to follow—adequate winter clothing. The 505th would soon find itself confronting the lead element of the 6th Panzer Army: *Kampfgruppe* (Battle Group) Peiper of the 1st *SS* Panzer Division, known as the *Leibstandarte Adolf Hitler*—Hitler's personal SS bodyguard unit, under the command of *SS* Lieutenant Colonel Jochen Peiper—in savage combat at a vital river crossing near Trois Ponts, Belgium.

After tangling with Peiper's notorious troops (*Kampfgruppe* Peiper was the very *SS*

unit responsible for the so-called "Malmedy massacre" at Baugnez), the 505th became a critical part of an American defensive perimeter centered on the town of Vielsalm, south of Trois Ponts, known as the "Vielsalm Goose Egg." The hamlet of Grand-Halleux lies north of Vielsalm and featured a bridge on the Salm River athwart N68, a critical roadway for the *SS* panzers (and also for the defending Americans' vehicles that were equally dependent on the Belgian road network). Thus, Grand-Halleux lay directly on the axis of advance of yet another formidable *SS* tank unit, the 9th *SS* Panzer Division, which hit the paratroopers' defensive perimeter a few days before Christmas.

The following—provided by Raymond Daudt, one of the survivors of the 505th's G Company, to his grandniece Jo Ann Gilpin—gives a first-hand account of what happened to Beaty and the men of his mortar squad at Grand-Halleux:

> "G" Company, led by Captain Isaacs, was positioned at Grand Halleux, Belgium. Isaacs sent Lt. George E. Clark's platoon to the east, across the bridge, where they set up defensive positions and an outpost about 300 yards outside [Grand-Halleux]. The outpost consisted of an 81mm mortar and five men, Sgt Willie Beaty from Tennessee, Pvt. William Sanchez from Puerto Rico, Pvt. Wilson Whicker, Pvt. Thomas, and my uncle, a young German-American from Payette, Idaho, Pvt. Raymond Daudt.
>
> It was on the morning of December 21, 1944, that thirteen-year-old Marcel Jeanpierre and his father left their home east of town, to see if they could find more information about what was going on. . . . Most of the houses in town had already been evacuated, and the Jeanpierre family was one of the few remaining families left. While Marcel's father conversed with an American soldier in German, a young Puerto Rican soldier, Pvt.

Sanchez, gave Marcel a chocolate candy bar. I'm sure this was quite a treat for a young Belgian boy in the middle of a war and a small act of kindness he would remember the rest of his life.

That afternoon, G Company set up [its] outpost near the [Jeanpierres'] home and later that evening some of the men of G Company settled into the [family's] home and spoke with Marcel's father. According to Marcel's account, Sgt. Beaty spoke with his father in German, but I have been told by members of the 505th that Sgt. Beaty didn't speak a word of German. The only one in the company that spoke fluent German was Pvt. Daudt, and he vividly remembers speaking with the young Belgian father.

At dawn on December 22, 1944, Ray [Daudt] and a few of the other soldiers left the outpost and went back into town. Ray was informed by locals that the SS were moving in on the ridge. According to Ray, he tried to tell his superiors, but they would not listen, him being just a young private and the information coming from locals. To protect the safety of the Jeanpierre family, Ray tried to talk the father into taking his family and leaving but he refused. By midday, Sgt. Beaty set up the outpost in a vacant house next door to the Jeanpierres. By this time, they were quite certain the SS were coming and didn't want the family in the middle of the firefight, even though they feared they would be anyway. By later that afternoon, Ray and Marcel's father were outside talking. Ray was still trying to convince the young father to leave but was reassured that the family would be safe from harm in the coal cellar. They then spotted a German lookout over the ridge. Sgt. Beaty ordered in artillery fire.

By 1700 that evening, it was beginning to get dark. Sgt. Beaty and his men continued to set up in the vacant house while the Jeanpierre family next door gathered around the stove with nothing but an oil lamp for light. Somewhere around 1915, the first sounds of machine gun fire pierced the air. Sgt. Beaty and his small group of men were taking on an entire battalion of Hitler's 9th SS Panzer Division. According to Ray's account, the Germans stormed down the hill lined up shoulder to shoulder. In the ensuing firefight, Sgt. Beaty was killed outside of the house by a grenade and Pvt. Sanchez was killed in the front doorway. The other [three] soldiers were somehow able to escape. Pvt. Ray Daudt was among those who survived.

As night fell, Ray continued to exchange fire with the SS. Then at some point during the night, as a light snow began to fall, he threw a grenade out the broken window and, as he puts it, "the shooting stopped." He seized upon this opportunity to make a run for it on his own. Ray ran the 300 yards to the [platoon's] CP, where his [platoon] leader called out: "What the hell is going on over there?" Ray replied: "What the hell do you think!" They then evacuated the CP and retreated across the bridge at Grand-Halleux as they were being pursued by their attackers. Just as Ray made it across the bridge and dove behind a small brick ledge, the bridge exploded. He was not expecting it, and he thought he was going to get his head blown off. Ray wasn't able to hear much for a few hours after this because he was so close to the blast. The destruction of the bridge basically stopped the advancing Germans. Those who tried to wade the river were promptly met with American firepower.[4]

It took a host of desperate firefights and bridge defense-and-demolition actions much like this one to halt the last major German offensive of World War II dead in its tracks. Willie B. Beaty is buried in the Storie Cemetery in the Little Crab community of Fentress County. Other East Tennesseans who fell at the Bulge were Marshall E. Masterson (Hamilton), John T. Davis (Roane), Fred W. Armstrong (Washington), Joseph D. McKinney (Roane), Charles E. McElyea (Knox), Andrew J. Scalf

(Greene), John M. Patrick (Sequatchie), and Reece Gass (Greene). Several of these men's accounts follow.

Private First Class Masterson was from Soddy (Hamilton), served with the 394th Infantry Regiment, 99th Infantry Division, and died on January 9, 1945, in the brutal combat for Elsenborn Ridge, located on the north shoulder of the Bulge. This poignant account by Brenda Korner-Carey describes Masterson's final moments:

> My father was the squad leader for Marshall E. Masterson during the Battle of the Bulge [at] Elsenborn Ridge. They were in battle for a month. During the battle, they were in a foxhole and were taking turns to get water. It was my father Fred Korner's turn to retrieve the water when Marshall said that he would get the water this time and that my dad could get it next time. When Marshall left the safety of the bunker (approximately 2 feet), a German 88 round hit him, and he disintegrated. Needless to say, this was very traumatic for my father, who has not gotten over it for 70 years. . . .

Marshall Masterson is buried at Dividing Ridge Church of God Cemetery, Soddy-Daisy, Hamilton County.

Private First Class Fred W. Armstrong was born in Sulphur Springs (Washington) on February 25, 1914. He enlisted in the Army on March 13, 1942, at Fort Oglethorpe, Georgia, and was sent to Camp Claiborne, Louisiana, for the reactivation of the 82nd Infantry ("All-American") Division on March 25, 1942. On August 15, 1942, the division was re-designated the 82nd Airborne Division, thus becoming the nation's first airborne division; the 325th Infantry, to which he was assigned, became the 325th Glider Infantry Regiment. In October 1942, Armstrong and the entire division went to

Fort Bragg, North Carolina, for airborne school. Afterwards, he completed glider training at the Laurinburg-Maxton Army Air Base, North Carolina, and was assigned to Company F, 2nd Battalion of the 325th.

Armstrong participated in the invasion of Sicily, Operation Husky, on July 9–10, 1943. His first battle would not be a glider drop, but a landing by sea. After Italy, the 325th trained in Ireland and England with the rest of the 82nd for the invasion of France. Armstrong's first combat glider assault was on "D+1," June 7, 1944, in the vicinity of Sainte-Mère-Eglise, to reinforce the parachute-landed regiments that dropped in there the morning before, on D-Day. On September 1, 1944, PFC Armstrong and the 325th conducted its fourth combat assault during Operation Market-Garden in the Netherlands, and all of his unit's objectives were taken. Such was not the case, however, for British and Polish paratroopers fighting north of the 82nd Airborne at Arnhem, the offensive's ultimate objective. Following the defeat and withdrawal of those Allied forces from Arnhem and Oosterbeek, marking the end of Operation Market-Garden, the 82nd's weary troops were sent to France on R&R.

At this point, Armstrong's next few weeks paralleled much of Sergeant Willie Beaty's experiences in his element of the 82nd Airborne. On December 18, two days after the Germans launched a surprise offensive through the Ardennes Forest, Armstrong and his unit joined the Battle of the Bulge. In savage combat at Baraque-de-Fraiture, Belgium, on December 23, 1944, during an engagement later known as the "Battle of Parker's Crossroads" after the senior-most American officer there, Major Arthur Parker, Armstrong was killed in action while he and Company F faced off against an-

Private First Class Reece Gass.

remains are being returned home to be re-buried in Tennessee. He still has family living in Greeneville and will be buried there on June 10, 2017. Gass was only 20 years old when his tank was hit by enemy fire on January 14, 1945. Gass was a member of Company E, 33rd Armored Regiment, 3rd Armored Division, moving from the Lomre area toward Cherain, Belgium, in a three-pronged advance against enemy forces, according to the DOD. Five tanks from the regiment were lost, including at least two from Gass' company.

A U.S. War Department investigator found a set of possible human remains in the remnants of a tank at Mont-le-Ban near Cherain in June 1947. All attempts to identify the remains were unsuccessful, and they were buried in the U.S. Military Cemetery Hamm, in Luxembourg, in March 1952 with a headstone reading, "Here Rests in Honored Glory a Comrade in Arms Known but to God."

Through the Defense POW/MIA Accounting Agency's disinterment program, historians were able to link the remains to one of three unaccounted-for service members, including Gass. The remains were disinterred on May 11, 2016. Scientists were able to match the remains with DNA from Gass' niece, allowing him to finally return to his Tennessee home. . . . Gass' name is listed on the Walls of the Missing at an American Battle Monuments Commission site along with other MIAs from WWII. A rosette will now be placed next to his name to show that he has been accounted for, the DOD said.[5]

other tank-equipped *SS* unit, the 2nd *SS* Panzer Division. He was thirty years old, and he was decorated with the Purple Heart. Armstrong had participated in six unit campaigns—Tunisia, Sicily, Naples-Foggia, Normandy, Rhineland, and the Ardennes-Alsace. He is interred at the Henri-Chapelle American Cemetery, Liège, Belgium. He also has a memorial marker at Fairview United Methodist Church Cemetery, Section 2, Row 2, Grave 17, in Jonesborough.

A June 8, 2017, report from WBIR-TV carried news of the DNA identification of still another World War II soldier, who was returned home for burial years after he fell in action:

A Greeneville soldier is finally returning home more than 70 years after he was killed in action in Belgium during World War II. The remains of Army Private First Class Reece Gass went decades without being identified. The Department of Defense was recently able to identify Gass, and his

Gass was buried in 2017 at Cross Anchor Cemetery in northern Greene County.

Finally, two GIs from East Tennessee, Sergeant Herbert C. Davenport Jr. (Greene) and Private First Class John W. Bliscerd (Loudon), were killed very close to the end of the war in Europe. Davenport was born on February 20, 1924, and enlisted on June 10, 1943. He served

Private First Class John W. Bliscerd.

as an NCO in the 513th Parachute Infantry Regiment, 17th Airborne Division, participating in Operation Varsity, the last big parachute jump across the Rhine and Weser Rivers in Germany, as Allied forces pressed further into central Germany. He was killed on March 30, 1945, near Bulden, Germany, not far from the city of Münster. He is buried at the Netherlands American Cemetery, Margraten, Netherlands. He was the recipient of several decorations, including the Bronze Star, the Purple Heart, the Combat Infantryman Badge, and the Parachute Badge with bronze arrowhead and bronze service star.

John Bliscerd was born in 1921 and called the Philadelphia community home; he enlisted on November 13, 1942. He served in the 736th Tank Battalion. At the time of his death, the 736th had crossed the Rhine River in support of the 83rd Infantry Division and reached the Elbe River on April 13, 1945. Bliscerd died on

April 15, 1945, and is interred at the Netherlands American Cemetery, Margraten, Netherlands. In 1945, as the war drew to a close, Nazi Germany was caught between the armies of the western Allies advancing from the west and the Soviet Union advancing from the east. On April 25,1945, these two forces linked up near Torgau on the Elbe, leading to a famous picture of the two victorious armies' soldiers shaking hands. On the day that Bliscerd died, Nazi Germany—and the war in Europe—had less than a month left; V-E Day was declared on May 7, 1945.

8

THE JAPANESE "HELLSHIPS"

Lasciate ogne speranza, voi ch'intrate
(Abandon all hope, ye who enter here.)

—*Dante's Inferno*

One particularly compelling, tragic, and often forgotten aspect of the war in the Pacific involved Allied POWs—many of them Americans—who, after suffering extended privation, torture, starvation, and disease in prison camps, became "friendly-fire" targets aboard the infamous Japanese "hellships." Not being identified as POW transportation vessels nor marked with Red Cross insignia, these vessels were often attacked and sunk by Allied submarines and aircraft, with most of their wretched occupants being killed in the process. The stories of the East Tennesseans consigned to these ships of woe are especially poignant, given the extreme suffering that they had already experienced during several years of harsh captivity.

All of the East Tennessee POWs who later found themselves on Japan's "hellships" were trapped in the Philippines as the Japanese Imperial Army advanced in early 1942. Allied troops retreated to the Bataan Peninsula and the nearby fortified island of Corregidor. Finally overrun and taken prisoner, many of the survivors were compelled to undertake the arduous sixty-five-mile Bataan Death March to their eventual prison camps, as previously described in several accounts in chapter 6.

Some three years later, many of the surviving POWs were herded onto unmarked Japanese freighters headed to Japan and its Korean and Manchurian provinces, where they would provide slave labor in factories and mines. Once at sea, Allied submarines and aircraft frequently targeted these ships—which were not marked as non-combatant vessels—completely unaware that their fellow service members were aboard. Among the best-known of the ships, in part because of the large number of American POWs they were carrying, were the *Arisan Maru*, the *Oryoku Maru*, and the *Shinyo Maru*. Twelve servicemen from nine East Tennessee counties perished when the *Arisan Maru* went down; two died aboard the *Oryoku Maru*; and five were lost with the *Shinyo Maru*—a death toll of nineteen in all.

The Japanese hellship *Oryoku Maru*. Courtesy of Fold3.com.

Private Waymon W. Sandidge was born in Cleveland (Bradley) in 1922. By the time he joined the military, he had moved to Blount County. He enlisted January 31, 1941, at Fort McPherson in Atlanta and was assigned to the 59th Coast Artillery Regiment, based in the Philippines and tasked with the anti-shipping and anti-aircraft defense of Manila Bay and Subic Bay. When Pearl Harbor was attacked on December 7, 1941, Japan also attacked the Philippines on the same day, which was December 8 across the International Date Line. The 59th Coastal Artillery defended the two bays until its troops were driven back to Corregidor and Bataan. Surviving on little or no food and running out of ammunition, the Americans held out on the Bataan Peninsula until April 9, 1942, and until May 6, 1942, on the fortress of Corregidor. After American and Philippine

forces surrendered, Sandidge was one of many forced to march approximately sixty-five miles without food and water. It is estimated that 5,000 to 11,000 died on the Bataan Death March, en route to the prison camps. Miraculously, Sandidge survived the march. He would not be so fortunate, however, after that.

On October 11, 1944, some 1,800 POWs were loaded onto the unmarked *Arisan Maru*, to be transported to Japan as slave laborers; among them, fatefully, was Waymon Sandidge. The freighter was eventually spotted 225 miles east of Hong Kong by the USS *Shark* (SS-314). The submarine torpedoed the *Arisan Maru* without knowing of its cargo of American prisoners. Only nine of the POWs survived. The *Shark*'s last message, received on October 24 by the USS *Seadragon* (SS-194), was that she had spotted a single freighter. The *Shark* itself was never heard from again. Five prisoners who survived and subsequently reached China stated that conditions on the *Arisan Maru* were so intolerable that the prisoners prayed for deliverance from their misery by a torpedo or bomb. Because many POWs had been rescued from the water by submarines after sinking the vessels in which they were being transported, US submarines were later instructed to search for Allied survivors in the vicinity of all sinkings of Empire-bound Japanese ships. In fact, the *Shark* may well have been sunk trying to rescue American prisoners of war.

After all attempts to contact *Shark* failed, on November 27, 1944, she was reported as presumed lost. A Japanese anti-submarine attack report received after the close of the war recorded an attack apparently made on the *Shark* on October 24, 1944, in Latitude 20° 41'N, Longitude 118° 27'E. Depth charges were dropped seventeen times, and the Japanese reported having seen "bubbles, and heavy oil, clothes, cork, etc." Several American submarines reported having been attacked on this date near the position given; in view of the fact that none reported the attack on the convoy as noted above, this attack was considered the most probable cause of the *Shark*'s loss.

Private Sandidge is listed as Missing in Action on the Tablets of the Missing at the Manila American Cemetery, Fort Bonifacio, Philippines. His awards include the Philippines Defense Medal with Bronze Star, Asiatic-Pacific Campaign Medal with Bronze Star, and the Purple Heart. Major Paul M. Jones (Bradley) was assigned to the 26th Cavalry Regiment, Philippine Scouts. An elite unit of the Philippine Army that was highly esteemed by US troops, the 26th Cavalry found itself engaged against the Japanese shortly after the initial

bombing of Manila and withdrew to the Bataan Peninsula per War Plan Orange. The surrender of the men found them pushed onto the Bataan Death March and into captivity as POWs. One of the nine *Arisan Maru* survivors reported that, after the torpedo struck the vessel, Major Jones acted to calm the men during the sinking. He also is remembered on the Tablets of the Missing at the Manila American Cemetery.

Others who went down with the *Arisan Maru* were Sergeant Bishop Lawson (Campbell), Private Alfred T. Davis (Cumberland), Private John W. Parker and Private Henry J. Wingfield (both Knox), First Sergeant Benjamin F. Harrison and Private First Class Conrad C. Perryman (both Loudon), Captain James A. Seay (Marion), Private David B. Lawson (Polk), and Staff Sergeant Herman R. Bouton (Washington).

Boatswain's Mate William Harrison Patrick (Knox) served aboard the USS *Canopus* (AS-9), the submarine tender assigned to Submarine Squadron 20 stationed in the Philippines. His ship, badly damaged by Japanese bombers, was scuttled and sunk in deep water on April 9, 1942. He was evacuated to Corregidor, "The Rock," located across the bay from Manila. There, Patrick was attached to the 4th Battalion Reserves (Provisional) of the 4th Marine Regiment and fought gallantly during the final battle for the island fortress. He was captured on May 6, 1942, the day that General Jonathan Wainwright was forced to surrender Corregidor to the Japanese, and Patrick was transferred to the mainland and interned at the Los Baños POW camp on the Philippine island of Luzon. On October 11, 1944, he boarded the *Arisan Maru* and was lost when that hellship met its fate. He was reported as buried at sea and is also memorialized at the Manila American Cemetery.

Staff Sergeant Frank Godsey (Cumberland), 698th Ordnance Company (Aviation), Army Air Forces, was also serving in the Philippines when the Japanese invaded. He was captured and survived the Bataan Death March, being imprisoned in the Cabanatuan POW camp until the Japanese decided to move him and 1,619 other POWs to Japan. They were loaded onto the hellship *Oryoku Maru* in Manila and departed from there on December 13, 1944. It was located the next day by aircraft of the USS *Hornet*, and the unmarked ship was repeatedly attacked as it moved up the west coast of Bataan. On December 15, the *Hornet*'s aircraft returned and sank the *Oryoku Maru* off the coast of Olongapo. Surviving POWs were allowed to jump overboard and swim to shore. Those that survived were loaded onto another hellship, the *Enoura Maru*, and the voyage continued to Takao Harbor, Formosa (now Taiwan). That ship was located there by planes from the *Hornet* and sunk on January 9, 1945. Staff Sergeant Godsey was not among the survivors placed on the *Enoura Maru*.

Second Lieutenant Jay M. Horowitz (Monroe), 93rd Bomber Squadron, 19th Bomber Group (Heavy), also perished with the sinking of the *Oryoku Maru*. He was awarded the Air Medal with Oak Leaf Cluster and the Purple Heart. Both he and Godsey, who was also awarded the Purple Heart, are remembered at the Manila American Cemetery. The following account, contributed by ETVMA Board member and fellow researcher Jeffrey Berry, describes the harrowing story and treatment of Horowitz.

Jay Malcolm Horowitz was, as his friends described him, the happy Jewish boy from Sweetwater, Tennessee. Born December 30, 1918, and raised in Brooklyn, New York, he was the son of Benjamin F. Horowitz and Ruth R. Cahn Horowitz. He was born of Russian, German, Austrian, and New York descent. He was one of two sons born to Ben and Ruth. His father was a clothing merchant in New York and moved to Sweetwater, Tennessee, where Jay was graduated from Sweetwater High School on May 23, 1936. By August 1936, he was enrolled at the University of Tennessee.

He was a senior in 1940 when he enrolled at the University of Miami at Coral Gables, Florida. He was one of forty-four who would become the inaugural class of 40-A (representatives of the United States Army Air Corps and Pan American Airways who had descended on Coral Gables for instruction on celestial navigation). His classmates would later go on to participate in Doolittle's Raid on Japan or lose their lives aboard B-17s defending their country. From August 12, 1940, to November 12, 1940, he studied and learned how to navigate using the stars. He earned his wings upon graduation and was stationed at Kirtland Field, Albuquerque, New Mexico. While there, the new airmen honed their bombing skills and kept a close ear to the radio and world events. War was in the air.

He and some of his classmates became part of the 93rd Bomber Squadron, 19th Bomber Group, Army Air Forces. Their orders in late October 1940 were to take the new fleet of B-17s to the Southwest Pacific Theatre, specifically Clark Field. While not as infamous as the attack on Pearl Harbor on December 7, 1941, the Japanese bombed Clark Field the very next day, on December 8, 1941. This air raid decimated the majority of the air fleet, and many of the undamaged planes were sent to Australia.

Without a plane to navigate, Jay remained in the Philippines and was not part of the evacuation to Australia. He occupied his time by helping keep the Japanese Imperial Army at bay until the United States forces were surrendered in April 1942. Jay would assist with artillery and other missions. Jay would eventually surrender to the Japanese and would begin his journey on [the] Bataan Death March. The march was a harsh, inhumane sixty-five-mile trail from the main island of Luzon to the prison camps at San Fernando. One survivor tells of the hot humid conditions without food and with little water. He remarked that, along the sixty-five miles, he never lost sight of dead American or Filipino soldiers who either died from starvation or exhaustion or were executed because they could not keep up due to fatigue and the conditions two which the prisoners were subjected. Jay survived.

Jay would be moved to the Cabanatuan Prison Camp, where he would watch many more friends and prisoners suffer and die over the next thirty-two months. The only correspondence that Jay was ever able to get out was during this time. The *Knoxville News Sentinel* reported on August 28, 1943, that Jay had penned a letter to his parents. He told them he was well and was treated fairly. One wonders if this was a comfort to his mother, or if she knew the truth behind the censored letter? Still, Jay survived.

On December 12, 1944, Jay was selected as one of 1,169 prisoners moved to Bilibid Prison in Manila. On the following day, the prisoners were marched through the streets of Manila to Pier 7 at Manila Bay. The civilians watched helplessly and feared the Japanese soldiers if they tried to offer even a small cup of water. Jay and the others were boarded on the *Oryoku Maru*, a Japanese cabin-type vessel designed for luxury travel. There were no markings to distinguish the ship from any other Japanese vessel, and anti-aircraft weapons were clearly visible. There were three cargo holds about twenty feet below the top deck. The prisoners were placed in the holds with no water or food, no air, and no restroom facilities. The men were back-to-chest with the next person. They were exhausted, emaciated, sick, and were experiencing temperatures at 100–110 degrees Fahrenheit. Some lost their senses and began to lash out at their fellow mates. Death began to take its toll. Jay survived.

At 3:00 a.m., the *Oryoku Maru* left port and headed out across Manila Bay toward the China Sea. It was at that point that the sound of aircraft engines pierced the night, as aircraft from the USS *Hornet* attacked the vessel with gunfire and bombs. The repeated attacks from the *Hornet* lasted until 4:00 p.m. that afternoon. Some of the bullets pierced the bodies of those below deck, yet Jay survived. They remained aboard the *Oryoku Maru* until the following day. No food; no water; men paralyzed with fear and others screaming out in agony. An announcement came, and the hatch was opened: "Officers first, then the others. You will swim to shore." Some of these tired, barely living men were forced to strip off their clothing and shoes; only their undergarments remained. They were forced off the ship into the water of Subic Bay. Some who were too weak to swim clung to debris in the water or drowned.

As the officers, including Second Lieutenant Jay Horowitz, led the way three hundred yards to shore, they were met by Japanese soldiers. The officers, who were told to go first, were met with machine gun fire. An astute lead pilot from the USS *Hornet* recognized the swimming bodies below as fellow Americans and called off the final bombing run for the moment, and many were saved. Despite the swim, the aborted air raid, and the machine gun fire, Jay survived.

Once on shore, the survivors were herded into tennis courts at the Olongapo Naval Station. The courts were surrounded by chicken wire. No food or medical aid was provided for the first two days. They were held on the tennis courts for five days and six nights, December 15–21, 1944, undernourished, exposed to the elements, and suffering from their captivity. One wonders whether, on a clear night, Jay looked to the heavens and for a brief moment lost himself in the stars that he was so acquainted with from his early days in the Armed Forces. When a roll call was taken on the tennis courts, it was determined that of the 1,619 prisoners who had sailed from Manila's Pier 7 on December 13, fewer than 1,300 remained. More than 300 American prisoners died in a thirty-eight-hour period from suffocation, starvation, drowning, and cold-blooded murder. Through the heat, starvation, exposure, and exhaustion, Jay endured.

From there, Jay and the survivors were loaded onto trucks and hauled back to San Fernando. After a couple of days there in the jail and jail yard, they were loaded onto boxcars so crowded that, again, there was no fresh air; 120 men were jammed into each boxcar. The eighteen-hour train ride ended at San Fernando La Union, a port on the China Sea. It was there that they would spend Christmas Day. Each prisoner was given one rice ball with compotes. Jay survived.

On December 27, 1944, the prisoners embarked on two different ships, the *Brazil Maru* and the *Enoura Maru,* which joined up with other ships heading for Formosa (present day Taiwan). They arrived on January 2, 1945, after

a journey with no food and cramped, unsanitary, and inhumane conditions. At this point, all prisoners were moved to the hold of the *Enoura Maru.* The hold had not been cleaned from the vessel's last voyage with men and horses. There, they remained for a week until the silence of the waves against the ship and the churn of the engine was interrupted again by a familiar sound, as bombs and gunfire filled the air and the hold of the ship. Between 350 and 400 men were killed, and many others were injured. There was no aid, no medicine, and no supplies except dirty rags. For three days after the raid, dead and dying men were held below deck. The dead were later removed and stacked on the pier like cordwood to be cremated, and the survivors were transferred to the *Brazil Maru.* It had been one month since they left Manila Bay. On January 13, 1945, weakened and worn from his journey, Jay still survived and boarded the *Brazil Maru.*

The *Brazil Maru* departed for Japan on January 13, 1945. Half of their number had died. The weather had changed and now Jay encountered the bitter winter cold. The soldiers were chilled, half naked, and their ranks diminished daily: ten to fifteen deaths per day in the beginning, reaching a maximum of forty dead per day a few days prior to arrival in Japan. Yet, Jay clung to life.

On January 23, 1945, after 1,021 days in captivity, the interpreter called: "Roll out your dead." The frail, emaciated, lifeless body of Jay Horowitz, the once happy boy from Sweetwater, was carried out on the deck of the ship. His clothing was stripped for the benefit of the survivors below, and a Navy corpsman cast him overboard into the cold water of the East China Sea. The sea received his remains, and his body slipped quietly under the water to his rest.

Private First Class Frank W. Hartsell.

On board the hellship *Shinyo Maru* were five East Tennesseans: Private Ben D. Gatliff (Knox), Second Lieutenant Harry R. Lafon Jr. and Sergeant Roy H. McPeters (both Roane), Technician Fifth Class James M. Offield (Sullivan), and Private First Class Frank W. Hartsell (Washington). Gatliff, who served with the 454th Ordnance Company (Aviation), was taken prisoner by the Japanese on Corregidor and was another survivor of the rigors of the Bataan Death March. He was one of 750 prisoners who were loaded onto the *Shinyo Maru*. The ship was torpedoed by the submarine USS *Paddle* (SS-263) on September 7, 1944, northwest of Mindanao. Only eighty-two POWs survived.

Second Lieutenant Harry R. Lafon Jr. was born in Virginia around 1919. He later lived in Harriman (Roane), Tennessee, and Harrodsburg, Kentucky. Lafon met Helen Frankie McCamish while they both were students at Lincoln Memorial University in Harrogate, Tennessee. They married on July 5, 1941, in Claiborne County. Lafon enlisted in the Kentucky National Guard at Harrodsburg. On November 25, 1940, when his tank company was federalized, Lafon went to Fort Knox, Kentucky, as a corporal. In early 1941, he was assigned to the 192nd Tank Battalion's Headquarters Company, when that company was formed with men from the four lettered (i.e., A through D) companies of the battalion. Lafon rose in rank from corporal to sergeant with that transition.

After training for nearly a year, Lafon was sent to Louisiana for maneuvers in late 1941. After the maneuvers at Camp Polk, he and the rest of the battalion learned that they were being sent overseas. At that time, those men who were twenty-nine years old or older were given the chance to resign from federal service. Lafon was commissioned a second lieutenant at this time.

Lafon arrived in the Philippines on Thanksgiving Day of 1941. He and the rest of the 192nd Tank Battalion were rushed to Fort Stotsenburg and assigned to tents along the main road between the fort and Clark Airfield, the principal air base on Luzon, located some forty miles northwest of Manila. At this time, D Company was attached to the 194th Tank Battalion. On December 8, 1941, Lafon lived through the Japanese air attack on Clark Field. He and the rest of D Company spent the next four months fighting a delaying action on Luzon to buy time for the United States to gear up for the war.

Thought of as being a man of courage, Lafon was apparently well-liked by D Company's enlisted men. Other members of the company later stated that, when he led his tanks into action, he stood up in the tank's turret and did not close the armored hatch for protection. On April 9, 1942, he became a prisoner of war. He took part in the Bataan Death March and was held at Camp O'Donnell. He was then sent to Cabanatuan. In October 1942, Lafon was selected for transport to the Davao penal colony on the island of Mindanao to work on a labor detail. The POWs on this detail worked on a farm and later built runways at Lasang, Mindanao. Lafon was sent to Davao on February 29, 1944, to work on a runway-building detail. Almost 650 POWs built the airfield at Lasang, while 100 POWs built an airfield south of Davao.

By June 6, 1944, it was apparent to the Japanese that it was just a matter of time before the Americans landed in the Philippines. To prevent the POWs' liberation, the Japanese ordered the *Tateishi Maru* to Lasang, in order to evacuate the men from Davao to Manila. On August 19, 1944, the POWs were marched shoeless to the Tabunco pier. The next day, they were packed into the *Tateishi Maru*'s stifling holds. On August 24, the *Tateishi Maru* arrived in Zamboanga, where it waited in port for ten days. The conditions in the ship's cargo holds were hot and steamy; the longer the POWs were in the holds, the worse the stench became. The only thing that the Japanese did to ease the conditions for the POWs was to let them on deck occasionally and spray them with salt water.

On September 4, the POWs were transferred onto another hellship, the *Shinyo Maru*, which sailed on September 7 at 2:00 a.m. as part of part of a convoy designated as C-076. Before it sailed, its hatch covers were secured so that the POWs could not lift them from below. Since the POWs had not heard any air raid alerts, they assumed that they were safe. However, on August 18, an American intelligence unit had intercepted the Japanese orders sending the *Shinyo Maru* to Zamboanga. Someone misinterpreted the deciphered message as saying the ship was to pick up military *personnel*, instead of military *prisoners*. Because of this mistake, the Navy sent the submarine USS *Paddle* to intercept the ship; the translation error was only later discovered in December 1944—long after the fact, and long after a resulting tragedy had already transpired.

At 7:37 p.m. on September 7, the *Paddle* spotted Japanese convoy C-076 off Mindanao's west coast, near Sindangan Point, and the sub promptly launched two torpedoes at the *Shinyo Maru*. A terrific explosion was observed, followed immediately by a second blast. Many of the POWs in the holds were bleeding and dying. Some of the prisoners successfully escaped the holds to jump overboard and swim toward shore. As they swam, the surviving Japanese fired at them. Others were shot as they attempted to escape from the holds. According to the surviving POWs, there was a tremendous crushing sound: the ship seemed to bend up in the middle and then sank into the water. Of the 750 POWs who boarded the ship, eighty-three were rescued by Filipino guerillas and returned to American forces in October 1944. It is not known if Lafon was one of the POWs who was shot by the Japanese while trying to escape one of the ship's holds, or if he died when the ship sank. All that is known is that Lafon died with the sinking of the *Shinyo Maru*.[1]

Sergeant Roy H. McPeters (Roane), Army Air Forces, was assigned to Headquarters, 27th Bomber Group (Light). This unit was caught in the Philippines and fought at Bataan as infantry before being captured and sent on the Bataan Death March. McPeters was captured on May 7, 1942, along with Technician Fifth Class James M. Offield (Sullivan). Like Lafon, both of them went down with the *Shinyo Maru*. They are listed on the Tablets of the Missing, Manila American Cemetery, Fort Bonifacio, Philippines.

Private First Class Frank W. Hartsell (Washington) was born on August 23, 1915, in the Lamar Community of Jonesborough (Washington) and attended Lamar School. He enlisted on November 4, 1940, at Fort George Wright in Spokane, Washington, while working as a farm hand. Hartsell was assigned to the 701st Ordnance Company (Aviation), 19th Bomb Group (Heavy), 16th Bomb Wing, 2nd Air Force. He was taken prisoner by the Japanese on May 7, 1942, when Corregidor fell. Hartsell was another POW aboard the *Shinyo Maru* when she was torpedoed. He was twenty-nine years old, and he is also listed on the Tablets of the Missing at the Manila American Cemetery.

The inscription on the Pacific War Memorial located at Corregidor provides an apt benediction for the dead of the *Arisan Maru*, the *Oryoku Maru*, and the *Shinyo Maru*, lost in the sinkings of those wretched "hellships":

> *Sleep, my sons, your duty done, for Freedom's light has come;*
>
> *Sleep in the silent depths of the sea, or in your bed of hallowed sod,*
>
> *Until you hear at dawn the low, clear reveille of God.*

9

THE TESTER BROTHERS OF WASHINGTON COUNTY

A Gold Star Family's Losses during World War II

A nation reveals itself not only by the men it produces
but also by the men it honors, the men it remembers.

—*President John F. Kennedy, 1963*

The loss of the five "Fighting Sullivan" brothers on the cruiser USS *Juneau* in the South Pacific and the deaths of the Hoback and Niland brothers on Omaha Beach inspired a nation and gave rise to a theme that was later popularized in the 1998 Steven Spielberg film "Saving Private Ryan." East Tennessee also had a trio of brothers who paid the ultimate sacrifice in the Second World War. The service and deaths of the three Tester brothers of rural Washington County—fallen in action in North Africa, France, and Germany, and buried side-by-side in Belgium—should not be forgotten.

Robert Denton "Dent" Tester, Glenn "Glen" William Tester, and James Earle Tester were three of seven sons born to Millard Franklin and Eliza Catherine (Walker) Tester. Five of the seven served in the United States Army during World War II, but three gave their all. These three were born in the New Victory Community of Telford, Washington County, near Jonesborough, which is the oldest town in the state of Tennessee. Robert was born on Christmas Day in 1910; Glenn was born on February 10, 1918; and James was born on August 26, 1920. The brothers were raised in a religious home, attended the New Victory Baptist Church, received a formal education and worked hard on their father's farm.

The oldest brother, Robert, was a jack of all trades and spent time as a poultry farmer, a carpenter, a woodworker and more. In the early 1930s, he moved to Ogle County, Illinois and worked on a dairy farm. He enlisted in the Illinois National Guard on February 12, 1941 and was assigned to Company I, 3rd Battalion, 131st Infantry Regiment. They were activated to federal service on March 5, 1941 and assigned to the 33rd Division. Later, Robert was reassigned to Company I, 3rd Battalion, 320th Infantry Regiment, 35th Infantry Division, and held the rank of Sergeant. Robert, while on a special assignment, was the first to fall. He died in the sinking of a transport ship: His

Sergeant Robert Denton "Dent" Tester.

Sergeant James E. Tester.

Private First Class Glenn Tester.

Majesty's Transport (HMT) *Rohna* on November 26, 1943, off the coast of Bougie, Tunisia in North Africa. (See chapter 5 for HMT *Rohna*'s sinking.) His body later washed ashore near Philippeville (now Skikda), Algeria. Robert was positively identified by the contents of his wallet and the extensive dental work that was done after he entered the Army. He was initially interred at the United States Military Cemetery, Constantine, Algeria in Plot B, Row 1, Grave 8. Robert was later reinterred in the United States Military Cemetery El Alia in Algiers, Algeria in Plot 12-N, Row 5, Grave 97. He was awarded the Purple Heart.

The next to fall was the youngest brother to serve, James, better known to his family and friends as Earle, who grew up doing farm work and odd jobs. After high school, he joined the Civilian Conservation Corps (CCC), a government-sponsored program and helped to build roads, schools, public parks, bridges, and provide general upkeep of government properties. After two years in the CCC, he enlisted in the Army on November 6, 1942 from Washington County. James served with Company E, 2nd Battalion, 22nd Infantry Regiment, 4th Infantry Division, and he also held the rank of sergeant. His baptism of fire came on June 6, 1944, D-Day, when he stepped off a LCI ("Higgins boat") onto Utah Beach. James was killed in action on September 17, 1944, near Brandscheid, Germany, as Allied forces approached Germany's westernmost edges of the Rhineland and its Siegfried Line fortifications. He was first interred where he rests now at the United States Military Cemetery Henri-Chapelle in Belgium, but in Plot C, Row 8, Grave 156. James was decorated with the Bronze Star Medal with V device for valor and Oak Leaf Cluster (indicating a second award) and the Purple Heart.

The last of the three brothers to perish was Glenn. He too, just like all his brothers, grew up working the farm. Afterwards, he tried his hand at logging, saw mill work, and as an automobile mechanic. Glenn married his childhood sweetheart, Marie, and they along with an older brother, Charles, moved to Paradise, California where they were employed in a woodworking plant. Later, they all moved to Bend, Oregon where Charles enlisted in the Army, followed by Glenn on July 15, 1943. Glenn served in Company I, 3rd Battalion, 142nd Infantry Regiment, 36th Infantry Division, and held the rank of private first class. He was first wounded in action on August 24, 1944, in Southern France. After a long hospital stay, he had only been back with his unit for a short time when he was killed in action in the vicinity of Oberhoffen-sur-Moder, Alsace, France on January

9, 1945. He was initially interred at the United States Military Cemetery in Épinal, France in Plot 2E, Row 23, Grave 4443. Like James, he too was recognized with a Bronze Star Medal with V device and the Purple Heart with Oak Leaf Cluster.

After the death of her husband, Millard, and her oldest son, Thomas Milton Tester, in 1942, the loss of three more sons must have been simply overwhelming to Mrs. Tester. She had to shoulder the responsibility of all the paperwork with the government after each son's death. After war's end, the three brothers' remains were all disinterred and relocated; the family opted not to seek to return their bodies to America but to leave them overseas. Thus, James Earle, Glenn William, and Robert Denton Tester, per their mother's written request, were reinterred side-by-side at the Henri-Chapelle American Cemetery located near Plombières, Belgium. Robert rests in Plot B, Row 14, Grave 20; Glenn in Plot B, Row 14, Grave 19; and James in Plot B, Row 14, Grave 18, just a section over from where he was originally interred. There are over 200 sets of brothers interred in American military cemeteries overseas, but this is the only group of three.

The Tester brothers are commemorated by memorial markers at New Victory Baptist Church and by Tennessee Historical Commission marker 1A-125 adjacent to Telford-New Victory Road, one mile from the family's homestead, commemorating the "supreme sacrifice of their lives in the European Theater of War." The oldest brother-in-arms, Charles Raymond Tester, rests in front of the memorial in the New Victory Baptist Church Cemetery. He passed away in 1991. The fifth brother to serve was Franklin George Tester, who was killed in the line of duty as a policeman in Panama in

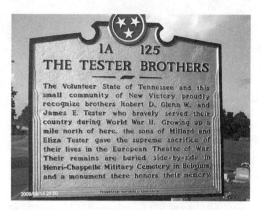

Tennessee Historical Commission marker 1A-125 adjacent to Telford-New Victory Road, one mile from the family's homestead

1956. He also is interred at the New Victory Cemetery, as is their mother, father, and youngest brother, Carroll Hamilton Tester. Carroll wanted to serve but was exempted from service due to his status as the family's last surviving son. He became the man of the house and kept the farm running and the "home fires burning." Carroll died in 2006.

One can only imagine the agony and lonliness felt by their family and rural East Tennessee community with the loss of these three young men and beloved brothers in the space of approximately one and one-half years.

10

A DIFFICULT HOMECOMING

The Challenges of Postwar Repatriation

We leave you our deaths. Give them their meaning.

—*Excerpted from the poem "The Young Dead Soldiers Do Not Speak" by Archibald MacLeish*

We have not forgotten, we will never forget, the debt of infinite gratitude that we have contracted with those who gave everything for our freedom.

—*René Coty, president of the French Republic*

Once the Second World War ended in Europe in May 1945 after the defeat of Nazi Germany and then, four months later, in Asia and the Pacific with Imperial Japan's surrender, the hard task of dealing with the American war dead then interred on foreign shores began in earnest. Much of that work would be undertaken by the American Battle Monuments Commission, which had been established by Congress in 1923 following the First World War. The ABMC was entrusted with designing, constructing, and maintaining permanent American cemeteries in foreign countries; establishing and maintaining US military memorials, monuments, and markers both at home and abroad; and, finally, controlling the design and construction of permanent US military monuments and markers by US citizens and organizations, public and private, and encouraging their maintenance.

In addition to grave sites, the ABMC's World War I and II cemeteries, together with three memorials on US soil, commemorate by name those American service members who were missing in action, lost, or buried at sea during World War I, World War II, the Korean War, and the Vietnam War. There are 207,637 US war dead from World War I and World War II so commemorated at ABMC sites; this includes 30,974 interments and 4,455 missing-in-action memorializations for World War I, and 93,218 interments and 78,990 MIA memorializations for World War II. Additionally, the names of 8,209 individuals listed as missing from the Korean War and 2,504 individuals missing from the Vietnam War are memorialized at ABMC's Honolulu Memorial, better known as the Punchbowl.

Understanding the need to acknowledge America's contribution to the war in Europe through commemorative cemeteries and memorials overseas, the federal government also respected the desire of many Americans to have their fallen family members returned to America. Under provisions of the law, families were entitled to select permanent interment of a loved one's remains in an American military cemetery on foreign soil or repatriation of the remains to the United States for interment in a national or private cemetery. The majority of families chose repatriation. Approximately 30 percent chose permanent interment in an ABMC cemetery.

The accounts to follow focus on a few case histories of East Tennessee family members who selected repatriation to America for their loved ones. They have become available recently, thanks to their online publication by the National Archives. These valuable records are known as the Individual Deceased Personnel File, or IDPF, and are, quite simply, a collection of documents created when a service member was declared missing in action and never recovered or died in the war. When one says someone "died in the war," this could alternatively mean that the casualty in question was killed in action; died as a POW; or died of wounds or disease while in military service. These IDPF files contain a wealth of information about these individuals and range from twenty pages to over one hundred. They often include, but are not limited to, the following items of information:

Location, time, date, and cause of death.

Location, time, date, and place of temporary burial. Sometimes, this was an isolated grave or an unknown location until the remains were located after the war.

Documents detailing burial, disinterment, and final burial information.

Handwritten letters from family members.

Letters from the military, congressmen, or US military-related organizations to the family.

Maps, search area testimony, and documentation, if the soldier's body was recovered from a crash site or not located immediately.

Dental and physical charts and information.

Stateside service training locations and dates.

These newly-released records are proving helpful in completing the online biographies for many of the service members on the East Tennessee Veterans Memorial's website.

At the onset of the process, family members would initially have received a form letter, explaining their options: either to leave their loved one in a military cemetery in Europe or in Asia and the Pacific, where their graves would be tended to in perpetuity under the ABMC's aegis, or to request that the remains be disinterred, repatriated to the United States, and reinterred in a public or private cemetery. One can easily imagine that, in many cases, the decision to request repatriation was made quickly and without much hesitation by the family. However, in other cases, as will be seen, that decision could become more complicated and confusing.

The American policy on repatriation was at odds with that of Commonwealth countries like Great Britain and Canada, who counted more than a million dead in the two world wars and who held that bodies should not be repatriated and that uniform memorials should be used to avoid class distinctions. Beyond the logistical nightmare of returning home so many dead bodies, under the Commonwealth's war graves

system, it was felt that repatriation would conflict with the feeling of brotherhood that had
developed between serving ranks. In essence,
the British Commonwealth policy was that one
should be buried as close as possible to where
one fell, nearby one's "mates."

In the conclusion to his 1947 book *Crosses
in the Wind*, a US Army Graves Registration
officer, Major Joseph J. Shomon, voiced this
question at the very time that families across
this nation were starting to make tough deci-
sions about repatriation:

> The issue of final burial is not closed.
> Many service men have been asked their
> opinion on the subject. Some did not want
> to think about dying; others thought about
> it seriously. Some wanted to be buried with
> their buddies where they fell; others wanted
> to be buried back home. One chaplain said,
> "The world is a lot smaller than it was in
> 1939 and we Americans may as well realize
> it. The bodies of our sons and husbands ly-
> ing overseas are the surest link we can have
> with the rest of the world." One American
> lieutenant in Germany said, "Well, if we're
> going to move them anyway, let's move them
> back to America."
>
> But we must ask the widows, the or-
> phans, the parents, the close relatives. Is it
> not their opinion, their decision, their sor-
> row that is all important? Is it not for them
> to say whether the dead should be brought
> home for burial or laid to rest in foreign soil?
> I think so.[1]

In the case of Staff Sergeant Willard
Adkins, who died in Germany in the Second
World War's waning days, his parents, then living in Pennsylvania, directed the Army to re-
patriate their son from the Margraten Military
Cemetery in the Netherlands,[2] where he was
first buried. This seemingly simple request set
in motion their son's long journey home to East
Tennessee for burial in the Jellico Cemetery in

Campbell County. The whole process, given the
extensive paperwork, could be lengthy; conse-
quently, the majority of reburials stateside did
not take place before 1948 and sometimes as late
as the early 1950s, as it took additional time to
identify skeletal remains using dental records
that had to be requested from the family. Less
than a month after her son's death, on May 10,
1945, Mrs. John Adkins sent the following letter
to the Army inquiry clerk assigned to her son's
file: "I received a letter from the commanding
office today telling me to write you for more information about my son, Willard Adkins, [who]
was killed in action April the 14th concerning
his grave number and disposition of his effects.
Will you please tell me if he can be shipped
back at any time?" In late August that same year,
his mother received this letter[3] in response to
her May 10 query (see below).

As soon as the family member designated
as next of kin had chosen repatriation for his or
her son or husband, the next step was the creation of a Disinterment Directive[4] (see below)
for that service member, in which the foreign
cemetery would be identified, along with plot,
row, and grave location. Moreover, the name
and address of the next of kin, as well as the
consignee—normally a local funeral home—
would be noted, along with the condition of
the remains. In the case of Willard Adkins,
this process, initiated in April 1948, some three
years after his death, was completed in late
August 1948. Embalming then took place before
the remains were sealed in a steel casket for
shipment back to the United States. The short-
age of steel following the war often slowed the
process of providing the necessary shipment
containers.

Once the service member's body had been
returned home, and possibly at the same time

```
SPQYG 293
Adkins, Willard
S. N. 6 964 170


                                              27 August 1945


     Mrs. John Adkins
     100 W. Elm Street
     Conshahocken, Pennsylvania

     Dear Mrs. Adkins:

          Acknowledgment is made of your letter requesting information
     regarding the death and personal effects of your son, the late Staff
     Sergeant Willard Adkins.

          The official report of interment shows that the remains of your
     son were interred in the U. S. Military Cemetery #1, Breuna, Germany,
     Plot D, Row 1, Grave 12.  This cemetery is located approximately
     fifteen miles northwest of Cassel, Germany.

          All burials of American personnel in Germany are being concentrated
     into established U. S. Military cemeteries not on German soil.  When a
     change in burial location has been made you will be fully advised of the
     new location.

          In view of the fact that the Army Effects Bureau,  Kansas City
     Quartermaster Depot, Kansas City 1, Missouri, has been designated to
     receive and ship the personal effects of our military personnel who
     die outside the United States, a copy of your letter has been forwarded
     to that office for a direct reply to you.

          At the outbreak of the war it became necessary to adopt the policy
     that the remains of our American dead overseas should not be returned
     to the United States until after the cessation of hostilities.

          Now that Japan has been defeated immediate plans are being for-
     mulated with a view to returning to the next of kin the remains of their
     loved ones.  This sacred duty will be carried out by the Government at
     its expense and insofar as practicable in accordance with the expressed
     wishes of the legal next of kin, who will be notified well in advance
     of the actual return of the remains.
```

Letter from the Army to Mrs. John Adkins.

as this return, a final government form, the Application for Headstone or Marker, had to be completed, so that the family could receive a memorial stone or bronze plate at no cost. The form, pictured below, for Willard Adkins would indicate that he was buried in January 1949 under a flat marble marker.[5] Again, the recent availability of these forms to researchers has facilitated our work and represents still another fitting and precious remembrance of those who made the ultimate sacrifice for their country.

The final part of the process was perhaps as grievously painful as the initial one. An important element in the settling of affairs for a deceased service member was the disposition of his remaining personal effects. These effects

Disinterment directive from the Army
for the body of Willard Adkins.

Order for a marker for Willard Adkins from the Army.

were carefully noted for return to the next of kin and, on occasion, sparked questions from family members over a variety of concerns, including the speed with which the effects were returned, the lack of a timely response, and also questions as to whether the personal effects actually belonged to their deceased relative.

Again, with Willard Adkins, the correspondence from beginning to end was lengthy, and the file on his personal effects ended up including eighty documents in all.

The shipment home of personal effects by the Army Effects Bureau in Kansas City, Missouri, would begin much earlier, usually within five to six months after the death, but for Willard Adkins's parents, there were immediate complications. In a letter written on September 10, 1945, Mrs. Adkins expressed her dismay about the first parcel, citing a cigarette lighter that was not his and a precious, homemade billfold that was missing (see below).[6] Approximately two months later in November, after a second shipment of personal effects, Adkins's father wrote about the lingering issues. His final words reflect his and his wife's inconsolable grief (see letter below).[7]

Parental grief turned to frustration, then anger over burial policies at Arlington National Cemetery in the unusual situation of First Lieutenant Douglas G. McMillin of Chattanooga (Hamilton), who was killed in action on August 29, 1944. McMillin served with the 380th Bomber Group, 529th Bomber Squadron (Heavy). He was flying on a B-24 bomber on a weather recon mission with his crewmembers in the Pacific when their plane crashed into the mountains of the island of Ceram in the Dutch West Indies. He was declared dead on July 5, 1944. He was eventually buried, along with members of his flight crew, in Arlington National Cemetery.

McMillin was graduated from the Virginia Military Institute in the class of 1940 and was commissioned in the Army Air Forces. He flew reconnaissance missions in North Africa, as well as over India and later from Australia, on a B-24 Liberator, before undertaking the mission in which he was killed. His IDPF file is

Letter from Mrs. John Adkins to the Army, first page.

Letter from Mrs. John Adkins to the Army, second page.

Letter from Mr. John Adkins to the Army.

voluminous, at more than three hundred pages, and reflects the consternation and activism of his parents and other family members concerning the memorial marker at Arlington that was constructed for him and his fellow crewmembers. At the same time, a close examination of his file reveals another important facet of the US military during World War II: specifically, that those who served in it often mirrored the social stratification of American society much more faithfully than those who have served in more recent US conflicts. Wealth and privilege were not an excuse to avoid enlistment and conscription in World War II. Nonetheless, the correspondence between McMillin's relatives and government agencies after their

First Lieutenant Douglas G. McMillin.

son's death exhibits a higher expectation of service and treatment than in the case of Willard Adkins's family, which was surely linked to the McMillins' social and political connections.

McMillin was the son of Mr. and Mrs. Edwyn W. McMillin of Chattanooga, and the husband of Martha Akin McMillin. He left behind a daughter, Martha Julia McMillin. At the time of her husband's death, Martha Akin McMillin's address of record, like that of her parents-in-law, was listed as the Richmond Hosiery Mills in Rossville, Georgia, about six miles due south of Chattanooga and just over the state line. The Richmond Mills were established in 1898 and were one of the largest and oldest textile mills in Northwest Georgia. The mill produced socks for men and women, and a unique section of the mill was dedicated to making hosiery for

"misses." The mill employed four hundred men, women, and children in 1910 and seven hundred by 1922. Although there is no direct evidence, the McMillins could very well have been the mill owners. However, the more significant factor in the plans for repatriation and interment of Douglas McMillin was that the lieutenant's father-in-law was Major General Spencer B. Akin, General MacArthur's chief signals officer throughout the war. He had, in fact, accompanied MacArthur from Corregidor to the initial Allied military government in occupied Japan after the close of World War II. Before Corregidor and Bataan fell, Akin's radio program, the "Voice of Freedom," broadcast to the world, three times daily, the news that the Philippines were holding. He was elevated to chief signal officer of the Army in 1947.[8]

After the remains of McMillin and his crewmembers were identified, they were shipped to Jefferson Barracks National Cemetery in St. Louis for interment in a group burial plot. Established for individual interments as far back as 1866, following the end of the Civil War, the St. Louis cemetery took on a new role during World War II as the central repository for group interments, often resulting from disasters when individual remains could not be identified. Among the more than 560 group burials—meaning two or more veterans in a common grave—are 123 victims of a 1944 Japanese massacre of POWs in the Philippines (see chapter 6 on Private Fred E. Vitatoe and the Palawan Massacre) and the remains of 41 unidentified Marines who perished in a helicopter crash in South Vietnam in 1968. Thirty East Tennesseans are currently buried at the Jefferson Barracks cemetery, the majority being airplane crewmembers. In McMillin's case, there was a request by his widow on December 19,

DEPARTMENT OF THE ARMY
OFFICE OF THE CHIEF SIGNAL OFFICER
WASHINGTON 25, D. C.

IN REPLY REFER TO

10 March 1950

Major General Herman Feldman
The Quartermaster General
Room 2087, Temporary Bldg B
Second and R Streets, SW
Washington, D. C.

Dear General Feldman:

    I would like to take this opportunity to express to you my sincere appreciation for the highly courteous and effective services that were rendered by your assistants in the group interment of my son-in-law, First Lieutenant D. G. McMillin, and the several others who were killed in action at the same time.

    I especially would like to commend the services that were rendered by Lieutenant Colonel Edward M. Brown of the Memorial Division, and Mr. Joseph J. Walsh, Superintendent of Arlington National Cemetery. The effectiveness of the arrangements was so outstanding that it is deserving of a commendation to be filed with their records. I voice the expressed opinion of all of the "nearest of kin" who were present. I hope that you will be kind enough to have this done for me.

                              Very sincerely yours,

                              S. B. AKIN
                              Major General, USA
                              Chief Signal Officer

Letter from Major General S. B. Akin to. Major General Feldman,
one of a series of letters described on pages 143–44.

1949, most likely supported by her father, that he and his flight crew be disinterred from Jefferson Barracks to be reburied together at Arlington. The directive was written on August 5, 1949, and by March 1950, McMillin and the others had been moved to Arlington. First, however, all of the other families would have to approve the move. Confirmation of that approval came in January 1950. Uppermost perhaps in the minds of McMillin's combined family unit was the proximity of Arlington to where General Akin lived and worked. Moreover, McMillin's widow and daughter had moved back to the Washington, DC, area and were living nearby. An additional factor would have been the prominence of Arlington as a distinguished military burial site. On March 10, 1950, General Akin wrote this note of thanks and commendation (see above).[9]

However, by 1951, new concerns were voiced by the family. McMillin's widow had remarried and moved to Raleigh, North Carolina, and a flat memorial stone had been installed at the graves of the crewmembers at Arlington. Both McMillin's father and his widow complained about the condition of the marker and the fact that it was not of the upright kind that was present elsewhere at the cemetery. There were also questions about the alphabetical order in which the names were listed, with the family suggesting that it should have been by rank, with First Lieutenant McMillin listed first. The family was also in touch with Tennessee senator Estes Kefauver, who served as their main contact with the Army Quartermaster General's office in Washington.

In a three-page letter addressed to Senator Kefauver on July 12, 1951, Mr. McMillin took to task the Quartermaster General's office for defending the use of the flat marker by asserting that the marker and the alphabetical listing of names "were in accordance with established policy, which has been approved by competent authority."[10] The Quartermaster General's office further stated that it "did not have the legal authority to replace the present headstone at government expense." In his challenge to this statement, McMillin wrote:

> If the United States Government is not financially able to supply a more fitting marker or monument for its soldier dead, then it should admit the fact frankly and ask the families of the dead to provide their own markers at their own expense. Certainly, if I had been notified in advance and had been advised of the type marker that was contemplated, I should have protested vigorously the burial of my son in Arlington Cemetery, and should have insisted upon being allowed to conduct the interment in my own family burial plot where I could have provided a suitable monument to his memory.

He concluded by citing a "Department of Army, Office of the Quartermaster General, 1 December 1947," pamphlet supporting his challenge: "My request is not for anything elaborate—merely a simple marker of the regulation type, standing in an upright position, as expressly provided for by Army regulations, and of a size and design suitable and fitting for the combined burial places of eight former Air Force service men. That request I do not consider an unreasonable one."

At the same time, General Akin, the dead officer's father-in-law, clearly appears to have been drawn into the controversy, because a series of letters were exchanged between Quartermaster General Herman Feldman and Akin prior to the July 12, 1951, challenge. In one letter, Akin wrote: "I completely understand your position in this matter, and I am sure you will

Original McMillin grave marker.

More recent McMillin grave marker.

General Akin, or perhaps it had proved impossible to reach the next of kin of the other crewmembers to obtain their unanimous approval (as required) for a special marker, for which they would have had to contribute the funds. Nonetheless, an upright granite marker now stands at Arlington in place of the previous one, with the eight names arranged alphabetically according to military protocol. The wishes of the family apparently prevailed in the end.

try to make it a closed instance." In a lengthier letter, Feldman addressed Akin by his first name (both men being major generals) and sought to reach a compromise by suggesting the erection of a suitable marker at private expense, "provided that all of the next of kin are in agreement and that the design of the marker is in accord with present regulations governing the erection of private headstones in national cemeteries."[11]

The IDPF file for Lieutenant McMillin concluded with documents regarding his personal effects and their disposition. There is no further correspondence concerning the grave marker at Arlington. Perhaps the McMillins gave up the matter after being persuaded by

11

THE "FORGOTTEN WAR"

Korea and the John Sadler Story

The wrong war, at the wrong place,
at the wrong time, and with the wrong enemy.

*—General Omar Bradley on the Korean War's
expansion into conflict with China, May 1951*

The Korean War represented the first major test of America's military during the Cold War. As only an armistice has bound the combatants since 1953, the Korean "police action" literally remains a war without end as of this writing. From the Pusan perimeter to the Inchon landing and the frozen desolation of the Yalu and Chosin Reservoir, numerous East Tennesseans served and perished between 1950 and 1953 on the Korean peninsula. The treatment of American prisoners by the Chinese and North Koreans and allegations of physical torture, mental abuse, and "brainwashing" are fairly well known. Less popularly known are violent uprisings by Communist prisoners against their US and South Korean guards. One of the victims of the most infamous of these incidents involving Chinese and North Korean POWs—in fact, the only American killed in an incident of that kind—was a teenager from Johnson City. John Sadler and the bloody revolt at the Koje-do POW camp, which came to play a critical role in the course of the Korean armistice talks, will be featured in this chapter.

A total of 444 East Tennesseans perished during the Korean conflict. While that is a smaller number than the number of casualties in Vietnam (667), the hostilities in and around Korea were of shorter duration than the conflict in Vietnam. Hamilton and Knox Counties led with the largest casualty number of 69 for each county, followed by Sullivan (28), Washington (21), and Carter (17).

PRISONERS OF WAR DURING THE KOREAN CONFLICT

The fate of Allied prisoners of war in Korea was, in several ways, even more precarious than was the case during World War II. In a conflict that was incredibly fluid, with multiple US military and United

Nations thrusts north, followed by North Korean and Chinese counterattacks pushing Allied troops back south (Seoul was captured once by North Korea, then recaptured by the Allies), along with a spider web of POW camps with spotty record keeping, the conditions and survival prospects of POWs were bleak.

The confinement of US military personnel in the POW camps located in North Korea essentially functioned in three phases: from the war's beginning in July 1950 until the entry of the Chinese Communist forces (CCF) into the war in November 1950; the winter of 1950–1951, when several temporary camps were created; and the institution of permanent camps. The North Korean People's Army (NKPA) at first had no formal POW system, just collection points, often with ramshackle huts for the POWs. During the summer and fall of 1950, the NKPA moved POWs to the rear on foot—often by what can only be called a "death march" reminiscent of what occurred on Bataan some eight years earlier—during which shootings and abuse of POWs were prevalent. For example, during one 120-mile forced march during November 1950, approximately 130 of 700 POWs died.

The first Chinese offensive in late 1950 resulted in the capture of several thousand US Army personnel and Marines. Like the NKPA, the CCF at that time had no established POW system. As an expedient, the CCF set up a temporary prison camp called the "Valley," located ten miles south of Pyoktong, North Korea, near the Yalu River. Primitive living conditions there resulted in the death of five to seven hundred of the one thousand POWs. American soldiers, most of them members of the 2nd Infantry Division captured at Kunu-ri in November 1950, were kept at a place called "Death Valley,"

thirty miles southeast of Pukchin, also near the Yalu River. Of that camp's two thousand prisoners, 40 percent died within three months. The remains of many POWs were never recovered for repatriation and interment back home. Their names are inscribed on the Tablets of the Missing, National Memorial Cemetery of the Pacific, Honolulu, Hawaii.[1]

Overall, Allied POWs died in sizeable numbers, especially during the war's first year. Lack of food, shelter, and medical care took a heavy toll, coupled with the fact that some prisoners were occasionally (much like the Japanese hell-ships' hapless inmates) the victims of "friendly-fire" airstrikes on the camps lying so close to the Yalu. During the winter of 1950–51, many American POWs recalled marching for days, seemingly sometimes in circles. Those prisoners who were weakened from battle, the cold, and lack of food and who could not keep pace with their fellow prisoners were often left to die or were executed outright by their Communist captors. Prisoners often carried and dragged one another through these marches. Approximately 3,000 of the 7,190 Americans captured in Korea died in captivity. This equates to a staggering mortality rate of approximately 43 percent, compared with Second

Corporal Paul E. Little's report of interment.

World War mortality rates for POWs held in German camps of 4 percent and, for POWs held by the Japanese, 34 percent.[2] And some of the American POWs were merely young teenagers.

Among those teenagers was Corporal Paul E. Little (Carter), who enlisted in the Army on August 3, 1948, from Johnson City, Tennessee, and recorded his date of birth as March 24, 1931. However, his actual date of birth on his grave marker, as requested by his mother, was October 29, 1934. Hence, Little was not even fourteen years old when he enlisted, and he was only fifteen when North Korea crossed the 38th parallel to attack South Korea in June 1950. Little was assigned to Company C, 65th Engineer Combat Battalion, 25th Infantry Division, and was captured by the Chinese at Hill 222 on November 27, 1950, during the Battle of the Chongchon River near Ipsok, North Korea. He was sent to POW Camp 5 in Pyoktong, North Korea, one of the Communists' prison camps in the infamous Valley, where he died at the tender age of sixteen.

Sergeant Frederick B. Bean (Knox) had attended Rule High School and was an employee of the Knoxville *Journal*. Bean entered the Army in December 1948 and received his basic training at Fort Jackson, South Carolina. He was transferred to Japan in August 1949 and to Korea in September 1950, where he was a member of Headquarters Company, 31st Infantry Regiment, 7th Infantry Division, serving as a reconnaissance scout. Bean was taken prisoner while fighting the enemy near Uisa-ni, North Korea, on November 29, 1950, during the Chosin Reservoir battle and died while a prisoner on February 12, 1951. His remains were not recovered. His name is inscribed on the Tablets of the Missing, National Memorial Cemetery of the Pacific, Honolulu, Hawaii.

A letter to the Bean family in July 1953 from the Defense Department explained that he had died from malnutrition during captivity. Bean was likely captured in a disaster for the Army's 7th Infantry Division, the destruction of "Task Force Faith," named for Lieutenant Colonel Don C. Faith, during which US forces were overrun by the Chinese. Isolated from the nearest American units of X Corps on the eastern edge of the Chosin Reservoir, the troops and vehicles of Task Force Faith were cut off and destroyed in extreme winter conditions. The relatively few survivors escaped south to join elements of the 1st Marine Division near Hagaru-ri, North Korea.

Similarly, Sergeant William C. Jenkins (Knox), also a member of Headquarters Company, 31st Infantry Regiment, 7th Infantry Division, was killed in North Korea on November 29, 1950, likely in the savage fighting involving Task Force Faith. Like Bean, his remains were not recovered, and his name is also inscribed at the National Memorial Cemetery of the Pacific

In the three years of the Korean War, 8,177 United States service members were designated as missing in action. At least 800 of these now rest in the National Memorial Cemetery of the Pacific in Honolulu, Hawaii. Remains of others rest forever at sea and on land in both North and South Korea. Thanks to the dogged efforts of researchers, military officials, behind-the-scenes diplomacy, and advances in forensic science, increasing numbers of MIA service members—some who were POWs and others who were killed in action—are being found. This has been especially true with the Korean conflict, as will be shown in the case of four East Tennessee veterans—Sergeant Bailey Keeton Jr. (Scott), Sergeant First Class Lewis G.

Sergeant Bailey Keeton Jr.

not immediately recovered, and his name was later inscribed at the National Memorial Cemetery of the Pacific. Sergeant Keeton was perhaps another victim of one of the grimmest and saddest incidents in modern US Army history, the destruction of Task Force Faith in early December 1950, the tragedy that apparently engulfed Sergeant Bean and Sergeant Jenkins, as well. This task force was the right-side "bookend" (the 1st Marine Division was the "left bookend") for the fighting at the Chosin Reservoir in late 1950. The long-lost remains of its commanding officer, Lieutenant Colonel Don C. Faith, were found, identified, and buried in Arlington National Cemetery in 2013. Faith was killed on December 2, 1950, in the vicinity of Hagaru-ri, North Korea. He was thirty-two years old at the time, having joined the military when he was just seventeen; he was officially labeled as killed in action.

Sixty-six years later, the remains of Keeton were finally located and identified via DNA sampling. As his remains were finally returned to East Tennessee for burial in June 2016, his brother, Ron Keeton, said of the "final farewell he thought he'd never get to give his brother in person": "He's coming out of a bitterly cold and unfriendly environment, to an environment that is warm and friendly. It's a good feeling. Even if it has been [sixty-six] years, it feels like he's coming home."[3] Sergeant Keeton is buried in the Hazel Valley Memorial Cemetery, Oneida, Tennessee.

Sergeant First Class Lewis G. Brickell of Chattanooga (Hamilton) was born on October 12, 1931, to Aary and Vera Thomas Brickell. He enlisted in the Army on August 15, 1949; in Korea, SFC Brickell served in Company D, 8th Engineer Combat Battalion, 1st Cavalry Division. He was listed as missing in action near

Brickell (Hamilton), Private First Class Lotchie J. R. Jones (Marion), and Corporal Sam C. Harris (Sullivan/Hawkins). However, the remains of many of those who lie at the National Memorial Cemetery of the Pacific are (to date) unidentified. The only potential means of positive identification is through DNA samples obtained from family members of the lost, and from other forensic records that only recently became available. A non-profit organization, the Korean War Project, based in Dallas, Texas, has been instrumental in the process of identifying these service members.

Sergeant Bailey Keeton Jr. of Scott County was a member of Company D, 1st Battalion, 32nd Infantry Regiment, 7th Infantry Division. He was listed as MIA while fighting in North Korea on December 2, 1950. He was presumed dead on December 31, 1953. His remains were

Sergeant First Class Lewis G. Brickell.

Private First Class Lotchie J. R. Jones.
Courtesy of Richard B. Tucker Sr.

Kaeson, South Korea, on September 4, 1950, and was presumed dead on December 31, 1953. His name was inscribed on the Courts of the Missing at the Honolulu Memorial. Brickell was decorated with the Purple Heart, the Korean Service Medal, the United Nations Service Medal, the National Defense Service Medal, the Korean Presidential Unit Citation, and the Republic of Korea War Service Medal. His remains were found, identified, and reunited with his loved ones in 2009. He was survived by his sister, Barbara Brickell Hobbs and her husband, Joe; his nephew, Lewis Hobbs; and his niece, Pamela Hobbs Burrows, all of Chattanooga. Brickell was buried in the Chattanooga National Cemetery with full military honors.

Private First Class Lotchie John Ray Jones (Marion) was born on December 12, 1932, and was a member of Company B, 1st Battalion, 8th Cavalry Regiment, 1st Cavalry Division. He was

taken prisoner while fighting the enemy near Unsan, North Korea, on November 2, 1950, and at the age of seventeen, died as a POW on February 28, 1951, at the at the Pyoktong POW Camp 5. His name is inscribed at the National Memorial Cemetery of the Pacific. A 2015 press release from the Tennessee Department of Veterans Affairs announced details of the discovery of Jones's remains:

> In September 1954, Chinese forces turned over remains recovered at POW Camp 5 and mistakenly identified as Delano B. Mulder. Efforts to correctly identify the

former prisoner of war in 1954 were unsuccessful. In 1956, the unidentifiable remains were interred at the National Memorial Cemetery of the Pacific . . . in Honolulu, Hawaii.

In 2014, the Joint POW/MIA Accounting Command's Central Identification Laboratory [located at] Joint Base Pearl Harbor-Hickam in Hawaii re-examined the records and determined resources to identify the remains designated as "X-14516" now existed. The unidentified remains were exhumed on July 10, 2014.

Researchers used chest radiographs, dental records and skeletal remains to confirm the remains were those of PFC Jones. "After decades of not knowing, the Jones family and Jasper community will finally get closure as they bring Lotchie home to rest," Haslam said. "We join the Jones family in recognizing the loss of a young Tennessean who gave the ultimate sacrifice for his state and country during the Korean War. Private First Class Jones was only a teenager when he gave his life in service to our country and his bravery will not be forgotten," Grinder said. "We are grateful that he will be laid to rest in his home state, where his name will be carved on his headstone and removed from the list of missing in action Tennesseans."[4]

Jones was survived by his brother M. V. Jones of Whitwell, Tennessee, and his sister Mamie Lou Wells of Jasper, Tennessee. He was buried at the Chattanooga National Cemetery.

Yet another Korean MIA soldier was Corporal Samuel C. Harris Jr. of Rogersville (Sullivan/Hawkins), whose name is also inscribed on the Courts of the Missing at the Honolulu Memorial. A 2009 *Knoxville News Sentinel* recounted the circumstances of Harris's death during the course of the savage Chinese-North Korean counteroffensive in November 1950 and the discovery of his remains. In doing so, it

Corporal Samuel C. Harris Jr.

also sheds light on some of the practical and scientific difficulties surrounding the recovery and identification of so many soldiers lost in Korea:

For decades, no one knew for sure what had happened to Army Corporal Samuel Carson Harris Jr. The kind and gentle soldier from East Tennessee had been stationed in Guam for a couple of years and was on the verge of ending his tour of duty when the Korean War broke out. Instead of heading home, Harris went off to war, and after a brutal battle in North Korea in November 1950, the young soldier was declared missing in action.

Much of the mystery behind his disappearance was finally solved April 3, 2009, when the U.S. Department of Defense disclosed that human remains found nine years ago in North Korea were positively identified as those of Harris and three other soldiers in his company. On April 10, 2009, more than a half-century after he had been set to return to his homeland, the Rogersville native was buried with full military honors at Arlington National Cemetery just outside of Washington. . . .

Pentagon officials said the remains of Harris and the other soldiers were found on a site overlooking the Kuryong River in P'yongan-Pukto Province, where U.S. soldiers were believed to be buried. Harris and the missing soldiers had been assigned to Company C, 65th Combat Engineer Battalion, 25th Infantry Division. The company came under intense enemy attack when it was occupying a position on a hill south of the Kuryong River, just east of what is known as Camel's Head Bend, on November 25, 1950. Two days later, Harris and the other men were reported missing in action.

A joint team of officials from the United States and the Democratic People's Republic of Korea recovered the human remains and non-biological evidence in 2000. Military scientists used DNA samples and dental comparisons to make a positive identification and were able to complete their work in September 2008. In Harris' case, a gold crown on the back of a broken front tooth helped to positively identify his remains. . . .

Harris was the second of six children born to Samuel Carson Harris Sr. and Maude Bates Harris of Rogersville. His siblings remember him as a friendly, gentle soul who experienced personal hardship at a very young age. When he was a toddler, Harris fell and hit his head on a metal bucket. Doctors inserted a steel plate in his head, but he was paralyzed for years. One day, when he was still a boy, the paralysis miraculously lifted. Just 21 when he died, Harris loved engineering and the Army and planned to make it his career. . . . [5]

THE PUNCHBOWL

Certain names given to battlefields and specific military undertakings tend to resonate in the collective imagination. Two that stand out indelibly in the case of the Korean conflict are the Punchbowl and Heartbreak Ridge. The Punchbowl was the name given to the bowl-shaped Haean-myon Valley in Gangwon Province of what is now South Korea by UN forces. The Punchbowl lies several kilometers south of the Demilitarized Zone (DMZ). After armistice negotiations broke down in August 1951, the UN Command launched a limited offensive in the late summer and early autumn to shorten and straighten sections of the lines, acquire better defensive terrain, and deny the enemy key vantage points from which it could observe and target UN positions. The Battle of Bloody Ridge took place west of the Punchbowl from August–September 1951; this was followed by the Battle of Heartbreak Ridge, northwest of the Punchbowl, from September–October 1951. At the end of the UN offensive in October 1951, UN forces controlled the line of hills north of the Punchbowl.[6]

The five East Tennesseans below sacrificed their lives during this series of bloody and savage engagements.

Corporal Billie R. Burkhart was born January 30, 1928, in Knoxville (Knox). He was the son of Ernest U. and Amy Ruth Mynatt Burkhart and attended Karns High School. He was employed by the East Tennessee Packing Company and was a member of Bethel United Brethren Church. Buddy, as he was known by his family and friends, was one of seven children who grew up in the Burkhart home on Francis Road. His siblings included brothers Clarence and Russell, and sisters Mildred,

Corporal Billie R. Burkhart.

fighting, elements of the 2nd Division would fight their way to the crest of the hill, only to be repulsed by the enemy with heavy machine gun fire, mortar fire, and grenades hurled at their advancing positions. It was during one of these advances that Burkhart was killed in action on Heartbreak Ridge. Corporal Burkhart's body was repatriated to the United States aboard the troop transport *Loma Victory*, which docked in San Francisco on December 20, 1951, just in time for Christmas. His family was notified of his body's arrival; the funeral was held on January 13, 1952, at Middlebrook Pike Baptist Church, with Burkhart being laid to rest in Lynnhurst Cemetery.

Sergeant Walter L. Seivers Jr. (Knox) was born on July 21, 1926, to Walter Louis Seivers Sr. and his wife Cleo. He attended Knoxville High School and was an employee of the White Stores grocery before entering the United States Army. Seivers was married in 1946 to Helen Lucille Davis. He was a veteran of World War II and was recalled to service in October 1950. He had been in Korea nine months with Company G, 3rd Battalion, 1st Marine Regiment, 1st Marine Division.

During Seivers's last days, the 1st Marine Division had driven north past the eastern tip of Hwachon Reservoir and had taken the objective of the deep circular valley in the mountains, the Punchbowl. A defensive line was established, and the Marines spent much of the summer there in their defensive positions. On September 5, 1951, the division was ordered to take the remainder of the Punchbowl. On September 13, 1951, the eighth day of fighting for the Punchbowl, Sergeant Seivers was killed by an artillery round that landed at his position. Like Corporal Burkhart, his remains were repatriated to the United States

Louise, Marie, and Evelyn. Buddy was twenty-two years old when he was drafted and sent to Korea. He had been in the service for ten months and had been overseas for six months with the 23rd Infantry Regiment, 2nd Infantry Division, when his unit was ordered to Heartbreak Ridge.

The Battle of Heartbreak Ridge was one of several major engagements in the Punchbowl. The attack started on September 13, 1951, when elements of the 9th Infantry and Corporal Burkhart's 23rd Infantry Regiments attacked North Korean positions. Hill 931 was the center of Heartbreak Ridge, and the battle for that hill was ongoing nine days later on September 22, 1951. Burkhart's regiment was engaged with the enemy; several times during that day of heavy

Private First Class Jackie D. Doyle.

on the very same voyage of the *Loma Victory*. His body was returned by rail to Knoxville, and his funeral services were held on January 20, 1952. Like Burkhart, Seivers was laid to rest at Lynnhurst Cemetery.

Private First Class Jackie D. Doyle (Knox) was one of eleven children born to Horace Eugene and Elizabeth Keith Doyle. He grew up in South Knoxville and was a member of Vestal United Methodist Church. He attended South High School until his family moved to old North Knoxville, and he continued his education at Knoxville High School. Doyle joined the Marine Corps Reserve and was called to active duty for service in Korea. He left Knoxville for training at Camp Pendleton, California, in September 1950. After training, he was assigned to I Company, 3rd Battalion, 5th Marine Regiment, 1st Marine Division. While in Korea, his

company was involved in the 1st Division's initial deployment to combat Communist troops, including the amphibious landings at Inchon and the retaking of Seoul. It was during the vicious and bitter winter warfare at the Chosin Reservoir that his company came under intense hostile attack. It was reported after the attack that I Company existed only on paper, with just twenty men left. Doyle was killed in action on December 1, 1950. He was initially listed as MIA the day after the battle. Exactly three years later, he was officially declared killed in action. He was not returned home for funeral services and burial until September 11, 1955. He was buried at Woodlawn Cemetery in Knoxville.

Another Knoxville resident killed in Korea was Private Luther E. Carr. He was born on September 26, 1933, attended Baxter Avenue Church of God, and was a student at Rule High School prior to entering the Army. He enlisted on December 26, 1950, and was sent overseas in May 1951. Private Carr was a member of the 23rd Infantry Regiment, 2nd Infantry Division. In June 1951, he was burned by an exploding bomb and hospitalized for a time. Private Carr later returned to his unit and was killed in action at Heartbreak Ridge, dying on September 13, 1951. Private Carr was repatriated to the United States and returned to Knoxville over the Southern Railway. He was buried at the Knoxville National Cemetery.

Monroe County lost two service members at Heartbreak Ridge as well: Sergeant Walter B. Smith of Sweetwater and Private First Class Ross M. Walker. Like Carr, Smith also served with the 23rd Infantry Regiment, 2nd Infantry Division. It was during one of the advances that Sergeant Smith was wounded by the enemy and was taken to the back of the lines to a field hospital. He died of those wounds on September 24,

1951. His body's journey back to the United States began aboard the troop transport ship *Loma Victory*—the same vessel that brought so many East Tennesseans' remains home—at the end of 1951. Smith was returned home on January 10, 1952, and he was buried at West View Cemetery in Sweetwater.

Ross M. Walker was also killed in action near Heartbreak Ridge on January 9, 1952, having been shot by a sniper while on patrol. He first enlisted in the Tennessee National Guard at Etowah, then he served in the Regular Army as an infantryman based at Fort Devens, Massachusetts, and at Fort Drum, New York. PFC Walker went to Korea on September 20, 1951, and was a BAR gunner with the 3rd Platoon, Company I, 3rd Battalion, 31st Infantry Regiment, 7th Infantry Division, the 31st Infantry being one of the units that lost so many troops in the destruction of Task Force Faith one year earlier. He was buried at Unicoi Cemetery, Tellico Plains.

A BUFFALO SOLDIER IN KOREA

Private Arthur O. Johnson was born on February 11, 1933, in Knoxville (Knox). He was a member of Logan Temple Church and a student at Austin High School before entering the United States Army. He was a member of the 24th Infantry Regiment, 25th Infantry Division. The 24th Infantry was one of the African American regiments known as the "Buffalo Soldiers"; founded in 1869, this regiment had served in the western United States before seeing combat in the Spanish American War. The 24th remained an all-black regiment through both world wars. At the Second World War's end, it was serving on occupation duty in Japan. In June 1950, when

the NKPA invaded South Korea, the 24th was ordered to Korea and participated in some of the earliest engagements of the Korean War around the Pusan perimeter on South Korea's southeastern tip.

Private Johnson joined the 24th Infantry while deployed in Korea and was killed in action while fighting the enemy in North Korea on July 17, 1951. His body was repatriated to Knoxville, and funeral services were held on June 5, 1953, at the chapel of Lillison & Mills Funeral Home. Private Johnson was interred in the Knoxville National Cemetery.

FLYBOYS OVER KOREA

Staff Sergeant George Washington Higgins was born on February 22, 1928, in Morristown (Hamblen) and was a crew member on a B-29A Superfortress heavy bomber with the 93rd Bomber Squadron, 19th Bomber Wing, based at Kadena Air Base on Okinawa. On April 12, 1951, while on a bombing mission over the western coast of North Korea, his aircraft was attacked by a Soviet-made MiG-15 jet fighter, and it was ditched. His remains were recovered.

First Lieutenant Medon ("Don") A. Bitzer was born on June 5, 1927, in New York City but moved with his family as a child to Johnson City (Washington). He first attended the Tennessee Military Institute and graduated from Castle Heights Military Academy in 1945 to become an enlisted member of the Army Air Force. After receiving an appointment to the Military Academy, Bitzer was transferred to the USMA Preparatory School, then located at Amherst College in Massachusetts. A West Point class of 1950 graduate, Bitzer was the pilot of a F-51D Mustang fighter-bomber with the

Staff Sergeant George Washington Higgins.

First Lieutenant Medon A. ("Don") Bitzer.

67th Fighter Bomber Squadron, 18th Fighter Bomber Group. On January 8, 1952, his aircraft received a direct hit by anti-aircraft fire, burst into flames, and crashed. His remains were not recovered. His name is inscribed on the Tablets of the Missing, National Memorial Cemetery of the Pacific. A tribute on the US Military Academy class of 1950 website provided a profile of his life, education, and military service:

Upon graduation Bitzer chose the Air Force and was assigned to Goodfellow Air Force Base, San Angelo, Texas, for basic flying school. Basic was completed in January of 1951, and Bitzer elected to become a conventional engine fighter pilot. . . . On 4 August 1951, at Craig Air Force Base, Se-

lina, Alabama, Don received his wings and orders to Korea. . . . [After he arrived] in the Far East Air Force, he was assigned to the famed 18th Fighter Bomber Group . . . the last operational fighter group flying F-51's. He was among friends in Korea, for seventeen of his USMA classmates and most of his flying school classmates were also assigned to the Mustang group at Wonju, Korea. Combat check-out and missions came slowly because of the lack of airplanes and the presence of bad weather.

The 67th Fighter Bomber Squadron, to which Bitzer was assigned, had a streak of heavy losses; and prior to his fifteenth mission he saw two of his classmates and four of his friends from flying school killed or taken prisoner by the Communists. On 8 January 1952, Bitzer was on his 15th mission, a dual purpose, two-target, fighter strike in North Korea. He dropped his bombs on the railroad deep in enemy territory; then on the return trip to his base, hit an important secondary target of supplies and personnel near the front lines, with his rockets and machine gun fire. As he broke away from the target after firing his first rocket, he and his aircraft were hit by enemy automatic weapons anti-aircraft fire. Because he was hit personally and was at a low altitude, he was unable to abandon his burning aircraft and crashed into the target area. Bitzer, like his older brother, Conrad, who was killed in World War II in Germany in 1945, found a "soldier's resting place beneath a soldier's blow" . . . part of the heavy price we have paid for our participation in two recent wars.[7]

Like Bitzer, First Lieutenant James M. Bellows Jr. (Knox) also flew a F-51 Mustang with the 18th Fighter Bomber Group in its 12th Fighter Bomber Squadron. He was born on June 11, 1929, and was killed in action on June 18, 1953. Bellows was flight leader on Mission Expire 17, a "MPQ" (a radar-controlled night-time) bombing mission. The fourth man in the flight could not release his bombs, so the flight turned north to attempt to jettison the unused bombs. After "salvoeing" the bombs and again turning south, the flight of four planes encountered intense AA fire; Lieutenant Bellows's aircraft was hit. His last transmission received over an emergency radio channel was: "I'm at 3,000 feet and am being shot at. I'll have to get out soon." Bellows crashed in his aircraft. The rest of the flight stayed to overfly the area until all were low on fuel, and only then did they withdraw. A ground party later recovered his body. The primary cause of the loss was attributed to enemy automatic weapons fire.[8] Bellows is buried at Berry Highland Memorial Cemetery, Knoxville.

Staff Sergeant Albert C. May, a native of Erwin (Unicoi), was born on November 20, 1920. He was a World War II veteran and in Korea was a member of the crew of a Curtiss C-46

First Lieutenant James M. Bellows Jr.

Staff Sergeant Albert C. May.

Captain Charles E. Wilhite.

Commando transport aircraft with the 21st Troop Carrier Squadron, 403rd Troop Carrier Wing. On April 29, 1952, he was participating in the evacuation of American wounded from Korea when his plane crashed into the sea near the beach en route from Seoul to Cho-do Island, killing all onboard. He was buried at Evergreen Cemetery in his hometown.

Captain Charles E. Wilhite was born on December 21, 1922, in Knoxville. He was a graduate of Knoxville High School, where he was a member of the football team and attended Second Methodist Church. The family home was in Fountain City, where he lived with his wife, June Mynatt Wilhite; son, Charles E., Jr.; and daughter, Rebecca. Wilhite had a passion for flying and was an observation pilot for the Tennessee National Guard's 191st Field Artillery Battalion. During World War II, he was an

Army Air Force pilot and rose to the rank of captain. He was a member of the Troop Carrier Command, where he transported troops and supplies to areas of operation in the European and the Central/South American Theaters. After the war, he returned to Knoxville; he was a flight instructor with the Knoxville Flying Service and a member of the Army National Guard's 278th Regimental Combat Team. Captain Wilhite returned to active duty in the latter part of 1950 and was an artillery liaison pilot with the Headquarters Battery, Division Artillery, of the 1st Cavalry Division. Wilhite and his fellow aerial observer flew a single-engined Cessna L-19 "Bird Dog" spotter airplane.

On October 25, 1951, after taking off from a frontline airstrip in North Korea, Wilhite spotted a prime area for enemy troop and artillery movements. When he returned to the same area later, an enemy artillery placement had been established, and Wilhite's L-19 was hit and caught fire. His observer parachuted to safety, but Wilhite did not escape, and he was killed when the aircraft crashed. The report of his death reached Knoxville just before Christmas 1951. Wilhite was returned to Knoxville over the Southern Railway on April 24, 1952; funeral services were held at Berry Funeral Home the following afternoon. He was laid to rest in Lynnhurst Cemetery with full military honors by Knoxville's American Legion Post 2.[9]

First Lieutenant Allan S. Bettis (Jefferson) was born on November 10, 1929. Much like James Bellows and Medon Bitzer, he piloted a F-51D Mustang in the 12th Fighter Bomber Squadron (the same squadron as Bellows) of the 18th Fighter Bomber Group. On April 13, 1952, after making a run to bomb rail lines six miles southeast of Chongju on the northwest coast of North Korea, his aircraft crashed after apparently taking antiaircraft fire. He was listed

Airman Second Class Earl W. Radlein.

ment succinctly reported that the bomber was shot down in flames about forty miles off the Siberian coast while on a "routine training mission." Only one member of the seventeen-man crew, Capt. John Ernest Roche of Washington, DC, was picked up by a US naval ship after eleven hours aboard a life raft dropped by an American rescue plane. Radlein's remains were not recovered.

Captain William K. Garmany of Chattanooga (Hamilton) was a veteran of World War II. In Korea, he was the pilot of a Vought F4U-5N Corsair night fighter with the Marine VMF(N) (Night Fighter Squadron)-513, Marine Air Group 12, 1st Marine Air Wing. On July 13, 1951, while flying a combat mission over the Sibyon-ni area of South Korea, contact with his aircraft was lost, and he was listed as MIA. He was presumed dead on December 15, 1953. His name is inscribed on the Tablets of the Missing,

as MIA, and he was presumed dead on December 31, 1953. Lieutenant Al Bettis's name is inscribed on the Tablets of the Missing, National Memorial Cemetery of the Pacific, Honolulu, Hawaii.

Airman Second Class Earl W. Radlein, of Chattanooga (Hamilton), was born on August 10, 1930. He was a crewmember of a RB-50 reconnaissance bomber (a modernized version of the B-29) with the Air Force's 91st Strategic Reconnaissance Squadron. On July 29, 1953, his plane was shot down by two Russian MiG-15 jet fighters over the Sea of Japan off the coast of Russia. Of the RB-50's loss, the State Depart-

Captain William K. Garmany.

First Lieutenant Robert Blaine ("Bob") Parker.

National Memorial Cemetery of the Pacific, Honolulu, Hawaii.

First Lieutenant Robert Blaine ("Bob") Parker was born on September 19, 1924, to Charles H. and Sarah Lyle Parker, and he was raised in the Lamar community of Jonesborough (Washington). He was a graduate of Lamar High School, class of 1943, and a veteran of World War II, having served in the Navy as an aviation ordinance man with VPB (Patrol Bomber Squadron)-148 in the Pacific Theater during 1944–1945. After the war, Parker applied to the Navy to become a pilot but was turned down. He reapplied later and was turned down yet again. After he applied to the newly-formed United States Air Force, he was accepted, and the Navy released him so that he could serve with the Air Force. After completing his training with recognition as a distinguished graduate, Parker finally became a pilot.

As a First Lieutenant, Parker was assigned to Detachment F, 3rd Air Rescue Squadron, Military Air Transport Service, reporting for Korean War duty on October 28, 1950. On November 28, 1950, an aerial reconnaissance mission was scheduled aboard the USS *Leyte* (CV-32), an *Essex*-class aircraft carrier, to film Chinese and North Korean troop movements along the border of those two countries. Composite Squadron 62 was assigned the task, and Ensign William George Wagner, call sign "WAG," would fly a F4U-1P Corsair photo plane on this mission. Upon reaching the border and starting his photo run, however, Wagner's aircraft was hit, and he had to bail out.

What happened next can only be described as reminiscent of the tragic conclusion of the Korean War-themed novel and movie, *The Bridges at Toko-Ri*, by James Michener. The 3rd Air Rescue Squadron was notified of Wagner's plight. Its men knew that this was going to be a very risky mission because of the distance they would have to cover, nearly all of it behind enemy lines, and because the lateness of the mission would place the rescue flight well into the hours of darkness. Parker's H-5G Dragonfly helicopter, Serial No. #49–2009, was not equipped for night flying and had a maximum range of 280 miles when fully fueled. Over 180 of those miles were to be flown that day behind enemy lines, so volunteers were requested. Parker volunteered, along with PFC Desmond Wilkerson, a medical technician, to rescue Ensign Wagner.

The mission was launched at 3:00 p.m., with two US Navy fighter aircraft assigned to fly cover. Upon reaching the Manchurian border, they located and rescued Wagner. On the return trip, however, the enemy lines kept shifting, forcing Parker to shift his flight path as well, depleting his scarce fuel in the process.

At 7:15 p.m. Parker radioed the escort fighters that he was out of fuel and had to land. He was only ten miles north of Airfield K-29 at Sinanju, North Korea. That was Parker's last radio transmission.

The remains of Parker, Wagner, and Wilkerson were discovered by a US Army patrol and interred at the UN cemetery at Pyongyang, North Korea. That, too, fell to the Chinese and North Korean forces just days after their burial, and Parker's remains were not returned to the United States until 1955. He now rests in Monte Vista Memorial Gardens, Johnson City, Tennessee. For his actions on that evening, Parker received the nation's second highest award for bravery and valor, the Distinguished Service Cross. He also received a Purple Heart, and the National Defense, Korean Service, United Nations, and Republic of Korea War Service Medals, along with all the honors he had received during World War II. His unit was also awarded the Republic of Korea Presidential Unit Citation.

Parker was twenty-six years old at the time of his death. He was married to Janelle, and they had no children. Parker's older brother was also an Air Force pilot, flying C-47 transports. Parker's Distinguished Service Cross citation reads:

> The President of the United States of America, under the provisions of the Act of Congress approved July 9, 1918, takes pride in presenting the Distinguished Service Cross Posthumously to First Lieutenant Robert Blaine Parker AFSN AO-18003, United States Air Force, for extraordinary heroism in connection with military operations against an armed enemy of the United Nations while serving as a Rescue Helicopter Pilot with Detachment F, 3d Air Rescue Squadron, in action against enemy forces in the Republic of Korea on 28 November 1950. Lieutenant

Parker departed Anju, Korea, and flew an unarmed helicopter more than ninety miles over enemy occupied territory in an attempt to rescue a naval pilot downed near the Manchurian border. Lieutenant Parker undertook this hazardous mission fully aware that hostile opposition could be expected and the return flight would tax the maximum range of the craft and involve night flying for which it was not equipped. Aided by two naval fighter aircraft in the area, he located the pilot, with utter disregard for possible sniper fire, landed the helicopter and effected the rescue. During the return flight, this mission was further imperiled by darkness, poor visibility and a dwindling fuel supply. Despite the odds against him, Lieutenant Parker bravely continued on until he reached friendly lines but crashed while attempting an emergency landing. Lieutenant Parker's extraordinary act of heroism in which he gave his life, and consummate devotion to duty reflect untold glory on himself and the noble traditions of the United States Air Force.

GALLANTRY IN ACTION

Corporal Lawrence E. Lett was born on August 21, 1932, in the Fountain City community of Knoxville (Knox). He was the son of Grant and Hazel Wells Lett and attended Central High School. He enlisted in the Marine Corps and served with the 1st Marine Division. While serving in Korea, he was killed in action by enemy gunfire on October 27, 1952. Lett was awarded the Navy Cross for valiant service to his country during the final moments of his life. His posthumous Navy Cross citation reads:

> The Navy Cross is presented to Lawrence Everette Lett, Corporal, U.S. Marine Corps, for extraordinary heroism while serving as a Squad Leader of Company I, Third Bat-

Corporal Lawrence E. Lett.

talion, First Marines, First Marine Division Reinforced, in action against enemy aggressor forces in Korea on 27 October 1952. Participating in an attack to recapture a vitally important sector of the main line of resistance which was previously overrun by the enemy, Corporal Lett fearlessly led his squad through intense enemy artillery, mortar and small-arms fire to reach his portion of the objective and single-handedly charged several enemy bunkers, hurling hand grenades and firing his rifle to rout the hostile troops. Although painfully wounded at point-blank range by hostile machine-gun fire from one emplacement, he succeeded in completely destroying the enemy position. When his men became separated from the platoon, he gallantly continued in the attack until the enemy was forced to withdraw and then reorganized his squad to assault a second objective. Throughout this action, he con-

stantly exposed himself to withering hostile fire and, moving into an enemy trench, courageously engaged three enemy soldiers in hand-to-hand combat until he fell, mortally wounded. By his indomitable fighting spirit, valiant leadership and marked fortitude in the face of heavy odds, Corporal Lett served to inspire all who observed him and contributed in large measure to the success of his squad in accomplishing its mission. His great personal valor reflects the highest credit upon himself and sustains and enhances the finest traditions of the United States Naval Service. He gallantly gave his life for his country.

The October 27, 1952, fight that cost Lett his life was not, however, his only act of heroism under fire. Lett had also earned the Silver Star for conspicuous gallantry during the Marines' earlier fight for Bunker Hill in late summer 1952. The Silver Star was posthumously presented to his family for his actions in that earlier engagement, and its citation follows:

The President of the United States of America takes pride in presenting the Silver Star (Posthumously) to Corporal Lawrence Everette Lett (MCSN: 1106261), United States Marine Corps, for conspicuous gallantry and intrepidity while serving as a Fire Team Leader of Company I, Third Battalion, First Marines, First Marine Division (Reinforced), in action against enemy aggressor forces in Korea, on 12 and 13 August 1952. When his fire team was cut off by an enemy attack during a patrol forward of friendly lines while the company was engaged in defending a vitally important hill position against a fanatical enemy force, Corporal Lett fearlessly led his patrol through a hostile trench and boldly engaged the enemy in hand-to-hand combat, inflicting heavy casualties on the opposition. Leading his men back to friendly lines, he reorganized his team and moved into positions on the platoon front, directing and encouraging his men throughout the remainder of the night in repelling a numerically superior enemy force. On the following morning, he aggressively led his group in an assault on an enemy bunker and, although twice painfully wounded during the ensuing hand-to-hand struggle, steadfastly remained in command throughout the successful assault on the enemy fortification, effectively covering the tactical withdrawal to friendly lines. Refusing medical aid until the more seriously wounded were attended, Corporal Lett, by his skilled leadership, indomitable fighting spirit and courageous initiative in the face of heavy odds, served to inspire all who observed him and upheld the highest traditions of the United States Naval Service.

He is buried at Lynnhurst Cemetery, Knoxville. An article by Mamie Nash in the *Knoxville News Sentinel* reported on the naming of a bridge in his honor:

> A 20-year-old United States Marine ran through intense artillery fire, single-handedly charged into enemy bunkers, and engaged three soldiers at once in hand-to-hand combat before succumbing to gunshot wounds sustained on the battlefield in Korea. Knox County Mayor Tim Burchett on Tuesday dedicated Connor Road bridge over Bull Run Creek in honor of this Knoxville-born Marine, Cpl. Lawrence E. Lett, who was killed in action on Oct. 27, 1952.
>
> "My family is very proud of what my uncle did," said Mark Lett, Cpl. Lett's nephew. "He was killed in action 63 years ago (Tuesday). This bridge dedication means a lot to us."

Lett was highly decorated posthumously for his actions, receiving the Navy Cross, Silver Star and Purple Heart, among many others. U.S. Sen. Bob Corker sent a letter to Lett's family for the occasion, recognizing the Marine's "great courage and service to our country during the Korean War."

"The service and sacrifice of Cpl. Lett represent the absolute best our country has to offer," Corker wrote. "We are privileged to live in the greatest nation in the world, and this is made possible by brave men and women such as Cpl. Lett."[10]

Corporal Billy C. Mosier (Johnson) was born on October 23, 1930, and was a combat medic with the Medical Company of the 21st Infantry Regiment, 24th Infantry Division. On January 3, 1951, near Uijongbu, South Korea, he was tending his wounded comrades under intense enemy fire. When a sniper made it impossible to work, he took the rifle of a wounded comrade and killed several of the enemy before being felled by another Communist sniper. He is buried at Acre Field Cemetery in Laurel Bloomery, Tennessee. For his valor, Corporal Mosier was awarded the Distinguished Service Cross. His citation follows:

> The President of the United States of America under the provisions of the Act of Congress approved July 9, 1918, takes pride in presenting the Distinguished Service Cross (Posthumously) to Corporal Billy Mosier, United States Army, for extraordinary heroism in connection with military operations against an armed enemy of the United Nations while serving as a Medical Aidman with the 21st Infantry Regiment, 24th Infantry Division. Corporal Mosier distinguished himself by extraordinary heroism in action against enemy aggressor forces in the vicinity of Uijongbu, Korea, on 3 January 1951. When the defensive positions of Company A were attacked by an estimated enemy battalion, supported by heavy mortar fire, Corporal Mosier voluntarily exposed himself to the intense enemy fire to administer aid to wounded soldiers. While treating a wounded man he heard a call for aid coming from a soldier approximately five hundred yards away. With complete disregard for his personal safety, he moved through the

Then Knox County Mayor Tim Burchett, center, talks with Mark Lett of the Knox County Veterans Office, left, and Eric Nash of the Marine Corps League during the 2015 dedication ceremony of the Connor Road bridge in memory of US Marine Cpl. Lawrence E. Lett on Tuesday. Lett was Mark Lett's uncle.

enemy fire to the wounded man and administered first aid as small arms fire struck all around him. When the enemy snipers continued to cover the area with fire making it impossible for him to evacuate the wounded man, he picked up the wounded soldier's rifle and moved forward to the crest of a hill from which he placed accurate fire on the enemy's position, killing several of them. He continued to fire on the enemy's positions until he was killed by an enemy sniper.

Private First Class Elmer E. Lewellyn (Sevier) was born on January 15, 1917. His Distinguished Service Cross citation for valorous action in the Korean conflict reads:

The President of the United States takes pride in presenting the Distinguished Service Cross Posthumously to Elmer E. Lewellyn ER06142686, U.S. Army, for extraordinary heroism in connection with military operations against an armed enemy of the United Nations while serving with Company E, 2d Battalion, 38th Infantry Regiment, 2d Infantry Division. Private First Class Lewellyn distinguished himself by extraordinary heroism in action against enemy aggressor forces in the vicinity of Oneamsong, Korea, on 13 January 1951. On that date, Company E was defending a key terrain feature in the Wonju area when a numerically superior enemy force launched several fanatical attacks against the company positions. In the initial attack, Private Lewellyn, a newly assigned replacement that had joined the company the preceding day, was thrown from his foxhole by the force of an enemy concussion grenade that exploded near his position. Quickly recovering from the shock of the blast, he crawled back to his position and aided in repulsing the attack by placing withering fire on the enemy. When the enemy troops rallied and launched a second attack, Private Lewellyn, heedless of the intense enemy fire, moved from one position to another in order to gain a better field of fire and thus inflict greater casualties on the enemy. Although seriously wounded during the second enemy assault, Private Lewellyn refused to retire for medical attention. When the enemy closed in for the third and final assault, Private Lewellyn leaped from his foxhole and stood fully exposed to the hostile fire, yelling taunts at the enemy and shouting words of encouragement to his comrades. During the final assault, enemy troops approached to within a few yards of Private Lewellyn's position, but he steadfastly refused to fall back and killed several enemy soldiers at his position before he fell mortally wounded. Inspired by the intrepid courage and self-sacrifice of Private Lewellyn, his comrades tenaciously held their positions, inflicted tremendous casualties on the enemy and successfully repelled the hostile assaults.

Lewellyn is buried at Mount Hope Cemetery in Bangor, Maine.

Private First Class Donald C. Vaughn of Knoxville (Knox) was born on April 12, 1931. His parents were Grant Edgar Vaughn and Bonnie Smith Vaughn; his siblings were Raymond Eugene, Ernie R., and Christine Imogene. Vaughn was a student at Gibbs High School and worked on his grandfather's farm before entering the Army in 1949. PFC Vaughn was a member of Company A, 1st Battalion, 21st Infan-

Private First Class Donald C. Vaughn.

try Regiment, 24th Infantry Division, and was killed in action while fighting the enemy near Chupari, North Korea, on July 8, 1951. His Distinguished Service Cross citation is as follows:

> The President of the United States of America, under the provisions of the Act of Congress approved July 9, 1918, takes pride in presenting the Distinguished Service Cross Posthumously to Private First Class Donald C. Vaughn ASN RA-14312142, United States Army, for extraordinary heroism in connection with military operations against an armed enemy of the United Nations while serving with Company A, 1st Battalion, 21st Infantry Regiment, 24th Infantry Division. Private First Class Vaughn distinguished himself by extraordinary heroism in action against enemy aggressor forces in the vicinity of Chupari, Korea, on 8 July 1951. On that date, Private Vaughn was a scout with the lead squad of Company A, which was on a reconnaissance patrol to determine the

strength and disposition of the enemy. Upon contacting the enemy, the lead squad immediately assaulted the hostile outpost and succeeded in neutralizing it. As the company moved forward to the base of their primary objective and another squad advanced to accomplish the next phase of the mission, Private Vaughn volunteered to go with them in their assault. As Private Vaughn reached higher ground, he observed that the hitherto hidden enemy platoons were moving out in a flanking movement aimed at encircling the friendly forces. Immediately, He ordered the patrol back and took up an exposed position to cover their withdrawal. Although his position was subjected to a deadly a crossfire from the enemy, Private Vaughn succeeded in pinning down the hostile forces with his intense and accurate rifle fire long enough for his comrades to reach safety before he was hit and mortally wounded.

Vaughn is buried at Roseberry Cemetery in Knoxville.

BROTHERS AT WAR IN KOREA

The Overbay Brothers of Sullivan County

Although they were almost nine years apart in age, two brothers from Kingsport (Sullivan), Charles M. and Jacob K. Overbay, were both killed in Korea within a year of each other. Jacob was born on September 4, 1922, and Charles was born on March 8, 1931. Each one served with the 25th (Tropic Lightning) Infantry Division: Jacob with its 35th Infantry Regiment, and Charles with its 14th Infantry Regiment. Jacob was serving as a Private First Class when he was killed, and Charles held the rank of Sergeant at the time he fell in action, just over one year after Jacob's death.

Jacob, as a dual-service soldier (a.k.a., a "two-war man"), was a decorated World War II veteran. He was killed in action on February 3, 1951, while fighting in South Korea, where he was a light weapons infantryman with the 35th Infantry. Charles entered the Army in January 1951 and was wounded in action in North Korea by an enemy land mine on March 7, 1952, dying of those wounds later that day. Both Charles and Jacob were married when they were killed. Charles's and Jacob's decorations included the Purple Heart, Combat Infantryman's Badge, Korean Service Medal, United Nations Service Medal, National Defense Service Medal, Korean Presidential Unit Citation, and Republic of Korea War Service Medal; Jacob's also included the World War II Victory Medal. Charles was buried in the Emory Methodist Church Cemetery in Sullivan County, and Jacob was buried at the Gunnings Cemetery, also in Sullivan County.

The Hyde Brothers of McMinn County

The tragedy of the Hyde family of Jefferson County began with the loss of one brother some five years before the start of the Korean conflict. Technician Fourth Class Arnold J. Hyde was the son of Marion Walter and Tina Miller Hyde. He was born in 1914 and raised on the family farm in Jefferson County. During World War II, his parents and his brothers Taylor, Charles, James, W. K., and Cecil Hyde moved to the community of Tranquility near Athens. Arnold enlisted in the Army on April 21, 1941, at Fort Oglethorpe, Georgia. He was promoted to the rank of Technician Fourth Class with the 813th Tank Battalion. He was killed in action on January 7, 1945, in France. T/4 Arnold J. Hyde is buried at the Épinal American Cemetery, Épinal, France. Arnold received the Silver Star for gallantry in action and the Purple Heart.

Tragedy returned to the Hyde family again as another brother, Sergeant James H. Hyde, was killed in Korea on December 30, 1951. James was born on March 21, 1918, and, like Arnold, he was a World War II veteran, having enlisted in 1939. In Korea, he served with Service Company, 15th Infantry Regiment, 7th Infantry Division. On December 30, 1951, he died of burns received when his tent caught fire as he slept near Yonchen, North Korea. In addition to his parents, he was survived by his wife, Helen Hyde; three-year-old daughter, Madoline Carol; and the four surviving brothers, Taylor, W. K., Cecil, and Charlie. Sergeant James Hyde's body was repatriated to his hometown in McMinn County and was laid to rest in Pond Hill Cemetery, Niota, Tennessee.

Sergeant Robert E. (Bob) Adams.

WASHINGTON COUNTIANS AND KOREA

Thanks to the efforts of retired US Air Force airman and historian Allen D. Jackson, the stories of many of Washington County's military personnel have been reconstructed in considerable detail. The especially noteworthy accounts of three of these men follow. Sergeant Robert E. Adams, Private First Class Odell Busler, and Corporal John F. Sadler all called Johnson City their home. As will be seen, the death of John Sadler has a special and unique historical relevance to the highly complex nature of the Korean War and the fraught peace via armistice that has followed for the last sixty-five years.

Robert E. ("Bob") Adams was born on March 1, 1929, to Tennessee Adams and Eva Mae Johnson, and the family lived in Midway, a small community between Johnson City and Jonesborough. He attended Midway School be-

fore enlisting in the Army and being assigned to duty in West Germany. He returned home after that assignment and reenlisted, hopefully enabling him to bring a very special German friend named Kitty home to Tennessee to be his wife. Before that could happen, however, he had to serve a tour of duty in Korea. Adams was assigned to Company E, 2nd Battalion, 9th Infantry Regiment, 2nd Infantry Division ("Indianhead") as a light weapons infantryman and was sent to Korea. A famous Regular Army regiment, the 9th Infantry had earned the nickname of "Manchu" for its exploits in China during the Boxer Rebellion and relief expedition in 1900.

Adams arrived in Pusan, South Korea, on July 23, 1950; his was the first unit to set foot on Korean soil from the United States after United Nations Resolution 84 of July 7, 1950, authorized UN military support to South Korea. The 9th Infantry went straight into defensive positions on the Pusan Perimeter along the Naktong River line, where its troops received their baptism of fire in the First Battle of the Naktong Bulge, August 5–19, 1950. After the UN forces' breakout from the Pusan Perimeter, the Manchus fought and took the Cloverleaf and Obong-Ni Ridge. They stayed there until September 1 when the last North Korean attempts to annihilate the Pusan Perimeter's defenders shattered the regiment, causing them to retreat temporarily. Sergeant Adams, along with eight hundred Manchus, reorganized with the 5th Marine Regiment, counterattacked, and retook both the Cloverleaf and Obong-Ni Ridge. They then started to push the North Koreans back to the Yalu River as part of the US Eighth Army.

Adams was wounded in the ankle on September 7 and returned to duty on October 27, 1950. He reentered the fight and likely thought—as did many other US, South Korean, and UN soldiers—that the war would soon be over. They believed that they would be home for Christmas, as Seoul had been liberated and UN troops neared the end of their push northward to the Yalu River and the North Korean-Chinese border. Those beliefs were crushed on November 25, 1950, when Communist Chinese forces attacked the Eighth Army near the Chongchon River. The 9th Infantry was one of the hardest hit units and could only account for approximately one-half of its assigned members at daylight on November 26, but Adams was one of those survivors. On November 30, the Manchus started to run what is now called "the Gauntlet." Adams was reported missing in action during the Battle of the Chongchon River (i.e., the Gauntlet), near Kunu-Ri, North

Korea, on December 1, 1950. A majority of the 1st and 2nd Battalions of the Manchus never made it out of the Gauntlet. Bob Adams was officially declared dead on December 31, 1953, as were many more Manchus. To date, his remains have not been located or recovered.

Sergeant Adams was twenty-one years old when he disappeared in the savagery and chaos of the Gauntlet. His brother Jack had served in the Army during World War II and was a German POW. After Sergeant Adams was declared missing, his family kept in contact with his fiancée, Kitty, in Germany, but that contact ended after he was declared dead, and she never made it to Tennessee. Adams is listed in the Tablets of the Missing, National Memorial Cemetery of the Pacific, Honolulu, Hawaii. He has memorial markers at Mountain Home National Cemetery, Monte Vista Memorial Gardens in Johnson City, and he is also commemorated

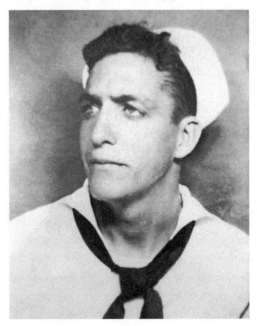

Private First Class Odell Busler.

at the Johnson City/Washington County and Jonesborough Veteran Memorial Parks.

Private First Class Odell Busler was born on August 25, 1928, in Ivy Hills, Haywood County, North Carolina to Jack (Jake) Busler and Ella Calahan, but he called Johnson City his home. Before enlisting in the Army and fighting in the Korean War, he was already a World War II veteran, having served with the United States Navy during that war.

Busler enlisted in the Navy on January 15, 1944, in Nashville, stating his date of birth as August 29, 1926. Actually, he was only fifteen years old when he enlisted. After basic training, he was shipped to Hawaii and placed in reserve. He was pulled from reserve status on May 9, 1944, and signed aboard the USS *PC-582*, a patrol craft and submarine chaser. Seaman Second Class Busler and his fellow crewmen helped keep convoys and the shores of Hawaii secure. They also performed a convoy escort mission to Saipan in the Mariana Islands of the western Pacific during July 1944. He was transferred and signed aboard the *PC-599*, another sub chaser, on June 19, 1945. He continued service with her and in Hawaii until the war ended, and he returned home to Tennessee.

When war broke out in Korea, Odell Busler was already in the Army. He had enlisted in the Army on June 11, 1946, at Fort Oglethorpe, Georgia at age seventeen; after basic training, he was assigned to the 7th Infantry Division in pre-war South Korea. Odell was transferred to the newly reactivated 5th Infantry Regiment on January 1, 1949, which was being stationed in South Korea to provide security while US personnel and troops were withdrawn from the country. On June 31, 1949, the 5th Infantry's withdrawal orders from South Korea took effect, and the regiment was transferred to Scho-

field Barracks, Hawaii. PFC Busler served in Company A, 1st Battalion, 5th Infantry Regiment, as a light weapons infantryman.

After hostilities erupted in Korea, the regiment returned there on July 25, 1950, and was attached to the 25th Infantry Division as part of Task Force Kean. It was re-designated the 5th Regimental Combat Team, earning a reputation as one of the most respected Army combat units of the Korean War. The 5th RCT reinforced the 25th Infantry and the 1st Cavalry Divisions on the Naktong River line. It was thrown into protracted combat, and while engaged in fierce fighting on the Pusan Perimeter-Southwest, near Chingdong-Ni, South Korea, on August 27, 1950, Busler was killed in action. Two days earlier, he had just

Corporal John F. Sadler.

turned twenty-two. He is interred at Monte Vista Memorial Gardens, Johnson City.

Corporal John F. Sadler was born on February 4, 1933, and was the son of David Milford Sadler and Ruth Leota Kelley. During the Korean fighting, he was assigned to Company A, 187th Infantry Regimental Combat Team, 11th Airborne Division, as a light weapons infantryman parachutist. His regiment was sent to Koje-do Island (now known as Geoje-do Island) off the southern coast of South Korea to suppress a violent and controversial uprising of Communist Chinese and North Korean prisoners of war. An Army historical report on the POW camp riots describes the American response to the melees of June 1952, which included the Communist POWs taking the US camp commandant prisoner and holding him hostage, as well as attacking American and South Korean troops with improvised weaponry:

> On the morning of 10 June [1952], [Brig. Gen. Haydon L. Boatner, assistant division commander of the 2d Infantry Division, the new commander of Koje-do] ordered Col. Lee Hak Koo [a senior North Korean officer interned in the camp] to assemble the prisoners of Compound 76 in groups of 150 in the center of the compound and to be prepared to move them out. Instead the prisoners brought forth their knives, spears, and tent poles and took their positions in trenches, ready to resist. Crack paratroopers of the 187th Airborne Regimental Combat Team wasted little time as they advanced without firing a shot. Employing concussion grenades, tear gas, bayonets, and fists, they drove or dragged the prisoners out of the trenches. As a half-dozen Patton tanks rolled in and trained their guns on the last 300 prisoners still fighting, resistance collapsed. Colonel Lee was captured and dragged by the seat of his pants out of the compound. The other prisoners were hustled into trucks, transported to the new compounds, fingerprinted, and given new clothing. During the two-and-a-half-hour battle, 31 prisoners were killed, many by the Communists themselves, and 139 were wounded. One U.S. soldier was speared to death and 14 were injured. After Compound 76 had been cleared, a tally of weapons showed 3,000 spears, 4,500 knives, 1,000 gasoline grenades, plus an undetermined number of clubs, hatchets, barbed wire flails, and hammers. These weapons had been fashioned out of scrap materials and metal-tipped tent poles by the prisoners.[11]

Sadler's unit had been sent in to secure Compound 76 of the Koje-Do prison camp. He was the soldier who was stabbed by a prisoner with a homemade spear, which severed an artery in his right leg; Sadler died as a result of this wound on June 10, 1952.

Almost unbelievably, Sadler was the only US forces member to be killed in action during this riot. The prisoners' uprisings had been precipitated in part by efforts taken by the UN forces to identify those North Korean and Chinese prisoners who did not want to be repatriated to their Communist homelands and help them relocate after the cessation of fighting to South Korea or Taiwan, respectively; this approach was aggressively challenged by the pro-Communist POWs, and the policy also became a major point of contention in the ongoing armistice negotiations at Panmunjon. The Koje-do riots, along with related allegations and observations (including by International Red Cross observers) of the rough handling of North Korean and Chinese prisoners, had a deleterious impact on the UN coalition's image and helped protract negotiations over prisoner exchanges during the armistice talks.[12] A final armistice agreement was only reached on

July 27, 1953, over one year after the Koje-do rioting. At the time of this writing, although that armistice still holds, the North Korean regime remains technically in a state of war with the United States, as peace has not been formally declared to this day between the two nations.

Sadler was nineteen years old at the time of his death in Koje-do. He is buried in Monte Vista Memorial Park, Johnson City.

12

VIETNAM
Selected Stories from the Conflicts in Indochina

... And in that time
When men decide and feel safe
To call the war insane,
Take one moment to embrace
Those gentle heroes
You left behind.

—US Army major Michael D. O'Donnell, written on January 1, 1970,
in Dak To, South Vietnam; Major O'Donnell was killed in action in 1970

Even before the Tonkin Gulf incident of autumn 1964 precipitated a wider "Americanization" of the fighting in Vietnam, East Tennesseans had already served, and died, in Indochina. While the Vietnam War polarized American society, numerous East Tennesseans fell in this conflict. This chapter will explore selected stories of service members who became casualties of this conflict, including several who died as North Vietnamese prisoners or who remain missing in action to this day.

As a relatively more recent conflict, the stories in this chapter have been enriched by the personal testimonies and remembrances of individuals who served with those who gave the last full measure of devotion in Vietnam, Laos, and Cambodia, and of surviving family members. These accounts of duty and bravery amply illustrate the wide-ranging experiences of those who served, and those who died, in combat in Southeast Asia.

A total of 669 men and one woman from East Tennessee were lost during the war in Vietnam. Hamilton County had the highest number of casualties with 120, followed by Knox County with 93. They were followed by Washington County (47), Sullivan (38); and Blount (34).

The names of all of those whose accounts are shared in this chapter are engraved on the Vietnam Veterans Memorial in Washington, DC.

ANDERSON

On April 26, 1970, Captain Samuel E. Asher was serving as the company commander of Company E, 2nd Battalion, 502nd Infantry, 101st Airborne Division, in Thua Thien Province, South Vietnam. Asher was killed that day by enemy artillery fire. This excerpt from an article by US Army colonel (retired) Wayne H. Morris, an Oak Ridge High School class of 1960 graduate and a former classmate and peer of Asher, recalled Asher's life, military service, and death in action, and the consequences of his death for his family:

Sam Asher was born on Nov. 3, 1941 in Oak Ridge, the oldest son of Earl and Helen Asher who had three boys. Sam tackled life in "the Ridge" with exuberance. Oak Ridge in the 50s was a great place for a young man to live. He thrived in this environment as a

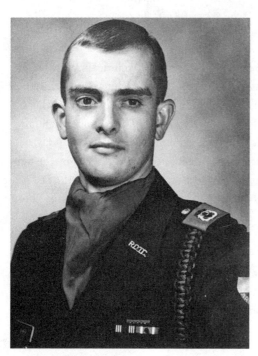

Captain Samuel E. Asher.

scholar, athlete, Boy Scout, lover of old cars and racing, girls, the Wildcat Den on Friday and Saturday nights and life in general! Sam's father was an independent electrical contractor and his mother a teacher in Oak Ridge School system. Sam was a skilled electrician and quite often worked for his father.

[After graduating from high school,] Sam attended Tennessee Tech, and, after one year, he transferred to UT where he quickly became a standout [Army ROTC] cadet and in his senior year was the student commander of the unit. Following graduation and commissioning, Sam entered Active Duty, attended Infantry Officer Basic, went to "jump" school and earned his airborne "wings," then completed the extremely difficult Ranger School at Fort Benning, Georgia.

Because of his record of service and his potential, Sam was selected to command a rifle company in the famous 101st Airborne Division. E Company, 2/502 Infantry was occupying a jagged hill known as Fire Base Veghel just SW of Hue, surrounded by regular North Vietnamese Army (NVA) troops, which were on the attack.

His recon platoon with 1st Lt. James Hill in command (now retired four-star General James Hill) was moving to reinforce Sam. On 26 April 1970, just two weeks after taking command, his mortar platoon was engaging the NVA when an enemy round hit and collapsed a bunker with Sam's soldier inside. Realizing the danger his soldiers were in he left his command bunker and raced to their rescue just as another enemy round landed beside him. Sam was killed instantly. Sam was awarded the Silver Star posthumously, our Nation's third highest award for heroism in the face of the enemy. He was interred in Woodhaven Memorial Gardens in Claxton with full military honors on 6th May 1970.[1]

Staff Sergeant Luther Eugene (Gene) Davis of Oak Ridge was born on April 11, 1947. He was married and had two sons, Larry and Lance. He served three tours in Vietnam; his final tour be-

Staff Sergeant Luther Eugene (Gene) Davis.

gan on August 15, 1969. He served as a pararescue specialist in the 37th Aerospace Rescue and Recovery Squadron, 3rd Air Rescue Group, 7th Air Force. While attempting to rescue a downed US Army helicopter in Kontum, South Vietnam, his own helicopter was attacked and crashed on April 14, 1970. On May 25, 1970, he died from injuries suffered in the crash. His death is listed as a result of hostile action. He was only twenty-three years old. He is buried in the Anderson Memorial Garden in Anderson County, Tennessee.

His brother, Tom Davis, advised that in May 1975, the Davis family attended a dedication of a building at Keesler Air Force Base in Mississippi named "Davis Manor" in his honor. Gene earned the Silver Star, three Distinguished Flying Crosses, fifteen Air Medals, and three Purple Hearts, among other awards and decorations. Davis's Silver Star citation follows:

The President of the United States of America, authorized by Act of Congress July 9, 1918 amended by an act of July 25, 1963, takes pleasure in presenting the Silver Star to Airman Second Class Luther E. Davis, AFSN 14912332, United States Air Force, for gallantry in connection with military operations against an opposing armed force as a Pararescue Specialist over North Vietnam, on 11 June 1967. On that date, Airman Davis flew as a rescue mission to recover two friendly pilots downed deep in hostile territory. Voluntarily descending on the rescue hoist, Airman Davis dangled hundreds of feet over dense bamboo jungle, which was heavily infested with hostile forces to cut the first survivor loose from his entangled parachute harness. As the helicopter encountered intense and accurate ground fire while hovering over the second survivor, Airman Davis responded immediately by delivering automatic weapon fire into unfriendly gun positions, thereby deterring the hostile forces and allowing the rescue effort to continue. By his gallantry and devotion to duty, Airman Davis has reflected great credit upon himself and the United States Air Force.

First Lieutenant Gary A. Glandon was born on April 17, 1940, to Mr. and Mrs. Charles Glandon and called Claxton his home. He was graduated from the University of Tennessee in 1964, where he was a cadet major in UT's Air Force ROTC detachment, and he went immediately into the Air Force after graduation. He was one of six Glandon sons to serve in the armed forces. Deployed to South Vietnam, he was a member of the 390th Tactical Fighter Squadron, based at the Da Nang airbase. On May 26, 1966, he was the weapons systems officer of a McDonnell Douglas F-4C Phantom II fighter-bomber on a bombing mission along the coast of South Vietnam about ten miles northeast of Qui Nhon in Binh Dinh Province.

First Lieutenant Gary A. Glandon.

trombone in the band. During summers he had a U-T job at Oak Ridge." After graduation, Lt. Glandon was stationed at Lackland AFB, Tex., and then at New Mexico bases before going to Vietnam in January. His mother said he usually had written home twice monthly but she hadn't heard from him for about six weeks before learning of his death. Besides his parents, he leaves five brothers, Max, Tony, Dan, Emil and Kenneth Glandon.

The following profile of Sergeant Fletcher M. Seeber Jr. was provided by Neil Wilson, US Marine Corps, 1965–1969 (South Vietnam, 1968–69), where he served as a member of Delta Company, 1st Battalion, 7th Marines:

> Fletcher M. Seeber, Jr., was born on March 1, 1946 in Frost Bottom, outside the small town of Oliver Springs located in the hills of East Tennessee. There were three brothers and three sisters in his family with Fletcher being the second-born of the three sons.
>
> After the 1962 football season at Oliver Springs High School, Fletcher was chosen

After making its second bombing run, his aircraft burst into flames and crashed. He was twenty-six at the time; his remains were not recovered. His name is inscribed on the Tablets of the Missing, National Memorial Cemetery of the Pacific, Honolulu, Hawaii. This excerpt from an article in the June 1, 1966, *Knoxville News Sentinel* provided further information on Glandon:

> The Claxton native was pilot of one of the two-man F-4C Phantom jet fighter-bombers. The Associated Press dispatch Thursday said the F-4C exploded in a freak accident when hit by its own bomb blast or another one while in a dive at only 200 feet. "We know our son's body could not be recovered," Mrs. Glandon said. "No, he wasn't married or engaged. He was always so busy he didn't take much time for girls. He graduated at Clinton High where he played the

Sergeant Fletcher M. Seeber Jr.

by his teammates to be one of the team captains for the 1963–1964 season. This was a well-deserved honor for Fletcher. While only about five foot nine and one hundred eighty pounds, Fletcher played at an intensity level far above his size. Sadly, his senior football season was not to be. On the opening play of the preseason Jamboree held at Harriman in August of 1964 Fletcher was to suffer a career-ending knee injury. His football playing days were over. Fletcher still took his responsibilities as a team captain to heart and continued to rally the team with his enthusiasm and leadership for the remainder of the season.

Little did they know at the time that four members from this team would eventually enter the Marine Corps and all would serve in a line company in Vietnam. One would be wounded, two would make it through unscathed and one, Fletcher, would lose his life. In June of 1964, soon after graduation, Fletcher along with three classmates enlisted in the Marine Corps. . . . He was also trained as a dog handler and had a German Shepherd as his partner. I was told by his brother years later that he was very attached to the dog and was very saddened when his tour was up and he had to rotate back to the states, leaving his dog behind.

Our paths crossed in early 1966 while we both served with the 6th Marine Regiment. Fletcher was with Bravo Company while I was a member of Alpha Company. The Marine Corps keeps a combat ready battalion in both the Caribbean Sea and Mediterranean Sea. This unit is called a Battalion Landing Team, and in this case we were members of BLT 1/6. After returning to Camp Lejeune, North Carolina, in August of 1966, it was almost a certainty that since I was only starting into my second year of a four-year enlistment that I was on my way to Vietnam. Fletcher on the other hand was into his final year of a three-year enlistment and it was unlikely that the Marine Corps would send him into combat. One day af-

ter liberty call had been sounded and the barracks was nearly empty, Fletcher and I were sitting on the stairs shooting the breeze when out of the blue the subject of Vietnam came up. Trust me—in the Marine Corps of 1966, Vietnam was always the topic at hand. I could tell that Fletcher had been thinking a great deal about what he was going to say before he spoke. "You know, I have been thinking about extending my enlistment so I can go to Vietnam with you," he said in a serious voice. It was apparent that this was no place for a frivolous reply so I said something to the effect that [he had] served his time and should go back home and continue his education or even start a family. It became quickly apparent this was not the response he had hoped for. "No," he said, "If I serve three years in the Marine Corps with an infantry MOS and don't serve in Vietnam, the people at home might think that I haven't done enough for my country." There wasn't much left for me to say other than, "Well, I think you have done what you have been asked to do."

Fletcher landed in Vietnam on his twenty-first birthday on March 1, 1967, as a squad leader with 3rd Platoon, Lima Company, 3rd Battalion, 9th Marines. His Battalion left Okinawa by ship and went directly into battle after they landed near the DMZ in the I Corps area of South Vietnam. His unit was in heavy contact with North Vietnamese Army. They were not fighting daytime farmers as in the earlier years of this conflict. The North Vietnamese had heavy supporting fire from North Vietnam and they came to stay. Fletcher's unit was in daily contact with the enemy. Only a week or so before his death, he was wounded by a piece of metal from an enemy grenade. After being treated in the bush, he returned to his squad.

Fletcher was killed in a grenade explosion on June 21, 1967.

BLEDSOE

Sergeant Joseph A. Oreto was born on August 22, 1947, and was a member of the Aero-Rifle Platoon, Air Cavalry Troop, 11th Armored Cavalry Regiment. His tour in Vietnam began on November 24, 1968. He was killed in action in Tay Ninh, South Vietnam. His Silver Star citation reads:

> The President of the United States takes pride in presenting the Silver Star Medal (Posthumously) to Joseph Anthony Oreto US51670676, Sergeant, United States Army, for gallantry in action while engaged in military operations involving conflict with an armed hostile force on 13 April 1969 while serving as Squad Leader with the Aero Rifle Platoon, Air Cavalry Troop, 11th Armored Cavalry Regiment, in the Republic of Vietnam. On this date while conducting a bomb damage assessment in a heavily-fortified enemy base camp, the platoon suddenly came under intense machine gun and anti-tank rocket fire from a well-concealed and well-entrenched hostile force. Sergeant Oreto and his lead squad were immediately pinned down in an open area directly in front of the enemy positions. Realizing the desperate situation he and his men were in, Sergeant Oreto single-handedly assaulted the nearest enemy bunker. While the hostile fire was concentrated on him, his men were able to maneuver into more secure positions. As he prepared to throw a hand grenade into the enemy bunker, he was fatally wounded by hostile fire. Sergeant Oreto's outstanding courage, unwavering devotion to duty and deep concern for the welfare of his men were in keeping with the highest traditions of the military service and reflect great credit upon himself, his unit and the United States Army.

Sergeant Joseph A. Oreto.

BLOUNT

Captain Johnny L. Bryant was from Maryville and was born on August 16, 1943. He served with the 334th Assault Helicopter Company (AHC), 145th Aviation Battalion, 12th Aviation Group, flying a Bell AH-1G Cobra helicopter gunship, and he was the recipient of three Distinguished Flying Crosses, two Bronze Star Medals, twenty-four Air Medals, two Army Commendation Medals, and four Purple Heart Medals. At the time of this writing, he is being considered for a Medal of Honor. He was killed in action on May 22, 1969, and was buried at Four Mile Cemetery in Blount County. Dale Dailey evokes the extraordinary service and achievements of his lost friend, as he describes one of Bryant's daring missions:

Captain Johnny L. Bryant.

I flew firefly missions [a specialized nighttime aerial mission, in which one helicopter illuminated a target area with powerful lights] regularly with Captain Bryant from mid-November 1968 through January 25, 1969 when he was shot down. I had been reassigned but still with the 334th AHC with Captain Bryant's return and did not have another opportunity to fly with him. I believe his "Crazy Joe" moniker came from his aggressive nature, one that served our firefly team well. I can share one mission memory with you, and it's a positive memory that I hold to this date.

We were called to a location to search for two LRRP [Long-Range Reconnaissance Patrol]/Rangers who became separated from their team after insertion when the team was ambushed. We were able to locate the two Rangers after a short search using our light to illuminate the area. We located both men concealed in a bomb crater. With hand motions—we had no radio communication with them—they signaled they were being

fired upon from a tree line to their immediate front. Captain Bryant immediately lowered his Cobra and hovered at about twenty feet directly above the two Rangers and fired his mini-guns into the tree line suppressing any aggression from that area. As we provided cover, the two Rangers were plucked from the ground using harnesses suspended from an additional helicopter called to the scene. The Rangers were flown back to their base, a twenty-minute ride, suspended from that harness. Quite the sight to see. The LRRP/Ranger company was so pleased with our effort that they wanted to meet our team and thank us personally. A group of us flew to Long Bien the next day for the meet. We were rewarded for our effort with LRRP rations: a ready to eat meal, and a treat from the C-Rations [we] normally consumed.

Sergeant First Class James L. Parker was a triple-war service veteran, having served in World War II, Korea, and Vietnam. He was born

Sergeant First Class James L. Parker.

Sergeant First Class Fred Calvin Russell.

to joining the military, he managed a service station. Following in the steps of his older brother, Russell enlisted on December 9, 1942, and served in World War II in the ETO and on occupation duty in Germany. After his European service, he continued serving in the Army and fought in the Korean War and the Vietnam War. In Vietnam, he served as a crewmember in the Howitzer Battery, 1st Squadron, 11th Armored Cavalry. He died at the age of forty-four on February 10, 1967, at Brooke Army Medical Center, Fort Sam Houston, Texas, from wounds caused by an explosive device in South Vietnam. His death is listed as a ground casualty. Family member David Love recalled Russell as follows: "From the recollections of my stepdad and his sisters, we understood that Calvin was climbing into a tank that was on fire to help one of the crew members out when it exploded,

on May 22, 1922, in Georgia. As a member of the Army, SFC Parker served his country until his death on April 3, 1967. He was forty-four years old and was married. Parker died from small arms fire wounds at Brooke Army Medical Center, Fort Sam Houston, San Antonio, Texas. He had served the country for twenty-two years. He was the husband of Lillie Mae Williams Parker, Durham, North Carolina, and the son of James and Viola Mills Parker of Georgia.

Sergeant First Class Fred Calvin Russell, another three-war veteran, was born in Maryville on October 16, 1922. His parents were William Fred and Sytha Jane Russell. His siblings were Mary Lou Russell, Ruby MacGregory, Nicholas Alexander Russell, Olivia McDonald, and Ruth Jobe. Russell grew up in Maryville and graduated from Lanier High School in 1941. Prior

Staff Sergeant Gordon L. Wheeler.

burning him severely; he died several weeks later." He is buried in Grandview Cemetery in Maryville, Tennessee.

Staff Sergeant Gordon L. Wheeler was born on August 16, 1931, in Maryville and died on March 8, 1969, in Quang Tri, Vietnam. Wheeler was a veteran of both the Korean and Vietnam Wars. In Vietnam, he served with the 50th Tactical Airlift Squadron, 314th Tactical Airlift Wing, 13th Air Force. Wheeler served his country for eighteen years until he was killed when his Lockheed C-130 Hercules transport plane crashed in Taiwan. He was thirty-seven and married. Wheeler was buried at Bethlehem Baptist Church Cemetery, Carthage, Moore County, North Carolina.

Captain William L. (Bill) Johnson.

BRADLEY

Captain William L. (Bill) Johnson was an "Army brat" who traveled and lived in many parts of the United States and Europe. Over the years, he came to know the Army and the soldiers who served in it and, through this knowledge, developed a love for the Army and a strong desire to serve his country. After graduation from high school, Johnson was admitted to the US Military Academy at West Point, the beginning of his service career. This recollection from friend and fellow officer Frank Thompson provided a portrait of Johnson's military career:

> Bill was quite successful as a cadet. This success, however, was flavored by an impatience born of anticipation and a desire to don the gold bars and crossed rifles of an Infantry Lieutenant. He could have had a much easier time at West Point had it not been for his roommates. . . .
>
> After graduation, Class of 1960, and attendance at the Infantry Basic, Airborne, and Ranger courses at Fort Benning, Bill joined the 504th Infantry of the 82d Airborne Division at Fort Bragg. Here, his already established reputation continued to grow. He soon became known throughout the division as an officer with an extraordinary capacity for hard work and hard play. When there was a job to be done, Bill knew no quitting time. When the job was done, Bill knew how to relax. He was one of the most popular officers in the division, on duty and off.
>
> Bill commanded the same respect as a Lieutenant as he had as a cadet at West Point. Subordinates found him a demanding leader but one with a sympathetic ear. His troops sought his help in all matters and found in his common sense and loyalty the answer to many of their problems. There was a special pride in being a member of Lieutenant Johnson's platoon, and he never let his men forget that they were Airborne troopers, and because they were, he expected more of them.

In preparation for an assignment to Vietnam, Bill was sent to the MATA[2] course at Fort Bragg where, according to his usual custom, he graduated near the top of his class. In Vietnam, Bill was assigned as advisor to an ARVN Ranger battalion, an assignment well suited to his training and to his aggressive nature. It was when this battalion was overrun by the Viet Cong on October 25, 1965, somewhere near Tuy Hoa, that Captain Bill Johnson was killed in action—serving his country in combat. He knew his job well, and he had confidence in his ability. He knew what he was doing in Vietnam, and he was always very proud to be an American. He loved the Army and his country. All of us who know him will always be inspired to a higher order of patriotism because of Bill's example.

Bill was buried with full military honors at Arlington National Cemetery on November 3, 1965. He is close to friends and classmates already on duty there. . . . When Bill was buried, he wore the Combat Infantryman's Badge, an award he always admired and respected. For me, the CIB is now a worthier symbol for Bill's having worn it, just as the Army is a better institution for his having served in it. All who know Bill will always remember him as a loyal friend, a patriotic American and a fine soldier.

Thompson concluded his tribute to Johnson with the following phrase from the traditional West Point cadets' song, "Benny Havens, Oh!": "May we find a soldier's resting place/ Beneath a soldier's blow".

CAMPBELL

Private First Class Roger M. Lay was born on May 9, 1948, and was originally from Milford, Ohio. He served his country in the Marine Corps as a rifleman in 3rd Platoon, D Company, 1st Reconnaissance Battalion, 1st Marine Divi-

Private First Class Roger M. Lay.

sion. His tour in Vietnam began on November 29, 1967. Less than two months later, on January 25, 1968, Lay was killed in Thua Thien Province, South Vietnam; he was nineteen years old. He is buried at Douglas Cemetery in Oswego, Campbell County, Tennessee. The following is a tribute to Lay provided to the ETVMA by former Marine aviator Chuck Nowotny, who flew Lay's patrol to his last mission:

I had occasion to insert the eight-man Quizmaster Team of the 1st Btn. 4th Platoon, Company C Force Recon into a small valley . . . just west of the 'Sông Ta Trach' River (a/k/a the South Branch of the Perfume River) just after 10:00 Hrs. The insertion was uneventful except that due to the very dense elephant grass that prevented the rear ramp from deploying on my CH-46A helicopter, *ergo*, I had to egress the team from the starboard-side hatch. As the team departed and since we were not taking fire and the team deployed directly beneath and in front of my .50 Cal., I grabbed my camera and snapped some photographs of the insertion and as we lifted from the LZ. After engaging in two other extractions elsewhere and after sustaining a fair amount of damage to the forward rotor blades during one of the emergency extractions and after about two hours of flying, we were low on fuel. After dropping off the last recon team at the Recon Pad at the 3rd [Marine Division,] we flew to the Phu Bai Airbase to refuel my now damaged and out-of-synch helicopter.

As I hot-refueled my bird, a mission was radioed informing us the initial team Quizmaster was in serious trouble with WIA's and needed an emergency extraction. We attempted three times to pull the team out each time received extremely heavy fire from large and small caliber weapons, only succeeding on the third attempt to locate the team and effect their successful extraction. Roger Lay was hit in the upper left chest area by a single shard of grenade shrapnel during the initial ambush laid by the NVA. The team held was heavily outnumbered and the LZ we'd dropped the team off in was teaming with hundreds of PAVN Soldiers apparently on their way to attack Hue city on January 31, the beginning of the Tet Offensive.

After 43 long years, I was able to finally contact the Lay family and put them in touch with the other men in his team and gave them the photos of Roger's last mission. There were four WIA's. . . . In October 2012 the surviving team and I had occasion to reunite in Hilton Head, South Carolina, where we dutifully remembered Roger's contribution and sacrifice for America with the honor and respect due a fallen Brother Marine.

CARTER

Lance Corporal John P. Avery was born on September 1, 1948, and was originally from Elizabethton. He served his country in the Vietnam War in the Marine Corps as a machine gunner in G Company, 2nd Battalion, 4th Marines, 3rd Marine Division. His tour in Vietnam began on June 19, 1967. On October 14, 1967, Avery was killed under hostile conditions from mortar fire in Quang Tri Province, South Vietnam. He was nineteen years old at the time of his death. He was buried in a small, private cemetery called the Forney Cemetery just across the street in Elizabethton from Highland Cemetery.

Major Dale Alonzo Johnson was born on September 17, 1929, and was originally from Elizabethton. He served his country in the Vietnam War in the United States Air Force as a pilot in the 333rd Tactical Fighter Squadron, 355th Tactical Fighter Wing, 7th Air Force. He was a sixteen-year veteran of the Air Force and had served in the Korean War when he began his tour in Vietnam. On October 27, 1966, Johnson

Lance Corporal John P. Avery.

Major Dale Alonzo Johnson in front of an F-105.

Specialist Fourth Class James W. Tuttle.

was piloting a Republic F-105D Thunderchief jet fighter-bomber that was shot down over North Vietnam; he was listed as Missing in Action, as his body was not recovered, but he was presumed dead. At the time he was shot down, he was thirty-seven years old. Johnson is memorialized at Arlington National Cemetery.

CLAIBORNE

Specialist Fourth Class James W. Tuttle was born on August 13, 1948, the son of James S. Tuttle and Willie Mae Tuttle, and was originally from Arthur, Tennessee. He served his country as an armor reconnaissance specialist

in G Troop, 2nd Squadron, 11th Armored Cavalry. His tour in Vietnam began on December 6, 1968. On April 29, 1969, Tuttle was killed under hostile conditions in Tay Ninh province, South Vietnam. He was twenty years old. He is buried at Shoffner Cemetery in Harrogate.

COCKE

Hospital Corpsman Third Class Michael Gerald Gibbs was born on June 23, 1945, and was originally from Del Rio, Tennessee. He served as a US Navy medical corpsman assigned to H&S Company, 3rd Battalion, III Marine Amphibious Force. On April 26, 1967, in Quang Tri Province, near the later bitterly contested hamlet of Khe Sanh, South Vietnam, Gibbs was serving as a medical corpsman with K Company, 3rd Battalion, 3rd Marines, 3rd Marine

Hospital Corpsman Third Class Michael Gerald Gibbs.

Division, when he was killed by fragmentation wounds in a battle with North Vietnamese forces. He was twenty-one. For the medical aid and dedication that he showed to his fellow soldiers despite his own grievous injuries, Gibbs was posthumously awarded the Silver Star. His citation reads:

> The President of the United States of America takes pride in presenting the Silver Star (Posthumously) to Hospital Corpsman Third Class Michael Gerald Gibbs, United States Navy, for conspicuous gallantry and intrepidity in action while serving as a platoon Corpsman with Company K, Third Battalion, Third Marines, Third Marine Division in connection with operations against insurgent communist forces in the vicinity of Khe Sanh, in the Republic of Vietnam, on 25 April 1967. Hospitalman Gibbs displayed exceptional valor in the heroic performance of his duties while engaged in intense conflict with a numerically stronger force of North Vietnamese Army regulars. Hospitalman Gibbs' platoon was leading the company assault upon the strongly fortified, heavily defended Hill 861, a strategic area commanding the approaches to Khe Sanh.

> As the assault commenced and advanced toward the crest of the hill, the lead platoon became subjected to intense enemy fire from small arms, automatic weapons and grenades. In the initial contact, the platoon sustained heavy casualties from the enemy's surprise fire and became temporarily halted. Heedless of his own personal safety and dangerously exposing himself to enemy fire, Hospitalman Gibbs, without hesitation or summons, advanced to the point of crisis to administer medical assistance to the wounded.

> While administering vitally needed aid to his fallen comrades and assisting them to areas of safety, Hospitalman Gibbs sustained a painful back wound. In spite of his wound, he returned to the front of his own accord and continued to treat casualties. He then received a more serious wound, which broke his leg. Physically unable to continue, Hospitalman Gibbs lay silent until darkness came, and he then allowed himself to be removed to the casualty collection point. Despite his wounds, Hospitalman Gibbs maintained an undaunted spirit and provided vitally needed medical aid to the critically injured and was a source of encouragement and inspiration to all who observed and served with him. On the morning of the 26th of April, while awaiting medical evacuation, Hospitalman Gibbs was mortally wounded during an enemy mortar attack. Hospitalman Gibbs' loyal devotion to duty and uncommon valor were an inspiration to his comrades and upheld the highest traditions of the United States Naval Service. He gallantly gave his life in the service of his country.

Gibbs was buried in Jonestown Cemetery, Del Rio, Cocke County.

CUMBERLAND

Staff Sergeant Beryl S. Blaylock was born on June 17, 1934, and was originally from Crossville. He served his country in the 772nd Tactical Airlift Squadron, 463rd Tactical Airlift Wing, 7th Air Force. He was a ten-year Air Force veteran when his tour in Vietnam began on March 19, 1968. A little over a month later, on April 26, 1968, Blaylock was killed in a plane crash in hostile conditions at Thua Thien province, South Vietnam; he was thirty-three years old. Blaylock is buried at Mapleview Cemetery in Smyrna, Rutherford County, Tennessee.

Blaylock died in the crash of a C-130B Hercules transport plane during Operation Delaware, which was intended to interdict Viet Cong activities in the A Shau Valley, west of Hue. This operation began on April 19, 1968; six days later, elements of the US Army's 1st Cavalry Division air-assaulted into an abandoned airstrip at A Luoi. The airfield was approximately one mile west of Highway 548, the primary road running through the A Shau Valley and part of the NVA's infiltration route through a jungle-covered and mountainous province of Laos and into a vital sector of South Vietnam. The entire area was a primary north-south artery of the Ho Chi Minh Trail, holding not only the Ho Chi Minh Trail's control center but also one of the largest NVA storage depots outside North Vietnam.

On April 26, flying with ceilings as low as three hundred to five hundred feet, C-130s from the Cam Ranh Bay, Bien Hoa, and Tan Son Nhut Air Bases were tasked with air-dropping supplies to the cavalrymen. The first twenty C-130s received anti-aircraft fire, and seven of them were hit. At 2:14 p.m., Major Lilburn R. Stow, pilot, Major John L McDaniel, pilot, and Sgt. Larry R. Todd, loadmaster, were three of an eight-man aircrew of the twenty-first C-130 (tail number 60–0298) to arrive overhead. Upon arriving, Major Stow established radio contact with ground control for landing instructions. Once cleared, the Hercules made its final approach, when it was hit heavily by NVA .51 caliber (12.7mm) and 37mm AAA fire, and its cargo was set afire. Major Stow attempted an emergency landing on the airstrip but hit trees, crashed, and exploded.

When the wreckage cooled, search-and-rescue (SAR) personnel were able to locate and recover the bodies of five of the eight men on board. They were unable to find any trace of either pilot or the aircraft's loadmaster. At the time the SAR mission was terminated, Lilburn Stow, John McDaniel, and Larry Todd were declared "Killed in Action—Body Not Recovered" (BNR). There is little doubt that Major Stow, Major McDaniel, and Sergeant Todd died in the loss of their aircraft, along with five other men. The crewmen killed in the incident were:

Maj. Lilburn R Stow (772nd Tactical Airlift Squadron)

Cpt. James J McKinstry (772nd Tactical Airlift Squadron)

Maj. John L McDaniel (772nd Tactical Airlift Squadron)

T/Sgt. Russell R Fyan (600th Photo Squadron)

S/Sgt. Beryl S Blaylock (772nd Tactical Airlift Squadron)

Sgt. Daniel J O'Connor (600th Photo Squadron)

Sgt. Larry R Todd (772nd Tactical Airlift Squadron)

A1C Kenneth L Johnson (772nd Tactical Airlift Squadron)

Major Elijah G. Tollett IV was born on August 30, 1930 and was originally from Chattanooga (Hamilton). The son of E. G. Tollett III,

Major Elijah G. Tollett IV.

The B-57 fuselage's tail scraped the surface first, then the body belly landed—belly slapped really. Landing gears-up, the fully fueled and armed bomber scraped along the runway flaming sparks like a high-speed but upside-down car sliding on its roof. Metal to runway, the scraping-screeching noise of a thousand fingernails on blackboards assaulted our ears. The bomber slid on the pavement from runway's center toward the right edge. God knows how, it bounced airborne again then immediately pancaked on the runway shoulder and plowed a shallow furrow for several hundred feet.

The bomber, still upright, rocked from left wing and settled onto the right bomb-laden wing. All was quiet as the cockpit opened and the pilot, Captain Leon Boyd Smith II, climbed out near the wing. Miraculously, [Major Tollett] followed him, both standing near the dipped wing, no doubt surprised to still be alive! A 500-pound bomb directly beneath the wing where they stood exploded. The first millisecond a glass-dome a hundred yards at its base and filled with white-fire engulfed the bomber. The next instant a massive concussion wave literally visible like a fog slapped sentry dogs and handlers to the ground. Seconds later the sound of worlds colliding assaulted and shook the airbase. Debris rained down from the heavens and a large chunk of fuselage crashed on the rim of a gouged red-earth crater.[4]

who was an attorney, judge, and legislator in the city of Crossville (Cumberland County), Major Tollett's grandfather was lieutenant governor of Tennessee and a judge of the Oklahoma Territory. His great-grandfather, Elijah Gore Tollett, was raised in the Sequatchie Valley of East Tennessee and moved to Crossville.

During Vietnam, Tollett served his country in the 13th Bomber Squadron, 6252nd Tactical Fighter Wing, 13th Air Force. He was a fourteen-year veteran when his tour of duty began. On January 12, 1966, Tollett was killed when his Martin B-57 Canberra jet bomber crashed under non-hostile conditions in Quang Nam province, South Vietnam. An eyewitness account of Tollett's death at the Da Nang Air Base in Vietnam follows:

He was thirty-five years old when he died in the explosion of the B-57 at Da Nang. Tollett is buried at Arlington National Cemetery.

FENTRESS

Private First Class Gasper A. Voiles was born on June 24, 1948, and served in the Marine Corps with F Company, 2nd Battalion, 9th Marines, 3rd Marine Division. He was killed in action

Private First Class Gasper A. Voiles.

Corporal John L. Mattock.

in Quang Tri, South Vietnam, on August 25, 1967. He was returned to his hometown and is buried at Fellowship Baptist Church Cemetery, Armathwaite, Tennessee.

GRAINGER

Corporal John L. Mattock was born on May 17, 1948, in Knoxville but grew up in Rutledge. Mattock was the son of Willie George and Bertha Mattock and was also survived by two sisters and one brother. He was a 1966 graduate of Rutledge High School and was a former employee of the Plaza Hotel in Miami, Florida. He attended Indian Ridge Baptist Church and Blaine Presbyterian Church. Mattock entered the Army on April 18, 1967, and went to Vietnam on October 2, 1967. He died on March 12, 1968, in Vietnam from burns received while a

passenger in a military vehicle when the vehicle hit a hostile mine. He was posthumously promoted to corporal. He was part of the HQ and HQ Troop, 3rd Squadron, 5th Armored Cavalry, 9th Infantry Division. Mattock was buried with full military honors at Indian Ridge Cemetery in Grainger County.

GREENE

Private First Class James D. Kelley was born on November 13, 1948, in Greeneville and served with Fox Company, 2nd Battalion, 7th Marines, 1st Marine Division. His tour of duty began on June 21, 1968. He was killed in action in Quang Nam, South Vietnam, by small arms fire on September 19, 1968. He was nineteen. He was buried at Greene Lawn Memory Gardens, Greeneville, Greene County, Tennessee. M. A. Lau, a friend and fellow veteran who served with him, shared this remembrance:

PFC James Daniel Kelley and I were good friends in Vietnam. We were in Fox Company, 2nd Battalion, 7th Marines, 1st Marine

ties and wounded in action. Disregarding his own safety, he fearlessly exposed himself to the intense hostile fire where he succumbed to his bullet wounds. His bold initiative and heroic efforts inspired all who observed him and contributed immeasurably to the accomplishment of Fox Company's mission. . . . [Fourteen] Marines died that day with PFC Kelley. . . . Jim, you will never be forgotten.[5]

HAMBLEN

Specialist Fourth Class Arthur W. Glover was born on September 14, 1939, and was originally from Morristown. He graduated from Bluff City High School in 1957 and worked for the Clark Radio Supply Co. in Bristol before entering the Army in February 1962. An article from the February 11, 1964, Kingsport *Times* reported how Glover died, the victim of an explosive device, likely hidden by Viet Cong guerrillas, which exploded during what seemed to be the most innocuous of pastimes, behind the lines in Saigon:

Mrs. Arthur J. Glover received a letter from her adopted son, shortly after she received a telegram notifying her he had been killed by a bomb in South Vietnam. In the letter, soldier Arthur Glover, 24, asked his mother to send his sweetheart flowers on Valentine´s Day. He had all we had, Mrs. Glover sobbed in a telephone interview. She said he was a very devoted son, and that she had received two letters from him during the past week. He always wrote cheerful letters, she said. Mrs. Glover said he talked about how hot it was in Vietnam, about his girl, Jean Harlow of Bristol, and what he planned to do when he was released from service. Glover was to return to the states in April, and his mother said he and Miss Harlow, 22, planned to marry then. . . . Glover was watching a softball game when a bomb exploded

Private First Class James D. Kelley.

Division, FMF. In June 1968, we both joined up with Fox Company in the Philippines. We completed several weeks of jungle warfare training and then we boarded the USS *Ogden* and headed for [Southeast] Asia via the South China Sea. We had no idea that we were heading straight into hell. Jim was born in Greeneville, Tennessee on November 13, 1948 and was only 19 and a half years old when he was killed in action. Jim had been in Vietnam for three months and had already participated in 4 or 5 major combat operations. PFC Kelley, who was a rifleman, showed extraordinary heroism on September 19, 1968, during Operation Mameluke Thrust, also known as Operation Dodge City. Fox Company was conducting a reconnaissance in force in Quang Nam Province when we encountered a large enemy force employing heavy automatic weapons and accurate sniper fire which pinned down elements of the company and caused numerous casual-

beneath the bleachers in Saigon, killing him and PFC Donald R. Taylor of Harrisburg, Pa., and injuring 23 others.

He was buried at Weaver Cemetery, Bristol, Sullivan County, Tennessee.

HAMILTON

Private First Class Bruce Ellis Armstrong was born on October 16, 1948, in Chattanooga, and he attended the Chattanooga State Technical Institute, from which his 1968 yearbook picture is gratefully acknowledged. Armstrong served his country in Vietnam with the Army's D Company, 3rd Battalion, 1st Infantry, 11th Infantry Brigade. His tour of duty began on July 19, 1969. Armstrong had been in Vietnam for slightly under eight months when he was criti-

Corporal Augusto J. Garcia.

cally wounded in hostile action in Quang Ngai Province, South Vietnam, on April 1, 1970; he died eleven days later on April 12, 1970, at the age of twenty-one. He is buried at Chattanooga National Cemetery.

Corporal Augusto J. Garcia was born on March 2, 1942, in Puerto Rico where he was also raised. Later, he moved to Tennessee, where he lived in Cookeville, attending Tennessee Technological University. He served his country in the Vietnam War as a four-year veteran of the United States Marine Corps with B Company, 1st Battalion, 27th Marines, 1st Marine Division. His tour in Vietnam began on July 17, 1967. Exactly one year later, on July 17, 1968, Garcia was killed by an explosive device in Quang Nam, South Vietnam, at the age of twenty-six.

Lieutenant Colonel Leslie Earl Harris Jr. was born in Gary, Indiana, on March 20, 1920. He grew up in Chattanooga and attended

Private First Class Bruce Ellis Armstrong.

Lieutenant Colonel Leslie Earl Harris Jr.

graduation in May 1950. He adopted her five-year-old son from her prior marriage, William Paul "Scooter" Harris.

Harris became a bomber pilot and was one of the first pilots trained in the B-50, the successor to the B-29 Superfortress. In 1951, he survived the crash of a B-50 in Britain. He served as a bomber pilot in the Korean War; after Strategic Air Command duty, he received an MBA from Georgetown University. He was also selected to attend the Air Force Command and General Staff College. He served as an assistant to the chief of Air Force Operations Planning and Training at the Pentagon for four years. He then began a tour in Vietnam, and his wife relocated to San Angelo while he was overseas.

Harris's Vietnam tour began on May 21, 1967. He was assigned as the operations officer for the 4th Air Commando Squadron (ACS), 14th Air Commando Special Operations Wing, 7th Air Force. On May 5, 1968, he was the commander of a Douglas AC-47D (a DC-3 transport modified to serve as a gunship, which planes were sometimes ironically known as "Puff the Magic Dragon" after the Peter, Paul, and Mary song) that was flying a "spooky" mission near Pleiku, supporting ground troops. The aircraft received ground fire and was shot down; all aboard the AC-47D perished. He was only two weeks away from completing his Vietnam tour.

Harris was buried with full military honors at the Fairmount Cemetery in San Angelo, Texas. His awards and decorations included the Air Force Pilot Wings, Silver Star, Legion of Merit, Distinguished Flying Cross, Bronze Star, Purple Heart, Air Medal, Air Force Commendations Medal, Air Force Longevity Medal with Three Arrow Heads, Good Conduct Medal, National Defense Service Medal with two stars, American Defense Service Medal, Korean Service Medal,

Baylor Preparatory School. He attended the University of Chattanooga during freshman year and, later, Purdue University. Enlisting in the US Army during World War II, Harris served in the China-Burma-India (CBI) theater in the Engineers, achieving the rank of master sergeant. Prior to the end of the war, he received a Congressional appointment from Representative Estes Kefauver of Tennessee to attend West Point. He entered the Academy in the fall of 1945 as a plebe, following three months' attendance at Cornell University taking preparatory classes. He was graduated from the USMA in the summer of 1949; due to his desire to fly, he took a commission in the Air Force. He was commissioned as a 2nd Lieutenant and, during flight training at Goodfellow Air Force Base in San Angelo, Texas, met his wife-to-be, May Hemphill, the granddaughter of the founders of Hemphill-Wells Department Stores. They married following his flight school

Staff Sergeant James E. (Jim) Bowman.

Master Sergeant James C. Helton.

and the United Nations Korean Service Medal, among others. He was survived by his wife and his son, who was a student at Texas A&M. Harris Hall at Goodfellow AFB was named in Harris's honor in 1985. His beloved wife May died in 2007 and now rests next to him.[6]

Staff Sergeant James E. (Jim) Bowman of Jonesborough (Washington County) was also killed in this same action. He was born on August 28, 1933. Bowman served alongside Harris in the 4th Air Commando Squadron, 14th Air Commando Special Operations Wing, 7th Air Force. He was thirty-four at the time of his death. He was buried at McInturff-Bennett Cemetery, Marbleton, Unicoi County, Tennessee.

HANCOCK

Master Sergeant James C. Helton was born on October 8, 1930, and served with the 5th Special Forces Group, the famed "Green Berets." His tour of duty in Vietnam began on November 28, 1966; he was a member of Special Forces Team A-255 when he was killed by small arms fire on April 17, 1967, near Plei Me in Pleiku Province, South Vietnam. He was thirty-six at the time of his death.

HAWKINS

Private First Class Thomas D. Bernard was born on May 30, 1947, and was from Rogersville. He was a member of B Company, 1st Battalion, 502nd Infantry, 101st Airborne Division. His tour began on March 7, 1968, and he was killed in action on June 16, 1968, in Thua Thien, South Vietnam. Bernard was buried at North Fork Baptist Church Cemetery, Rogersville. Friend and relative Gary Beal remembered Bernard this way:

Tommy and I are distant cousins. He was born in 1947 in the small Tennessee community of Beech Creek. He was a victim of rheumatic fever, falling two school years behind. We entered the Army together, 20 September 67, and went to Fort Campbell for Basic Training. He then went on to Infantry Training at Fort Polk. We were able to write in RVN, and Tommy never had an unkind word to say to anyone, even the NVA. We fought together in the Tet Offensive, only being concerned for myself and his buddies in the 101st Airborne division at Hue. He was KIA June 1968. Tommy was awarded the Bronze Star, Purple Heart and Combat Infantryman Badge, 11 total military awards from the United States and RVN.[7]

Fellow soldier Bill Foreman was with Bernard on the day he died:

I was there when he died. We were sweeping through a village. Bernard was making his way through a bamboo hedgerow when he triggered a booby trap. I went to see if there was anything I could do to help. One of our medics got there first and did all he could, but there was no hope. . . . We had spent a fair amount of time swapping stories. There was always plenty of time for that. He was a farm boy from the south. I remember him telling me how to gain maximum cooperation from a balky horse. Seemingly an otherwise gentle sort, he said you had to beat the **** out of a horse to get it to go along with your agenda. Not exactly a horse whisperer. I miss him.

Sergeant First Class Luther V. Gilreath was born on July 6, 1932, in Surgoinsville. He served with C Company, 1st Battalion, 7th Cavalry, 1st Cavalry Division during the battle of the Ia Drang Valley near Pleiku in October and November 1965. This was the first major US combat engagement of the Vietnam War. The battle was documented in the book *We Were Soldiers Once . . . and Young,* by retired lieu-

Sergeant First Class Luther V. Gilreath.

tenant general Harold G. (Hal) Moore, who was Gilreath's battalion commander. Gilreath died in the Ia Drang valley on November 16, 1965, in the savage fighting for Landing Zone X-Ray. Moore recalled Gilreath as "a tall, slender paratrooper who hailed from Surgoinsville, Tennessee," and who was serving as the platoon sergeant of First Platoon, Charlie Company. Moore further related how, after recovering the body of the Second Platoon leader, Moore and his battalion's command sergeant major, Basil Plumley, located Gilreath's body and brought him back to the landing zone (the infamous LZ X-Ray) to begin the long journey home.[8] Gilreath is buried at the Fort Benning Post Cemetery in Georgia.

JEFFERSON

Private First Class William L. Mott of Jefferson City was born on September 14, 1949, and died on January 29, 1969, in Vietnam. The son of Willie W. Mott and Polly A. Mott, he enlisted in the Marine Corps on January 8, 1968; arrived in Vietnam on July 21, 1968; and was assigned for duty with the Sniper Platoon, HQ Company, 7th Marines, 1st Marine Division. During Operation Linn River, the men of E Company, 2nd Battalion, 26th Marines were in their defensive perimeter near the Da Hoa An village complex in the Dien Ban district of Quang Nam Province, when they were hit with incoming enemy rifle fire. Mott, who had been attached to the unit as a scout-sniper, was hit and killed by the hostile fire. Fellow Marine scout-sniper Jay Taylor's 2009 book, *Point of Aim, Point of Impact*, devoted a chapter to Mott, whom he called "a big kid from Tennessee with a thick southern accent." Taylor added that Mott and he "hit it off right away."[9] Mott was buried at Jefferson Memorial Gardens Cemetery, Jefferson City.

JOHNSON

Corporal Donald T. Sluder was born on February 22, 1947, and was from Mountain City. He served with B Company, 7th Engineering Battalion, 1st Marine Division, arriving in Vietnam on September 10, 1967. He died of wounds slightly over a month later on October 18. He was twenty years old. The 7th Engineer Battalion's command chronology (war diary) for October 1967 contains the following entry: "090915H B-7 1st Plt. Two men using a pick to break asphalt on Route 1 at BT 039628 struck

Corporal Donald T. Sluder.

booby-trapped grenade, resulting in two WIA, both medivaced [*sic*]. The two wounded men were Corporal Don Sluder and Jerry Baker. Baker was the more seriously injured, but it was Cpl. Sluder who died nine days afterwards, on 18 October 1967, apparently due to complications from a blood clot. As far as can be determined, Jerry Baker recovered—there is no one named Baker in the casualty database who satisfies the circumstances."[10]

This remembrance provided to the ETVMA is by Sluder's fellow veteran, Rich Hafer:

> This is what I remember of the day he and Jerry Baker got hit. We arrived out on Highway 1 early that morning to finish some repairs we had started the day before. We should have been more alert as the usually heavily traveled road was empty of traffic that morning—nothing—zip. . . . As everyone

was gathering tools to start the job, Smith and I grabbed the pick and shovel, leaving the jackhammer work for someone else. As Smith and I headed towards a hole in the road, to start cleaning out the loose materials, Cpl. Roman barked out, "Hey, you two, get your asses over here. Smith and Hafer, you two are running the jackhammer today." After pleading our case with Roman, we reluctantly handed over our tools to Sluder and Baker, who proceeded to the pothole in the road. As Cpl. Roman started the air compressor, the engine took off with a roar. At this moment, Sluder stuck his pick into the pothole, which was booby-trapped. With the noise of the air compressor we never heard the explosion, just the thud and vibration. We quickly turned, only to see both men, like in slow motion, fall back. . . . Sluder died, but I'm not sure when, if it was the same day or a day later at Da Nang Hospital. We have had conflicting reports on this. Jerry Baker, the last I heard, was in a hospital in Japan but he seems to have just disappeared. Some say he lost his life as a result of these injuries, but no one can confirm this. Sluder was due to rotate back to the states 10 days prior to this tragedy but chose to extend his duty in Vietnam by six months. Isn't it strange how life can be? It gives you all these roads to travel; choose the wrong one and you end up a statistic. . . .

Dick Phaneuf's recollection essentially confirmed Hafer's account and added further details:

In the morning, when they started again [after taking an overnight break on the road work], the VC had hidden one of our frag grenades down under the debris in one of the holes. When Sluder and Baker removed the debris, the grenade blew. I was leaving the company that day and stopped by at China Beach hospital on the way. When I saw Baker in the hospital that afternoon, all I could see was one of his eyes, for the

bandages on his head and face and his body had stitches and clamps up the stomach. He was apparently pretty close to the grenade because he had blast injuries in addition to the fragments. . . . Sluder, on the other hand, was sitting up in bed with two medical guys picking fragments out of his legs. We talked normally and he looked pretty good in spite of being peppered by the little pieces of wire that our grenades put out. He did have one busted eardrum also, 'cause he couldn't hear me on one side of the bed. I was shocked later to hear that a blood clot had killed him, and I never heard what happened to Baker.

Sluder is buried at Phillippi Cemetery, Mountain City, Tennessee.

KNOX

Staff Sergeant Michael R. Conner was born on September 17, 1947. His tour of duty began on October 25, 1969, and he served with Detachment 2, 6994th Security Squadron, 7th Air Force. He died on April 22, 1970, at the age of twenty-two in Thua Thien, South Vietnam, in the crash of a Douglas EC-47 electronics airplane, call sign "Cap-53." The shoot-down of Cap-53 on April 22, 1970, was recounted by Conner's fellow crewmember, Danny E. Russell:

Our crew consisted of Lt. George M. Wall, pilot, Lt. Nasipak, co-pilot, Capt. Carl Lemon, navigator, SSgt. Edward J. Mosely, flight engineer, all with 362nd TEWS [Tactical Electronic Warfare Squadron] and Ron Lawlor was our 203; Phil was in charge of the back-end crew, consisting of SSgt. Michael R. Conner and myself. Mike and I were in charge of scheduling, and we were really excited about flying together and we had made it a point to handpick this crew to fly with.

Mike had just recovered from a broken finger and I had just come off DNIF [duty

Staff Sergeant Michael R. Conner.

not involving flying] due to hernia surgery. . . . We took off after our normal routine and flew an uneventful mission. I think we took off about 3:30 AM with a six-hour mission. It was the kind that you knew who you were after and where he was supposed to be, but he just didn't come up. We joked back and forth, saying he knew WHO was up here and he was afraid to come up with all the EXPERTS up here ready to copy.

About 10 minutes before time to RTB [return to base], he [the enemy] came up and we asked the AC for permission to stay on site to get him. Permission [was granted], so we dug in and did our thing. Capt. Lemon got on him and directed the plane into position, I think we had a fix on him when KABOOM. Reports say we got hit with 37mm [antiaircraft fire] but I looked down and saw at least a 4-inch hole right next to the Doppler set. Capt. Lemon was the only one hit. I think a piece of shrapnel went through close to his elbow—not too much blood and he did an excellent job. He hung right there and

between him and Phil, they got out the MAYDAY and gave our exact position.

Rescue was Johnny on the spot, and other than me trying to clean my pants, I think everyone did a fine professional job. Our first intent was to get to sea because the damage was to the rear end control and the front-end crew didn't have a lot of options. We lost one engine immediately and the other one was smoking pretty bad, so going over the mountains was out. Next, I think they tried for a landing strip, but rescue said it was VC controlled.

Next option was to bail out, so Mike and I went to the jump door and tried to open it. Jammed due to the concussion. We tried and tried, and finally the door just fell off!!!!!! We looked at each other and both agreed we were way too low to jump, and about that time, Lt. Wall looked back at us expecting the back end to be clean and ordered us to strap in and prepare for crash landing. As we went forward, Mike was ahead of me and he automatically went to my seat, so I took his rear seat. I had just buckled in and looked out the left window to see the wing hit a tree and break loose. I honestly don't know if I was knocked out or not, I did realize that something very heavy was on me when I tried to move, one of the consoles had broken loose and had landed on me. As I got free, I started hearing moans and groans, so I knew someone else had made it also.

As we slowly started to unpile each other, I discovered my good friend Mike, who had gone forward and had taken my seat, was killed. To this day I still ask GOD why. This man was married and all he could do is talk about his wife and the baby they were about to have. Upon reaching the hospital I learned that Capt. Wall has also been killed in the crash. Ron, Phil and Capt. Lemon were all accounted for and visually seen. I never saw Lt. Nasipak or SSgt Mosely.

After returning to base and starting to work we learned that Mike's widow had given birth to a son one month to the day after the crash. Mike Jr. was born 22 May 1970. We took up a collection and started a college fund for him, and I must say 63 guys gave till it hurt. I'm so proud of them.

Upon returning stateside, Phil and I and Alan Brack and his wife went to Tennessee to visit the widow and son who never got to see Daddy. Mike's parents and his widow's parents also attended.[11]

Conner was buried in Woodhaven Memorial Gardens, Claxton, Anderson County.

Senior Master Sergeant Paul Leonard Foster was born on November 20, 1945, and was a graduate of Knoxville's Young High School, class of 1963. He served with the 606th Air Commando Squadron, 56th Air Commando Wing, 7th Air Force. He died on December 29, 1967, at the age of twenty-nine in Laos.

On December 29, 1967, Captain Carlos Cruz, pilot, Captain William Potter, navigator, and Staff Sergeant Foster, aerial gunner, comprised the crew of a World War II-vintage, twin-engine Douglas A-26A Invader that de-

parted Nakhon Phanom Airfield in Thailand on an operational mission to interdict NVA activity in an area of Laos adjacent to the DMZ separating the two Vietnams. Shortly before this flight, Laotian premier Prince Souvanna Phouma had reported the incursion of North Vietnamese troops into his country, stating that communist forces had launched a general offensive against Royal Laotian forces in southern Laos. While North Vietnam denied fielding troops, ample intelligence refuted the North's claims. At 1:58 p.m., as the A-26 bomber made an attack pass on its target, it was struck by enemy ground fire and crashed on the east side of a mountain with a jungle-covered valley continuing on to the east. The crash site was approximately three miles southeast of Ban Nam, twenty-three miles northwest of Muang Xepon, Savannakhet Province, Laos, twenty-five miles west of the Lao/South Vietnamese border, and fourteen miles south of the DMZ.

Cruz, Potter, and Foster were among almost six hundred Americans who disappeared in Laos. While the Laotians admitted holding "tens of tens" of living American prisoners of war, these men were never negotiated for, either by direct negotiation between the two countries or through the Paris Peace Accords—which ended the Vietnam War—since Laos was not a party to that agreement.

In early 1993, a joint American/Laotian field team excavated the Invader's crash site. In addition to aircraft wreckage and personal effects, the team recovered human remains later identified as those of Carlos Cruz, William Potter, and Paul Foster. All three are now buried together in Arlington National Cemetery.[12]

Specialist Fourth Class Donald A. Sherrod was born on June 2, 1943, the son of F. J. and Mariana Ancker Sherrod and the husband of

Senior Master Sergeant Paul Leonard Foster.

Barbara Sherrod. He was a 1952 graduate of East High School and a member of Fifth Avenue Baptist Church, and enlisted in the United States Army in 1963. While serving in South Korea, Sherrod volunteered for service in Vietnam. Sherrod left Knoxville on January 6, 1966, to start his tour of duty with A Company, 1st Battalion, 7th Cavalry Regiment, 1st Cavalry Division, which had fought under Lieutenant Colonel Hal Moore's command in fall 1965 at the Ia Drang Valley, where SFC Luther V. Gilreath was killed. Sherrod was killed in action on August 8, 1966.

On August 1, 1966, units of the 1st Battalion, 7th Cavalry, were once again inserted into the Ia Drang Valley on a search-and-destroy operation codenamed Paul Revere II. Although evidence of the enemy's presence was found during the first week, 1/7 Cav had little enemy contact. That changed shortly after noon on August 8 when A Company made contact with a large enemy force near LZ Juliet. A Company's 3rd Platoon was "on point" and made the initial contact with North Vietnamese troops. They aggressively pursued and were immediately hit by several enemy heavy and light machine-guns, cutting them off from the rest of the company. Most of the 3rd Platoon was able to exfiltrate back to the company perimeter, where A Company found itself under heavy attack. By 3:00 p.m., after artillery and air strikes, the NVA broke contact and withdrew. But A Company paid a high price: twenty-five dead, including Donald A. Sherrod, and thirty-six more wounded. His Silver Star award citation reads:

> For gallantry in action: on 8 August 1966, Specialist Sherrod distinguished himself by exceptional heroism in action, while serving as a rifleman with Company A, 1st Battalion, 7th Cavalry during a search and clear operation in the Republic of Vietnam. As the company was setting up a perimeter, Specialist Sherrod noticed several enemy soldiers trying to penetrate a weak spot in the defense. Leading the men of his fire team, Specialist Sherrod advanced to a key position, firing his individual weapon and throwing hand grenades. His action so inspired his soldiers that they joined him at the position. During the engagement, Specialist Sherrod was wounded, but continued to fight and lead in the defense. Constantly maneuvering from man to man to offer encouragement and assist the wounded, Specialist Sherrod fell mortally wounded as he attempted to render aid to another casualty. His truly outstanding bravery and devotion to duty significantly contributed to the success of the company defense. Specialist Sherrod's courageous action under fire is in keeping with the highest traditions of the military service, and reflects great credit upon himself, his unit, and the United States Army.

Private First Class David S. Whitman.

He was buried on August 18, 1966, at Berry Highland Memorial Cemetery in Knoxville with full military honors.

Private First Class David S. Whitman was born in Knoxville on May 25, 1949, and began his tour of duty in Vietnam on January 20, 1969. He was killed in action February 27, 1969, at the age of nineteen in Quang Tri, South Vietnam. He was a member of G Company, 2nd Battalion, 9th Marines, 3rd Marine Division. He was buried in Knoxville National Cemetery on March 11, 1969. A brief article in the *Knoxville News Sentinel* on March 5, 1969, provided an account of his short life:

> Pfc. Whitman had barely escaped death three weeks ago, according to a letter, one of two his parents received yesterday, the same day they learned he was killed. The young man reported he had been rescued by helicopter during a narrow escape, after which his unit was given two days of rest before being sent back to the front lines on patrol. Pfc. Whitman joined the Marine Corps as a volunteer last summer after graduation from Austin-East. He finished his basic training at Camp Pendleton, Calif., and spent Christmas with his family. He died February 27 of a gunshot wound in the stomach, his father said.

LOUDON

Corporal John H. Simpson was born on August 1, 1945, and was originally from Loudon. He served as a machine gunner in B Company, 1st Battalion, 1st Marines, 1st Marine Division. On May 13, 1967, at the age of twenty-one, Simpson was killed in action in Quang Nam Province, South Vietnam. He was buried at his family plot in Loudon. The following is a story about Simpson shared with the ETVMA by his relative, Joe Harrison:

Corporal John H. Simpson.

John Harrison Simpson, cousin to Benjamin F. Harrison [who was] killed in WWII, grew up in Loudon and graduated from Loudon High School, after which he entered the University of Tennessee with plans to follow his father and study law. After two years at the University, Johnny volunteered for the U.S. Marines. He was selected the outstanding member of his basic training class and then volunteered to serve in Vietnam. He was killed in action and is buried in his family plot near their Loudon home. Johnny was descended from a sixth-generation Tennessee family whose members served in both the American Revolution and the War of 1812.

MARION

Corporal John D. Martin was born on January 22, 1948. He was from Jasper, where he

Corporal John D. Martin.

attended Marion County High School, graduating in 1967. For all who knew him, according to his memorial program, he was courteous, kindly, modest, and thoughtful, and he "will long be remembered as one of Marion County High School's natural athletes. He excelled in football, basketball, and baseball. His preparation for professional baseball was interrupted by his call to enlist. . . . Willingly and courageously he fought for his country."

Martin served with the 3rd Platoon, A Company, 1st Battalion, 502nd Infantry, 101st Airborne Division. His tour of duty started on January 7, 1969. Just six months later, he was killed in South Vietnam on July 8, 1969, at the age of twenty-one. He is buried at Chattanooga National Cemetery. Classmate Michael Bible remembered Martin this way: "John David and I played football together at Marion County High. He was by far the best athlete on our team [in] football, basketball and track and

later minor league baseball. Segregation didn't go easy in Tennessee in the mid-60s, but our football team was so happy to see John David arrive. We later found out that he had just as much class as a human being as he did as an athlete. What a loss for us all."

MCMINN

Specialist Fourth Class Danny R. Roberts was born on April 17, 1949, in Etowah. A member of Company C, 2nd Battalion, 1st Infantry, 196th Light Infantry Brigade, American Division, his tour of duty began on August 20, 1969. He was killed in action on February 4, 1970, near Quang Tin, South Vietnam. Tyler Harper, who served as Roberts's platoon leader, wrote: "I was there when he was killed. He was within 25 yards of me and two other men when he was hit by a NVA soldier on the opposite side of a hedgerow we were going through. Danny was a brave man and good soldier. My job was

Specialist Fourth Class Danny R. Roberts.

easier thanks to men like Danny. Danny was a hero who was always taking risks to protect other men." Roberts is buried at Shady Grove Cemetery, Tellico Plains, Monroe County, Tennessee. His cemetery marker includes the text of a letter that Danny wrote to his family and friends, which reads:

> I want this put on the largest stone at the head of my grave.
>
> To whom it may concern: I lived on this here climate 20 years. The first 19 were full of excitement and pleasure, then it happened, I got drafted into the Army and sent to Vietnam to fight a useless war. With God's help I'll make it to Heaven. I've done spent my time in Hell. Take heed, dear friends, I died needlessly, along with a lot of my comrades, but I did my best. This is a cruel world that we live in. Even though, I consider myself the luckiest guy that ever lived. Because of you, my many dear friends and relatives and because I had the greatest mom and dad in the world. Goodbye for now, we'll meet again though on that great judgment morning. May God bless and keep all of us and bring everlasting peace.

MEIGS

James T. Davis was drafted into the Army on October 25, 1966. Shortly after he completed basic training in Louisiana, he was promoted to sergeant and received orders for Vietnam. On February 15, 1968, during some of the heaviest fighting of the Tet Offensive, Davis fell to enemy fire as a result of multiple shrapnel wounds.[13]

MONROE

Corporal James E. Self was from Madisonville and was born on October 4, 1947. He served

Corporal James E. Self.

with A Battery, 2nd Battalion, 13th Artillery, II Field Force Artillery. His Vietnam tour of duty started on February 9, 1968, and ended when he was killed by hostile fire in Tay Ninh on August 22, 1968, at the age of twenty. Self was buried at Sunset Cemetery, Madisonville. Fellow veteran William E. Novakovic provided this appreciation of his buddy:

> [Self] was assigned as a cannon crew non-commissioned officer, which would have him performing duties as gunner, assistant gunner, or section chief. As the unit had 24-hour firing responsibility, SP4 Self would have found himself performing any of these interchangeable responsibilities.
>
> A Battery operated out of the many fire support bases in Tay Ninh Province during 1968. No matter which base they were occupying, the sight of Nui Ba Dinh, the Black Virgin Mountain, was always present. No

matter which fire support base they occupied near Nui Ba Dinh, A Battery received random sniper, mortar, and, rocket fire.

Corporal James Self was killed by small arms fire, presumably sniper rounds, six months into his tour with A Battery. . . . Unit veterans from Service Battery always commented that resupplying A Battery with ammunition, rations, and equipment was a dangerous task. A Battery seemed to be assigned to the most dangerous locations in III Corps during 1968–1970. A Battery seemed to be located in the center of a bull's-eye target in the middle of Indian Country. Resupply of A Battery was always a dicey assignment because of the fire support missions A Battery drew during those years.

Corporal James Self was assigned to a unit accustomed to dangerous assignments. He served in a leadership role with a 105mm howitzer crew for six months. Our veterans speak highly of the gun crew leaders, many of whom were drafted into the Army like James Self. Life at the fire support bases in Tay Ninh Province was filled with ever-present danger of shelling and ground attack. Leaders like Corporal Jim Self set the example for the men in their crews. The gun crews of A Battery, B Battery, and C Battery all had men like Jim Self leading by example. Small wonder why the Red Dragon Clan earned the reputation of being General Ewell's Fire Brigade in II Field Force Artillery.[14]

MORGAN

Sergeant Clarence E. Barnes served with B Company, 1st Battalion, 2nd Infantry, 1st Infantry Division. He was born on August 16, 1943, and his last residence was in Harriman, Roane County. His tour in Vietnam began on December 20, 1965. He was killed by enemy fire on April 11, 1966 at the age of twenty-two. He was buried in Roane Memorial Gardens Cemetery, Rockwood, Roane County.

Sergeant Clarence E. Barnes.

POLK

Sergeant First Class Jeptha J. (Jeppie, or to his troops, "Pop") Payne of Copper Hill was more than twice the age of the men who served under him. Born on August 25, 1919, and nearing retirement after twenty-one years in the Army, he knew that his son, Specialist Fourth Class Larry Payne, stationed at Fort Meade, Maryland, would not have to go to Vietnam as long as he was there, owing to a Department of Defense regulation restricting family members' combat service.[15] The elder Payne served with A Company, 14th Engineering Battalion, 45th Engineering Group, 18th Engineering Brigade. His tour of duty began on January 11, 1967; he was killed in action on August 16, 1968. He was one of twenty men killed when NVA/VC

much family meant to SSG Payne and . . . he took care of us kids in the unit."

Sergeant First Class Jeptha J. Payne.

forces penetrated the perimeter of LZ Nancy in Quang Tri Province, South Vietnam. He was forty-eight. He was buried at Mobile Cemetery, Epworth, Fannin County, Georgia.

Carl Meier, who served in Payne's unit, paid this tribute: "I remember you as a man that extended his tour to keep his son out of war. I remember that you were back in country less than two weeks when we were overrun on August 16, 1968. I remember that night and I remember how you died." Likewise, Michael Swift, who served with him, recalled that the NVA regular troops who stormed LZ Nancy on the night of August 15–16 "far exceeded our strength," adding: "I knew Pop Payne as a gentle dad to all of us. I was 19. I know he extended his tour there to keep his son out of [Vietnam]. If I remember correctly, he had recently returned from the states. [I know] how

RHEA

Staff Sergeant James R. "Sandy" Potter was born on February 21, 1947, and was from Daisy, Tennessee. He served as a scout team member of D Troop, 1st Squadron, 4th Cavalry, 1st Infantry Division, and began his tour in Vietnam on June 4, 1969. He was killed in a helicopter crash on September 11, 1969, at the age of twenty-two in Tay Ninh Province, South Vietnam. He is buried at Hamilton Memorial Gardens, Hixson, Hamilton County, Tennessee. Fellow veteran David De la Rocha remembered Potter as a "Dark Horse hero":

Staff Sergeant James R. (Sandy) Potter.

He was part of the Big Red One's elite Dark Horse scout teams that flew recon missions in the Big Red One's area of operation. On this day, Sergeant Potter was a crew chief in the back seat of a Loach [Hughes OH-6], an observation helicopter being piloted by scout pilot Bill Jones. The scout team was being escorted by a Cobra helicopter or gunship. It was the Loach's job to scout a certain area and if the Loach drew fire from the ground, the Cobra gunship would then come in from out of altitude, usually at 1,500 feet, and take out the enemy target. On this day the scout ship would be working an area known as the Razorback area or Nui Tha La. The area was also a staging area for the enemy to bring in men and materiel into Vietnam from Cambodia. While scouting the area, the scout pilot Bill Jones reported seeing men and movement down below his Cobra gunship. The gunship next reported that the scout ship was taking heavy enemy fire from below and was hit and going down. The Loach went down after being hit by the enemy fire and burst into flames after hitting a tree on the way down, which punctured the fuel tank. The pilot was able to make it out of the wreck severely burned and was lifted out of the area by the Cobra crew who took heroic measures and landed near the wreck with the enemy still lurking around the downed Loach. Sergeant Potter unfortunately was killed in the hail of enemy gunfire that brought down the Loach. Rest in Peace, Sergeant Potter.[16]

ROANE

Private First Class Bradley K. (Keith) Watts was born on January 19, 1948, and was originally from Harriman, Tennessee. He served as an infantryman in E Company, 51st Infantry, Americal Division. He began his tour in Vietnam on August 3, 1968. A little over a month later, on September 16, 1968, Watts was killed in action

Private First Class Bradley K. (Keith) Watts.

under hostile conditions in Quang Nam province, South Vietnam. He was twenty years old. Watts was buried in Dyllis Cemetery, Roane County. The following is a tribute by Neil Wilson, a classmate and fellow Vietnam veteran:

Both Keith and myself attended the same small high school in the small town of Oliver Springs in the hills of East Tennessee. While the wall reflects Keith as being from Harriman, Tennessee, that was only his mailing address; he attended and graduated from Oliver Springs High School in 1966. I graduated in 1965. I can still picture in my mind the tall, lanky teenager from those days. We were both members of the Future Farmers of America. I left for the Marines after graduation and had lost touch with Keith. By 1968, I knew he was both in the Army and in Vietnam. I was headed for home late on a Friday night in September of 1968 from Camp Lejeune, North Carolina with a set of orders for Vietnam. When I started getting close to the Tennessee state line, I began fiddling with the radio, trying to pick up a Knoxville radio station. As soon as one came in, the announcer said, "East Tennessee soldier is killed in Vietnam." For some reason that I still can't explain, I knew the name would be Keith Watts. It was. I pulled over to the side of the road for a short pause.[17]

SCOTT

James D. West was born in Oneida on August 20, 1948, and grew up in Scott County's Foster Crossroads community. He enlisted in the Marine Corps in Ohio, where he was working at the time. Captain A. C. Slater, his company commander, wrote West's parents the following account of their son's death on May 15, 1967, from wounds sustained in a firefight:

> The untimely death of your son, Lance Corporal James D. West, at 2:35 p.m. on May

Lance Corporal James D. West.

15, 1967, at the Station Hospital NSA, near the city of Da Nang, in Quang Nam Province, Republic of Vietnam, is a source of great sorrow to me and to his many friends in Company "A."

As you know, James was an automatic rifleman in our second platoon. On the afternoon of May 13, our company was assigned a search and destroy mission in the area near Phu An. James' platoon was our lead element of this operation. As they moved out to their objective, they were fired on by a large force of Viet Cong. There was a heavy exchange of fire and James fell seriously wounded. A corpsman rushed to his side and quickly administered first aid. Within minutes he was flown by helicopter to a field hospital where he received the best medical care possible. James's courage and calmness just prior to his evacuation to the hospital led us to believe he was going to be all right. It was a great shock to us all when we were informed by the hospital that James had passed away. . . .

Even though James had been with us only a short time, he became very highly respected and well-liked by his fellow Marines. It is a privilege and an honor to be associated with such persons as your son, and my personal grief is great when such a fine man must pass from us. You can be sure that his many friends share in your sorrow at this sad time.

SEQUATCHIE

Sergeant Walter L. Clark was born on April 21, 1947. He was with Company C, 1st Battalion, 8th Infantry, 4th Infantry Division. He was killed on October 29, 1967, while conducting a search-and-destroy operation northwest of Ban Me Thuot in the Central Highlands of Vietnam. He was killed at the age of twenty by "friendly fire," when a round fell short. He was survived

Sergeant Walter L. Clark.

Specialist Fourth Class Dannie A. Carr.

by seven sisters and one brother. Clark was buried in Hillside Cemetery, Belleville, Wayne County, Michigan.

SEVIER

Specialist Fourth Class Dannie A. Carr was born on June 30, 1947, and was originally from Sevierville. He served as an infantryman in B Company, 2nd Battalion, 7th Cavalry, 1st Cavalry Division. He was a one-year veteran of the Army when his tour began on November 5, 1968. On July 3, 1969, Carr was killed by artillery fire under hostile conditions in Tay Ninh Province, South Vietnam. He was twenty-two years old. He is buried at Zion Grove Cemetery in Sevier County, Tennessee.

Private First Class Randy R. Cogdill was

Private First Class Randy R. Cogdill.

born on December 5, 1947, and was the son of Mr. and Mrs. Claude W. Cogdill. He was originally from Sevierville. He served as an infantryman in D Company, 1st Battalion, 27th Infantry, 25th Infantry ("Tropic Lightning") Division. His tour in Vietnam began on October 8, 1967. Twenty days later, on October 28, 1967, Cogdill was killed under hostile conditions in Tay Ninh Province, South Vietnam, at the age of nineteen. He is buried at Shiloh Memorial Cemetery in Pigeon Forge, Tennessee. His friend and fellow casualty John Coon provided this recollection of his buddy to the ETVMA: "We were both shot, standing side by side on that terrible day; I survived and you did not, God only knows why? As long as I live, you will not be forgotten."

Harry G. Hodges was a construction equipment operator with the 9th Naval Construction Battalion, one of the units of the Navy's "Seabees." He was born on October 10, 1947, and was from Sevierville. He was killed in action on January 14, 1968. He is buried at Boyds Creek Cemetery, Sevier County. Hodges's Silver Star citation for valor reads as follows:

Seabee Harry G. Hodges.

The President of the United States of America takes pride in presenting the Silver Star (Posthumously) to Equipment Operator Constructionman Harry G. Hodges (NSN: B-320923), United States Navy, for conspicuous gallantry and intrepidity in action while serving with the Security Platoon, Headquarters Company, United States Naval Construction Battalion NINE, in connection with operations against hostile forces in the Republic of Vietnam. During the early morning hours of 14 January 1968, while on duty as sentry in a defensive position at a construction site near Da Nang, Constructionman Hodges and a companion were attacked by the enemy, with a grenade being thrown into their position. Disregarding his own safety by electing not to vacate the position, Constructionman Hodges unhesitatingly placed himself between his comrade and the grenade and attempted to throw the grenade out of the position. Unable to clear the grenade before it exploded, Constructionman Hodges sacrificed his life to save that of his fellow Seabee. His gallant efforts and bold initiative in the face of extreme danger were in keeping with the highest traditions of the United States Naval Service. He gallantly gave his life for his country.

SULLIVAN

Kingsport native Lance Corporal William F. Dykes was born on November 5, 1946, and was the son of Mr. and Mrs. Earl V. Dykes of the Bloomingdale community. Dykes was graduated in 1966 from Ketron High School and enlisted in the Marine Corps in October 1966. He served with A Company, 1st Battalion, 4th

Lance Corporal William F. Dykes.

First Lieutenant James L. Tarte.

Marines, 3rd Marine Division. His tour in Vietnam began April 13, 1967; he was twenty years old when he was killed on October 29 of that same year, having been wounded by a grenade during action in the Phue Thien province of South Vietnam. He had been in Vietnam for only eight months when he was killed. He was buried at Oak Hill Cemetery in Kingsport. To compound his family's tragedy, his first cousin, Daniel L. Gregg, was also killed in Vietnam, one year later.

Kingsport native First Lieutenant James L. Tarte was born on November 2, 1945, and served with A Company, 4th Battalion, 47th Infantry Regiment, 9th Infantry Division. His tour in Vietnam began on January 4, 1968, and he was killed by enemy fire August 24, 1968, in Dinh Tuong Province, South Vietnam. He was twenty-two and was buried at Oak Hill Cemetery in Kingsport.

UNICOI

Air Force veteran and researcher Allen Jackson contributed the following account of Army aviator Donald R. Cook.

Chief Warrant Officer Two Donald R. Cook was born in Bakersville, Mitchell County, North Carolina on August 19, 1946, the only child of Mack Donald Cook and Cora Evelyn Newton. His family moved to Johnson City (Washington) in 1955. Cook was graduated from Boones Creek High School, class of 1964. After graduation, he moved to Unicoi (Unicoi), Tennessee; he attended Milligan College for two years and East Tennessee State University for one. While at Milligan College, he became an ordained minister in the Apostolic Pentecostal Church and a guest minister at many churches in Eastern Tennessee and Western North Carolina.

Chief Warrant Officer Two Donald R. Cook.

Cook enlisted in the Army in November 1968. While attending Basic Training at Fort Polk, Louisiana, he filed paperwork to become a warrant officer and was accepted for flight school. He attended the Army's Primary Helicopter Center (Class 69–39) at Fort Wolters, Mineral Wells, Texas, and then the Warrant Officer Rotary Wing Aviation Course (Class 69–41) at Hunter Army Airfield, Savannah, Georgia.

Cook returned home on leave in December 1969 to be with his wife and family. He gave the Sunday sermon at the Church of the Lord Jesus Christ in Bakersville, North Carolina, on the Sunday before he left for Vietnam. His tour of duty began on January 20, 1970; he was assigned to the 498th Medical Company (Air Ambulance), 67th Medical Group, 44th Medical Brigade, 1st Logistic Command, as a "dustoff" [air medevac] pi-

lot. He was based at Lane Army Heliport in An Son, Binh Dinh Province, South Vietnam, and also flew missions out of LZ Uplift in Qui Nhon and LZ English in Bong Son. Cook mostly flew in support of the 173rd Airborne Brigade. He had already been shot down twice while flying rescue missions for the 173rd before the night of October 26, 1970.

At approximately 7:45 p.m. that evening, while at LZ Uplift, an urgent request was received for dustoff/medevac support from Forward Support Base Washington, a mountaintop artillery base at an altitude of 1,400 feet. Even though the FSB was covered in clouds, fog, light rain, and darkness, Don, as aircraft commander, volunteered to go and get the soldier and was airborne within two minutes of the call. Flying a UH-1H Iroquois ("Huey") helicopter, tail number 67–17765, Don attempted to reach the base from the west, carrying a crew of four and one observer; due to lack of visual references to the ground because of the flight conditions, he aborted and moved over to the east. While hovering up the eastside, he requested the base maintain constant illumination on the mountainside via mortar-launched aerial flares during his approach. As he approached within 150 meters of the FSB, illumination was lost due to a dud round; another round was immediately fired, but it too was a dud, and Cook lost all visual reference. He attempted to turn right, away from the mountain, when his chopper lost altitude. The Huey's left skid caught a tree, causing it to nose forward and slam into a large rock formation. Cook and two members were thrown out as it rolled down the mountain and came to rest on its right side between another rock formation and two large trees. The observer on the mission crawled from the wreckage as sole survivor just before it burst into flames with the crew chief still aboard.

Cook completed 1,915 missions racking up 1,227 flight hours, 710 of them combat flight hours while airlifting 1,333 patients.

His awards include the Distinguished Flying Cross, Bronze Star, Air with numeral twenty-four device, National Defense, Vietnam Service, Vietnam Campaign with three Bronze Stars, and Gallantry Cross with Palm (Republic of Vietnam) Medals, and the Combat Medical Badge. He was also promoted to Chief Warrant Officer Two posthumously. A memorial service was held for him and his crew at a little church that overlooks Lane Army Heliport and the An Son Valley, ten miles northwest of Qui Nhon. Cook rests at Evergreen Cemetery, Section Lower E, in Erwin, Tennessee. He was married to Toni Margo Whitson, and they had no children.

Specialist Fourth Class Bobby J. Shelton was born on May 7, 1944, and was from Flag Pond. In Vietnam, he served as a Scout Dog Handler with the 38th Scout Dog Platoon, 2nd Battalion, 14th Infantry Regiment, 25th Infantry Division. He was killed at the age of

Specialist Fourth Class Bobby J. Shelton, possibly with "Paddy.".

twenty-three on September 29, 1967, in Binh Duong Province, South Vietnam. Shelton was buried at Harris Cemetery in Unicoi County. The Bronze Star citation for Shelton's brave deed follows:

[Shelton] distinguished himself by heroic actions on 29 September 1967 in the Republic of Vietnam. On this date Specialist Shelton was serving as a Scout Dog Handler attached to the Second Battalion, Fourteenth Infantry conducting a search and destroy operation in the Ho Bo Woods. At approximately 1330 hours on this date SP4 Shelton was working his Scout Dog in advance of the company's point element when the dog gave a strong alert to the left front of the company. With complete disregard for his personal safety, SP4 Shelton advanced farther in front of the company in order to determine the source of the alert. Reaching a hedgerow, he broke through without waiting for the point element to precede him. As he came to the other side of the hedgerow his Scout Dog again alerted. Again, with complete disregard for his personal safety, SP4 Shelton, knowing that enemy contact was imminent, exposed himself in order to warn the elements of the company that followed him that enemy contact was imminent. As he did this, the enemy opened fire with automatic weapons mortally wounding him. SP4 Shelton's heroic actions in the performance of his duty saved the elements behind him from being ambushed by the Viet Cong force. This outstanding display of aggressiveness, devotion to duty, and personal heroism is in keeping with the highest traditions of the military service and reflects great credit upon himself, his unit, and the United States Army.

Fellow veteran Denis McDonough contributed to the ETVMA the following clipping from an unidentified publication as to the effects of Shelton's death on his assigned scout dog, Paddy:

Dog Is Bewildered During Memorial. Men of the 25th [Infantry Division's] 38th Scout Dog Platoon gathered recently to pay tribute to one of their members killed in action against the Viet Cong. The saddest member of all of them never said a word but glanced repeatedly at the weapon and beret of his master. Held at the 1st Battalion, 27th Infantry Wolfhound's chapel, the service was in memory of Sp4 Bobby J. Shelton of Flag Pond Tenn., who was killed while on a search and destroy operation deep in the Ho Bo Woods. Paddy, his dog, took it hardest of all, said Plt. Leader First Lieutenant John Anderson. All morning he wandered around looking for him. Paddy was trained at Lackland Air Force Base in Texas and was one of the dogs to arrive with the unit in Vietnam in July of 1966. Paddy has been on continuous combat operations with the 25th Div since that time. Shelton was a product of the 38th [Platoon's] own training program given at the unit's Cu Chi base camp. The program accepts volunteers from the division and trains them to be combat dog handlers. Paddy will be retrained to another master, says Anderson, but it takes a while to adapt to someone new.

Private First Class Garry K. Cook.

UNION

Private First Class Garry K. Cook was born on May 4, 1947, was from Sharps Chapel and was the son of Owen Thomas and Ida June Johnson Cook. His tour of duty in Vietnam began on January 7, 1967, with A Company, 2nd Battalion, 28th Infantry Regiment, 1st Infantry Division. Cook died of wounds on February 28, 1967, at the age of nineteen in Binh Duong, South Vietnam. He is buried at Johnson Cemetery, Sharps Chapel, Union County.

WASHINGTON

Specialist Fourth Class Floyd W. ("Jason") Lamb Jr. was born in Greeneville on October 4, 1949, the son of Floyd Watsel Lamb Sr., an Army veteran of World War II, and Bonnie Bell Waddle. He grew up in the Chuckey community and was a member of the Boy Scouts of America. He was graduated from Lamar High School, class of 1967. Jason was a member of the Beta Club and graduated second in his class. Lamb was assigned to Company B, 1st Battalion, 46th Infantry Regiment, 198th Light Infantry Brigade, 23rd Infantry Division, better known as the Americal Division, as a light weapons infantryman.

His tour of duty in Vietnam began on December 10, 1969. Lamb was killed in action

Specialist Fourth Class Floyd W. ("Jason") Lamb Jr.

Major Homer L. Pease.

while participating in a search-and-clear operation in the Nui Yon Thon Mountains, approximately eight miles southwest of Tam Ky City, Quang Tin Province, South Vietnam, on May 4, 1970. At 8:30 a.m., Lamb received a fatal fragmentation wound when a concealed enemy explosive device was detonated. For his actions, he received the Bronze Star, Purple Heart, Army Commendation, National Defense, Vietnam Service, and Vietnam Campaign Medals. Lamb rests in the Liberty Freewill Baptist Church Cemetery, Chuckey, Tennessee. He was twenty years old and a member of the Liberty Freewill Baptist Church. Lamb was married, with no children.

Researcher and Air Force veteran Allen Jackson contributed the following account of another Upper East Tennessee military officer

with a remarkable life story and military career cut short:

At an early age, the future Major Homer L. Pease moved to his new home at 1100 East Chilhowie Avenue in Johnson City, Tennessee. He was a strapping, free-willed, freckle-faced, red-headed lad, whose dream was to become a United States Marine. After World War II began, Pease wanted to join up, but he knew he was too young. In early 1942, he went by himself to the Marine Corps' recruiter and was turned away. Undeterred, Pease went back to the recruiting office, to the Army recruiter—this time, it was said, with a gentleman from Kentucky whom his uncle had hired to pose as Pease's father. This time, he was accepted. Pease volunteered to join the newly-formed paratroopers. Pease's mother thought that he had run away. Perhaps, in a way, he had, but she never dreamed it was to the Army.

After Pease completed his airborne

training and qualified as a paratrooper, he was shipped to England, and he was assigned to the 101st Airborne Division. Pease jumped into Normandy on the morning of June 6, 1944, and fought the Germans throughout D-Day and the days thereafter, until he was wounded. He received a Purple Heart and a Bronze Star for his valor. While healing up in England, he missed his unit's jump into Holland during Operation Market Garden; he rejoined them soon afterwards. He next fought the Germans during the Battle of Bulge in the fighting for Bastogne, when the Germans completely encircled his unit. After the siege of Bastogne was lifted, it was on to Germany; at Berchtesgaden (Hitler's Eagle Nest), he was again wounded, and at this time his real age was discovered. Pease was only fifteen: he had lied about his age and had joined up at age thirteen. With another Purple Heart in hand, reduced in rank from sergeant to private, he came home to Johnson City to recover—but his story does not end here.

Pease attended Science Hill High School but still longed to be a soldier. On March 2, 1946, at the age of sixteen, Pease went back to the recruiting office and rejoined the Army for another two-year hitch. After getting to his unit at Fort Bragg, North Carolina, and after his military records caught up with him, his commanding officer reviewed them and him. Homer was informed that he was not going to be "busted" for fraudulent enlistment, but that he was being sent back home—again. Pease pleaded his case to stay on active service, pointing to his Bronze Star, two Purple Hearts, Airborne badge, and Combat Infantryman's Badge. His CO was impressed, but his mind was made up; he essentially advised Pease that he had done his duty and that it was time for Pease to return home, play football, and get an education. Pease took his commander's advice to heart. He returned to Science Hill, played football (defensive tackle, number 96), and was a Junior ROTC cadet.

After graduation, Pease joined the Tennessee Army National Guard and was selected to further his education. Pease attended both East Tennessee State University (ETSU) and Milligan College. He volunteered for the ROTC Program at ETSU but did not complete it. He was also a member of Phi Beta Chi and the Veterans Club. Upon graduation, class of 1954, he was given a commission as a second lieutenant in the Tennessee Army National Guard. Pease did a lot of jobs during his twelve years after high school but staying active in the Guard and training with the Reserves was first and foremost, whether it was drilling with his troops, driving a "deuce and a half" (2 1/2-ton truck) wide-open through downtown Johnson City, or firing mortar rounds into Boone Lake.

In 1960, Pease decided to run for office as state representative for Johnson City. That year, nine party members in Washington County were arrested for voter fraud; Pease was one of them. At the end of the trial, he was acquitted, but his dream of a public service career was over. The judge essentially advised Pease that he would be better served by going back into active service with the Army. Pease took the judge's advice, and he returned to the Guard to submit paperwork to change his status to active duty in the Army.

This request was granted, and, as a first lieutenant, Pease was assigned to Fort Knox, Kentucky. He was assigned to an armored unit and worked as a maintenance officer. One of Pease's new duties was to test newly acquired armored vehicles and write detailed reports on their performance and durability. In 1965, he volunteered to be a military advisor in Southeast Asia, more specifically, Vietnam.

Pease was accepted by the Military Assistance Command, Vietnam (MACV), but first he had to complete the US Army Ranger course and learn French. He completed both courses and became a Ranger at the age of thirty-six. He arrived in Vietnam on March 14,

1966, after a short stop to visit family in California. Then-Captain Pease was assigned to MACV's Military Advisory Team 93 and was further assigned to an Army Republic of Vietnam (ARVN) regiment. On November 19, 1966, at Ba Tri, Kien Hoa Province, South Vietnam, Pease was leading an ARVN ground combat operation, and when the bullets starting flying, he was not as lucky as he had been in World War II. At the age of thirty-seven, Pease died on that field of battle. For his actions and bravery, he was recognized with the Silver Star and promoted posthumously to major. He was sent home by the Army to Johnson City, for the third and final time. Pease is buried at the Monte Vista Memorial Gardens, Section F, Lot 37, Space 4. He was the son of Jesse Mae Raulston and had one daughter.

First Lieutenant Harry R. Stewart was born in Johnson City on October 3, 1941, and was the youngest son of Mr. and Mrs. Fred H. Stewart. He was a member of the First Evangelical

First Lieutenant Harry R. Stewart.

United Brethren Church and was graduated from Science Hill High School, class of 1960. While working in a movie theater, he enlisted on September 28, 1960. After five years as an Army enlisted man, Stewart applied for Officer Candidate School (OCS) and was accepted. He was graduated from Infantry OCS, Class 1–66, at Fort Benning, Georgia, and was promoted to second lieutenant on January 14, 1966.

Stewart was assigned to Company C, 2nd Battalion, 27th Infantry Regiment, 25th Infantry Division. While at Fort Ord, California, he was assigned as a training officer. Harry met the love of his life, Mary Michelle Hall, daughter of the base commander, and they were married on October 5, 1966. After a leave in Johnson City in November 1966, he left for and arrived in South Vietnam on December 14, 1966, and was promoted to first lieutenant shortly thereafter. As platoon leader for Company C's 3rd Platoon, Harry Stewart was killed by an enemy grenade during combat in the Kien Hoa Province, South Vietnam on March 10, 1967. He was twenty-five years old and was awarded the Purple Heart. Stewart is interred at the Andrew Johnson National Cemetery in Greeneville.

In one of his very last letters, Stewart wrote his family: "Last, but not least, thank you and everyone else for remembering me in their prayers. Don't waste that precious stuff on my safe return. That is already decided. Ask instead, that I do my job well and that God be with me in the performance of my duties. Ask that I have the wisdom, the skill, the courage, the strength, the leadership, the endurance, and the will that this job requires. All else will take care of itself."

13

REMEMBERING THE EAST TENNESSEE WOMEN WHO SERVED

For I have loved many people and many places and many things, and best of all, I have loved life, especially American life. And if I can say one thing in truth, it is that to my friends and my convictions I have brought all the loyalty and integrity of which I was capable.

If I die violently, who can say it was "before my time?" I should have dearly loved to have had [a family], but if that is not to be, I want no one to grieve for me.

I was happiest in the sky. . . . Think of me there and remember me, I hope, as I shall you.

—An excerpt from a letter to her family, written in January 1942, by Tennessean and Women's Auxiliary Ferrying Squadron pilot Cornelia Fort. Killed in a mid-air collision in March 1943, she was the first female pilot to die on active duty.[1]

Among the service personnel recognized by the East Tennessee Veterans Memorial, four names stand out prominently, those being the names of the four East Tennessee women who died in military service. One of these women was the sister of another East Tennessee service member, who, like her, died during World War II. Their service and sacrifices are recounted in this chapter.

Second Lieutenant Jane M. Blevins was originally from Oneida (Scott) and was born on September 1, 1922. Her brother, Technician Fifth Class Howard K. Blevins, was a German POW after being captured in Sicily on July 11, 1943. He survived the war, only to be killed in a vehicle accident in 1956.

Blevins entered the Army as a nurse on February 8, 1944. She received her nurse's training at Erlanger Hospital in Chattanooga, graduating in May 1943. She then had nursing duty at Oak Ridge, Tennessee. After training at Denver, Colorado, Amarillo, Texas, and Brigham City, Utah, she was sent to the China-India-Burma ("CBI") Theater in December 1944 as part of the Army Nurse Corps. Her last duty station was as an operating room nurse for the 20th Field Hospital. She was killed in an airplane crash traveling to Ledo, India, on March 4, 1945. She was one of twenty-five passengers aboard a C-47 transport (the militarized version of the DC-3 passenger and cargo airplane) that crashed while attempting to land at Ledo.

She was initially buried in the American Military Cemetery at Kalaikunda, India. Her remains

US Army nurses coming ashore in Normandy, France, during World War II.
Courtesy of the Army Medical Department Center of History and Heritage.

were later returned stateside, and she was buried on June 8, 1948, in the City Cemetery, Somerset, Kentucky, where her parents were then living.[2]

Private Vilena L. (Velma) Cannon was born on November 14, 1921, in Greene County. She was a member of Piney Grove United Methodist Church. Cannon was graduated from Greeneville High School on May 24, 1940, where she was a member of the National Beta Club and received recognition for outstanding character and achievement. She joined the Women's Army Corps ("WAC") when she was twenty-one years old, enlisting on January 22, 1943, at Fort Oglethorpe, Georgia, in order to serve as an aviation cadet.

Cannon died in service on June 29, 1943, while undergoing surgery for a brain tumor at Fort Devens, Massachusetts. She was returned to her hometown of Greeneville and was buried at the River Hill Cemetery on July 4, 1943.

Lieutenant (j.g.) Julia M. Zecchini was born on October 8, 1915, in Newcomb, Tennessee (Campbell). She attended Jellico High School. In 1931, she was a member of the 6th District Champion Girls Basketball team from the school. By 1935 she was a student nurse at St. Mary's Memorial Hospital in Knoxville. Details about her early military service appear sparse, but in late 1942, she was a passenger on the cargo ship USS *Talamanca* (AF-15), en route to join the US Naval Mobile Hospital No. 4 in Auckland, New Zealand. From the nature of this assignment, she most likely had to provide nursing care for the many seriously wounded Marines, sailors, and aircrews who had been

Second Lieutenant Jane M. Blevins.

Lieutenant (j.g.) Julia M. Zecchini.

evacuated during the August 1942–February 1943 Guadalcanal Campaign and the frequent and vicious ensuing naval and aerial battles in and around the Solomon Islands and Ironbottom Sound.

Zecchini died at the US Naval Hospital in Memphis of sodium fluoride poisoning on her twenty-ninth birthday—October 8, 1944—having been stationed after her service in New Zealand at the nearby Millington Naval Air Station. Her younger brother, Peter Zecchini, had died a year before, as he was lost in the 1943 sinking of the transport *SS Dorchester*. His own story can be found in chapter 5, "Lost at Sea and in the Air."

Currently, the Zecchini family represents the only East Tennessee family with siblings of both genders to be commemorated on the East Tennessee Veterans Memorial. The deaths of both Julia and Peter must have been a special tragedy for this Italian-American immigrant, coal-mining family of Campbell County.

Specialist Fifth Class Belinda Sue Taylor was born Belinda Sue Cotton on May 30, 1946, in Chattanooga (Hamilton). At an early age, she was adopted by William J. and Fannie Posey Taylor of Chattanooga. She had one sibling, James Edward Taylor. Taylor was educated in the Hamilton County schools and attended Clifton Hills Elementary, East Lake Elementary, East Lake Junior High School, and Chattanooga City High School. She lived in Rock Springs, Georgia, during her second and third grade years. Belinda's adoptive mother died while Belinda was in school, and her father remarried. Belinda soon left home and often lived with friends during her senior year. She sometimes found residence with Mr. and Mrs. Robert Madison Lanham, Mr. Lanham being a Chattanooga attorney. She briefly worked as a

Specialist Fifth Class Belinda Sue Taylor.

she was killed in an automobile accident in Heidelberg on June 2, 1967. Taylor was returned to Chattanooga, and her funeral services were held on June 12, 1967. She was buried in the Chattanooga National Cemetery, with full military honors.

clerk at L. O. Griffin and Associates, a collections agency in Chattanooga, before joining the Army.

Taylor enlisted in the Army on February 23, 1965, in Knoxville. She took basic training at Fort McClellan, Alabama, from February to June 1965 and then entered the WAC's eight-week Clerical Training School from July to September 1965. Her first assignment was to Fort Myer, Virginia, where she served as a clerk typist with the Department of Army's Military Personnel Management Team SF-2910 in Washington. Taylor left for West Germany on July 19, 1966, and was an administrative specialist assigned to Company B, 7th Army Headquarters, in Heidelberg, West Germany. She was promoted to specialist fifth class on October 11, 1966. Taylor had served for two years when

14

NON-COMBAT TRAGEDIES AND LINGERING MYSTERIES

He will swallow up death in victory;
and the Lord God will wipe away tears from off all faces.

—*Isaiah 25:8*

While some may think that only combat-related deaths are represented on the memorial, this is not the case. In recognition of the fact that many service members died from non-combat causes, the memorial also honors military service casualties and wartime casualties who have fallen for various reasons. Whether in troop train wrecks, from disease (as was the case with the victims of the Spanish influenza on 1918–1919), in training or logistics-related accidents, or (as in two tragic cases) death by shark attack or by execution after a court martial, this chapter's vignettes will address the memorial's recognition of such casualties.

WORLD WAR I

Private First Class Ray T. Parker was born near Pikeville (Bledsoe) and was twenty-three years at the time of his death. He moved with his family to Cumberland County when he was young and for many years resided at Dayton Spur, a suburb of Crossville. Parker farmed and did construction work prior to his entry into the service. He enlisted at Jefferson Barracks, Missouri, on October 4, 1916 in the Regular Army. He served on the Mexican border with a provisional ambulance company and then with the Ambulance Company of the 1st Division ("The Big Red One") and the Medical Department of the 1st Division's 28th Infantry Regiment while in France. His division was the first to land there and, in due time, became known as one of the best fighting units of the AEF.

Parker was severely wounded in action on July 19, 1918. A few months later, he returned stateside and was assigned to the Army Medical Department's General Hospital 6, Fort McPherson, Georgia, where he was stationed at the time of his death, which resulted from his being struck by a mail train.

His records also reveal that he had been kicked by a horse during his service, but his parents had never been apprised of this injury. Parker's remains were buried in the city cemetery just on the outskirts of Crossville.

Apprentice Seaman John S. Good (Hamblen) was born June 14, 1896, in Milligan, Tennessee and volunteered for the Navy on June 18, 1918. He was assigned to the Naval Training Station at New Orleans, Louisiana, for his preliminary training. He was on duty there until November 4, 1918, when he drowned in the Mississippi River while assisting in raising a sunken tugboat. His burial place is unknown.

Private James L. Scoggins, Supply Company, 321st Infantry Regiment, 84th Division, was born on November 11, 1893, in Ooltewah (Hamilton) and died on May 10, 1918, as a result of a train wreck at Camp Jackson, Columbia, South Carolina. The train was leaving for Camp Sevier, Greenville, South Carolina when a wooden passenger coach carrying Scoggins and other troops was derailed from a railroad trestle and plunged down an embankment. He is buried at the McDonald Cemetery, McDonald, Tennessee. Also killed in the same accident was Private Jess Reno of the same regiment. He was born August 20, 1894, in Soddy (Hamilton) and is buried at the Soddy Presbyterian Cemetery.

Private James and Private Alfred Cantwell were two of fifteen children of Wiley and Margaret Russell Cantwell who resided in Sneedville (Hancock). Robert Mathis (born July 6, 1893, also from Sneedville) was a cousin of James (born January 22, 1983) and Alfred (born April 28, 1887). James and Alfred were in the timber business before they entered the Army. All three—James, Alfred, and Robert—left Sneedville together for the war. While in the Army, their troop train stopped in St. Joseph, Missouri, on January 14, 1918. The three relatives spent the night in a hotel. The bodies of James, Alfred, and Robert, the victims of suffocation from a faulty gas stove, were found

Private Alfred Cantwell.

Private James Cantwell.

the next morning, January 15, by their fellow servicemen.

Their bodies were returned by train to Lone Mountain. Family members were at the station to pick up the bodies of their loved ones. They transported them back to Sneedville by horse and wagons through rugged trails with very deep snow. All three were buried side by side in the Cantwell Family Cemetery, which is next to the Cantwell home place. Wiley, the father of James and Alfred, died—according to Cantwell family history—from a broken heart, only six months after his sons' funeral.[1]

Wagoner George L. Mowry was born in Knoxville (Knox) on May 18, 1896. He entered the service in October 1917. As a member of Battery D, 5th US Field Artillery, he received his military training at Fort Oglethorpe, Georgia. He sailed for overseas duty with the AEF in January 1918, and Mowry took part in all engagements of his command, which (as part of the divisional field artillery component of the "Big Red One," the 1st Division) included service at Montdidier-Noyon, the Aisne-Marne offensive, at St. Mihiel, the Meuse-Argonne offensive, and in the Lorraine and Picardy regions of France. He was killed accidentally on May 4, 1919, as a result of a pistol shot while serving on occupation duty in the Rhineland area of western Germany. He died at the age of twenty-three. Mowry was initially buried at Dernbach, Germany, and, after his body was repatriated, now is buried at the Knoxville National Cemetery.

Petty Officer (Water Tender) Earnest Ely (Knox) enlisted in the Navy on August 1, 1907, in Knoxville. He was assigned to the destroyer USS *Dale* (DD-4) after he had completed his preliminary sea training. He took part in the naval attack on Vera Cruz, Mexico, which was bombarded and occupied in response to the

arrest and detention of American sailors by Mexico at the port of Tampico in 1914. He lost his life on May 31, 1917, when he was killed by a shark in Manila Bay. His body was recovered. He had received two medals and was serving in his third enlistment. At the time of Ely's death, the *Dale* was on patrol at the entrance to Manila Bay from June 30 to August 31, 1917 before heading to Gibraltar. He is buried at Knoxville National Cemetery.

Sergeant James O. Huff.

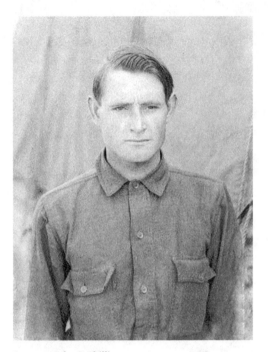

Sergeant John E. Phillips.

Sergeant James O. Huff was born on May 24, 1893, at Euchee (Meigs), Tennessee, and was assigned to the 323rd Infantry Regiment, 81st Division. He was killed in a railroad accident on September 17, 1918, at the age of twenty-four and is interred at the Meuse-Argonne American Cemetery, Romagne, France.

Corporal Bascom Breeden from Archville (Polk) died on August 13, 1918, and was buried at Greasy Creek Cemetery, Polk County. He served with the 44th Company of the Marine Corps. He was one of three Marines killed and one wounded in a skirmish with bandits in Seibo Province, Santo Domingo (now the Dominican Republic). A number of bandits were killed or captured in this firefight. Bascom and the other dead Marines were initially buried at San Pedro Macoris, Santo Domingo.

Sergeant John E. Phillips was born on De-cember 6, 1893, in Washington County and died on January 1, 1918, in Jonesborough of an accidental gunshot wound. As Christmas 1917 approached, Phillips, like many of the 117th Infantry Regiment of the 30th Division, were given leave from their training post at Camp Jackson, South Carolina, to return home to their families for the holidays. He and his father went hunting on New Year's Day 1918, and John slipped and fell. As he hit the ground, his weapon discharged, severing the artery in his leg below the knee causing him to bleed to death. John was twenty-five years old. He is buried at the Oliver Cemetery, Washington County, Tennessee.

Of all the deaths and casualties remembered on the plinths of the East Tennessee Veterans Memorial, the loss of one supply ship and its crew, in particular, remains an unsolved mystery of near-legendary proportions. Among its vanished crew were three Knox County citizens.

Hospital Apprentice Second Class James M. Wheeler (Knox) enlisted in Nashville, Tennessee, on July 24, 1917. He shipped aboard the collier (coal supply ship) USS *Cyclops* (AC 4). The ship departed Barbados March 4, 1918, and disappeared into the Western Atlantic near the infamous "Bermuda Triangle" with 306 crewmembers and passengers. It was declared lost on June 14, 1918. The ship's disappearance is one of the great mysteries of the sea, has formed one of the enduring mysteries of the Bermuda Triangle, and represents the single largest loss of life in United States naval history outside of combat. It is often speculated that the *Cyclops* sank in an unexpected storm, although as its wreckage remains lost, the actual cause of the ship's fate may never be known. Also lost from Knox County aboard the *Cyclops* were Fireman Third Class Joe Parks and Fireman

USS *Cyclops.*

Third Class W. Archie Pope. It is remarkable that three Knox Countians were lost with the *Cyclops*'s disappearance.

Seaman Second Class Porter Lee St. John was born at Bluff City (Sullivan) on July 2, 1897. Both his parents died before Porter was ten years old, and he remained in the home with his five brothers and sisters. St. John served on the armed yacht and patrol vessel USS *Winchester* (SP-156). While the ship was near City Island, New York City, he was serving with the starboard wire crew. The wire that they were handling became fouled in the vessel's rail and carried away a section about four or five feet long. In attempting to free the wire, St. John lost his footing, fell overboard through an opening in the rail, and drowned on February 17, 1919. He is buried at the Saint John Cemetery, Sullivan County.

WORLD WAR II

Captain James Sullins ("Sully") Varnell Jr., born December 9, 1921, in Charleston (Bradley), enlisted in the Army Air Forces on March 28, 1942, at Chattanooga. He was a fighter pilot in the European Theater of Operations, stationed in Italy. He was sent overseas in the summer of 1943 and began by flying mainly British-supplied Supermarine Spitfires, then was moved to the 15th Air Force, flying North American P-51 Mustangs. Varnell downed seventeen German planes over the next three months. Once his tour of duty expired, he was rotated home to train other pilots. Ironically, he was killed in a flying accident on April 9, 1945, near Pinellas Field, Florida, less than a month before V-E Day ended the conflict in Europe. Varnell was one of the most highly-ranked Mustang aces of World War II. He was recognized with

Captain James S. (Sully) Varnell Jr.

Technician Fifth Class Curtis D. (Dale) Pearson.

Sergeant Leon F. Russell.

the Silver Star, Distinguished Flying Cross, and Air Medal with fifteen Oak Leaf Clusters and was buried at Calhoun Community Cemetery, McMinn County. He was twenty-three at the time of his death.[2]

Sergeant Leon F. Russell, LaFollette (Campbell), was born on March 15, 1913, and died on May 1, 1944, at Camp Beale in Yuba County, California. He was a member of Company A, 321st Infantry Regiment and is buried at Pond Cemetery, Demory, Campbell County. He, along with Staff Sergeant James A. Tummins, Elizabethton (Carter), who was born March 13, 1921, were killed in the explosion of a land mine or experimental "booby trap" used in advanced infantry training at the Camp Beale training facility. He is buried at Green Hill Cemetery, Etowah, McMinn County.

Technician Fifth Class Curtis D. (Dale)

Pearson was born on January 28, 1922, in Johnson County and served with Headquarters Company of the 414th Infantry Regiment. His basic training was at Camp Adair, Oregon, where Pearson received a thirty-day notice that he would be sent to Camp Carson, Colorado, for training. While at Camp Carson, Dale and a buddy were given a weekend pass. They were returning to base when the motorcycle they were riding was hit head-on by a civilian automobile driving on the wrong side of the road. Both soldiers were killed, with Pearson dying on July 9, 1944. He was twenty-two years old. He is buried at the Elk Mills Christian Church Cemetery, Elk Mills, Tennessee.[3]

Technician Fourth Class Jessie E. Bean, Chattanooga (Hamilton), and his wife, Etna Deering Bean, were both killed October 17, 1943, in a tourist cabin fire in Tullahoma. At the time he was based at Camp Forrest in Tullahoma and served with the 239th Engineer Battalion. He and his wife are buried in the same plot at the Chattanooga National Cemetery. She had been visiting him for the weekend.

Staff Sergeant Clarence A. Dacus of Chattanooga (Hamilton), born November 23, 1920, was killed by injuries sustained in an airplane accident, approximately six miles outside of Middlesboro, Kentucky, on November 10, 1945. He enlisted in the United States Army on July 30, 1941. At the time he enlisted, he had completed high school and was a semi-skilled welder and flame cutter. He was stationed with the 240th Army Air Force Base, 17th Bombardment Operational Training Wing in Sioux City, Iowa, and was on a training and inspection flight from Middlesboro, Kentucky, to Knoxville when the B-25 Mitchell medium bomber in which he was traveling encountered fog and bad weather over the Cumberland Mountains. The bomber crashed into the side

Staff Sergeant Clarence A. Dacus.

of a mountain, killing all five aboard. The B-25 was piloted by Colonel Norris Perry, originally of Sedro Wooley (Washington) and, coincidentally, a Knoxville resident during the war. The following is an excerpt of the USAAF's official accident report, describing the accident:

> The pilot had intended making a flight from Bowman Field to Knoxville, Tenn. . . . [I]n as much as the pilot did not possess a current instrument card, he was briefed upon the route by the Operations Officer. Shortly before the crash, the plane was observed flying very low along a valley in the Cumberland Mountains approximately 55 miles from Knoxville and in a southeasterly direction. The plane entered a cul-de-sac with a high [2600-foot] mountain directly ahead. . . . The Pilot apparently began pulling up as he noticed the steepening incline.
>
> Approximately 200 feet up the slope,

the plane began shearing off treetops. The pilot must have maintained a very high angle of attack as the plane kept climbing for approximately 500 more feet before the main impact. With the main impact, the plane exploded and the engine landed 50 feet higher. All of the occupants were killed instantly. At the time of the crash, observers stated that the top of the mountains were in the overcast and visibility was very low.

Staff Sergeant Dacus is buried at Forest Hills Cemetery, Chattanooga.

Aviation Machinist's Mate Able Smith, Ooltewah (Hamilton), was injured due to a boxing accident on March 17, 1943, at the Navy's Cabaniss Field, Corpus Christi, Texas, dying of intracranial injury the next day at the US Naval Hospital at the air field. He was buried at the McDonald Cemetery, Ooltewah, Tennessee.

Private First Class Alvin R. Rollins, Chattanooga (Hamilton), 306th Quartermaster Railhead Company, was born December 5, 1924. He was inducted on June 15, 1943, at Camp Forrest (located in Tullahoma), Tennessee. Rollins died under extremely grim circumstances, under the aegis of the Army's military justice. An Army report detailed the circumstances

Burial plot in France where Private First Class Alvin R. Rollins is buried.

leading to his arrest, trial, and subsequent fate as one of the ninety-six GIs sentenced to death and executed in the ETO during the Second World War:

> Private First Class Alvin R. Rollins (colored), age 20, was charged with the murder of Private First Class John H. Hoogewind and Sergeant Royce A. Judd, Jr., white American soldiers by shooting them with a pistol at Troyes, France. On the evening of February 23, [the] accused broke restriction at his camp and went to an off-limits café in Troyes, France. While he was there, the two deceased military police arrived in a patrol car. He endeavored to evade the military police when they entered the café and had an altercation with them concerning his knowledge that the café was off limits. Ultimately, he was forcibly ejected from the café and placed in the jeep for the purpose of taking him to military police headquarters. No sooner had the jeep started than the accused drew a pistol and fired on the police in the jeep and fled leaving the two military police fatally wounded. The general court-martial found the accused guilty on March 13, 1945 and sentenced him to be hanged. No evidence of previous convictions was considered. The confirming authority confirmed the sentence on April 29, 1945, and the accused was hanged at Loire Disciplinary Training Center, Le Mans, Sarthe, France, on May 31, 1945.[4]

A footnote to Rollins' story is that his hangman was most likely Master Sergeant John C. Woods. Woods was assigned to the facility where Rollins was executed and was responsible for the hanging of at least twenty-three soldiers. Woods gained international fame in October 1946 by serving as the hangman for the International Military Tribunal at Nuremberg, where he executed ten senior German generals and civilian officials convicted of crimes against humanity, crimes against peace, and war crimes.[5]

ETVMA researcher Astrid van Erp corroborated the details of the cemetery plot where Rollins is buried at the Oise-Aisne American Cemetery and Memorial in France. The cemetery in which Rollins was laid to rest is maintained and groomed by caretakers, although it is hidden from view and kept separate from the nearby four plots for the honored dead of World War I. Unlike the marble monuments and inscribed standing headstones of the regular plots, Plot E, where Rollins is buried, contains nothing but ninety-six flat stone markers, arranged in four rows, and a single small granite cross. The markers are the size of index cards and have nothing on them except sequential grave numbers engraved in black. No American flag flies over this section, and the numbered graves literally lie with their backs turned to the hallowed ground of the main cemetery, which is located across the street. Visitors are not encouraged, and its existence is not mentioned on the cemetery website or guide pamphlets. The dead of Plot E, while once American servicemen, were all executed in accordance with military justice for a variety of offenses. Thus, under military burial practices, they are buried as US servicemen but lie without the full honors typically afforded to deceased American service members.

Seaman Second Class Isaiah Ash Jr. (Hamilton) was born in 1925 and died in California as a result of the infamous Port Chicago munitions disaster. On the evening of July 17, 1944, at the Port Chicago naval munitions base located on San Francisco Bay, the largest stateside military disaster of World War II occurred, killing 320 men and injuring another 390 men on the base. Two transport ships, the S.S. *E. A. Bryan* and

the S.S. *Quinault Victory*, were completely destroyed. The small town of Port Chicago, only thirty miles from San Francisco, also suffered tremendous damage. Chunks of smoldering metal weighing hundreds of pounds and even undetonated bombs rained down upon the community, damaging over 300 structures and injuring over 100 people. Miraculously, none of the bombs exploded, and no residents of the town of Port Chicago were killed. By sheer size of the blast, the Port Chicago explosion was as large as a five-kiloton atomic bomb. No cause for the explosion was ever officially determined.

Of the 320 men who lost their lives on the base, 202 of them were black; of the additional 390 men injured, 233 were black. Many of these African American naval seamen volunteered in the United States Navy expecting—and some even hoping—to see combat action on the front lines of the war. They went through segregated boot camp, applied to training schools, and graduated as full seamen in the United States Navy. Many of the African American ammunition handlers and stevedores had voiced their concerns about appropriate safety while loading ammunition.

Fifty enlisted black men, including one with a broken arm, were tried for mutiny. The men stated they were willing to follow orders but were afraid to handle ammunition under unchanged and unsafe circumstances. All fifty were found guilty of "mutiny" under US naval regulations and were sentenced to fifteen years' imprisonment. Review of their sentences brought reductions for forty of the men to sentences of two to eight years. An appeal by prominent African American lawyer (later justice of the US Supreme Court) Thurgood Marshall of the NAACP was denied. In 1944,

225

the Navy announced that blacks at ammunition depots would be limited to 30 percent of the total work force. The next year, the Navy officially desegregated; in January 1946 the fifty "mutineers" were released from prison but had to remain in the Navy. They were sent to the South Pacific in small groups for a "probationary period" and were then gradually released.[6]

Captain Thomas B. Drinnen was a medical doctor in Knoxville (Knox) who entered the Army on July 15, 1942. He trained at Fort Rucker, Alabama, and then moved to Memphis where he served with the 48th General Hospital unit at Kennedy General Hospital (later the Kennedy VA Hospital). His unit left for Europe in late December 1943 or early January 1944, a few months before D-Day. They were stationed in Swindon, England. On February 24, 1944, Captain Drinnen was accidently killed by carbon monoxide from a water heater in the small metal barracks in which the unit lived. His body was interred in Swindon until after the war and was then repatriated to Knoxville. At his death, he left three small sons, Gary L. Drinnen, age eight; Tommy Drinnen Jr., age six; and Daniel B. (Danny) Drinnen, age two. Tommy and Danny became medical doctors and served in Knoxville and Dickson, Tennessee, and Gary received a PhD in education.

In January 2010, his family found the letters that Captain Drinnen had written to his wife and sons on his voyage to England and then as he settled into life there. They had been stored in an old barn for over sixty years. The last letter is dated the day before his death. Because the boys were very young, and their grieving mother did not talk very much about their father, this collection of about thirty-five letters gave his sons new knowledge about the personality of a devoted dad and husband.[7] Cap-

First Lieutenant Joseph R. McCready.

tain Drinnen is buried in Asbury Cemetery, Knoxville.

A July 30, 1942, article in the Alton (Illinois) *Evening Telegraph* chronicles the death of First Lieutenant Joseph R. McCready; as is the case here, in many instances involving training accidents or deaths in transit, the details of how the service member died were often scarce:

> Jerseyville relatives of Lieut. Joseph McCready of Knoxville, Tenn., were notified Tuesday evening that he had been killed in service at a camp near Falmouth, Mass. Lieut. McCready was the son of Mr. and Mrs. J. H. McCready of Knoxville, Tenn. His mother, before her marriage, was Miss Bernice Richards, daughter of the late Mr. and Mrs. William P. Richards of Jerseyville.

Her father was postmaster at Jerseyville for a number of years and was in business in this city for many years as a member of the firm of Richards and Manning. Details of the manner in which Lieut. McCready was killed were not obtained. . . . He was married last April and is survived by his widow, his parents and two sisters, Miss Margaret McCready and Miss Janet McCready. His father saw service in the first World War and attained the rank of Captain. . . . Lieut. Joseph McCready was born during the last war and was twenty-five years of age at the time of his death.[8]

McCready was educated at the University of Tennessee, and his picture is from UT's 1940 yearbook. He is buried at Saint James Cemetery, Phelps County, Missouri.

Captain William H. Lansdon (McMinn) was born March 27, 1901, and died as a non-battle casualty on September 12, 1942, the victim of what can only be described as a freak car accident at an Army post in Minnesota. According to his obituary in a Boise, Idaho, newspaper, Lansdon was commanding a military police company at Camp Ripley, Minnesota, and was driving in a rainstorm when wet weather brought thousands of frogs onto the highway: "The surface became slippery. The car skidded, overturned three times, and threw Capt. Lansdon clear. He was killed instantly." Lansdon is buried at Morris Hill Cemetery, Boise, Ada County, Idaho.

Sgt. Clyde J. Ellis (Monroe) was born on July 15, 1915, and entered the service in June

Captain William H. Lansdon.

Sgt. Clyde J. Ellis.

227

1941. He served with Battery C, 54th Anti-Aircraft Training Battalion. He died on May 27, 1942, in San Diego, California, from complications following jaundice. He was the second Monroe County man to die in World War II. His untimely death ended the marriage plans of his fiancée, Miss Eva Nell Curtis, aged eighteen, of Tellico Plains. He had written her that he would be able to take leave in June and would return from Callan Field, San Diego, California, for the ceremony. Miss Curtis said his last message was: "Honey, you are always in my heart. Bye, Dear." He is buried in Old Coker Creek Cemetery in Coker Creek, Tennessee.[9]

Private John Robert "Bobby" Stahr (Sullivan) was born in Pawnee, Illinois, on February 7, 1919. He enlisted on July 15, 1943, and was attached to the 292nd Engineers. He died in Taylorville, Illinois, on July 15, 1945, at St. Vincent's Hospital at 7:15 p.m. after falling from a bridge under construction at Palmer, Illinois, on June 26, 1945. Private Stahr was on a thirty-day furlough from Camp Custer, Michigan, at the time of his fatal fall.

Private First Class Oscar A. Dulaney Jr. was born on July 1, 1917, in Johnson City (Washington). He died on January 23, 1945, in Orangeburg, Rockland County, New York. He was a graduate of Science Hill High School, class of 1937. He was a member of the Citizenship Club and a Junior ROTC cadet. Dulaney enlisted in the Army on March 15, 1942, and completed training with a Glider Infantry regiment at Camp Mackall, North Carolina. On January 13, 1945, Dulaney received movement orders to Camp Shanks, New York, via train, to prepare to deploy overseas. He arrived on January 19 and, as he was debarking from the train, his feet slipped out from under him on the slick depot floor, and his head struck the train's metal stairs. He was transported to Camp Shanks's

Private First Class Oscar A. Dulaney Jr.

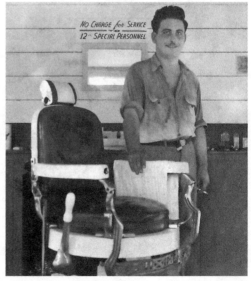

Ship's Serviceman (Barber)
Second Class William J. Brien Jr.

post hospital, where he died of his head injuries at the age of twenty-seven.

Ship's Serviceman (Barber) Second Class William J. Brien Jr. was born on April 10, 1922, in Lebanon, Russell County, Virginia, but he considered Johnson City his home. His father, a World War I Navy veteran, moved to Johnson City while Brien was very young. His father was a barber by trade and owned two barber shops in Johnson City, so Brien followed in dad's footsteps. While cutting hair, he heard the stories of the World War I veterans; when the next world war broke out, he too joined the Navy, in April 1942.

During basic training, the Navy decided to utilize his civilian trade, and they made him a barber as well. He was assigned to the 12th Special Naval Construction Battalion (NCB), "The Boxcar Battalion," a "Seabee" unit. While on leave in Johnson City, Brien's father told him he could take the barber chair in which he had learned to cut hair to war with him. They contacted the Navy, which gave its permission; the Navy supposedly shipped the chair to California, so it could travel with him and his unit to the Pacific in December 1942. In 1945, Brien served with the 12th Special NCB on the Russell Islands and on Okinawa. While on Okinawa, the island was hit by Typhoon Louise, and the hut that housed William's barber chair was lost to the sea. Somewhere off the coast of Okinawa rests a one-time Johnson City barber chair.

On returning to the United States in November 1945, Brien was driving men to their out-processing appointments when his vehicle was hit by a bus. His leg was badly mangled; while hospitalized, a blood clot broke loose, and he died that same day, November 19, 1945. He was buried in Oak Hill Cemetery, Johnson City. Brien was twenty-three at the time of his

death. His grave marker was placed on November 17, 2010, and a full military service conducted on November 19, 2010, sixty-five years to the day of his death. His grave was unmarked until that day.

KOREA

Private First Class Gene Wiggins (Anderson) was born on March 25, 1931. He was assigned as a furnace fireman at Camp Drum, New York, with the 191st Field Artillery Battalion. On January 13, 1952, he was found unconscious in his barracks' boiler room and died at the station hospital of carbon monoxide poisoning. He was awarded the National Defense Service Medal and was buried at Sunset Cemetery in Clinton, Tennessee.

Airman Third Class Garry R. Russell (Fentress) was born on June 9, 1936, and died on April 12, 1955. He enlisted on August 5, 1954. He served with the 306th Tactical Hospital at MacDill Air Force Base, Tampa, Florida. He died at the age of eighteen at Jamestown due to a car accident. His car ran off the road, and he was thrown out. He was buried at Upchurch Cemetery, Fentress County.

Private First Class Floyd A. Snyder (Johnson) was born on September 21, 1931, and died on December 7, 1951, at San Bernardino, California. The local newspaper, the *San Bernardino County Sun*, reported on the freak accident that claimed his life:

> A team of U.S. Army Doctors lost a 15-hour surgical battle to save the life of Pfc. Floyd A. Snyder Jr., 20, of Carderview, Tenn., yesterday, after the soldier was crushed by a 46-ton tank during a routine training problem at Camp Irwin.

The young tankman was a member of the 141st Tank Battalion, which arrived recently at the Army's new armored combat training area from Ft. Campbell, Ky., for an intensive five-week combat workout. According to the public information spokesman, a board of inquiry has been appointed to determine how the soldier fell beneath the tracks of the M-46 "General Patton" tank as the unit neared the completion of a tactical exercise.

The death of the Tennessee draftee was the first casualty as the result of a training accident in the six months since Camp Irwin was reactivated to prepare tank men for combat under realistic battle conditions.[10]

Major Eugene P. Miller, from Bristol (Sullivan), was born on April 19, 1917, and was a member of the 8202nd Army Unit, Korean Military Assistance Group. He developed hemorrhagic fever and was taken to the 121st Evacuation Hospital, where he died July 19, 1951. He is buried at the Ogden City Cemetery, Ogden City, Utah.

Airman Second Class Billy G. Elliott was born on March 11, 1930, in Johnson City (Washington) and served with the 53rd Strategic Reconnaissance Squadron (Medium), Weather, 9th Weather Group, US Air Force. He was operator of a dropsonde (a kind of an expendable weather-tracking device) on a WB-29 Superfortress, serial number 44–62277. On September 18, 1953, en route to Kindley Air Force Base, Bermuda, one of the four-engined weather-recon aircraft's giant propellers broke loose and slammed into the adjacent engine, starting a fire that spread to the airplane's wing. The pilot lost control, and the WB-29 crashed into the Atlantic Ocean, one-hundred fifty miles off Charleston, South Carolina. Elliot's remains were not recovered; he has a memorial marker at Mountain Home National Cemetery, Mountain Home, Tennessee.

First Lieutenant George E. Sims was born in Johnson City (Washington) on July 28, 1927,

Major Eugene P. Miller.

Airman Second Class Billy G. Elliott.

and served with the 3625th Training Wing, US Air Force. He flew over one hundred combat missions during the Korean War. When his tour of duty there was up, he was reassigned as a flight instructor with the 3625th Training Wing at Tyndall Air Force Base (AFB), Florida. He typically flew a Lockheed T-33A Shooting Star jet trainer. On the morning of May 20, 1953, although Sims had already logged his required monthly flight hours, his friend First Lieutenant Thomas J. Wood Jr. asked Sims to go up with him to get in his flight hours. On their return flight to Tyndall AFB, fourteen miles northwest of Panama City, Florida, their plane exploded in mid-air. Sims was the recipient of the Distinguished Flying Cross and was buried at Arlington National Cemetery along with his friend Lieutenant Wood.

Major Carl S. Cross.

VIETNAM

Air Force Major, Vietnam veteran, and noted jet test pilot Carl S. Cross was from Chattanooga (Hamilton) and was born on August 16, 1925. Cross was killed at San Bernardino, California, at the age forty on June 8, 1966 when the experimental bomber aircraft for which he was the copilot, the North American XB-70 Valkyrie, was struck by an F-104 Starfighter airplane during a "photo op" for General Electric, the manufacturer of the XB-70's turbojet engines. Both aircraft crashed. The pilot of the XB-70, Al White, managed to escape the stricken airplane in his ejection pod; however, Cross, incapacitated by the G-forces pressing on him, was unable to start the ejection sequence of his new, complex pod ejection system, and he went down with the XB-70. He was buried at Forest Hills Cemetery, Chattanooga, Tennessee.

The pilot of the F-104, Joseph Walker, was

also lost in the crash. Unfortunately, the name of Major Cross has been all but overshadowed by the names of his fellow test pilots. Both of Cross's fellow test pilots, Walker and Alvin ("Al") White, had come from the more well-known X-15 test program. Walker was a veteran of twenty-five flights in the X-15 and holder of the world's speed and altitude records.

Major Carl Cross made the ultimate sacrifice in the pursuit of aviation conquests. Not only did this collision cost the country two fine test pilots, but it doomed the XB-70 test program, and any further progress that it might have made in aviation was halted. One can only ponder the fact that this tragedy and waste was, in large part, the result of a marketing request for advertising photos.

Captain Wallace A. Kell was born on April 25, 1937, and raised in Copperhill (Polk), Tennessee. He was graduated from Copperhill High School, where he was the valedictorian of the class of 1955. He then was graduated in

231

Captain Wallace A. Kell.

aboard, which collided with an Air National Guard Republic F-84 Thunderjet fighter. Three persons died in the collision; Kell was twenty-nine. He was survived by his wife, Annette Thorpe of Johnson City, Tennessee, daughter Catherine Martin of Atlanta, Georgia, son Michael Kell of Austin, Texas, and four grandsons. Kell is buried at Arlington National Cemetery.[11]

the class of 1959 from Tennessee Technological University with an engineering degree. While there, Kell was cadet commander of the Army ROTC cadet detachment. Following his graduation, a Regular Army commission in the infantry led to service with the Army Rangers, Army Airborne, and Army Aviation. Kell spent July 1965 to June 1966 with the 119th Army Aviation Company (the "Headhunters") in Vietnam. The 119th was designated for that period of time as the best aviation unit in the Army.

Kell was killed in a mid-air collision during a training exercise near Montgomery, Alabama, on December 20, 1966. The crash involved an aircraft from Fort Rucker, a Bell UH-1 Iroquois ("Huey") helicopter with Kell and another man

15

WAR IN THE MIDDLE EAST
Accounts from the Persian Gulf, Afghanistan, and Iraq

[In] the end, of course, a true war story is never about war. It's about sunlight. It's about the special way that dawn spreads out on a river when you know you must cross the river and march into the mountains and do things you are afraid to do. It's about love and memory. It's about sorrow. It's about sisters who never write back and people who never listen.

—*Tim O'Brien, The Things They Carried*

At the time of this writing, the memorial honors four East Tennesseans who fell in the Persian Gulf, twenty-one who died in Afghanistan, and thirty-nine who have fallen in Iraq. Besides regular Army, Navy, Air Force, and Marine personnel, many of those who served in the days and conflicts following September 11, 2001, were reservists or National Guard troops. The deaths of "citizen-soldiers" like these, during the time of an all-volunteer military, will be one apparent theme of this chapter. Another recurring fact will be the number of deaths incurred in these wars caused by the hated "IED," the improvised explosive devices often used by both Iraqi and Afghan insurgents. To date, five courageous East Tennesseans have been awarded the Silver Star for valor during these three conflicts.

THE PERSIAN GULF (DESERT SHIELD/DESERT STORM)

Specialist Fourth Class John B. Stephens was born in Salem County, New Jersey, on March 8, 1965. He was the son of William J. Stephens and Charlotte Stephens. After Stephens's father died when he was a child, the family relocated to Morristown (Hamblen). Stephens was graduated from Morristown West High School with the class of 1983. He was active in the Navy JROTC program while attending Morristown West High.

Stephens enlisted in the Army on July 7, 1983, and attended basic training and AIT at Fort Sill, Oklahoma. From November 1983 through January 1986, he was an ammunition handler in Garlstedt, West Germany, with the Service Battery, 4th Battalion, 3rd Field Artillery, 2nd Armored Division. In January 1986, he returned stateside to serve as an ammunition handler for the 6th Student Company of the Ordnance Missile and Munitions Center and School at Redstone Arsenal, Huntsville, Alabama. This assignment lasted until December 1986, when he would return to West Germany. Next, Stephens was a heavy weapons gunner with the 11th Armored Cavalry Regiment, the famed "Black Horse" regiment, headquartered in Fulda near the inter-German border. He remained with the 11th ACR until May 1990. Stephens

Specialist Fourth Class James D. Tatum.

returned home in June 1990 and joined the Army Reserves as a transport driver with the 418th Quartermaster Battalion at Fort Campbell, Kentucky. His unit was activated in December 1990 to participate in Operations Desert Shield and Desert Storm. While participating in Operation Desert Storm, Stephens was killed on March 27, 1991, when the five-ton truck he was in rolled over as the vehicle made a right-hand turn. Stephens' body was repatriated to his childhood home in Penns Grove, New Jersey, and buried at Eglington Cemetery in Clarksboro, New Jersey, on April 2, 1991.

Specialist James D. Tatum, a native of Riceville (Monroe), was born on December 5, 1968. The son of Ray Neal and Debbie Tatum, he was a 1987 graduate of McMinn County High School and a member of Oak Grove Baptist Church. After graduation from high school, James joined the Army and served three years as a petroleum specialist in the Quartermaster Corps. He was employed by Wright Brothers Construction as a mechanic's helper and was a member of the Army Reserve.

Tatum reported for duty with the 23rd Replacement Detachment, Army Reserves, at Fort Lee, Virginia, on January 31, 1991. He was activated and sent with the 475th Quartermaster Group headquartered in Pennsylvania to Dhahran, Saudi Arabia. The following is an account from the 14th Quartermaster Detachment, a water purification unit beefed up by Tatum's 23rd Replacement Detachment, chronicling his death in one of the most infamous episodes of the 1991–1992 Gulf conflict: Saddam Hussein's Scud ballistic missile campaign against Saudi Arabian and Israeli targets:

> The 14th Quartermaster Detachment, a United States Army Reserve water purification unit stationed in Greensburg, Pennsyl-

vania was mobilized for service in Southwest Asia on January 15, 1991. The unit arrived at Fort Lee, Virginia three days later to conduct intensive mobilization training in preparation for deployment to Saudi Arabia. For the next thirty days, detachment soldiers trained 18 hours a day on the Reverse Osmosis Water Purification Unit (ROWPU) water purification system and common soldier tasks. The unit, augmented by 35 filler personnel from other active Army and reserve units, arrived in Dhahran, Saudi Arabia on February 19, 1991. The detachment's soldiers were quartered in a warehouse that had been converted to a temporary barracks. There they waited for the arrival of unit equipment and movement to a field support location.

At 8:40 p.m. (1240 p.m. EST) on February 25, 1991 parts of an Iraqi SCUD missile destroyed the barracks housing members of the 14th Quartermaster Detachment. In the single, most devastating attack on U.S. forces during that war, 29 soldiers died and 99 were wounded. The 14th Quartermaster Detachment lost 13 soldiers and suffered 43 wounded. Casualties were evacuated to medical facilities in Saudi Arabia and Germany.[1]

James Tatum was twenty-two years old. Tatum's remains were repatriated back to his hometown of Riceville, and funeral services were held on March 4, 1991, at Oak Grove Baptist Church. He is buried at Oak Grove Cemetery.

Captain Daniel E. Graybeal, from Johnson City (Washington), was born on November 13, 1965. Graybeal served with the 50th Medical Company (Air Ambulance). He was killed in action as the result of a helicopter crash in Iraq during Operation Desert Storm on February 29, 1991. He was twenty-five. He is buried at Mountain Home National Cemetery, Johnson City.

Senior Master Sergeant James B. May II was the son of Sam D. and Jane May of Jones-

Senior Master Sergeant James B. May II.

borough (Washington). He was born in Johnson City on May 23, 1950, and was graduated with the class of 1968 at Jonesborough High School. May joined the Air Force and served from 1968–1991. He was stationed with the 33rd Fighter Wing and the 51st Fighter Wing at bases in Tampa, Florida; Ubon, Thailand; Zaragoza, Spain; and Eglin Air Force Base in Florida. May was last stationed at Hurlburt Field in Galveston from 1979–1991 with the 16th Special Operations Squadron. He was married to Master Sergeant Christina L. May, also in the Air Force; they had a son, Scott, and a daughter, April, all of Fort Walton Beach, Florida.

May was a gunner aboard a Lockheed AC-130H Spectre gunship and was deployed to the Persian Gulf to participate in Operation Desert Storm. The gunship would seek out enemy targets and neutralize them or direct other aircraft to the enemy location. On January 31, 1991, May's Spectre gunship, call sign "Spirit 03," was providing support for Marine ground forces defending the Saudi Arabian town of Khafji from an onslaught by Iraqi armored units. Spirit 03 was the last of three Spectre gunships on station, providing close-air support for the embattled Leathernecks in Khafji. As it was about to end its patrol, Sprit 03 received an urgent call for fire support from the Marines, who needed an Iraqi FROG missile battery destroyed:

> Despite the risk of anti-aircraft artillery fire, and the greater danger of the morning sun casting light on the circling gunship, the crew of 'Spirit 03' chose to remain and destroy the position requested." "Spirit 03" did what it had been asked to do, it destroyed the target designated by the Marines who were under fire, but that action came at a heavy cost. An SA-7 "Grail" man-portable surface-to-air missile was fired by the Iraqis at the now in-the-early-morning-light-visible AC-130 in the sky over Khafji.

> The missile found its target and at 0635 hours the aircraft sent out a "mayday" distress call and then crashed into the waters of the Persian Gulf. . . . All [fourteen] crewmembers were killed.

> The bravery and dedication of Spectre resulted in the destruction of 21 enemy fuel trucks, 10 armored personnel carriers, and 2 antiaircraft artillery sites during the Battle of Khafji. The crew of Spirit 03 was awarded the Silver Star and Purple Heart medals. The actions of the aircrews played a decisive role in the retaking of Khafji and its subsequent control for the duration of hostilities.[2]

May had completed the qualifications for senior master sergeant and was promoted posthumously. After the crash, the crew was officially listed as MIA. After the Gulf War ended and the POWs held by the Iraqis were returned, the Air Force discovered the wreckage of "Spirit 03" in the Persian Gulf's waters off Khafji. The standard military protocol was to bury the crew's remains recovered in a centralized National Cemetery, such as Jefferson Barracks National Cemetery.[3] However, at the request of the families of the fourteen crewmen, each family was allowed to bury their loved ones in their home towns. May was buried by his family at Barrancas National Cemetery in Pensacola, Florida. His Silver Star citation follows:

> The President of the United States of America . . . takes pride in presenting the Silver Star (posthumously) to Master Sergeant James B. May II, United States Air Force, for gallantry in connection with military operations against the forces of the Republic of Iraq, while serving as Gunner of AC-130H Spectre Gunship "Spirit 03" of the 16th Special Operations Squadron, U.S. Air Force Special Operations Command, in action against the Iraqi Army near Khafji, Saudi Arabia, on 31 January 1991. On that date, while performing an Operation DESERT STORM AC-130H armed reconnaissance mission, Sergeant May was tasked to engage a free rocket over ground missile site. As the right scanner, Sergeant May assisted the aircrew by calling evasive maneuvers to the pilot as he began firing 40 and 105 millimeter munitions at the target. While engaging the target, the aircrew received heavy fire from numerous anti-aircraft artillery sites. His courageous and aggressive attack continued while under unceasing anti-aircraft artillery fire preventing a missile attack on allied coalition forces. The actions of Sergeant May aided the allied forces in repelling the Iraqi Army incursion south into the Saudi Arabia border town of Khafji. The professional competence, aerial skill, and devotion to duty displayed by Master Sergeant May in the dedication of this service to his country reflect great credit upon himself and the United States Air Force.[3]

AFGHANISTAN

Anderson

Corporal Jason D. Hovater, whose hometown was Lake City, now known as Rocky Top, was born on August 10, 1983. He was the son of Gerald and Kathy Hovater, one of six brothers and one sister, and he was a member of the Lake City Christian Fellowship. He served in Afghanistan with C ("Chosen") Company, 2nd Battalion, 503rd Infantry Regiment (Airborne), 173rd Airborne Brigade Combat Team, based in Vicenza, Italy. Shortly after 4:00 a.m. on July 13, 2008—five days after his platoon of Chosen Company, led by First Lieutenant Jonathan P. Brostom, had arrived at a largely unfinished

Corporal Jason D. Hovater.

outpost in the hamlet of Wanat, located in the Nurestan province of Afghanistan—some two hundred Taliban fighters "let loose a torrent of rocket-propelled grenade fire, destroying the base's anti-tank missile system and its mortar tubes. Then they trained their guns on the observation post." He was twenty-four when he fell in action. An abbreviated account by reporter Greg Jaffe of the savage fight that cost Hovater his life follows:

> The rocket-propelled grenade and rifle fire was so intense that most of the soldiers spent the opening minutes of the battle lying on their stomachs, praying that the enemy would run out of ammunition. They had been in the tiny Afghan village of Wanat, near the Pakistani border, for four days. The command post of their remote base was still just a muddy hole surrounded by sandbags. The radio crackled. About 50 yards from the base's perimeter, nine U.S. soldiers manning an observation post were on the verge of being overrun. Several soldiers were already dead.
>
> "We need to get up there!" screamed 1st Lt. Jonathan Brostrom, the platoon leader at the main base. He and Spec. Jason Hovater grabbed as much ammunition as they could carry and someone popped a yellow smoke grenade to cover their movement. The two soldiers sprinted into enemy fire. It was a predictable reaction from the 24-year-old lieutenant. . . . When Brostrom joined the military, his father, a retired colonel and career aviator, had tried to steer him away from the infantry and toward flying helicopters. "I don't want to be a wimp," the son chided his father.
>
> Brostrom and Hovater dove into the observation post. A sergeant who was too hurt to fight handed Brostrom his M240 machine gun. As the lieutenant turned to set up the weapon, someone spotted an insurgent: "He's inside the [expletive] wire!" Nine U.S. soldiers were killed and 27 were wounded

during the July 13, 2008, attack, which raged for several hours and was one of the bloodiest of the Afghan war. Among the dead was Brostrom [and Hovater].

. . . .

[Brostom and Hovater] were killed within minutes of their arrival [at the OP]. With the enemy closing in, Stafford, McKaig and Sgt. Matthew Gobble—woozy from a loss of blood—abandoned the observation post. In the chaos, they accidentally left behind Sgt. Ryan Pitts, who could hear the enemy fighters barking orders just a few feet away. He whispered into a radio that he was alone and out of ammunition.

"I knew this was going to be it," he later told an Army historian. Soldiers at the main base called to him over the radio, but Pitts didn't answer. The wounded sergeant couldn't afford to let the enemy hear him. Another team of reinforcements sprinted to the observation post, pulled rifles and ammunition off their dead comrades, and fired back at the insurgents. An hour into the battle, Apache helicopters arrived and swung the momentum in favor of U.S. troops.

Brostrom's friend, Brandon Kennedy, arrived at Wanat a short time later to find soldiers coated in sweat and blood. Thick clouds of smoke spewed from burning Humvees. "I had been in firefights before, but this was totally different," he said. "It was like a movie." It fell to Kennedy to escort [his friend's] body back to the United States. He asked a sergeant who had done it before what to expect. "It is always the same," the soldier replied. "The moms just want to know about their son. They want to know what kind of man he was. The dads want to know how their son died. They want someone to explain to them what happened."[4]

Hovater's Silver Star citation follows:

The President of the United States of America . . . has awarded the SILVER STAR to CORPORAL JASON HOVATER, 173D AIR-

BORNE COMBAT TEAM. For Gallantry in action on 13 July 2008 at Wanat, Afghanistan while assigned as a Rifleman with Company C, 2d Battalion, 503d Infantry Regiment, 173d Airborne Brigade Combat Team in support of Operation Enduring Freedom. Corporal Hovater volunteered to reinforce an isolated platoon observation post and moved with his platoon leader to that position while under heavy direct fire from insurgent forces in nearby buildings. After arriving at the observation post, Corporal Hovater engaged the enemy with his personal weapon while also assisting in the emplacement of a mounted weapon. Corporal Hovater's actions ensured that the position was defended from enemy fire and helped prevent it from being overtaken by enemy forces. Corporal Hovater demonstrated courage and unparalleled dedication in the face of imminent and mortal danger. Corporal Hovater's actions reflect

Staff Sergeant Christopher M. Ward.

distinct credit upon himself, the 173d Air-borne Brigade Combat Team and the United States Army.

Hovater is buried at the Knoxville East Tennessee State Veterans Cemetery. He was married to his wife Jenna for approximately six weeks before he deployed.

Staff Sergeant Christopher M. Ward, twenty-four, of Oak Ridge, was the son of Joyce Marie Scott Ward and Michael H. Ward and was born on April 20, 1988, in Arcadia, Florida. He attended DeSoto County High School until his sophomore year, where he first became involved with JROTC. He moved to Oak Ridge with his mother and attended Oak Ridge High during his junior year and enlisted in the Army at age seventeen. He was assigned to the 5th Squadron, 7th Cavalry Regiment, 1st Armored Brigade Combat Team, 3rd Infantry Division, Fort Stewart, Georgia, during Operation Enduring Freedom. Ward died April 6, 2013, in Kandahar, Afghanistan, of wounds suffered when insurgents attacked his unit in Zabul, Afghanistan, with a vehicle-borne improvised explosive device ("IED"). His decorations included the Bronze Star and Purple Heart.

Blount

Sergeant First Class William M. Bennett, thirty-five, of Seymour (Blount), was a 1986 Heritage High School graduate, the senior medic on a twelve-man Army Special Forces team group that specialized in Middle East operations, and the father of an eight-year-old son when he was killed in a predawn raid on enemy forces on April 7, 2003, about thirty miles west of Fallujah, Iraq. Bennett entered the Army in December 1986 and completed Combat Engineer training at Fort Leonard Wood, Missouri. He completed Army diver training in 1989 at the

Sergeant First Class William M. Bennett.

Naval Diving and Salvage Training Center at Panama City, Florida; then, he was assigned to the 7th Engineer Detachment, Fort Kobbe, Panama, where he participated in Operation Just Cause from December 1989 to January 1990. After deploying in 1991 to participate in Operation Desert Storm, Bennett volunteered for Special Forces training in 1992. In 1994, he graduated from the Special Forces Medical Sergeants Course at Fort Bragg, North Carolina. Bennett went on to study Arabic at the Army's John F. Kennedy Special Warfare Center and School at Fort Bragg. He was assigned to the 5th Special Forces Group in July 1995, and he participated in numerous overseas deployments to include combat operations in Afghanistan in support of Operation Enduring Freedom.[5] His Silver Star citation reads:

> Sergeant First Class William M. Bennett, United States Army, was awarded the Silver

Star (Posthumously) for conspicuous gallantry and intrepidity in action while serving with Operational Detachment Alpha 583 (ODA-583), 3d Battalion, 5th Special Forces Group (Airborne) in support of Operation IRAQI FREEDOM in Iraq, on 7 April 2003. Sergeant First Class Bennett's performance as a member of a two-detachment direct action force was exemplary. His selfless dedication to his fellow Soldiers served as an example for others. Sergeant First Class Bennett's willing sacrifice of his own life proved instrumental in saving the lives of his fellow warriors. Sergeant First Class Bennett's gallant actions and dedicated devotion to duty, without regard for his own life, were in keeping with the highest traditions of military service and reflect great credit upon himself, his unit, and the United States Army.

Bennett was survived by his wife, Allison, his son, Seth, and his parents, Leonard and Kathleen Bennett. He was the recipient of the Silver Star, Purple Heart, Bronze Star with Valor, and Army Commendation Medal. He is buried at Oak View Cemetery, Walland, Blount County.

Staff Sergeant Travis W. Nixon, whose parents and relatives live in Blount County, was born in Shreveport, Louisiana, on January 2, 1981. He was a 1999 graduate of St. John-Endicott High School in St. John, Washington. He enjoyed playing the saxophone in the concert and jazz bands and was an avid sportsman. He also enjoyed being part of the swimming team, as well as track, football, baseball, and basketball. He was a member of the Future Farmers of America for four years, and he enlisted in the Army the summer before his senior year of high school began. Nixon was killed on October 29, 2005, while in action in Afghanistan in support of Operation Enduring Freedom. The Department of Defense announced he died from injuries sustained north of Lwara, Afghanistan,

Staff Sergeant Travis W. Nixon.

when his patrol was attacked by enemy forces using small-arms fire and rocket-propelled grenades. He was then serving as a member of the 2nd Battalion, 504th Parachute Infantry Regiment, 1st Brigade, 82nd Airborne Division, Fort Bragg, North Carolina. He was twenty-four when he died, and he was survived by his wife, Wendy Taylor Nixon, his parents, Nicky and Mary Margaret Nixon, and other relatives. His body was returned to Raleigh, North Carolina, and was laid to rest at Raleigh Memorial Park in Wake County, North Carolina. An article in the *Moscow-Pullman Daily News* recounted:

> [Sergeant Nixon] was nearing the end of his third overseas deployment with the United States Army when an enemy ambush surprised his squad while on patrol near Lwara

on the Pakistani border. 'My understanding is that he was squad leader. He died making sure his squad got to safety in an ambush,' said Frank Watson, Nixon's high school football coach and teacher. "I was not surprised Travis would do that. If his job was to lead his men, he would lead his men the best way he knew how. . . ." "You should've seen his grin," said Watson, who described Nixon as a little kid, a rusty-headed, freckle-faced kid, with grins way back to his ears. . . . [Nixon's mother] Maggie was a bus driver for the school district and would drive the team to games. . . .

Watson said, "That wasn't a number that was killed. That was Travis Nixon, and he was one of ours.

"He was more than a number."[6]

Carter

Army master sergeant Jefferson Donald (Donny) Davis was from Watauga and was born on October 22, 1962. Davis was a 1981 graduate of Elizabethton High School, where he played on the football and basketball teams. He also attended Lees-McRae College in Banner Elk, North Carolina, where he played on the football team and studied nursing at East Tennessee State University. In August 1984, Davis enlisted as a medical specialist and served in Korea for three years. Davis is remembered by his friends for his fondness for motorcycles. He was assigned to the 3rd Battalion, 5th Special Forces Group, at Fort Campbell, Kentucky. Davis was one of three Special Forces soldiers and five Afghan opposition fighters from the Northern Alliance who were killed on December 5, 2001, when a two thousand-pound, satellite-guided bomb from a B-52 bomber missed its intended target north of Kandahar and landed on his detachment's position.

His awards and decorations include the Purple Heart, two Meritorious Service Medals, two Army Commendation Medals, the Defense

Master Sergeant Jefferson Donald (Donny) Davis.

of Saudi Arabia Medal, the Liberation and Defense of Kuwait Medal, the Special Forces Tab, the Ranger Tab, and the Combat Infantryman Badge, among others. Captain Jason Amerine commanded the Special Forces A-team that was hit and said that he did not want his men remembered as a detachment that was taken out by an errant bomb: "They cannot be remembered that way. They are the best that America has to offer."[7]

Davis' remains were repatriated to his hometown of Elizabethton, and he was laid to rest at Happy Valley Memorial Park, Elizabethton. He was the son of William Lon and Linda Curd Davis, Watauga, and the husband of Mi

Kyong Yu Davis. He was the father of two children. Davis' Silver Star citation reads:

> The President of the United States of Amer-
> ica takes pride in presenting the Silver Star
> (Posthumously) to Master Sergeant Jeffer-
> son Donald Davis, Unites States Army, for
> gallantry in the face of overwhelming odds
> and direct hostile aggression as the Team
> Sergeant of Operational Detachment Al-
> pha 574 (ODA-574), 3d Battalion, 5th Special
> Forces Group (Airborne), on 5 December
> 2001, in support of Operation Enduring Free-
> dom in Afghanistan. Master Sergeant Davis'
> exceptional courage, dedication to mission
> and personal sacrifice directly contributed
> to the current success of both Chairman
> Harmid Karzai and the Northern Alliance's
> defeat of Taliban Forces. Master Sergeant
> Davis' remarkable performance and selfless
> commitment to his fellow comrades in arms
> serves as the standard for others to emu-
> late. Master Sergeant Davis' actions while
> engaged in combat operations during Oper-
> ation Enduring Freedom reflects great credit
> upon himself, the 5th Special Forces Group
> (Airborne), and the United States Army.

The medal was presented posthumously to
Donny Davis' widow by Major General Geoffrey C. Lambert on December 13, 2001.

Cumberland

Sergeant Alex Van Aalten was born on September 2, 1985. He moved with his family to
Monterey, Tennessee, at an early age and spent
much of his life there. Van Aalten was a strong
Christian and a leader. Before he was deployed,
he taught karate to children and attended Trin-
ity Assembly as well as Cookeville First Assembly. He also liked to go rock climbing and
four-wheeling and was involved in his church
youth group. He loved serving his country.
Van Aalten signed up for the Army soon after

Sergeant Alex Van Aalten.

graduation from high school and went to basic
training at Fort Benning, Georgia. He was a
member of the 508th Parachute Infantry Regiment, 82nd Airborne Division. His tour of duty
in Afghanistan began in January 2005, and he
was scheduled to be there for fifteen months.
June 2007 would have marked his third year
in the Army, and he had signed up to serve
for another six years. Van Aalten was a machine gunner on a Humvee; his assigned duty
on April 20, 2007, the day he perished, was to
drive insurgents out of an Iraqi town so that the
village's citizens could freely vote. He and his
wife had been married for about two years before he died in action; he was twenty-one when
he died. In July 2009, a Senate Joint Resolution
designated the bridge between Monterey, Tennessee, and Interstate 40's exits 300 and 301
the "Sgt. Alex Van Aalten Memorial Bridge"
in his honor. Van Aalten is buried in Arlington
National Cemetery.

Greene

Staff Sergeant Rusty H. Christian.

Staff Sergeant Rusty H. Christian of Greeneville was born on November 15, 1985, and died of wounds sustained when enemy forces attacked his unit with an IED in Tarin Kowt, Afghanistan, on January 28, 2010, during Operation Enduring Freedom. He was twenty-four years old and was assigned to the 2nd Battalion, 1st Special Forces Group, Joint Base Lewis-McChord, Tacoma, Washington. He is buried at Arlington National Cemetery.

Hamilton

Sergeant Patrick K. Durham, twenty-four, of Chattanooga, died on August 28, 2010, in Babur, Afghanistan, of wounds suffered when insurgents attacked his unit with an IED. Durham was a member of the 1st Battalion, 320th Field Artillery, 2nd Brigade Combat Team, 101st Air-

Sergeant Patrick K. Durham.

borne Division (Air Assault), Fort Campbell, Kentucky. He left behind his wife, Kristy W. Durham, two sons, Elijah and Jordan, and one daughter, Cheyenne. He is buried at Francis Cemetery, Marion County, Tennessee.

Johnson

Specialist Frederick Z. (Fred) Greene, age twenty-nine, of Mountain City, lost his life on November 5, 2009, from injuries sustained at the US Army base in Fort Hood, Texas, during an infamous "active shooter" event at that Army base. Greene was in the line of fire when a disgruntled US Army major and psychiatrist opened fire on his fellow soldiers. He was one of thirteen who died in the Fort Hood shooting. Greene had earned the rank of Specialist 4. He was a combat engineer and a father of two, who was raised by his grandparents in Mountain City. Greene graduated from Johnson County High School and was a former employee at the

Specialist Fourth Class Frederick Z. (Fred) Greene.

Knox

Lieutenant Colonel Frank D. Bryant Jr. was from Knoxville and was born on August 13, 1973. Bryant was graduated from Karns High School in 1991, winning a state trophy that year. He was graduated from the Air Force Academy in 1995, where he was captain of the wrestling team and most valuable player. Bryant had piloted an F-16 on more than a dozen bombing missions in Baghdad, Iraq, including one in support of a surprise raid on Saddam Hussein. He was assigned to the 56th Operations Group, Luke Air Force Base, Arizona, beginning in August 2007. Colonel Bryant was one of eight airmen who were killed on April 27, 2011, in a mass shooting incident at the Kabul International Airport while Bryant was supporting Operation Enduring Freedom, having been stationed in Afghanistan since June 2010 as part of the 438th Air Expeditionary Advisory Group. His

A. C. Truss plant in Mountain City. He joined the Army in May 2008. He had been awarded the National Defense Service Medal, the Global War on Terrorism Service Medal, and the Army Service Medal and was qualified as an expert on the M-4 carbine. He was a member of the 510th Engineering Company, 20th Engineer Battalion, 36th Engineer Brigade, based at Fort Hood.

Greene is buried at Bakers Gap Cemetery, Butler, Johnson County. On April 19, 2013, the Tennessee state legislature passed Public Chapter No. 482, designating the bridge spanning Goose Creek on State Route 67 in Mountain City, Tennessee, located west of such route's intersection with US Highway 421, the "Specialist Frederick Green Memorial Bridge" to honor the memory of this remarkable young man who lost his life in the pre-deployment tragedy at Fort Hood, Texas.

Lieutenant Colonel Frank D. Bryant Jr.

Specialist Fourth Class Jonathan M. Curtis.

sachusetts, and grew up in Belmont, Massachusetts. His parents said that he attended a special education program at Belmont High School, but eventually left the school, earning his diploma from a correspondence school. Curtis joined the Army in 2004; as his parents later reported, he "defied doubters" by completing basic training. He was then assigned to the 1st Battalion, 502nd Infantry Regiment, 2nd Brigade Combat Team, 101st Airborne Division (Air Assault). He died from combat wounds inflicted by a motorcycle-carried IED driven by an insurgent suicide bomber on November 1, 2010, in Kandahar, Afghanistan. Curtis and another soldier, Private First Class Andrew N. Meari, were guarding the entrance of Combat Outpost Sanjaray when the suicide bomber tried to run the gate and get into the outpost. Although sacrificing his own life,

fellow officers called the loss "devastating." "He excelled in everything he did and gave his life defending the nation he served for sixteen years," Brigadier General Jerry D. Harris Jr., commanding general of the 56th Ops Group, stated. Bryant received his Air Force wings in 1997. He received his commission as a lieutenant colonel in July while serving in Afghanistan as an adviser to the budding air force there. His decorations included the Bronze Star, the Purple Heart, the Defense Meritorious Service Medal, two Air Force Commendation Medals, and the Air Force Achievement Medal.[8] Bryant is buried at Arlington National Cemetery.

Specialist Fourth Class Jonathan M. Curtis was born on June 3, 1986, in Cambridge, Mas-

Private First Class Patrick S. Fitzgibbon.

Corporal Kristopher D. (Daniel) Greer.

Curtis' actions (and Meari's) saved the lives of seven fellow soldiers. He was the husband of Samantha Foust Curtis of Knoxville; the father of an infant daughter, Tessa-Marie Curtis; and the son of Philip and Pamela Curtis. Curtis had been inducted as a Distinguished Member of his regiment; his decorations and awards included the Purple Heart, Bronze Star, Army Achievement Medal, Army Good Conduct Medal, National Defense Service Medal, Afghanistan Campaign Medal, Iraq Campaign Medal, Global War on Terrorism Service Medal, Army Service Ribbon, Overseas Service Ribbon, and Comb. He is buried at the Highland Memorial West Cemetery in Knoxville.[9]

Private First Class Patrick S. Fitzgibbon (nicknamed "St. Paddy") of Knoxville was the eldest of six children. He was born on March 30, 1990. He was funny, a bit of a rebel, and a huge practical joker. Making other people laugh was a big part of Fitzgibbon's life, and he especially enjoyed making comedy videos. He was attending South Doyle High School when, in his senior year, he decided to drop out and obtain his GED. A member of the Junior ROTC in school, he decided to "get his life together" and, following in a cousin's footsteps, he enlisted in the Army in December 2008. He graduated from basic training at Fort Benning, Georgia, and is remembered by his fellow soldiers there as a crack-up who was always finding a way to break the tension. Transferred to Fort Carson, Colorado, he deployed to Afghanistan in May 2009, having been assigned to the 1st Battalion, 12th Infantry Regiment, 4th Brigade Combat Team, 4th Infantry Division. He was one of three soldiers killed when insurgents attacked their patrol with IEDs and rocket-propelled grenades on August 1, 2009. Fitzgibbon's medals included a posthumous Bronze Star and the National Defense Service Medal, Afghanistan Campaign Medal with Campaign Star, Global War on Terrorism Service Medal, and the Army Service Ribbon. Survivors include his father, Donnie Fitzgibbon, his stepmother, Trish Fitzgibbon, and mother, Tonya Brown. He is buried at Sherwood Memorial Gardens, Alcoa, Blount County.[10]

Corporal Kristopher D. (Daniel) Greer of Ashland City, Tennessee, died on August 8, 2010, of wounds received two days earlier while in combat in Helmand Province, Afghanistan. Born on October 29, 1984, he was twenty-five. He was assigned to the 4th Combat Engineering Battalion, 4th Marine Division, Marine

Corps Forces Reserve, based in Knoxville. Greer joined the Ashland City Fire Department as a volunteer and became a full-time employee two years later. He joined the Pegram Volunteer Fire Department in July 2001 and volunteered there for four years before transferring to Ashland City's fire service. He was survived by his wife, Stacy Bennett Greer of Ashland City, son, Ethan Douglas Greer of Ashland City, father, Kris Greer and his wife, Mary Jo of Russellville, Kentucky, and mother, Gina Foster Breeden, of Pegram, Tennessee. His decorations included the Marine Corps Reserve Medal, National Defense Service Medal, Afghanistan Campaign Medal, Global War on Terrorism Medal, Armed Forces Reserve Medal, and Sea Service Deployment Ribbon. He is buried at the Middle Tennessee State Veterans Cemetery in Nashville.

Senior Airman Tre F. Porfirio of St. Mary's, Georgia, died on November 28, 2010. He succumbed to injuries after being wounded in Afghanistan in the previous year. Born on Oc-

Senior Airman Tre F. Porfirio.

tober 8, 1988, in Knoxville, Porfirio was an altar boy at Holy Ghost Catholic Church and was a Junior ROTC cadet at Bearden High School; he later moved and was graduated in 2007 from Camden County High School, Kingsland, Georgia. Upon completion of high school, he entered the US Air Force and served with its 88th Communication Squadron. Porfirio was a devoted father, fun-loving brother, and dedicated son.

While serving in Afghanistan, Porfirio was shot three times in the back, making it necessary for Army surgeons at Walter Reed Army Medical Center in Washington, DC, to remove his pancreas via an innovative medical procedure to stimulate the production insulin in his liver. Although the surgery went well and was groundbreaking in its own right, Tre Porfirio ultimately died from complications just over a year after he was wounded, on November 28, 2010, at the age of twenty-two:

> The Knoxville-born serviceman's father, Karl Porfirio, said Thursday that the past year "has been rough." "I keep calling him a boy, but he's a man," Karl Porfirio said, his voice cracking. "He's my boy, but to everybody else he's a man. A senior airman in the United States Air Force." . . .
>
> While Porfirio had lived in northern Georgia for the last six years, his father knew Knoxville is where his son would want to be. . . . "His grandmother is here, and his brother's here. I could have laid him to rest in Arlington (National Cemetery), and some people probably think I'm crazy to not bury him there, but Knoxville is his home. He was born here," the father continued. "I'm pretty sure this is where he would want to sleep."[11]

He was survived by his son, Landon Porfirio, and his father, Karl Porfirio of St. Mary's, Georgia. He is buried at the Knoxville East Tennessee State Veterans Cemetery.

Sergeant First Class Carlos Santos-Silva.

Sergeant First Class Carlos Santos-Silva was born at a military base in Wiesbaden, West Germany, on November 4, 1977, and lived the life of an "Army brat" before enlisting in the Army in August 1996. Santos-Silva began his career as a medical supply specialist with the 101st Airborne Division (at one point, his father, a brother, and he were all simultaneously stationed at Fort Campbell), and he later became an infantryman with the 10th Mountain Division at Fort Drum, New York. He served on three deployments with the 10th Mountain: the first to Kosovo in August 2001, and two more in Iraq. He joined the 82nd Airborne Division in February 2009 and was killed in Afghanistan on March 22, 2010, by the blast of an IED while patrolling in southern Afghanistan's Kandahar province. At the time of his death, he was serving with Com-

pany C, 2nd Battalion, 508th Parachute Infantry Regiment, 4th Brigade Combat Team of the 82nd Airborne. He was thirty-two when he died. His father, a retired command sergeant major living in Knoxville, paid his son this tribute: "I'll always remember him as a better soldier than I was. I looked forward to seeing him finish his career and achieve levels higher than I did," and added, "He loved what he was doing, and he treated his soldiers like sons. . . . He would have been coming home in three weeks on leave, but he delayed that so he could be there for [he and his wife's] twelfth anniversary."[12]

Santos-Silva's decorations include the Bronze Star with Oak Leaf Cluster, Meritorious Service Medal, Purple Heart, Army Commendation Medal, Army Achievement Medal, Army Good Conduct Medal, National Defense Service Medal, Kosovo Campaign Medal, and the Afghanistan Campaign Medal. He left behind a wife, Kristen; a nine-year-old son, Cameron; and his parents, CSM (Retired) Francisco and Monika Santos-Silva, of Knoxville. He is buried in Arlington National Cemetery.

Private First Class Tommy Chance Young served with Company C, 4th Battalion, 31st Infantry Regiment, known as the "Polar Bears." He was born on May 28, 1982, and was killed in a helicopter accident at Fort Drum, New York, on March 11, 2003. He is buried at the East Tennessee State Veterans Cemetery in Knoxville. His father, Tommy Young Sr., shared the following account of his brief life with the ETVMA:

> My son PFC Tommy Chance Young [was] in Operation Anaconda right after 9/11 after serving in Afghanistan. My son was killed in a Blackhawk crash at Fort Drum, NY, and I am hoping that my son will not be forgotten for fighting for our country. . . . I hope and pray that his name will be put with the other fallen heroes, for he was a 20-year-

Private First Class Tommy Chance Young.

Specialist Fourth Class Nathan E. Lillard.

old veteran. No one made my son join the U.S. Army. He did it on his own, and when it was time for my son to be called up for Operation Anaconda, he didn't say no. He went with pride and didn't back down. He spent his 19th birthday over there fighting for our freedom, so please don't forget him.

McMinn

Specialist Fourth Class Nathan E. Lillard hailed from McMinn County. Lillard was born in East Ridge on August 18, 1984, and was a longtime resident of Athens before moving to Lenoir City. Lillard spent his junior and senior years at Lenoir City High School, where he graduated in 2003 and joined the Army. Lillard later lived in Knoxville and worked in the warehouse at Modern Supply on Lovell Road, but he left

his civilian job to reenlist in the Army in November 2006. He arrived at Fort Campbell, Kentucky, in August 2009. When deployed to Afghanistan, he served as a member of A Company, 1st Battalion, 327th Infantry Regiment, 1st Brigade, 101st Airborne Division (Air Assault), Fort Campbell, Kentucky. Lillard was killed in the Watahpur District, Kunar Province of Afghanistan, by small-arms fire on November 14, 2010, during Operation Bulldog Bite, an effort to root out insurgents and weapons in rugged terrain near the Pech River. He was twenty-six at the time he died; four other soldiers of the 327th died alongside him. Lillard's death made him the first graduate of Lenoir City High School killed in the Afghan conflict.[13]

His awards and decorations included the National Defense Service Medal, Global War on Terrorism Service Medal, Army Service Medal, NATO Medal, and the Combat Infantryman Badge. His survivors include his mother, Helen Marie Trentham Hyatt of Athens, his stepfather, Edward C. Hyatt of Lenoir City, one brother, Eric, and his fiancée, Leonarda Beoddy, of Sweetwater. He is buried at McMinn Memory Gardens in Athens.

Monroe

Private First Class Robert Kelsey Repkie died on June 24, 2010, at Forward Operating Base Farah, Afghanistan, of injuries sustained from a non-combat related incident. He was twenty. He was assigned to the 782nd Brigade Support Battalion, 4th Brigade Combat Team, 82nd Airborne Division, Fort Bragg, North Carolina. Repkie was born on March 13, 1990, and attended Sweetwater High School in Monroe County before leaving to earn his GED. He then joined the Army, where he was serving with the 82nd Airborne. Repkie was due home during the summer of 2010, and he had already made plans to go camping with his family. He was survived by his father, Russell Repkie, and his mother, Linda Haney. His decorations and awards included the Army Achievement Medal, National Defense Service Medal, Afghanistan Campaign Medal with Campaign Star, Global War on Terror Service Medal, Army Service Medal, Overseas Service Medal and the NATO Medal. He is buried at Arlington National Cemetery.

Lance Corporal Franklin N. Watson of Vonore died on September 24, 2011, while conduct-

Lance Corporal Franklin N. Watson.

ing combat operations in Helmand Province, Afghanistan. He was twenty-one. He was assigned to Company D, 4th Combat Engineer Battalion, 4th Marine Division, Marine Corps Forces Reserve, based out of Knoxville. Watson was born on April 6, 1990. He graduated from Sequoyah High School in 2008. Teachers and coaches remember a vibrant young man and a proven leader on the football field. After graduation, he worked as a deputy in the Monroe County Sheriff's Department and patrol officer for the Madisonville Police Department. He joined the Marine Corps Reserve in July 2010. Survivors include his mother and stepfather, Stacy and Jack Couch, and his father and stepmother, Troy N. Jr. and Katie Watson. He is buried at the Hiwassee Church of God Cemetery, Madisonville, Monroe County.

Private First Class Robert Kelsey Repkie.

Sevier

Private First Class Zachary S. Salmon was born on August 31, 1989, in Cincinnati, Ohio, and originally lived in Hebron, Kentucky, near Cincinnati, but moved with his mother to Pigeon Forge when he was fourteen. He graduated from Pigeon Forge High School in 2008 and joined the Army in March 2010. He served as a member of Troop A, 1st Squadron, 32nd Cavalry, 1st Brigade Combat Team, 101st Airborne Division (Air Assault), out of Fort Campbell, Kentucky. He died on January 12, 2011, in Afghanistan, at the age of twenty-one. Salmon was survived by his father, Steven Salmon, mother, Renee, and son, Noah Salmon. He is buried at Riverview Cemetery in Aurora, Indiana. His decorations included the National Defense Service Medal, Global War on Terrorism Service Medal, Army Service Ribbon, and the Combat Action Badge.[14]

Sullivan

Sergeant First Class Jason O. B. Hickman was a 1992 graduate of Dobyns-Bennett High School in Kingsport and joined the Army in April 1999. Hickman had served as an engineer at Fort Bragg, North Carolina, and in a recruiting battalion in Wisconsin. He had also served in Iraq before joining the 25th Infantry Division, based at Fort Richardson, in May 2008. The brigade deployed to Afghanistan in February and March 2009. He was assigned to A Company,

Private First Class Zachary S. Salmon.

Sergeant First Class Jason O. B. Hickman.

Brigade Special Troops Battalion, 4th Brigade Combat Team (Airborne), 25th Infantry Division. Hickman died in Afghanistan at the age of thirty-five after his combat post was hit by a vehicle carrying an explosive. A Fort Richardson, Alaska, spokesman said Hickman was wounded at Combat Outpost Bowri Tana. The outpost was attacked by insurgents firing small arms and was struck by the bomb-carrying vehicle. Hickman died later that night en route to Forward Operating Base Salerno. His decorations and awards included the Bronze Star and Purple Heart. He is buried in Tahoma National Cemetery in Kent, Washington.

Unicoi

Senior Airman Benjamin D. White of Erwin was born on October 16, 1985, and was the son of Anthony White and Brenda Shelton. He was graduated from Science Hill High School in

Senior Airman Benjamin D. White.

2004 and had attended East Tennessee State University for several semesters before enlisting in the Air Force in July 2006. He had always wanted to join the Air Force, and once he reached that goal, White felt a sense of purpose, as though he was doing what he was meant to do. White was assigned to the 48th Rescue Squadron, Davis-Monthan Air Force Base, Tucson, Arizona. He died on June 9, 2010, near Forward Operating Base Jackson, Afghanistan, alongside three other airmen, in the crash of a HH-60G Pave Hawk search-and-rescue helicopter. White was twenty-four when he died. He is buried at Mountain Home National Cemetery in Johnson City.

IRAQ

Anderson

Sergeant First Class James D. Connell Jr. was born on June 11, 1966, and was from Lake City, now known as Rocky Top. A platoon sergeant in the Army's 10th Mountain Division, Connell was killed on May 12, 2007, during his second tour of duty in Iraq. He was forty years old and was one of five soldiers killed when his patrol came under attack near Mahmudiyah, Iraq. He is buried at Arlington National Cemetery.

A May 14, 2007 article in the *Knoxville News Sentinel* by Darren Dunlap provides this account: "On two weeks' home leave, recovering from a shrapnel wound, not long before his return to service in Iraq, he had visited Lake City Middle School to tell the students about his duties and the military, talking both to his 12-year-old son Bryan's and 14-year-old daughter Courtney's classes. Courtney added, 'He's a hero.' She said that during her father's leave, he took each of his three children out of school for

Sergeant First Class James D. Connell Jr.

four-hour ambush and firefight by insurgents south of Balad Ruz, Iraq. Kennedy was Anderson County's first resident to die in Operation Iraqi Freedom. He was described by his father as "the consummate soldier," and his wife elaborated:

> [Kennedy] "felt that going over there and doing what he was doing was right because it was for his family and it was for his country," [his wife] Tiffany Kennedy said during a press conference on the carport of the family's modest home in the Scarboro community.... [She] last spoke with her husband by phone [and] they communicated daily by e-mail, phone or instant messenger. Their conversations centered on their children and life in Oak Ridge, she said.
>
> "We never discussed anything he was doing," she said. "He loved his children," she said. "This is the hardest on them. They all understand what happened." ... Tiffany Kennedy said she learned of her husband's death Monday when a military chaplain arrived at her door. "About the only words that went through my mind at that time were, 'Oh God, why Stephen?' That was pretty much it."[16]

one day to spend the day with them. He took his oldest son, 16-year-old Nick, horseback riding in the Smokies. He took Bryan to Knoxville Center and to a movie. "In the back bedroom of the Connell home, Connell's father, James Sr., looked at pictures from his son's most recent military leave.... The pictures appeared one at a time, an electronic slide show from just one week ago when the family had celebrated Bryan's birthday."[15]

Sergeant First Class Stephen C. Kennedy was from Oak Ridge and was born on April 6, 1969. Kennedy first enlisted in the Marine Corps in 1988, after graduation from high school in Bremerton, Washington, and he served in Operations Desert Shield and Desert Storm. He joined the Tennessee Army National Guard in 1998, serving in the Lenoir City detachment of the 278th Regimental Combat Team. He departed for Iraq in November 2004 as a non-commissioned officer of D Company, 1st Squadron, 278th Regimental Combat Team. He was killed in action on April 4, 2005, in a

SFC Kennedy left behind his parents, Bob and Jo Kennedy; his wife, Tiffany; and four children, three sons, aged fifteen, twelve, and ten, and a three-year-old daughter, at the time he died. Kennedy is buried at the East Tennessee State Veterans Cemetery. The Lenoir City Armory in Loudon County, where he trained and trained others in the 278th, now bears Kennedy's name.

Staff Sergeant Daniel M. Morris, a Clinton native, died on November 25, 2006, when a roadside bomb exploded next to his Humvee in Iraq's Diyala Province. He was twenty-eight and was born on May 15, 1978. He had re-enlisted for a second tour of duty. He planned to become a minister. Morris served as an infantryman and was assigned to A Company, 1st Squadron, 1st Cavalry Regiment, based at Fort Hood, Texas. Morris was a seven-year veteran on his second tour of duty in Iraq. He was a 1996 graduate of Clinton High School and a member of Lakeview Baptist Church in Clinton. Morris was survived by his daughter, Alexys Morris, of Pigeon Forge. Other survivors included his father and mother, Glenn and Amy A. Morris, his sister Cassidy, and brother Adam, all of Clinton. He is buried at Oak Ridge Memorial Park.

Blount

Private Michael H. Ferschke Jr. was born in Woonsocket, Rhode Island, on November 13, 1985, and enlisted in the Marine Corps on Oc-

Private Michael H. Ferschke Jr.

tober 7, 2003, from his hometown of Maryville. After "boot camp" at the Marine Corps Recruit Depot at Parris Island, South Carolina, Ferschke reported to the School of Infantry at Camp Lejeune, North Carolina, where he was assigned the primary Military Occupational Specialty (MOS) of basic rifleman. After that training, he reported to the 2nd Reconnaissance Battalion, 2nd Marine Division, at Camp Lejeune. While there, he attended the Amphibious Reconnaissance School and Basic Airborne Course and was reassigned as a Reconnaissance Marine. In March 2005, he was reassigned to the 3rd Reconnaissance Battalion, the 31st Marine Expeditionary Unit, based in Okinawa, as a member of its Amphibious Reconnaissance and Deep Reconnaissance Platoons. Ferschke also served in billets as radio operator and as an assistant team leader before being assigned to his final duty as Team Leader, Team One, 1st Platoon, Company A, 3rd Recon. He was killed in action in Iraq on August 10, 2008, while conducting a house-to-house search. Ferschke's decorations and awards include the Purple Heart and Combat Action Ribbon, the Iraqi Campaign Medal, Global War on Terrorism Medal, Good Conduct Medal, Sea Service Deployment Ribbon (with two stars in lieu of a third award), and the National Defense Medal. Ferschke was survived by his parents, Michael and Robin Ferschke; brother, Raymond L. Ferschke; sister, Alissa Bridgman; his wife of only one month, Hotaru N. Ferschke of Okinawa, and a child.

He is buried in Knoxville's East Tennessee State Veterans Cemetery. As his casket was laid to rest, twenty-two doves, representing each year of his life, were released skyward by his wife and mother. Michael Casteel, Maryville High School's assistant principal during Ferschke's high school years, recalled him "as someone who was quiet yet outgoing and who had a wide spectrum of friends." "He could find the good in a lot of people," Casteel added, and "from the beginning, he knew what he wanted to do, to join the armed forces, the Marines. He fulfilled that exact dream."[17]

Bradley

Private First Class James W. Price of Cleveland was assigned to the 4th Battalion, 5th Air Defense Artillery Regiment, 1st Cavalry Division, Fort Hood, Texas. He was killed on September 18, 2004, when an IED destroyed his vehicle in Baghdad. He was twenty-two. Price was born on July 22, 1982, and attended Bushnell High School in Bushnell, Florida, where he was a tuba player in the band and

Private First Class James W. Price.

participated in track. He then attended Chattanooga State Community College. He joined the Army as a communication specialist and served three-and-a-half years on active duty. Though he was a native of Grand Forks, North Dakota, he lived most of his life in Florida. He was survived by his mother, Darlene Howell; a sister, April; and a brother, Joseph. Price was given full military honors and was decorated with the Purple Heart and the Bronze Star for his actions. He is buried at Sunset Memorial Gardens, Cleveland, Bradley County.

Sergeant David T. Weir of Cleveland was a career military man doing what he wanted to do and what he felt needed to be done. He was born on September 22, 1982, and was a 2001 graduate of Bradley Central High School, where he played football as number 24. His favorite sport was football, and he also enjoyed camping and the outdoors and was a member of Waterville Baptist Church. He was a history buff who studied all of the wars and knew the times and dates of each one. He was killed on September 14, 2006, in Baghdad, in what US military officials described as a running gun battle with insurgents with alleged ties to Al Qaeda. He served with the 1st Squadron, 61st Cavalry Regiment, 4th Brigade Combat Team,

Sergeant David T. Weir.

101st Airborne Division (Air Assault), based at Fort Campbell, Kentucky.[18] He was survived by his wife, Alison Weir; his son, Gavin; his parents, Charles Lynn and Jackie Weir; three brothers, Chris, Jeff, and Tim Weir; a sister, Missie Burgraff; and grandmother, Beulah Weir. He was decorated with the Purple Heart and Bronze Star. He is buried at the Chattanooga National Cemetery.

Carter

Staff Sergeant Stephen R. Maddies of Elizabethton was born on November 3, 1965, and was the son of Roosevelt and Sharon Maddies. He attended Catskill Elementary, then Carnegie Junior High, and was graduated from Carson High School in Carson, California. He also attended Victory Faith Center Church in Wilmington, California. His family and friends were close to his heart, and he was full of life, love, and humor. Maddies made loyal friends wherever he went, and he loved Tennessee, his adopted state.

Maddies was a twenty-year veteran, with a career that spanned fifteen years of active duty in the United States Army and five years with the Tennessee Army National Guard. His Army career included two tours in Korea; one tour in

Staff Sergeant Stephen R. Maddies.

Kuwait with the 82nd Airborne Division during the Gulf War; and tours in Bosnia and Honduras. His first tour in Iraq in 2004 was with the Bristol-based F Troop, 278th Armored Cavalry Regiment. Maddies volunteered to return to Iraq for a second tour of duty. He earned his Master Parachutist Wings while serving with the 82nd Airborne Division at Fort Bragg, North Carolina, and was already a decorated warrior when he redeployed to Iraq. He was serving his second tour there when he was killed on July 31, 2007, just eighteen days before he was slated to return home.[19] He was forty-one and a member of the Tennessee Army National Guard's 473rd Counter-Rocket Artillery and Mortar Platoon, 278th Armored Cavalry Regiment, headquartered in Columbia, Tennessee.

He is buried at Riverside National Cemetery, Riverside, California. On April 15, 2008, Tennessee governor Phil Bredesen signed a bill from the Tennessee legislature honoring the memory of Sergeant Maddies of Elizabethton with a memorial bridge located in Wilson County. The Stephen R. Maddies Memorial Bridge was dedicated on July 11, 2008, and is located at Franklin Road (State Route 840) in Wilson County.

Lieutenant Colonel Joseph T. McCloud was born on December 14, 1966, and was from Elizabethton, although his family moved away when he was only two years old. The family first went to Atlanta and later to the Detroit, Michigan, area where he was graduated from Grosse Pointe High School. He was an outstanding athlete, even as a young boy, and made the All-City team in football in Detroit playing linebacker for the Grosse Pointe team. He also stood out as a center fielder in Colt League baseball for teenagers. After graduating from high school, he went to the University of Tennessee, where he studied liberal arts and history. He graduated from UT in 1989 and enlisted in the Marine Corps just in time for Operation Desert Storm, during which he served on the USS *Missouri*. He also served on the battleship during action in Somalia. He was accepted to attend Officer Candidate School. His most memorable moment on board the *Missouri* came at Pearl Harbor, Hawaii, when the captain selected him to escort President George H. W. Bush on the fiftieth anniversary of the bombing of Pearl Harbor.

After obtaining his commission via OCS, McCloud was assigned as an infantry officer. One of his assignments was with the Navy and Marine Corps News, where he produced a weekly television program that was broadcast to sailors and Marines around the world. After the terrorist attacks on the World Trade Center and the Pentagon, McCloud served in the Philippines. He died on December 3, 2006, under non-hostile circumstances, when a CH-46 helicopter airlifting him and fourteen others crashed near Lake Qadisiyah, Iraq. He was thirty-nine. McCloud served almost seventeen years with the Marines and had begun his tour in Iraq in September. He is buried at Arlington National Cemetery.[20]

Campbell

Sergeant First Class Gregory B. Hicks was born on July 7, 1960, and grew up in the Duff community of Campbell County. Less than a month after he graduated from Wynn High School in 1986, the seventeen-year-old enlisted in the Army. He was a nineteen-year Army veteran when he was deployed to Iraq with Company B, 1st Battalion, 9th Cavalry Regiment, 1st Cavalry Division, of Fort Hood, Texas. On January 8, 2004, on his second war in Iraq (having served

during Operation Desert Shield/Desert Storm in 1990–1991), Hicks and eight other soldiers were killed in the crash of a UH-60 Black Hawk medical transport helicopter. The thirty-five-year-old native of Duff was heading home to the United States to have surgery after suffering shrapnel wounds to his face and knee damage. Military officials believe the UH-60 Black Hawk chopper was probably shot down by enemy insurgents. His mother, Flora Hicks, learned of her son's death when she received a phone call from Gregory Hicks's wife in Texas. "She was looking forward to having him come home and getting his surgeries taken care of so they could get out and travel with the kids," Flora Hicks said. At the time of his death, he was the second East Tennessee soldier killed during Operation Iraqi Freedom and the third to die in overseas combat since September 11, 2001. At the time of his death, SFC Hicks had decided to retire from the Army in sixteen months. He and his wife Melinda had a son, Chris, and a daughter, Jennifer.[21] Hicks was buried at the Fort Riley Post Cemetery in Geary County, Kansas.

Staff Sergeant Alfred Barton Siler, originally of Duff, Tennessee, was born on November 27, 1971, and was a 1989 graduate of Jellico High School. He was an eight-year veteran of the Tennessee Army National Guard, Troop A, Support Squadron, 278th Regimental Combat Team, stationed in Knoxville. Siler had joined the military a few years after graduating from high school and was a welder in civilian life. He enjoyed four-wheeling and outdoor activities. Most pictures of Siler in Iraq show him surrounded by children, often holding stuffed animals for them. He was killed in action on May 25, 2005, at the age of thirty-three, when the Humvee he was riding in swerved to avoid

Staff Sergeant Alfred Barton Siler.

Church of God; he was buried following the service at Marlow Cemetery in Caryville. In June 2006, the Tennessee Army National Guard Armory in Jacksboro was named in honor of Siler.

Claiborne

Staff Sergeant Terry William Prater, age twenty-five, of Speedwell, was born on August 13, 1981. The 1999 graduate of Powell Valley High School was a member of the Centex Bass Hunters and of the Baptist faith. Prater grew up in eastern Kentucky before moving with his mother to Tennessee during high school, said his father, Terry D. Prater of Floyd County, Kentucky. Prater had received the Silver Star for jumping on another soldier to protect him from a grenade in August 2004, saving his buddy's life in the process. He was injured in the attack and also received a Purple Heart for the injuries he sustained. However, he returned to Iraq after recovering from several injuries

a person and hit another vehicle in Tuz, Iraq. He was the turret gunner on the Humvee and lost his life when the Humvee flipped during the ensuing accident. He was scheduled to return home within a month and looked forward to being with his family and friends. Siler had already bought tickets to take his three-year-old daughter, Mikkah, to Disney World over the summer of 2005. He could not wait to get home and hold his little girl. He was going to take her to the beach, and they were going to go fishing and just hang out, his brother, Jason, said. Siler told his brother that he could not wait to have some biscuits and gravy and a cold beer.[22]

Siler's body was repatriated to Tennessee, and funeral services were held at the LaFollette

Sgt Prater Receives Silver Star

Staff Sergeant Terry William Prater.

incurred in the grenade's blast. On March 15, 2007, in Baghdad, Iraq, Prater died along with four other soldiers when their vehicle struck an explosive. They were assigned to the 1st Squadron, 8th Cavalry Regiment, 2nd Brigade Combat Team, 1st Cavalry Division, Fort Hood, Texas.

Thinking of his friend's service and sacrifice, the soldier whom Prater had saved in 2004, retired Sergeant Tim Ngo, said, "The [hand] grenade landed on the other side of me, and he covered me up," and added, "Each and every day I live will be in honor of him. I'll live each day, each minute, as if it's the first time." At the time of Prater's death, one of his brothers was serving with the 82nd Airborne Division in Afghanistan. Prater's Silver Star citation is as follows:

> The President of the United States of America . . . takes pleasure in presenting the Silver Star to Sergeant Terry William Prater, United States Army, for conspicuous gallantry and intrepidity in action while serving as Team Leader for RED Platoon, Company C, 1st Battalion, 153rd Infantry Regiment, Task Force 1–9 Cavalry, 1st Cavalry Division, during combat operations in support of Operation Iraqi FREEDOM, on 5 August 2004 in Iraq. Sergeant Prater's courage, dedication to mission accomplishment, and outstanding performance during Operation Iraqi FREE-DOM is in keeping with the finest traditions of the military service and reflects great credit upon himself, the Headhunter Task Force, 3rd GREYWOLF Brigade, 1st Cavalry Division, the Multi-National Corps Iraq, and the United States Army.

Prater was survived by his mother, Cheryl Hurley; father, Terry Darrell Prater; wife, Amy Prater; son, Bryson; daughter, Madisen; and brothers, Shane Prater and Ilas Hurley. His ashes were scattered across Norris Lake, where he loved to go fishing with his son.[23]

Cumberland

Lance Corporal Stephen F. Dearmon of Crossville was born on May 5, 1987. He attended Crossville High School for three years, where he was on the wrestling team, before graduating from Cookeville High School. In addition to wrestling, he was a member of several clubs, including Students Against Violence. Following his high school graduation, he joined the Marine Corps and served with the 2nd Marine Logistics Group at Camp Lejeune, North Carolina. He became a USMC photographer after graduating from the Defense Information School in Fort Meade, Maryland, on April 10, 2008. He died at age twenty-one on April 3,

Lance Corporal Stephen F. Dearmon.

Sergeant Morgan W. Strader.

2009, as a result of a non-hostile incident in Anbar Province, Iraq. His survivors included mother and stepfather, Robin and Steven Hartke; father, William Dearmon; grandparents, Larry and Maryellen Bedford and Irene Dearmon; and sister and brother-in-law, Tiffany and Zack. Dearmon's decorations included the National Defense Service Medal, the Global War on Terrorism Service Medal, and the Iraq Campaign Medal. He is buried at the Knoxville East Tennessee Veterans Cemetery.

Sergeant Morgan W. Strader was born on July 18, 1981, in Danville, Indiana, the son of Gary Strader and Linda Morgan. He lived in Brownsburg, Indiana, through age fourteen, spending time most summers with his grandparents, Onza and Estelle Morgan, in Tennessee, fishing, hunting, and hiking the Cumberland Plateau. He moved to Patch Barracks in Stuttgart, Germany, in August 1995 with his

mother and stepfather and enjoyed activities such as soccer and the Rod and Gun Club. He returned to the United States to live in Crossville in 1998 and was a member of Cumberland County High School's class of 2000. While a student there, he was a cross-country runner and wrestler. He was a member of First United Methodist Church in Crossville. Strader joined the Marines in July 2000. He served with the 2nd Platoon, Kilo Company, 3rd Battalion, 1st Marine Regiment, 1st Marine Division, 1st Marine Expeditionary Force, Camp Pendleton, California. Strader was serving on a tour of duty in Iraq and was killed in action on November 12, 2004, while fighting in the Second Battle of Fallujah. He died while protecting a convoy that his platoon was escorting. A memorial service was held on November 17, 2004, and Strader was buried four days later in the Hebbertsburg Cemetery in Crab Orchard, Indiana.[24]

In 2005, the Cumberland County High School sponsored an Army JROTC detachment. The lead JROTC company was named the Strader Company in honor and memory of Sergeant Strader for several years.

Greene

Specialist Brandon M. Read, twenty-one, of Hopkinsville, Kentucky, formerly of Greeneville and DuBois, Pennsylvania, was killed in action on September 6, 2004, while serving with the Army in Iraq. He was born on June 5, 1983, in Panama City, Panama and was a son of Michael Read of Greeneville, and R. Kelli Courtright Read of Hopkinsville. Read was killed in Qayyarah West, Iraq, after a roadside bomb exploded near his truck. He was with the 125th Transportation Company from Lexington, Kentucky, when the bomb detonated

Hamilton

Specialist Brandon M. Read.

Private First Class Travis F. Haslip was the first Hamilton County resident killed in Operation Iraqi Freedom. Haslip was born on March 21, 1987, in Pontiac, Michigan, and raised in Tennessee. He attended Ooltewah Adventist Church and Collegedale Academy, as well as Chattanooga State. Haslip grew up in Ooltewah with his mother, stepfather, and older sister. He attended Ooltewah Adventist School through the eighth grade but moved to Michigan for about a year in 2003 and 2004. After high school, Haslip joined the Army in December 2005. He took basic training at Fort Benning, Georgia, and afterward was assigned to A Company, 1st Battalion, 5th Cavalry, 1st Cavalry Division. He joined Alpha Company in

Private First Class Travis F. Haslip.

near a convoy. The Army told his mother that Read had volunteered to exchange places with another soldier while they were on a dangerous convoy mission. He was serving as a machine gunner on his vehicle when the blast occurred.

Read was a 2001 graduate of Greeneville High School and attended Walters State Community College. He worked for the Walmart distribution center in Hopkinsville and was a member of the US Army Reserves. His family noted that he enjoyed computers and spending time with family, and that he was an avid fan and successful player of the "Everquest" multiplayer computer game. He was survived by his parents and his brother, Jaymon Cody Read, of Greeneville. He is buried at Arlington National Cemetery.

June 2006 and immediately began training with the "Annihilators" in preparation for deployment to Iraq. In October 2006, Haslip deployed with Alpha Company and the 1–5 CAV's "Black Knights" for Operation Iraqi Freedom. Haslip and five other soldiers were killed on May 19, 2007, in Baghdad when an IED detonated near their vehicle. His decorations and awards included the Army Achievement Medal, National Defense Service Medal, Global War on Terrorism Service Medal, Army Service Ribbon, and the Basic Marksmanship Badge. He is buried at the Chattanooga National Cemetery.

Sergeant James D. Stewart was born on January 20, 1976, in Fort Oglethorpe, Georgia. He died on June 21, 2005, in Iraq when he was killed by an IED that destroyed the truck he was

Sergeant John M. Sullivan.

Sergeant James D. Stewart.

driving in a convoy. He was twenty-nine and served with the 57th Transportation Company. Stewart's commanding officer told his mother that he had just minutes earlier swapped out the mission with another soldier. Stewart was five when he moved with his sister, Marilyn, to St. Petersburg, Florida. He finished his high school years at Dixie Hollins High School in St. Petersburg and was in JROTC. He spent eleven months in Kuwait before going to Iraq. He is buried at Bay Pines National Cemetery, Pinellas County, Florida.

Sergeant John M. Sullivan of Hixson served with the 2nd Battalion, 17th Field Artillery, 2nd Brigade Combat Team, 2nd Infantry Division, Fort Carson, Colorado. He died on December 30, 2006, when his Humvee was struck by a roadside bomb in Iraq. He was twenty-two. The

2003 Soddy Daisy High School graduate was just days away from returning home from his second tour of duty in Iraq. He was scheduled to arrive on January 10, 2007, to see his son, who was born just hours after he died. He had volunteered for the patrol that claimed his life when a fellow soldier got sick. During his first tour in Iraq, Sullivan was hurt when a roadside bomb—yet another IED attack, apparently—hit his truck. He earned the Purple Heart for his injuries sustained in this incident, but he refused to accept the honor because the decoration ceremony would have kept him in Iraq, and he wanted to be with his family in Tennessee. He was of the Baptist faith, and he loved music and working on his "low-rider" truck.[25] He is buried in the Chattanooga National Cemetery and was posthumously decorated with the Purple Heart and Bronze Star.

Knox

Captain Marcus R. Alford Sr. was a graduate of South Doyle High School and Carson-Newman College, and was a member of First Calvary Baptist Church in Lonsdale and of that church's choir. He was born on February 9, 1988, and was from Knoxville. Alford's school friends described him as a "bright, fun-loving" young man who spent four years in the school's ROTC program and earned the title of "Wittiest" from his senior class, and who landed a helicopter on South-Doyle's lawn during a visit to his alma mater in December 2008. One childhood friend recalled: "All he really ever talked about was being in the Army and flying helicopters. He always knew someday he'd be up there doing what they were doing, and he couldn't wait." He served with the 1st Squadron, 230th Air Cavalry, of the Tennessee Army National Guard. Alford and his co-pilot, CWo2

Captain Marcus R. Alford Sr.

Billie Jean Grinder, were killed while supporting Operation Iraqi Freedom on February 21, 2010, in the non-combat-related "hard crash" of their Bell OH-58D Kiowa Warrior helicopter near Qayyarah Airfield West, about thirty miles south of Mosul.[26]

Besides his parents, Michael Alford and Karen Ray, Alford left behind two children, Mya Alford and Marcus Alford Jr.; he was South-Doyle High School's fourth former student killed since the start of the wars in Iraq and Afghanistan. On June 21, 2010, Tennessee governor Phil Bredesen signed a bill from the Tennessee legislature honoring the memory of Captain Marcus Ray Alford Sr. with the dedication of a memorial bridge to him. The Marcus Alford Sr. Memorial Bridge was dedicated on October 12, 2010. It runs over Oak Grove Road in Wilson County and is located 2.5 miles west on State Road 840 from the Interstate 40 and State Route 840 interchange near Lebanon. Marcus Alford is buried in Knoxville's East Tennessee State Veterans Cemetery.

Sergeant Eric A. Fifer.

before he left that he was afraid this one would not end well, that he knew he was going somewhere really dangerous . . . [and] there was something unsettling about his last message, sent the night before he left for what would be his final mission." "He was always a joker, and usually signed his e-mails 'Eric Fifer, Regular Guy. But this time, there was none of the joking stuff, and he just signed it 'Eric Fifer.' My sister told me she was struck by that, too." His father, Bruce E. Fifer of Ninety-Six, South Carolina, a retired Army officer, added: "We both knew the dangers (of Iraq), but we didn't discuss that very much . . . [t]he only advice I gave him was to stay alert, keep his eyes open and his head down."[27] Fifer's decorations included the Army Service Ribbon, Global War on Terrorism Service Medal, National Medal, and the Purple Heart. He is buried at the Mattox Cemetery, Walden Creek, Sevier County.

Sergeant Eric A. Fifer was born in Columbus, Georgia. He attended Bonny Kate School and South-Doyle Middle School in Knoxville. He completed his senior year at South-Doyle High School, then went directly into the Army. He served in both Iraq and Afghanistan and left on September 1, 2005, for his second deployment to Iraq. His last e-mail message before being killed in action in Iraq at the age of twenty-two was: "Family, friends, I love you all," four days before being fatally wounded in a firefight when his dismounted patrol was attacked with small-arms fire in Haqlaniyah. At the time of his death, Fifer was the fourth East Tennessee soldier to die in Iraq. According to his mother, Nancy Fifer of Knoxville, he "may have had a premonition. He told one of his friends right

Specialist Fourth Class Christopher T. Fox.

Specialist Fourth Class Christopher T. Fox was born on October 7, 1986, in Memphis. He attended Hamilton High School and then the Dr. Benjamin L. Hooks Job Corps Training Facility in Arkansas, where he received carpentry training and his GED. Fox joined the Army in March 2005 and was sent to Fort Benning, Georgia, for basic training. After training, he was assigned to Fort Carson, Colorado, to B Company, 1st Battalion, 68th Armor Regiment, 3rd Heavy Brigade Combat Team, 4th Infantry Division. Fox served his first tour in Baqubah, Iraq, from November 2005 until January 2007. During this time, he received a Purple Heart for wounds received from the explosion of an IED. He returned to Iraq for a second tour in 2008.

Fox was killed on September 29, 2008, at age twenty-one, in Adhamiyah, when he encountered small-arms fire while conducting a dismounted routine patrol. Fox had been approached by local children requesting water from the soldiers. After receiving permission to retrieve water bottles from a vehicle, he was shot by a sniper. His death occurred one week before his twenty-second birthday. His decorations and awards included the Bronze Star Medal and two Purple Hearts. Fox is buried at the Crittenden County Memorial Park, Marion, Arkansas.

Army Specialist Fourth Class G. Daniel (Dan) Harrison, Knoxville, was born on October 19, 1982. Daniel graduated from Carter High School in 2001; attended Pellissippi State Community College; and worked at Sears, Wolf Camera, Lift Truck Sales, and Ed Financial before joining the Army on February 19, 2003. Harrison was assigned to the 293rd Military Police Company, 385th MP Battalion, 3rd Infantry Division, based at Fort Stewart, Georgia. An Associated Press story recalled that his infectious

Army Specialist Fourth Class G. Daniel (Dan) Harrison.

sense of humor and what was described as his "grizzled-veteran shtick" helped defuse the tensions of serving in Iraq for his fellow MPs: "'He would talk about Vietnam like he was there, back in Nam,' said Spc. Joshua Curl, Harrison's roommate. 'He would buy water guns from the Iraqi kids and come in, guns blazing. We acted like a bunch of kids on our downtime, but when it was time for business, everybody was on it.'"[28] On December 2, 2004, some nine months after his MP company had deployed to train Iraqi policemen and MP units, Dan Harrison lost his life coming to the aid of his fellow soldiers in a firefight in Mosul with Iraqi insurgents on December 2, 2004. He was behind the machine gun of a Humvee providing suppressing fire to US troops under attack by a group of Iraqi insurgents and was shot in the chest. Harrison is buried at the Knoxville East Tennessee Veterans Cemetery.

Cryptologic Technician–Technical Seaman Daniel K. Leonard died unexpectedly on July 23, 2006. He was survived by his parents, Kim and Eileen Leonard, and his sister, Rebekah Leonard. Onboard memorial services were held on July 31, 2006, on the amphibious assault ship USS *Tarawa*. He is buried at the Knoxville East Tennessee Veterans Cemetery.

Corporal William A. Long was killed after an attack in Buritz, Iraq, on June 18, 2005. He died from injuries sustained the previous day, when he was conducting a mounted patrol and his Humvee was attacked by enemy forces using rocket-propelled grenades. Long was assigned to the Army's 2nd Battalion, 69th Armor

Corporal William A. Long.

Regiment, 3rd Brigade, 3rd Infantry Division, Fort Benning, Georgia. He was twenty-six when he died. Long is buried at Arlington National Cemetery. The following is an excerpt from an article about Long's interment at Arlington Cemetery, where he had been assigned as a member of the Old Guard's burial-honors detachment before volunteering to serve in Iraq. He was one of the first US dead of the fighting in Iraq to be buried at Arlington:

> "Arlington National Cemetery is probably the most sacred ground in the country," his stepfather, Lee Cordner of Lilburn, Ga., said in an interview. . . . Long, 26, received the standard honors military burial: six military pallbearers in dress uniforms, a U.S. flag-draped coffin, seven soldiers firing simultaneously three times each, a bugler playing "Taps." The flag was precision-folded in midair by 12 hands and presented to his mother.
>
> Beyond that, about 60 other members of the 3rd Infantry Division, the highly disciplined honor guard, attended. Many lowered their heads, a couple wiped their eyes. All saluted during "Taps."
>
> Also, Chaplain Douglas Fenton, formerly assigned to Arlington cemetery with Long, made a special trip to the burial. He read a Bible verse and shared some personal memories of Long. Then he hugged Long's mother, stepfather and Elizabeth Jackson of Raleigh, N.C., Long's fiancée. . . .
>
> He could have remained at Arlington National Cemetery's military honors unit and kept away from danger in the Middle East. But he re-enlisted last year so he could see active duty in Iraq, his stepfather said. He went to Iraq in January.[29]

Master Sergeant Michael L. McNulty died on June 17, 2005, at the age of thirty-six in Qaim, Iraq. He was born on October 12, 1968, in Knoxville. He was a Green Beret with the US Army

Master Sergeant Michael L. McNulty.

Special Operations Command. McNulty is buried at Arlington National Cemetery. Jeffrey Gaunt of the Elgin, Illinois *Daily Herald* contributed this account on June 23, 2005:

> Master Sgt. Michael McNulty was at his most compassionate in moments like these. When tragedy struck, he was the family's rock. The one who could wipe away their tears, recalled McNulty's sister-in-law, Amy Lessing. "If you were feeling down, he'd pull you off to the side," Lessing said. "He was always there for you." But now the family will have to go it alone.
>
> The former Larkin High School [in Elgin, Illinois] student was killed Friday during combat operations in western Iraq, the Department of Defense said this week. McNulty was 36. "He was just a great person," Lessing said. "An all-American. This is too young for him. This is way too young." McNulty was living with his wife, Paula, and four children in Southern Pines, North Carolina, about 120 miles from Gastonia, where he was born. One of nine kids, he graduated

from Larkin in 1986 with his twin brother, Sean, who also serves in the military.[30]

McNulty was posthumously promoted to the rank of master sergeant. He was awarded more than twenty medals in his career, including three Bronze Stars, the Humanitarian Service Medal, and the Purple Heart.

Specialist Fourth Class Michael J. Rodriguez was born on May 30, 1986, in Syracuse, New York; he later called Knoxville home, attending Central High School in Fountain City. His friends recalled his prankish but loving sense of humor. In 2005, Rodriguez joined the Army and was assigned to Bravo Troop, 5th Squadron, 73rd Cavalry, 82nd Airborne Division at Fort Bragg, North Carolina, to become a paratrooper. He was killed in action in Iraq on April 23,

Specialist Fourth Class Michael J. Rodriguez.

Petty Officer Second Class Christopher E. Watts.

2007, at the age of twenty, dying in a suicide bombing in As Sadah, in Iraq's Diyala Province. Rodriguez was awarded the Purple Heart, Bronze Star, Combat Action Badge, and the Good Conduct Medal. He is buried at the Knoxville East Tennessee State Veterans Cemetery.[31]

The following Associated Press article recounted the life and death of a Knoxville sailor, Petty Officer Second Class Christopher E. Watts, who was twenty-eight years old at the time he died. Watts was a crewman on the USS *Firebolt*, and was killed on April 24, 2004, when a small boat he was boarding exploded near an Iraqi oil terminal:

> A sailor killed in Iraq during a suicide attack at an oil terminal is being remembered as a down-to-earth person not prone to fanfare. . . .
>
> [Petty Officer Watts] was one of three servicemen to die in the attack April 24 in

the northern Persian Gulf. The three were part of a seven-person boarding team from the *Firebolt* who were conducting maritime interception operations. A sailing vessel known as a dhow approached the Iraqi Khawr Al Amaya Oil Terminal and exploded as the men went to inspect it. . . . Chilhowee Hills senior pastor Dr. Tony Crisp said Watts died for a worthy cause.

"There is no higher calling than to give our lives, as Americans, for the cause of freedom." Watts joined the Navy in 1995 following in the footsteps of his father and grandfather. A Jordanian militant with links to al-Qaida claimed responsibility for the attack.[32]

Watts was buried at the Cedar Grove Baptist Church cemetery in Maryville.

Corporal Luke C. Williams of Knoxville was born on August 12, 1970. He served with the 3rd Squadron, 7th Cavalry Regiment, 2nd Brigade, 3rd Infantry Division, out of Fort Stewart, Georgia. He was killed at age thirty-five in Baghdad on September 5, 2005, when his vehicle accidentally rolled over into a ditch. Williams had worked for seven years at a local Kroger supermarket in Knoxville before enlisting in order to better himself and provide for a better life for his family. He was survived by his wife, Teresa (who had just returned from her own tour of duty in Iraq), a daughter, and a son. He is buried at the Knoxville East Tennessee State Veterans Cemetery.

Loudon

Lance Corporal William C. Koprince Jr. was serving his third overseas deployment with the 2nd Marine Regiment, 2nd Marine Division, and his second tour in Iraq, when he was killed by an IED on December 27, 2006, in the city of Habbaniyah during Operation Iraqi Freedom. He was twenty-four. He was born in Dearborn,

Lance Corporal William C. Koprince Jr.

Monroe

Staff Sergeant Ryan E. Haupt served with the 1st Battalion, 68th Armor Regiment, 3rd Heavy Brigade Combat Team, 4th Infantry Division, based at Fort Carson, Colorado. Haupt was from Monroe County. He was born on June 6, 1982, and was killed by an IED in Baqubah, Iraq on October 17, 2006. Haupt was a member of his unit's sniper section; an expert on the .50 caliber Barrett sniper rifle, he and three other soldiers of his team were killed by the IED's blast. He was twenty-four at the time of his death and had enlisted from Phoenix, Arizona. He is buried at Queen of Heaven Catholic Cemetery, Hillside, Cook County, Illinois. Haupt was posthumously decorated with the Combat

Michigan, on September 16, 1982, to William and Bernice Koprince. Koprince moved with his parents and sister to Lenoir City in 1991. At the time of his death, he was only five weeks away from coming home.

His mother Bernice Koprince has said her son was a prankster, loved Johnny Cash, and did not say much but, when he did speak, was funny and insightful. He is buried at Kingston Memorial Gardens, Lawnville, Roane County, Tennessee. On September 13, 2014, a sign was dedicated near his home town of Lenoir City, renaming the portion of Interstate 75 located between mile markers 81 and 83 in Koprince's memory.

Staff Sergeant Ryan E. Haupt.

Sergeant Joseph D. (Joey) Hunt.

olina, to Master Sergeant Sonny and Beverly (Jeffers) Washam. He joined the Marines in June 2003, serving with the 6th Marine Regiment, 2nd Marine Division. In 2004, he was sent to Afghanistan, serving seven months. In August 2005, Washam was next sent to Iraq, where he was killed on February 14, 2006, by a suicide bomber. He was survived by three sisters, Michelle Washam, Lilly Washam, and Misty Day; and two brothers, Technical Sergeant Donny Washam of the US Air Force and Sergeant Dustin Washam of the US Army. Washam had two sons, Ryan and Andrew. His uncle, Private First Class Denny L. Washam, was also a Marine and was killed in Vietnam on December 8, 1968. Both were twenty-one when they died. He is buried at Fairview Memorial Gardens, Huntsville, Scott County.

Sevier

Victoir P. Lieurance of Seymour was born on December 6, 1970, and died on August 22, 2005, while serving in Iraq with the 3rd Squadron, 278th Regimental Combat Team of the Tennessee Army National Guard. He is buried in Atchley Seymour Memory Gardens, Seymour. His brother, Henri (Hank) Lieurance, provided the following tribute:

> Sgt. Victoir P. Lieurance, 34, died in Samarra, Iraq, while conducting patrol operations when an improvised explosive device detonated near his HMMWV [i.e., "Humvee"]. He was assigned to the Army National Guard's 3rd Squadron, 278th Armored Cavalry Regiment, Sparta, Tennessee. His family has a strong military background—his father Andre Lieurance served 26 years in the Navy, his mother Karen served 20 years in the Navy, and his sister Jonette Owens, served 8 years in the Army.
>
> Victoir Lieurance was a professional. His name floated through the ranks in Tennes-

Infantryman's Badge, the Purple Heart, and the Bronze Star. He left behind his wife, Nannette.

Joseph D. (Joey) Hunt was from Monroe Country and served with the 3rd Squadron, 278th Armored Cavalry Regiment of the Tennessee Army National Guard. He held the rank of sergeant and was killed on August 22, 2005, in Iraq. He is buried at Sweetwater Valley Memorial Park. On May 19, 2006, Tennessee governor Phil Bredesen signed a bill from the Tennessee legislature honoring the memory of Hunt with a memorial bridge. The Sergeant Joseph D. Hunt Memorial Bridge was dedicated September 28, 2007, and is located on State Road 840 at the West Fork of Stones River in Rutherford County.

Scott

According to family member Sonny M. Washam, Corporal Rusty L. Washam was born on February 11, 1985, at Fort Bragg, North Car-

Sergeant Victoir P. Lieurance.

Sergeant Paul W. Thomason III.

see's National Guard as the best of the best Bradley guys in the state. He was no stranger to war. After serving in the Gulf War in the 90s, fate found Vic back in Iraq in 2004–2005. A father, husband and son of a Naval family, Vic never shrugged his calling, deploying in the summer of 2004 to serve with Knife Troop at FOB O'Ryan in Iraq's triangle of death.

His sense of humor, which some would argue bordered on the absurd, was found on a daily basis as he patted his fellow comrades on the rear and called them "honey." He was well known by his captain as an almost constant planner of pranks during those times he was inside the wire.

Beyond his antics was a man who loved his family. As he sat outside the bunker the night before his death, he talked about his recent leave back in the United States and longed for the day he would rejoin his wife and children.

If there was anything he'd like to have seen in Iraq, it was camels. But there had never been any time for that—not during the Gulf War and not during Operation Iraqi Freedom.

Minutes before his death, a herd of camels crossed the road in front of his patrol. Hundreds of them—including some rare white camels—seemed to come out to greet Vic Lieurance and the other soldiers.

Then-Staff Sgt. John McCullouch will never forget his words to Vic that day.

"Here's your camels, Vic."[33]

Sergeant Paul W. Thomason III was born on October 21, 1967, and was from Talbot. He was a 1986 graduate of Sevier County High School and was employed by Ampad in Morristown. He served with the 2nd Squadron, 278th Regimental Combat Team, Tennessee Army National Guard, and was killed by an IED on March 20, 2005, in Kirkuk. He is buried at Knob Creek Cemetery, Seymour. On May 19, 2006, Tennessee governor Phil Bredesen signed a bill from the Tennessee legislature honoring the memory of Sergeant Thomason with a memorial bridge located on State Route 840 in Rutherford County, Tennessee.

Sullivan

Chief Warrant Officer Two Alexander S. (Scott) Coulter was born on May 1, 1968, and was from Bristol. He served with the 124th Signal Battalion, 4th Infantry Division, based at Fort Hood, Texas. He was "a good all-around guy—the best of the crop," in the words of his grandmother. Coulter, who grew up in Bristol and was stationed at Fort Hood, was killed on November 17, 2003, when his vehicle struck a homemade land mine while en route to Baquba, Iraq. CW2 Coulter had joined the Army in 1987 after graduating from high school and had served in Somalia, Bosnia, and Operation Desert Storm. Coulter met his wife Robin while both were stationed in Germany. They had been married

Chief Warrant Officer Two Alexander S. (Scott) Coulter.

for twelve years. He had two daughters, Shenna and Hannah, and a stepdaughter, Cindy. Family and friends had been hopeful that Coulter would remain safe. "He said he was doing all right, and that he didn't have to go out real often," said his grandmother, Mrs. Stuart Coulter. CW2 Coulter is buried at the Fort Sam Houston National Cemetery, San Antonio, Bexar County, Texas.

Corporal Robbie G. Light was born on September 24, 1984, in Kingsport. He was the son of Robert and Beverly Light. He was a 2002 graduate of Sullivan South High School. Light entered the military on May 15, 2003, in Knoxville. He received basic combat training at Fort Knox, Kentucky. Light also completed AIT at Fort Knox and became a tank crewman. After the completion of his training, he was assigned to C Troop, 1st Squadron, 10th Cavalry Regiment, 2nd Brigade, 4th Infantry Division (Mechanized), based at Fort Hood, Texas. He deployed in support of Operation Iraqi Freedom in 2003, and in October 2004, Light was assigned to C Company, 1st Battalion, 67th Armor Regiment, 2nd Brigade Combat Team, 4th Infantry Division. He was then deployed a second time to Iraq in December 2005, serving as an M1A2 Abrams tank driver. Light was killed in action on May 1, 2006, just south of Baghdad, Iraq, after driving over an IED. Light was survived by his wife, Elizabeth, and his daughter, Ashlyn, of Gray, Tennessee, as well as his parents. He is buried at the Light Family Cemetery in Kingsport.

Corporal Michael R. Speer of Davenport, Iowa, grew up in southeastern Kansas in Redfield, a small town with a population of 140 people. He graduated from Uniontown High School in 1997, where he was a member of the football team and was regarded by his class-

Corporal Michael R. Speer.

The 1st Marine Division posted this tribute, written by Corporal Shawn C. Rhodes, on April 21, 2004:

CAMP MAHMUDIYAH, Iraq—Sgt. Michael R. Speer, 24, was leading 2nd Platoon, Company F, 2nd Battalion, 2nd Marine Regiment on a combat mission in Lutafiyah, Iraq when he was killed in action April 9.

Speer was the first Marine from the Camp Lejeune-based battalion killed in action since the beginning of their deployment in March. He was posthumously promoted to sergeant. To Marines who knew Speer, he was "Poppa."

His battalion held a memorial ceremony in his honor April 19. The ceremony was packed with Marines from his platoon and those who called Speer a friend. The simple ceremony started with a Bible reading. Marines followed with stories of the Kansas Marine and how Speer impacted their own lives.

"I went to boot camp with Speer," said Cpl. Adam M. Magnuson, a Las Vegas Marine assigned to Headquarters Company, 2nd Battalion, 2nd Marine Regiment. "He was just as bad as a drill instructor, believe me. He always made sure everyone was giving their all. He knew how to yell, so you didn't want him to catch you slacking off."

Magnuson and Speer were both assigned to the School of Infantry together. The two seemed inseparable when their order assigned them both to the same battalion. "We were both sent to 2/2 after SOI," Magnuson explained. "My brother was also there, and sure enough, he and Speer ended up roommates." Getting to know Speer's family and spending time with them was a common occurrence during liberty for Magnuson.

Speer's magnetic personality is what drew people to him most, Magnuson said. If he walked in a room, you wanted to talk to him, to see how he was doing and see what he had to say about whatever was going on. "When he spoke to you, it wasn't like he

mates as being a quiet leader. Soon after, he moved to Davenport, Iowa, where he enlisted in the Marine Corps in January 2001. Speer planned to leave the service and spend more time with his new wife, Eliza. They were married on August 16, 2001, and planned to start a family and buy a house. Speer was a great storyteller and had a way of telling stories that made them come to life. A strong man who did not fold in the face of adversity, Speer never showed weakness in front of his Marines; many of those same Marines believed that was because he had no weaknesses. Corporal Speer was killed at the age of twenty-four by hostile fire in Lutafiyah, Anbar Province, Iraq, while on his second tour of duty on April 9, 2004.

was just hearing you," Magnuson said. "You could tell he was really listening. He was a great person to talk to about anything."

The ceremony concluded with a roll call. The platoon sergeants of Company F were called and answered "Present!" Speer's name was called and returned with only silence. His name was barked again and again with no answer from the fallen warrior. Taps was sounded for Speer. The battalion's Marines paid their final respects to Speer before leaving by saluting an upturned rifle, helmet, and boots.[34]

Speer was survived by his wife, Eliza, who resides in Tennessee. He is buried at Mountain Home National Cemetery, Johnson City.

Unicoi

Sergeant First Class Mark O. Edwards was born in Detroit, Michigan, on September 17, 1964. He began his military career on August 10, 1983, training as a tank crewman. Following his initial training and subsequent graduation, he was stationed in Germany for the next eighteen months. After completing active duty, Edwards

Sergeant First Class Mark O. Edwards, with Iraqi children.

enlisted in the Tennessee Army National Guard on July 1, 1986. He was assigned as a tank crewmember to Company H, 2nd Battalion, 278th Armored Cavalry Regiment in Erwin, where he continued to work, learn, and train and eventually reached the position of tank commander.

Edwards and his company were mobilized in support of Operation Iraqi Freedom III on June 17, 2004. After intense training at Camp Shelby, Mississippi, and the National Training Center, Fort Irwin, California, Edwards was deployed to Forward Operating Base Bernstein near the city of Tuz, Iraq, where he lost his life in the line of duty on June 9, 2005, due to non-combat-related causes. At the time of his death, Edwards was forty years old, having served twenty-two of those years in the military. He left behind a wife, Kimberly; a son, Mark Andrew; and a stepdaughter, Whitney Dayton. He is buried at Mountain Home National Cemetery in Johnson City.

On May 19, 2006, Tennessee governor Phil Bredesen signed a bill from the Tennessee legislature honoring the memory of Sergeant Edwards of Unicoi with a memorial bridge located on State Route 840 in Rutherford County, Tennessee. The Tennessee legislature, by joint resolution signed by Governor Phil Bredesen on June 18, 2007, also named the Tennessee National Guard Armory located at 615 S. Main Avenue in Erwin (Unicoi County) in memory of Edwards.

Washington

The Associated Press provided this account of the life and service of Private First Class David L. Potter, a twenty-two-year-old ETSU student living in Johnson City, who died in Baghdad of non-combat-related injuries on August 7, 2004, five months after arriving in Iraq, while serving

Private First Class David L. Potter.

David Potter originally enlisted as a reservist to pay for college, recruiter Sgt. Rusty Hicks said. But Hicks said Potter thought about it becoming a career. Potter requested active duty, and the Army sent him to basic training at Fort Leonard Wood, Mo., followed by intelligence training at Fort Huachuca, Arizona.

"He said the reason he put on his uniform was so we could sleep safely at night," his brother said. "That's what he said kept him going."[35]

Potter is buried at Atchley Seymour Memory Gardens, Seymour. He was survived by his father and stepmother, Carlton and Beverly Potter; his mother and stepfather, Apryl and Kenneth Hicks; and his two brothers, Carlton and Benjamin.

with the 115th Forward Support Battalion, 1st Cavalry Division of Fort Hood, Texas:

> The Army announced the death of 22-year-old Pfc. David L. Potter of Johnson City on Monday. They released no information about Saturday's death except that it was "non-combat related" and under investigation. . . .
>
> David Potter was born [on January 15, 1982] in Portsmouth, N.H., but graduated from Gatlinburg-Pittman High School in Sevierville and enlisted in February 2003. He had been living in Johnson City as a sophomore art student at East Tennessee State University. He was not married.
>
> "My father was in the Air Force, and I was in the Army," Carlton Potter said. "He felt like he wanted to try it and do what we had done."

16

THE ROLL OF HONOR

The Names Listed on the East Tennessee Veterans Memorial

WORLD WAR I

Anderson County

ARMY

- CALVIN ASLINGER
- EDWARD W. BOWLING
- BRATCHER BROWN
- JAMES E. CARDEN
- JOHN M. COX
- FRED L. DUNAWAY
- EMIT M. EDMONDS
- WILLIAM E. FOSTER
- ETHEL GAMBLE
- JOHN B. GAMBLE
- JOHN W. GILREATH
- CHARLES L. HATMAKER
- SAMUEL S. E. HENNING
- HENRY M. JEFFRES
- WILLIAM A. LOY
- MILBERN MELTON
- CLIFFORD NEWPORT
- EARL C. PARROTT
- SAWYER PATTERSON
- CAREY G. PETERSON
- DAWN W. PHILLIPS
- OTIS SHARP
- BERT WALLER

NAVY

- CODA L. GILES
- JOHN W. REEVES

Bledsoe County

ARMY

- VICTOR L. ANGEL
- JOHN ARNETT
- AMOS L. AUSTIN
- JAMES H. CURTIS
- SAMUEL C. DYER
- BURETT HAMILTON
- ALFRED HILLIS
- DAVID H. MCMILLON
- SHERMAN MILLER
- CHARLIE SIMMONS
- GEORGE R. SWAFFORD

MARINE CORPS

- THOMAS W. AULT

Blount County

ARMY

- WILLIAM R. BURCHFIELD
- GEORGE H. L. BURNS
- GRAYSON CAYLOR
- SAMUEL CRISP
- WALTER CRISP
- JOHN DOCKERY
- J. AULS FAGG
- LONNIE FRENCH
- JAMES GARDNER
- THOMAS W. GODDARD
- DAVID M. GOURLEY
- MILTON L. HARPER
- LUKE LAWSON
- WISDOM LEE
- ERNEST R. LINGINFELTER
- EMERSON J. LONES
- FRED D. LOVE
- CLAUDE O. LOWE
- LEONARD F. MARINE
- CHARLES C. MEEKS
- MURPHY J. MYERS
- W. PRUETT MYERS
- WILLIAM A. MYERS

- DAVID E. OTT
- WILLIAM M. PAYNE
- WALTER ROGERS
- PLEAS RUSSELL
- R. LLOYD STERLING
- JOHN P. TALLENT
- HARRISON TOWNSEND
- CHARLES A. WALKER
- HENRY L. WEBB
- ANDERSON A. WILBURN
- CLAUDE M. WILLIAMS
- HOBART D. WILLOCKS

NAVY

- J. ROY GIBSON
- CECIL F. GODDARD

Bradley County

ARMY

- CALVIN C. CLIMER
- ROBERT DAUGHERTY
- FRED FARMER
- OLLIE F. GOINS
- JAMES O. HANEY
- CARTER H. HICKS
- JOHN F. KEYS
- PETER LINGERFELT
- J. HARVE MITCHELL
- THOMAS L. MOORE
- THOMAS O. ROY
- HARRY A. SEYMOUR
- EDWARD C. TAYLOR
- CALVIN M. WHEELER
- JOYCE WINKLER

NAVY
- J. FRANKLIN BARNES
- CHARLES N. TATUM

Campbell County

ARMY
- GEORGE W. AYERS
- MILLARD BAIRD
- SAMUEL F. BENNETT
- CLEMENTE BOCCIA
- FORREST L. BRADLEY
- ROBERT F. BROYLES
- ERNEST C. CARPENTER
- CHARLES E. COOPER
- CLINTON F. DELIUS
- FRANK HARDEN
- HARVE HATMAKER
- JOSEPH L. HOUSLEY
- LLOYD HOUTS
- JAMES H. LAYNE
- JAMES MARCUM
- ERNEST MOZINGO
- GEORGE MYERS
- JOHN F. MYERS
- SAWYER PATTERSON
- JAMES PAUL
- CAREY F. PETERSON
- TRAVIS ROBINSON
- ANDY SILER
- BEN H. SINGLETON
- TILMAN T. VOYLES
- LUTHER WARD
- HENRY S. WILSON
- ALBERT H. WYNN

NAVY
- JAMES T. HUDDLESTON
- SIDNEY MCDONALD
- WILLIAM E. NUNNALLY

MARINE CORPS
- ROBERT VITATOE

Carter County

ARMY
- CHARLES H. ALBERTSON
- LAWRENCE F. ALLEN
- HENRY F. ANGEL
- FREDRICK BARLOW
- SAMUEL M. BOWERS
- ELBERT BOWMAN
- CHARLES E. COOK
- JOHN DAYTON
- WALTER DELOACH
- WILLIAM S. DUGGER
- JAMES R. GEISLER
- SMITH GRINDSTAFF

- LAWSON J. HAMBY
- WALTER H. HEATON
- ROBY HENDRIX
- FRED C. HICKS
- BERNIE HILTON
- CLAUDE HOPSON
- EDWARD INGRAM
- JOHN INGRAM
- CLARENCE JOHNSON
- CHARLES S. LACEY
- ORVILLE E. LEWIS
- WALTER LYONS
- GEORGE B. MARKLAND
- BASCOM MCKINNEY
- CLAUDE MCKINNEY
- WILL MILLER
- MILBURN MOFFITT
- JESSE NAVE
- LONNIE PRITCHETT
- CLIFTON ROARK
- CHARLES F. ROE
- ROBERT L. SCOTT
- FRED SHATLEY
- CECIL SMITH
- STACY SMITH
- BLAN S. STOUT
- ROSS C. TUCKER
- WILLIAM M. WARD
- PAUL WILLIAMS
- ROTHSEY E. WILLIAMS
- TYLER WILSON
- WILLIAM E. WILSON
- DANIEL WRIGHT

NAVY
- EDWARD MILLER

Claiborne County

ARMY
- LENARD T. BREWER
- LEVI W. BROOKS
- ROBERT B. CARPENTER
- FRED CAWOOD
- OSCAR P. CUPP
- LAFAYETTE DAY
- SAMUEL H. DUNCAN
- MAJOR G. ELLISON
- JAMES I. FRANCISCO, JR.
- CARBEN A. KECK
- ARTHUR V. KIBERT
- WILLIAM LASLEY
- WILLIAM H. LEACH
- BALLARD C. LYNCH
- ESTEL W. LOOP
- HARVEY MIRACLE
- HAGAN MOORE
- WILLIAM F. MOORE

- WILLIAM C. PARKEY
- LEWIS F. PEARSON
- ONIE SANFORD
- GEORGE W. SINGLETON
- HENRY V. SOARD

Cocke County

ARMY
- OBEY L. ALLEN
- SAM ARCHER
- WILLIAM AUSTIN
- FRED BARNETT
- JOHN BAXTER
- C. OTTO BOYER
- WILLIAM BRITT
- GEORGE R. CLARK
- ERNEST N. ELLISON
- WILLIAM M. FISH
- GUY B. GILLESPIE
- WILLIAM HALL
- BEN HOLDWAY
- HOBART M. HOLT
- WILLIE JAMES
- ROBERT JOHNSON
- MARVIN H. LEE
- CARTER F. MCFEATURES
- ROBERT MALOY
- WILLIAM H. MESSER
- EDWARD NOLEN
- HERMAN B. OTTINGER
- LUTHER REESE
- KIFFIN Y. ROCKWELL
- BURNETT SMITH
- JESSE SPROUSE
- LAWRENCE M. TALLEY
- JAMES C. TRANTHAM
- REUBEN H. TURNER

Cumberland County

ARMY
- ARTHUR T. ALLISON
- URIOUS I. BURGESS
- WILLIAM W. CAMPBELL
- JAMES E. CAUDILL
- NEAL G. CLIFTON
- VIRGIL FORD
- WILLIAM GODSEY
- ERNEST B. HENRY
- PHILLIP HOWARD
- THOMAS R. JORDAN
- MILO L. LEMERT   MOH*
- ALLEN LEWIS
- JAMES F. LINKOUS
- J. JACK LODEN
- JAMES T. MCCORMICK
- JAMES B. NORRIS
- JIMMIE G. NORRIS

* Medal of Honor recipients are listed with the abbreviation *MOH*.

JOHN NORRIS
RAY T. PARKER
JOSEPH PATTON
JOHN V. REESE
WILLIAM J. B. SHERRILL
WILLIAM M. WILSON
ARTHUR G. VAN WINKLE

NAVY
SAMUEL J. BRISTOW

Fentress County
ARMY
EVERETT ALLRED
WILLIAM H. ANDERSON
VIRGIL G. BEATY
WAYNE S. BEATY
JAMES W. BLACK
VIRGIL BOWDEN
LOYD O. COOPER
FRANCIS M. DAVIS
ROSCOE FOWLER
MACK GREEN
HENRY L. HICKS
G. BENTON HUGHES
HENRY H. JONES
ALDER H. MILLSAPS
MINIS L. REAGAN
GEORGE W. L. SIDNER
W. ALFRED STEPHENS
BIRDIE M. TURNER
VAN WILLIAMS
ALVIN C. YORK   MOH

Grainger County
ARMY
JAMES T. ACUFF
ROBERT T. BISHOP
JOE BUNCH
HUGH T. CLEMENT
FRANK S. FRAZIER
JAMES A. HAMMER
JOHN P. HIGGS
THOMAS A. HODGES
JAMES L. KECK
WILLIE STRATTON
STERLING VAUGHN
JAMES S. WRIGHT

Greene County
ARMY
JOHN W. ADAMS
ELLIS M. BANKS
JOE BEARD
CARL D. BRANDON
GEORGE E. BROWN
CECIL C. BROYLES

EDGAR C. BURKEY
ERNEST C. CARTER
OLA K. CARTER
WALTER O. CARTER
ALBERT D. CUTSHALL
CHARLIE T. DUNCAN
ROBERT L. DYER
JOHN W. FRY
ROY GARDNER
ROWDY GENTRY
CURTIS GIRDNER
WILLIAM E. GIRDNER
WILLIAM W. GOSNELL
JOSEPH W. GOURLEY
DANIEL S. HAIRE
SENTER HANEY
OSCAR B. HARRISON
BENJAMIN F. HICE
NOAH G. HIPPS
JAMES E. HOUSE
ANDREW J. JOHNSON
VESTUS KESTERSON
RALPH L. LIVINGSTON
WILLIE A. LOLLAR
CLARENCE MCAMIS
WALEN MCNEES
JOHN A. MALONE
SAMUEL J. MALONE
ROBERT F. MITCHELL
JOSEPH W. OVERHOLSER
GEORGE W. RHEA
HORACE T. RICKER
WILLIAM G. B. ROLLINS
CONNIE H. SAUCEMAN
EVERETT L. SHELTON
WILLIAM SHEPHERD
CHARLES W. STARNES
EDWARD C. STYKE
JULIUS B. TARLTON
HARRY C. TUCKER
CALVIN J. WARD   MOH
JAMES H. WHITE
GEORGE H. WILHOIT
JOHN D. YEARWOOD

NAVY
JOHN MCNABB

Hamblen County
ARMY
TIP M. ALLEN
WILLIAM F. BLACKWELL
WILLIAM BUSHONG
DONALD E. CARDWELL
ALONZO CARTER
WILLIAM CARTER
BRUCE M. COLBOCH

SIMON COLE
MARCUS N. DELIAS
IDOL ESTES
GRADY HARRIS
CHARLES E. SMITH   MOH
EDWARD R. TALLEY   MOH
JAMES M. WEST

NAVY
GEORGE R. DONALDSON
JOHN S. GOOD

Hamilton County
ARMY
JOHN F. ACUFF
STEPHEN C. ALLISON
FRANK H. ATLEE
LEONARD BELL
PHILIP M. BERRY
CLIFFORD A. BLANTON
LEMUEL H. BOGART
CHARLES H. BOICE
LAKE C. BOYD
WALTER BROWN
JESSE BROYLES
CLEVELAND BRYANT
ROBERT G. BUCHANAN
CARLTON BURRELL
LIONEL L. CAMP
SANFORD G. CARTER
RUFUS W. CHENOWETH
CHARLES L. CLARK
FRANK H. COOPER
AUSTIN CRAFT
WILL CUMMINGS
VERNAL DAVENPORT
MALLIE L. DAVIS
THURMAN C. DAVIS
JOHN H. DAYTON
EARL T. DEMPSEY
JOHN DENNIS
GROVER C. DENT
GEORGE G. DILLARD
RALPH DOBBINS
JOHN DONAHOO
MARSHALL B. DUDDERAR
ED EDMERSON
BENJAMIN W. ELBON JR.
LUTHER EVANS
WILLIAM D. FARIS
RUFUS S. FERGUSON
LEONARD I. FRANK
JAMES M. FREEMAN
THOMAS J. FREEMAN
FRED W. FRITTS
JOSEPH F. GAFNEY
WILLIAM N. GARRISON

WILLIAM C. GEORGE
GEORGE E. GERBER
JAMES H. GHOLSTON
CURTIS GIVENS
CLIFFORD B. GRAYSON
HUGH T. GREGORY
WALLACE L. HAGAN
ANGUS HAGLER
EDWIN S. HALE
WILLIAM E. HAMILTON
CLIFFORD C. HANCOCK
CLAUDE L. HARMON
JOHN W. HAYNES
JAMES N. HAZLEHURST
ROBERT J. HENDERSON
ARTHUR W. HICKS
JOHN D. HICKS
SAMUEL B. HOGE
AUGUST B. HOLDAM
ALBERT M. HORN
CARL HOUSTON
HENRY HOUSTON
JESSE HUDSON
JAMES HUMPHREY
GEORGE T. HUNT
JESSE P. HUNT
JOHN W. JILLSON
ESKAR L. JOHNSON
JAMES A. JOHNSON
JOHN JONES
ABE L. KENNEDY
JOSEPH G. KUNTZ
XAVIER T. KUSS
LEVERE KYLE
WILLIAM LAWLAH
IRA M. LAWSON
CLAUDE LEVI
GEORGE W. LEVI
WILLIAM H. LIGHT
AUGUSTINE B. LITTLETON
JAMES C. LODOR
PAUL LOMENICK
JAKE F. LONG
JUNE LOTT
BEAUFORD MCCULLOUGH
CLYDE MERONEY
JAMES T. MICHAELS
HOMER MOORE
THOMAS W. MORELAND
WILLIAM A. OHLS
ALFRED ORR
SAMUEL D. PICKLESIMER
WILLIAM F. RAMSEY
CARLETON H. RANDALL
JESS RENO
JACOB P. ROBB
ALFRED P. ROCK

JAMES L. SCOGGINS
HARRY E. SMITH
JOHN P. SMITH
MARVIN H. SMITH
NATHAN SMITH
JOHN SPRINGER
CHARLES STEVENSON
DAVIS K. SUMMERS
CARL A. G. SUNDSTROM
ALBERT SYKES
CHARLES H. TALIAFERRO
ARETUS G. TAYLOR
CHARLES TORAN
RAYMOND THOMSON
CHRISTOPHER S. TIMOTHY JR.
JESSE TUCKER
JOHN E. UPTON
E. WARREN VICKERY
MATTHIAS M. WAGNER
CLAUDE T. WALKER
ZANNIE WARE
WILLIAM M. WHITE
RAY WILSON
JOHN J. WOMBLE

NAVY
FLOYD M. CATE
OSBORNE L. COLVILLE
GORDON DEWEES
JOHN HENLEY
ELMER H. KELL
GEORGE B. LEAMON
LAWRENCE O. LONGLEY
FRANCIS A. MASON
JAMES MCISAAC
JAMES C. PRICE
EDWARD E. REAVELY
HERSCHEL S. TAPP

MARINE CORPS
THOMAS B. ANDERSON
NATHAN BREWER
FLOYD EDGE
ROBERT L. ELY
CARL E. HARRISON
HERBERT L. HILL
CLARENCE R. HIXSON
FRED R. LOSEY
JOHN H. MISHLER
CLIFFORD O. WALLER

Hancock County
ARMY
JOE ADAMS
RIDLEY S. AMYX
SAMUEL H. BOLTON
ERNEST BURKE

ALFRED CANTWELL
JAMES CANTWELL
DAN FLETCHER
ROBERT L. FROST
NEIL GREEN
ROBERT MATHIS
WILLIAM PURKEY
THOMAS SUTTON
LEONARD T. TRENT
PETE WILLIAMS
ELBERT WOLFE

Hawkins County
ARMY
EVAN BALL
ALPH BROOKS
LEWIS H. BROOKS
FRED CLIFTON
JOHN F. COMPTON
FRANK R. DAVIS
CLAUDE FANSLER
JAMES C. FLOYD
JAMES B. GLADSON
DAN R. HAMILTON
HOBART HUDGENS
BUD LAWSON
WILLIAM P. LAWSON
HARRY LIGHT
CLAUDE LONG
SAMUEL K. MOLSBEE
CHARLES C. MOORE
HAROLD L. MOWL
ANSON J. PARK
ORDLEY PARVIN
BROWNLOW REYNOLDS
LUTHER ROBINSON
AUSTIN ROGERS
PRESTON A. SPITZER
COY C. TUNNELL

NAVY
ZOLLIE D. CHRISTIAN

Jefferson County
ARMY
CHARLIE ALLEN
FRANK H. BAILEY
W. BUFORD BISHOP
JOHN F. BROWN
AMOS CHRISMAN
BRITTON CLUCK
WALTER M. FOSTER
MARSHALL T. FRENCH
JIM GANN
EMERY J. GRAY
WILLIAM P. HICKMAN
JOHN H. HILL

Marshall N. Hopkins
Floyd T. Koontz
Howard T. Mann
Jacob Manning
Gallion Mitchell
Charles C. Patterson
J. Lloyd Reneau
Sam W. Reneau
Estle R. Skeen
Roscoe M. Slaton

Marine Corps
William E. Line

Johnson County
Army
Joseph Cowan
John W. Forrester
Glen Greer
J. Elbert Grindstaff
Thurmon E. Hawks
Ross Hawkins
Wiley Hines
Joseph R. Mains
Jade Martin
Sam McGuire
Earl Matney
Lon H. Miller
D. Clate Owens
Albert C. Payne
James H. Poe
Rufus A. Potter
Clinton H. Reeves
Nicholas E. Wallace
Millard F. Warren
Don S. Williams

Navy
Ray E. Wilson

Knox County
Army
Christopher C. Acklin Jr.
Thomas D. Adcock
Lillard E. Ailor
James C. Andes
Walter R. Armstrong
Charlie Arnold
Joseph A. Bayless
John L. Bentley
John W. Black
Ralph E. Boles
William L. Bowling
Richard H. Boyd
William E. Britton
Robert L. Brock
Bruce Burkhart

Lyman C. Butler
Thomas M. Cain
John M. Carr
Arthur E. Caton
Charlie A. Clark
Lawrence W. Cockrum
Warren A. Congdon
William N. Cooper
Roger H. Cross
Thomas Curtis
James R. Daniel
Thomas L. Davis
Richard H. Dickson
Mayfield Dorsey
Roscoe H. Duggan
Merritt Dunbar
Jackson C. Earle
Patrick N. B. Earle
William H. Eckel
Louis Fasio
Willard Fleming
John J. Flenniken
Alvin Fowler
David French
William P. Gaddis
John Gaines
Arthur W. Gibbons
Hubert Goines
Lena F. Groner
Charles B. Hackney
Jessie F. Hall
Walter R. Harper
Clarence Harrison
Jess H. Hellard
George S. Hembree
Callie M. Hickey
Lee L. Hickey
Kenney J. Huff
Adrian O. Jett
Dewey M. Johnson
John H. Johnson
Charles D. Johnston Jr.
George H. M. Jones
James E. Karnes   MOH
Leo Keith
Arl B. Kelly
Fred Key
Adrian W. Kidd
Richard F. Kirkpatrick
Albert R. Kline
Edward W. Lane
John A. Langford
Floyd S. LaRue
Alison L. R. Laugherty
Jesse H. Long
Hugh Luttrell
Samuel A. McCarty

Reuben McDaniel
Charles R. McGuire
Charlie H. McInturff
William A. McMillan
James S. Matthews
John C. Meeh
Hicks R. Meltabarger
George F. Miller
Oliver Miller
Claude L. Mingle
Rolfe Moody
Cleo Morris
Harrison Moulden
George L. Mowry
Ody Mulvany
George A. Ogle
Roy O. Palmer
Morris L. Parks
Robert S. Parks
William Parris
James M. Payne
William L. Phibbs
Claude B. Phillips
Frank Reed
Charles H. Rich
Oscar Rider
Mack Rose
Frank R. Russell
Earl C. Sanders
George Seymore
Lee Sharp
Samuel O. Shoemake
Hubert C. Sisk
Mack H. Smith
James B. Snyder
Loney E. Sparks
Taylor C. Stone
Roy L. Sweet
James M. Tillery
Sherman H. Turner
Alvie Underwood
Grant Vandeventer
George E. Waitman
Spencer Wallace
Fred L. Williams
Sam Wohlford
Richard Wyatt
Carrick H. Yeager

Navy
John H. Balthrop
Francis Burdet
Walter W. Burkhart
Earnest Ely
William H. Jackson
James E. Johnston
Robert H. Leonard

Arthur J. McClinton
Joe Parks
W. Archie Pope
C. McGhee Tyson
James M. Wheeler

Marine Corps
William T. Bayless
Dan M. Blankinship
Harry R. Bohanan
William H. Boothe
Frank W. Daniel
Edgar E. Johnson
Samuel S. Jones
Burlie G. Mynatt
Andrew D. Reed

Loudon County
Army
Elmer L. Anthony
James W. Blair
John R. Cabe
Thomas G. Cagle
John H. Ferguson
William N. Johnson
Roe Jones
John Malone
Eugene R. Phibbs
Ira E. Presswood
Grover C. Propes

Navy
Earnest M. Milsaps

Marion County
Army
Malcolm Burnett Jr.
Vince R. Choat
Claude D. Crumbliss
Joseph Dennis
Robert A. Dykes
Dallas P. Ewton
John H. Finney
Robert A. Gamble
Archie Gilbreath
Grover C. Goins
James Harrison
John I. Kilgore
Walter G. Layne
Lawrence D. Lewis
Eastly Maxwell
Andrew Reynolds
Bertice Roberts
Ransom E. Sampley
William A. Sharp
Lacy O. Smith

Luther L. Smith
Aaron Westmoreland

McMinn County
Army
Lewis B. Adams
Reese Adams
Arthur N. Bacon
Charles E. Boone
Robert T. Burgess
Albert A. Carlock
James Carpenter
Charlie Clark
James R. Cooley
James D. Daugherty
Hobart E. Emerson
James B. Foster
Will F. France
Rankin D. Gay
Jasper Gerald
Joe Gossett
Lloyd E. Gregory
William J. Humphreys
McKinley E. Johnson
Roy B. Johnson
Oscar Kibble
Dewey A. Ledford
Lee L. Liner
John C. Long
John Looney
William R. McKay
Arvel Maynor
Riley O. Murphy
Herbert L. Payne
William I. Roberts
John Shelton
Jesse Sims
Gilbert W. Smith
Charles E. Stansbury
Roy A. Thompson
Bryant S. Trew
Oscar Vaughn
Jake Visage
Roe West
John E. Wilkins
Josephus B. Wilson
Claude Womac
James M. Yates

Meigs County
Army
Albert C. Burton
James F. Collins
Charlie Fitch
Ben J. Gates
Samuel M. Hill

James O. Huff
Edgar W. Lane
Bratcher H. Long
Wilbur Moore
William H. Powers
William R. Ratledge

Navy
Grundy B. Johnson

Monroe County
Army
Fred R. Allen
Willie E. Brookshear
Horace Burger
Columbus L. Clark
Harden E. Clark
David Davis
Lem E. Emert
Willie M. Goad
Willie Greer
David C. Hickey
Meredith G. Jenkins
Bedford B. Lunsford
John McClendon
Thurber McConkey
Joe McGhee
Robert L. Miller
William H. Milligan
Levi S. Morehouse
Anon L. Moser
Benjamin Nichols
Horace R. Raper
Frank A. Ray
William S. Scruggs
Albert B. Simpson
Dan W. Snider
James H. Taylor

Marine Corps
William E. Giles

Morgan County
Army
Martin C. Brown
Joseph H. Carson
John Daugherty
John W. Fletcher
Mark Hambright
Harrison B. Jackson
Bert M. Jones
George W. Kennedy
Joe Nance
A. C. Peters
Daniel Pitman
Isham D. Robbins

Oscar Williams
David H. Wilson

Navy
Ernest R. Johnson

Polk County
Army
James Adams
Thomas C. Cate
Lewis E. Chatham
James A. Collins
Roy C. Curtis
Virgil Green
Isham N. Houk
Harvey Hughes
Gilliam H. Hyde
Sam Key
Arthur Lee
Oscar R. Liner
James L. Loden
Ben H. McClary
William C. McNelley
Joseph C. Runyon
Bert E. Russell
Leonidas Taylor
Ephriam Thompson
Carl L. Weber

Navy
William T. Fritts
Carl F. Graham

Marine Corps
Bascome Breeden

Rhea County
Army
Fred W. Brady
Tom Bruce
John Garrison
Alvin Gill
Fred C. Guth
Leroy Hudson
Clint B. Miller
Charles R. Sharp

Roane County
Army
Hobart M. Bailey
Albert A. Bowman
Jessie Branan
Jennings Brown
George D. Bryant
John H. Burchfield
Clarence Butler

Tillman Butler
Ulys Coker
Joe J. Davis
Arthur B. Douglas
Joe H. Evans
Charley Galyon
Charley W. Graves
Oscar Hampton
Edward H. Hickey
Joseph T. Jones
George McClure
Edgar L. McKinney
Monterville Mee
Ralph B. Newman
Sam Ooten
Thurlow M. Price
John J. Rayburn
Will W. Renfro
Marion Robinson
Curtis E. Smith
Clifford T. Stegall
Harvey S. Teeter
George E. West
Tom R. West
Elbert J. Woody
James Y. Wright

Navy
Clarence A. Howard
Reuben R. Wallin

Scott County
Army
William Blevins
William Brown
William Chitwood
Huffman Davis
Burl Dyer
Guy D. Fryar
James Gibson
Robert M. Hughett
Clovus Jeffers
Elsic Lawson
Hugh T. Lewallen
Hett Phillips
Lawrence Phillips
Onva K. Phillips
Lonus Reed
Fred Sexton
Mitchel Sexton
Jesse Slaven
Sherman Stanley
Edson L. Toomey
Jasper York

Marine Corps
Eugene Sharpe

Sequatchie County
Army
Anderson Elliot
Lida M. Hackworth
Mark Harvey
Victor S. Johnson
Willie K. Swanger
Claude C. Williams

Sevier County
Army
Lavator L. Allen
Amos Atchley
Victor Blazer
Ashley J. Cate
Hugh C. Clabo
Robert P. Clabo
Benjamin J. Cogdill
Pleas H. Cooper
Arthur W. Dickey
Luna W. Enloe
Meek Feezel
John F. Fine
John W. Fleming
John O. Fox
Joshua Freeman
Ollie Harden
Arlie Hardin
Miles P. Hurst
Plina C. Hurst
William H. Keener
Daniel I. King
Odell Lane
Henry R. McMahan
James M. McMahan
Leander H. Messer
Walter Newman
Arlie H. Ogle
Samuel A. Ogle
Bruce S. Smallwood
Wesley Stinnett
Richard Z. Trentham
Von C. Underwood
Charley Wells
Walker B. Wells

Navy
David C. Quarrels

Marine Corps
Bert D. Gann
James A. Marshall

Sullivan County

ARMY

ROBERT A. ANDERSON
JAMES L. BARR
BALLARD BURDINE
WILLIAM CARNAHAN
WILL R. CARR
EDWARD L. CARROLL
GEORGE W. CLOUD
SHERMAN COMBS
JESSIE G. COMPTON
ISAAC CROSS
ROBERT CRUSENBERRY
EDGAR FEATHERS
JAMES L. GLOVER
JOHN L. GODSEY
EARL D. GRIMSLEY
HAGAN HAMMOND
CLIFFORD HARDY
VALDRIE D. HAWK
JOE HAWKINS
JOHN S. HENRY JR.
CHARLES L. HICKS
GEORGE HUMPHREY
GEORGE B. HUNIGAN
WILLIAM F. JONES
JAMES KETCHEM
JERRY KETRON
VERLIN P. KING
PAUL E. MASSIE
CLYDE C. MORTON
SAM E. MYERS
ERNEST L. PENN
FREDRICK L. PEOPLES
JAMES W. RAGAN
JOHN ROSENBAUM
FRANK SLAGLE
ERIE STEADMAN
EDWARD N. STREET
ALEX SWINEY
JOE S. TAYLOR
JAHUE TILLISON
JOSEPH TRIBBLE

ALBERT WAMPLER
JOSEPH E. WARREN

NAVY

BRUCE R. ALLEY
JOSEPH S. BACHMAN
PORTER L. ST. JOHN
DAVID G. VANCE

MARINE CORPS

PATRICK H. DAVIS

Unicoi County

ARMY

GARRETT EDWARDS
JOHN GREEN
HOBERT HARRIS
HARRISON HOPKINS
WILLIAM A. JONES
LINA McCOURRY
PAUL MASTERS
WILLIAM M. MOORE
DOUGLAS PENLAND
JAMES H. PRICE
JAMES W. TEAGUE

Union County

ARMY

GEORGE D. CALDWELL
CHARLES M. GOSE
McKINLEY W. HANSARD
BERNIE LETT
THOMAS M. PHIPPS
LINDSAY ROUSE
MONROE STINER
GEORGE R. WYRICK

Washington County

ARMY

JOHN W. ARMSTRONG
ROY C. BACON
HUBERT BARRON
GEORGE BOWMAN
JOHN R. BOWMAN
ALEXANDER BROWN

FRED R. CAMPBELL
EMMETT COLE
BERNIE DANIELS
GILFORD DENTON
JOE FULKERSON
WESLEY M. FURCHES
CLAUDE GREEN
LESTER P. HARRIS
CHARLIE A. HELTON
HOBART B. JONES
RAYMOND JONES
WILLIAM A. KEEZEL
JOHN J. KELLEY
PAUL D. KELLY
THURMAN J. LEACH
HOBART M. LEONARD
PATRICK LOVELESS
WILLIAM H. McCRACKEN
HENRY J. McMACKIN
WALTER E. McNEESE
RALPH B. MATHERLY
JAMES MILLER
WALTER R. MILLION
ORVILLE T. MITCHELL
JOSEPH L. MOORE
HARRY D. MORRIS
VIRGIL C. MOTTERN
JOHN E. PHILLIPS
WILLIAM PHILLIPS
JAMES L. SEARCY
WILLIAM SHORT
LAWRENCE C. SMITH
GEORGE F. ST. CLAIR
EDIE B. WADE
ROY B. WRIGHT
GEORGE YOUNG

NAVY

WILLIAM N. CHINOUTH
ROBERT L. MILLER
DAVID E. C. PUGH

MARINE CORPS

STEVE P. CARSON

WORLD WAR II

Anderson County

ARMY/ARMY AIR CORPS

CARL A. ALLEN
BERL G. AULT
EARL J. AULT
GLENN E. BILLINGSLEY
WILBER L. BRADFORD
CLYDE W. BRUMMETT

G. B. BUNCH
COLLINS O. BUTLER
MEREDIETH L. CARTER
CYRIL J. CHADWELL
JOHN C. CLIFFORD
RAY T. COLLINS
CARL R. COOK
FORREST M. COOK

DAVID L. DISNEY
HENRY C. L. DISNEY
ROBERT D. DISNEY
MACK DUNCAN
ROWE C. EAGER
HAROLD C. ELLENBURG
MALCOLM L. ELLIOTT
CLIFTON R. FOSTER

Carl E. Foust
James R. Foust
William W. Gault
Ray Gilbreath
Virgil Goodman
Homer A. Goodykoontz
James V. Gross
J. W. Hamilton
Leonard L. Harness
Carl R. Hendrix
John W. Horner
Erwin F. Huckaby
James C. Huffines
Cecil Humphrey
Clifton Jarnigan
Joseph A. Jett
R. Paul Johnson
Paul K. King
John E. Lewis
Ellis F. Long
Arthur L. Lowery
Thomas Manuel
Willard Marlow
Carl G. Martin
Walter Mayton
Ralph E. Melton
Charles E. Merritt
Benton B. Mitchell
Troy E. Mitchell
William W. Mitchell
Albert L. Moneymaker
Norman E. O'Neal
C. Kenneth Patterson
Clifford E. Phillips
Harry K. Phillips
Meredith J. Phillips
John A. Pickman
Paul W. Pickrell
William A. Queener
John E. Richardson
Raleigh C. Seiber
Harry G. Sharp
Lyndall E. Smiddy
James W. Stooksbury
Reuben E. Tallant
James D. Tucker
Eugene B. Wallace
Cecil Ward
Lawrence Ward
William C. Weisgerber
Eugene White
Blaine E. Williams
Elbert M. Williams
Sherrill R. Williams
James W. York

Navy
Robert M. Allen
William R. Bush
William Byrd
Norman C. Draper
Robert M. Maxwell
William C. McKenzie
John C. Owen Jr.
Joyce C. Phillips
James H. Sharp
Elmer H. Shubert
George E. Skeggs
Charlie F. Weatherford

Marine Corps
Joe K. Alderson
James E. Barlow
Elmer A. Merritt
James T. Smith

Bledsoe County
Army/Army Air Corps
Monroe H. Bayless
Ray Brewer
Robert L. Brewer
Melvin C. Brock
James E. Cagle
James C. Childress
A. B. Collier
Ernest H. Corvin
Joe R. Cunningham Jr.
Ed C. Davis
John C. Farmer
William C. Farmer
John D. Fisher
James P. Graham
Claude W. Hale
Mose N. J. Hamilton
Ernest D. Hancock
Carl K. Hitchcox
Samuel C. Hitchcox
William P. Jolley
Bernard W. McReynolds
Claude M. Mills
Ralph E. Moore
Charles M. Riggs
Greer Rigsby
Clyde J. Smith
Manis Swafford
Willard L. Turner
Elmer F. Walker
Samuel J. Washington
Arthie V. Whitson

Navy
Billy B. Bayless
James I. Blaylock

George H. Mansfield
Clifford Rhea
George N. Sanders Jr.
B. Henry Smith
Robert F. Swafford

Coast Guard
Henry F. Lester

Blount County
Army/Army Air Corps
Carl E. Adams
Howard E. Baker
Willie Barker
Ray Barrett
Paul K. Beck
James A. Bennett
Roscoe M. Best
Harvey W. Boling
James E. Bowers
Carl J. Branton
David H. Briggs Jr.
Cledith Brown
James K. Brown
John R. Broyles Jr.
Denvil Burgess
Robert G. Campbell
Charles D. Carroll Jr.
Fred P. Caylor
Archabald H. Chandler
Silas J. Chapman
William O. Chums
Alex M. Clabough
J. Brent Clemmer
Wilbur C. Connatser
Troy W. Cope
Horace C. Costner
Tollton E. Coulter Sr.
Henry O. Cox. Jr.
Owen G. Cox Jr.
Paul Z. Crabtree
William P. Crisp
James E. Davis
Paul F. Davis
John C. Dugger
John A. Dunlap
Ollie P. Dunn
Birch England
John H. Evans
John W. Farr Jr.
Roy E. Freeman
Charles E. French
William W. French Jr.
Ode J. Garner
Stephen V. Gibson
James H. Giffin
Wade Graham

Freeman A. Greene Jr.
David R. Guy
Harvey E. Hall
John H. Hammonds
Kenneth C. Hargis
Claude E. Hembree
Conrad J. Hembree
Fred J. Henry
Herman M. Hicks
James S. Hill
Jasper E. Hill
William H. Hudgens Jr.
Raymond C. Huffstetler
Paul E. Humphrey
Sam A. Humphrey
Lester L. Hunt
Luther C. Hurst
Burl D. Huskey
Charles O. Irwin
Obie Jenkins
Floyd H. Jones
Vernon L. Jones
Edward L. Kellar
William B. Keller
Paul A. Kerr
Jesse B. Kirkland
Arthur G. Kiser
Robert O. Kitchin
Rudolph F. Klarer
George Koons
Ralph Lambert
Fred Lewis
Marvin H. Long
Audley E. Lynn
Obed L. McCollum
William C. McConnell
William H. McCulley Jr.
Howard B. McGill
P. L. Morehead Jr.
Glenn S. Morton
Robert D. Mosier
Howard K. Moss
James V. Myers
William G. Onks
William L. Orr
Eather E. Patterson
James D. Pemberton
Jack L. Phelps
Mort J. Potter
Charles T. Presley
Oscar R. Proffitt
Harold Rathbone
Clifford Reagan
Roy A. Reno
Earl L. J. Rhyne
George Riggs Jr.
Warren B. Robinson

Thomas E. Rodgers
Henry M. Rowland
Lacy W. Rueter
Charles V. Russell
Waymon W. Sandidge
Sanford Sloan
Eugene W. Smith
W. Roy Smith Jr.
John S. Stafford
William A. Stanfield Jr.
Roy D. Steele
Horace S. Stephens
Ray F. Stiles
Clell R. Stinnett
Henry T. Stinnette
Howard P. Sullivan
Bennie Summey
Wendell F. Swanson
Jack M. Thames
Ross H. Thompson
James S. Todd
Raymond B. Wade
Alvin Welch
James L. Widner
George K. Wright
Samuel N. Yearout Jr.
William R. Young

Navy
Donnas H. Boyd
Samuel T. Byers
William B. Carpenter
W. C. Jack Dunn Jr.
John R. Eaves Jr.
Arnold H. Ferguson
George E. Goodman Jr.
John W. Griffitts
K. Howard Hicks
Robert L. Kinnaman
Carl S. McFee
Thomas M. McGee Jr.
Joe L. McGhee
Carl W. Miller
Marvin R. Mizell
Robert B. Moore
Robert H. Norris
J. Wayne Pierce
Elmer H. Russell

Marine Corps
J. R. Blair
Harold D. Burch
Clarence J. Carver
Marion B. Cooper
Abraham L. Hill
Kenneth H. Owens
James L. Rhyne
Julian C. Stinnett

Merchant Marines
Max M. Pearson

Bradley County
Army/Army Air Corps
George H. Bean
John D. Bell
Walter R. Bigham
James D. Blankenship
Frank L. Boyd
John B. Brock
Hoyt Buckner
Andrew J. Carr
Jarius Casada
Harold E. Chadwick
Reeldon R. Chambers
Dennis S. Crisp
Albert G. Cross
Doyle C. Davenport
Hubert Davis
Carl T. Duff
Jessie J. Edwards
C. L. Elmore
J. M. Farmer
Charles R. Finnell
Earl J. Freeman
James R. Gee
Edward R. Gibson
Howard G. Goodner
Roy E. Gregg
Archibald R. T. Hambright
Tipton Hancock
Chester L. Haney
William G. Hargis
Gideon S. Hawk Jr.
Henry O. Hewett
Roland J. Hickey
James L. Hicks
William R. Hill
Charles E. Hixson
Robert Holland
John E. Hood
Paul B. Huff   MOH
Ben F. Huffine Jr.
Paul M. Jones
Robert J. I. Jordan
Eugene D. Kimsey
Fred A. King
George King
Clarence L. Lawson
W. David Lee
L. J. Lewis
William Longwith
Joseph L. Mackey
Boyd L. Martin
Jesse C. Maupin
Joe McClanahan

CLAUDE F. MCNABB
FRED R. MCNABB
D. L. MESSER
JESSIE C. MINNIS
ROY G. MOORE
VERNARD R. MURRAY
ALEXANDER C. NEWTON
RAY H. OGLE
JAMES P. O'NEAL
GEORGE H. PARKS
FLOYD T. PATTERSON
JESSE W. POTEET
JESSIE W. PULLIN
BILLY K. RAINEY
JAMES W. ROBBINS
LOYD W. ROBERTS
JESSIE RODLEY
WILLIAM H. ROGERS
GLENN R. SKELTON
HAROLD E. SPICER
HARVEY E. STEPHENS
R. M. T. SWAFFORD
COURVILLE B. TARPLEY
JAMES S. VARNELL JR.
ARCHIE M. WALLACE
PAUL WARE
MILBURN K. WATTENBARGER
WILLIAM V. WEAVER
WALLACE H. WELCH
W. H. WESTMORELAND
GEORGE WHITMIRE
DALLAS M. WILLET
CARL C. WILLIAMS
JESSE T. WILLIS
CLAUDE J. WOMBLE
HOMER R. YOUNG

NAVY
JAMES B. BARRETT
FRENCH A. FINNELL
CHARLES W. LEGARDE
JOHN H. MADDOX
CARL W. ROGERS
SELMAR B. WELCH

MARINE CORPS
WILBURN K. GASTON
HORACE E. HAWK JR.
RAYMOND MCCANN

MERCHANT MARINES
EMORY CASS
HARRY W. GUINN
HOWARD UPCHURCH

COAST GUARD
WILLIAM A. MULLINAX

Campbell County
ARMY/ARMY AIR CORPS
CONLEY E. ADAMS
WILLARD ADKINS
JOHN E. ANDERSON
CLAYTON ARTIS
LEMAN D. BALL
JOHNIE M. BATES
WILLIAM E. BELL
LEWIS B. BOLTON
HERNDON C. BOWMAN
JAMES F. BRANAM
WILLIS BRANAM
PAUL BRASHEARS
HENRY E. BRASSFIELD JR.
FREDRICK W. BRUCE
JORDAN C. CARROLL
CHARLES CHADWELL
JAMES M. CHILDRESS
LEE M. CLOTFELTER
HUBERT COLE
ROSS COLLINGSWORTH
WENDELL D. COPELAND
DAVID H. CREEKMORE
ARTHUR CROSS
ARCHIE A. DALTON
WILLIAM G. DAVENPORT
ROY W. DAVIS
CHARLES W. DILBECK
CHARLIE DOUGLAS
CLYDE A. DOUGLAS
HENRY L. DOUGLAS
HAZEL H. DUNCAN
MARION E. DUNCAN
CHARLIE EVANS
OWEN H. EVANS
BILLIE V. FRANKLIN
EDD FUSTON
BYRON L. GOINS
ROY GOODMAN
LONNIE E. GRADY
ELIHUE GREEN JR.
ARVEL H. HALL
CARL G. HATFIELD
WILLIAM C. HATFIELD
ROY L. HATMAKER
WILMER W. HATMAKER
ANDREW J. HAWKINS
EARL E. HAYES
MAYNARD W. HEATHERLY
PAUL E. HEATHERLY
WOODROW HEATHERLY
JAMES I. HENSLEY
JOHN L. HUDDLESTON
KLEETIS C. IVEY
VERNON IVEY
JAMES C. JEFFERS

JOSEPH E. JOHNSON
WILLIE T. JUSTICE
LEWIS KING JR.
ALVIN H. LAMB JR.
GEORGE F. LAMB
JAMES T. LAND
WAYMON R. LAWHORN
G. BISHOP LAWSON
JAMES F. LEACH
ARLIE LONG
QUINCY H. LONG JR.
JAMES D. LONGMIRE
LONNIE LYNCH
VERDIA LYONS
CHARLES H. MARPLE
LAWRENCE L. MCCARTY
SHIRLEY MCGHEE
CAL MILLER
WALTER C. NELSON
LOYD W. NICHOLS
LEE R. NORMAN
BARTON W. OWENS
WILLIAM M. PARKER
GEORGE W. PARTIN
FRED K. PAUL
THOMAS E. PERKEY
WILLIAM E. PETITT
JACOB H. QUEENER
JOHN C. RICHARDSON
WILLIAM W. RIDENOUR
EARL ROACH
WARREN G. ROADEN
WILLIAM F. ROBBINS
HOMER L. RODEHEAVER
LEON F. RUSSELL
HENRY C. SCOTT
CHARLES V. SHARP
CLYDE SHOFFNER
MARTIN SILER
GILMORE W. SMITH
OVA SMITH
HARLEY F. SPRADLIN
OSCAR M. STEVENS
JAMES W. STEWART
ELWOOD J. STINER
JAMES E. STONE
MILTON G. SUTTON
CARL W. THOMPSON
VENIS R. TODD
JAMES H. WALDEN
JAMES R. WALDEN
ERIC W. WARMING
EUKLE WELCH
JOSEPH B. WHITE
ROBERT T. WILLIAMS
ARCHIE WILSON
JAMES F. WILSON

THOMAS W. WILSON
LEONARD B. WOODS
MILLER D. YOAKUM

NAVY

JOSEPH ARNETT
ELMER M. AYERS
HOWARD E. DAUGHERTY
DANIEL H. DISNEY JR.
GENERAL P. DOUGLAS
JOE GAYLOR JR.
WILLIE HALE
SHIRLEY O. LOWE
ROBERT G. MCGHEE
J. V. RUSSELL
JAMES T. SHEPHERD
JOSEPH H. SILER
WALTER TACKET
JULIA M. ZECCHINI

COAST GUARD
PETER T. ZECCHINI JR.

Carter County

ARMY/ARMY AIR CORPS

SHONA K. ALDRIDGE
GRANT E. ALLEN
CLYDE T. ANGEL
ALLISON A. ARROWOOD
PAUL T. BARNETT
BARNEY C. BENNETT
HARVEY C. BIRCHFIELD
JOHN S. BIRCHFIELD
JOHN S. BOWERS
SAMUEL M. BOWERS
FELIX R. BREWER
BASCOM BRYANT
HERMAN BUCHANAN
JAMES L. BUCKLES
JOHN S. BUCKLES
PAUL BURNETT
CLAY BYERS
JUNIOR R. CALLOWAY
HARRISON C. CARVER
JAMES C. COGGINS JR.
FARRELL R. COLLINS
EARL P. COOKE
PAUL B. CRABTREE
STANLEY A. CURRY
KENNETH W. DAVIS
ROBERT C. DAVIS JR.
ROBERT L. DAVIS
ROBERT DELOACH
WILLIAM T. DELOACH
WILLIAM E. DENNEY
ROBERT C. DUFF
ELDRIDGE S. EDENS

GEORGE S. ELLIS
THURMAN H. ESTEP
CHARLES B. FRANKLIN
JAMES FREEMAN
KARL F. GRINDSTAFF
IRA J. HARDIN
HOWARD R. HEATON
LEON HELTON
MERLIN B. HICKS
ROBERT H. HILTON
AVERY HOPSON
FRANK HOPSON
CLIFFORD B. HYDER
FREDERICK S. JENNINGS
JOHN P. KEYS
GLEN E. KUHN
ALVIN D. LAMBERT
WALTER J. LANG
GEORGE E. LAWS
JOHN O. LEWIS
ROBINSON LEWIS
HOWARD E. LITTLE
JAMES B. LITTLE
FRANCE E. LOTHERY
HARRY C. MARKLAND
TOMMY E. MCKEEHAN
DANA MCKINNEY
DAVID R. MCQUEEN
IRA L. MEREDITH
THOMAS R. MICHAEL
DELMAR D. MILES
AVERY R. MILLER
DAVID R. MILLER
HERMON MILLER
JOSEPH W. MORRELL
LLOYD H. MORRELL
HARRY K. NAVE
L. HERSCHEL NAVE
ROBERT R. NORMAN
EVANS E. OVERBEY
C. DALE PEARSON
ELWYN S. PERRY
ALVIN L. PIERCE
WALTER D. PIERCE
JACK L. PLEASANT
LEONARD B. PRITCHARD
RAYMOND F. RANGE
CLARENCE G. ROE
MARTIN E. ROSENBAUM
JOHN E. RUSSELL
WALTER M. SHIELDS
ELMER J. SHULL
PAUL E. SHULTZ
KALE SIMERLY
STEWART R. SIMERLY
BROADWAY V. SIMS
JACK A. SLAGLE

ANTIE E. SOUDER
LEWIS H. STARNES
LONZIE J. STOUT
CAMERON C. TAYLOR
FRED TAYLOR
HENDRIX C. TAYLOR
PHIL S. TAYLOR
STOKES M. TAYLOR
WILLIAM T. TAYLOR
GEORGE W. TEN EYCK
PHILLIP TOLLEY
ROY TOLLEY
WILLIAM A. VANCE
AMON D. WAGNER
WILLIAM B. WAGNER
CLARENCE W. WALKER
JAMES W. WALKER
LLOYD WARD
ROBERT WATSON
RALPH M. WATTENBARGER
PAUL E. WHITE
CLYDE WHITEHEAD
T. W. WHITEHEAD
WILLIAM H. WHITSON
TILLMAN H. WILLIAMS
MARK P. WILSON

NAVY

WILLIAM V. CAMPBELL
CLARENCE C. CARDEN
CLEVE J. CLAWSON
RHUDY L. HINKLE
WESLEY J. HOLDEN
OLIN JACOBS
ODEN D. JOHNSON
WORLEY S. MARKLAND
LOUIS MCKEEHAN
ALBERT R. MOORE
JAMES W. MUNSEY JR.
GARNETT B. NUTTER
JAMES E. PEOPLES
BRUCE W. PERRY
GEORGE W. PERSINGER
WARREN C. PRICE
ROBERT D. RAINWATER
RAY R. SMITH
CLAUDE SWANNER
L. T. STOUT
JESSE J. TAYLOR
WILLIAM L. TREADWAY JR.
FRANK E. VERRAN
ERNEST E. WALKER
ROY S. WILLIAMS

MARINE CORPS

CHARLES W. CLAMON
LLOYD E. CARVER

HUGHES W. GOBBLE
DILLARD L. KERLEY
JOSEPH E. PAYNE
STEWART WHITEHEAD

Claiborne County
ARMY/ARMY AIR CORPS
WILLIAM J. AYE
LEE BERRY
SHERMAN H. BRADEN
LOWELL E. BROCKMAN
COLONEL A. BROOKS JR.
WESLIE L. BROOKS
HARRY L. BUIS
CLEO CAIN
ROY L. CAMPBELL
BILL G. CLARK
ATHEL J. CLINE
MILLARD O. CLINE
ROSS T. COLLINGSWORTH
GEORGE J. DAVIS
HAROLD D. DOUGLAS
EDWARD G. DOUGLAS
NEIL ENGLAND
JOHN R. ENGLAND
NATHAN E. FISHER
AUSTIN S. FRANCISCO
LONNIE E. GRADY
LLOYD M. GRAVES
ERNEST GRIFFEN
JAMES E. HAMBLIN
JAMES C. HARMON
ROY F. HATFIELD
HENRY A. HOPPER
SAMUEL L. HOUSTON
NEIL E. INGLE
RALPH C. JORDAN
CLAUDE B. KEYES
KELS LAWS
CONLEY M. LEACH
AUSTIN M. LONG
JOHN MANNING
TOM MESSER
CARL MINTON
JOHN H. MIRACLE
OWEN MONEY JR.
JIM C. MYERS
MAYNARD L. NUNN
EDWIN E. OVERTON
CORDELL PARTIN
EVERETT W. PIERCE
LLOYD J. POWERS
AARON RAINS
GEORGE W. RAMSEY
CARL R. REECE
KENNETH B. ROBINSON
VERNON W. ROBINSON

JAMES M. ROGERS
ERNEST E. SEAL
ELVERT E. SHIFLET
EDWARD R. SHUGART JR.
ROY W. SIVILS
RILEY L. SUTTON
CLYDE S. TAYLOR
CECIL C. TERRY
CLARENCE TINNEL
LOUIS W. TREECE
HAROLD C. TURPIN
WILLIAM WEAVER
DANIEL M. WEAVER
HAROLD W. WELCH
PAT M. WILLIAMS
HORACE F. WILSON
A. F. WOLFENBARGER
WOODROW W. WRIGHT
JOHN D. YEARY

NAVY
WILLIAM BROOKS
HOUSTON E. EDWARDS
ROSCOE L. FORTNER
ROBERT N. JOHNSON
LILLON B. LYNCH
JAMES T. LYNCH JR.
JAMES C. OSBORNE
CHARLES H. PATTERSON
HARRY L. PHELPS
AUBURN C. SHARP
KERMIT C. TAYLOR
OTIS M. THOMPSON

Cocke County
ARMY/ARMY AIR CORPS
ESTON A. BAXTER
HAL H. BAXTER
OLIVER F. BAXTER
JOSEPH A. BROWN
SWANNIE H. BURKE
JAMES D. BUTLER
OLIVER R. BUTLER
ALBERT M. CAMPBELL
HUGH M. CAMPBELL
HUGH J. CARLISLE JR.
CLEVE H. CARVER
DARIUS R. CODY
KENNETH O. CROWE
LUTHER L. CURETON
TOM W. DANIELS
RICHARD W. DOVER
WILLIAM S. FOSTER
LUCAS GENTRY
CHARLES E. GILES
ELMER J. GILES
ROY C. GREENE

MILBURN B. HALL
J. C. HAWK
CHARLES F. HODGE JR.
HOLLIS J. HOLT
IVAN F. HOLT
ROY A. JOHNSON
MANYARD LACKEY
RALPH LAWS
TROY W. LAWS
Y. J. LEATHERWOOD
CLIFFORD LEWIS
MANSON MATHES
HOWARD H. MATHIS
CHARLES L. McGAHA   MOH
LUTHER S. McGAHA
JOHN W. M. McMAHAN
JAMES F. McMILLON
LLOYD R. McNABB
ALBERT M. OLSAKOVSKY
JESS W. O'NEIL
JOHN W. OTTINGER
ORDWAY H. PADGETT
GLENN H. PEARCE
FRED F. PHILLIPS
LESTER PHILLIPS
SAMUEL E. PHILLIPS
ZACK PHILLIPS
IKE F. PRICE
JAMES L. RAGAN
WALTER I. RAMSEY
ISAAC N. REECE
J. D. SHELTON
ARTHUR M. SHULTS
NEIL L. SHULTS
J. D. SMELCER
ELMER F. S. STAHLMAN
CHARLES M. SUGGS
WILLIAM R. WALLER
DAVID A. WILLIAMS
RAY WOODY

NAVY
ROBIN E. ALLEN
MITCHELL BOLEY
DALLAS A. BROWN
OSCAR SAMPLES
JOSEPH L. SPRATT
ROBERT SUTTLES
CLYDE WILLIAMSON

MERCHANT MARINES
FREDRICK R. C. STOKELY

Cumberland County
ARMY/ARMY AIR CORPS
JESSE C. ANDERSON
DOYLE B. ASHBURN

Sidney S. Barnes
Lloyd M. Barnett
Emmit L. Bolin
Clarence E. Bow
Andrew J. Bristow
Roscoe C. Brown
Douglas W. Burnett
Cecil G. Buttram
Jack Cannon
Walter Copeland
Harvey W. Coulter
Robert F. Daggett
Alfred T. Davis
Oscar W. Dixon
Cecil Elmore
General A. Elmore
James C. Fox
Frank Godsey
Wiley H. Hedgecoth
Willa Hood
Charles W. Hyder
Benton E. Jolley
James T. Kerley
Granville R. Kimbro
Conrad E. Kindrick
James D. King
David D. Lawson
S. Jack Lephew
Robert H. Lewis
James E. Losey Jr.
James E. Lowe
Andrew C. McCoy
Haskel E. McHaney
Carvel E. Moles
Donald V. Mooneyham
Olen R. Moore
Roy E. Nealon
Everett L. Norris
John Padgett
M. Luther Patton
John R. Pippin
Ernest C. Pugh
Charles C. Ray
Charles E. Scarbrough
James W. Scarbrough
Everett Smith
Lawrence B. Smith
Roy E. Smith
Noble T. Stevens
Charles M. Storie
Casto A. Swafford
Lester L. Tabor
Beecher L. Templeton
James H. Troutt
Hollis W. Welch
J. Mason Wood
Doyle P. Woody

Navy
Chester E. Hamby
Marshall L. Hassler
Clay L. Kilgore
Fred M. Rockwell
George F. Smith
John J. Smith
Thomas L. Turner
Albert V. Welch Jr.
Benjamin H. West Jr.

Marine Corps
James A. Finney
Everett R. Kerley
Robert L. Parsons
Clayton Robbins

Fentress County
Army/Army Air Corps
John D. Allred
Willard T. Allred
Lester E. Anderson
Lonzo E. Atkinson
Chester H. Beaty
William M. Beaty
Willie B. Beaty
Elmo Bertram
Normal Bilbrey
Fred J. Blevins
Don Bowden
Elzie Brown
Roy Carney
Andrew B. Chambers
Guy M. Choate
Houck H. Choate
Willie C. Choate
George W. Clark
Coleman B. Clemons
Lelon L. Cobble
Lindsey Cody
Clarence O. Cook
Caleb F. Crabtree
Charlie W. Crabtree
Delmer E. Crouch
Earl D. Davis
Willard C. Dossett
Walter Franklin
Edwin F. Frazier
Milton Hatfield
Noah P. Hensley
Walter C. Hicks
Lonzie W. Hurst
Raymond W. Hurst
Joe C. Isabell
Hurstle Jones
Lonnie W. Jones
Joe H. Ledbetter

William D. Mullinix
William K. Murray
Ivan E. Overstreet
Thomas L. Owens
Woodrow W. Owens
Carlie E. Perry
Thomas D. Pierce
Earnest C. Price
Charlie C. Ramsey
Willie R. Ramsey
Ergo T. Robbins
Ralph Slaven
Bethel Smith
John T. Smith Jr.
Quentin Smith
Marrion E. Stephens
James M. Summers
Ethridge Turner
Willard M. Upchurch
Ralph L. Wheaton
David M. Williams
Clarence E. Wilson
Haskel D. Winningham
Warren D. Wright
Walter E. York

Navy
Edgar B. Atkinson
Walter M. Ledford
Asby C. Linder
Egbert C. Norman
Cosby A. Tinch

Grainger County
Army/Army Air Corps
Paul E. Atkins
Thomas O. Beeler
Ray K. Beets
Clarence C. Cantwell
Thomas A. Chichester
Donald W. Cockrum
James H. Coffey
Jack T. Collette
Haskell Dalton
Willis R. Dalton
R. R. Douglass Jr.
Zenas N. Estes
Faine M. Doyal
Robert M. Foley
Sam M. Harrell
James Harville
Albert E. Isbell Jr.
Edward C. Jones Jr.
Ford L. Kitts
Dreuey Mallicoat
Dudley O. Nash
Doyle W. Needham

Neil G. Reagan
Henry E. Scearce
Fred H. Slaton Jr.
James V. Stalans
George L. Sweatt
Charlie M. Sykes
James C. Trent
Marvin Walker

Navy
William J. Greer
Thomas W. Hall
George E. Jones
Bernard F. Long
Horace J. Long
Carl D. Patterson

Greene County
Army/Army Air Corps
Theodore Aldridge
Bryson Ayers
Alex Bailey
Henry B. Baker
Joel R. Barlow
John R. Baskette
W. Emory Baughard
David F. Bible
Harry Blankenship
Ray F. Bowser
Charles F. Bradburn
Jack Brooks
George R. Brown
Marcus W. Brown
Henry L. Broyles
Raymond L. Broyles
Fay Cannon
Velma L. Cannon
Paul B. Carter
Eugene A. Chandler
William A. Cook
Clifford Cooter
Howard L. Cornwell
George D. Cox
Estel H. Crum
Hubert M. Cutshaw
Herbert C. Davenport Jr.
Billie B. Davis
Earl K. Dean
William T. Dean
Haskell C. Dearstone
Pelham E. DeWitt
George W. Dobbs
Roy L. Dolinger
David P. Duck
Wallace H. Dunbar
James R. Erwin
Henry Farnsworth

Clinton A. Franklin
Reece Gass
James F. Gray
James R. Gregg
Coleman Gunter
Herschel O. Hamblin
Charles E. Haney
Robert S. Haren
J. Carter Harmon
Estell G. Harris
Donald E. Hensley
David P. Hice
Johnny Hipps
Cannon Holt
Corbett Hope Jr.
Norville E. Ingle
John S. Irvine Jr.
Ralph Jackson
Robert W. Jennings
Fred Johnson
Herbert H. Johnson
Dale A. Jones
Derice O. Jones
Nick G. Jones
William J. Jones
William H. Justis
W. Carter Kenney
Elijah Kidwell
James S. Kilday
Fred M. Killion
Clyde V. Knisley Jr.
Raymond R. Lawing
Winston Lawing
Arlyn L. Lones
Clyde T. Long
Hamlin P. Lowry
William P. Malone
Earl W. McAmis
Christopher C. McIntosh
John C. Miller
Ellis A. Moore
James Moore
John T. Moore
Raleigh B. Moore
James V. Murray
Lacy C. Myers Jr.
Paul E. Myers
Clarence A. Nanney
Jay Neal
Sylvester Norton
Roscoe L. Ottinger
Lewis F. Pardue
Grady Parker
Oscar R. Payne
Arthur C. Phillips
Ralph G. Phillips
Herman B. Pierce

Eugene Raby
Wiley E. Rader
Elmer E. Ramey
James G. Ramsey
Vaughn Reaves
Walter P. Renner
Clinton O. Ricker
Johnny C. Ricker
R. B. Ricker
Howard B. Ross
J.B. Rupert
Andrew J. Scalf
Ralph Scalf
Charles Shannon
Edgar Shepherd
Vern C. Shipley
Eugene Smith
Ralph W. Smith
Robert L. Smith
George D. Starnes
Frank Tame
Neal D. Thomas
Glen E. Tweed
Cleve H. Tweed
Richard Vaughn
Doyle D. Verran
Elgin T. Webb
Jacob A. White
Jess W. White
James C. Wilhoit
Charles W. Willett
Gurdine Wills
Jessie D. Wills
Horace J. Wood Jr.
Hugh E. Wright
Emory C. Yokely

Navy
Calvin C. Broyles
J. Glenn Chase
W. Newton Conway
Troy B. Fillers
Robert C. George
Rupert Greenlee
Ralph J. Gray
Charles R. Hartman
J. M. Franklin Hartman
Kenneth T. Lamons
George M. Ledbetter
Hooper E. McFarland
Dale McKay
Charlie H. Morrison
Charles M. Park
J. V. Poe
Billy F. Purgason
Roland O. Rich Jr.
Ernest M. Stokley

HUBERT D. THORNBURG
CHARLES W. WATTENBARGER

MARINE CORPS
RALPH E. CANNON
JAMES L. CHASE
JAMES E. COSLEY
EARL F. FAIR
ELBERT L. KINSER   MOH
ROBERT B. MCINTOSH
OTTIE B. SENTELLE

Hamblen County
ARMY/ARMY AIR CORPS
ORBEN B. ALLEY JR.
LILBERN M. BALES
EARL BREEDEN
CECIL BROWN
CLIFFORD BRYAN
MILLARD CAMERON
WILLIAM F. CAMERON
JAMES R. CAMPBELL
FRENCH E. CLAIBORNE
WAYLAND E. CORNWELL
FLOYD A. CROSS
CHARLES T. DARNELL
DAVID K. EDWARDS II
GEORGE G. EVANS
JACK J. FINE
JOHN H. FRANKLIN JR.
BOYD M. FULLINGTON
THOMAS W. GILLEY
HORACE A. GRAY
ROBERT GREENE
JOHN F. HAY
CLURE H. HODGE
JOHN W. HORTON
CECIL HUX
LEROY HYDER
JOE F. JOHNS
JAMES F. E. JOHNSON
PERRY D. JOLLAY
KYLE B. JONES
WILLIAM W. KREIS
CLYDE H. LAMPKIN
DEWEY K. LEDBETTER
FRANK MCKINNEY
WALTER R. MCKINNEY
TED MCMAHAN
EUGENE L. MOYERS
CLARENCE NOE
EUGENE H. NOE
WAYNE D. PRATT
ALBERT RAUSCHER
ERNEST E. ROBERTSON
ROBERT L. SEAL JR.
EARL H. SEALS

JOE SHOCKLEY
LEONARD R. SHOUN
GEORGE W. SHULTZ
BUFORD C. SIMMONS
RALPH H. SMITH
JAMES C. TALLEY
CLYDE L. THOMAS
HAROLD L. VICKERS
JAMES A. WALDROP
LYNN R. WALKER
JAMES C. WEST
BENJAMIN F. WICE
JAMES D. WILDER
JOHN A. WILLIAMS
HAROLD F. WOLFE
LAWRENCE B. WYATT
GLEN M. YOUNT

NAVY
RHEA O. BOYD
JOHN S. DALTON
HAROLD W. MASSENGILL
JAMES R. MORGAN
CLYDE NEWBERRY JR.
JAMES M. ROBERTSON

MARINE CORPS
JESS E. HARVILLE

MERCHANT MARINES
ERNEST C. LOWRY

Hamilton County
ARMY/ARMY AIR CORPS
JOHN E. ABBOTT
ROBERT S. ABEEL JR.
RUFUS ABERCROMBIE
RICHARD H. ADAIR
JAMES A. ADAMS
JOHN T. ADAMS
WILLIAM C. ADAMS
HOUSTON C. AKINS
WILLIAM E. ALEXANDER
ALTON W. ALLEN
JAMES H. ALLEN
MICHAEL M. ALLISON
ROBERT L. AMIEL
HENRY APPLIN
JOE N. ARMSTRONG
JAMES A. BACON JR.
EDWARD A. BAGWELL
FRED BAILEY JR.
GROVER C. BAILEY
LEONARD D. BAILEY
BOBBY K. BAKER
WILLIAM T. BALES JR.
ALBERT BARBEE

FLOYD W. BARKER JR.
HUBERT O. BASS
RALPH T. BASS JR.
ROBERT W. BAUMGARDNER
JAMES E. BAZEMORE
O. EARL BAZZELL
GEORGE H. BEAN
JESSIE E. BEAN
JAMES J. BEENE JR.
JAMES E. BELL
JAMES T. BELL
WILLIS E. BELL
JAMES D. BENDER
GRAHAM R. BETTS
BERLIN BIGGS
CARL C. BLAKE
WILLIAM BLAKE
JAMES W. BLANCETT
H. M. BLANCHARD II
WILLIAM L. BONE
HAROLD K. BONINE
RAYMOND J. BORK
EDWARD F. BOSS
GEORGE BOSTON
JAMES R. BOYD
G. TERRELL BRAND
BERNARD A. BRANNON
CLAUDE BREWER
HUGH H. BREWER JR.
GEORGE T. BRIGHT
NALL BRIGHT
CLIFFORD BROWN
DANIEL H. BROWN JR.
JESSE J. BROWN
JOE L. BROWN
WILLIAM J. BROWN
CHARLES D. BURKHART
GROVER BURNETT
WILLIAM H. BURNS
BUOL BURT
SAMUEL A. BUSH
WADE H. BUTLER JR.
JOHN C. BYAS
JOHN B. CALDWELL
CHARLES H. CAMPBELL
FRED H. CAMPBELL
R. A. CARMICHEAL
ROY D. CATE
LEONARD O. CHADWICK
ROBERT W. CHAMBERLAIN
COY CHAMBERS
DAVID C. CHAMBERS
LUTHER CHAMBERS
DAVID J. CHAMBLISS
FRED D. CHANDLER
THOMAS W. CHANDLER
JACK CHILDERS

G. STOKES CHRISTIANS

BEN H. CHURCH

HERMAN CLARK JR.

JACK L. CLARK

OTHA CLARK

DELMON J. CLAYTON

PAUL W. CLAYTON

WARREN G. CLIFT

WILLIAM R. CLIFT

GEORGE W. CLINE

JAMES R. COFFELT

FRED N. COLEMAN

OLON H. COLEMAN

LEONARD R. COLVILLE

ANTHONY CAMPOSANO

CHARLES M. CONLEY

JOHN W. CONLEY

GLENN W. CONNELLY

SAM R. CONNELLY JR.

CARL W. COOKE

CHARLES H. COOLIDGE   MOH

JOHNNIE B. COPE

WILLIAM M. COPE

BILLY J. COX

CHARLES T. CRANE

ROBERT L. CRANE

WILLIAM G. CRAWLEY

ROBERT W. CREIGHTON

JAMES R. CROCKETT

JESSE J. CROSS JR.

VICTOR L. CULBERSON

C. R. CUNNINGHAM JR.

CLAUDE M. CURTIS SR.

PAUL W. CURTIS JR.

CLAUDE B. CUZZORT

CLARENCE A. DACUS

MARVIN N. DANSBY

HENRY C. DAUGHTERY JR.

CLIFFORD M. DAUGHERTY

CLYDE J. DAVIS

HERBERT C. DAVIS

JOHN H. DAVIS

RONALD A. DAVISON

JOHN H. DEAN

PAUL J. DEAN

HARRY T. DENNEY

HOYT E. DIXON

LEE E. DOBSON

CLEVELAND B. DOE

BENJAMIN J. DOMINIK

DAVID DUBROW

EULISS L. DUGGAN

GEORGE R. DUNCAN

FRED A. DURHAM

HENRY C. EARL

CHARLIE L. EARLY

ERNEST L. EARLY

ERNEST ECHOLS

RICHARD E. EDWARDS

RICHARD D. ELMORE

EARL W. ELSEA

VERNON O. ENDERS

CHARLES E. ETTER

SAMUEL M. FANBURG

RAYMOND W. FETTERMAN

JOHN H. FICKEN JR.

EUGENE H. FINCH

WILLIAM T. FINDLEY

GLENN D. FISCHER

ADAM FRANKLIN

CLYDE J. FRIDDELL

ROBERT J. FRIST

JAMES A. FULLER

THURMAN S. L. GADDIS

CLAUDE R. GARMANY JR.

WALLACE B. GARNER

ERFURT J. GENTRY

JEFF R. GIBBS

GERALD W. GLEDHILL

WILLIAM D. GOODLET

FRANK D. GOODWIN JR.

HARRIS A. GOULD

LOUIS E. GRAHAM

ADAM S. GRANT

FREDERICK M. GRAYSON

JAMES P. GREENE JR.

ROY W. GREGORY

ROBERT L. GRISWOLD

FRANK H. GROOMS

MILTON GROSS

GEORGE M. GUY

MARION O. HAGAN JR.

CALVIN H. HALE

THOMAS E. HALE

JOHN D. HALL

ROBERT L. HALL JR.

SAMUEL N. HALL

JACK W. HAMMEL

ROBERT G. HAMPTON

OSCAR HANDLY JR.

ARRY J. HANES

C. ROBERT HANKINS

SAMUEL F. HANSSARD JR.

TOMMIE M. HARDEN

WALTER HARDYMAN JR.

HARRY L. HARPER

TENNYSON C. HARRELL

CAMPBELL L. HARRIS

HAROLD L. HARRIS

BETHEL HARRISON

CLARENCE J. HAWKINS

JOHN W. HAWKINS

WARREN H. HAYDEN

L. G. HENSLEY JR.

SAMSON HERSHFIELD

LEON HICKMAN

KENNETH D. HICKS

WILLIAM HICKSON JR.

EDWARD E. HILDEBRAND

NEWTON M. HILLIARD

CHARLES HILTZ

FLOYD L. HIPP JR.

WALLACE H. HIXON

RICHARD E. HOLLAND

HERBERT N. HOLLIS JR.

WILLIAM K. HOLMES

WALTER A. HOLT

HENRY R. HOWARD JR.

WILLIAM H. HOYT JR.

THOMAS O. HUDSON

EVAN P. HUGHES

RAYMOND V. HUNTER

HAROLD W. HUTCHERSON

KENNETH L. JACKSON

LEONARD L. JAMES

GRADY L. JOHNSON

RICHARD H. JOHNSON JR.

JULIAN S. JOHNSTON

BERT E. KAYLOR

JOHN KEEF

ALBERT G. KELLY

EUGENE D. KELLY

OLA B. KELSO JR.

REUBEN L. KILLIAN

RICHARD H. KIMBALL

JOHN M. KING

WILLIAM C. KINLEY

JOHN M. KIRKLAND

CHARLES B. KRAUSE

JOHN L. LACKEY

EUGENE H. LAMBDIN

J. P. LANCASTER JR.

MELVIN O. LANCASTER

RAYMOND F. LANCASTER

EARL E. LANDRETH

JAMES W. LANIER

DEWEY A. LAPPIN

T. C. LAWHORN

JAMES L. LAWSON

KIRK E. LAWSON

FRED T. LEDFORD

RAYMOND O. LEDFORD

RALPH H. LEVERETTE

EDDIE L. LEVI

ROBERT D. LEVY

LAKE LEWIS

MARVIN N. LEWIS JR.

DONALD R. LINAM

BENJAMIN F. LINGERFELT JR.

CHARLIE R. LITTLE

JOHN A. LLEWELLYN

Joe W. Loftis Jr.
Clarence W. Long
Donald L. Long
Eulis R. Long
William H. Lowery
Willard L. Lowman
Brents M. Lowry Jr.
Harry M. Lupher Jr.
Ballard Lyerly
Henry M. Madaris Jr.
Jewel C. Maddox
Wilson Maddox
Harold G. Manning
Leslie A. Manning
George Mannon
Theodore G. Martin
William L. Massey
Marshall E. Masterson
Charles E. Matthews
George R. Maupin
Oliver E. Mayo
William K. Mayo
Walter R. McBee
J. Nelson McBrayer
Johnnie V. McClelland
C. K. McClure Jr.
Homer McClure
John W. McCluskey
Louis S. McCullohs
Robert C. McGee
William T. McKenna Jr.
Douglas G. McMillin
Gano E. McPherson Jr.
L. A. McWhorter Jr.
John T. McWilliams
Lawrence W. Medlin
Elmer L. Miles
Albert Miller
Gaines I. Milligan
James B. Milligan
Clark W. Mills
W. Scott Milne
David T. Minor
Homer J. Mitts Jr.
James L. Moody
Clarence Mooneyham Jr.
Frank Moore
Thomas J. Moore Jr.
Travis L. Moore
Walter B. Moore Jr.
James S. Morgan
Joe D. Morris
Robert C. Morrison Jr.
Henry B. Mosely
James W. Moyer
George D. Mullins
Marion E. Murphy Jr.

Hadley Neff
Henry A. Nichols
Clarence E. Nolan
Gerkin C. Norris Jr.
Berlin G. Oakes
Thomas D. Oles
Ernest D. O'Neal
George E. Orr
Robert F. Pace Jr.
Mack C. Pardue Jr.
Charles H. Park
Norman R. Parlier
Groover W. Partin
Robbins Patton
Charles C. Payne
Harold Payne
Hobson A. Pearson
Harvey O. Pennington
David W. Peters
Mamerd E. Phillips
James E. Pickett
Reed B. Pickett
Jack E. Pinion
William E. Pinion
Layton W. Pippin
Fred Poole
James H. Pratchard
Charlie W. Presly
Hoyt C. Prince Jr.
H. Kenneth Pryor
Hubert Pullins
Willard M. Radford
Robert B. Randle
James W. Rawlings
George W. Ray
Charles R. Reeves
Marvin K. Rex
Charles E. Rhodes
Everette E. Ricketts
Carl F. Roberson
Carson M. Roberts
Noah B. Roberts
Paul A. Roberts
William R. Roberts
William J. Robinson
Lester C. Rogers
William A. Rogers
William B. Rogers
Alvin R. Rollins
Robert S. Romines
Albert L. Rose
John S. Rose
Sanford G. Roy
L. Raymond Runyan
James W. Russell
Thomas J. Ryan Jr.
Ernest J. Sampley

Cleo Sanders
Frank T. Saunders Jr.
David O. Schoocraft
Richard A. Scoggins
Jasper N. Scott
Simeon J. Seals
Charles R. Seay
John B. Selman
William H. Settles
Charles T. Severs
Robert M. Shannon
John E. Sharp
Frank E. Shell
Wallace B. Shipplett
James G. Sims
John G. Sims
James Sivley
William J. Sizemore
Charles E. Skipper
Willis A. Smartt Sr.
Willard D. Smiddie
Albert Smith
Edward M. Smith
Ernest R. Smith
G. H. Miller Smith
Gene M. Smith
G. Hershell Smith
Gordon D. Smith
Johnnie C. Smith
Lawrence D. Smith
Malcolm H. Smith
Russell R. Smith
William R. Smith
Woodrow W. Smith
Samuel Spector
Floyd M. Spray
Robert A. Springer
Horace F. St. Johns
Wales O. Standifer
William T. Standifer
Carlyle L. Stevens
George M. Stewart
Leroy M. Sullivan
Edward G. Taliaferro
James S. Tallent
Beacher F. Taylor
Carl P. Teague
J. B. Thomas
Walter H. Thompson
George P. Toft
Orville M. Tollett
Floyd A. Tudor
James L. Turner Jr.
Thomas O. Tyner Jr.
Alvin W. Vanzant
Albert I. Vanzant Jr.
William T. Walden

MILES N. WALKER
WILLIAM A. WALKER
FRED J. WALLEY
HENRY P. WALLEY
B. GLENN WARBINGTON
JOSEPH S. WATTLES
CHARLES A. J. WEBSTER
JAMES T. WESTFIELD
WILLIAM C. WHEAT JR.
VERNON E. WHEELER
JOSEPH L. WHITEHEAD
WILLIAM P. WILHOITE
THOMAS J. WILKINS
CLARENCE E. WILLIAMS
DEXTER D. WILLIAMS
W. L. WILLIAMSON JR.
EDWARD T. WILSON
MANUEL B. WILSON
ROLAND B. WOFFORD
JOE C. WOLFE
THOMAS F. WOODHEAD
RAYMOND E. WRIGHT
W. GARNETT WRIGHT

NAVY

ISAIAH ASH JR.
JOHN C. BAKER
ALBERT J. BANTHER
WILLIAM R. BARGER
OTIS B. BARNES
HARRY F. BAUER
ERNEST F. BENNETT
JOHN H. BINNS
GARNET H. BOWLIN
MARSHALL S. BOYD
ROBERT L. BRINKLEY
RALPH W. BROOM
ALEX J. BROWN
JOHN S. BUCKNER
JOHN W. BURDEN
HOMER L. CAIN
CLIFFORD E. CAMP JR.
WILLIAM B. CARROLL
WILLIE F. DAVIS
SAMUEL H. DEAKINS
JAMES P. DEAN
JAMES L. DEATHERIDGE
WILLIAM E. DORSEY
JOHN H. DOTSON
FRANK B. EARP JR.
VAN L. EASTLAND
JAMES H. FOSTER
ANDREW J. GANDY
PAUL F. GOODMAN
DONALD H. GREENE
JAMES R. GRISWOLD
ROGER W. GUNN

PAUL A. HANES
EDWARD E. HARRIS
J. D. HARRIS JR.
WILLIAM P. HEMPHILL JR.
ANDREW J. HOLLOWAY
CARL D. HOUSER
FRANCIS P. HUBBUCH
LAWRENCE H. JACKSON
WILLIAM G. JAMISON
HENRY C. JOINER
FREDERICK D. JONES
ALEX M. KENDRICK
REUBEN G. KERBY
CHARNOLD A. KERLEY
GORDON B. LANE
GEORGE S. LEWELLYN
JAMES R. LONDON
EDWARD J. MATHERLEY
WILLIAM F. McKIBBEN
HARRISON E. McMILLEN
LUTHER MILLER JR.
WENDELL T. MOFFITT
JERRY S. MONDS
BARNEY C. MORGAN
LESTER C. MULLINS
PERRY L. OLIVER
MILO G. PARKER JR.
GRAHAM S. PARTEN
K. C. PATTERSON
SAMUEL W. PEEBLES JR.
FRANK H. PENNYBACKER
GROVER G. PHILLIPS
JAMES H. REAVLEY
ALPHONZO REESE
JOHN L. RIGSBY
BILL E. RITCHIE
JOE W. ROBERTS
ELMER E. ROBINSON
ERNEST L. ROSS
RALPH J. SAGESER
POWELL T. SATERFIELD
ANTHONY B. SHIRLEY JR.
GEORGE W. SHOEMAKER
JULES J. SIMS
ABLE L. J. SMITH
HORACE L. SMITH
CLYDE E. STEPHENS
WILLIAM R. STUBBLEFIELD
WILLIAM E. STULCE
WILLIAM L. THOMAS JR.
ROBERT H. THORPE
FRED W. TITTSWORTH
NEAL TROTTER JR.
ERNEST E. ULRICKSON
JOHN E. WAGNER
WOODROW WASHINGTON JR.
NORMAN E. WILLIAMS

JAMES C. WILSON
JOSEPH R. WILSON
ROBERT E. WILSON
WALTER A. WITT JR.
LAWRENCE C. WOMACK

MARINE CORPS

A. C. ADAMS
MICHAEL E. AMAR
JOSEPH H. ARNOLD
ERIAL W. BLEDSOE
JOE W. BROWNING
ROBERT W. CALLAHAN
THOMAS H. COOPER
HUGH S. DANIEL
DALMOS E. ELDRIDGE
WILLIAM F. ELDRIDGE
W. HARDING ELSEA
CAREY A. EVANS
JAMES C. FINE
JAMES H. FOLEY JR.
THOMAS F. HAYES
WILLIAM J. HERRIOTT
AARON F. JACKSON
JAMES R. JENNINGS III
WINFRED C. JONES
FREDERICK C. KNITTLE
DAN M. LAMB
HARRY C. LANG
CHARLES E. LYNN
ROBERT L. MANNING
CLYDE E. McDANIEL
JAMES E. McMILLAN
JOSEPH I. McWHORTER
RALPH M. MILLER
ANDREW D. MYNATT
LEON E. O'DANIEL
WILLIAM H. ODELL JR.
THOMAS E. PARK
JOHN J. POE
BETHEL A. D. RICH
CARLTON L. SATTERFIELD
WILLIAM E. SATTERFIELD
WILLIAM G. SIMMONS
LEWIS O. STARR
JAMES P. WALSH

COAST GUARD

BURL D. UNDERWOOD

MERCHANT MARINES

JOHN S. BUCKNER

Hancock County

ARMY/ARMY AIR CORPS

JOE T. BARNES
EARL L. BLOOMER

ELLIS S. BOWLIN
EUGENE H. BREWER
JOE E. CARPENTER
PAUL H. GREENE
EDGAR A. EDENS
HAMMIE F. MOORE
ALLEN H. PRIDEMORE
CLURE D. SINGLETON
JOHNNIE R. SMITH
J. D. WALLEN
LAWRENCE W. WILLIS
EARL S. YOUNT

NAVY
ANDY G. JOHNSON

MARINE CORPS
WILLIAM F. CAVIN

Hawkins County
ARMY/ARMY AIR CORPS
FRED E. BALL
CHARLES R. BLEDSOE
JESSE J. BLEDSOE
WILLIAM H. BOYD
GEORGE H. BREWER
LEROY BROBECK
RUDOLPH BURTON
ERNEST G. BYRD
ROBERT R. CALDWELL
LAWRENCE E. CARMACK
JOHNNY D. CARMICHAEL
RAYMOND CARPENTER
EVERT K. CARTER
MARION G. COLLIER
JAMES T. COOPER
HARVEY CRAWFORD
CHARLES D. DALTON
JACK H. DAVIS
PATRICK H. DAVIS JR.
SHERRILL A. DAVIS
DENZEL D. DYKES
LEE O. EPPS
FRANCIS P. EVERHART
JOHN J. FERRELL
GRIFFETH H. FORT
EARL J. GILLEY
LOYD GOINS
O. B. GREENWAY
JAMES E. GROSS
CLAUDE C. HENEGAR
CARL E. HENSLEY
WILLIE G. HERRON
CARL M. HICKMAN
THOMAS J. HILL
JOHN W. HODGES
HENRY C. HOLT

CARL E. HUGHES
HUBERT L. HUGHES
CHARLES R. JEFFERS
LESTER JONES
MILLARD LAWSON
WILLARD R. LEE
JAMES E. LIGHT
ROBERT K. LOONEY JR.
MILLER K. MANIS
CHARLES R. MARSH
TROY E. MARSHALL
J. D. MAYO
ANDREW McCLOUD
MACK R. MELLON
JOSEPH C. MOONEY
FRANK H. NOE
FRED PRATT
LEWIS E. PRICE
SILAS M. PRICE JR.
WESTERN PRICE
CARRY A. QUILLEN
GALE M. RICHARDSON
CALVIN C. ROWLAND
SIMS A. ROWLAND
CHARLES H. RUSH
BILL H. RUSSELL
ROY L. RYANS
RAY R. SCISM
WILLIAM L. SENSABAUGH
DELMA SMITH
ELMER L. SMITH
FLOYD B. SMITH
JAMES B. SMITH
LUTHER R. SMITH
JAMES H. SULLIVAN
HERBERT H. SWOFFORD
RICHARD B. THOMPSON
CARL H. TRENT
CLINTON A. TRENT
WILLIAM L. TRENT JR.
EUGENE WALKER
RUFUS R. WEBB
HEISKELL M. WILLIAMS

NAVY
LEWIS E. CHRISTIAN JR.
WILLIAM E. McCRAVY

MARINE CORPS
PAUL E. ARMSTRONG
WILLIAM J. BAILEY
JOSEPH C. BREWER
JESS W. BRIGHT
GALE W. CHARLES
HENRY N. DICKENSON
J. DEWEY MARSH

COAST GUARD
ERNEST O. GILLENWATERS

Jefferson County
ARMY/ARMY AIR CORPS
BURL W. AILEY
ROBERT L. ARNOLD
GUY E. BAILEY
JAMES C. BAILEY
ALVIN L. BALLINGER
WILLIS W. BETTIS
JOHN W. BILLS
JAMES O. BLACK
RAYMOND H. BOLIN
PAUL R. BREWER
BENJAMIN H. BRITT
CHARLES A. BROGDEN
DOYLE L. BROWN
THOMAS E. BURCHFIELD
JAMES L. CAIN
GEORGE A. CANNON
JAMES C. CARMICHAEL JR.
MELVIN M. CARTER
WINFORD D. CATE
JOHN B. CLEVENGER
THOMAS C. COCKRUM
JAMES C. COLEMAN
GILBERT N. COUCH JR.
HOUSTON N. COX
NEIL W. DENISTON
CHARLES A. ELWOOD JR.
ARLEY B. FRENCH
JAMES N. FRYE
ROBERT B. HAWORTH
JAMES T. HAYES
OLIVER L. HECK
EARL E. HICKLE
JACK L. HILL
HALMOND L. HOWARD JR.
ROY T. JAYNES JR.
GEORGE R. K. JENKINS
CLAUD JOHNSON
ROY R. KANIPE
LUTHER W. KEIRSEY
JOHN P. KERR
WILLIAM C. KIMBROUGH
WILLIAM A. LOVE
GEORGE T. MALONE
EARL H. McCOIG
MAX MILLER
JAMES C. MORGAN
THOMAS S. MORIE
RAY T. MURPHY
JOHN F. MURRAY
GEORGE F. NELSON
ROY J. NEWMAN
HERMAN H. PERKEY

CASLEE E. PRUITT
PAUL E. PRUITT
JAMES F. RECTOR
JAMES H. REESE
SAMUEL F. RENEAU
WILLIE G. RENEAU
WILLIAM F. REPASS
CHARLES E. RINES
LYLE B. ROACH
ZACK ROMINES
JOSEPH A. SHELL
PRESTON K. SMITH
WILLIAM H. SMITH
JOHN A. STILES
WILLIE L. STUBBS
IRA K. SWAGGERTY JR.
BLAIR A. TALLEY
THOMAS E. TAYLOR
RALPH THOMAS
NORMAN J. TIPTON
JAMES D. TRACY
JOHN H. UNDERWOOD
JAMES L. VANCE
CLARENCE B. VARNELL
JAMES S. VAUGHT
CLAUDE VINEYARD
JOHN H. WALSTON
RAY E. WALTERS
LESTER B. WEBB
ROBERT Y. WHEELER
WILLIAM R. WILES
GEORGE E. WILKERSON
HERBERT G. WILLIAMS

NAVY
PAUL M. BROOKS
J. H. DONALD ELLISON
URSTLE C. KECK
HAROLD D. LACY
WILLIAM C. LOONEY
JOHN C. OWEN JR.
JAMES W. REPASS JR.
BUFORD M. STALLINGS

MARINE CORPS
TOM B. CHRISMAN
JAMES L. MOYERS
PAUL E. PRATT

COAST GUARD
LOUIS M. GOAN

Johnson County
ARMY/ARMY AIR CORPS
GEORGE F. BARRY
WAYNE D. BROOKS
WILLIAM A. CORNETT JR.

JOHN W. COX
CECIL D. CULVER
LEE L. DICKENS
JOSEPH S. DILLENGER
CARROL B. EVANS
JAMES L. EVANS
JAMES E. FORRESTER
ALFRED D. FRITTS
RAY C. FRITTS
J. C. GENTRY
WALTER W. GENTRY
AVERY M. GREER
JOHN H. HAMILTON
DELMAR L. HAND
NELSON O. HARMON
ARTHUR B. HODGE
RODERICK B. HORN
LUTHER JENKINS
VICTOR E. KIRBY
BYRON C. LEWIS
BASIL P. LITTLETON
BURMAN H. MAINE
CECIL M. MAY
WILLIAM D. MCCLOUD
JAMES W. MCCOY
JAMES W. MOREFIELD
WILLIAM R. NOLAND
WALTER B. PAYNE
JOSEPH F. PENNINGTON
JAMES S. PHILLIPPI
DWIGHT L. SHUPE
JOE B. SNYDER
FLOYD G. STOUT
JOE V. TESTER
W. WADE WAGNER
CHARLES E. WATERS
RALPH E. WHITELEY
D. W. WILSON JR.
WILLIAM J. WRAY

NAVY
DALLACE D. CABLE
WALLACE H. CABLE
ALVIN B. CLAWSON
DALLAS EGGERS

Knox County
ARMY/ARMY AIR CORPS
JAMES L. AARON
GEORGE ADAMS
JAMES G. ALLEN JR.
IVAN A. ANDES
CARL J. ANDERSON
CALVIN L. ANTHES
SAM M. ARMETTA
RALPH G. ARMSTRONG
JAMES C. ATCHLEY

JOHN D. AUSTIN
HERBERT C. BABELAY
JAMES L. BADGETT
HARTSELL L. BAILES
GILBERT H. BAILIE
FRANK H. BALL JR.
JOHN G. BANNER
WALTER M. BANNER
WILSON B. BARKER JR.
JAMES A. BARRICKMAN
FRED B. BATES
JOHN L. BEAN
JOHN E. BELL
WILLIAM R. BEST
CHARLES H. BLACK
JOHN H. BLACKBURN
EARL L. BLAIR
LESTER F. BLALOCK
WALTER N. BLAUFELD JR.
GRADY H. BLAZIER
WILLIAM W. BONNER
NICHOLLS W. BOWDEN JR.
GEORGE L. BOWERMAN
JACK L. BOWERS
JAMES A. BREEDEN
PAUL U. BREWER
RAYMOND U. BRIGHT
ARCHLIOUS B. BROGDON
MAYFORD D. BROOKS
CLOFUS R. BUNCH
JAMES L. BURGIN
THOMAS H. BURGIN
WALTER E. BURNETT JR.
GERALD C. BURTON
JOHN T. BYERLY
CHARLES W. BYRD
LEE R. CAPPS
EDWARD B. CARROLL
JAMES W. CASH
HOWARD M. CASTLEBERRY
JOE E. CATHEY
FRANK H. CAYLOR JR.
ROBERT L. CHAMBERS JR.
ROBERT P. CHANDLER JR.
WILFRED T. CHANDLER
JOHN N. CHILDRESS
WILLIAM CHRISMAN
FRANK M. CLABOUGH
LESTER G. CLARK
WYMAN K. CLARK
CHARLES R. CLARKE JR.
ROY E. CLAYTON
ESLEY CLEMONS JR.
EUGENE B. CLIFTON
GEROME CLINE
HENRY T. CLOWERS
SHELLEY C. COFFEY

297

HECTOR COFFIN III
ALVIN W. COFFMAN
PAUL C. COILE
LEROY H. COLE
W. F. COLLINGSWORTH JR.
NOAH V. COLLINS
RICHARD H. COLVIN
CECIL COMBEST
JAMES R. CONNER
HOMER C. CONWAY
MELVIN O. COOPER
OTIS E. COOPER
RAYMOND L. COOPER
ROY K. COPPENGER
CLYDE R. CORUM
EDWARD F. COTHREN JR.
DAVID M. COULTER
LESTER W. V. COVINGTON
MATT T. COWARD
MARION B. COX
MONROE H. COX
BROWN A. CRAIG
JOHN H. CRUM
CLIFFORD C. CRUZE
KENNETH A. CRUZE
WILLIAM H. CRUZE
HERBERT B. CUMMINGS
HARRY L. CURNUTT
WILLIAM T. DALTON JR.
WALTER E. DAVIS
WILLIAM J. DAVIS
WARREN M. DEMARCUS
FRANCIS T. DEVANE
BOYD R. DERREBERRY
STEWARD R. DICKEY JR.
EDGAR C. DODSON
WALTER E. DOOLEY
HUGH W. DOUGLAS
THOMAS B. DRINNEN
EARL S. DUNN
HOLLIS E. DUNN
HARLESS DYER
PORTER H. DYER
CHARLES B. EASLEY
MURRELL W. ECKLE
SAM L. ELLIS
JAMES A. ELLISON
KARL R. ELZA
CLIFFORD L. FAIN
EARL F. FARMER
RALPH H. FAULKNER
FRANK J. FEEMAN
LINCOLN A. FIELDEN
JOHN FINE
FRED C. FORD
WALTER A. FORD
CHARLES E. FOX

JAMES H. FORD
LOUIS O. FOX
DAVID FRANCIS
LOUIS FRANCIS JR.
PHILIP FRANCIS
PAUL A. FREELS
RICHARD L. FURGERSON
RALPH E. GADDIS
FREDERICK A. GAMBLE
LESTER J. GARDNER
BEN D. GATLIFF
EDWARD R. GENTRY
FRED H. GEYER III
JAMES D. GILBERT
JAMES D. GILBERT
JAMES C. GLOVER
LEWIS F. GODDARD
ARTHUR L. GOOLSBE
HUGH S. GOSNELL
HAROLD R. GOSSAGE
RALPH E. GRAVES
VIRGIL R. GRAVES
MILLARD C. GRAY
JACK GREEN
LONNIE GREEN JR.
ONIE J. GRODEMAN
EDWARD C. GROOMS
EUGENE GROSCLOSE
NORMAN GUNN
ELMER B. HACKWORTH
JACK HAIRE
LAWRENCE F. HAIRE
FRANCIS L. HALL
J. GRAYSON HALLIBURTON III
FRANK HAMILTON
LEROY J. HANSARD
EARNEST HANSON
WILLIAM R. HARBISON
WILLIAM E. HARMON
EDWARD L. HARRIS
JAMES D. HARRIS
JULIUS HARRIS
VERNON M. HARRIS
KENNETH B. HART
CHARLES HATMAKER
CHARLES W. HAYES
CLIFFORD H. HEADRICK
GEORGE L. HEATH
CHARLES HEDGECOCK
EDWARD L. HENDERSON
CHARLES H. HENLEY JR.
ULYSSES S. HENRY
JOHN R. HENSLEY
ROSCOE O. HENSLEY
BILLY F. HEWITT
JAMES G. HICKS JR.
KARL K. HICKS JR.

ROBERT C. HOARD
WALTER M. HORNER
CHARLES R. HUDSON
JACK D. HUFF
JAMES C. HULL
C. C. FRANKLIN HUNDLEY
JOHN D. HUNT
THOMAS J. HUNT
ALBERT P. HURST
WALTER HUSKEY
WENDELL P. IMES
CHARLES B. IRWIN
MURRELL D. IVENS
JOHN K. JARNIGAN
ROBERT M. JENKINS
SAMUEL E. JETT
ARTHUR E. JOHNSON
EDWARD F. JOHNSON
JOHN W. JOHNSON
JOHN B. JOHNSON
CHARLES D. JOHNSTON
GLEN E. JOINER
HUGH J. JONES JR.
ROY D. JONES
WILLIAM M. JULIAN JR.
ELMER KECK
EDWARD F. KEESLING
BENJAMIN H. KELLEY JR.
EDWARD KEMP JR.
JAMES C. KENNEDY
WILLIAM A. KENNEDY JR.
DWIGHT C. KEY JR.
BERT L. KIDD JR.
WILLIAM L. KILLIAN
ORVILLE R. KING
WILLIAM J. KIRBY
LEROY KLINE
WALTER B. KNIGHT
WILLIAM W. KREIS
WILLIAM C. LAMBERT
JAMES T. LAND
ANDERSON F. LANE JR.
MCKINLEY B. LANE
RUDOLPH L. LANE
WALLACE LAUDERBACK
WESLEY T. LAWSON
JAY V. LEDGERWOOD JR.
EDGAR F. LENNON JR.
CLARENCE H. LILLY
GEORGE E. LINDLEY
LEWIS N. LINDSEY
ALMER D. LISTER
HOWARD E. LONG
JAMES D. LONG
ODELL LONG
ALVIN M. LOWE
ROMIE E. LOY

JOHN A. LYLE JR.
HOYLE E. MAJORS
GEORGE H. MANNING
JAMES E. MANUEL
JOHN D. MAPLES
PAUL MAPLES
SHERMAN W. MAPLES
FRANCIS J. MARTIN
JACK H. MARTIN
JAMES W. MARTIN
WILLIAM H. MARY JR.
ORBIN L. MASON
CECIL L. MCCLOUD
ROBERT S. MCCOOK
ARTHUR R. MCCOY
BERNEY H. MCCOY
EARL C. MCCOY
PAUL C. MCCOY
JOE R. MCCREADY
HUGH H. MCCUTCHAN JR.
C. J. MCDANIEL JR.
JAMES V. MCDANIEL
WILSON J. MCDONALD
CHARLES E. MCELYEA
RAYMOND S. MCELYEA
MILOUS MCENTYRE
RALPH L. MCFALL
TROY A. MCGILL   MOH
TOMAS J. MCHARRIS
BILL A. MCMILLAN
BAYLESS C. MCMILLAN
ALFRED L. MEADOWS
JAMES O. MERRIMAN
CHARLES A. MERRITT
MARVIN L. MERRITT
JAMES R. MILLER
LEROY MILLER
LOGAN C. MILLER
LOYD W. MILLER
ROBERT R. MILLER
ROBERT W. MILLS
RICHARD MINCH
WILLIAM E. MINTON
DONALD M. MITCHELL
TROY A. MONDAY
RAYMOND E. MOORE
D. G. MORRISSEY JR.
JOE MOSS
ELMER E. MULLINS
ALVA C. MURPHY
DEWEY C. MURPHY
JAMES A. MURRIAN JR.
WILLARD E. MYERS
JACK W. NAUGHER
WILLIAM R. NEELY
WILLIAM H. NELSON
LUTHER L. NEWCOMB

WILLIAM H. NEWMAN
FRANK S. NORRIS JR.
JOHN A. NORRIS JR.
HOWARD V. NORVELL
SAMUEL L. OGDEN
CLAUDE L. OGLE
JUNIOR F. OTT
CHARLES D. OTTINGER
HORACE D. A. OWENS
CHARLES W. PACK
JOHN W. PARKER
ROY M. PARKER
WAYNE A. PARKEY JR.
RAYFORD C. PASKELL
HENRY C. PATRICK III
GLENN W. PATTON
ROSS W. PERRIN JR.
ROSS H. PETERSON
CLAUDE J. PETTIFORD
LAMBRETH A. PHIFER
ROBERT M. PHILLIPS
CARL E. PIERCE
JOHN H. PINKERTON
CLIFFORD H. PITTS
WILLIAM E. PORTER
W.H. PORTERFIELD
SAMUEL K. PRATER
GEORGE W. M. PRATT
WILLIAM O. PRATT
JAMES H. PRESNELL JR.
ALBERT T. PRIDEMORE
KENNETH R. RADER
JOE RAMSEY
GEORGE E. RAY
CHARLES F. RENFRO
WILLIAM H. RENFRO
RALPH B. RICHEY
ROBERT H. RIMMER JR.
HAROLD E. ROBERTS
JOHNSON F. ROBERTS
THOMAS T. ROBERTS
JOE A. ROBINSON
ARTHUR F. ROCHAT
ALLAN L. ROCHE
HOWARD O. ROMINES
EUGENE W. N. ROOP
CARL B. ROSE
CHARLES H. ROSE JR.
JACK W. ROSE
EARL RUTHERFORD
J. D. SANDERS
JOHN W. SANDS
ROY M. SATTERFIELD
FRANK C. SCARBROUGH
HARRY E. SCARLETT
JAMES C. SCRUGGS
VIRGIL R. SEEBER

WILLIS G. SHANKLES
FLOYD J. SHARP JR.
LOU G. SHEDDAN JR.
JAMES E. SHIPLEY
ROBERT SHORT
CLEO H. SHULER
ELMER SINGLETON
JAY M. SINK JR.
THOMAS G. SISSON
BEAUFORD L. SMELSER
CLARENCE A. SMELTZER
DANIEL B. SMITH
EUGENE A. SMITH
GEORGE SMITH JR.
HOYLE J. SMITH
JOHN R. SMITH
KENNITH L. SMITH
NELSON W. SMITH
PEYTON M. SMITH JR.
WILLIAM K. SMITH
KENNETH H. SNYDER
FRANK D. SOLOMON
PLES J. SOLOMON
FRED H. SOTHERLAND
LEMUEL C. SPURGEON
ELBERT P. STALCUP
JOHN D. STALLINGS
WALTER F. STANDRIDGE
CLINTON G. STEVENSON
GEORGE B. STEWART
HORACE E. STEWART JR.
JAMES M. STILL JR.
PAUL S. STOUT
WILEY O. STROUP
FRED SUFFRIDGE
THEODORE SUNDERLAND
EDWARD C. SWAGGERTY
ROBERT E. SWAGGERTY
WILLAFORD S. SWAN
J. H. SWANNER
HAROLD E. TALBOTT
ROBERT L. TALLEY
ARBETH L. TAYLOR
CHARLES TAYLOR
FORREST D. TAYLOR
B. H. TESTERMAN JR.
LEROY R. THOMAS
CHARLES L. THOMPSON
CHARLES T. THOMPSON
ADRIAN M. TINDELL
CHARLES E. TIPTON
HOWARD W. TIPTON
MARL A. TIPTON
HARRIS C. TONKIN
DAVID D. TOWNSEND
LLOYD E. TROUTT
JOBE TROXLER

HARRIS A. TUCKER
WILLIS N. TUCKER
CHARLES A. VALENTINE
CARL A. VINEYARD
JOHN A. WAGGONER
SAMUEL H. WAGGONER
NOBLE D. WAGONER
MILLARD WAKEFIELD
ROBERT C. WALLACE JR.
ROBERT T. WALLACE
JACK L. WALLER
HARRY R. WAYLAND
ROY L. WEBBER
DANIEL F. WELCH
J. C. WEST
WARREN J. WEST
HAROLD H. WHITE
WILLIAM W. WHITE
JACK E. WILLIAMS
JAMES B. WILLIAMS
CHARLES T. WILSON
HERMAN C. WILSON
WILLIAM L. WILSON
HENRY J. WINGFIELD
ELBERT G. WOOD JR.
RAYMOND W. WORSHAM JR.
CHARLES R. WRIGHT JR.
CHARLES A. WRIGHT
LEONARD WRIGHT
WADE E. WRIGHT
JAMES R. WYATT

NAVY
PAUL A. ANDERSON
JOHN J. ANGLE
KARL P. BAUM
JEROME BERNSTEIN
BALDWIN BOONE
JAMES L. BRIDGES
ROBERT L. BROWDER
SAM W. BROWN
CHARLES W. BRUMLEY
EARNEST V. BRYANT
SEDRIE B. BULL
PRESTON L. BUNCH
PAUL R. BURNETTE
SAMUEL CANTRELL
EARL CHEATHAM
BOBBY E. CLOUD
PAT L. CROSS
CLAUDE B. CULVAHOUSE
BERNARD H. DAVIS
CHARLES L. ECHOLS JR.
CLARENCE F. EDMUNDS
WILLIAM G. ESSEX
CHARLES E. EUBANKS
RICHARD D. FOUST

JAMES F. FROST
JAMES W. GREENE
ELIJAH H. HAGGARD JR.
CECIL M. HENLEY
EARL O. HENRY
ARNETT L. HODGE
HARRY HUBBS JR.
CLAUDE R. HUFFMAN
JAMES E. HURST
MARTIN L. JEANES
ANDLEY E. JOHNSON
STANLEY F. JONES
HAROLD P. JORDAN
HERBERT JULIAN
JOHN A. KELLER
GORDON B. KING
J. LESTER LLEWELLYN
JAMES F. LOWERY JR.
MILFORD C. MARTIN
ROBERT H. MCMAHAN
JOHN B. MCPHERSON
JAMES E. MEDLEY
JARVIS B. MELLON
GLENN E. MILLER
WHITMAN S. MILLER
FORD P. MITCHELL
KYLE C. MOORE
ALBERT K. MURRIAN
KENNETH J. MYERS
JAMES P. MYNATT
CLIFFORD S. NUCKLES
ALEXANDER A. OGLESBY
EDWARD S. OSBORN
JAMES C. PARKER
WILLIAM E. PARSLEY
WILLIAM F. PASCHAL
WILLIAM H. PATRICK
LEELON T. PHILLIPS
ROY PRATER
WILLIAM RICE
BENJAMIN T. RICKETTS
CLAUDE W. ROBERTS
HAROLD L. ROSE
JOSEPH R. SAMPSON
LEON H. SAPANAS
WILTON E. SCHMIDT
HARRISON D. SHAW
LEROY SHELBY
JACK T. SHIRLEY
ELDON SINGLETON
CLARENCE E. SMITH
JAMES A. SMITH
THOMAS J. STILES
CARL J. STRONG
GLENN A. TILLETT
CAREY L. UNDERWOOD
FRED E. WARE

EARL L. WARREN
BRUCE E. WEAVER
BUDDY J. WELLS
JOHN F. WHILLOCK
DAVE E. WILLIAMSON
THEODORE WOLFENBARGER
JOHN W. WOOD JR.

MARINE CORPS
WESLEY H. BAKER
PETIE H. BARBER
PHILLIP L. BEELER
CHARLES M. BLAIR
ALEXANDER BONNYMAN JR.   MOH
CHARLES W. BRAY
JOHN H. BROWN
WILBERT F. CARMICHAEL
JAMES A. COCKRUM
CECIL A. COPPOCK
GENE W. COX
HERBERT L. DAVIS
CALVIN C. DAY
FRED W. DONALDSON
ORVILLE A. DUNAWAY
PAUL J. FITZGERALD
LLOYD C. GOOLSBE
EDWARD W. HERRON
OWEN E. HOOVER
JAMES R. HUTCHENS JR.
NEWTON T. JAMES JR.
JACK W. KELLEY
JOHN R. LILLY
ROBERT J. LUSK
JOHN W. MAHAN
RICHARD P. MCCURRY
C. LAWRENCE MCNEIL
GEORGE M. PARRISH JR.
BILL N. POPE
BENJAMIN S. PRESTON JR.
JOHN ROGERS
MACK E. SANDERS
CARL J. SENTELL
ROBERT C. SMITH
CECIL V. STONE JR.
RALPH E. VISE
GLENN A. WATSON
ROY C. WILKERSON

Loudon County
ARMY/ARMY AIR CORPS
VIRGIL L. BIVENS
JOHN W. BLISCERD
GORDON L. BROOKSHEAR
MAYNARD L. CARMACK
WILLIAM W. COOPER
SHERMAN L. CUMMINGS
EDWARD H. CUNNINGHAM

RAYMOND J. DAVIS
GLEN L. DIXON
CLARENCE E. EASTER
ROBERT J. FRANCIS
GEORGE E. FRENCH
RAYMOND C. HAIR
GEORGE W. HALZEL
CHARLES A. HARP
BENJAMIN F. HARRISON
DWIGHT E. HARVEY
LUTHER D. HASKINS
HAROLD E. HEDRICK
JAMES U. HOUSLEY
ARTHUR B. HOUSTON
HENRY M. HUFF
JAMES R. HUFF
WILLIAM E. ISBILL
KENNETH H. JAYNES
JAMES R. JOHNSON
JAMES A. JULIAN
JOHN E. LANE
CHARLES W. LARGE
JOE C. LETT
ALLEN C. LUTTRELL
JOHN J. LUTZ JR.
NUEL W. MCDONALD
SAMUEL MCINTURFF JR.
ROY A. MILLS
IVAN F. MORELL
OLIVER MORTON
ALLEN A. MURR
GEORGE J. NICHOLS
JAMES W. OODY
W. N. PERKEY JR.
JOHN T. PERKINS
CONRAD C. PERRYMAN
HENRY E. O. PHIBBS
KENNETH R. PICKELL
GEORGE W. PURDY
OLA B. QUILLEN
CLETIS F. RATLEDGE
ROGER D. SCARBROUGH
WILLIAM A.N. SHELTON
MCDONALD SHUBERT
JAMES P. SMITH
ROY SPARKS JR.
ROBERT V. TURPIN
BEN VIARS
JOE A. VINYARD
ORAN L. WATTS
WALTER E. WELLS
JAMES A. WOODY

NAVY
ROBERT L. BAILEY
THOMAS E. BARGER
PAUL R. CAMPBELL

GRANT U. DAWN
ROY T. EDMONDS
JOSEPH K. HARPER
JOSEPH C. HELTON JR.
LAWRENCE N. JACKSON
RAYMOND R. LOVELACE
PAUL B. VAUGHN JR.

MARINE CORPS
WILLIAM H. HENSON
WAYNE J. KING
WILLIAM H. LIMBURG

Marion County
ARMY/ARMY AIR CORPS
GARLAND S. ANDERSON
VINCENT S. AYCOCK
NORMAN T. BAYNE
WILLIAM T. BLANSETT
EDWARD F. BLANSETT
ROBERT L. BROWN
ESTLE L. COLVIN
LANCLE B. CONDRA
RAYMOND H. COOLEY   MOH
BUFORD G. COOPER
GILBERT H. COPPINGER JR.
JOHN L. CURTIS
PAUL G. CURTIS
TOMMY DAVIDSON
JOHN P. DAWKINS
CLARENCE A. DURHAM
CHESTER G. FLOYD
JAMES H. FLOYD
ARTHUR K. GOINS
HERMAN C. GRIFFITH
WILLIAM R. HARRIS
SAM T. HASKEW
SAM B. HENRY
SILAS L. JENKINS
GEORGE T. JOHNSON
OSCAR JONES
JACK R. KEITH
HARLIE E. KILGORE
WILLIAM R. KILGORE
FRED A. LAWSON
ALEX H. LOFTY JR.
CHARLES L. MASON
HOMER J. MELTON
NUBERT R. MILES
HUBERT MURRAY
OSCAR OWENS
JAMES G. PARKER
WILLIAM A. PEARDON
NEILL M. RAY
ROBERT L. RIDGE
RICHARD ROBERSON
HENRY E. ROGERS

JAMES A. SEAY
HOMER L. SLAUGHTER
HAROLD H. SPEARS
HOLDMAN L. TANNER
WILLIAM G. THOMAS
WILLIAM W. TROXELL
JAKE WALDEN
JAMES R. WEST
LLOYD D. WHITE
J. T. WIGGINS
MACK W. WILEMAN

NAVY
T. BENTON ALLEN
LESLIE G. ALLEY
GRADY L. DAVIS
CHARLES S. HALEY
OLIVER HASS
RALPH H. HOLLOWAY
THOMAS H. JORDAN
ALBERT A. LEGG
CLIFFORD C. OWENSBY
ROBERT C. PENNINGTON JR.
AULTON N. PHILLIPS SR.
WAYMON L. POPE
HENRY E. SMITH
CHARLES W. TALLEY

MARINE CORPS
HENRY ANDREGG JR.

McMinn County
ARMY/ARMY AIR CORPS
VERNELL ANDERSON
JOEL T. ARMSTRONG
JAMES W. BATES
LAWRENCE BAYLESS
JACKSON R. BOHANNON
JAMES A. BOWERS
CLAUDIE BREWER
WILLIAM C. BROCK
JACK K. BROWN
AMOS O. BUCKNER
JAMES P. BURNETT
CHARLES S. BURNETTE
EUGENE CANTRELL
DENVER R. CASTEEL
JOHNNIE CASTEEL
KENNETH H. CASTEEL
ARTHUR R. CLAYTON
CLAYTON H. DAVIS
JAMES R. DAVIS
JOHN A. DERRICK
ROBERT DITMORE
VERNON L. DOCKERY
JOHN L. ELLIOTT
GLEN B. EVANS

Clarence T. Filyaw
James E. Giles
Ruel H. Goodman
Earl S. Green
James C. Guffey
Albert L. Harrell
Oliver H. Hicks Jr.
David L. Hutsell
Paul H. Hutsell
Arnold J. Hyde
James T. Ingram
Samuel B. Isbell
Junior L. Jackson
Kinnie E. Jamerson
David N. Jerless
Cyril W. Jones Jr.
James C. Lane
Charles H. Lankford
Edwin K. Lankford
William H. Lansdon
Ralph A. Lattimore
H. Royston Lawson
Johnnie E. Liles
John A. Liner
Clarence E. Lipps
Hugh V. Lipps
Harry D. Long
Arlie E. Malone
Benjamin F. McCamish Jr.
Hilburn McCormick
Harry McMahan
William F. McNutt
Robert J. Melton
William C. Miller
Edward Montgomery
Frank C. Newberry
J. David Oliphant
Earl Oliver
Hubert F. Padgett
William L. Philpott
Earl A. Powers
William M. Reasonover
Frank Richesin
George A. Riden
Walter L. Rose
Paul W. Rucker
Robert E. Shell
Ancil U. Shepherd
Joseph E. Simpson
Robert L. Smith
Wince L. Solsbee
Odis C. Stanfill
James T. Sykes
Albert G. Taylor
Joseph W. Todd
James A. Tummins
James F. Turner Jr.

Ralph A. Wall
Jeff D. Watts
Everett B. West
Paul W. Williams
James G. Williamson
Dewey E. Womac
Vester M. Young
Walter D. Zimmerman

Navy

Lawrence M. Amburgey
Robert J. Atchley
Kenneth O. Burger
Malcolm R. Cobb
W. Elmer Greenwell
Kermit W. Hodges
Howard L. Hyde
James R. Lewis
Joseph G. Rowden
Paul S. Sims
William C. Sitzlar
Taylor K. Vaughn
Charles R. Ware
O. James Williams

Marine Corps

Dexter C. Arden
Harry L. Clayton
Paul O. Gunter
Eugene S. Helton Sr.
William S. Holder
Hershel P. McMillan
Hobert T. Price
Raymond F. Ray

Meigs County

Army/Army Air Corps

Raymond Brown
Lonzo E. Campbell
Willard F. Crisp
Charles B. Davis
Hubert R. Finney
Herman B. Gentry
Willard D. Grubb
William P. Jolly
Howard Kennett
Norman W. Lane
Willie C. Long
Raymond C. McKinney
James R. Patterson
J. Woodrow Powell
Jesse Price
George E. Rice
Carson L. Ricks
James Rogers Jr.
John H. Runyan Jr.
James O. Wilson

Navy

Earl R. Ford

Monroe County

Army/Army Air Corps

Shirley J. Allen
Warren H. Bailey
Matt C. Berry
William R. Bowers
James H. Breeden
Buster K. Brown
Joseph A. Brunner
Robert H. Bryson
John B. Burleson
Michael C. Callahan
Lee H. Cardin
Gilford R. Carson
Jack I. Clevenger
Donnie Cline
William E. Collis
Melvin L. Crain
Hubert W. Crowder
Fred O. Curtis
Archie A. Dalton
Robert L. Davis
Robert O. Dotson
Francis E. Dupes
Hugh D. Eller
Clyde J. Ellis
Glenn B. Frank
Carl B. Freeman
John W. Freeman
Virgil D. Freeman
Enos B. Gardner
Wesley R. Garren
Gola G. Gibby
James C. Gray
Maxwell O. Green
William F. Hanley
Gordon M. Harris
James R. Hawkins
Francis V. Henry
William B. Hicks
Denver Hollingshead
Jay M. Horowitz
Joe C. Howard
Oscar J. Huey
Melvin L. Ivens
Elmer O. Jones
James N. Jones
Samuel T. Jones
Willie J. King
Homer E. Kirkland
Milburn L. Long
Raymond C. Mason
Ralph A. McNabb
Robert C. Melton

CHARLES W. MORGAN
WILLIAM G. NOBLITT
THEODORE D. NORWOOD
THOMAS E. PEARSON
KERMIT PETITT
JOE S. PHILLIPS
FREDERICK K. PLYLEY
CLAUDE POWELL
JOSEPH H. RANDOLPH
JAKE ROSE
MACK R. ROWAN JR.
WALLACE S. SAYNE
LUTHER R. SHOPE
WARREN J. SLOAN
WRAY R. SLOAN
LOUIS D. SMITH
W. F. STARRITT JR.
VERNON F. STEWART
LUTHER SUTTON
ARTHUR B. TALLENT
GUY TALLENT
HERBERT W. TENNYSON
CLINTON W. THOMAS
JOHN E. THOMAS
REED THOMPSON
LUTHER L. TRUE
THEODORE L. WATSON
CLYDE WEBB
CHARLES R. WHITE
L. ARNOLD WILKERSON
HORACE L. WILKINS
LABERN WILLIAMS
ROBERT P. WILSON
JAMES A. WINTON
ARRANTS R. WOOD
CHARLES E. WOODS

NAVY
VIRGIL CARRINGER
MARVIN R. JONES
HAROLD W. UPTON
WINSTON H. WATSON
LESTER M. WHALEY
JAMES C. WISEMAN

MARINE CORPS
WOODROW LEONARD
H. RICHARD MCCASLIN
MARION A. SHEWMAKER

MERCHANT MARINES
WILLIAM L. KIZER

Morgan County
ARMY/ARMY AIR CORPS
CARL A. AKINS
WILBURN BARDILL

AMOS BOSELEY
WILLIAM R. BROCK JR.
WALTER D. BYRD
EDD CZARNEY
BENJAMIN B. DUNCAN
BILL EVANS
JULIAN L. EVANS
WALTER J. FAIRCHILD
RAYMOND A. FRANCIS
MARYVILLE R. GALLOWAY
CHARLES O. GRIFFITH
ALBERT E. HALL
BOYD HALL
BRUCE HAMBY
FRED R. HAMPTON
ERNEST C. HARGIS
NORMAN J. HAWN
HUBERT C. HUNT
KENNETH R. HURTT
DANIEL L. JACKS
HORACE JACKSON
COVELY JONES
WILLIAM H. KREIS
EGBERT R. LARUE
KENNETH E. LARUE
EUGENE A. LAYMANCE
OTHO LILES
WALTER G. MADEN
LESLIE L. MATHESON
C. EUGENE MAYTON
WILLIE O. MCCARTT
CHARLES W. MCDANIEL
ROBERT H. MCGILL JR.
DAVID E. MCPETERS
FREDRICK O. MELHORN JR.
JOHN F. MORGAN
LEON D. PEMBERTON
GEORGE W. H. PENNINGTON
CLAY H. PHILLIPS
NELSON RICH
WILLIS H. RUSSELL
CLYDE SEABOLT
STANLEY J. SNOW
ROY E. VITTATOE
WILLIAM R. WEBB
WILBUR R. WELCH
MILTON WHALEY
JOHN E. WOODS
THOMAS WORMSLEY

NAVY
GEORGE W. BAUGHMAN
REX D. BOARDMAN
JEFF L. BYRD JR.
MARVIN L. CROMWELL
ARNOLD MORTON
CHARLES E. VENABLE

MARINE CORPS
EDWARD R. BUNCH JR.
CARLETON RUSSELL

Polk County
ARMY/ARMY AIR CORPS
JAMES T. AILOR
EUGENE ANDERSON
W. T. BAXTER
WILLIAM H. BEAVER
ROBERT L. BEAVERS
J. WALLACE BOGGS
WINSTON E. BROWN
D. G. CAMPBELL
MARTIN H. CAMPBELL
CHARLES C. CARLTON
KENNETH CASADA
JAMES W. CHANCEY
JAMES H. CLONTS
CHARLES W. COLE
FRED D. COLEMAN
AUSTIN P. DALE
JAKE E. DALE
GLENN O. DALTON
GEORGE W. DENMAN
EUGENE DOCKERY
FRANKIE B. ENSLEY
RASSIE L. FANNIN
CHRISTOPHER C. FARNER
REED J. GASTON
ROY E. GOODE
CALVIN A. GRAY
EDSEL N. GRIFFIN
RAYMOND A. HALE
WILLIAM G. HAREN
RUPERT E. HARPER
MAYFORD L. HEDRICK
WILLIAM B. HOLDEN
J. D. JONES
DAVE B. LAWSON
ROBERT H. LAWSON
JOE E. MAXWELL
GARLAND MAY
GERALD D. MCGEE
JOSEPH H. MILLER
CLAUDE T. PANTER
CLEASTON A. PATTERSON
HOYT H. PAYNE
DEBLANC RAMSEY
JOSEPH A. RAMSEY
CHARLES W. RUNNION
CALVIN W. SISSON
LUTHER C. TRIPLETT
S. N. WATERS
FLOYD W. WOODY

NAVY
- JOHN W. BAILEY
- MAX H. COLE
- HARLE H. GREEN
- NIGAL H. MARLETTE JR.

MARINE CORPS
- FRANK O. BOGGS
- HAROLD W. DAILEY
- BYRD W. EVERETT
- MILLARD C. HOOD
- JOHN I. KERNS

Rhea County

ARMY/ARMY AIR CORPS
- WILLIAM M. ATKINS
- JOHN C. BAKER
- JAMES H. BALES
- ARNOLD F. BLAKE
- JAMES BOLES
- ROY BOLES
- ELLIS C. BYRON JR.
- JACK E. BYRON
- DAVID A. CLINGAN
- HARRY L. COBBLE
- WILLIAM C. COFER
- CHARLES E. COLVIN
- WARREN G. H. DEVAULT
- JOE E. DODSON
- EUGENE EDINGTON
- CHESTER EDMONDSON
- JAMES F. EVANS
- TILLMAN L. FILYAW
- JAMES L. GALBRAITH
- JOHNNY J. GALLAGHER
- EARL GRASHAM
- RUSSELL F. GRAHAM
- JAMES O. HALE
- COY HARRIS
- JAMES F. HEISKELL
- CLAUDE D. HICKEY
- HASKELL HILL
- RALPH F. HOOD
- ALFRED D. KINCANNON
- HAROLD S. KNIGHT
- JOHN S. LEUTY JR.
- WALLACE C. LLOYD
- EUGENE MCCLENDON
- BRUCE MCCLENDON
- DALLAS T. MCCLURE JR.
- ELZIE MCCUISTON
- GEORGE N. MCCUISTON
- LAWRENCE MILLER
- WILLIAM H. MILLER
- OTHA D. MINCY
- CARL E. MIZE
- WALLACE F. MONTGOMERY

- EDWARD OLDHAM
- CLYDE M. POTTER
- ROBERT W. REED
- JONES REVIS
- SEABORN M. RODDY
- JAMES H. RUNYAN
- F. A. SCHLEMMER
- LEONARD L. SEDMAN
- JOHN E. SHARP
- JOE F. SHREVE
- JAMES C. SMITH
- RAYMOND H. SNYDER
- THOMAS D. TANKERSLEY
- RALPH C. TAYLOR
- ISAAC A. THOMAS
- FRANCIS D. VILLENEUVE
- ARNOLD E. WILKEY
- JESSIE J. WILSON

NAVY
- WILLIAM H. CARNEY JR.
- KENNETH J. SNEED
- WALLACE F. SNEED
- JAMES U. WILLIAMS

MARINE CORPS
- ORAL G. DAY
- GORDON L. GRIFFITH
- D. SPENCE KINCANON

Roane County

ARMY/ARMY AIR CORPS
- SIDNEY P. ARNOLD
- KENNETH W. BLEDSOE
- HARLIE J. D. BODINE JR.
- JAMES M. BRADSHAW
- HOMER H. BRITTON
- EDWARD R. BUTLER
- PRICE W. CARROLL
- BILLIE CARTER
- JOHN M. CLACK
- SAMUEL P. COLE JR.
- ROBERT L. COLLETT
- THOMAS R. COLLETTE
- SAMUEL J. COLYER
- CLARENCE A. CONANT
- DELES T. COOPER
- NOEL D. COPENHAVER
- JAMES R. DANIELS
- JAMES A. DAVIS
- JOHN T. DAVIS
- WALTER DAVIS
- WILLIAM F. DELANEY
- R. P. DELOZIER
- CORNELL DILLON
- WESLEY A. EASTER
- CHARLES W. EATON

- EARL H. EDWARDS
- CHARLES E. EVANS
- RALPH L. FEEZELL
- CLYDE FORRESTER
- JOHN R. FRANCIS
- CLIFFORD FRANKLIN
- EDD H. FRANKLIN
- WILLIAM N. FULKS
- GEORGE E. GALLAHER
- JOHN E. GALYON
- GEORGE F. GIBSON
- ERNEST P. GOFORTH
- WILLIAM GOLDSTON
- ARTHUR L. GOLLIHER
- CREED I. GOLLIHER
- CASPER W. HINDS
- WALTER W. HOLLAND
- CARL E. HUMAN
- BILLIE J. JARNAGIN
- CHARLES E. JARNAGIN
- WILLIAM N. KELSEY
- HERBERT L. KERLEY
- PHILLIP C. KINDRED
- THOMAS M. LADD
- HARRY R. LAFOND
- PETE M. LANE
- JESSE E. LAWHON
- JOE C. LIVELY
- JACK MARSHALL
- ERNEST E. MCCOY
- JOSEPH D. MCKINNEY
- ROY H. MCPETERS
- JAMES A. MILLSAPS
- HOMER L. MONEYMAKER
- EUGENE B. MOORE
- J. C. MOORE
- JOHN F. MURRAY
- CARL NEWBY
- JEWEL PARKS
- MAURICE B. PARRISH
- RAY G. PATTERSON
- GEORGE D. PLEMONS
- ISAAC D. PRIVETTE
- BERT RABY
- HUGH P. RAINS
- R.L. RENFRO
- MIKE ROBINETTE
- TOMMIE W. ROSE
- JAMES W. RYANS JR.
- EDD SANDERS
- ROBERT C. SCANDLYN
- HUGH L. SHUBERT
- PAUL D. SHUBERT
- CARSON K. SIMPSON
- HENRY M. SIMPSON
- NEWTON A. SITZLAR
- JOHN H. SMITH

CHARLES W. STOUT
HARRY F. STRICKLAN
ALBERT TAYLOR
ELMER L. THOMAS
GEORGE E. THOMPSON
RALPH L. TINDALL
PAUL S. TURNER
TED E. VITATOE
JOHN F. WALLS
CURTIS E. WHITSON
OTHER C. WOOLVERTON

NAVY
JOHN C. BRENNAN
ANDERSON F. BROWN JR.
HENRY E. BRYANT JR.
JOE G. CAMPBELL
GEORGE W. CHAPMAN
WILLIAM G. CHRISTIAN
JAMES D. CHRISTMAS JR.
FLOYD B. EAST
HOYT H. HAMLETT
JESSE J. HILL
KINDRED B. JOHNSON
CHARLES F. KELSO
JAMES A. PIERCE
JOSEPH W. PLEMONS
HAROLD G. RUFFNER
JAMES D. SMITH

MARINE CORPS
JOHN K. COFFMAN
JAMES R. GAMBLE
HOYTE B. GRANSTAFF
CYREL E. MILLER

Scott County
ARMY/ARMY AIR CORPS
AUGRIE ADKINS
FRANCIS L. ALLEN
LONUS A. ASHBURN
ORA J. BLAW
JANE M. BLEVINS
RALPH BLEVINS
BILLIE B. CARROLL
RICHARD L. CHAMBERS
WILLIE C. CLARK
FRED COTTON
JAMES CRABTREE JR.
CLINTON E. CROSS
MARLIE CROSS
MILLARD CROSS
FLOYD DAUGHERTY
ETHAN DAVIS
GEORGE M. DAY
KELSIE O. DUNCAN
VERNON W. DUNCAN

RAY DYKES JR.
MARION C. ELLIS
ALBERT EPPERSON
OLIVER R. EVANS
T. HARRY EVANS
HURSTLE L. GOAD
SAM J. GOAD
JAMES F. GOINS
JOHNNIE E. GOOCH
ROBERT W. HALL
HOUSTON HAMBY
TOM C. HENDERSON
CLAUDE V. HENSLEY
DILMON JEFFERS
OLIVER JEFFERS
MURRY C. LASTER JR.
JAMES A. LAWHORN
JUNIOR LAWSON
EUGENE D. LEWALLEN
HURST LEWALLEN
WARREN H. LEWALLEN
HAROLD E. LLOYD
JAMES M. LOVETT SR.
ARCHIE D. LOWE
COLVY B. MADDEN
GEORGE C. MARCUM
HOMER S. MARCUM
MEARL MASSEY
JOHN F. MILLSAP
HOWARD P. MORRIS
VIRGIL L. NEAL
FRANK A. NEELY
BURL NEWPORT
GEORGE B. NEWPORT
HOBERT OWENS
RALPHARD PAYNE
EARL PHILLIPS
JAMES E. PHILLIPS
DAVID E. ROSSER
ARTHUR SEXTON
WOODROW W. SHARP
JOHN R. SLAVEN
WILLIAM S. STANFILL
OSCAR STANLEY
AUDNEY TERRY
JAMES A. TERRY
THERON C. TERRY
HOWARD THOMPSON
HERMAN TRAMELL
CLARENCE B. WEST
JOHN H. WEST
RAY WEST
CORDELL WILMOTH
GEORGE WILSON
MACK H. YANCY
DANA T. YORK

NAVY
HOLLIS F. BELL
RALPH W. COOK
BEN O. LAY
KERMIT ROBBINS
WILLIAM A. SEXTON
HERBERT M. SMITH

MERCHANT MARINES
PAUL E. FOSTER

Sequatchie County
ARMY/ARMY AIR CORPS
WALTER L. ALLEN
THOMAS H. CAMP
JAMES FULTZ
PAUL W. HEARD
LLOYD O. HIXSON
EDWIN W. KILGORE
JAMES E. LOWERY
JOHN MCCOY PATRICK
ISAAC D. ROBERTS
J. C. SWANGER
OSBIN WORLEY

NAVY
GRADY L. DAVIS
DELER D. JOHNSON
THOMAS L. MERRIMAN
ROY OWENSBY
WOODROW W. VON ROHR

Sevier County
ARMY/ARMY AIR CORPS
WOODROW W. ADAMS
CLARENCE E. ALLEN
HUGH H. ALLEN
JOHNNIE H. BAILEY
REECE H. BAKER
MARION A. BATSON
YANDELL BAXTER
ROBERT C. BIGGS
JOHN C. BLAZER
CARROLL B. BRYAN
JOHN F. CARVER
JOHN R. CATE
JAMES W. CAUGHRON
WILLARD B. CAUGHRON
ALFRED C. EMERT
HAROLD C. FOX
TALMADGE FRAZIER
ANDREW H. GRAVES
ROY G. GREEN
CLYDE E. HELTON
FRANK V. HENRY
GLENN H. HENRY
JESSIE R. HENRY

Joe E. Henry
John R. Henry
Robert T. Hillard
Clell Huskey
Samuel T. Huskey
Troy E. Huskey
Lloyd E. Jenkins
Chester R. A. Keeler
Roy D. Kelley
George A. King
Raymond King
William E. Kirkland
Melvin Lane
Burnette Lewelling
Buford M. Loveday
Frank E. Manis
Joe L. McCarter
Richard F. McFalls
Hermitt McGaha
Roy V. Montgomery
James Murphy
Wayne L. Myers
Lyman Newman
Beecher B. Ogle
James E. Ogle
Robert C. Parton
Ralph C. Petty
Lones E. Proffitt
Bill Ramsey
Ernest Reagan
James N. Rector Jr.
Lon D. Robertson
Lloyd M. Robertson Jr.
Robert M. Robertson
Charles A. Rolen
Ralph S. Romines
William C. Rudd
Chester W. Shultz
James R. Shultz
Charlie E. Sise
Charles W. Sizemore
John R. Smelcer
William R. Smith
Winfred G. Smith
Fred W. Tarwater
Luther C. Thurman
Dott Trentham
Hubert R. Turner
Luther Ward
Amos H. Webb
Cleo Webb
A. D. Whaley
Hollen W. Whaley
Silas J. Whaley
Omide T. Williams
O. Lavator Williams
Ray E. Worth

Navy
James W. Bailey
Charlie L. Burnett
Carl H. Flynn
James C. Flynn
Ernest L. Howard
Creed C. McCarter
Carl A. Ogle
Walter H. Smith
Fred J. Spicer
Add Tritt

Marine Corps
Luther E. Caughron
Allen Cole

Sullivan County
Army/Army Air Corps
Clyde J. Adkins
Clyde M. Amos
Isaac R. Anderson
Lloyd G. Anderson
James E. Arnold
Clyde E. Ashworth
Claude J. Austin
John I. Baker
Charley H. Ball
Willard R. Ball
Armon B. Banner Jr.
William H. Barnes
Clyde R. Begley
Charles R. Benfield
George R. Bennett
James F. Bentley Jr.
Jim Biggerstaff
Audie H. Bishop
Hiram C. Bloomer
Lester C. Booher
Wayne H. Bowers
Darwin E. Bowman
Jack V. Boyd
Bill M. Bradley
Lewis Brown
Whitsel R. C. Brown
Harlan L. Bryan
Walter A. Buckles Jr.
James T. Campbell
Hubert A. Camper
George W. Carmack
Clyde Carroll
James E. Carroll
Harrison B. Carter
Jesse H. Church
Thomas J. Church
Henry C. Clark
Willie L. Clark
Victor W. Clees

Carl H. Collins
Arthur R. Combs Jr.
Joseph L. Combs Jr.
Bill G. Comerford
Earl Conkin
Earnest Conkin
Orville L. Cox
Leeroy Crawford
Roy A. Crawford
Sammie L. Crawford
Charlie L. Cross
Fred C. Cross
Herbert G. Cross
Lester G. Cross
Eugene Darter
William H. Davenport
Max W. Denton
Donald C. Devault
Dual F. Dishner
Thomas T. Dooley
Mack N. Droke
Ferd A. Dunn
Samuel M. Dykes
William E. Ellison
Paul A. Fansler
Paul B. Fields
Joe H. Fleming III
Charles T. Fletcher
Kenneth W. Foster
James E. Frye
Charles W. Fuller Jr.
John Furge
William A. S. Furlow
Howard P. Geisler
Robert B. Gentry
John B. Gilley
Cary L. Gray
William L. Griffin
Jasper C. Grills
H. L. Gutman
Ralph M. Hammond
Paul F. Harkleroad
Lloyd R. Harmon
Nev A. Hauk
Albert L. Hawkins
Stephen T. Haworth
Marvin H. Helbert
Joe F. Henard
Harry C. Hensley Jr.
Carl H. Hickman
Billie F. Hicks
Carl K. Hicks
William R. Hilton Jr.
Dave C. Hinkle
James H. Hodge
Sylvester J. Huffman
Beverly W. Izlar

Douglas E. Johnson
Robert J. Johnson Jr.
Samuel P. Jones
Walter E. Jones
Samuel J. Kyle
Earl C. Lane
Thomas A. Larimer
Alonzo Ledbetter
Joseph H. Lee
Ralph R. Lethco
Beecher J. Lewis
Milburn R. Light
Roy E. Light
Ernest E. Ligon
Hassell H. Martin
Delmar A. McCracken
Chambliss P. McDowell
Miles M. Mitchell
W. P. Mitchell Jr.
Andrew F. Moles Jr.
William D. Moody
James C. Moore
Thomas H. Morgan Jr.
George A. Morrell
Guy W. Morrison
Joseph D. Neal
John H. Neely
Rex C. Newman
Frank L. Nickels
Ralph H. Nunn
James M. Offield
Thurman H. Olinger
Glen S. Oliver
Robert H. Osborne
Elbridge W. Palmer
Thomas L. Peters
William B. Peters
Zackrie T. Peters
Carl E. Pettigrew
R. O. Phillips Jr.
Lewis G. Plummer
Samuel E. Poore
Walter H. Preston
Kemp G. Price
James W. Rader
James C. Rainey
Carlos Ringley
James E. Roe
Henry C. Rogers
Arthur L. Rutherford
John P. Senter
Edward J. Sheets
Robert S. Shoaf
Paul D. Slater
John R. Stahr
Howard P. Steadman
Oscar M. Stewart

Wayne S. Stewart
Charles J. Strong
Bruce O. Tester
William C. Thomas
George T. Tipton
James R. Todd
Doffice E. Trent
Haskell Turner
Ernest L. Vance
Charles W. Vicars
Hubert L. Wagner
Jackson A. Walker
Norman F. Walker
Robert T. Wallace
Samuel V. Walling
Kenneth F. Walsh
Floyd J. Wampler
Carl E. Weaver
Clarence Webb
Roy E. Wheeler
Wilbur C. White
Ben J. Widner
Clifton E. Williams
Ralph B. Wininger
Jack D. Yates

Navy
Charles G. Abell
Floyd H. Bolling
Charles D. Byrd
Victor E. Clasby
Donald E. Coffey
Marion D. Colvard
Bobby J. Cox
Howard F. Crawford
Warren H. Crim
Nealous M. Dalton
Arthur M. Denton
Nat Ferrell
Wray J. Franklin
John C. Gillenwater
Levi Guy Jr.
Francis E. Horne
Lewis W. Hughes
Claude E. Jarrett
Douglas E. Jones
Edmund B. Kneisel
Robert A. Koontz
Walter T. Malcolm Jr.
Carlus B. Moore
William E. Neil
Charles D. Norris
James J. Overbay
Robert S. Owens Jr.
Fred C. Parsons
Wilburt J. Vicars
Stuart H. Wallace

James K. Weaver
Fleet F. Willis

Marine Corps
Houston Chastain
Aaron H. Dempsey
Paul K. Duncan
Joseph I. Fleenor
James E. Gentry
Orville D. Kitzmiller
Jerrel L. Musick
Thomas B. Neal
Carl E. Patrick
Fred O. Russell
Joseph P. Smith
Warren G. Snapp
Joseph L. Vance
George B. Wampler Jr.

Unicoi County
Army/Army Air Corps
Robert Bailey
Alfred Banks
Charles B. Baxter
Bob Beam
Albert Bennett
Robert L. Bennett
William R. Buchanan
Walter R. Caton
Bernard C. Chapman
Gus Cousins
Charles W. Day
Charles E. Duncan
Mills Edmonds
Plem Edwards
Roy English
Kelly L. Epley Jr.
Paul E. Farmer
James H. Foster
William T. Gilbert
Dwight L. Guinn
Woodward Harris
Elmer C. Harvey
Luther E. Hensley
Orville F. Hensley
Howard W. Hurt
Howard Huskins
Bruce Johnson
Dwight L. Keever
William A. Ledford
Harley E. Lewis
Paul T. Loyd
Joseph D. Love
Robert E. Martin
Harley G. Masters
Ralph C. McIntosh
Wade H. McLain

JOSEPH P. MCLAUGHLIN
JOHNIE J. MEADOWS
ROBERT M. MOON
RUFUS S. MOORE JR.
LEE R. MORGAN
RUSSELL NICHOLS
WILLIAM F. NIEMEYER
IVAN A. OSBORNE
GLEN W. PACK
MILLARD F. PARSLEY JR.
CLARK PETERSON
LESTER L. PULLEY
WALTER L. RICE JR.
EARL D. RYBURN
SIMON P. SHELTON
CLARENCE C. STOCKTON
JAMES STRICKLAND JR.
LEONARD W. TAYLOR
CARROLL B. TILSON
ROY C. TINKER
LATTIE TIPTON
J. VANDERGRIFT
HUGH L. WALDROP
MARVIN L. WILLIAMS
RALPH WILSON
CLYDE R. WISHON

Navy
KEITH ADKINS
OSCAR J. BENNETT
CURTIS D. CLARK
FINNIE C. CLARK
HUBERT D. COPP
DALLAS P. EDMONDS
FRED B. HOWELL
DONALD L. KEPLINGER
DANAH R. MCCURRY
CLAUDE R. MCINTURFF
THOMAS S. MCINTURFF
HUGH P. PRINCE
EUGENE H. STREET
JACK M. TURNER
EDWARD M. VOGEL
PAUL WILLIAMS
FRED D. WILSON

Marine Corps
RALPH BURGESS

Union County
ARMY/ARMY AIR CORPS
HENRY I. BREWER
EDWIN B. BUTCHER
GLENN C. FIELDS
JAMES L. HAYNES
FRED KISER
JOE R. MUNSEY

JAMES W. NORRIS
COSTER PETERS
JAMES R. REAGAN
HERMAN E. ROGERS
JAMES D. SHIFLET
OATY L. SMITH
ELMER O. WELCH
FRANCIS A. WILLIAMS
HARVEY H. WOLARD

Navy
GLEN L. BRIDGES
ESTLE J. GRAVES
LEROY SHELBY

Marine Corps
JOHN H. MILLER JR.

Washington County
ARMY/ARMY AIR CORPS
LYON E. AGEE JR.
JAMES F. ALLEN
FRED W. ARMSTRONG
LINNIE ARROWOOD
CARROLL W. BAILEY
ROBERT A. BALLE JR.
JOHN H. BARNETT
CONRAD C. BITZER
JOHN BOGGS
CHARLES R. BOONE
HERMAN R. BOUTON
JACK BOWMAN
CECIL A. BRANSCOM
JOHN C. BRATTON
EARL E. BROOKS
HARRY BROYLES
JACOB S. BROYLES
BENNIE B. BURGESS
ROBERT E. BURLESON
LESTER A. BUTLER
WILLIAM T. CANNON JR.
CHARLES B. CAREY
EMMETTE B. CARTER
JAMES H. CHRISTIAN
CHARLES W. CLOYD
CLARENCE C. CORPENING JR.
EARL G. CORZINE
JOE M. COX
DEWEY E. CROWE
HENRY R. CROWDER
JIM M. CRUMLEY
EDWARD M. CUTSHALL
CECIL H. DALE
KENNETH A. DALTON
WILLIAM B. DAVIS
RICHARD S. DEAKINS
ARGYL L. DEPEW

FRED T. DIGGS
OSCAR A. DULANEY JR.
PARIS L. DULANEY
RALPH L. DUNN
GLENN EDWARDS
LAWSON FAIR
EUGENE H. FEATHERS
BUCKLEY E. FRAZIER
ROBERT C. GARDEN
JOHN R. GARLAND
JOHN E. GREENE
MAYNARD F. GREENE
FRANK A. GRINDSTAFF
ROBERT P. GUINN
WELDON H. HAMMITT
LAWRENCE A. HARRISON
WILLIAM H. HARRISON JR.
GILBERT L. HARROWER
FRANK W. HARTSELL
SCOTT HERRIN
WILLIAM L. HITE
JAMES C. HOLTSINGER
CLAUDE HONEYCUTT
LUM HONEYCUTT
CLAUDE L. HUFFINE
JAMES L. ISENBERG
SWAYNE C. JOHNSON
WILBER L. JOHNSON
JAMES C. JOINES
ERNEST E. JONES
JOHN C. KELSEY
JOHN P. KEPLINGER
CARL R. KEYS
JAMES H. KINCADE
WILEY G. KING JR.
ROGER W. KIRKPATRICK
WILLIAM M. KITCHEN
LLOYD R. LEONARD
CHRISTIAN LEQUIEU
FRED R. LEWIS
JOHN H. LOCKNER
WARREN H. MACK
GEORGE W. MARKLAND
BERYL L. MARTIN
ZEBULON P. MARTIN
W. E. MCCARTT JR.
JAMES B. MCKAMEY
FRED M. MCPAUL
HERMAN E. MILHORN
ELMER MILLER
PAUL J. MILLER
ELWOOD P. MINNICK
GLENN H. MITCHELL
JAMES W. MULLINS
ROBERT G. MURR
LUCAS M. NEAS
JOSEPH W. NICHOLS

GEORGE D. OWENS
AMOS J. PARSONS
BILLY B. PAYNE
HIAWATHA L.E. PERRY
ORDWAY PERRY
HOWARD L. PETERSON
HENRY POORE
FOY L. PRICE
DAVID S. RENFRO
HOWARD H. ROGERS
JOHN S. RUSH
PARKS W. SAMS JR.
CHARLES W. SAYLOR
CLYDE G. SCALF
FRED G. SHEETS
ALONZO E. SHELTON
WALTER A. SHEPHARD
KENNETH B. SMALLWOOD
EARL SMITH
VIVIAN C. SPEER
BILLY SOUTH
FRANK B. ST. JOHN
CHARLES E. STANSBERRY
WASTEL W. STEVENS
ROBERT STILLS
JOSEPH A. SUMMERS JR.

VERLEY TATE
CLARENCE E. TAYLOR
CLIFFORD H. TAYLOR
FRED TAYLOR
GLENN W. TESTER
JAMES E. TESTER
JAMES D. TESTER
ROBERT D. TESTER
KENNETH R. THOMPSON
JESSE D. TILSON
JAMES M. TIPTON
ROSCOE D. TOMLINSON
WALTER R. TREADWAY
NILES VAUGHN
MACK C. WHITTEMORE
JAMES H. WILLENS
CLIFFORD A. WISHON
HARRY A. WOMACK

NAVY
NELSON F. ANDREWS
MILLER W. BEALS
WILLIAM J. BRIEN
CARL E. COPLIN
RICHARD E. CORUM

CLYDE W. COX
ANDREW C. DILLS JR.
JAMES A. DYER
CARL M. FERGUSON
EDWIN HINES
NEFF L. LAWS
LOREN B. OWENS
ALLEN K. PAINTER
HENRY W. PATTON
CHARLES P. PETERS
PAUL E. SAYLOR
JIM TAYLOR
WILLIAM R. WEAVER

MARINE CORPS
HOWARD T. BAWGUS
BERNIE T. BYRD JR
RAY M. JOHNSON
WILLIAM C. RUNYON
JOSEPH H. STEWART
WORLEY M. WALTERS
JOHN W. WHEELOCK

MERCHANT MARINES
JOHN E. COLE
JONES G. HINE

KOREA

Anderson County
ARMY
LEWIS BROGANS
WALTER R. BRUMMETT
ALBERT CARTER
JACK HOHMAN
ROBERT L. JENNINGS
RAYMOND L. JONES
WILLIAM KILLINGSWORTH
JAMES E. LOWERY
JOE S. MULLINS
WILLARD G. PALM
MYREL PHILLIPS
GRADY D. REESE
ROBERT L. ROGERS JR.
WARREN WEST
GENE WIGGINS

MARINE CORPS
CLAY HARNESS

Bledsoe County
ARMY
ANDREW A. LADD

HAROLD D. MCMILLON
HENRY C. PRUITT
ALVIN S. RIGSBY

MARINE CORPS
EDWARD STRIBLING

Blount County
ARMY
CLIFFORD J. BORING
FRED H. GOSSETT
RAY F. HENRY
JACK E. KING
DANIEL R. LAMBERT
GENE E. LILLARD
WILLIAM R. STINNETT
COLUMBUS H. THACKER
WILEY J. TIPTON
WENDELL H. WALKER

MARINE CORPS
JAMES R. MCNEILLY
CHARLES D. ORR

Bradley County
ARMY
JOHN M. COFER
JAMES L. EVANS
WILLIAM D. JOHNSON
PAUL T. MCCRACKEN
JACK C. MANIS
ARTHUR D. RODDY
RALPH F. UNDERWOOD
ROY L. WHALEY

NAVY
CALVIN R. JOHNSON

Campbell County
ARMY
BILLY A. ARNOLD
JEROME J. BROOKS
OSCAR FILYAW
RAYMOND E. HALL
DEWEY W. LAMBDIN
GIBSON LOUDIN JR.
ALBERT MCNEELEY
EARNEST MOSER

THOMAS MYERS
HARLEY NORMAN
WILLIE PARTIN
DONALD G. SMITH
HERBERT WARD
RUBIN B. WILSON
J. LELDON YORK

Carter County

ARMY

BERNIE B. BRITTON JR.
RAZOR J. CAMPBELL
ROSCOE C. CAMPBELL
JOHN E. CARVER
MATHEW G. COLE
RAY M. GUESS
EARL LEWIS
PAUL E. LITTLE
JOE P. MCKEEHAN
WILLIAM C. NIDIFFER
BILLY B. NORRIS
RAYMOND PIERCE
JOE D. SIMERLY
GRADY STANLEY
ROBERT M. TRIVETT
NOAH H. TYREE JR.
WILLIAM E. WILSON

AIR FORCE

JAMES R. HOLLYFIELD

Claiborne County

ARMY

FOSTER L. ALSTON
PAUL T. BUNCH
DEAN R. MCNEW
AARON MORGAN
GENERAL H. PARTIN
EARL E. SEALS
GENERAL J. WILSON

MARINE CORPS

ALFRED J. TROVILLO

Cocke County

ARMY

HAROLD J. CARR
Y. J. CRUM
ISAAC D. FORD
WILLIAM E. GOODRUM
ARTHUR GROOMS JR.
ROME H. HANCE
FRANK MOORE
JESSE E. SPROUSE

NAVY

JOHN D. CARMICHEAL

MARINE CORPS

JOHN D. WILLIAMS

Cumberland County

ARMY

BOBBY G. ANDERSON
LINCOLN ELMORE
JOE L. FORD
CARSON L. PARSONS JR.
HOMER PROFFITT

AIR FORCE

WINFRED D. MORGAN

Fentress County

ARMY

LEONARD J. DISHMAN
STANLEY R. LOWE
JACK D. PARKER
ROBERT L. SHEPPARD
JAMES B. UPCHURCH
HERBERT C. WHITED
JOHN L. YOUNG

MARINE CORPS

HERSHEL B. GOODING

Grainger County

ARMY

GEORGE G. BOOKER
DELMAS G. HAYES
JAMES O. JOYCE JR.
GLENN V. ROACH

Greene County

ARMY

GEORGE G. CAMPBELL
HUGH L. CANNON
SAMUEL H. COUCH
WARD A. DOBSON
GILBERT H. FORTNER
JAMES M. GABY JR.
KENDRICK HAMPTON
CHARLES M. KEITH
TOMMY R. KELLEY
BROWNLOW MCINTOSH JR.
FREDRICK E. STONE
IRA L. VAUGHN
DELMAR R. WARD
WILLIAM E. WILSON

Hamblen County

ARMY

JAMES A. BLAIR
ROBERT C. ESTES
WILLIAM E. GOAN
JAMES B. HONEYCUTT
RALPH E. LOWE

PORTER W. TAYLOR
JOHN F. WRIGHT

AIR FORCE

GEORGE W. HIGGINS

Hamilton County

ARMY

HUGH R. ARENDALE
JOHN H. BOND
JOHN E. BRANCH
LEWIS G. BRICKELL
ALVIN B. CAMPBELL
ROBERT X. CARTER
JOHN M. CORBETT
THOMAS V. CRAZE
AUGUST B. CROSS JR.
RICHARD B. DICKSON
GEORGE DORMAN
WILLIE J. FAGAIN
TROY L. GENTRY
SAMUEL F. GILL JR.
CLIFFORD GOTHARD
RUDOLPH HARRIS
JAMES L. HAWKINS
HOMER HICKMAN
FLOYD L. HODGE
JAMES L. HOWARD
HAROLD S. JACKSON
HAROLD JARMON
CLIFFORD L. JENKINS
SAM JONES
JAMES W. KEITH
WILLIAM C. LAZENBY
HAROLD LEWIS
WALLACE R. LOVELADY
WALLACE R. LUSK
HORACE M. MANER
CHARLES L. MARTIN
GEORGE H. MATTHEWS
JAMES L. MENATOLA
CLAUDE F. MOORE JR.
FRANK MOORE JR.
JOHN J. MORROW
RAY T. PEVEHOUSE
GEORGE PICKETT JR.
THOMAS E. PRIVETT
JAMES R. RICHMOND
BILLY J. RIDGE
HILLARD RUTHERFORD
FREDERICK SHADDEN
CARL G. SHANNON
ALTON E. SHIRLEY
JAMES L. TABOR
WILLIE E. THOMAS
HAROLD V. THORNHILL
JOSEPH T. TOCCO
GEORGE W.T. TORBETT

JAMES N. TWITTY
ROY S. UNDERWOOD
JAMES O. VARNELL JR.
GLENN W. VAUGHN

MARINE CORPS
PAUL T. BAKER
DENVER I. CHAMBLISS
PAUL N. DEVRIES
RICHARD W. DURHAM
CHARLES FOSTER
WILLIAM R. FRAZIER
WILLIAM K. GARMANY
LEE R. HYCHE
REGINALD V. JOHNSON
VIRGIL E. STEPHENSON
EDWARD A. WILLIAMS

AIR FORCE
WILLIAM R. KIMBRO
JAMES W. LUNSFORD
EARL W. RADLEIN JR.
BEVERLY A. SWINGLE

Hancock County
ARMY
J. L. MATHIS

Hawkins County
ARMY
JAMES E. BEGLEY
JAMES B. CREECH
JAMES R. DAVIS
JOHN N. FREEMAN
RICHARD J. RIMER
HENRY F. WEST
DENNIS W. YANKEE

MARINE CORPS
ROY L. FISHER
W. JULIAN GRIGSBY JR.

AIR FORCE
WILLIAM C. CLICK

Jefferson County
ARMY
DENNIS BROCK
JACK A. HORNER
BURNETT H. INGRAM
R. STANLEY RINES
BOBBY G. WALKER

AIR FORCE
ALLAN S. BETTIS
JAMES A. HALL

Johnson County
ARMY
AVERY G. BISHOP
DORAN L. CANTER
VESTAL R. COWAN
LYNDBURG DICKENS
GEORGE W. DUNN JR.
JAMES D. GAMBILL
JAMES D. GENTRY
RAY GENTRY
EULIS G. GRACE
TOMMY J. JOHNSON
BILLY C. MOSIER
CHARLES E. OSBORNE
FLOYD A. SNYDER JR.
HARRY L. WILSON

MARINE CORPS
ROBERT F. ROBBINS

Knox County
ARMY
JACK K. AMYX
FREDERICK B. BEAN
CHARLES P. BEELER
HUGH H. BREWER
ROBERT M. BUCKNER
BILLIE R. BURKHART
LLOYD R. CABE
LUTHER E. CARR
BRUCE W. CLEVENGER
EDWARD E. COLLINS
ESTLE L. COLLINS
HOMER R. COSTNER
CARL E. DEFORD
BILL B. GASS
JOE P. GIBBS
MARTIN L. GOINS
GEORGE W. HALL
WILLIAM B. HATTON
ISHAM C. HEWGLEY JR.
JAMES C. HIBBEN
MATTHEW HUNNICUTT
HERBERT K. IDOL
WILLIAM C. JENKINS
ARTHUR O. JOHNSON
ERNEST M. KELLY
LEE O. KERR
DAVID C. KNIGHT
JACK D. LANIER
ARVIL LEMONS
VAUN A. LOVEDAY
DONALD E. MCMURRAY
RALPH A. MCPHERSON
HARRY L. MILLER
WALTER B. MILLS
JOHN L. NAYLOR
CHARLES L. NIX

CHARLES B. OWENS
ERNEST G. PARKER
CLYDE M. PINKSTON
DAVID V. RADCLIFFE
DONALD R. RADER
PAUL R. REED
BOBBY L. RIGGS
JAMES D. ROGERS
RAYMOND L. SMITH
WILLIAM R. TAYLOR
LESTER P. THURMAN
DONALD C. VAUGHN
WILLIAM VERMILLION
ROBERT J. VINYARD
ARTHUR T. WALDROP
JOHNNIE T. WARREN
GLEN L. WATSON
EDWARD T. WEAVER
CHARLES E. WILHITE
GEORGE H. WILLIAMS
SAM D. WILLIAMS
EMERSON J. WRIGHT

MARINE CORPS
WILBURN D. BUCKNER
JACK S. DAVIS
JACKIE D. DOYLE
REUBEN LEONARD
LAWRENCE E. LETT
SAM Q. MILLER
ALBERT C. OWEN
J.B. POLAND
WALTER L. SEIVERS JR.
JOHN E. TROTTER

AIR FORCE
JAMES M. BELLOWS JR.
WILLIAM R. BRISCOE JR.

Loudon County
ARMY
ROBERT R. HEATON
JACK MOORE
ROY L. MUNSEY
ZEB W. VANCE JR.
HENRY L. WATSON

MARINE CORPS
JOE W. MALONE JR.

Marion County
ARMY
DEWITT CAMPBELL JR.
RAY E. DUKE   MOH
LOTCHIE JONES JR.
CHARLES L. LANSDELL
GILBERT L. MCCURRY
JAMES E. ROGERS JR.

JAMES W. STEPHENS
WILLIAM M. STEPHENS
JAMES W. STEWART
JAMES W. TALLEY
JAMES H. TANNER

MARINE CORPS
JAMES L. ALLISON

AIR FORCE
HUGH A. GRIFFITH JR.

McMinn County
ARMY
STARL L. BANKS
TOMMY BUCKNER
DAVID H. GRISHAM
JAMES H. HYDE
GROVER G. JENKINS
CALEB JOHNKINS JR.
JAMES J. KIRKLAND
JAMES T. PRUEITT
THOMAS L. SISSON
JAMES E. STEPHENSON

MARINE CORPS
RICHARD E. HARRIS

AIR FORCE
JACK M. BROCK

Meigs County
ARMY
DAVID C. GORDON
WILLIAM E. SCOTT

Monroe County
ARMY
AVERY E. BURNETT
ROBERT A. GREEN
PARRION R. HARRIS
CHESTER S. HICKS
JAMES H. RABY
WILLIAM R. SLOAN
WALTER B. SMITH
ROSS M. WALKER

AIR FORCE
WESLEY E. TALLENT
JOHNNY S. TEAGUE

NAVY
TUBBY B. WATSON
ALLEN L. WRIGHT

Morgan County
ARMY
CHARLES ASHLEY
REUBEN W. FREYTAG
WALTER C. HAAG
DEAN B. JOHNSON
RAYMOND C. LAMANCE
GEORGE C. WALLS
LESTER J. WARD

MARINE CORPS
FRANK WATSON

Polk County
ARMY
DOYLE R. BROWN
RUFF G. QUEEN
RAY C. UNDERWOOD

Rhea County
ARMY
CHARLES T. SHIPLEY
RAYMOND BROOKS

Roane County
ARMY
JAMES E. ALTUM
HEARL E. BULLENS
LUTHER B. DANNEL
DAVID L. FERGUSON
LESTER A. KINDRED
THOMAS H. MULLINS
BOYD RUCKER
JOHN E. RUMMEL
ARNOLD G. SMITH
RALPH A. THOMPSON
PAUL L. WRIGHT

MARINE CORPS
E. JACK WITT

NAVY
JOHN A. COLLETT

AIR FORCE
WILBURN C. SNOW

Scott County
ARMY
CHARLES CORDER JR.
BAILEY KEETON JR.
ROY W. MATTHEWS
WILLIS WATTERS

MARINE CORPS
ROY E. CROSS

Sequatchie County
ARMY
ARTHUR W. ALLEN

Sevier County
ARMY
GEORGE E. BARNES
NORMAN E. FLYNN
ELMER E. LEWELLYN
JOHN R. SEAGLE

MARINE CORPS
LEE R. COLE

Sullivan County
ARMY
ARLIE P. BARRETT
HUVILLE E. BEAR
PAUL A. BENTON
LAWRENCE E. CARRIER
GEORGE W. COPAS
MARSHALL L. COX
HOWARD M. CROSS
RICHARD C. DAVIDSON
JOHN L. DUTRA
GEORGE D. ELKINS
RALPH E. GARRETT
GEORGE C. HAGIE
MARSHALL L. HARRISON
SAM C. HARRIS JR.
WESLEY C. LAWSON
HERMAN MANIS
EUGENE P. MILLER
JOHN C. MYERS
CHARLES M. OVERBAY
JACOB K. OVERBAY
FOSTINE R. RUTLEDGE JR.
J. D. THOMPSON
RICHARD L. TURNER
JAMES W. WHITE

MARINE CORPS
JOHN D. BOWYER

NAVY
JOSEPH D. WITHERSPOON

AIR FORCE
VERLIN F. TODD
GEORGE H. WYMAN

Unicoi County
ARMY
LEWIS R. CALLAHAN
VERNON C. HARDIN
CHARLES W. HOPSON
CECIL POORE

AIR FORCE
  ALBERT C. MAY

Union County
ARMY
  ROY E. ROE
  STINER WRIGHT

Washington County
ARMY
  ROBERT E. ADAMS
  ODELL BUSLER
  FRANK L. DEADERICK

DALLAS HONEYCUTT
DAYTON F. ISLEY
NATHAN E. JACKSON
GEORGE E. JOHNSTON
RALPH G. JONES
RAYGER G. ROBERTS
JAMES F. SADLER
BOBBY L. TRUELOVE
ALFRED WHITSON

MARINE CORPS
  JOHN D. HICKS
  POWELL H. MCELHENNEY

AIR FORCE
  MEDON A. BITZER
  BILLY G. ELLIOTT
  J. RAY GREENWAY JR.
  ROBERT B. PARKER
  GEORGE E. SIMS
  CHARLES E. WEST
  WILLIAM E. WILLIAMS

NAVY
  CHARLES H. MCGEE

VIETNAM

Anderson County
ARMY
  SAMUEL E. ASHER
  MICHAEL R. BAKER
  GERALD W. DAVIDSON
  JOHN T. DAVIS
  KENNETH J. DAVIS
  GARY L. EDWARDS
  DALLAS E. GREEN
  GOMER D. HOSKINS JR.
  BENJAMIN LEE IV
  JOHN H. PATE JR.
  BILLY J. PATTERSON
  JOHNNIE H. PATTERSON
  HOYLE TERRY JR.
  GARRY L. WEAVER

MARINE CORPS
  JEFFERSON T. BARNETT SR.
  JOSEPH K. BRADLEY
  EDWARD D. DISON
  WILLIAM E. HAGGARD
  ACIE D. HALL
  RONALD E. HIBBARD
  PHILLIP E. MINTON
  FLETCHER SEEBER JR.
  GREGORY J. WEBER

AIR FORCE
  LUTHER E. DAVIS
  GARY A. GLANDON
  JOHN T. WELSHAN

Bledsoe County
ARMY
  BOBBY D. LEWIS
  BILLY F. MOONEYHAM

ARNOLD G. OAKES
JOSEPH A. ORETO

Blount County
ARMY
  DANNY E. BLEVINS
  JOHNNY L. BRYANT
  WALTER T. BRYANT
  JOHN H. BURGESS JR.
  DONALD C. COULTER
  DONALD L. DOTSON
  JAMES L. DUNLAP
  RICHARD L. DUNLAP
  DAN G. FEEZELL
  WAYNE O. GAY
  THOMAS J. GRINDSTAFF
  GORDON A. HAWKINS
  WILLIAM C. HOPPER
  LEONARD H. MANTOOTH JR.
  JACK W. MILLER
  JAMES L. PARKER
  MONTE L. PAYNE
  JAMES A. PETTITT
  ERVIN PROCTOR
  JOHN D. RHODES III
  JOHNNY L. ROBERTS
  JAMES H. ROULETTE
  F. CALVIN RUSSELL
  CLAUDE A. WILLIAMS
  WAYNE C. WILLIAMS

NAVY
  JOHN R. CUNNINGHAM
  LEROY POPLIN

MARINE CORPS
  GERALD E. CUNNINGHAM
  HENRY D. CUSTEN
  EARL A. JENKINS

OSCAR R. PARROTT
ROBERT L. ROGERS
LARRY G. WHITEHEAD

AIR FORCE
  GORDON L. WHEELER

Bradley County
ARMY
  LARRY A. BRANAM
  JAMES L. DANIEL
  WILLFORD L. DYER
  JOHNNY HICKEY
  WILLIAM L. JOHNSON
  DENVER A. LONGWITH JR.
  JOHN R. MUNGER
  JAMES K. PARKER
  DENNIS M. POTEET
  JIMMY R. WOLFE

Campbell County
ARMY
  RONNIE J. DAUGHERTY
  WILLIAM D. DAUGHERTY
  ERNEST GIBSON
  LONNIE L. GIBSON
  GEORGE G. HEATHERLY
  ROBERT J. HUDDLESTON
  MARVIN D. LAMBDIN
  JOHN E. LAY
  BILL B. LONG
  EARNEST L. LOWE
  REECE L. MARPLE
  DICKIE W. REAGAN
  CLAUDE D. REID
  LONNIE J. ROBBINS
  ARLIE SPENCER JR.
  DANIEL E. WALDEN

MARINE CORPS
JAMES W. HUNLEY
ROGER M. LAY

UNKNOWN
JERRY E. PERKINS
CARL L. RUSSELL

Carter County
ARMY
JAMES M. CORNETT
JAMES D. DUGGER JR.
BILLY J. ELLIS
JAMES C. GILBERT
WILLIAM L. GREENWELL
FREDDIE R. GUINN
FLOYD S. HARMON
JOHN P. ISAACS
LARRY J. LYONS
JAMES H. MARKLAND
GARY D. MURRAY
HERMAN H. PAYNE
ELBERT F. PRICE JR.
SAM E. STOUT
CLIFFORD M. TAYLOR
THOMAS C. TREADWAY
ROY H. WILSON
ALLEN L. WINTERS

MARINE CORPS
JOHN P. AVERY
ROBERT L. SHAFFER
WILLIAM J. WILLIAMS

AIR FORCE
CHARLES E. FULTON
DALE A. JOHNSON
HERBERT A. KEHRLI

Claiborne County
ARMY
LEON E. BARNARD
THOMAS A. BARRETT
JESSE L. ELLIS
KARL W. LAWSON
CHARLES M. LEONARD
DON SMITH
RAY TAYLOR
JAMES W. TUTTLE

AIR FORCE
ROBERT B. JOHNSON
LARRY D. LOVE

Cocke County
ARMY
CARL EALY

LEN M. JENKINS
DANIEL J. MCMAHAN
THOMAS H. MESSER

NAVY
MICHAEL G. GIBBS

MARINE CORPS
CHARLES R. RAINES
CHARLES C. ROBERTS

Cumberland County
ARMY
JOE D. BROWN
SEAN P. DODSON
FREDERICK A. HASSLER
JESSE B. HAYES
LYNN C. HAYES
NELSON P. HENRY
JOHNNY A. LEE
THEODORE TAYLOR JR.

NAVY
JERRY B. EDMONDS JR.

MARINE CORPS
ALLAN L. ELMORE
WILLIAM H. ELMORE JR.
JACK L. SUTTON
MOSES C. TABOR
TROY T. THREET

AIR FORCE
BERYL S. BLAYLOCK
ELIJAH G. TOLLETT IV

Fentress County
ARMY
BOBBY R. BROWN
JERRY A. CAMPBELL
DAVID A. CRABTREE
LARRY T. OWENS
OSWALD C. SOUTH JR.
WILLIAM O. VAUGHN

NAVY
GEORGE R. CRABTREE

MARINE CORPS
GASPER A. VOILES

Grainger County
ARMY
JOHN L. MATTOCK
MACEY L. RUCKER

Greene County
ARMY
ROBERT L. ALEXANDER
CHARLES H. AYRES
WILLIAM CUTSHAW
DONALD J. FILLERS
PHILIP R. FINK
JIMMY R. HARRISON
BOBBY E. HUNT
WILLIAM F. MALONE
CHARLES O. NEAL
HARVEY L. PROFFITT JR.
FRANK T. SHELTON
HAROLD C. STILLS
DONNIE J. SWATSELL
OLIVER N. THOMPSON

MARINE CORPS
JAMES O. JAYNES
RONALD H. JUSTIS
JAMES D. KELLEY
ROBERT MASON
RAE K. RIPPETOE

Hamblen County
ARMY
JON A. ALLEN
JIMMY D. COURTNEY
ARTHUR W. GLOVER
STEVEN J. POPKIN
BOBBY J. QUINN
WILLIAM B. REAMS JR.
ROY E. SOUTHERLAND
CHESTER W. WILSON

MARINE CORPS
G. MICHAEL COUCH
CHESTER A. MOLLEY

Hamilton County
ARMY
BRUCE E. ARMSTRONG
WILLARD D. ARNOLD
TIMOTHY H. ARTMAN
JAMES H. BASS JR.
WADE L. BROOME
RONDAL L. BURNS
WILLIAM L. BYRD
RAYMOND G. CLARK
BILLY B. DAY
WILLIE W. DAVE JR.
RONALD L. DELONG
CARL C. DEVORE
BILLY R. FARRIOR
CALVIN FIELDER
LONNIE A. FLOYD
WILL L. D. FOWLER

HARRY B. FRANK JR.
JESSIE J. GARTH
JIMMY R. GRIFFIN
ROBERT E. GUTHRIE
ROBERT E. L. HAMILTON
ROY G. HARRIS JR.
JOHN W. HAYNES
HAROLD C. HEDDEN JR.
MANUEL A. HICKS JR.
RANDALL L. HIXSON
MELVIN T. HUFFINE
DANNY L. JOHNSON
EMANUEL JONES JR.
LARRY C. JORDAN
JAMES K. KEITH III
GLENN H. KELLEY
VIRGIL KIRKLAND JR.
THOMAS E. LAYNE JR.
LARRY D. LEAMON
MARVIN E. LIVELY
RAYFON LOFTON
FREDDIE L. LONG
ROBERT LOONEY
GEORGE W. MARTIN
WILLIAM H. MARTIN
THOMAS W. MATTHEWS JR.
ROBERT L. MCARTHUR
HOMER L. MEDLEY
RAPHNELL J. MERONEY
JOHN M. MIZELLE
DANIEL E. NELMS
WALTER W. NUNLEY JR.
HOWARD P. PETTY
SAMUEL H. PIERCE JR.
ROBERT E. POE
JOHN R. PRINCE
DONALD I. PRINGLE
JOE D. RAMEY
WILLIAM D. REVIS SR.
JOHN A. ROGERS
CARLTON ROSS
WILLIE SHELTON
THOMAS F. SHIPLEY
JOSEPH W. SHORT
KENNETH E. SHRUM
GORDON R. SKYLES
CHARLES E. SMITH JR.
KENNETH L. STANCIL
THOMAS A. STEPHENS
JAMES D. SWINDELL
CHARLES J. SWINT
RUDOLPH SWOOPE
CLIFTON TANKSLEY
BELINDA S. TAYLOR
GEORGE D. TAYLOR
TOMAS C. TUCKER
ROGER C. VIPOND

JAMES F. WATSON
LANCE D. WORKMAN

NAVY
NATHAN L. INGLE
S. RUSSELL MCGEE III
JAMES G. NASH
DAVID G. PETTY
JOHN C. PODY III

MARINE CORPS
JERRY L. BELL
BILLY J. BENNETT
JAMES A. BENTON
JEFFERSON C. CHESNUTT
A. JACKIE DUCKETT
JOHN P. ELLIS
GEORGE A. ESSARY
JAMES D. FINNEY
AUGUSTO J. GARCIA
FRED S. LEA
ROBERT T. MCJUNKIN
GEORGE E. NAYLOR
SAMMY G. PATTERSON
WILLIAM L. PEMBERTON
WILLIAM H. PLESS
FRANKLIN D. RATLIFF
JOHN D. REYNOLDS
TOMMY L. TAYLOR
JOHN A. TEMPLETON
HAYWOOD W. TIPSY JR.
THOMAS C. TUCKER
JOHNNIE L. VAUGHT JR.
JOHN H. WALKER JR.
RONNEL L. WAUGH
DAVIS T. WEBSTER
RONALD L. WRIGHT
DARYL M. YOKELY

AIR FORCE
DONALD F. CASEY
CARL S. CROSS
WAYNE E. FULLAM
JAMES T. GRAY
LESLIE E. HARRIS JR.
SAMUEL L. JAMES
C. PARKS MCCALL
WILLIAM T. MCPHAIL
ARTHUR E. NORMAN
LAWRENCE B. TATUM
ROBERT D. TUCKER

UNKNOWN
LAVERNE EAST
NORMAN M. HUFFINE

Hancock County
ARMY
JAMES C. HELTON
LARRY L. SEXTON

Hawkins County
ARMY
THOMAS D. BERNARD
CONLEY A. BRADSHAW
BILLY R. COURTNEY
GALE V. CRAWFORD
FREDDIE D. FORD
LUTHER V. GILREATH
ELGIE G. HANNA
THOMAS A. LAWSON
JAMES P. RICHARDS
GARY S. ROWLETT
DAVID P. SPEARS

MARINE CORPS
DON E. ALLEY
ROY M. BROOKS
GARY M. CARTER
THOMAS G. RICHMOND

Jefferson County
ARMY
MACK L. FRANCE JR.
JAMES R. RAINWATER
JOHN W. WATKINS

MARINE CORPS
W. LARRY MOTT
JAMES A. RUSSELL III

AIR FORCE
RONALD H. KNIGHT

Johnson County
ARMY
TONY L. GRIFFITH
RONALD R. KING
MICHAEL P. OLIVER
DALLAS D. ROBINSON
EDSEL W. STEAGALL

MARINE CORPS
WORLEY W. HALL
DONALD T. SLUDER

Knox County
ARMY
LEEVERNE R. ACHOE
JOHN B. BALITSARIS
LARRY W. BARNARD
WILLIAM B. BISHOP II
WILLIAM A. BLACKBURN

LARRY G. BRADLEY
JAMES A. BRADY SR.
FREDERICK P. BROYLES
JAMES E. BYRD JR.
WARREN D. CAMPBELL
BENJAMIN V. CHILDRESS JR.
GEORGE E. CLARK JR.
JESSE J. COFFEY
STERLING E. COX
JAMES W. DIAL
JAMES M. DICKEY
WILLIAM W. FORD
LENNIS C. GENTRY
THOMAS H. GOODMAN JR.
ALBERT R. HANKINS
VERNON L. HEADRICK
LEONARD T. HIGDON
RAYMOND L. HILL
STEPHEN J. HUSKEY
LENNIS G. JONES JR.
THOMAS M. KENNEDY
ROBERT H. LANE JR.
WAYNE T. LONG
PAUL E. MAPLES
JIMMY A. MARCUM
DAVID H. MARINE
ROBERT L. MCCARTER
JAMES R. MCNISH
C. EDWARD MERRIMAN
JOHN H. MORGAN
EDWARD L. NEAL
ROBERT D. NELSON
DONALD E. NIPPER
JERRY L. NOE
BOBBY G. OLIVER
CHARLES O. REED
WILBERT REED
ANDERSON N. RENSHAW III
ALLEN H. ROBERTSON
VICTOR R. SCHEELER
WILLIAM H. SCOTT
JOHN D. SEXTON
DONALD A. SHERROD
BOYD W. SMITH
GARY D. SMITH
JERRY L. SMITH
JACKIE C. WALKER
GARY F. WALLACE
JAMES H. WATSON
ALVIN E. WILES
JAMES S. YODER

NAVY
TOMMY E. HILL
ROBERT L. LANE
THOMAS L. MCCARTER

JAMES C. NEWMAN JR.
ROGER M. SMELSER

MARINE CORPS
DAN S. ALLEN
BRUCE W. BLAKELY
GARLAND C. BOBBITT
HAROLD G. CURTIS
WILLIE F. DAIL JR.
MICHAEL D. DAWSON
BILLY J. HARRISON
RAY A. HAYES
SAM R. JONES
GERALD E. KING
DONALD R. LUMLEY
JAMES R. MCLEMORE
ROBERT A. MCLOUGHLIN JR.
CHARLES H. PILKINGTON JR.
ROBERT L. ROEBUCK
JOHN R. RUGGLES III
ROBERT W. SAUNDERS
JAMES D. TRAVIS JR.
JOHN W. VAN SANT
RODGER A. VANDERGRIFF
THOMAS A. VARNER JR.
JERRY L. WEAVER
DAVID S. WHITMAN
LABON R. WILLIAMS
CHARLES W. WOOLIVER
MELVIN R. WRIGHT

AIR FORCE
MICHAEL R. CONNER
PAUL L. FOSTER
WAYNE MONEYMAKER
ROY D. PRATER
FREDERICK M. RADER III

Loudon County
ARMY
WILLIAM E. BRIDGES JR.
BENNY C. BURNS
HARVEY C. CRABTREE JR.
DENNIS T. HAYWORTH
DANNY E. KING
H. ALLEN LOVE
JOHN E. MCCARRELL
CARL PARTON
MITCHELL W. STOUT
JAMES G. SUITS
MARION F. WALDEN JR.
JOHN W. WILSON

NAVY
HUBERT TUCK JR.

MARINE CORPS
LARRY E. FOSTER
JOHN H. SIMPSON
SCOTT W. THORNBURG
LARRY D. WEBB

AIR FORCE
JAMES C. KROUSE

UNKNOWN
RICKEY M. THOMAS

Marion County
ARMY
PAUL P. CABE
BILLY DODSON
BOBBY G. GAMBLE
BILLY J. KENNEDY
GARY B. KILGORE
DILLARD R. LAYNE
JOHN D. MARTIN
RONALD D. MELTON
GARY E. PERKINS
CHARLES A. RAULSTON
GLEN H. ROLLINS
TERRY WELCH
JAMES K. WOODARD

MARINE CORPS
HUGH S. LASTER
CLIFTON MOSES

AIR FORCE
EDWARD R. SITZ

McMinn County
ARMY
CLUSTER L. BEARFIELD
RONNIE F. BRANAM
JEROME A. BROWDER JR.
JAMES D. CASTEEL
HERSHEL L. GOSSETT
FREDDY GREENE
JOSEPH V. MARTIN
CHARLES T. OWEN
JOE A. REED
DANNY R. ROBERTS
FREDDIE M. SHERLIN

MARINE CORPS
JOSEPH O. CLINE III
GERALD T. DOBBS
LARRY R. HARRIS
EDWARD G. SHARPE

AIR FORCE
MILLARD L. BLEDSOE

Meigs County

ARMY
BILLY R. COURTNEY
JAMES T. DAVIS
HERBERT D. HORNER
LEE R. MCELHANEY
WILLIAM A. SHELTON

Monroe County

ARMY
LARRY R. ARWOO
CAREY E. BEST
JAMES A. BORDEN
J. C. DAVIS
STEVE J. DOCKERY
FREDDY L. GRAY
RON J. HAYNES
THOMAS E. LATHAM
HAROLD E. LEE
JAMES E. SELF
WINSTON O. SMITH
JAMES C. THOMASON
CLARENCE E. WATSON
TOMMY R. WILSON

Morgan County

ARMY
REXIE L. ARMES
CLARENCE E. BARNES
DAVID W. HOLMES
ROBERT A. LOVELACE
DONALD R. MATHIS
HERBERT ROBERTS JR.
DENNIS W. VAUGHN
JOHN D. WARD JR.

Polk County

ARMY
LESLIE H. CANTRELL
WALLACE A. KELL
WILLIAM A. KIMSEY JR.
HUBERT A. MEREDITH
WILLIAM D. MORROW
JEPPIE J. PAYNE
DONALD R. ROBINSON

Rhea County

ARMY
BILL J. JOHNSON
JOHNNY L. PELFREY
RANDALL E. PERRY
JAMES R. POTTER

MARINE CORPS
JACKIE K. REED
DAVID SMITH

AIR FORCE
ROY L. MAYNOR

Roane County

ARMY
JAMES E. CUNNINGHAM
JERRY R. FERGUSON
ALVIN F. GUNTER
EVERETT W. JOHNSON JR.
JAMES W. KNIGHT
ALBERT A. LADD
JERRY A. MCFALLS
DON M. O'SHELL
RICHARD L. PATTERSON
ESTEL D. SPAKES
RALPH R. SPRINGS JR.
WILLIAM O. STEED
DAVID W. STOUT
BRADLEY K. WATTS

NAVY
MICHAEL L. FERGUSON
BILLY W. MCGHEE

MARINE CORPS
DAVID L. BELL
CHARLES D. STRINGFIELD

Scott County

ARMY
RALPH BYRD
WILLIAM L. COFFEY
DOYLE FOSTER
JOE E. GRIFFITH
PHILLIP E. IRELAND
TOMMIE KEETON
DONALD E. MADDEN

MARINE CORPS
JAMES L. CHAMBERS
MICHAEL D. TERRY
DENNY L. WASHAM
JAMES D. WEST

Sequatchie County

ARMY
WALTER L. CLARK
GORDON R. SKYLES

MARINE CORPS
DOVER L. LOCKHART

Sevier County

ARMY
CARROLL D. ABBOTT
DANNIE A. CARR
RANDY R. COGDILL
HOBART E. COVINGTON
GARY R. FOX
ALTON L. HORNBUCKLE
MICHAEL C. VICKERY

NAVY
HARRY G. HODGES

MARINE CORPS
THOMAS G. GAINES
ESTEL HUSKEY
JERRY MCCARTER

AIR FORCE
EDDIE MANIS

Sullivan County

ARMY
JESSE H. ARCHER
DAVID W. BARNETT
KARL A. BROWN
JASPER D. CLARDY
JOHN W. DINGUS JR.
DONALD F. FLETCHER
DAVID L. HANN
MICHAEL E. HARR
JIMMY L. HENRY
HERBERT D. HORNER
LAWRENCE J. HUMPHREY
JIMMY L. JONES
KENNETH E. LOCKHART
GEORGE W. MCREYNOLDS
ROY W. NEAL
WILLIAM G. POOLE III
ROBERT G. PRICE
JAMES E. REED
FRED L. RICHARDSON
DENNIS W. SMITH
CARL C. SPANGLER
ROBERT B. STAFFORD
JAMES L. TARTE
STEPHEN J. TORBETT
DOUGLAS B. WADE
DAVID C. WILLIAMS
GARRY L. WORLEY

NAVY
JACK E. LUNTSFORD

MARINE CORPS
ADRIAN L. ALLEN
CHARLES H. DUTY
WILLIAM F. DYKES
DANIEL L. GREGG
CHESTER S. HUGHES
CHARLES M. MCKINNEY
JOSEPH L. MEADE
WILLARD F. MORELOCK
WILLIAM J. ROBERTS
RANDALL D. YEARY

Unicoi County
ARMY
DONALD R. COOK
DAVID L. EDNEY
DONALD L. GRUBB
BOBBY G. HAYNES
DOYLE HOLCOMB
DOUGLAS L. JONES
JOHNNY W. OGLE
BOBBY J. SHELTON
EUGENE W. WILSON

MARINE CORPS
RICHARD W. BANNISTER
JAMES J. BRITT
MICHAEL TOLLEY
ALLEN E. WHITE

Union County
ARMY
GARRY K. COOK
DONNIE L. DAMEWOOD

Washington County
ARMY
HAROLD G. AYERS
NILON K. BACON
ALVIN K. BROYLES JR.
DARYL C. CULVER
GARY A. CURTIS
LARRY G. CURTIS
DANNY M. ERWIN
CHARLES J. FORD
EUGENE D. FRANKLIN
CHARLES H. GOBBLE
JOHN A. HARLAN
ARTHUR G. HENSLEY
KENNETH R. HODGE
ROBERT G. HODGES
JAMES E. HYLMON
CECIL B. JONES JR.
RAY M. K. JONES
HAROLD B. KING
FLOYD W. LAMB JR.
BENNIE E. MCCORKLE
FULTON B. MOORE III
BILLY J. NAVE

HOMER L. PEASE
MICHAEL D. RIDDLE
ALLEN T. ROGERS JR.
HOBERT T. ROLLINS
MARVIN SHELL
THOMAS D. SNYDER
HARRY R. STEWART
EDDIE B. STORY
GARY L. TINKER
THOMAS W. TRUELOVE
GORDON O. WALSH

MARINE CORPS
JAMES D. BOWERS
KIRBY W. BRADFORD
KENNETH L. HINNANT
ARNOLD B. JACKSON
ANDREW M. LARSON
JAMES H. LEDFORD
LARRY D. MILHORN
JOHN E. WEST JR.
DORSEY B. WILLIAMS
HAROLD W. WILSON
EARNEST L. WITT

AIR FORCE
JAMES E. BOWMAN
LOUIS R. TAYLOR

PERSIAN GULF

Hamblen County
ARMY
JOHN B. STEPHENS

McMinn County
ARMY
JAMES D. TATUM

Washington County
ARMY
DANIEL E. GRAYBEAL

AIR FORCE
JAMES B. MAY II

IRAQ

Anderson County
ARMY
JAMES D. CONNELL JR.
STEPHEN C. KENNEDY
DANIEL M. MORRIS

Blount County
ARMY
WILLAM M. BENNETT

MARINE CORPS
MICHAEL H. FERSCHKE JR.

Bradley County
ARMY
JAMES W. PRICE
DAVID T. WEIR

Carter County
ARMY
STEPHEN R. MADDIES

MARINE CORPS
J. TRANE MCCLOUD

Campbell County
ARMY
GREGORY B. HICKS
ALFRED B. SILER

Claiborne County
ARMY
TERRY W. PRATER

Cumberland County
MARINE CORPS
   STEPHEN F. DEARMON
   MORGAN W. STRADER
   GREENE COUNTY
   BRANDON M. READ

Hamilton County
ARMY
   TRAVIS F. HASLIP
   JAMES D. STEWART
   JOHN M. SULLIVAN

Knox County
ARMY
   MARCUS R. ALFORD SR.
   ERIC A. FIFER
   CHRISTOPHER T. FOX
   G. DANIEL HARRISON
   WILLIAM A. LONG
   MICHAEL L. MCNULTY

   MICHAEL J. RODRIGUEZ
   LUKE C. WILLIAMS

NAVY
   DANIEL K. LEONARD
   CHRISTOPHER E. WATTS

Loudon County
MARINE CORPS
   WILLIAM C. KOPRINCE JR.

Monroe County
ARMY
   RYAN E. HAUPT
   JOSEPH D. HUNT

Scott County
MARINE CORPS
   RUSTY L. WASHAM

Sevier County
ARMY
   VICTOIR P. LIEURANCE
   PAUL W. THOMASON III

Sullivan County
ARMY
   ALEXANDER S. COULTER
   ROBBIE G. LIGHT

MARINE CORPS
   MICHAEL R. SPEER

Unicoi County
ARMY
   MARK O. EDWARDS

Washington County
ARMY
   DAVID L. POTTER

AFGHANISTAN

Anderson County
ARMY
   JASON D. HOVATER
   CHRISTOPHER M. WARD

Blount County
ARMY
   TRAVIS W. NIXON

Carter County
ARMY
   JEFFERSON D. DAVIS

Cumberland County
ARMY
   ALEX VAN AALTEN

Greene County
ARMY
   RUSTY H. CHRISTIAN

Hamilton County
ARMY
   PATRICK K. DURHAM

Johnson County
ARMY
   FREDERICK Z. GREENE

Knox County
ARMY
   JONATHAN M. CURTIS
   PATRICK S. FITZGIBBON
   CARLOS M. SANTOS-SILVA
   T. CHANCE YOUNG

MARINE CORPS
   KRISTOPHER D. GREER

AIR FORCE
   FRANK D. BRYANT JR.
   TRE F. PORFIRIO

McMinn County
ARMY
   NATHAN E. LILLARD

Monroe County
ARMY
   ROBERT K. REPKIE

MARINE CORPS
   FRANKLIN N. WATSON

Sevier County
ARMY
   ZACHARY S. SALMON

Sullivan County
ARMY
   JASON O.B. HICKMAN

Unicoi County
AIR FORCE
   BENJAMIN D. WHITE

OTHER MILITARY OPERATIONS

Blount County
AIR FORCE
- MICHAEL S. CARPENTER
- PRESTON E. PRESLEY
- JAMES W. RIDOUT III
- EDWARD J. SCHULTZ

Hamilton County
MARINE CORPS
- DAVID A. WYATT

NAVY
- RANDALL S. SMITH

Knox County
ARMY
- H. LENN BLEVINS
- ROBERT E. BRANNUM
- DANIEL E. COLE
- GLEN M. HAYNES
- THOMAS J. WILLIAMS JR.

NAVY
- CARTER M. DEAN

AIR FORCE
- CHARLES T. MCMILLAN II

McMinn County
ARMY
- JERRY L. HANEY

Rhea County
ARMY
- RICHARD H. THURMAN

AFTERWORD

The Sorrow, the Pity, and the Lasting Memories of War

Dear God, let us exchange our memories—
I will recall the beginning, you will remember the end.

—*Abraham Sutzkever*

Among the shared threads of war and remembrance across all conflicts, the most poignant has to be the ongoing, enduring sense of loss, and the void so often experienced by family, friends, and loved ones of those fallen in military service. These sentiments transcend place, generation, and time, and they are certainly not unique to Americans or East Tennesseans, although each person's memory and senses of pain and absence are, clearly, individually held and keenly felt. This comes across very strongly in reading the postings on the Veterans Memorial's website, which has come to be a place for family, friends, "battle buddies," and loved ones to leave their memories and condolences for so many of East Tennessee's military dead.

Although space must limit the authors' ability to capture in this book each of those recollections and tributes—many of them extremely heart-rending—for the over 6,200 men and women memorialized on the Veterans Memorial, this afterword is intended to capture and reflect something of the ongoing sensations of love, loss, and "time ripped out of time" experienced to the present day by many, including children and relatives not yet born at the time the serviceman perished. Accordingly, these are—and can be—merely samples. The reader is encouraged to visit the ETVMA website for more condolences, reminiscences, and memories for so many others of East Tennessee's fallen service members.

Brenda Korner-Carey's father described to her his buddy Marshall E. Masterson's death on January 9, 1945, at Elsenborn Ridge during the Battle of the Bulge. In providing her father's account to the ETVMA, Ms. Korner-Cary included his response when she told him of her plans: "This morning, I told him what I had done in researching Marshall, and that I had contacted [the ETVMA]. He actually smiled and approved of my action. He said, 'Marshall, my dear friend . . . he was a good soldier.' It broke my heart because of the pain that he has held in. Not wanting to share his experience, even with other soldiers. This is so rare for him to even utter Marshall's name, out of reverence to this young man. . . . I think it is doing [my father] good to see that Marshall is in a place where he is being cared for and honored."

Winston H. Watson of Madisonville, lost in the USS *Indianapolis*' sinking so near the Second World War's end, was fondly remembered by his sister, Mrs. Clyde T. Atkins: "He professed faith in Christ at an early age and joined the Notchey Creek Baptist Church. He always loved his church, and Sunday School. He was a Christian, honest, kind and true. . . . He was a good husband, a true father, a real son and brother."

Jack Sherrod, the brother of Specialist Fourth Class Donald A. Sherrod who was killed on August 8, 1966, near LZ Juliet in the Ia Drang Valley, wrote on what would have been his brother's 67th birthday in 2010: "My brother was awarded the Silver Star for the action where he died, and he got the Bronze Star with the 'V' device, and, of course, the Purple Heart. I have the awards and citations that came along with them as well as the flag that draped his coffin. He was a guy who could be very funny, and our family got many laughs from his antics. It took many years experiencing life to fully understand what he gave up and what so many others sacrificed. . . . When my brother died, part of my mom died also, and she was proud to be his mom—she died in 1994."

The following is from former Marine Neil Wilson, as sent to the ETVMA in 2001, about his friend and "battle buddy" Sergeant Fletcher M. Seeber Jr., killed in action on June 21, 1967:

Many years later, I was told by his brother that Fletcher had related to his sister that he somehow felt obligated to go to Vietnam with the young Marines that he had been training for the past year. In any case we changed subjects and within a matter of days I received orders to the Philippines

for an eighteen-month tour. I lost contact with Fletcher and I assumed that he had gotten out in June 1967 when his enlistment was up. On [June 22], 1967, I got a copy of the *Pacific Stars and Stripes* newspaper and glanced quickly at the front page where they listed the deaths in Vietnam by state and hometown. Oliver Springs, Tennessee, leapt from the page. Even now, nearly thirty-four years later, I can still remember the eerie realization that I knew the name of the person without having to look. I did not look. I threw the paper on my bunk and walked outside for an hour or so. When I came back, I picked it back up and sure enough it read: Sergeant Fletcher M. Seeber, Jr., killed on June 21, 1967. Marines do cry. . . .

In Alaska, his brother Kenneth, who was serving in the Air Force, was told of the death of his brother. His unit leader told him not to wait for the Red Cross request but to hop a cargo plane coming through later that night heading for Dover, Delaware. When Kenneth got on board the giant plane, he and the loadmaster were the only two people in the large cargo bay. After take-off, when Kenneth got up to stretch, he glanced to the rear of the cargo bay. It was then he noticed all of the boxes. There was no mistaking what they were. They were aluminum containers used to transport the dead military personal back to the United States from Vietnam. He strolled slowly back to them, and he noticed they all had tags attached to them. When he got to the first one, he slowly reached out and moved the tag to where he could read what was written on it. The name at the top read *Sgt. Fletcher M. Seeber, USMC*. The loadmaster walked back and asked him if he was okay. Kenneth turned and softly replied: "This is my brother." The airman said, "I'm sorry, take all the time you need." So, for part of his final journey home, Fletcher was not alone.

322

Fletcher's final resting place is very near where he was born in Frost Bottom. He rests between his mother and father and near his brother Jerry. Jerry followed his brother into the Marine Corps after Fletcher's death. He would also serve in Vietnam in a Marine heavy artillery battery. He died of a heart attack in 2000. There are no monuments to Fletcher in his hometown. No bridges carry his name. . . . Nothing at or near the high school football field where he was the captain of his team bears witness to his sacrifice.

The following tribute to Corporal Augusto J. (Jose) Garcia, killed on July 17, 1968, in South Vietnam, is from Cristy Garcia McDaniel, his daughter: "My Dad met my mother while attending Tennessee Tech University. . . . He majored in and loved music and the arts. He was killed just weeks before he was scheduled to come home. I never got the privilege of meeting him, but I know he would have been a wonderful father and he has been my guardian angel for the past 31 years. Thanks, Dad. Love, Cristy."

Garcia's nephew, Jose Agustin Mendez Garcia, added: "My uncle, although a long-time resident of Tennessee, was in fact born and raised in Puerto Rico. He left behind a wife and a daughter, as well as both his parents, two brothers, a sister (my mother), and a host of other loved ones. He was well loved and is well remembered by us all. May he rest in peace."

And, Michael Brown, Garcia's college roommate, recalled his dear friend in a posting sent to the ETVMA on a Veterans Day: "Jose was one of my college roommates and close friends. We were music majors together at Tennessee Tech. His funeral was the day following my wedding. What a graphic example of the price of freedom Jose and so many others paid.

I will always treasure my memories of him as a gentle and kind young man with a great sense of humor and a heart of gold. On this Veterans Day, I pause to remember and give thanks."

Shirley Bowman Kelly, the widow of Air Force Staff Sergeant James E. Bowman, killed on May 5, 1968, in the crash of his AC-47 "Spooky" near Pleiku, provided the following in his memory:

Today, May 5, 2008, marks the 40th anniversary of my husband's death. . . . I still get cold chills writing these words! For a very long time, I could not speak of this event when I met new people nor read a written word about this country and this horror of war which devoured mine and my children's lives. . . . He was 34 years old, career Air Force and the father of two lovely daughters, ages 9 and 13. We were high school sweethearts. He was the most popular boy in our small high school, the team's star quarterback and everyone's friend. He was his parents' only child, his grandmother's favorite grandson. He had been in Viet Nam four months, when his plane was shot down. His parents, grandparents and family are all gone now, as well as my family. Our daughters are grown up and some how we have managed to go on, but we have never forgotten, nor has his memory dimmed in our hearts.

Bowman's daughter, Kitty Holt, shared the following memories of Bowman:

Although my father was taken away from me [when I was] at the tender age of 12, I have never forgotten him nor the morals that he instilled in myself and my sister, Connie. We used to love going fishing at Watauga Lake until the early morning. Mom would fuss at him for bringing me home so late. I always loved doing things with my dad. When my family traveled I would sit behind my dad and would call him my angel. I know in my heart that he is with me every day and is very proud of me and my sister. I have missed him every single day since May 5, 1968. James E. Bowman was a great soldier, a loving father and a wonderful husband.

David L. Summers wrote this about his Army comrade Sergeant Joseph A. Oreto, who fell in Tay Ninh, South Vietnam, on April 13, 1969:

Tony arrived in the platoon late in 1968 and was assigned to the 4th squad [of the Aerorifle Platoon, or "ARP," a helicopter-borne infantry platoon]. On missions, this platoon consisted of 28 soldiers, and in many cases less. The ARPs would engage the enemy in combat and cut off all routes of escape. They would do snatch missions, bomb damage assessments, and rescue downed pilots. Tony was a first-class individual, with a great sense of humor that manifested itself in the toughest of times. He was dedicated to his fellow soldiers and was a consummate leader. His call sign was *Raider 64*. For 33 years, I have wanted to contact his family and tell them about Tony in this period of his life. I feel blessed to have known him and feel that with his death the world was deprived of one of its finest men.

Debra Wheeler Marion, one of six children and the eldest daughter of Staff Sergeant Gordon L. Wheeler, who was killed on March 8, 1969, in Quang Tri, Vietnam, fondly remembered her father:

Wow, it seems like a lifetime since I heard of your death. I still remember seeing the military car driving up to the house, and I remember asking Mom what [they were] doing. I remember it as if it happened yesterday. All of your children are now grown, and most of us have our own children and grandchildren. Mom passed away in June of 2001, and I miss her too! I think of you often and think that the younger children would have benefited so much if they could have known you . . . they only have memories from a made-up father. I have tried to tell

them over the years that we had some good times together as a family and that you were a great father at those times. . . .

Several of us older children visited Tennessee a couple of years ago and were able to visit your sister, Margie. She has since passed away. I was very surprised this year when I received a package in the mail and Sissy, Margie's daughter, had mailed me pictures of you as a young boy. I truly enjoyed seeing you in those happy, carefree times. I'll always love you, and miss you, Dad.

The family of Army Specialist G. Daniel Harrison, killed in action on December 2, 2004, provided the following: "He will always be our hero. . . . Daniel, our first-born son, was very precious to us. When Daniel was just a few weeks old, he learned to smile—an infectious smile that stayed with him throughout his life. It was a smile that will always be engraved on our hearts. Daniel's enthusiasm and love for life touched many people. Daniel's death is an inconceivable loss to our family. However, this loss strengthens the bond of love we feel for each of you. The Word of God tells us in John 15:13, 'Greater love hath no man than this, than a man lay down his life for his friends.'"

The mother of Joseph D. Hunt of Monroe County, killed in Iraq on August 22, 2005, recalled her lost son: "Joey Hunt, as he is remembered by us, was our oldest child. He lived in Sweetwater all his life. He loved sports of any kind and the outdoors. He leaves behind two beautiful little boys. . . . When he was called upon to go to war, he went gladly, eager to serve his country. He related many stories to us about his time in Iraq and kept in touch as often as possible. Just a few weeks from coming home, his Humvee was hit by a roadside bomb. He was much loved and is greatly missed by all who knew him."

Kathleen Ann Hovater, the mother of Corporal Jason Hovater who fell in action on

July 13, 2008, at Wanat, Afghanistan, remembered her son

> as a man of God, a psalmist of the Lord. His presence when he entered a room was unmistakable. All attention would land on him. He was taught piano at age five. His dad showed him three chords, and the boy literally took off playing music. One fond memory was after watching the movie "Robin Hood" with Kevin Costner, Brian Adams came on and played "(Everything I Do) I Do It for You," and Jason ran to the piano and played the song from memory in its entirety. He could hear a piece one time and play it from memory. He gave his life for his country. But he could have been more effective setting "creation free" with his songs of life to the Lord. . . . He was a joy to all who knew him. He had a great sense of humor. We choose to see him through God's eyes playing on the best praise team ever with a great cloud of witnesses!

Each of these recollections is, of course, just a microcosm of the wellspring of feelings and remembrances held by so many across East Tennessee and this nation. The ETVMA is enormously grateful for the contributions and sharing of reminiscences—many deeply personal—of so many who have added their memories and condolences to the memorial's website over the years.

The ETVMA and the authors acknowledge, with the deepest gratitude, each of these contributions, and the families, friends, service buddies, and loved ones who sustained and nurtured for so long the lives and souls recounted in this book.

Soldier, rest! thy warfare o'er,

Dream of fighting fields no more;

Sleep the sleep that knows not breaking,

Morn of toil, nor night of waking.

—*Sir Walter Scott, "Soldier Rest! Thy Warfare O'er"*

The bugle never more will blow

Across the camping ground.

And men for welcome mail from home

Will never crowd around.

It is silent now. No guns are heard

The war for them has fled.

And now they are immortal:

The battalion of the dead.

And each of these mute crosses

Is a symbol, stark and white,

Of hopes, of plans and treasured dreams,

Which now have taken flight.

Out to the blue horizon stretch

The rows in solemn state.

And join the shafts of sunlight

Stretching up to heaven's gate.

They died because they know that man

Was destined to be free.

And freedom's price is often death,

Men far beyond the sea,

So there they lie, as heaven paints,

With cosmic bars of red,

That silent final camp of

The battalion of the dead.

—*Army Corporal O. Arthur Hertel, "The Battalion of the Dead,"*
written while serving in France during World War II

NOTES

PREFACE

1. See Chapter 5.
2. See www.fold3.com (last accessed June 27, 2018).

ACKNOWLEDGMENTS

1. Readers can visit the ETVMA's website at www.etvma.org.
2. Available at www.wbir.com/local/service-and-sacrifice (last accessed June 27, 2018).

1. UNCOMMON VALOR

1. Each of the Medal of Honor citations provided in this chapter may be accessed from the official website of the Congressional Medal of Honor Society, www.cmohs.org; and from the US Army Center of Military History website, http://www.history.army.mil/moh/ (both accessed on June 27, 2018). See also Committee of Veterans Affairs, US Senate, *Medal of Honor Recipients, 1863–1978*, 96th Cong., 1st Sess., February 14, 1979, available at https://www.fold3.com/image/1/310761214 (last accessed June 27, 2018).
2. Ward's postwar life has elements of tragedy that may resonate with many veterans and survivors of war. His family members have recounted that the Calvin Ward who came home from the war was not the same man who left. It is believed that he suffered from post-traumatic stress disorder (PTSD) (undiagnosed, as was common for many survivors of the Great War, in a time when medical and psychiatric care was less advanced), alcoholism, and depression, which contributed to his death in 1967—ironically on a day when his longtime friend and co-Medal of Honor recipient Buck Karnes was being honored. See John M. Jones Jr. and Kristin Buckles, "Memory Of John Calvin Ward Honored In Hawk's Resolution," *Greeneville* (TN) *Sun*, February 25, 2012, available at https://www.greenevillesun.com/news/memory-of-john-calvin-ward-honored-in-hawk-s -resolution/article_33a49b99-c1a9-5dcb-ba7e-ad20f6f353cd.html (last accessed June 27, 2018).
3. Michael E. Miller, "'Golden' Ending: How One Man Discovered His War Hero Grandfather's Long Lost Grave," Washington Post, July 2, 2015, https://www.washingtonpost.com/news/morning-mix/wp/2015/07/02/golden -ending-how-one-man-discovered-his-war-hero-grandfathers-long-lost-grave/?utm_term=.779a506b7cc5; and "Remains of WWII Medal of Honor Winner, Unidentified for 72 Years, Coming Home," *Chicago Tribune*, Sept. 24, 2015, http://www.chicagotribune.com/news/nationworld/ct-alexander-bonnyman-marine -coming-home-20150924-story.html (both accessed June 27, 2018).
4. The bloody fighting on Okinawa—resulting in 49,151 US casualties, including over 7,450 dead, versus 100,000 dead Japanese—was largely seen by America's military leadership as a precursor of what would happen when the Japanese mainland was invaded. See Joseph H. Alexander, *Storm Landings: Epic Amphibious Battles in the Central Pacific* (Annapolis, MD: Naval Institute Press, 1997), 172–92; Williamson Murray, "Armageddon Revisited," *Military History Quarterly* (Spring 1995): 6–11; Stanley L. Falk, "A Nation Reduced to Ashes," *Military History Quarterly* (Spring 1995): 54–63; Rod Paschall, "Tactical Exercises: Olympic Miscalculations," *Military History Quarterly* (Spring 1995): 62, 63; Edward J. Drea, "Previews of Hell," *Military History Quarterly* (Spring 1995): 74–81; Peter Maslowski, "Truman, The Bomb, and The Numbers Game," *Military History Quarterly* (Spring

1995): 103–7; and Thomas B. Allen & Norman Polmar, "Gassing Japan," *Military History Quarterly* (Autumn 1997): 38–43.

2. THE MEN OF THE 30TH DIVISION IN WORLD WAR I

1. For more of the history of the 30th Division and its subordinate units, to include the 117th and 119th Infantry Regiments, see Elmer A. Murphy and Robert S. Thomas, *The Thirtieth Division in the Great War* (Lepanto, AR: Old Hickory Pub. Co., 1936); Mitchell A. Yockelson, *Borrowed Soldiers: Americans Under British Command, 1918* (Norman, OK: Univ. of Oklahoma Press, 2008); and "History of Old Hickory," www.30thinfantry.org /history.shtml (last accessed June 27, 2018).
2. Nelson L. Robinson, ed., *St. Lawrence University in the World War, 1917–1918: A Memorial* (Canton, NY: St. Lawrence Univ., 1931), 110.
3. Robinson, ed., *St. Lawrence University*, 110–11.

3. EARLY MILITARY AVIATORS

1. The photo of Rockwell standing by his Nieuport 17 biplane is from the North Carolina Museum of History (Photograph, accession no. H.1947.30.2., 1916, North Carolina Museum of History).
2. Kiffin Y. Rockwell and Paul Ayres Rockwell, eds., *War Letters of Kiffin Y. Rockwell: Foreign Legion and Aviator France, 1914–1916* (Garden City, NY: Doubleday, Page and Co. Country Life Press, 1925), 70 (citing letter to his mother, September 8, 1915).
3. Charles Bracelen Flood, *First to Fly: The Story of the Lafayette Escadrille, The American Heroes Who Flew for France in World War I* (New York: Atlantic Monthly Press, 2015), 36.
4. Flood, 31–32.
5. Flood, 164.
6. Glenn Tucker, "Rockwell, Kiffin Yates," NCPedia.org, http://ncpedia.org/biography/rockwell-kiffin-yates (last accessed June 27, 2018).
7. Flood, 190.
8. Amy McCrary, "WWI Aviator Remembered in Naming of Knoxville Airport," *Knoxville* (TN) *News Sentinel*, Aug. 28, 2016, 12E.
9. McCrary, 12E.
10. Capt. Reese T. Amis, ed., *Knox County in the World War: 1917, 1918, 1919* (Knoxville, TN: Knoxville Lithographing Co., 1919), 78.
11. McCrary, 12E.
12. McCrary, 12E.
13. McCrary, 12E.

4. EAST TENNESSEANS IN WORLD WAR I AND THE GREAT INFLUENZA EPIDEMIC

1. *The American Experience: Influenza 1918*, PBS/WGBH television documentary (broadcast Jan. 2, 2018).
2. *Report of the Surgeon General, US Army, to the Secretary of War*, vols. I and II (Washington, DC: GPO, 1919); "Influenza Pandemic of 1918," US Army Medical Department, Office of Medical History, http://history .amedd.army.mil/booksdocs/wwi/1918flu/flu1918intro.htm (last accessed on June 27, 2018); David Tschanz, "Plague of the Spanish Lady," *Military History Online* (Dec. 11, 2011), http://www.militaryhistoryonline.com /wwi/articles/plagueofspanishlady.aspx (last accessed June 27, 2018).

3. Tschanz, "Plague of the Spanish Lady."

4. Appreciation is expressed to Leo York for sharing this account with the ETVMA.

5. The accompanying photo is provided courtesy of his grandnephew, Paul Smith.

6. Appreciation is expressed to Pat Kelly for sharing this account and the Henry Forte letter with the ETVMA.

5. LOST AT SEA AND IN THE AIR

1. Appreciation is expressed to the Hon. Robert P. Murrian for providing this information to the ETVMA.

2. See James E. Wise and Scott Baron, *Soldiers Lost at Sea: a Chronicle of Troopship Disasters* (Annapolis, MD: Naval Institute Press, 2003), 146–47; Rohna Survivors Memorial Association website, https://rohnasurvivors .org/the-memorial/ (last accessed June 27, 2018).

3. Excerpt from Northern Miyazaki's Nature Preservation Association Journal, "Tsuchibinoki," no. 2, *The War Is Over* ("Sobosanchu B-29 Tsuiraku Hiwa"), by Hiroshi Kudo, president of Northern Miyazaki's Nature Preservation Association (on file with the ETVMA).

4. Acknowledgment of the grave marker photo is hereby provided to Vadis Sagadraca.

5. Thomas Childers, *Wings of Morning: The Story of the Last American Bomber Shot Down Over Germany in World War II* (Reading, MA: Perseus Books, 1995), 5–8.

6. Childers, 21, 192–202, 237, 240–41, 243.

7. Childers, 203–10.

8. Childers, 3–4, 231.

9. Childers, 254; Neely Tucker, "The 10 Lost Lives of the Black Cat," Washington Post, July 30, 2005, https:// www.washingtonpost.com.

10. Tucker, "The 10 Lost Lives of the Black Cat."

11. For more, see "USS Bush—DD529" website, www.ussbush.com (last accessed June 27, 2018).

12. Appreciation is expressed to Gary Moncur for sharing this information with the ETVMA. For further information on the 303rd Bomb Group, see http://www.303rdbg.com/index.html (last accessed on July 1, 2018).

13. See Tonya Allen, "The Sinking of SS Leopoldville," U-Boat.net website, http://uboat.net/articles/21.html (last accessed June 27, 2018).

14. J. Edwin Smith, "In Search of a Memory," *Atlanta* (GA) *Weekly* (*Atlanta Journal and Atlanta Constitution*), June 21, 1987, 1, 4–7, 12–13.

15. For more on Typhoon Cobra and its consequences, see Jack Williams and Bob Sheets, *Hurricane Watch: Forecasting the Deadliest Storms on Earth* (New York: Vintage, 2001); Bob Drury and Tom Clavin, *Halsey's Typhoon: The True Story of a Fighting Admiral, an Epic Storm, and an Untold Rescue* (New York: Grove Atlantic/Atlantic Monthly Press, 2006); C. Raymond Calhoun, *Typhoon, the Other Enemy: The Third Fleet and the Pacific Storm of December 1944* (Annapolis, MD: Naval Institute Press, 1981); and Hans Christian Adamson and George Francis Kosco, *Halsey's Typhoons: A Firsthand Account of How Two Typhoons, More Powerful than the Japanese, Dealt Death and Destruction to Admiral Halsey's Third Fleet* (New York: Crown Publishers, 1967).

16. Find-a-Grave entry for General Preston Douglas, https://www.findagrave.com/memorial/23730501 /general-preston-douglas; and "Seaman 1st Class General P. Douglas, U.S. Navy, k1943," Douglas Archives, http://www.douglashistory.co.uk/history/generaldouglas.htm (both accessed June 27, 2018).

17. Earl Henry Jr., "Earl Henry Bird Prints," https://www.earlhenrybirdprints.com/about/ (last accessed June 27, 2018).

18. Henry, "Early Henry Bird Prints."

19. Sam Venable, "The 'Other' Roger Tory Peterson," *Knoxville News Sentinel*, July 29, 2012, www.knoxnews.com /news/columnists/sam-venable-the-other-roger-tory-peterson-ep-360345509–356814081.html (last accessed June 27, 2018).

20. "One Who Survived: Seaman Heyn's Story, From the Naval Archives of World War II," *American Heritage* 7, no. 4 (June 1956), http://www.americanheritage.com/content/one-who-survived (last accessed June 27, 2018).

21. Jacey Fortin, "Wreck of the Juneau is Found, 75 Years After 5 Brothers Perished," *New York Times*, Mar. 22, 2018, https://www.nytimes.com/2018/03/22/world/asia/uss-juneau-sullivan-brothers.html (last accessed June 27, 2018).

22. Paul W. Wittmer and Charles R. Hinman, "Pickerel (SS-177)," originally from "U.S. Submarine Losses World War II," NAVPERS 15,784 (1949), reprinted at www.oneternalpatrol.com/uss-pickerel-177-loss.html (last accessed June 27, 2018).

23. Randy Keener, "Holiday is Time to Remember Unsung Heroes like Dooley," *Knoxville* (Tenn.) *News Sentinel*, May 24, 1998, p. A1.

24. For more on these and other "Silent Service" losses, see the On Eternal Patrol website, http://www.oneternalpatrol.com/wwii.htm (last accessed June 27, 2018).

25. The vessel accompanying the *Grampus*, USS *Grayback*, was itself reported missing by the Navy in March 1944. Seventy-five years later, *Grayback*'s wreck was discovered off Okinawa. John Ismay, "Navy Submarine Missing Since World War II Is Found Off Okinawa," *New York Times*, Nov. 11, 2019, p. A-6.

26. For more on this battle and the fight of the *Samuel B. Roberts*, see *The Dictionary of American Fighting Ships*; James D. Hornfischer, *The Last Stand of the Tin Can Sailors: The Extraordinary World War II Story of the U.S. Navy's Finest Hour* (New York: Bantam Books, 2004); and John Wukovits, *For Crew and Country: The Inspirational True Story of Bravery and Sacrifice Aboard the USS* Samuel B. Roberts (New York: St. Martin's Press, 2013).

27. Appreciation is expressed to Weaver's family members, Ann D. Ashley, Jackie Weaver Dennison, and Betty Weaver Malone, for providing this information to co-author Jack McCall, who is related to James Kenneth Weaver by marriage.

6. PRISONERS OF WAR IN WORLD WAR II

1. "Can You Take It?," Stalag Luft I Online website, http://www.merkki.com/poetry.htm (last accessed June 27, 2018).

2. Appreciation is expressed to Dave Jones for this photograph.

3. See East Indies Camp Archives, www.indischekamparchieven.nl (last accessed June 27, 2018).

4. "Edwards Died in Jap Prison, Wife Learns," *Portsmouth* (NH) *Herald*, Oct. 30, 1945, p. 1.

5. Appreciation is expressed to his brother, Howard Clyde Thornburg, for providing this information to the ETVMA.

6. See Hampton Sides, *Ghost Soldiers: The Forgotten Epic Story of World War II's Most Dramatic Mission* (New York: Doubleday, 2001), 20; Historical Report, US Casualties and Burials at Cabanatuan POW Camp # 1, Washington, DC: Defense POW/MIA Accounting Agency, http://www.dpaa.mil/Portals/85/Documents/Reports/U.S.Casualties_Burials_Cabanatuan_POWCamp1.pdf?ver=2017-05-08-162357-013; and Suzanne Stamatov, "Cabanatuan Prisoner of War Camp-1942," NewMexicoHistory.org, http://newmexicohistory.org/people/cabanatuan-prisoner-of-war-camp-1942 (both accessed June 27, 2018.)

7. *Kingsport* (TN) *News*, July 9, 1943.

8. Lisa Beckenbaugh and Heather Harris, archival research memorandum, "Casualties of the Philippines POW Camps, O'Donnell and Cabanatuan and the History of their Burials," Defense Prisoner of War/Missing Personnel Office, Oct. 13, 2005 (revised Mar. 2, 2010), p. 3, http://www.historicfarnam.us/cemetery/images/Cabanatuan_History.pdf (last accessed June 27, 2018).

9. Sides, *Ghost Soldiers*, 7–17; V. Dennis Wrynn, "American Prisoners of War: Massacre at Palawan," *World War II Magazine* (Nov. 1997), www.historynet.com/american-prisoners-of-war-massacre-at-palawan.htm (last accessed June 27, 2018).

10. Appreciation is expressed to his sister, Fern M. Lavind, for providing this information to the ETVMA.
11. Appreciation is expressed to his nephews, Harold L. Badgette Jr. and Lennon K. Badgette, for providing their contributions to the ETVMA for this account.

7. THE GIs' GREAT CRUSADE IN EUROPE

1. Appreciation is expressed to family member Wendell Harkleroad for providing this information to the ETVMA.
2. Interview with Benjamin C. Franklin, November 19, 2004, Veterans Oral History Project, Center for the Study of War and Society, University of Tennessee (on file with the ETVMA).
3. Fred Brown, "Son Excited to Honor Father He Never Knew," *Knoxville* (TN) *News Sentinel*, Sept. 9, 2006, p.1
4. See "Paratroopers of the 505th Parachute Infantry Regiment: This Page Is Dedicated to Francis X. Schweikert," 505th Regimental Combat Team website, www.505rct.org/album2/schweikert_f.asp; and Jo Ann Gilpin, as told by Raymond Daudt, "The Battle of Grand Halleux," 505th Regimental Combat Team website, www.505rct .org/upload/Grand-Halleux.pdf (both accessed June 27, 2018).
5. "Greeneville WWII Soldier Coming Home, Decades Later," WBIR TV transcript, https://www.wbir.com /article/news/local/greeneville-wwii-soldier-coming-home-decades-later/51–445120467 (last accessed June 27, 2018).

8. THE JAPANESE "HELLSHIPS"

1. The information on the *Shinyo Maru*'s sinking comes from the Proviso East High School, Maywood, Illinois, Bataan Commemorative Research Project, www.bataanproject.com; and the On Eternal Patrol website, www .oneternalpatrol.com (both accessed on June 27, 2018). For more on the ghastly conditions at the Davao camps, read John D. Lukacs, *Escape from Davao: The Forgotten Story of the Most Daring Prison Break of the Pacific War* (New York: Simon and Schuster, 2010).

10. A DIFFICULT HOMECOMING

1. Joseph James Shomon, *Crosses in the Wind* (New York: Stratford House, Inc., 1947), 159.
2. The Margraten cemetery, coincidentally, was established by Major Shomon's Graves Registration unit in 1944–1945; Shomon, 61–133.
3. Willard Adkins, 6964170, Individual Deceased Personnel File, no. 32.
4. Willard Adkins, 6964170, Individual Deceased Personnel File, no. 6.
5. Willard Adkins, 6964170, Individual Deceased Personnel File, Application for Headstone or Marker, December 13, 1948.
6. Willard Adkins, 6964170, Individual Deceased Personnel File, nos. 47–48.
7. Willard Adkins, 6964170, Individual Deceased Personnel File, no. 43.
8. For more on General Akin and his career, see Hiroshi Masuda, *MacArthur in Asia: The General and His Staff in the Philippines, Japan and Korea* (Ithaca, NY: Cornell Univ. Press, 2009), 14–15; and Michael Robert Patterson, entry for "Spencer B. Akin, Major General, United States Army," Arlington National Cemetery website, http://www.arlingtoncemetery.net/sbakin.htm (last accessed June 27, 2018).
9. Douglas G. McMillin, 389311, Individual Deceased Personnel File, no. 47.
10. Douglas G. McMillin, 389311, Individual Deceased Personnel File, nos. 153, 155, and 157.
11. Douglas G. McMillin, 389311, Individual Deceased Personnel File, no. 163.

11. THE "FORGOTTEN WAR"

1. For details of the POW camps of this war and the treatment and fate of US and Allied prisoners of the North Koreans and Chinese, see Raymond B. Lech, *Broken Soldiers* (Urbana and Chicago: Univ. of Illinois Press, 2000); the Korean War POW/MIA Network website, http://www.koreanwarpowmia.net/Prison_Camps /POW_Camps.htm (last accessed Apr. 10, 2018) and Defense POW/MIA Accounting Agency, http://www .dpaa.mil/Our-Missing/Korean-War/Maps/ (last accessed June 27, 2018).

2. Lech, 1–2.

3. Mike Blackerby, "Home After 66 Years," *Knoxville* (TN) *News Sentinel*, June 24, 2016, p. 1A.

4. "Jasper Soldier Missing Nearly 65 Years Will Be Laid To Rest at Chattanooga National Cemetery," Tenn. Dept. of Veterans Affairs press release, Mar. 2, 2015, https://www.tn.gov/veteran/news/2015/3/2/jasper -soldier-missing-nearly-65-years-will-be-laid-to-rest-at-chattanooga.html (last accessed June 27, 2018).

5. Michael Collins, "Remains of Long-Lost ET Soldier Found," *Knoxville* (TN) *News Sentinel*, Apr. 4, 2009, p. 1.

6. For more on this battle, see Joshua W. Montandon, "Battle for the Punchbowl: The U. S. First Marine Division's 1951 Fall Offensive of the Korean War" (Master's thesis, Univ. of North Texas, 2007), https://digital. library.unt.edu/ark:/67531/metadc3938/ (last accessed June 27, 2018); Charles R. Smith, ed., *U. S. Marines in the Korean War* (Washington, DC: History Division, Headquarters, US Marine Corps, 2007), 413–75.

7. "USMA Class of 1950: Medon Armin Bitzer—No. 17778—5 June 1927–8 January 1952," https://www.usma1950 .com/memorial/medon-armin-bitzer (last accessed June 27, 2018).

8. See Roll of Honor, Truckbusters from Dogpatch website, www.truckbustersfromdogpatch.com/index .php?id=86 (last accessed June 27, 2018).

9. Appreciation is expressed to Charles E. Wilhite Jr., Captain Wilhite's son, for providing this biographical information to the ETVMA.

10. Mamie Nash, "Bridge Named for Soldier KIA in Korea," *Knoxville* (TN) *News Sentinel*, Oct. 28, 2015, p. 4A.

11. Walter G. Hermes, *Truce Tent and Fighting Front: The United States Army in the Korean War* (Washington, DC: Center of Military History, US Army, 1992), 259–60, http://www.history.army.mil/books/korea /truce/ch11.htm (last accessed June 27, 2018). For more on the Koje-do riots and their aftermath, see Allan R. Millett, "War Behind the Wire: Koje-Do Prison Camp," *MHQ* (Winter 2009): 46–61; and Lawrence Malkin, "Murderers of Koje-do!," *MHQ* (Summer 1993): 88–97.

12. Hermes, *Truce Tent and Fighting Front*, 233–57.

12. VIETNAM

1. Wayne H. Morris, "Sam Asher's Short but Full Life, Honors all East Tennesseans," *The Courier News* (Clinton, TN), Aug. 31, 2016.

2. I.e., Military Advisor Training Academy, a course to train officers and NCOs selected to serve as military advisors to other nations as part of foreign military assistance. In Vietnam, the term "military advisor" was often rendered as *co van*, said to mean "trusted friend" in Vietnamese.

3. Frank Thompson, "William Leroy Johnson," US Military Academy, Class of 1960 memorial website, http:// www.west-point.org/class/usma1960/Johnson_WL-Memorial.html (last accessed June 27, 2018).

4. See "B-57 Canberra, 0–33876," Vietnam Security Police Association Inc. website, http://www.vspa.com /dn-b57–02–1966.htm (last accessed June 27, 2018).

5. "James Daniel Kelley," Virtual Wall, Vietnam Veterans Memorial website, http://www.virtualwall.org/dk /KelleyJD01a.htm (last accessed June 27, 2018).

6. Appreciation is expressed to Billy M. Brown, a member of the Permian Basin Vietnam Veterans Memorial in Midland, Texas, for providing this information to the ETVMA.

7. "Thomas D. Bernard," Vietnam Veterans Memorial Fund website, http://www.vvmf.org/Wall-of-Faces/3734

/THOMAS-D-BERNARD?page=2 (last accessed June 27, 2018).

8. Harold G. Moore and Joseph L. Galloway, *We Were Soldiers Once . . . And Young: Ia Drang-The Battle that Changed the War in Vietnam* (New York: Random House, 1992), 103, 167.

9. Jay Taylor, *Point of Aim, Point of Impact* (Bloomington, IN: AuthorHouse, 2011), 42–57.

10. "Donald Ted Sluder," Virtual Wall, Vietnam Veterans Memorial website, http://www.virtualwall.org/ds /SluderDT01a.htm (last accessed June 27, 2018).

11. Appreciation is expressed to Danny E. Russell for providing his recollections, and to Mike Belli for submitting his own remembrances of Michael Conner to the ETVMA. See also "361st Expeditionary Reconnaissance Squadron," USAF Orders of Battle website, http://usafunithistory.com/PDF/0300/361%20 EXPEDITIONARY%20RECONNAISSANCE%20SQ.pdf (last accessed June 27, 2018), p. 3.

12. For more, see Michael Robert Patterson, "Paul Leonard Foster, Senior Master Sergeant, United States Air Force," Arlington National Cemetery website, http://www.arlingtoncemetery.net/plfoster.htm (last accessed June 27, 2018).

13. Appreciation is expressed to Dot Gallaher for providing this information to the ETVMA.

14. "James Edward Self," Virtual Wall, Vietnam Veterans Memorial website, http://www.virtualwall.org/ds /SelfJE01a.htm (last accessed June 27, 2018).

15. For more on the general history of this policy, see the account of the sinking of the USS *Juneau* in chapter 5.

16. Appreciation is expressed to David De la Rocha for providing this recollection to the ETVMA.

17. "Bradley Keith Watts," The Wall-Vietnam Veterans Memorial website, http://www.thewall-usa.com/guest .asp?recid=54845 (last accessed June 27, 2018).

13. REMEMBERING THE EAST TENNESSEE WOMEN WHO SERVED

1. Rob Simbeck, *Daughter of the Air: The Brief Soaring Life of Cornelia Fort* (New York: Grove Press, 1999), 237–38.

2. Appreciation is expressed to E. Sharon Hodges for providing this information.

14. NON-COMBAT TRAGEDIES AND LINGERING MYSTERIES

1. Appreciation is expressed to Kenneth Cantwell for providing this information to the ETVMA.

2. John L. Frisbee, "Valor: Ace Among Aces," *Air Force Magazine* (Jan. 1993, available at http://www.airforcemag .com/MagazineArchive/Pages/1993/January%201993/0193valor.aspx (last accessed on June 27, 2018).

3. Appreciation is expressed to Phil Pearson for providing this information to the ETVMA.

4. Along with the more well-known Private Edward D. Slovik, who, of the ninety-six, was the only one executed for desertion in the face of the enemy and who was also the first U.S. soldier executed for desertion since the Civil War. For more on the execution of Slovik and U.S. executions in the ETO, see William Bradford Huie, *The Execution of Private Slovik* (New York: Duell, Sloane & Pierce, 1954); Joseph Connor, "Who's to Blame for Private Eddie Slovik's Death?," *World War II Magazine*, available at http://www.historynet.com /whos-to-blame-for-private-eddie-sloviks-death.htm (last accessed on June 27, 2018). The special cemetery where PFC Rollins is buried forms a portion of the Oise-Aisne cemetery, maintained by the ABMC; it is also the cemetery where the more well-known Private Slovik is buried.

5. French L. MacKlean, "The Fifth Field: Master Sergeant John C. Woods," available at www.thefifthfield.com /sgt-john-c-woods/sgt-woods-post (last accessed on June 27, 2018).

6. Robert L. Allen, The Port Chicago Mutiny (Berkeley, CA: Heyday Books, 2006); Leonard F. Guttridge, Mutiny: A History of Naval Insurrection (Annapolis, Md.: Naval Institute Press, 1992), at 211–20; American Merchant Marine at War website, www.usmm.org/portchicago.html (last accessed June 27, 2018).

7. Appreciation is expressed to his middle son, Thomas B. Drinnen Jr., for providing this information to the ETVMA.

8. "Lieut. McCready Killed," *Alton* (IL) *Evening Telegraph*, July 30, 1942, p. 10.

9. Appreciation is expressed to Joy Locke for providing this information to the ETVMA.

10. "Army Doctors Lose Battle to Save Man's Life," *San Bernardino County* (CA) *Sun*, Dec. 8, 1951, p. 17.

11. Appreciation is expressed to his son, Michael Kell, for providing this information to the ETVMA.

15. WAR IN THE MIDDLE EAST

1. Army Quartermaster Foundation, "14th Quartermaster Detachment," https://www.qmfound.com /article/14th-quartermaster-detachment/ (last accessed June 27, 2018).

2. "In Memory of 'Spirit 03' Jan. 31, 1991," Shadowspear: Special Operations website, posted Jan. 31, 2014, available at https://www.shadowspear.com/vb/threads/in-memory-of-spirit-03-jan-31–1991.19898/ (last accessed on June 27, 2018).

3. See chapter 10 for more on these types of crew burials.

4. Greg Jaffe, "The Battle of Wanat: Inside the Wire," *Washington Post*, Oct. 4, 2009, http://www.washington post.com/wp-dyn/content/article/2009/10/03/AR2009100303048.html (last accessed June 27, 2018). See also Michelle Tan, "Hard-Hit C Company Suffers Another Agonizing Blow," reprinted in *Military Times* Honor the Fallen website, https://thefallen.militarytimes.com/army-cpl-jason-d-hovater/3630790 (last accessed June 27, 2018); and Hugh G. Willett, "ET Soldier Memorialized," *Knoxville* (TN) News Sentinel, July 22, 2008, p.7.

5. Bryan Mitchell, "Tears for a Soldier," *Knoxville* (TN) *News Sentinel*, Dec. 24, 2003, p. A1; Bryan Mitchell, "'Great' Soldier Is Laid to Rest," *Knoxville* (TN) *News Sentinel*, Sept. 21, 2003, p. A1; Green Beret Foundation, "William M. Bennett, SFC," https://www.greenberetfoundation.org/memorial/william-m-bennett/; and "Sgt. 1st Class William M. Bennett," TogetherWeServed.com website, https://army.togetherweserved.com/army /servlet/tws.webapp.WebApp?cmd=ShadowBoxProfile&type=Person&ID=33991 (both accessed on June 27, 2018).

6. Kate Baldwin, "More Than a Number," *Moscow* (ID)-*Pullman* (WA) *Daily News*, Nov.1, 2005, reprinted at Iraq War Heroes website, http://www.iraqwarheroes.org/nixont.htm (last accessed June 27, 2018).

7. Appreciation is expressed to Brenda Normandin for providing this biographical information to the ETVMA.

8. Michael Robert Patterson, "Frank D. Bryant, Jr., Lieutenant Colonel, United States Air Force," Arlington National Cemetery website, http://arlingtoncemetery.net/fdbryantjr.htm (last accessed June 27, 2018).

9. Obituary, Jonathan M. Curtis, *Knoxville* (TN) *News Sentinel*, Nov. 7, 2010, https://www.legacy.com /obituaries/knoxnews/obituary.aspx?n=jonathan-m-curtis&pid=146506377; and Associated Press, "Parents: Soldier Stopped Suicide Bomber, Saved Comrades," reprinted in Military Times Honor the Fallen website, https://thefallen.militarytimes.com/army-spc-jonathan-m-curtis/4997756 (both accessed on June 27, 2018).

10. J. J. Stambaugh, "Honored as a Hero," *Knoxville* (TN) *News Sentinel*, Aug. 10, 2009, p.1; Associated Press, "Knoxville Bridge Dedication for Soldier Killed in Afghanistan," reprinted in Military Times Honor the Fallen website, https://thefallen.militarytimes.com/army-pfc-patrick-s-fitzgibbon/4221822 ; and Obituary, PFC Patrick S. "St. Patty" Fitzgibbon, *Knoxville* (TN) *News Sentinel*, Aug. 9, 2009, https://www.legacy.com /obituaries/knoxnews/obituary.aspx?page=lifestory&pid=131071253 (both accessed on June 27, 2018).

11. Nash Armstrong, "Airman to be Buried Here Today; 'Knoxville Is His Home,' Father of Serviceman Says," *Knoxville* (TN) *News Sentinel*, Dec. 3, 2010, p. A01.

12. Associated Press, "Soldier Was on His Fourth Deployment," reprinted in *Military Times* Honor the Fallen website, https://thefallen.militarytimes.com/army-sgt-1st-class-carlos-m-santos-silva/4555079; and Michael Robert Patterson, entry for "Carlos M. Santos-Silva, Sergeant First Class, United States Army," Arlington

National Cemetery website, http://www.arlingtoncemetery.net/cmsantos-silvia.htm (both accessed on June 27, 2018).

13. Todd South, "Soldier With Local Ties Killed in Afghanistan," *Chattanooga* (TN) *Times Free Press*, Nov. 18, 2010, http://www.timesfreepress.com/news/news/story/2010/nov/18/soldier-with-local-ties-killed-in -afghanistan/34906/; and Heidi Vogt, "Details Given on Deadly Attack in Kunar Province," Associated Press, reprinted in *Military Times* Honor the Fallen website, https://thefallen.militarytimes.com/army-spc-nathan-e -lillard/5070430 (both accessed June 27, 2018).

14. Carrie Whitaker, "The Most Mundane Thing, He Made Fun," Cincinnati Enquirer, reprinted in *Military Times* Honor the Fallen website, https://thefallen.militarytimes.com/army-pfc-zachary-s-salmon/5475561; and Fallen Heroes Project, "Zachary S Salmon," https://www.fallenheroesproject.org/united-states/zachary-s-salmon/ (both accessed June 27, 2018).

15. Darren Dunlap, "Lake City Soldier Killed in Attack," *Knoxville* (TN) *News Sentinel*, Apr. 14, 2007, p. 1.

16. Bob Fowler, "He Was the Consummate Soldier," *Knoxville* (TN) *News Sentinel*, Apr. 7, 2005, p. A1.

17. Robert L. Wilson, "Sgt. Michael Harvey Ferschke Jr., 1985–2008," *Knoxville* (TN) *News Sentinel*, Aug. 19, 2008, p.1; and "Maryville Marine Killed in Iraq," reprinted in *Military Times* Honor the Fallen website, https:// thefallen.militarytimes.com/marine-sgt-michael-h-ferschke-jr/3675924 (both accessed June 27, 2018).

18. B. Jay Johnson, "Cleveland Mourns Death of Young Soldier in Iraq," *Cleveland* (TN) *Bradley News*, reprinted in Iraq War Heroes website, http://www.iraqwarheroes.org/weir.htm (last accessed June 27, 2018).

19. Entry, Find-a-Grave website, "Sgt. Stephen Roosevelt Maddies," https://www.findagrave.com /memorial/20741948/stephen-roosevelt-maddies (last accessed June 27, 2018).

20. Leef Smith, "Mourners Honor Selfless Marine," *Washington Post*, Dec. 16, 2006, http://www.washingtonpost .com/wp-dyn/content/article/2006/12/15/AR2006121501749.html; and Michael Robert Patterson, entry for "Joseph Trane McCloud, Lieutenant Colonel, United States Marine Corps," Arlington National Cemetery website, http://www.arlingtoncemetery.net/jtmccloud.htm (both accessed June 27, 2018).

21. Associated Press, "Loss of Soldier Son Crushes Family," reprinted in *Military Times* Honor the Fallen website, https://thefallen.militarytimes.com/army-sgt-1st-class-gregory-b-hicks/256999 (last accessed June 27, 2018).

22. Jim Balloch, "Soldier, Father Honored," *Knoxville* (TN) *News Sentinel*, June 5, 2005, p. B1; Bryan Mitchell, "Campbell Guardsman Dies in Iraq," *Knoxville* (TN) *News Sentinel*, May 27, 2005, p. A1; entry on Find-a-Grave website, "Sgt. Alfred Barton Siler," https://www.findagrave.com/memorial/15453722/alfred-barton-siler (last accessed June 27, 2018).

23. Obituary, Terry W. Prater, Legacy.com, http://www.legacy.com/Obituaries.asp?Page=LifeStory &PersonId=149068359; and Associated Press, "Retired Soldier Says Slain Former Comrade Saved His Life in Iraq," reprinted in *Military Times* Honor the Fallen website, https://thefallen.militarytimes.com/army-staff -sgt-terry-w-prater/2632389 (both accessed June 27, 2018).

24. Entry on Find-a-Grave website, "Sgt. Morgan William Strader," https://www.findagrave.com/memorial /12624446/morgan-william-strader (last accessed June 27, 2018).

25. Obituary, "Sullivan, John Michael: Soddy-Daisy High Graduate Was Serving Second Tour of Duty in Iraq," The Chattanoogan.com (Chattanooga, TN), Jan. 4, 2007, http://www.chattanoogan.com/2007/1/4/99197 /Sullivan-John-Michael.aspx (last accessed June 27, 2018).

26. Matt Lakin, "2 Tenn. Pilots Die in Chopper Crash." *Knoxville* (TN) *News Sentinel*, Feb. 24, 2010, p. 1.

27. Entry on Find-a-Grave website, "Sgt. Eric Andrew Fifer," https://www.findagrave.com/memorial/12085455 /eric-andrew-fifer; and Associated Press, "Knoxville Soldier Among Two Killed in Attack in Iraq," reprinted at M*ilitary Times* Honor the Fallen website, https://thefallen.militarytimes.com/army-sgt-eric-a-fifer/1163701 (both accessed on June 27, 2018).

28. Associated Press, "Fort Stewart Honors Knoxville MP Killed in Iraq," reprinted at *Military Times* Honor the Fallen website, https://thefallen.militarytimes.com/army-pfc-george-d-harrison/542124 (last accessed June 27, 2018).

29. Richard Powelson, "Soldier Killed in Iraq Returns to Arlington for Final Time," *Knoxville* (TN) *News Sentinel*, June 28, 2005, p. A1.

30. Jeffrey Gaunt, "Ex-Elgin Resident Dies in Iraq Combat," *Elgin* (IL) *Daily Herald*, June 23, 2005, sec. 1, p. 1, https://dailyherald.newspaperarchive.com/daily-herald-suburban-chicago/2005–06–23/page-179/ (last accessed June 27, 2018).

31. Entry on Find-a-Grave website, "Spec. Michael J. Rodriguez," https://www.findagrave.com/memorial/19081323 (last accessed June 27, 2018). Photographs are courtesy of Elizabeth Reed.

32. Associated Press, "Fallen Sailor Remembered as Down-to-Earth," reprinted at *Military Times* Honor the Fallen website, https://thefallen.militarytimes.com/navy-signalman-2nd-class-sw-christopher-e-watts/257226 (last accessed June 27, 2018).

33. Appreciation is expressed to Henri Lieurance for providing these remembrances of his brother.

34. Cpl. Shawn C. Rhodes, "Battalion Memorializes Camp Lejeune Marine," 1st Marine Division, Camp Pendleton, CA, Apr. 21, 2004, https://www.1stmardiv.marines.mil/News/News-Article-Display/Article/540588/battalion-memorializes-camp-lejeune-marine/ (last accessed June 27, 2018).

35. Associated Press, "Soldier Killed in Iraq Felt Duty to Serve," reprinted at *Military Times* Honor the Fallen website, https://thefallen.militarytimes.com/army-pfc-david-l-potter/297318/ (last accessed June 27, 2018).

GLOSSARY

A1C	Airman First Class
A-26	Douglas twin-engined medium bomber and attack aircraft, officially nicknamed the "Invader."
AA	Anti-aircraft (also sometimes called "ack-ack" during the two World Wars). In the context of the 82nd Airborne Division, it stands for that division's nickname, the "All-Americans."
AAA	Anti-aircraft artillery (also sometimes called "triple-A").
AAF	US Army Air Forces, the predecessor of today's US Air Force. Prior to 1941, known as the Air Army Corps.
ABDA	American-British-Dutch-Australian joint command in East Asia in early 1942.
Abrams	The M1-series Abrams main battle tank, armed with either a 105mm (in the original, M1 version) or 120mm (in the later, M1A1 and M1A2 versions) main gun.
AC	Navy acronym for a collier vessel.
AC-47	See entry for "C-47."
AC-130	See entry for "C-130."
ACR	Armored Cavalry Regiment.
ACS	Depending on the context, either (1) Air Commando Squadron, or (2) Assistant Chief of Staff.
ADA	Air Defense Artillery, the modern term for anti-aircraft; see "AA" and "AAA."
AEF	American Expeditionary Forces; General John J. Pershing's command in Europe during World War I.
AFB	Air Force Base.
AFS	Air Force serial (or service) number.
AH-1	Two-man Bell attack helicopter-gunship, officially nicknamed the "Cobra."
AHC	Assault (or Attack) Helicopter Company
AIT	Advanced Individual Training.
AK	Acronym for a cargo ship.
AKA	Acronym for an attack cargo ship, used to support amphibious landings.
AO	Acronym for a fleet-class oiler/oil tanker.
Americal	Army's 23rd Infantry Division
ARP	Aero-rifle platoon; sometimes used in airmobile/air cavalry units in Vietnam.
ARVN	Army of the Republic of Vietnam, i.e., the South Vietnamese army.
ASN	Army serial (or service) number.
AWOL	Absence without leave.
B-17	Boeing four-engined heavy bomber, nicknamed the "Flying Fortress," used by US Army Air Forces during World War II.

B-24	Consolidated four-engined heavy bomber, nicknamed the "Liberator," used by both the Army Air Forces and the Navy (called the PB4Y in Navy service) during World War II.
B-25	Douglas twin-engined medium bomber of World War II, known as the "Mitchell." Several Marine medium bomber squadrons also used the Mitchell, called "PBJ" by the Marines and Navy.
B-29	Large, four-engined Boeing heavy bomber, nicknamed the "Superfortress," used by the Army Air Forces for long-range bombing of Japan in 1944–1945 and again during the Korean War; a modernized version used in the later stages of the Korean War and through the 1950s was the B-50. The reconnaissance version was the RB-29, and the weather squadrons' version was the WB-29.
B-50	See entry for "B-29."
B-57	Martin twin-engined jet bomber nicknamed the "Canberra," used by the Air Force in the 1960s. A reconnaissance and intelligence model was the RB-57.
BAMC	Brooke Army Medical Center, in San Antonio, Texas.
BAR	30 caliber Browning Automatic Rifle. Really a light machine gun, the 19.5-pound BAR resembled a large rifle mounted on a folding bipod, which was attached to the front of the barrel, and fired a 20-round clip.
Battery	Artillery equivalent of a company; usually commanded by a captain.
BB	Acronym for battleship.
BCT	Depending on the context, either Basic Training, or (2) Brigade Combat Team.
Big Red One	The Army's 1st Infantry Division, for its self-explanatory unit insignia.
BLT	Marine Corps acronym for battalion landing team.
BNR	Body not recovered.
Boondocks	Military slang for rough terrain, particularly if woody or jungled, and derived from a Filipino word for mountain or hill.
Boot	Nickname for a new Marine recruit undergoing basic training at "Boot Camp."
Buffalo Soldier	A member of one of the Army's historically all-black infantry and cavalry regiments.
C-47	Douglas twin-engined cargo and troop transport; the military version of the DC-3 airliner. Its heavily armed, attack version used by the Air Force in and after Vietnam was the AC-47, sometimes known as "Spooky" or "Puff the Magic Dragon" because of its nighttime operations in support of ground troops.
C-46	Curtiss twin-engined cargo and troop transport, sometimes called the "Commando."
C-130	Lockheed four-engined cargo and troop transport, officially known as the "Hercules" or, less formally, as the "Herc." Its heavily armed, attack version used by the Air Force as the successor to the AC-47 is the AC-130 gunship, called the "Spectre."
CA	Acronym for heavy cruiser-class warships.
Cav, CAV	Cavalry.
CB	Acronym for a Naval Construction Battalion. See "Seabee."
CBI	China-Burma-India theater of operations of World War II.
CCF	Chinese Communist Forces, i.e., the Communist Chinese army.
CL	Acronym for light cruiser-class warships.

CO	Commanding officer (the "old man;" an endearment never expressed to his face, however).
Cobra	See "AH-1."
CP	Command post.
Cpt., CPT	Captain.
Catalina	Consolidated PBY twin-engined seaplane, used by the US Navy during World War II.
Corpsman	Navy combat medical technician assigned to serve as a medic in a Marine unit and most often called simply "Doc."
Corsair	Chance-Vought F4U single-engined fighter-bomber; the Corsair was a mainstay of US Marine and Navy fighter units beginning in February 1943 and through the Korean conflict.
Cpl., CPL	Corporal.
CSM	Command Sergeant Major; typically, the highest rank of non-commissioned officer. The Army's most senior NCO is the Command Sergeant Major of the Army.
CV	Acronym for fleet-class aircraft carriers. A CV(N) is a nuclear-power aircraft carrier.
CVE	Acronym for escort-class aircraft carriers (sometimes called "baby flattops" or "jeep carriers").
CVL	Acronym for light aircraft carriers.
CW, CWO	Chief Warrant Officer.
Dauntless	Douglas SBD single-engined dive bomber, with a two-man crew, used by US Marine and Navy bomber squadrons during World War II.
DD	Acronym for destroyer-class warships.
DE	Acronym for destroyer-escort class warships.
Death Valley	Nickname for infamous Communist POW camp located near the Yalu River in North Korea.
Deuce-and-a-half	A 2 1/2-ton cargo truck.
DMZ	Demilitarized zone; typically used to refer to either the longstanding armistice line between North and South Korea, or the similar zone that formerly stood between the border of South and North Vietnam.
DNIF	Duty not involving flying; Air Force term.
Doc	Nickname for any military surgeon, doctor, medic, or Navy corpsman.
Dogface	Nickname, usually applied to Army infantrymen but also applied to other troops in other combat services; derived from the stubbly-bearded and haggard appearance of soldiers after several days or weeks in combat.
Doughboy	Popular nickname for Army troops during (and sometimes after) the First World War. The expression is variously thought to be a corruption of the Spanish word *adobe* due to the dusty tinge of troops' uniforms while on the march in the western United States; or from the soldiers' love of doughnuts and other deep-fried goodies; or the doughnut-like shape of their uniform buttons.
Dropsonde	A disposable, aircraft-dropped instrumentation pod used by Air Force and Navy weather squadrons for taking meteorological measurements.
Dustoff	Aerial medical evacuation helicopter, or a mission/sortie of the same.
88	88mm German dual-purpose (anti-aircraft and anti-tank) cannon used during World War II. A version of this high-velocity and highly accurate artillery piece was the main armament of the Germans' feared Panzer VI Tiger and King Tiger model heavy tanks.

EM	Enlisted man.
ETO	European Theater of Operations of World War II.
ETVMA	East Tennessee Veterans Memorial Association.
.45	Colt .45 caliber M1911A1 automatic pistol.
.50	Browning M2 heavy machine gun. Often fitted on a portable tripod for ground usage (in the M2-HB—"heavy-barrel"—model) or on an M2 pedestal with water-cooled jacket for AA use or on vehicular mounts, the .50 caliber machine gun was often used for AA defense but was originally designed as an antitank weapon.
.51	Soviet-made 51-caliber (12.7mm) heavy machine gun.
F-4	McDonnell Douglas Air Force, Navy and Marine jet fighter-bomber, known as the "Phantom."
F-51	See "P-51."
F-80	Lockheed P-80 "Shooting Star," the first jet fighter used operationally by the Army Air Forces and later relabeled as the F-80. A trainer version was the T-33.
F-84	Republic turbojet fighter-bomber of the early Cold War period; it was known as the "Thunderjet."
F-86	North American jet fighter aircraft, and the nemesis of the Soviet, Chinese and Korean MiG-15s in Korea; known as the "Sabre," it was one of the Air Force's first supersonic warplanes.
F-101	North American supersonic jet bomber escort and fighter-bomber, which served the Air Force during the 1950s and early 1960s; known as the "Voodoo."
F-104	The Lockheed "Starfighter," a single-engine, supersonic jet interceptor, which later became widely used as an attack aircraft. A unit of F-104s was based at Knoxville's McGhee Tyson Air Force Base in the early 1960s.
F-105	Republic jet fighter-bomber used by the Air Force extensively in Vietnam and known as the "Thunderchief," or more simply, the "Thud."
F4U	See entry for "Corsair."
FA or FAF	Field artillery.
FCO	Fire control officer.
Field Force	One of several United States Army Corps-level commands in South Vietnam during the Vietnam War.
Flak	A synonym for AA and AAA, or the shell bursts from such weapons; from the German *flieger* [or, *flug*] *abwehrkanone*, "air defense cannon."
FMF	Fleet Marine Force, the administrative and command designation used for the Marine Corps "in the field"; that portion of the Marine Corps made up of all deployed field units, from Corps and Division level downwards to the ship detachments on board US Navy vessels.
FO	Forward observer.
FOB	Forward Operating Base.
FROG	NATO acronym for Free Rocket Over Ground, Soviet Model 9M21 short-range artillery rocket system.
FSB	Forward Support Base.
GI	Nickname for Army troops (derived from the Army acronym for "government issue").
Garand	.30 caliber M1 semiautomatic rifle.

Grail	Soviet/Russian-made SA-7 man-portable anti-aircraft missile.
Gunner	Marine Corps rank equivalent to that of an Army warrant officer.
Gunny	Marine Nickname for a Gunnery Sergeant (Marine NCO rank comparable to an Army Sergeant First Class or E-7).
GySgt	Gunnery Sergeant, Marines' NCO rank about Staff Sergeant.
HHB	Headquarters and Headquarters Battery; Artillery equivalent to "HHC."
HHC	Headquarters and Headquarters Company.
HHT	Headquarters and Headquarters Troop; Cavalry equivalent to "HHC."
H&S	Headquarters and Service.
Heartbreak Ridge	Ridged area located northwest of the Punchbowl in South Korea and the site of heavy combat during the Korean War.
HEMTT	Heavy Expanded Mobility Tactical Truck, an eight-wheel drive, ten-ton tactical truck serving several logistics functions.
HMMWV	See "Humvee."
HQ	Headquarters.
Huey	See "UH-1."
Humvee	High Mobility Multipurpose Wheeled Vehicle, a four-wheeled series of light tactical, personnel and cargo vehicles made by AM General; the successor to the famous "Jeep" 1 1/4-ton utility vehicle.
IED	Improvised explosive device.
Indianheads	The Army's 2nd Infantry Division.
Inf., INF	Infantry.
Iroquois	See "UH-1."
JPAC	Joint POW/MIA Accounting Command. Jolly Green, or Jolly Green Giant Sikorsky HH-53 and MH-53 long-range combat search-and-rescue helicopter, also sometimes used for special operations missions due to its range, carrying capacity, and endurance.
JPAC CIL	Joint POW/MIA Accounting Command, Central Identification Laboratory
JROTC	Junior ROTC, for high-school students.
Kamikaze	Japanese suicide plane or its pilot. Means "divine wind," in honor of a medieval typhoon that destroyed an invading Chinese fleet and saved Japan from foreign occupation.
KIA	Killed in action.
KMAG	Korean Military Assistance Group; the Korean-era counterpart of MAAG in Vietnam.
Kriegie	In the ETO, an Allied prisoner-of-war nickname for themselves, from the German *kriegsgefangener*, "war prisoner."
LCI	Landing Craft, Infantry. Nicknamed the "Elsie-Eye"; by 1944, some LCIs were converted to light gunboats [(LCI(G)s] or rocket-launching platforms for 3.5-inch bombardment rockets, several of which were used to support the landings on Normandy, Guam, Iwo Jima, and Okinawa.
LCM	Landing Craft, Medium (also called a Higgins boat, after its inventor).
LCP	Landing Craft, Personnel (early-model Navy landing craft, without a bow ramp for unloading troops).
LCpl, LCPL	Lance corporal; the Marine Corps' equivalent of PFC.

LCT	Landing Craft, Tank.
Loach	Hughes OH-6 scout/observation helicopter.
LRRP	Long-range reconnaissance patrol.
LST	Landing Ship, Tank. (Due to their bulkiness, the acronym for these vessels was also said to stand for "Long, Slow Target.")
Lt., LT	Lieutenant.
Lt. Col., LTC	Lieutenant colonel.
LVT	Landing Vehicle, Tracked; sometimes also called an "Alligator" during World War II, or variously, an "amtrac" or "amphtrack" (for amphibious tractor).
Leatherneck	Nickname for US Marines; derived from a heavy leather collar often worn by early US Marines in the late 1700s and early 1800s to help ward off saber blows to the neck.
Liberator	See entry for "B-24."
Lightning	See entry for "P-38."
Luftwaffe	The German Air Force, both during World War II and in the years after 1955.
LZ	Landing zone.
mm or MM	"Millimeter" and "caliber" refer to the diameter of a gun's bore, measured at the mouth of the barrel, caliber being this measurement in inches or fractions of inches (i.e., .30 caliber being equal to .30 of an inch in diameter). US weapons were gauged in millimeters, calibers, and inches (the latter mainly for naval ordnance), with caliber usually being used for small arms (i.e., machine guns, rifles and pistols), and millimeters for larger guns (20mm and up). Note, by way of example, that .50 caliber is equal to 12.7mm.
M1	Depending on the context, this refers to (1) the .30 caliber Garand rifle (see entry for "Garand"); (2) the smaller .30 semi-automatic carbine; or (3) the M1-series Abrams main battle tank, armed with either a 105mm or 120mm main gun.
M4	Depending on the context, either the (1) "Sherman" medium tank of World War II and Korea, or (2) a shortened, carbine version of the M16 rifle.
M14	7.62mm semiautomatic rifles, used in the early days of Vietnam, is was the success to the M1 Garand. Modified versions remain in service as a sniper rifle.
M16	5.56mm assault rifle; the Army's replacement for the M14.
M60	7.62mm machine gun.
M249	5.56mm squad light machine gun, also called the SAW, for "squad automatic weapon."
MAAG	Military Assistance and Advisory Group; the US military advisors to South Vietnam's forces.
MACV	Military Assistance Command Vietnam; the successor to MAAG.
Maj., MAJ	Major.
Manchus	The Army's 9th Infantry Regiment, so-called for its service during the Boxer Rebellion and the relief mission that followed in China in 1900–1902.
MATA	Military Advisor Training Academy, a course to train officers and NCOs selected to serve as military advisors to other nations' as part of foreign military assistance.
MCSN	Marine Corps serial (or service) number.
MEU	Marine Expeditionary Unit: the smallest Marine air/ground task force in the Fleet Marine Force, and typically used for amphibious landings as an expeditionary quick reaction force.

MIA	Missing in action.
Mickey	American nickname for British-made H2X navigational and bombing radar.
MiG	Soviet/Russian aircraft designer-manufacturer, typically of fighter aircraft; Russian abbreviation for the firm's two chief designers' last names, Mikoyan and Gurevich. MiG-15 jet fighters were common threats to USAF pilots in Korean skies. MiG-17, MiG-19, and MiG-21 jet fighters were the enemy aircraft most encountered by US airmen over North Vietnam.
MOS	Military Occupational Specialty; a soldier's primary skill or "trade."
MP	Military Police.
MPQ	Radar-controlled nighttime air mission.
Mitchell	See entry for "B-25."
Msgt., M/Sgt, MSG	Master Sergeant.
NATO	North Atlantic Treaty Organization.
NCB	See "Seabees."
NCO	Noncommissioned officer (i.e., corporals and all grades of sergeant in the Army, Air Force, and Marine Corps, and in the Navy, the petty officer grades).
NKPA	North Korean Peoples' Army.
NMCP	See "Punchbowl."
NSN	Navy serial (or service) number.
NVA	North Vietnamese Army.
OCS	Officer Candidate School.
OD	Depending on the context, the Ordnance Corps; Officer of the Day (i.e., a duty officer); or Operational Detachment (the last, an Army Special Forces term for its "A-Team" detachments.).
Oflag	See "Stalag."
OP	Observation post.
P-38	Lockheed P-38 twin-engined fighter-bomber, used by US Army Air Forces during World War II.
P-47	Republic single-engined fighter-bomber; known officially as the "Thunderbolt" and unofficially (due to its barrel-like engine) as the "Jug," it saw active service in World War II.
P-51	North American single-engined fighter-bomber, known as the "Mustang;" it saw active service in both World War II and Korea, and it was known as the F-51 by the USAF during the 1950s.
PAVN	People's Army of Vietnam, i.e., the North Vietnamese Army (also, "NVA").
PBY	See entry for "Catalina."
PC	Patrol craft.
PFC	Private First Class.
Plt., PLT	Platoon.
POW	Prisoner of war.
P/Sgt, PSG	Platoon Sergeant; the Marine equivalent to the Army's Sergeant First Class.
Polar Bears	Army's 31st Infantry Regiment, so-called for its service in the Allies' intervention in Russia at the end of the First World War, 1918–1921.

GLOSSARY

PRC-25	Man-portable, backpack-style radio of the Vietnam era. An improved later version was the PRC [pronounced "prick"]-77.
PT	Acronym for—depending on the context—either (1) physical training, or (2) patrol torpedo boat.
PTO	Pacific Theater of Operations, during World War II.
Punchbowl	Nickname for—depending on the context—either (1) the National Memorial Cemetery of the Pacific because of its location in a bowl-shaped volcanic crater, near Honolulu, Hawaii, or (2) the bowl-shaped Haean-Myon Valley just south of the DMZ in South Korea.
R&R	Variously, either "refitting and recuperation" or "rest and recreation."
RA	Regular Army
RAF	British Royal Air Force.
RB-50	Reconnaissance and intelligence-gathering version of the B-50 bomber; see "B-29."
RCT	Regimental combat team; typically, an infantry regiment, reinforced with artillery, and sometimes tank, support, so as to be a stand-alone, "all-arms" tactical unit.
Recon	Contraction of "reconnaissance."
ROK	Republic of Korea, i.e., South Korea.
ROTC	Reserve Officers Training Course, for college and university students.
ROWPU	Reverse osmosis water purification unit; a modern water purification device.
RTB	Return to base.
S1C	Seaman First Class.
SBD	See entry for "Dauntless."
SCUD	Soviet-designed ballistic missile; used by various nations, including Iraq and North Korea, it can carry a nuclear, biological, chemical, or conventional warhead.
Seabees	Members of a US Navy Construction Battalion ("CB" or "NCB").
Semper Fi	A popular Marine saying, derived from the Marine Corps' motto, Semper Fidelis ("Always Faithful").
Sgt., SGT	Sergeant.
S/Sgt., SSG	Staff sergeant.
Sfc., SFC	Sergeant First Class.
Shellback	Anyone who has been initiated during a crossing of the Equator.
Shooting Star	See "F-80."
Skipper	A popular Marine and Navy nickname for a ship's or unit's commanding officer.
Sp/4 orSP4	Specialist Fourth Class; an Army rank equivalent to corporal.
Spc.	Specialist
Spectre	See "C-130."
Springfield	M1903 .30 caliber bolt-action rifle. Also called the "03" for short.
Squadron	The cavalry unit equivalent of a battalion.
S.S. or SS	Acronym for—depending on the context—the following: (1) steamship, a steam-powered merchant vessel; (2) the standard Navy acronym for submarines (a SSN is a nuclear submarine; a SSBN is a ballistic missile-armed nuclear submarine); or (3) Schutzstaffel, German for "protection squadron," Hitler's elite guard and the black-suited paramilitary arm of the Nazi Party.

SSU	Special Service Unit, being a subordinate unit of the United States Army Ambulance Corps Service, the Army's World War I ambulance units.
Stalag	German POW camps; "stalag" is an abbreviation of the German *stammlager*, itself an abbreviation of *kriegsgefangenenmannschafts-stammlager*, "standing (or permanent) camp for enlisted men prisoners of war." Officers-only POW camps were called Oflags, for *offizierslager*, "officers' camp," while POW camps established by the *Luftwaffe* solely for captured air force personnel were termed Stalag Luft.
.30	Caliber of bullet used for the BAR, Springfield, and Garand rifles and also for the M1917 and M1919 light machine guns. A smaller .30 caliber round was used by the M1 carbine.
T4, T/4	Technician Fourth Class (later, Specialist Fourth Class).
T-33	Lockheed two-seater jet training aircraft, based on the F-80 fighter.
TBF	Grumman Avenger single-engined Navy torpedo and attack bomber used during World War II. Also extensively made by Eastern Aircraft, a subsidiary of General Motors, whose variant was called the TBM.
TEWS	Tactical electronic warfare squadron; Air Force term.
Troop	The cavalry unit equivalent of a company-sized formation.
Tropic Lightning	Army 25th Infantry Division.
Tsgt., T/Sgt.	Technical Sergeant.
U-boat	German submarine (from *unterseeboot*, "undersea boat").
UH-1	Bell utility and transport helicopter, officially known as the Iroquois but nicknamed and almost universally known as the Huey (from its original designation as HU-1, "helicopter, utility"). It can also serve as a gunship.
UH-60	United Technologies (Sikorsky) medium-lift utility helicopter, officially known as the "Blackhawk." The Air Force model is the HH-60.
USA	United States Army.
USAACS	United States Army Ambulance Corps Service.
USAF	United States Air Force.
USAT	United States Army Transport.
USCG	United States Coast Guard.
USMA	See "West Point."
USMC	United States Marine Corps.
USN	United States Navy.
USS	United States Ship, the designation for all official Navy (as opposed to Army or Merchant Marine) vessels, both combat and non-combat.
VB	Acronym for Navy fighter squadron.
VC	Viet Cong; from the Vietnamese *Việt Nam Cộng-sản* ("Vietnamese communist"), also known as the National Liberation Front for South Vietnam; the guerilla and military forces backed by the North Vietnamese regime, as distinguished from the PAVN regular troops of the North Vietnamese.
"V" device	Small V-shaped device added to the ribbons of US decorations and medals under certain conditions to indicate the medal is being awarded for valor in combat.

VF	Acronym for Navy fighter squadron.
VFW	Veterans of Foreign Wars.
VMF	Acronym for Marine Corps fighter squadron.
VN	Vietnam.
VPB	Acronym for Navy patrol bomber squadron.
WAC	Women's Army Corps.
West Point	The United States Military Academy, located at West Point, New York.
WIA	Wounded in action.
Wildcat	Grumman F4F single-engined fighter; the Navy's principal fighter aircraft in the early stages of World War II.
WO	Warrant Officer.
Wolfhounds	The Army's 27th Infantry Regiment.
X-15	North American experimental rocket-powered aircraft, flown by Air Force and NASA test pilots for high altitude and sub-space scientific research.
XB-70	North American experimental supersonic, long-range jet bomber, known as the "Valkyrie," tested between 1964–1969.
XO	Executive officer (second-in-command). Also often called the "Exec."
Zero	Allied codename for Mitsubishi A6M-series single-engined Japanese fighter.

SELECTED BIBLIOGRAPHY

With the hundreds (if not thousands) of books available on many of the themes raised in this book and on the history of the American military, American military units, and naval ships since the First World War, what follows is, of necessity, a selective list of books for those readers who may be interested in further reading on the wars, battles, and engagements, and aspects of the military experience, as touched upon in this book.

WORLD WAR I

American Battle Monuments Commission. *American Armies and Battlefields in Europe: A History, Guide, and Reference Book.* Washington, DC: Government Printing Office, 1938.

Amis, Reese T., ed. *Knox County in the World War: 1917, 1918, 1919.* Knoxville, TN: Knoxville Lithographing Co., 1919.

———. *History of the 114th Field Artillery.* Nashville, TN: Benson Printing Co., 1920.

Bacon, William J. *History of the Fifty-Fifth Field Artillery Brigade, 1917–1918–1919.* Nashville, TN: Benson Printing Co., 1920.

Barry, John M. *The Great Influenza: The Epic Story of the Deadliest Plague in History.* New York: Viking, 2004.

Blair, Dale. *The Battle of Bellicourt Tunnel: Tommies, Diggers and Doughboys on the Hindenburg Line, 1918.* Barnsley, UK: Frontline/Pen & Sword Books, 2011.

Berg, A. Scott, ed. *World War I and America: Told by the Americans Who Lived It.* New York: Library of America, 2017.

Birdwell, Michael E., ed. *Tennessee's Experience during the First World War.* Knoxville: University of Tennessee Press, 2020.

Budreau, Lisa M., and Richard M. Prior, eds. *Answering the Call: The U.S. Army Nurse Corps, 1917–1919: A Commemorative Tribute to Military Nursing in World War I.* Washington, DC: Office of the Surgeon General, US Army, Borden Institute, Walter Reed Army Medical Center, 2008.

Carroll, Andrew. *My Fellow Soldiers: General John Pershing and the Americans Who Helped Win the Great War.* New York: Penguin Press, 2017.

Clark, George B. *Devil Dogs: Fighting Marines of World War I.* Novato, CA: Presidio Press, 1999.

Coffman, Edward M. *The War to End All Wars: The American Military Experience in World War I.* Lexington, KY: University Press of Kentucky, 1998.

Conway, C. B., and George A. Shuford. *History, 119th Infantry, 60th Brigade, 30th Division U.S.A., Operations in Belgium and France, 1917–1919.* Wilmington, NC: Wilmington Chamber of Commerce, 1920.

Crosby, Alfred W., Jr. *America's Forgotten Pandemic: The Influenza of 1918.* 2nd ed. New York: Cambridge University Press, 2003.

Eisenhower, John S. D. *Yanks: The Epic Story of the American Army in World War I.* New York: Simon and Schuster, 2001.

Ellis, John. *Eye-Deep in Hell: Trench Warfare in World War I*. Baltimore: Johns Hopkins University Press, 1976.

Falls, Cyril. *The Great War*. New York: G. P. Putnam's Sons, 1959.

Faulkner, Richard S. *The School of Hard Knocks: Combat Leadership in the American Expeditionary Forces*. College Station: Texas A&M University Press, 2012.

Flood, Charles Bracelen. *First to Fly: The Story of the Lafayette Escadrille, The American Heroes Who Flew for France in World War I*. New York: Atlantic Monthly Press, 2015.

Gilbert, Martin. *The First World War: A Complete History*. New York: Henry Holt, 1994.

Gilbert, Oscar E., and Romain Cansiere. *First to Fight: The US Marines in World War I*. Havertown, PA: Casemate Publishers, 2017.

Hall, James Norman, Charles Nordhoff, and Edgar G. Hamilton. *The Lafayette Flying Corps*. Boston: Houghton Mifflin Company, 1920.

Haythornewaite, Philip J. *The World War One Source Book*. London: Arms and Armour Press/Cassell, 1992.

Keegan, John. *The First World War*. New York: Alfred A. Knopf, 1999.

Lengel, Edward G. *Never in Finer Company: The Men of the Great War's Lost Battalion*. Boston: Da Capo Press, 2018

———. *Thunder and Flames: Americans in the Crucible of Combat, 1917–1918*. Lawrence: University Press of Kansas, 2015.

———. *To Conquer Hell: The Meuse-Argonne, 1918*. New York: Macmillan, 2008.

Mason, Herbert Molloy, Jr. *The Lafayette Escadrille*. New York: Random House, 1964.

Murphy, Elmer A., and Robert S. Thomas. *The Thirtieth Division in the Great War*. Lepanto, AR: Old Hickory Publishing Co., 1936.

Nelson, James Carl. *I Will Hold: The Story of USMC Legend Clifton B. Cates, From Belleau Wood to Victory in the Great War*. New York: Caliber, 2016.

Persico, Joseph E. *11th Month, 11th Day, 11th Hour: Armistice Day, 1918: World War I and Its Violent Climax*. New York: Random House, 2004.

Rockwell, Kiffin Y. *War Letters of Kiffin Y. Rockwell: Foreign Legion and Aviator France, 1914–1916*. Edited by Paul Ayres Rockwell. Garden City, NY: Doubleday, Page & Co. Country Life Press, 1925.

Royall, Sam F. *History of the 118th Infantry, American Expeditionary Force, France*. Columbia, SC: The State Co., 1919.

Simmons, Edwin H., and Joseph H. Alexander. T*hrough the Wheat: The U.S. Marines in World War I*. Annapolis, MD: Naval Institute Press, 2008.

Toland, John. *No Man's Land: 1918, The Last Year of the Great War*. Garden City, NY: Doubleday, 1980.

Yockelson, Mitchell A. *Forty-Seven Days: How Pershing's Warriors Came of Age to Defeat the German Army in World War I*. New York: NAL/Caliber, New American Library, 2016.

———. *Borrowed Soldiers: Americans Under British Command, 1918*. Norman: University of Oklahoma Press, 2008.

Winter, Jay, and Blaine Baggett. *The Great War and the Shaping of the 20th Century*. New York: Penguin Books, 1996.

WORLD WAR II

General

Bradley, John H., Jack W. Dice, and Thomas E. Griess. *The West Point Military History Series—The Second World War: Asia and the Pacific*. Wayne, NJ: Avery Publishing Group, 1989.

Brokaw, Tom. *The Greatest Generation*. New York: Random House, 1998.

Calvocoressi, Peter, and Guy Wint. *Total War: The Story of World War II*. New York: Ballantine Books, 1974.

Childers, Thomas. *Soldier from the War Returning: The Greatest Generation's Troubled Homecoming from World War II.* Boston: Houghton Mifflin Harcourt, 2009.

Cooper, Belton. *Death Traps: The Survival of an American Armored Division in World War II.* Novato, CA: Presidio Press, 1998.

Devlin, Gerard M. *Paratrooper! The Saga of the U.S. Army and Marine Parachute and Glider Combat Troops during World War II.* New York: St. Martin's Press, 1979.

Gilbert, Martin. *The Second World War: A Complete History.* New York: Henry Holt, 1989.

Hastings, Max. *Inferno: The World at War, 1939–1945.* New York: Alfred A. Knopf, 2011.

Jablonski, Edward. *Airwar: An Illustrated History of Air Power in the Second World War.* 2 vols. Garden City, NY: Doubleday, 1971.

———. *Flying Fortress: The Illustrated Biography of the B-17s and the Men Who Flew Them.* Garden City, NY: Doubleday, 1968.

Johnson, Charles W., and Charles O. Jackson. *City Behind a Fence: Oak Ridge, Tennessee, 1942–1946.* Knoxville: University of Tennessee Press, 1981.

Keegan, John. *The Second World War.* New York: Viking Press, 1989.

McManus, John C. *Deadly Sky: The American Combat Airman in World War II.* New York: NAL Caliber, 2016.

———. *The Deadly Brotherhood: The American Combat Soldier in World War II.* Novato, CA: Presidio Press, 1998.

Morison, Samuel Eliot. *The Two-Ocean War: A Short History of the United States Navy in the Second World War.* New York: Little, Brown and Co., 1963.

Weinberg, Gerhard. *A World at Arms: A Global History of World War II.* New York: Cambridge University Press, 1994.

European Theater

Ambrose, Stephen E. *Citizen Soldiers: The U.S. Army from the Normandy Beaches to the Bulge to the Surrender of Germany.* New York: Simon and Schuster, 1997.

———. *D-Day, June 6, 1944: The Climactic Battle of World War II.* New York: Simon and Schuster, 1994.

———. *Band of Brothers: E Company, 506th Regiment, 101st Airborne: From Normandy to Hitler's Eagle's Nest.* New York: Simon and Schuster, 1992.

Ardery, Philip. *Bomber Pilot: A Memoir of World War II.* Lexington, KY: University of Kentucky Press, 1978.

Atkinson, Rick. *Battle of the Bulge.* New York: Henry Holt, 2015.

———. *The Guns at Last Light: The War in Western Europe, 1944–1945.* New York: Henry Holt, 2013.

———. *The Day of Battle: The War in Sicily and Italy, 1943–1944.* New York: Henry Holt, 2007.

———. *An Army at Dawn: The War in North Africa, 1942–1943.* New York: Henry Holt, 2002.

Baumer, Robert W. *Old Hickory: The 30th Division: The Top-Rated American Infantry Division in Europe in World War II.* Guilford, CT: Stackpole Books, 2017.

Beevor, Anthony. *Ardennes 1944: Hitler's Last Gamble.* New York: Viking, 2015.

———. *D-Day: The Battle for Normandy.* London: Penguin Books, 2009.

Blumenson, Martin. *Bloody River: The Real Tragedy of the Rapido River.* College Station: Texas A&M University Press, 1970.

———. *Anzio: The Gamble that Failed.* Philadelphia: J. B. Lippincott, 1963.

———. *Breakout and Pursuit.* Washington, DC: Dept. of the Army, Office of Chief of Military History, 1961.

Childers, Thomas. *Wings of Morning: The Story of The Last American Bomber Shot Down Over Germany In World War II.* Reading, MA: Perseus Books, 1995.

DePuy, Trevor N., David L. Bongard, and Richard C. Anderson. *Hitler's Last Gamble: The Battle of the Bulge, December 1944–January 1945.* New York: HarperCollins 1994.

D'Este, Carlo. *Fatal Decision: Anzio and the Battle for Rome.* New York: HarperCollins, 1991.

Dugan, Jame, and Carroll Stewart. *Ploesti: The Great Ground-Air Battle of 1 August 1943*. New York: Bantam, 1963.

———. *World War II in the Mediterranean, 1942–1945*. Chapel Hill, NC: Algonquin Books, 1990.

———. *Bitter Victory: The Battle for Sicily, 1943*. New York: Dutton, 1988.

———. *Decision in Normandy: The Unwritten Story of Montgomery and the Allied Campaign*. New York: Dutton, 1983.

Eisenhower, John S. D. *The Bitter Woods: The Dramatic Story, Told at All Echelons, from Supreme Command to Squad Leader, of the Crisis that Shook the Western Coalition: Hitler's Surprise Ardennes Offensives*. New York: G. P. Putnam's Sons, 1969.

Eisner, Peter. *The Freedom Line: the Brave Men and Women Who Rescued Allied Airmen From the Nazis During World War II*. New York: William Morrow, 2004.

Freeman, Roger A. *The Mighty Eighth: A History of the Units, Men and Machines of the US 8th Air Force*. Garden City, NY: Doubleday, 1970.

Hastings, Max. *Armageddon: The Battle for Germany 1944–45*. New York: Macmillan, 2004.

———. *Overlord: D-Day and the Battle for Normandy*. New York: Simon and Schuster, 1984.

Kershaw, Alex. *The Longest Winter: The Battle of the Bulge and the Story of World War II's Most Decorated Platoon*. Boston: Da Capo Press, 2004.

———. *The Bedford Boys*. Boston: Da Capo Press, 2003.

Kurzman, Dan. *No Greater Glory: The Four Immortal Chaplains and the Sinking of the Dorchester in World War II*. New York: Random House, 2004.

MacDonald, Charles B. A *Time for Trumpets: The Untold Story of the Battle of the Bulge*. New York: Bantam Books, 1984.

———. *The Last Offensive*. Washington, DC: Dept. of the Army, Office of Chief of Military History, 1973.

———. *The Mighty Endeavor: American Armed Forces in the European Theater in World War II*. New York: Oxford University Press, 1969.

———. *The Battle of the Huertgen Forest*. Philadelphia: J. B. Lippincott, 1963.

———. *The Siegfried Line Campaign*. Washington, DC: Dept. of the Army, Office of Chief of Military History, 1963.

McManus, John C. *The Dead and Those About to Die: D-Day: The Big Red One at Omaha Beach*. New York: NAL Caliber, 2014.

———. *September Hope: The American Side of a Bridge Too Far*. New York: New American Library, 2012.

———. *The Americans at Normandy: The Summer of 1944—The American War from the Normandy Beaches to Falaise*. New York: Forge, 2004.

Miller, Donald L. *Masters of the Air: America's Bomber Boys Who Fought the Air War Against Nazi Germany*. New York: Simon and Schuster, 2006.

Miller, Edward G. *A Dark and Bloody Ground: The Hürtgen Forest and the Roer River Dams, 1944–45*. College Station: Texas A&M University Press, 1995.

Schultz, Duane. *Into the Fire: Ploesti, the Most Fateful Mission of World War II*. Yardley, UK: Westholme Publishing, 2007.

Toland, John. *The Last 100 Days: The Tumultuous and Controversial Story of the Final Days of World War II in Europe*. New York: Random House, 1966.

———. *Battle: The Story of the Bulge*. New York: Random House, 1959.

Ward, Ray. *Those Brave Crews: The Epic Raid to Destroy Hitler's Ploesti Oil Fields*. Waverly, NY: Weldon Publications, 2003.

Weigley, Russell F. *Eisenhower's Lieutenants: The Campaigns of France and Germany, 1944–45*. Bloomington: Indiana University Press, 1981.

Whiting, Charles. *Bloody Aachen*. New York: Stein and Day, 1976.

The Pacific Theater

Adams, Captain Henry H. *1942: The Year that Doomed the Axis*. New York: Warner Paperback Library, 1973.

Alexander, Joseph H. *Storm Landings: Epic Amphibious Battles in the Central Pacific*. Annapolis, MD: Naval Institute Press, 1997.

———. *Utmost Savagery: The Three Days of Tarawa*. Annapolis, MD: Naval Institute Press, 1995.

Ballard, Robert D., with Rick Archbold. *The Lost Ships of Guadalcanal*. New York: Warner/Madison Press Books, 1993.

Bergerud, Eric. *Touched with Fire: The Land War in the South Pacific*. New York: Viking, 1996.

———. *Fire in the Sky: The Air War in the South Pacific*. Boulder, CO: Westview Press, 1999.

Bilek, Tony, and Gene O'Connell. *No Uncle Sam: The Forgotten of Bataan*. Kent, OH: Kent State University Press, 2003.

Drury, Bob, and Tom Clavin. *Halsey's Typhoon: The True Story of a Fighting Admiral, an Epic Storm and an Untold Rescue*. New York: Grove Atlantic/Atlantic Monthly Press, 2006.

Dull, Paul. *A Battle History of the Imperial Japanese Navy*. Annapolis, MD: Naval Institute Press, 1978.

Feifer, George. *Tennozan: The Battle of Okinawa and the Atomic Bomb*. New York: Ticknor and Fields, 1992.

Frank, Richard B. *Guadalcanal: The Definitive Account of the Landmark Battle*. New York: Random House, 1990.

Hastings, Max. *Retribution: The Battle for Japan, 1944–45*. New York: Alfred A. Knopf, 2008.

Hornfischer, James D. *The Fleet at Flood Tide: America at Total War in the Pacific, 1944–1945*. New York: Bantam Books, 2016.

———. *Neptune's Inferno: The U.S. Navy at Guadalcanal*. New York: Bantam Books, 2011.

———. *The Last Stand of the Tin Can Sailors: The Extraordinary World War II Story of the U.S. Navy's Finest Hour*. New York: Bantam Books, 2004.

Hoyt, Edwin P. *The Glory of the Solomons*. New York: Stein and Day, 1983.

Leckie, Robert. *Strong Men Armed: The United States Marines vs. Japan*. New York: Da Capo Press, Inc., 1997.

Lukacs, John D. *Escape from Davao: The Forgotten Story of the Most Daring Prison Break of the Pacific War*. New York: Simon and Schuster, 2010.

Manchester, William. *Goodbye, Darkness: A Memoir of the Pacific War*. Boston: Little, Brown, 1979.

Michno, Gregory F. *Death on the Hellships: Prisoners at Sea in the Pacific War*. Annapolis, MD: Naval Institute Press, 2001.

Miller, John J., Jr. *Cartwheel: The Reduction of Rabaul*. Washington, DC: Dept. of the Army, Office of Chief of Military History, 1959.

———. *Guadalcanal: The First Offensive*. Washington, DC: Dept. of the Army, Office of Chief of Military History, 1949.

Newcomb, Richard F., with Peter Maas. *Abandon Ship! The Saga of the U.S.S. Indianapolis, the Navy's Greatest Sea Disaster*. New York: HarperCollins, 2001.

Prange, Gordon W., with Donald M. Goldstein and Katherine V. Dillon. *At Dawn We Slept: The Untold Story of Pearl Harbor*. New York: McGraw-Hill Publishing, 1981.

Schultz, Duane. *Hero of Bataan: The Story of General Jonathan M. Wainwright*.New York: St. Martin's Press, 1981.

Scott, James M. *Rampage: MacArthur, Yamashita, and the Battle of Manila*. New York: W. W. Norton and Co., 2019.

———. *The War Below: The Story of Three Submarines That Battled Japan*. New York: Simon and Schuster, 2013.

Shaw, Henry I., Jr. *The United States Marines in the Guadalcanal Campaign*. Washington, DC: Headquarters, US Marine Corps/Govt. Printing Office, 1962.

Shaw, Henry I., Jr., and Douglas T. Kane. *The Isolation of Rabaul: History of U.S. Marine Corps Operations in World War II*. Washington, DC: Historical Branch, G-3 Division, Headquarters, US Marine Corps/Govt. Printing Office, 1963.

Sides, Hampton. *Ghost Soldiers: The Forgotten Epic Story of World War II's Most Dramatic Mission*. New York: Doubleday, 2001.

Spector, Ronald H. *Eagle Against the Sun: The American War with Japan*. New York: Vintage Books, 1985.

Stanton, Doug. *In Harm's Way: The Sinking of the USS Indianapolis and the Extraordinary Story of Its Survivors*. New York: Henry Holt, 2001.

Toll, Ian W. *Pacific Crucible: War at Sea in the Pacific, 1941–1942*. New York: W. W. Norton, 2011.

———. *The Conquering Tide: War in the Pacific Islands, 1942–1944*. New York: W. W. Norton, 2015.

Whitman, John M. *Bataan: Our Last Ditch*. New York: Hippocrene Books, 1990.

Winslow, Walter G. *The Fleet the Gods Forgot: The U.S. Asiatic Fleet in World War II*. Annapolis, MD: Naval Institute Press, 1982.

Wukovits, John. *For Crew and Country: The Inspirational True Story of Bravery and Sacrifice Aboard the USS Samuel B. Roberts*. New York: St. Martin's Press, 2013.

Korea

Blair, Clay. *The Forgotten War: America in Korea*. New York: Times Books, 1988.

Center of Military History, US Army. *Korea 1950*. Washington, DC: Dept. of the Army, Center of Military History, 1997.

Dorr, Robert F., Jon Lake, and Warren Thompson. *Korean War Aces*. London: Osprey Publishing, 1995.

Fehrenbach, T. R. *This Kind of War: The Classic Korean War History*. Herndon, VA: Brassey's US, Inc., 1994.

Goulden, Joseph C. *Korea: The Untold Story*. New York: Times Books, 1982.

Gugeler, Russell A. *Combat Actions in Korea*. Washington, DC: Dept. of the Army, Center of Military History, 1954. Revised edition, 1984.

Halberstam, David. *The Coldest Winter: America and the Korean War*. New York: Hyperion, 2007.

Hammel, Eric M. *Chosin: Heroic Ordeal of the Korean War*. New York: Vanguard Press, 1981.

Heinl, Robert D. *Victory at High Tide: The Inchon-Seoul Campaign*. Philadelphia: Lippincott, 1968.

Hoyt, Edwin P. *The Day the Chinese Attacked: December 1, 1950*. New York: McGraw-Hill, 1990.

———. *The Bloody Road to Panmunjom*. New York: Stein and Day, 1985.

———. *On to the Yalu*. New York: Stein and Day, 1984.

———. *The Pusan Perimeter*. New York: Stein and Day, 1984.

James, D. Clayton, with Anne Sharp Wells. *Refighting the Last War: Command and Crisis in Korea, 1950–1953*. New York: Free Press, 1993.

Langley, Michael. *Inchon Landing: MacArthur's Last Triumph*. New York: Times Books, 1979.

Latham, William C., Jr. *Cold Days in Hell: American POWs in Korea*. College Station: Texas A&M University Press, 2012.

Lech, Raymond B. *Broken Soldiers*. Urbana: University of Illinois Press, 2000.

Marshall, S. L. A. *The River and the Gauntlet: Defeat of the 8th Army by the Chinese Communist Forces, November 1950, in the Battle of the Chongchon River*. New York: William Morrow and Co., 1953.

———. *Pork Chop Hill: The American Fighting Man in Action, Korea, Spring, 1953*. New York: William Morrow and Co., 1956.

Miller, John, Jr., Owen J. Curroll, and Margaret E. Tackley. *Korea 1951–53*. Washington, DC: Dept. of the Army, Center of Military History, 1954. Revised edition, 1997.

Smith, Charles R., ed. *U.S. Marines in the Korean War*. Washington, DC: History Division, Headquarters, US Marine Corps, 2007.

Toland, John. *In Mortal Combat: Korea, 1950–1953*. New York: William Morrow, 1991.

Vietnam

Alexander, Ron and Charles W. Sasser. *Taking Fire: The True Story of a Decorated Chopper Pilot*. New York: St. Martin's, 2001.

Allen, Michael J. *Until the Last Man Comes Home: POWs, MIAs, and the Unending Vietnam War*. Chapel Hill: University of North Carolina Press, 2009.

Alley, J. Lyles (Bud). *The Ghosts of the Green Grass: The Journey of the Second Battalion, Seventh Cavalry into the Hell of the Ia Drang Valley in 1965*. Signal Mountain, TN: Codi Publishing, 2015.

Ballentine, David A. *Gunbird Driver: A Marine Huey Pilot's War in Vietnam*. Annapolis, MD: Naval Institute Press, 2008.

Bergerud, Eric M. *Red Thunder, Tropic Lightning: The World of a Combat Division in Vietnam*. Boulder: Westview, 1993.

Bowden, Mark. *Hue 1968: A Turning Point of the American War in Vietnam*. New York: Atlantic Monthly Press, 2017.

Bradley, Mark Phillip. *Vietnam at War*. New York: Oxford University Press, 2009.

Broughton, Jack. *Going Downtown: The War Against Hanoi and Washington*. New York: Orion, 1988.

Bryan, Courtlandt D. B. *Friendly Fire*. New York: Putnam, 1976.

Butler, David. *The Fall of Saigon*. New York: Simon and Schuster, 1985.

Caputo, Philip. *A Rumor of War*. New York: Holt, Rinehart, and Winston, 1977.

Clancy, Tom, with Tony Zinni and Tony Koltz. *Battle Ready*. New York: Putnam, 2004.

Clarke, Bruce B. G. *Expendable Warriors: The Battle of Khe Sanh and the Vietnam War*. Westport, CT: Praeger, 2007.

Coram, Robert. *American Patriot: The Life and Wars of Colonel Bud Day*. Boston: Little, Brown, 2007.

Cutler, Thomas J. *Brown Water, Black Berets: Coastal and Riverine Warfare in Vietnam*. Annapolis, MD: Naval Institute Press, 1988.

Denton, Jeremiah A., with Ed Brandt. *When Hell was in Session*. New York: Reader's Digest Press/Crowell, 1976.

Downs, Frederick, Jr. *The Killing Zone: My Life in the Vietnam War*. New York: Norton, 1978.

Drez, Ronald J., and Douglas Brinkley. *Voices of Courage: The Battle for Khe Sanh, Vietnam*. New York: Bullfinch, 2005.

Ebert, James R. *A Life in a Year: The American Infantryman in Vietnam,1965–1972*. Novato, CA: Presidio Press, 1993.

Eggleston, Michael A. *Dak To and the Border Battles of Vietnam, 1967–1968*. Jefferson, NC: McFarland, 2017.

Engelmann, Larry. *Tears Before the Rain: An Oral History of the Fall of Saigon*. New York: Oxford University Press, 1990.

Fields, Kenny Wayne. *The Rescue of Streetcar 304: A Navy Pilot's Forty Hours on the Run in Laos*. Annapolis, MD: Naval Institute Press, 2007.

Goldsmith, Wynn. *Papa Bravo Romeo: U.S. Navy Patrol Boats at War in Vietnam*. New York: Ballantine, 2001.

Grant, William T. *Wings of the Eagle: A Kingsman's Story*. New York: Ivy, 1994.

Hackworth, David H., with Julie Sherman. *About Face: The Odyssey of an American Warrior*. New York: Simon and Schuster, 1989.

Hammel, Eric. *Marines in Hue City: A Portrait of Urban Combat, Tet 1968*. St. Paul: Zenith, 2007.

———. *Ambush Valley: I Corps, Vietnam—The Story of a Marine Infantry Battalion's Battle for Survival*. Novato, CA: Presidio Press, 1990.

———. *Khe Sanh, Siege in the Clouds: An Oral History*. New York: Crown, 1989.

Hampton, Dan. *The Hunter Killers: The Extraordinary Story of the First Wild Weasels, the Band of Maverick Aviators Who Flew the Most Dangerous Missions of the Vietnam War*. New York: William Morrow, 2015.

Hastings, Max. *Vietnam: An Epic Tragedy, 1945–1975*. New York: Harper, 2018.

Hawk, Amy Shively. *Six Years in the Hanoi Hilton: An Extraordinary Story of Survival and Courage in Vietnam.* Regnery History, 2017.

Herbert, Anthony. *Soldier.* New York: Holt, Rinehart and Winston, 1973.

Herr, Michael. *Dispatches.* New York: Alfred A. Knopf, 1977.

Herring, George C. *America's Longest War: The United States and Vietnam, 1950–1975.* 4th ed. New York: McGraw-Hill, 2002.

Herrington, Stuart. *Peace with Honor? An American Reports on Vietnam, 1973–75.* Novato, CA: Presidio, 1983.

Holloway, James L., III. *Aircraft Carriers at War: A Personal Retrospective of Korea, Vietnam, and the Soviet Confrontation.* Annapolis, MD: Naval Institute Press, 2007.

Howes, Craig. *Voices of the Vietnam POWs: Witnesses to their Fight.* New York: Oxford University Press, 1993.

Hubbell, John G. *P.O.W.: A Definitive History of the American Prisoner-of-War Experience in Vietnam, 1964–1973.* New York: Reader's Digest Press, 1976.

Hughes, Larry. *You Can See a Lot Standing under a Flare in the Republic of Vietnam.* New York: Morrow, 1969.

Johnson, Tom A. *To the Limit: An Air Cav Huey Pilot in Vietnam.* Washington, DC: Potomac Books, 2006.

Jones, Gregg. *Last Stand at Khe Sanh: The U. S. Marines' Finest Hour in Vietnam.* Boston: Da Capo Press, 2014.

Karnow, Stanley. *Vietnam: A History.* New York: Viking, 1983.

Kinney, Katherine. *Friendly Fire: American Images of the Vietnam War.* New York: Oxford University Press, 2000.

Kovic, Ron. *Born on the Fourth of July.* New York: McGraw-Hill, 1976.

Lehrack, Otto J. *No Shining Armor: The Marines at War in Vietnam, An Oral History.* Lawrence: University Press of Kansas, 1992.

Mangold, Tom, and John Penycate. *The Tunnels of Cu Chi: The Untold Story of Vietnam.* New York: Random House, 1985.

Maslowski, Peter, and Don Winslow. *Looking for a Hero: Staff Sergeant Joe Ronnie Hooper and the Vietnam War.* Lincoln: University of Nebraska Press, 2005.

McAdams, Frank. *Vietnam Rough Riders: A Convoy Commander's Memoir.* Lawrence: University Press of Kansas, 2013.

McCain, John, with Mark Salter. *Faith of My Fathers: A Family Memoir.* New York: Random House, 1999.

Melson, Charles D., and Curtis G. Arnold. *U.S. Marines in Vietnam: The War That Would Not End, 1971–1973.* Washington, DC: History and Museums Division, Headquarters, US Marine Corps, 1991.

Michel, Marshall L. *Clashes: Air Combat Over North Vietnam 1965–1972.* Annapolis, MD: Naval Institute Press, 1997.

Miller, John Grider. *The Bridge at Dong Ha.* Annapolis, MD: Naval Institute Press, 1989.

———. *The Co-Vans: U.S. Marine Advisors in Vietnam.* Annapolis, MD: Naval Institute Press, 2000.

Moore, Harold G., and Joseph L. Galloway, *We Were Soldiers Once . . . And Young: Ia Drang-The Battle that Changed the War in Vietnam.* New York: Random House, 1992.

Murphy, Edward F. *The Hill Fights: The First Battle of Khe Sanh.* New York: Presidio/Ballantine, 2003.

———. *Semper Fi—Vietnam: From Da Nang to the DMZ, Marine Corps Campaigns, 1965–1975.* Novato, CA: Presidio Press, 1997.

Nichols, John B., and Barrett Tillman. *On Yankee Station: The Naval Air War Over Vietnam.* Annapolis, MD: Naval Institute Press, 1987.

Nolan, Keith W. *The Battle for Saigon: Tet 1968.* New York: Pocket Books, 1996.

———. *Sappers in the Wire: The Life and Death of Firebase Mary Ann.* College Station: Texas A&M University Press, 1995.

———. *The Magnificent Bastards: The Joint Army-Marine Defense of Dong Ha, 1968.* Novato, CA: Presidio Press, 1994.

———. *Into Cambodia: Spring Campaign, Summer Offensive, 1970.* Novato, CA: Presidio Press, 1990.

———. *Death Valley: The Summer Offensive, I Corps, August 1969*. Novato, CA: Presidio Press, 1987.

Oberdorfer, Don. *Tet!* New York: Doubleday, 1971.

Olds, Robin, Christina Olds, and Ed Rasimus. *Fighter Pilot: The Memoirs of Legendary Ace Robin Olds*. New York: St. Martin's Press, 2010.

Philpott, Tom. *Glory Denied: The Saga of Jim Thompson, America's Longest-Held Prisoner of War*. New York: Norton, 2001.

Pisor, Robert. *The End of the Line: The Siege of Khe Sanh*. New York: W. W. Norton, 1982.

Robbins, Glenn. *The Longest Rescue: The Life and Legacy of Vietnam POW William A. Robinson*. Lexington: University Press of Kentucky, 2013.

Schemmer, Benjamin F. *The Raid*. New York: Harper and Row, 1976.

Sharp, Arthur G. *The Siege of LZ Kate: The Battle for an American Firebase in Vietnam*. Mechanicsburg, PA: Stackpole, 2014.

Sheehan, Neil. *A Bright Shining Lie: John Paul Vann and America in Vietnam*. New York: Random House, 1988.

Sherwood, John Darrell. *Fast Movers: Jet Pilots and the Vietnam Experience*. New York: Free Press, 1999.

Smith, Eric McAllister. *Not by the Book: A Combat Intelligence Officer in Vietnam*. New York: Ivy Books, 1993.

Spector, Ronald. *After Tet: The Bloodiest Year in Vietnam*. New York: Free Press, 1993.

Stanton, Doug. *The Odyssey of Echo Company: The Tet Offensive and the Epic Battle to Survive the Vietnam War*. New York: Scribner, 2017.

Stanton, Shelby L. *The Rise and Fall of an American Army: U.S. Ground Forces in Vietnam, 1965–1973*. Novato, CA: Presidio, 1985.

Stockdale, Jim, and Sybil Stockdale. *In Love and War*. Annapolis, MD: US Naval Institute, 1990.

Taylor, Jay. *Point of Aim, Point of Impact*. Bloomington, IN: AuthorHouse, 2011.

Tonsetic, Robert L. *Days of Valor: An Inside Account of the Bloodiest Six Months of the Vietnam War*. Philadelphia: Casemate, 2007.

Villard, Erik. *The 1968 Tet Offensive Battles of Quang Tri City and Hue*. Washington, DC: US Army Center of Military History, 2008.

Ward, Geoffrey C., with Ken Burns and Lynn Novick. *The Vietnam War: An Intimate History*. New York: Alfred A. Knopf, 2017.

Ware, Ezell, and Joel Engel. *By Duty Bound: Survival and Redemption in a Time of War*. New York: Penguin, 2005.

Wilkins, Warren K. *Nine Days in May: The Battles of the 4th Infantry Division on the Cambodian Border, 1967*. Norman: University of Oklahoma Press, 2017.

Willbanks, James H. *The Tet Offensive: A Concise History*. New York: Columbia University Press, 2006.

Wolff, Tobias. *In Pharaoh's Army: Memories of the Lost War*. New York: Knopf, 1994.

Yarborough, Thomas R. *A Shau Valor: American Combat Operations in the Valley of Death, 1963–1971*. Havertown, PA: Casemate, 2016.

Zaffiri, Samuel. *Hamburger Hill: May 11–20, 1969*. New York: Presidio/Ballantine, 1988.

The Gulf War of 1991–92, Iraq and Afghanistan, and Conflicts after the Cold War

Atkinson, Rick. *Crusade: The Untold Story of the Persian Gulf War*. Boston: Houghton Mifflin, 1993.

Bowden, Mark. *Blackhawk Down: A Story of Modern War*. New York: Grove Press, 1999.

Carroll, Andrew. *Operation Homecoming: Iraq, Afghanistan, and the Home Front, in the Words of U.S. Troops and Their Families*. New York: Random House, 2006.

Chandrasekaran, Rajiv. *Imperial Life in the Emerald City: Inside Iraq's Green Zone*. New York: Vintage Books, 2006.

Clancy, Tom, and Frederick M. Franks Jr., *Into the Storm: A Study in Command*. New York: Putnam Publishing Group, 1997.

Coyne, James B. *Airpower in the Gulf*. Arlington, VA: Air Force Association, 1992.

Diamond, Larry. *Squandered Victory: The American Occupation and the Bungled Effort to Bring Democracy to Iraq*. New York: Henry Holt, 2005.

Dorr, Robert F. *Desert Storm Air Victory*. Stillwater, MN: Motorbooks International, 1991.

Franks, Tommy, with Malcolm McConnell. *American Soldier*. New York: Regan, 2004.

Friedman, Norman. *Desert Victory: The War for Kuwait*. Annapolis, MD: Naval Institute Press, 1991.

Gordon, Michael R., and Bernard E. Trainor. *Cobra II: The Inside Story of the Invasion and Occupation of Iraq*. New York: Pantheon, 2006.

Hutchinson, Kevin Don. *Operation Desert Shield/Desert Storm: Chronology and Fact Book*. Westport, CT: Greenwood Press, 1995.

Jones, Seth G. *In the Graveyard of Empires: America's War in Afghanistan*. New York: W. W. Norton and Co., 2009.

Junger, Sebastian. *War*. New York: Twelve, 2010.

Kaplan, Robert D. *Imperial Grunts: On the Ground with the American Military, from Mongolia to the Philippines to Iraq and Beyond*. New York: Knopf Doubleday Publishing Group, 2006.

Keegan, John. *The Iraq War*. New York: Alfred A. Knopf, 2004.

Lansford, Tom. *9/11 and the Wars in Afghanistan and Iraq: A Chronology and Reference Guide*. Santa Barbara, CA: ABC-CLIO, 2011.

Mansoor, Peter R. *Baghdad at Sunrise: A Brigade Commander's War in Iraq*. New Haven, CT: Yale University Press, 2008.

Meisner, Arnold. *Desert Storm Sea Victory*. Stillwater, MN: Motorbooks International, 1991.

Murray, Williamson, and Robert H. Scales Jr. *The Iraq War: A Military History*. Cambridge, MA: Belknap Press of Harvard University Press, 2005.

Packer, George. *The Assassins' Gate: America in Iraq*. New York: Farrar, Strauss and Giroux, 2005.

Palmer, Michael. *On Course to Desert Storm: The United States Navy and the Persian Gulf*. Washington, DC: Naval Historical Center, 1992.

Pritchard, Tim. *Ambush Alley: The Most Extraordinary Battle of the Iraq War*. New York: Random House, 2005.

Robinson, Linda. *Tell Me How This Ends: General David Petraeus and the Search for a Way Out of Iraq*. New York: Public Affairs, 2008.

Romesha, Clinton. *Red Platoon: A True Story of American Valor*. New York: Dutton, 2016.

Sanchez, Ricardo S., with Donald T. Phillips. *Wiser in Battle: A Soldier's Story*. New York: HarperCollins, 2008.

Schwartzkopf, H. Norman, Jr., with Peter Petre. *It Doesn't Take a Hero*. New York: Bantam Books, 1992.

Stanton, Doug. *Horse Soldiers: The Extraordinary Story of a Band of U.S. Soldiers Who Rode to Victory in Afghanistan*. New York: Scribner, 2009.

Thomas, F. Allen, Clifton Berry, and Norman Polmar. *CNN: War in the Gulf*. Atlanta, GA: Turner Publishing, 1991.

Woodward, Bob. *Bush at War*. New York: Simon and Schuster, 2002.

———. *Plan of Attack*. New York: Simon and Schuster, 2004.

———. *State of Denial*. New York: Simon and Schuster, 2006.

Zucchino, David. *Thunder Run: The Armored Strike to Capture Baghdad*. New York: Grove Press, 2005.

Military Cemeteries, Graves Registration, Gold Star Mothers, the ABMC, and Memorialization

American Battle Monuments Commission. *American Armies and Battlefields in Europe: A History, Guide, and Reference Book*. Washington, DC: Government Printing Office, 1938.

Atkinson, Rick. *Where Valor Rests: Arlington National Cemetery*. Washington, DC: National Geographic Books, 2007.

Bigler, Philip. *In Honored Glory: Arlington National Cemetery: The Final Post*. 4th edition. St. Petersburg, FL: Vandamere Press, 2005.

Budreau, Lisa M. *Bodies of War: World War I and the Politics of Commemoration in America, 1919–1933*. New York: New York University Press, 2010.

Dolski, Michael R. *D-Day Remembered: The Normandy Landings in American Collective Memory*. Knoxville, TN: University of Tennessee Press, 2016.

Hawley, Thomas M. *The Remains of War: Bodies, Politics, and the Search for American Soldiers Unaccounted for in Southeast Asia*. Durham, NC: Duke University Press, 2005.

Nishiura, Elizabeth, ed. *American Battle Monuments: A Guide to Military Cemeteries and Monuments Maintained by the American Battle Monuments Commission*. Detroit, MI: Omnigraphics Inc., 1989.

Peters, James Edward. *Arlington National Cemetery, Shrine to America's Heroes*. Bethesda, MD: Woodbine House, 2000.

Poole, Robert M. *On Hallowed Ground: The Story of Arlington National Cemetery*. New York: Walker and Co., 2009.

Ruck, Tom. *Sacred Ground: A Tribute to America's Veterans*. Washington, DC: Regnery Publishing, 2007.

Shomon, Joseph James. *Crosses in the Wind*. New York: Stratford House, 1947.

Sledge, Michael. *Soldier Dead: How We Recover, Identify, Bury, and Honor Our Military Fallen*. New York: Columbia University Press, 2005.

Wise, James E., and Scott Baron. *Soldiers Lost at Sea: A Chronicle of Troopship Disasters*. Annapolis, MD: Naval Institute Press, 2003.

The Medal of Honor, Its Recipients and its History

Collier, Peter, and Nick Del Calzo. *Medal of Honor: Portraits of Valor Beyond the Call of Duty*. 3rd edition. New York: Artisan 2011.

DeKever, Andrew J. *Here Rests in Honored Glory: Life Stories of Our Country's Medal of Honor Recipients*. Bennington, VT: Merriam Press, 2008.

Mikaelian, Allen, and Mike Wallace. *Medal of Honor: Profiles of America's Military Heroes from the Civil War to the Present*. New York: Hyperion Books, 2003.

Murphy, Edward F. *Vietnam Medal of Honor Heroes*. New York: Presidio Press/Random House, 2005.

Widener, Robert. "Who Was the Most Decorated U.S. Serviceman of WWI?" *VFW Magazine* 99, no. 3 (Nov./Dec. 2011): 38–41.

Willbanks, James H. *America's Heroes: Medal of Honor Recipients from the Civil War to Afghanistan*. Santa Barbara, CA: ABC-CLIO, 2011.

General Books on the US Military, Branches of Service, and the Military Experience

Alexander, Joseph H. *A Fellowship of Valor: The Battle History of the United States Marines*. New York: HarperCollins, 1996.

Ambrose, Stephen E. *Duty, Honor, Country: A History of West Point*. Baltimore: Johns Hopkins University Press, 1966.

Asprey, Robert B. *War in the Shadows: The Guerrilla in History*. 2 vols. Garden City, NY: Doubleday, 1975.

Atkinson, Rick. *The Long Gray Line: The American Journey of West Point's Class of 1966*. Boston: Houghton Mifflin, 1989.

Carroll, Andrew. *War Letters: Extraordinary Correspondence from American Wars*. New York: Scribner, 2001.

Clancy, Tom, with Carl Stiner and Tony Koltz. *Shadow Warriors: Inside the Special Forces*. New York: G. P. Putnam's Sons, 2002.

Coffman, Edward M. *The Regulars: The American Army, 1898–1941*. Cambridge, MA: Harvard University Press, 2004.

Huebner, Andrew J. *The Warrior Image: Soldiers in American Culture from the Second World War to the Vietnam Era*. Chapel Hill, NC: University of North Carolina Press, 2008.

Howarth, Stephen. *To Shining Sea: A History of the United States Navy, 1775–1998*. Norman, OK: University of Oklahoma Press, 1999.

Hynes, Samuel. *The Soldiers' Tale: Bearing Witness to Modern War*. New York: Penguin Books, 1997.

Lewis, Adrian. *The American Culture of War: A History of American Military Force from World War II to Operation Iraqi Freedom*. New York: Routledge, 2006.

McCarthy, James P., and Drue L. Berry, eds. *Air Force*. Westport, CT: Hugh Lauter Levin Associates, Inc., 2002.

McManus, John C. *Grunts: Inside the American Combat Experience, World War II to Iraq*. New York: NAL Caliber, 2010.

Schultz, Howard, and Rajiv Chandrasekaran. *For Love of Country What Our Veterans Can Teach Us About Citizenship, Heroism, and Sacrifice*. New York: Borzoi Books/Alfred A. Knopf, 2014.

Sheeler, Jim. *Final Salute: A Story of Unfinished Lives*. New York: Penguin Press, 2008.

Simmons, Edwin H. *The United States Marines: A History*. 4th edition. Annapolis, MD: Naval Institute Press, 2003.

Wheeler, James Scott. *The Big Red One: America's Legendary 1st Infantry Division from World War I to Desert Storm*. Lawrence, KS: University Press of Kansas, 2007.

Wilson, George C. *Mud Soldiers: Life Inside the New American Army*. New York: Scribner's, 1989.

INDEX